ENVIRONMENTAL ECONO
and Natural Resource Ma

Necessary decisions about natural resources and the environment pit the present against the future, development against nature, and certain benefits against uncertain consequences. The resulting importance of careful economic analysis heightens the need for high-quality educational materials for the next generation of decision makers.

With *Environmental Economics and Natural Resource Management* we aim to provide the most user-friendly textbook on the market. The fourth edition pairs the story-based narrative and visual emphasis of previous editions with new policy initiatives and the latest developments in the field. The expanded set of visual aids includes scores of color photographs and illustrations unmatched in other texts.

In this book students will discover environmental policies from around the world, practical approaches to resource-use dilemmas, techniques for environmental dispute resolution, and ample coverage of hot topics including:

- tradable emissions permits
- solar and wind energy
- recycling policies
- global environmental initiatives.

This innovative textbook serves students of environmental economics, ecological economics, and natural resource management. Instructors receive access to an online *Instructor's Guide* with answers to the practice problems and downloadable slides of the figures and tables in the book.

David A. Anderson received his B.A. from the University of Michigan and his M.A. and Ph.D. from Duke University. His other books include *Favorite Ways to Explore Economics* and *Economics by Example*. He is the Paul G. Blazer Professor of Economics at Centre College.

ENVIRONMENTAL ECONOMICS and Natural Resource Management

Fourth Edition

David A. Anderson
Centre College

Routledge
Taylor & Francis Group
LONDON AND NEW YORK

First published 2014 by Routledge
2 Park Square, Milton Park, Abingdon, Oxon, OX14 4RN

Simultaneously published in the USA and Canada by Routledge
711 Third Avenue, New York, NY 10017

Routledge is an imprint of the Taylor & Francis Group, an informa business

British Library Cataloguing in Publication Data
A catalogue record for this book is available from the British Library

Library of Congress Cataloging in Publication Data
Anderson, David A.
Environmental economics & natural resource management /
David A. Anderson. -- 4th edition.
pages cm
1. Environmental economics. 2. Natural resources--Management.
I. Title. II. Title: Environmental economics and natural resource management.
HC79.E5A5137 2013
333.7--dc23
2013015400

ISBN 978-0-415-64095-4 (hbk)
ISBN 978-0-415-64096-1 (pbk)

Typeset in Century Schoolbook
by David A. Anderson
Printed by Ashford Colour Press Ltd

For Donna, Austin, and Ally

Contents

Part III
Policy and Procedure

Chapter 15

Chapter 16

Preface

Environmental economics is unique among course offerings. Like the arts, the environment serves as a basis for cultural identity and a fount for social welfare. As in the natural sciences, students of environmental economics seek a better understanding of the natural world. Yet the study of environmental economics holds special importance because it speaks directly to practices and policy decisions that determine our fate. Economic tools address the specifics of what products best serve society, what regulations are appropriate, what incentives are optimal, and what resources should be conserved.

Humans have the capacity to protect, alter, or destroy natural resources on a grand scale. Regulators confront trade-offs between lives and profits, and can be guided by greed or emotion, if not by informed approaches. Economic analysis reveals that the value of human life is not infinite and the optimal amount of pollution is not zero, but that ignorance of economic insights results in undervalued lives and excessive pollution. The purpose of this book is to make the tools of economic analysis readily available to college students interested in the environment or natural resources.

Most people are aware of debates surrounding environmental assets. Relatively few are familiar with the economic way of thinking. Even fewer know the means by which to weigh short-term costs against long-term benefits, or the costs and benefits of, say, biodiesel as an alternative fuel. When information is lacking, critical environmental policy is more easily swayed by questionable arguments. It may be inhuman to be dispassionate, but economic theory provides opportunities to displace emotions with concrete criteria. The challenge, then, is to apply the most valid methodology earnestly and honestly. This book explains relevant techniques and points out likely missteps.

The fourth edition of *Environmental Economics and Natural Resource Management* retains the story-based narratives and visual emphasis of the previous editions, updated with contemporary policy initiatives from around the world and discussions of the latest developments in the field. As visual aids, an expanded array of full-color photographs, diagrams, and graphs impart new perspectives on global environmental and resource issues. "Reality Checks" in each chapter delve more deeply into the application of economic principles in the real world. Review problems and "websurfing challenges" reinforce understanding, and suggested Internet links and additional readings serve students whose interests have been stirred. Some of the more challenging models appear in appendices to grant instructors the flexibility to cover them or not. Above all, this textbook addresses the critical objectives of environmental and economic literacy with policy-oriented, application-based content that is easy to follow.

Although ethical dilemmas surround environmental economics, criteria for deciding right from wrong receive little coverage in many textbooks. The need for education on ethical considerations is punctuated by daily headlines about corruption and severe abuses of the environment. The allocation of scarce resources involves moral quandaries over the treatment of humans, wildlife, and future generations of the same. Chapter 16 of this textbook explains secular ethical theories and highlights the role of ethics in environmental policy.

While alarm about resource scarcity earned economics a reputation as the "dismal science," there is hope for a marriage between growing consumer demands and progress on environmental fronts. The navigation of economic growth through sensitive environmental waters requires deliberate practices and a firm understanding of the relevant theory and evidence. May reading this book be a meaningful step along that journey.

General Overview

This textbook is divided into three parts. The chapters in the first part introduce environmental economics and provide a review of the more useful tools in the field. The second part lays out current areas of interest and concern, and explains alternative approaches to problem solving and the attainment of efficiency. Although the topic of environmental policy appears throughout the text, the third part emphasizes policy and public-sector oversight. Because decisions regarding natural resources cannot escape the realm of ethics, the final chapter provides a foundation in environmental ethics.

One cannot discuss or apply environmental economics appropriately without adequate knowledge of the underlying concepts and definitions. Without an understanding of the food chain, one cannot appreciate the economic value of plankton. Not knowing the meaning of hedonic pricing, one cannot speak intelligently about estimating the value of biodiversity. For this reason, the opening sections of most chapters contain definitions and perhaps a taste of chemistry, biology, or political science. The alternative would be to assume that readers have taken and remember all of those classes that complement environmental and natural resource economics—an expectation I would not want applied to myself!

Part I Building a Foundation

Chapter 1 The Big Picture

This chapter presents an overview of compelling environmental economics issues and gives readers a sketch of what is ahead in the text and why it is important. Nine key areas within the field are briefly highlighted: market failure, waste and recycling, environmental ethics, sustainable development, biological diversity, environmental degradation, alternative energy sources, population and economic growth, and natural resources management. The chapter provides less-than-subtle hints that the forthcoming tools of economics will address each of these issues.

Chapter 2 Efficiency and Choice

This chapter covers the primary tools of economic analysis, explaining marginal analysis, expected value calculations, supply and demand, and consumer choice. It is written as a comprehensive review for students who have seen most of this material in other courses, and to serve as a reference for students who encounter applications of this material later in the text and want to re-read the underlying concepts.

Appendix Efficiency in Greater Detail

This appendix provides a mathematically rigorous explanation of efficiency criteria.

Chapter 3 Market Failure

This chapter explains why the invisible hand might not always yield an efficient outcome. The sources of market failure—externalities, public goods, imperfect information, and imperfect competition—are explained in detail, including graphical analysis and real-world examples. In addition to foreshadowing the policy solutions of the second section, this chapter presents the Coase Theorem using numerical examples.

Chapter 4 The Role of Government

Chapter 4 analyzes the role of government in stemming market failure. Discussions address the need for government, the solutions government brings, and some of the pitfalls of both public and private approaches to externalities. The chapter also identifies opportunities to gain by substituting regulation for liability risks, and outlines key environmental agencies and legislation.

Chapter 5 Trade-offs and the Economy

Many of the most difficult questions in this field deal with long-run versus short-run benefits, and financial versus environmental gains. This chapter explains the tools of discounting and their applications. The chapter then covers methods for weighing economic growth against environmental degradation, and explores prospects for economic growth that are consistent with environmental goals.

Part II Issues and Approaches

Chapter 6 Environmental Quality

This chapter explains measures and determinants of environmental quality, including air quality, water quality, light pollution, and noise pollution. Case studies of solutions include policy, education, technology, product substitution, and market-based incentives. Tradable pollution permits are introduced, and receive more thorough coverage in Chapter 12.

Chapter 7 Energy

This chapter addresses traditional and alternative sources of energy, with attention to the trade-offs between various options, political and economic barriers, and future prospects. A case study of twenty-first century automotive technology provides a backdrop for discussions of the politics, pawns, and big players in energy-policy debates.

Chapter 8 Sustainability

This nebulous but conceptually attractive approach provides a guiding question for every activity that affects the environment: For how long can this activity be sustained? This chapter considers the appropriate application of the sustainability criterion and examines promising opportunities for sustainable development.

Chapter 9 Population, Poverty, and Economic Growth

This chapter covers demographic trends and their relationships to the environment. Past theories, including the work of Malthus and Kuznets, are coupled with more recent perspectives on municipal waste generation and the determinants of resource use. The chapter concludes with a discussion of how current and proposed government policies affecting poverty and economic growth are likely in turn to affect the environment.

Chapter 10 Biodiversity and Valuation

This chapter addresses optimal levels of biodiversity, issues of species prioritization, and the valuation of natural resources. Methods for estimating the marginal value of specific species are explained, with references to the current literature. Topics include the interpretation of market prices, contingent valuation, hedonic pricing, and the travel cost method.

Chapter 11 International and Global Issues

This chapter describes the aspects of environmental economics that transcend national boundaries. It covers attempts at international cooperation and the associated organizations and agreements. Topics include the CITES and Kyoto treaties, global warming, acid rain, natural disasters, global scarcity, poaching, and the strengths and weaknesses of international law.

Part III Policy and Procedure

Chapter 12 Perspectives on Environmental Policy

Building on the review of marginal analysis in Chapter 2, this chapter explains the application of cost-benefit analysis to major environmental policy initiatives. With an even-handed approach, the chapter presents the concerns of business firms and environmental guardians, discusses the specific marginal gains and losses, and explores the efficient reconciliation of relevant needs and wants. Case studies include congestion pricing and a thorough discussion of tradable emissions permits.

Chapter 13 Natural Resource Management: Renewable Resources

Although many of the chapters in this text pertain to natural resource management, Chapters 13 and 14 have a narrower focus. Chapter 13 introduces a model of renewable resource use that serves as a basis for policy discussions in this and the following chapter.

Chapter 14 Natural Resource Management: Depletable and Replenishable Resources

Models of depletable, recyclable, and renewable resource use appear in a single chapter, in which differences among the treatments can be easily identified and explained. For simplicity and brevity, one representative resource from each group is selected for a case study. Topics include consensus research findings and the optimal size and timing of harvests.

Appendix Intertemporal Allocation and Hotelling's Rule

The Appendix offers a rigorous explanation of optimal allocation across periods and a derivation of Hotelling's rule to supplement the rule's introduction in the chapter.

Chapter 15 Environmental Dispute Resolution

The field of environmental economics harbors many opportunities for disagreement. Liberals and conservatives battle over policy. Businesses and communities battle over growth. Owners of natural resources battle over use restrictions, liability, and conflicting ownership claims. How these disputes are resolved often determines the allocation of natural resources and the state of environment preservation. This chapter emphasizes efficient mechanisms for dispute resolution, including "cake-cutting" techniques, mediation, arbitration, and offer-of-settlement devices.

Chapter 16 Morals and Motivation

At the core of many environmental economics debates are moral issues involving the appropriate treatment of flora, fauna, fellow humans, and future generations of all the above. This chapter considers the motives behind our behavior; in essence, the elements of our utility functions. General ethical theories are followed by narrower discussions of deep ecology, social ecology, and ecofeminism. The chapter concludes with several alternative "tests" for whether particular actions that affect the environment are acceptable.

Acknowledgments

It was my pleasure to work with Lindsey Hall, Simon Holt, Andy Humphries, and Robert Langham on the development of the fourth edition. I am indebted to David Martin, Mark Smith, and Anne Lubbers for valuable discussions. Sarah Howard, Nathan Olsen, John Takach, and Ashley Vinsel provided research assistance. My parents, my wife, and my children are to thank for providing inspiration and practicing patience. For thoughtful comments and checks of accuracy I am grateful to the following reviewers:

Kathleen P. Bell
University of Maine

Allan Collins
West Virginia University

Jay R. Corrigan
Kenyon College

Bob Cunningham
Alma College

Molly Espey
Clemson University

Christina Fader
University of Waterloo

Sue E. Hayes
Sonoma State University

S. Aaron Hegde
California State University, Bakersfield

Andrew T. Hill
Washington College

Joe Kerkvliet
Oregon State University

Rajaram Krishnan
Earlham College

Charles Krusekopf
Austin College

John B. Loomis
Colorado State University

Allan MacNeill
Webster University

Frederic Menz
Clarkson University

Gretchen Mester
University of Oregon

Jeffrey A. Michael
Towson University

Diane K. Monaco
Manchester College

Brian Peterson
Manchester College

Margaret A. Ray
Mary Washington College

George D. Santopietro
Radford University

Eric C. Schuck
Colorado State University

Davis F. Taylor
College of the Atlantic

Kenneth N. Townsend
Hampden-Sydney College

Cees Withagen
VU University Amsterdam

Anonymous reviewers from:
University of Durham (UK)
University of Texas
University of Nevada
Southern Oregon University
Webster College
Bates College

ENVIRONMENTAL ECONOMICS and Natural Resource Management

1 The Big Picture

The motivation to study environmental economics is all around you. From a window you might see trees and grasses that require moderate temperatures and clean water to survive. Your body requires the same, as do the sources of the natural fibers in your clothing, the wood in your desk, the pages in this book, and the food you ate for breakfast. Even the oxygen you breathe comes from plants. It takes 300 to 400 plants of average size to produce enough oxygen to keep you alive.[1] *While the environment sustains your life, you enjoy manufactured goods, electricity, housing, and travel at the environment's expense. Environmental economics is about making wise decisions about trade-offs such as these.*

Natural resources *are those components of nature that humans find useful. Some natural resources, such as trees and fish, can be harvested sustainably with proper management. Others are available for extraction only once. The minerals used to make your frying pan, bicycle, and washing machine come from nonrenewable sources, as do the petroleum-based synthetics in your backpack and shoes. The tools of* ***natural resource management*** *address critical decisions of whether, when, and how to tap supplies of the Earth's raw materials.*

Economists use the goal of efficiency to guide decision making. They ask the question: What would maximize the net benefit to society? Yet the cost-benefit comparisons that can lead to efficiency are often absent or flawed. Pollution costs seldom enter into private decisions about whether to drive another mile or build another factory. The benefits of habitat protection are often neglected in cost-benefit analyses of development projects. And as a matter of law, the costs of implementing some environmental regulations are not weighed against the

1 See www.newton.dep.anl.gov/newton/askasci/1993/biology/bio027.htm.

benefits.[2] The opportunities to improve current approaches, and the environment's broad relevance to individuals, firms, and wildlife, make the study of environmental economics and natural resource management important and exciting. This chapter highlights nine major issues to whet your appetite for the discussions that follow.

Market Failure: Can We Trust the Free Market?

In 1776, Scottish economist Adam Smith wrote that self-interested individuals operating in a free market could achieve efficiency as if guided by an "invisible hand." Given these words from one of the founding fathers of economics, why would anyone want to meddle with the market? Unfortunately, as Smith himself seems to have understood, the conditions required for free-market efficiency are seldom fully met. This section introduces four issues that motivate assistance from the not-so-invisible hands of policymakers.

What you don't know can hurt you.

When producers hold inside information about product-related dangers, consumers may overindulge in risky products. A lack of information can also lead consumers to under-consume products with unrecognized benefits. That's why government agencies step in to require hazard-warning labels on insecticides and teach consumers the benefits of eating vegetables. For such products, consumption closer to the efficient level can result from cautions, education programs, and other forms of information sharing that tend not to arise out of a free market.

Competition underpins efficiency.

The European Commission fined computer-chip maker Intel $1.33 billion for alleged anti-competitive actions and abuse of its market dominance. Why the large fine? Because a lack of competition generally leads to higher prices, lower quality, and smaller quantities. When barriers prevent competitors from entering a market, a small number of firms may become powerful and threaten efficiency. The challenge is for the government to limit market power while promoting innovation and permitting adequate incentives for entrepreneurs.

Side effects matter.

Externalities are effects felt beyond or "external to" the people causing the effects. When individuals decide how many cigarettes to smoke or how many trees to plant in their yards, they may not consider the costs or benefits conveyed on others. This common form of neglect results in too many purchases of goods like cigarettes that cause detrimental *negative externalities*, and too few purchases of goods like trees that generate beneficial *positive externalities*. The environment often bears the burden of inefficiencies that arise due to externalities. In this book you will learn how externality problems can be addressed with taxes, subsidies, and property rights that help people feel for themselves—or *internalize*—the effects of their own behavior.

2 The U.S. Environmental Protection Agency is not permitted to consider implementation costs when determining national ambient air quality standards under the Clean Air Act. See http://supreme.justia.com/us/531/457/.

If someone pays to clean the water, everyone benefits. But who wants to be the one who pays?

Free riders cause the underprovision of public goods.
Public goods are goods whose benefits: (1) can be received by more than one person at a time; and, (2) cannot be kept from people who did not pay for them. Streetlights, TV signals, and military protection are classic examples. Public goods present problems because individuals can *free ride* on the purchases of other people by receiving benefits from goods they did not pay for. As a result, too few public goods are purchased. Many goods and services related to the environment suffer from the same free-rider problem. Consider efforts to remove toxins from rivers and lakes. Large numbers of people benefit from these efforts, regardless of their personal contribution. Free riders would rather have someone else pay to make the water safe, so too few people pitch in for cleanups. In such cases, the government can tax beneficiaries and use the revenue to fund cleanups among other public goods. This textbook elaborates on the threats to free-market efficiency and explains the pros and cons of market intervention.

Waste and Recycling: Where Can We Put It All?

People buy a lot of stuff, so sooner or later there's a lot to throw away. In a typical year, the average child in Australia receives almost $500 worth of toys, and the average Canadian buys $2,900 worth of clothing. Worldwide, consumers purchase $1.5 trillion worth of home furnishings and appliances each year. In many countries including the United States, the number of *landfill* disposal sites is decreasing while the volume of waste is increasing. As disposal sites near cities fill up, waste must be transported greater distances at a higher environmental cost. Beyond that are problems with groundwater contamination from landfills and ash toxicity from waste incineration.

Trash bins in Mexico guide users to sort organic and inorganic items as the first step in coping with large volumes of waste.

Approaches to growing waste problems include incentives for waste reduction and recycling, advances in landfill safety, improved waste-management systems, and efforts to generate energy out of waste. Some solutions come from firms, such as PepsiCo's redesigned water bottle that cut plastic use by 75 million pounds per year. Other solutions come from local governments. Almost 7,100 U.S. communities have adopted *pay-as-you-throw* programs that encourage waste reduction by having people pay by the bag for waste sent to the landfill. Chapter 9 explains more solutions to the mounting waste problem.

Sustainable Development: How Long Can This Last?

Before we decide how to dispose of things we must decide how to make things. Some production processes can be continued long into the future; others cannot. We obtain most of our energy from nonrenewable oil and coal reserves. We use stocks of old growth forests, groundwater, and fertile topsoil at unsustainable rates. We send harmful emissions into the air and water faster than they can dissipate, so they collect and increase in concentration. The unsustainable path of most modern development has inspired attempts to alter that path. For example, the Leadership in Energy and Environmental Design (LEED) rating system provides guidelines for socially responsible building design and acknowledges developers who endeavor to protect the environment.

Economists have developed ways to assess the values of animal species.

Recent innovations in industries that include forestry, mining, cement, transportation, and energy represent progress toward sustainability. But many questions complicate the issue: How much progress is enough? What value should we place on the welfare of others? Should we act, as philosopher John Rawls suggests, so that we would be indifferent between living now or in the future? Our behavior influences the wellbeing of future generations. We must decide the toll we will take on their quality of life.

Biological Diversity: What Is a Flamingo Worth?

Biological diversity, or **biodiversity**, refers to the variety of ecosystems, species, and genetic differences within species. Biodiversity is in conflict with development, which comes at the cost of lost habitat for wildlife.

The advancement of human civilization has ushered in a dramatic increase in the rate of extinctions, now estimated to occur at 100 to 1,000 times the natural or "background" rate of between 1 and 10 extinctions per year. This impels us to consider the value of biological diversity, the value of industrial progress, and the best way to balance our conflicting interests.

Wildlife provides benefits to humans, including natural beauty, recreational opportunities, medicinal cures, and the air we breathe. To use human-centered benefits such as these as the basis for decisions is to take an **anthropocentric** approach. An **ecocentric** approach includes recognition that wildlife has value in and of itself. Proponents of this approach argue that even in the absence of human life, plants and animals are worthy of preservation. Although economists understand both of these bases for decision making, most concentrate on the sufficiently challenging question of what biodiversity is worth to humans, rather than the more daunting task of assessing the value of biodiversity apart from human interests.

Economists have developed primarily anthropocentric techniques for estimating the values of wilderness areas and animal species including everything from slugs to *Homo sapiens*. While more or less imperfect, these methods provide superior alternatives to throwing up our hands and saying we cannot determine the values, which in the past has led policymakers to use values of zero or infinity. Chapter 10 will explain several specific ways to place values on biodiversity.

Environmental Degradation: How Much Pollution Is Too Much?

Under a zero-pollution policy, we couldn't drive accident victims to the hospital, build homes, or produce most goods. In fact, to live is to pollute. Animals, including humans, emit hydrogen (H_2), methane (CH_4), hydrogen sulfide (H_2S), nitrogen (N_2), and carbon dioxide (CO_2) in the processes of breathing, eating, and digesting.

Industrial exhaust systems send CO_2 and other emissions into the atmosphere, contributing to pollution and global climate change. Controversy rages over what levels of pollution are acceptable and what will happen to jobs if tighter controls are instituted. Economic tools help to answer these questions.

Even setting these essential emissions aside, the optimal level of pollution is positive because the benefits from the most important sources of pollution, such as hospitals and basic housing, outweigh the negligible effects of the first few puffs of smoke out of cars and smokestacks.

As we carry industrial development to new levels, the challenge from a societal standpoint is to distinguish areas where further development is appropriate from those where another tree should not fall and another product should not roll off the assembly line. Is there evidence that we have gone too far? Should we conduct further research, or take new action against global climate change and similar threats? Despite apparent confusion among politicians, the answers to these questions are clearer than you might think.

Alternative Energy Sources: Why Aren't They Here?

Over the last half-century, the Internet has connected the world, spaceships have landed on Mars, and computers have found their way into virtually every reasonably affluent home. Yet advancements in alternative energy production have been modest at best. Why isn't there a hybrid car in every garage? Why aren't there solar panels on every rooftop or windmills on more mountaintops? Why did we develop the perfect fat substitute before the perfect fossil fuel substitute? Economic principles help to explain the contrasting growth rates in these industries. Complicating factors include politics, imperfect information, high start-up costs, and the profit-maximizing strategies of firms that compete with clean energy sources. At the same time, there is reason to be optimistic about the future. In the words of Karl R. Rabago, Managing Director of the Rocky Mountain Institute:

Despite the barriers of politics and inertia, the availability of clean-energy technology feeds optimism for increased implementation. Wind power is now the fastest growing sector of power generation, with solar fuel cells close behind. The pictured wind turbines collect energy outside of Lincoln, Nebraska.

> *In spite of all the problems, the growth of clean energy options including generation, efficiency and energy management continues at a brisk if oft-overlooked pace. Wind is the fastest growing sector of generation, with photovoltaics not far behind. Fuel cells for both stationary and mobile applications will become fully commercial before the end of the decade. Thousands of megawatts worth of efficiency have been put to work. The linkage between information technologies and the energy sector is strong and growing. In all, the ground floor for an exciting and clean energy revolution is solid.*[3]

3 Written for this textbook.

Population and Economic Growth: Are We Doomed to Starvation?

Doomsayers have predicted our demise for centuries. In 1798, economist Thomas Malthus heard that the population of the United States was doubling every 25 years. In contrast, he estimated that food supplies would increase by a fixed amount each year. Malthus's famous conclusion was that population growth would out-pace growth in food supplies, meaning that starvation was in our future. Since then, advancements in technology and exploration have spoiled predictions of doom, as the world has produced unprecedented quantities of food, fuels, and all other essentials.

New discoveries and technological improvements aren't the only things that help ward off shortages. The market mechanism increases prices for goods that become short in supply, and higher prices motivate suppliers to find ways to produce more. Higher prices also lead consumers to desire less. Both of these incentives decrease the likelihood of shortages. Of course, sooner or later we must confront the many binding resource constraints of the Earth, and this will force difficult questions on society. How can trends in consumption be reversed? If population control is part of the solution, should it be mandated or self-imposed? What is the ideal population? What role should more-developed countries play in the population-control strategies of less-developed countries? Economists have theories and opinions on each of these weighty questions, some of which might surprise you.

Natural Resource Management: When Should I Harvest My Elms?

Shakespeare said that the world is a stage and we are just players. In some other respects, the world is a farm and we are just farmers. As consumers, voters, or cultivators ourselves, we all influence decisions about whether and when to harvest the Earth's crop of wildlife and its stock of minerals. When farming our vast forests and oceans, we must also decide how many trees and fish to reap, how to bring them to market, and how to reseed the land and waters. Indeed, these issues apply to water itself. Only about 2.5 percent of extractable groundwater is available on a renewable basis. Decisions about these resources must be made in light of their repercussions for current and future generations. This is the task of natural resource management.

Beyond questions of whether, when, and how to harvest natural resources is the issue of how to manage access to resources that are not privately controlled. Harvests of fish from the world's oceans started to decline in the 1990s due to past overfishing, pollution, and inadequate regulation. When those with access to natural resources do not feel the effects of their decisions because they do not own the resources they are depleting, their actions may be inefficient and harmful to society. The challenge is to find ways to provide incentives for everyone to use natural resources responsibly. This can mean limiting access, enacting policies of resource restoration, or creating punishment schemes that surmount the difficulties of monitoring the remote areas where many of our most valued natural resources are. This text presents models of natural resource management and methods for encouraging responsible resource use by those who lack private incentives for compliance.

Environmental Ethics: What Can We Do? What Must We Do? What Should We Do?

Ethical issues are intertwined with many an environmental and natural resource dilemma. It is never easy to place the welfare of society above personal interests. While pollution-control efforts tug on our purse strings, the act of polluting pulls on our moral fiber. Is it ethical to build homes in the remaining wilderness areas? How much trash generation is acceptable? Do we have a moral responsibility to recycle? How much value should we place on sustainable development for the sake of future generations? What right do we have to eliminate species of wildlife? And what ethical issues should we consider when planning our contributions to the planet's population?

Some ethical quandaries stem from uncertainty over the appropriate goal for society. We seek happiness and satisfaction, but what trade-offs should be made between maximizing the total amount of satisfaction in society, equality in satisfaction across individuals, equality of satisfaction across generations, and merit-based distributions of satisfaction? Scholars have also suggested a number of approaches to individual ethical dilemmas, such as whether to purchase material goods that detract from the environment or whether to sell products that may cause harm to consumers. While reading Chapter 16 you will have the opportunity to consider these questions and others of your own, and to apply various morality tests to the dilemmas you face.

Conclusions

A pod of 26 whales beached itself on the coast of Scotland in 2012. Half of the whales died. Similar beachings are common in Australia, the United States, and elsewhere. Among the possible causes is military sonar, which can temporarily deafen these mammals or cause them to surface too rapidly. Despite common misconceptions, economics covers far more than money and applies to myriad environmental issues such as this. Economics provides tools to deal with trade-offs between, for example, the benefits of military training and the possibility of serious harm to marine animals. In this textbook you will learn how economists place values on wildlife, factor in elements of uncertainty, and seek efficient solutions to environmental and natural resource problems.

More broadly, **economics** is the study of the allocation of scarce resources among

Whales and dolphins beach themselves in Marion Bay, Australia. Military sonar and global climate change are among the possible reasons. Economic analysis helps policymakers weigh the costs of noise and air pollution against the benefits of sonar and economic growth.

Photo by Liz Wren, courtesy of the Tasmania Parks and Wildlife Service

competing ends. With most environmental assets being scarce, economics applies to most cases of tension between developmental progress and environmental health. The stakes are high, and mistakes can have profound repercussions.

There are several views on environmental and natural resource policy. Some people accept the status quo and feel it is unnecessary to use natural resources more efficiently. Other people seek lower environmental standards and fewer limits on natural resource depletion, asserting that the problems are exaggerated and that financial resources could be better spent creating jobs or lowering taxes. Still others push for progressive environmentalism. They believe that a lack of foresight could take us so far down a path of environmental neglect that the damage will be regrettable and irreversible. Who is right? This textbook and this course can help you make your own informed decisions about the proper allocation of environmental assets.

This chapter introduced the intrigue and import of environmental and natural resource economics. As you read more, you will discover answers to many of the questions presented here, although these answers tend to spawn new questions: Given optimal pollution levels, how can factories be monitored to prevent excesses? How can improved techniques for natural resource management be implemented? How can we find the self-discipline required to do the right thing? Do not be afraid of new questions; be afraid of not knowing what the important questions are. Deliberate thought and debate will lead to new answers and still more questions, with each round bringing greater levels of understanding and new opportunities to improve the quality of life.

Problems for Review

1. What approaches does your college take to reduce the volume of waste generated on campus? If you could implement one additional waste-reduction policy, what would it be?

2. List five consumer goods that you have purchased recently. For each, note the source of a raw material that went into that good. For example, a computer mouse is made from plastic by the petrochemical industry, which extracts its raw material (oil) from below the Earth's surface.

3. In your opinion, does society take an anthropocentric or an ecocentric view of natural resources when deciding on policies for preservation? Explain which view you think we *should* take and why.

4. What criterion does John Rawls suggest for decisions about how to act? Would you favor limits on gasoline use in the present under this criterion?

5. What is the source of energy for the building you are in or closest to? What barriers prevent more energy from being obtained from clean sources?

6. Is the optimal level of pollution zero? Why or why not?

7. What four broad categories of problems can prevent free markets from allocating resources efficiently?

8. What has prevented the starvation predicted by Thomas Malthus and others?

9. In what ways are we all farmers?

10. Beyond the examples of ethical issues mentioned in this chapter, list two more ethical issues related to the environment that you face on a regular basis.

websurfer's challenge

Find five websites devoted to the environment (not including those listed under Internet Resources in this book). For each site write down:

1. The name or URL.
2. An environmental insight you learned from the site.
3. A connection between the insight listed for item 2 and environmental economics as discussed in this chapter.

Internet Resources

Australian Department of the Environment, Water, Heritage and the Arts:
www.environment.gov.au

Environmental and Natural Resource Economics News, Opinion and Analysis:
www.env-econ.net

Environment Canada:
www.ec.gc.ca

Environmental Education Station:
web.centre.edu/econed

European Environment Agency:
www.eea.europa.eu

Indian Ministry of Environment and Forests:
www.envfor.nic.in

New Zealand Ministry for the Environment:
www.mfe.govt.nz

Singapore Ministry of the Environment and Water Resources:
http://app.mewr.gov.sg

South African Department of Environmental Affairs and Tourism:
www.environment.gov.za/

U.S. Environmental Protection Agency:
www.epa.gov

Further Reading

Anderson, David A. *Treading Lightly: The Joy of Conservation, Moderation, and Simple Living*. Danville, KY: Pensive Press, 2009. A collection of specific solutions to resource scarcity that minimize the associated trade-offs.

Dietz, Rob, and Dan O'Neill. *Enough Is Enough: Building a Sustainable Economy in a World of Finite Resources*. San Francisco: Berrett-Koehler, 2013. A deep discussion of what happens when markets fail and what can be done about it.

Smith, Adam. *The Wealth of Nations*. New York: Prometheus Books, 1991. One of the books that started it all—the study of economics, that is. Smith discusses the efficiency of markets as mentioned in this chapter.

Stavins, Robert N. (ed.). *Economics of the Environment: Selected Readings*. New York: Norton, 2012. A collection of 17 new papers on many of the issues introduced in this chapter, written by contemporary stars of environmental economics.

Van Kooten, G. Cornelis, and Erwin H. Bulte. *The Economics of Nature: Managing Biological Assets*. Malden, MA: Blackwell, 2000. Provides a rigorous approach to environmental economics for those who want to see the calculus.

Phnomphone Sirimongkhon

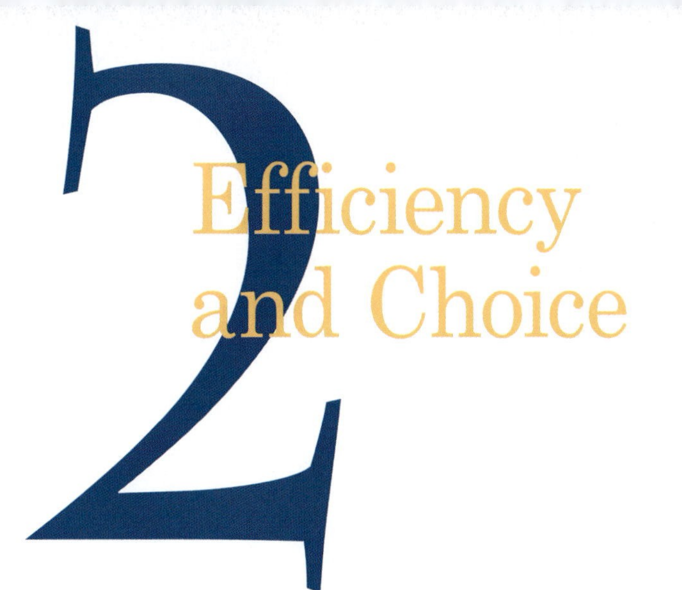

2 Efficiency and Choice

Even the best things in life—hikes in the woods, chocolate consumption, kisses—end voluntarily when they do not end by necessity. Naturally, it's all a matter of economics. A golden rule of economics is that every action should continue until the additional benefit of going on falls below the additional cost. Adherence to this rule, when all additional (or marginal*) costs and benefits are measured accurately,[1] yields the largest net benefit from the activity. This rule is appropriate for decisions ranging from when to wake up in the morning to how many toxic industrial sites to clean up. The implications and applications of this rule are striking; the same cannot be said about its frequency of use in the policy arena. This chapter reviews many of the tools of marginal analysis, supply and demand, consumer choice, and expected value calculations. Familiarize yourself with these concepts because they will appear at the core of many of our discussions.*

Surprisingly to some, economists see beyond money in their calculations of efficiency. Hikers, chocolate lovers, and kissers don't go on hiking, eating, or kissing forever, but the costs and benefits they weigh as they decide when to stop may have little to do with money. While soaking up the joys of acceptance and affection, kissers may also be thinking about the increasing likelihood of a roommate entering the dorm room, about their own fear of commitment, about not appearing too eager, or about the large and growing opportunity cost of not being able to spend the time studying environmental economics. Of course, they may also get caught up in the moment and neglect some of the costs. That's a problem in environmental economics too! Economic models of efficiency aren't all about money.

1 Measurement failures and omissions are addressed in Chapter 3 and later chapters.

Some models consider how individuals maximize **utility**—*an abstract measure of happiness. Others consider* **social welfare**, *which is the collective well-being of society. These models can account for the importance of joy, sorrow, love, guilt, spite, disease, free time, and anything else of interest or ill favor. In fact, to omit any significant influence on happiness, monetary or otherwise, would be to jeopardize the integrity of the models.*

Scrutinizing Efficiency

Italian economist Vilfred Pareto provided a well-accepted criterion for efficiency: **Pareto efficiency** is achieved if no one can be made better off without making at least one person worse off. Suppose you have two cans of soda and no pizza, and your friend has four slices of pizza and no soda. If you would both be happier with one can of soda and two slices of pizza, the initial allocation is not Pareto efficient. An exchange of one of your sodas for two of your friend's pizza slices would be mutually beneficial. If no additional change could make at least one of you better off without making the other worse off, you have achieved Pareto efficiency!

An efficient outcome maximizes the net gain for society, but the achievement of efficiency implies nothing about what happens to that gain. There are differing schools of thought about the objective when dividing benefits. For example, the **utilitarian** goal is to maximize the sum of everyone's utility. The **egalitarian** goal is to divide benefits evenly among members of society. And the **Rawlsian** goal is to maximize the utility of the least-well-off person. Efficiency alone does not ensure any such outcome. In theory, the maximized gain can be divided to satisfy any of these objectives. What happens in practice is another matter.

Suppose there are two possible sites for a new landfill, one in a low-income area and one in a wealthy area. The property needed to build the landfill in the low-income area would cost $300,000; the property needed for the landfill in the wealthy area would cost $2 million. There are presently 30 families living on each of the sites, all of whom would need to move elsewhere if their site were chosen for the landfill. Near each site are an additional 100 families that would not be relocated, but would face risks of groundwater contamination, property devaluation, odor, flying debris, and ugliness. If the landfill provides benefits that exceed the associated costs, and if the price of the land accurately reflects the cost to society of using that land, then the net gain is maximized by placing the landfill where the land has the lowest price.

The decision of where to place the landfill might not be as clear-cut as it seems. A careful assessment of the best solution for society will include at least two other considerations. First, there is nothing about the *creation* of net benefits that causes the benefits to be allocated so as to satisfy societal goals. For example, the 30 relocated families might not receive appropriate compensation for their emotional and financial costs of moving. Those who are not relocated might not be compensated for their unsavory neighbor and for related losses in property value.

The NIMBY (not in my backyard) effect makes it difficult to find locations for new landfills. Economists seek efficient solutions that maximize the net gain for society.

And most of the benefits from the landfill might go to the people in the wealthy area, including the owners of the sanitation companies that send their trash to the landfill in the low-income area. If the goal is to provide equitable outcomes for the broader wellbeing of society, a second step of *distributing* the benefits must follow. Economists generally focus on efficiency and leave decisions about equity to others. A good policymaker understands that both equity and efficiency are important to social welfare.

A second consideration is that the property valuations are driven by the incomes and wealth of the people interested in living in these areas. Although some people who desire to live in the wealthy area might pay far more for property in that area than anyone would pay for property in the low-income area, it is not necessarily the case that the loss of happiness or "utility" as the result of relocation would be larger for the wealthy people than for the low-income people. It is possible that people in the low-income area receive much of their happiness from the history, community, and unique geographical features associated with their location, and not from anything money can buy. If the low-income people derive greater utility from their property than the wealthy people gain from the wealthy area, and if the amount of money the wealthy people are willing to pay is inadequate to compensate the low-income people for their relatively large losses, placement of the landfill in the low-income area will not maximize social welfare.

Another caveat about the search for efficiency as commonly conceived is that, although it is not all about money, it does tend to be centered around people.

In other words, efficiency targets are anthropocentric. Natural resources and the environment are considered in calculations of efficiency, but generally in terms of their value to humans. For example, U.S. Fish and Wildlife Service officials considered human interest in the endangered San Francisco garter snake when placing limits on the expansion of the local train service, but they did not consider the snakes' interests in snake preservation, in rail lines, or in humans for that matter.[2] If they did, the present tallies of snakes, rail lines, and humans would be quite different. Given conflicting interests, humans tend to do that which is best for humans. This isn't surprising, but it is important to understand when seeking context for outcomes described as "efficient," "optimal," or "the best possible."

Despite these limitations, most economists embrace the goal of efficiency. While efficiency guidelines do not resolve the equity question, they can accomplish the important first step of maximizing the size of the "pie" to be divided. The landfill example showed that practical applications of efficiency may have more to do with maximizing net monetary benefits than utility. However, the virtual impossibility of comparing utility across people complicates more direct attempts to maximize utility. For example, if I say I'm really happy and you say you're really happy, do we really know that we are equally happy? In the landfill story, it may be impossible to determine which group would lose more utility if forced to move. As discussed in later chapters, applications of efficiency are also limited by the difficulty of measuring all of the costs and benefits associated with an action. Nonetheless, there are many situations in which adequate data are available. And while efficiency criteria tend to be anthropocentric, it may be only fitting because our goals tend to be equally self-serving.

Cost–Benefit Analysis

Media reports lamenting drops in the gross domestic product or celebrating increases in the number of housing starts can leave the impression that boundless increases in production and development would necessarily be a good thing. Addressing environmental issues with the goal of economic efficiency improves upon more simplistic views that production should be maximized or pollution should be minimized. The best outcome for society is neither the highest possible level of production nor zero pollution. An all-out effort to make as much output as possible would decrease social welfare because output maximization at all costs would result in smoke-blackened skies, failing health, the end of leisure time, and the eradication of wildlife. But some pollution is better than none. Chapter 1 explained that to live is to pollute. No food, shelter, or medicine could be produced without creating some pollution.

To determine whether contemplated pollution, production, or anything else is worthwhile, the benefits can be weighed against the costs. The U.S. Environmental Protection Agency (EPA) estimated that the benefits of Clean Air Act regulations between 1990 and 2020 will be $2 trillion and the costs will be

2 See Wilson (2000).

$65 billion.[3] If this Act were an all-or-nothing proposition, we would want to take it all because the benefits outweigh the costs. Some decisions are about *how much* of an activity to engage in. For example, how many trees should be harvested? How much carbon dioxide should be released? And how many regulations should be added to the Clean Air Act? For decisions about how much, economists advise comparisons between the *additional* benefits and costs of each additional unit. The additional cost of one more unit is called the **marginal benefit** (*MB*); the additional cost of one more unit is called the **marginal cost** (*MC*). If the marginal benefit of a unit exceeds the marginal cost, that unit is worthwhile. Crandall, Rueter, and Steger (1996) noted that the marginal benefits of incremental policies within the Clean Air Act were not compared with the marginal costs in the EPA's initial cost-benefit analysis of the Act. The EPA (Brenner and Morgenstern, 1996) responded that "there is no doubt that a marginal analysis of the benefits and costs of the act, perhaps even on a provision-by-provision basis, would have been more informative than an analysis of the total benefits and costs." Subsequent Regulatory Impact Analyses evaluated the costs and benefits of individual regulations within the Clean Air Act and found them to be worthwhile.

With the appropriate data, the comparisons of marginal benefits and marginal costs that constitute **marginal analysis** can be used to determine the efficient stopping point for all sorts of activities. Consider the decision of how many whales to "harvest" from the sea each year. The International Whaling Commission

Photo by David Ellifrit, courtesy of the Center for Whale Research, www.whaleresearch.com

These orcas promote tourism. The global whale-watching industry generates over $2 billion in revenues and employs about 13,000 workers.

3 See www.epa.gov/oar/sect812/prospective2.html.

Figure 2.1
An Efficient Whale Harvest

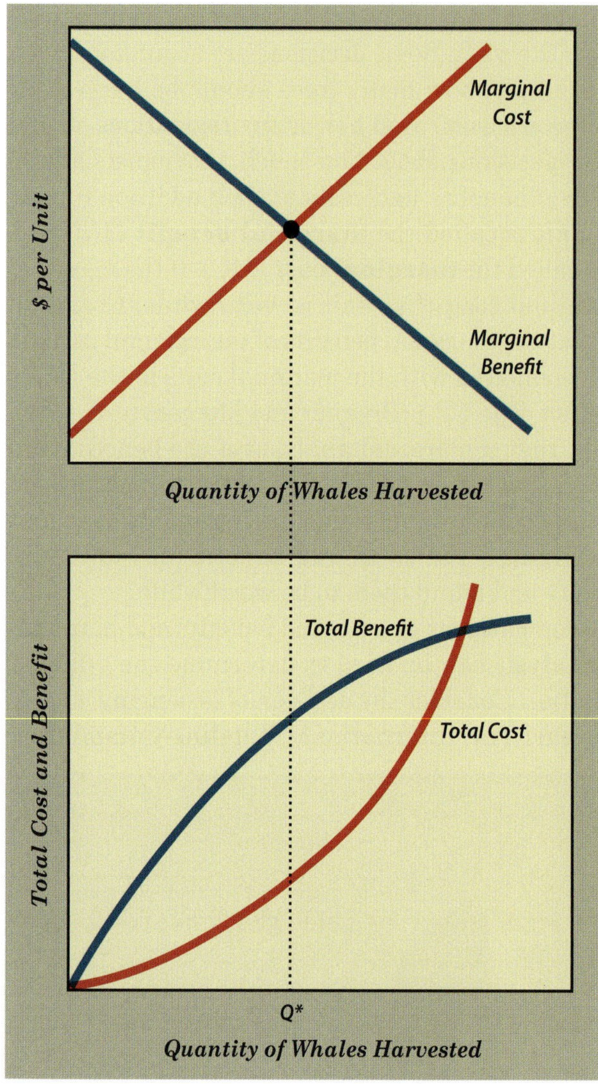

Efficiency is achieved if whales are harvested until the marginal cost equals the marginal benefit. An efficient whale harvest maximizes the net benefit, which is the difference between the total benefit and the total cost.

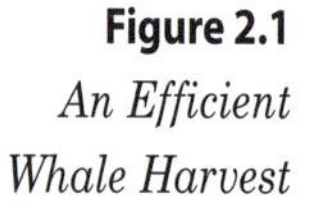

governs whaling around the world, and many countries, including Norway, the United States, and Japan, permit limited whaling. The marginal benefit from the first few whales harvested is high, as they allow for scientific research and the subsistence of native cultures that rely on whaling. The marginal benefit from harvesting whales declines as labs get enough research subjects, native cultures get plenty of whale oil to last through the winter, and whale meat lovers are satiated. The blue line in the top graph of Figure 2.1 illustrates the decreasing marginal benefit from "harvested" whales.

As the whale population decreases, potential costs include the loss of genetic variation and herd viability, and the associated risk of extinction. Expanded whale harvests increase losses to future generations of whale processors and eaters, present and future generations of whale watchers, and workers in the multibillion-dollar whale-watching industry, among others. Another cost involves imbalance in the ecosystem. Some whales eat large quantities of squid and fish.[4] The loss of a few whales would not break the food chain, but excessive whale harvests could leave populations of whale prey unchecked. An overabundance of the types of fish that whales eat could lead to the decimation of smaller marine life that those fish eat. In turn, other species that eat the same smaller marine

4 This is particularly true of toothed whales. Baleen whales eat small fish, krill, and plankton. See: www.enchantedlearning.com/subject/whales/anatomy/diet.shtml.

organisms would face inadequate food supplies, and as each domino falls, so does the next.

When legal whaling activity reaches a significant volume, poaching problems ignite because the limited legal trade in whale meat provides a cover for illegal whaling activities. If there were no legal trade in whale meat, any whale meat discovered would clearly be illegal. As more and more legal whale meat enters the markets, shipments of whale meat appear less and less suspect, and black-market whale exporters are more likely to succeed with large-scale activities. In each of these examples, the costs associated with the marginal whale harvest grow as more whales are harvested. This increasing marginal cost of harvested whales is illustrated by the marginal cost curve in Figure 2.1.

Types of Efficiency

The equation of marginal cost and marginal benefit forms the basis for several specific types of efficiency. What constitutes cost and benefit differs depending on who is making a decision. Efficiency for firms typically means maximizing profit. The marginal benefit to a firm is marginal revenue—the additional revenue received by selling one more unit of a good. Firms equate their marginal revenue with their marginal cost of production to find the profit-maximizing level of output. Notice in Figure 2.1 that marginal benefit equals marginal cost at Q^*,the same quantity at which total benefit and total cost are the furthest apart. For a firm, producing at Q^* means producing where the difference between total revenue and total cost is as large as possible, and that difference represents profit. The marginal benefit for individuals is **marginal utility**, the additional utility received from one more unit. Like the marginal benefit of harvesting whales, the marginal utility received from most goods diminishes as consumption increases, because additional units serve decreasing needs and wants. Individuals should continue each activity until the value of marginal utility equals the marginal cost.

For an economy to achieve efficiency, it must answer three fundamental questions: "What will be produced?"; "What resources will be employed?"; and "Who will receive the final goods and services?" This section describes the associated types of efficiency. The appendix to this chapter provides a more rigorous approach to these issues and explains why, in a competitive market filled with rational, utility-maximizing consumers and profit-maximizing firms, economic theory predicts that all three types of efficiency will be achieved.

What Goods and Services Should Be Produced?

Our deeper foray into efficiency begins with the question of what goods and services to produce given the available resources. **Allocative efficiency** or **output efficiency** is achieved when the available inputs are allocated to make the socially optimal mix of outputs. Figure 2.2 illustrates a **production possibilities frontier** (PPF)—a locus of output combinations that can be produced when all inputs are used efficiently. In this two-good model, allocative efficiency is achieved by selecting society's most favored combination of the two goods among all of the combinations along the frontier.

Consider the set of inputs—land, labor, and capital[5]—that could be allocated either to create snowmobile paths or to provide bear habitat in the national parks. The creation of snowmobile paths can require the clearing and grooming of trails and the construction of toilet facilities, shelters, and parking areas. Successful bear protection involves not only land, but preliminary research, the closing of campgrounds, the formation of planning groups, and the development of interactive computer models.[6]

Note that bears do not hibernate the way that, for example, hedgehogs and ground squirrels do. Bears go into a relatively light sleep that makes them particu-

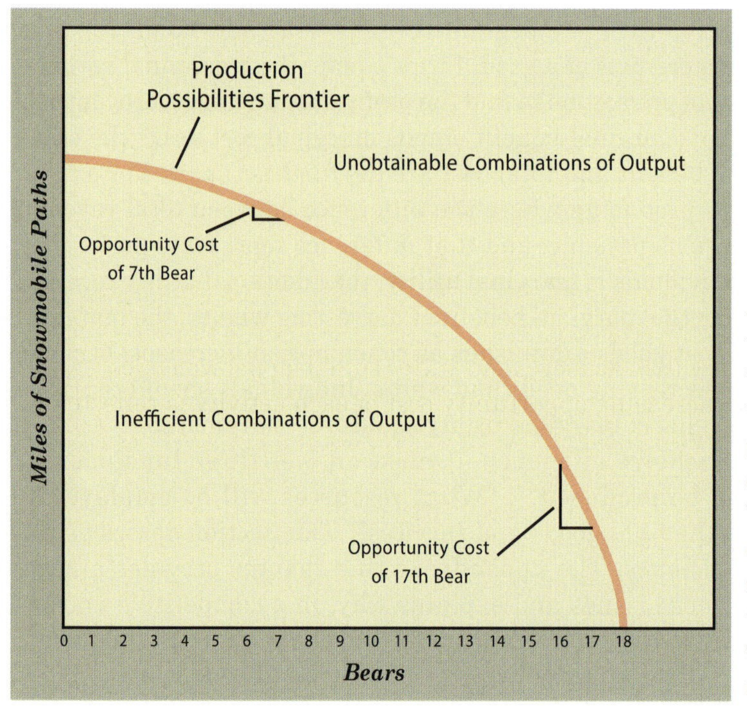

Figure 2.2
A Production Possibilities Frontier

A production possibilities frontier represents all the combinations of two goods that can be provided using every available input efficiently. The opportunity cost of each good increases as the quantity increases due to the use of more resources that are specialized for making the other good.

5 Capital is equipment, machines, and other manufactured goods used in the production of goods and services.

6 See www.canadianrockies.net/Grizzly/sci_pol1.html.

larly vulnerable to disturbance. Noise from nearby snowmobiles can cause a bear to burn critical stores of energy, lose its cubs, or abandon its den.[7] Difficult decisions must be made about the amount of land, ranger time, and capital resources to devote to snowmobiles and bears among other forms of wildlife. In the United States, 28 national parks in the lower 48 states and all of Alaska's national parks devote resources to snowmobiles. Bears are also common in many national parks.

In the process of providing snowmobile paths, opportunity costs will be minimized by starting with resources that are better suited for snowmobiles than for bears. The first land designated for snowmobile paths will be far from rugged bear country, and might have existing hiking trails with little need for maintenance and infrastructure. Likewise, the first land set aside for bears will be in forested backcountry where rocks and streams make life difficult for snowmobilers but wonderful for bears. The opportunity cost of each good will increase as more territory is converted from one type of use to the other. Each additional mile of snowmobile path must encroach into increasingly pristine wilderness areas, displacing more bears and requiring more labor and capital to clear trails and install infrastructure. Likewise, additional bear habitat comes at an increasing opportunity cost, as more land better suited for snowmobiles is used for bears instead. The increasing opportunity cost of each activity is reflected in the shape of the production possibilities frontier. Looking again at Figure 2.2, notice the steady increase in the miles of snowmobile path lost (the vertical drop) per bear as the number of bears increases along the PPF, as illustrated for the seventh and seventeenth bear. Going in the other direction along the PPF, the number of bears lost per mile of snowmobile path grows as the path length increases.

Society's allocation of resources between two goods is efficient when the rate at which we would willingly trade one good for the other equals the rate at which available inputs and technology allow us to trade one for the other as indicated

7 See www.nrmsc.usgs.gov/products/03PODRUZ.PDF.

reality check

The Efficiency of Drugs, Sex, and Partying Until You Puke

How common are applications of efficiency criteria in the real world? They're out there, but not everywhere. Sometimes marginal analysis is difficult to carry out because there is little basis for the estimation of marginal cost and marginal benefit. For example, a crime such as parking illegally can be efficient if the benefit of making it to an important interview exceeds the cost of the likely punishment. However, criminals often overestimate the efficient level of crime due to ignorance of the repercussions of their behavior, heat-of-the-moment decisions, perceptions of invincibility, and drug-induced irrationality (see Anderson, 2002). Sexual activity sometimes exceeds the efficient level for similar reasons, contributing to the 19 million new cases of sexually transmitted diseases and the nearly 3 million unwanted pregnancies in the United States each year. Addictions to drugs, sex, food, or anything else can also result in the neglect of cost-benefit analysis. Yet addictions may not always be irrational. Economists including Gary Becker and Kevin Murphy (1988) discuss the possibility of rational addiction.

Sometimes marginal costs are understood firsthand but quickly forgotten. You may have heard people say "never again" in the midst of experiencing the marginal cost of mountain climbing, throwing up due to alcohol consumption, or giving birth to a child. For better or worse, the same people are often found paying the marginal cost again, despite their earlier assertions that it exceeded the marginal benefit.

At times, the absence of cost-benefit analysis can be deliberate. In 2001 the U.S. Supreme Court upheld federal air-quality standards, which, in accordance with the Clean Air Act of 1970, do not take compliance costs into account. The quest for economic efficiency is sometimes imperfect, and sometimes absent. Nonetheless, many economists think efficiency is the best target among the available alternatives.

by the slope of the production possibilities frontier. If these rates are not equal, society can achieve a higher level of satisfaction by reallocating some resources to more of one or the other good. For instance, suppose that at our current position on the PPF, one fewer mile of path would free up enough resources to provide habitat for three bears, and that one mile of snowmobile path makes society as happy as two bears. By creating one fewer mile of path, we could gain the two bears needed to maintain our level of happiness, plus one more bear, leaving us better off. Conversely, if giving up five bears would make us as happy as one mile of path, and moving along our PPF we could give up five bears and gain two miles of path, then we should give up five bears and gain two miles of path—more than enough to be as well off as before. These adjustments along the PPF should continue until the rate at which we are willing to substitute one good for another equals the feasible rate of substitution given our production possibilities, at which point allocative efficiency is achieved.

With What Resources Should Goods and Services Be Produced?

With an efficient allocation of resources, it is not possible to produce more of one good or service without producing less of another. The attainment of this goal is referred to as **productive efficiency** or **technical efficiency**. Productive efficiency is necessary to achieve a position on the production possibilities frontier. Without productive efficiency, an economy finds itself at a point below its production possibilities frontier, missing opportunities to make more of either or both goods without giving up any of either good.

Hydroponic tomatoes are grown without soil.

Using hydroponic techniques, plants can be grown without soil. The plants are given the water and nutrients they require while the roots rest in a growing medium such as perlite, vermiculite, coconut fiber, gravel, sand, or air. While conserving on soil, hydroponic farming does require the use of greenhouses and workers. Suppose that at the current level of hydroponic tomato cultivation, output would be unchanged if three workers were removed and one additional greenhouse were added. The number of tomatoes grown would remain the same because the easing of space constraints with the added greenhouse would make up for the smaller number of workers. In orchid production, on the other hand, suppose the same number of orchids could be grown with one fewer greenhouse and one more worker. Assuming that workers and greenhouses are transferable between tomato and orchid propagation, the exchange of one tomato worker for one orchid greenhouse would allow more tomatoes to be grown with no loss of orchids. The new orchid worker would exactly make up for the loss of a greenhouse, and the new tomato greenhouse would make up for the loss of *three* workers, whereas only *one* was lost. The tomato producers would then have two more workers than are needed to maintain the current production level. The two additional workers could continue to produce tomatoes and thereby increase production. Alternatively, the two workers could be allocated to the production of orchids to increase orchid production, or they could be split between the two industries to produce more of *both* goods. Given these opportunities for gains without losses, the initial allocation of resources led to a point within the production possibilities frontier and did not achieve productive efficiency because more of one or both goods could be produced without making less of either good.

As with orchids and tomatoes, most goods and services can be produced with a variety of input combinations. Clothing can be hand sewn or machine sewn. A road through the forest can be forged by many workers wielding machetes, a few workers operating bulldozers, or various combinations of these inputs. In every case, productive efficiency can be improved if the rate at which one input can be substituted for another differs among producers. The appendix to this chapter explains how, according to economic theory, profit-maximizing decisions by individual firms will result in productive efficiency across all firms and products.

Who Will Receive the Final Products?

If the right mix of goods and services is produced with the right combination of inputs, the final efficiency hurdle is to get the output to the right consumers. **Distributive efficiency** is achieved when no allocation of goods or services could make anyone better off without making someone worse off. As with the other types of efficiency, distributive efficiency comes down to a comparison of trade-offs. Suppose we've made medicines to treat malaria and tuberculosis (TB)—diseases that kill over a million people each year—and distributed them between Kenya and Tanzania. If consumers in Kenya are willing to exchange 50 malaria treatments for one TB treatment, and consumers in Tanzania are willing to exchange 100 malaria treatments for one TB treatment, both countries can be made better off by an exchange of one TB treatment from Kenya for a quantity of malaria treatments from Tanzania that exceeds 50 but falls short of 100. For example, if 75 malaria treatments from Tanzania were exchanged for a TB treatment from Kenya, the Tanzanians would give up 25 fewer malaria treatments than what the TB treatment is worth to them, and the Kenyans would receive 25 more malaria treatments than what the TB treatment is worth to them.

As Tanzanians receive more TB medicine and lose malaria medicine in the process of exchange, their willingness to pay for TB medicine will decrease. In Kenya, with more malaria medicine and less TB medicine, the willingness to pay for TB medicine will increase. Mutually beneficial exchange can continue until the number of malaria treatments each country would exchange for a TB treatment is the same for each country, at which point distributive efficiency is achieved. The appendix to this chapter explains distributive efficiency in greater detail.

Supply and Demand

Supply and demand curves are the cornerstones of economic modeling. What's so special about these lines? For starters, under the right conditions, supply reflects marginal cost, demand reflects marginal benefit, and allocative efficiency is achieved at the market equilibrium where the quantity supplied equals the quantity demanded. This section provides a brief overview of supply and demand curves and highlights their role in the story of efficiency.

A **demand curve** represents the relationship between the price of a good or service and the quantity demanded within a given period. Figure 2.3 illustrates Eric's demand curve for pads of recycled notebook paper. Because a first pad of paper would give Eric $5 worth of utility, his demand curve has a height of $5 at the quantity of one. Eric would receive $3 worth of marginal utility from a second pad, so $3 is the height of his demand curve at the quantity of two. Similarly for each unit, the height of his demand curve is determined by the largest amount he would be willing to pay for that pad of paper.

If the price of pads of recycled paper is $6, Eric will buy zero pads, because even the first one is only worth $5 to him. If the price is $4.50, he will purchase one and receive $0.50 worth of **consumer surplus**, which is what economists call the difference between the most a consumer would pay for a purchase and the actual amount paid. If the price is $2.50, Eric will purchase two units, because each of the first two units is worth more to him than the price. His consumer surplus with a price of $2.50 will be $5.00 – $2.50 = $2.50 for the first pad, plus $3.00 – $2.50 = $0.50 for the second pad, for a total of $3.00. In general, to find the quantity Eric would purchase at any given price, begin by drawing a horizontal price line with the height of the price, as shown in Figure 2.3 for a price of $2.50. Then draw a vertical line down from the intersection of the price line and the demand curve to the quantity axis to find the quantity. Consumer surplus is the area below the demand curve and above the price line.

The market demand curve for pads of recycled notebook paper holds the same information for all the consumers in the market that the individual demand curve does for Eric. It indicates the total number of pads that would be sold at each price, and for each quantity its height is the number of dollars' worth of marginal utility that the last pad would provide to some consumer. The market demand curve is found by adding all of the individual demand curves horizontally, meaning that at each price, the quantities demanded by each of the individuals in the market

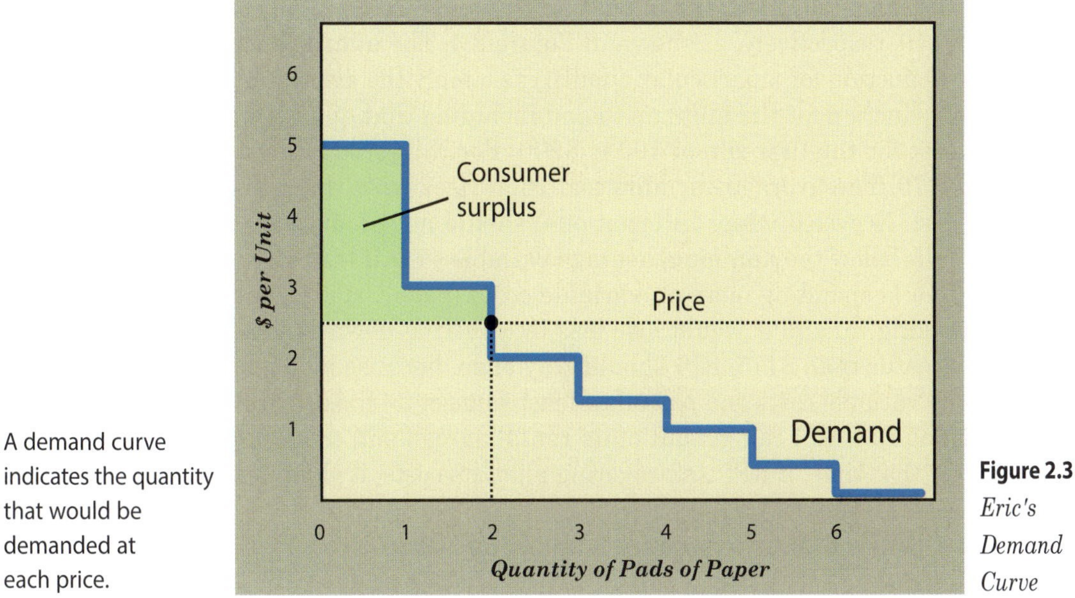

A demand curve indicates the quantity that would be demanded at each price.

Figure 2.3 *Eric's Demand Curve*

Figure 2.4 *RPI's Supply Curve*

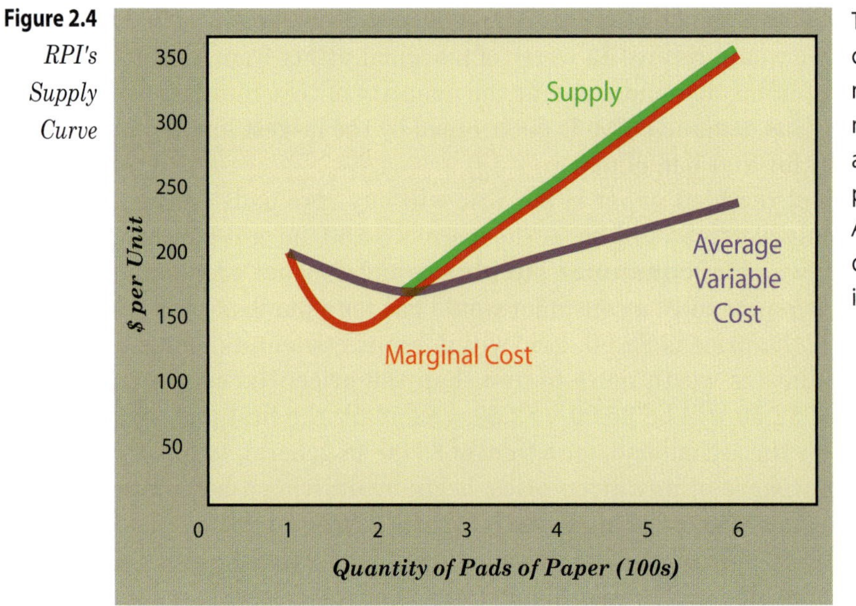

The supply curve for a competitive firm is the marginal cost curve above minimum average variable cost (*AVC*). When price falls below minimum *AVC*, the firm should shut down immediately to cut its losses.

are added up to find the total quantity demanded in the market. Suppose Eric and Margaret are the only consumers in the market, and at a price of $2.50, Eric demands two pads and Margaret demands three. The market demand at that price is 2 + 3 = 5 pads.

The **supply curve** indicates the relationship between the price of a good or service and the quantity supplied within a given period. Suppose that Recycled Paper International (RPI) pays a fixed rent of $1,000 per week for its manufacturing plant. Recycled notebook paper is made in runs of 100 pads at a time, and the marginal costs of the first six runs are $200, $150, $200, $250, $300, and $350, respectively, as shown in Figure 2.4. The **average variable cost** (*AVC*) of production for a particular quantity is simply the average of the marginal costs of production for the units up to and including that quantity. The average variable cost for the first run of 100 is $200. For the second run it is ($200 + $150)/2 = $175. The average variable cost then rises with the ever-increasing marginal cost. Recycled Paper International should not produce at all if the market price falls below the minimum average variable cost. If the price per 100 is below $175, RPI is spending more on variable costs (paper, spiral binders, labor) than it is taking in, and it would lose less by shutting down immediately. If the price is greater than $175, RPI should stay open, because by doing so it can cover all of its variable costs and pay off at least some of its fixed rental cost of $1,000. In the long run, RPI can get out of its rental agreement, so all of its costs are variable. At that time, if RPI isn't covering all of its costs, it should shut down to minimize losses. (May RPI RIP.)

If RPI chooses to produce at all in this competitive market, it should produce

When the market is in equilibrium, the marginal benefit equals the marginal cost. The market equilibrium is thus efficient *if* all marginal costs and benefits are included and measured accurately.

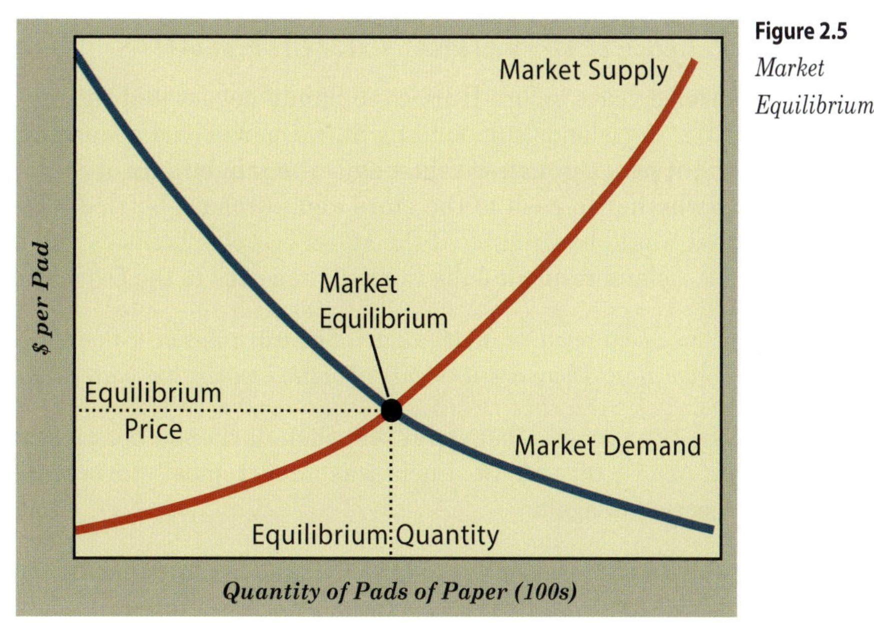

Figure 2.5 *Market Equilibrium*

until the marginal cost rises to equal the market price. For example, if the market price is $2.25 per pad ($225 per hundred), RPI should produce the first three runs, all of which bring in a price in excess of the marginal cost. This difference between the price and the marginal cost is called **producer surplus**. RPI should not produce the fourth run, which has a marginal cost of $250 and brings in $225. Thus, for a competitive firm, the supply curve that indicates the most that will be produced at any given price is coincident with the marginal cost curve above minimum average variable cost. The market supply curve is found by adding all of the individual firm supply curves horizontally, meaning that at each price, the quantities supplied by each of the firms in the market are added up to find the total market supply.

Monopolies do not have a supply curve, because rather than taking the market price as given, they charge as much as the market demand will allow for the quantity that equates marginal cost and marginal revenue. Since a supply curve indicates one particular quantity that would be produced at each price, and the quantity a monopoly would produce for a particular price changes when the demand curve changes, one cannot pin down a supply curve for a monopoly.

Market equilibrium occurs where market supply equals market demand, as shown in Figure 2.5. Knowing that the demand curve represents the dollars' worth of marginal utility gained from each additional unit, and the supply curve represents the marginal cost of each unit, we can now share Adam Smith's glee in discovering that the market equilibrium brings marginal benefit and marginal cost together to yield an efficient level of output (barring market failure, as discussed in Chapters 1 and 3).

Expected-Value Calculations

Twelve years before Hurricane Sandy devastated the eastern United States in 2012, the islands surrounding St. Lucia received a warning that Hurricane Joyce might pass through within a day. The inhabitants of St. Lucia faced the decision of whether to rush to the store and purchase bottled water and other supplies that would be valuable if the storm crippled utilities and supply routes. At 6:50 A.M., island resident Julie Connolly reported to the Caribbean Hurricane Network:

> *St. Lucia remains in denial, with no warnings or watches issued as of Saturday morning. There is still plenty of bottled water and batteries in the store.*

The sky turned a beautiful red, then darkened before scattered showers swept in. As of 8:00 A.M., St. Lucia was on a tropical storm watch. At 8:30 A.M., Julie reported in again:

> *Not many visible preparations being made here on the island, but it is early yet.*

Stores closed. Prepared or not, people would have to live with their decisions.

The citizens of St. Lucia waited behind boarded windows to learn the verdict on Joyce's visit. By midday, the clouds had parted and the sun sparkled through. Hurricane Joyce passed south of St. Lucia with only minimal impact on the island. At 12:30 P.M., Julie shared the good news:

> *It is another beautiful sunny day here. Looks like lucky St. Lucia will continue its streak of missing storms. Now, what to do with all this bottled water!?!*

This section describes how to find the expected value of a course of action that could have several different outcomes. Storms may or may not make landfall, tropical species may or may not hold the remedies for long-fought diseases, levees may or may not prevent waterfront homes from falling to floods, and indeed, few things in life are certain. We must often base our decisions on estimated probabilities and expected values.

Returning to Julie of St. Lucia, suppose that upon weighing the projections of meteorologists, past experience, and the unfolding story in the skies, Julie estimated a 5 percent chance that all supply lines would be cut by the storm and she wouldn't have access to running water for a week, a 15 percent chance that only minor supply lines would be cut and she wouldn't have running water for a day, and an 80 percent chance that the storm would not harm the supply lines. It would be worth $1,000 to Julie to avoid the loss of water for a week. Without water, she and her family would be desperate for a drink, and unable to cook, clean, flush toilets, provide for pets, and so on. For similar reasons, Julie would be willing to pay $100 to avoid the relatively minor loss of water for a day.

To find the expected value of a course of action, add, for each possible outcome, the estimated probability of that outcome multiplied by the value of that outcome:

reality check

How Much Is That Animal Worth?

Chapter 10 discusses the need for policymakers to include the value of wild animals in cost-benefit and expected-value calculations. Automakers must estimate the value of *Homo sapiens* when conducting expected-value calculations for safety devices. If lives were to be saved at any cost, a fleet of heavily armored tanks would not suffice for typical automobile customers because more money could always be spent to reduce the number of traffic casualties further. During the Iraq war, with roadside bombs killing large numbers of personnel, some of the military vehicles were not outfitted with life-saving armor that cost around $75,000 per vehicle. If lives were worth, say, $1 trillion, a modification that had a one-in-one-billion chance of saving a life would have an expected value of $1,000. Would you buy it? The fact that many consumers are unwilling to pay amounts less than $1,000 for features like antilock brakes and side-impact air bags that offer a greater than one-in-one-billion chance of saving lives suggests that people do place a finite value on life, even when it is their own.

Automakers have gotten into trouble by underestimating the cost of accidents resulting from the omission of safety devices. The most famous case involves a decision by the Ford Motor Company in the 1970s not to equip its car called the *Pinto* with metal baffles or rubber bladders that would have cost between $1 and $11. The parts would have prevented hundreds of burns and deaths caused by fuel tanks that ruptured in rear-end collisions. In the expected-value calculations used to decide that the part was not worth its cost, Ford used a $200,000 figure for the value of life, and $67,000 for the value of a serious burn injury. In 1978, when a jury awarded $128 million to a severely burned 16-year-old boy, Ford learned that its calculations had been as faulty as its fuel tanks.

$$\text{Expected Value} = \begin{pmatrix}\text{Probability}\\ \text{of Outcome 1}\end{pmatrix}\begin{pmatrix}\text{Value of}\\ \text{Outcome 1}\end{pmatrix} + \begin{pmatrix}\text{Probability}\\ \text{of Outcome 2}\end{pmatrix}\begin{pmatrix}\text{Value of}\\ \text{Outcome 2}\end{pmatrix} + \ldots$$

For Julie, the expected value of bottled water was the 5 percent chance of major damage times the $1,000 value of having water in that event, plus the 15 percent chance of minor damage times the $100 value of having water for a day, plus the 80 percent chance of no damage times the zero value of bottled water when running water is steadily available:

$$\text{Expected value of water} = (.05)(\$1{,}000) + (.15)(\$100) + (.80)(\$0) = \$65$$

Julie should compare the expected value of bottled water with the cost of bottled water when deciding whether or not to make the purchase. If a stock of water sufficient for these contingencies would cost less than $65, Julie should invest, unless she has a penchant for risk-taking. Similar calculations are useful to inform decisions regarding the protection of wildlife that might go extinct, policies on global climate change, and, as discussed in the Reality Check above, investments in rubber bladders and metal baffles to protect gas tanks from exploding.

Summary

If you are wise, you have decided to study today until the marginal benefit of studying no longer exceeds the marginal cost. That is the path to efficiency and the maximization of net benefits. Efficiency for firms means maximizing profit by equating marginal revenue and marginal cost. Efficiency for individuals means maximizing utility by equating the value of marginal utility and marginal cost. The fundamental economic questions of what, how, and for whom to produce are answered by satisfying the criteria of allocative efficiency, productive efficiency, and distributive efficiency, respectively. In a perfectly competitive market in the absence of market failure, the equation of supply and demand is synonymous with the equation of marginal cost and marginal benefit, and yields all three types of efficiency. Caveats apply. The reckless assessment of costs and benefits can cause environmental missteps. Those who gain the most from a good may not be those who are willing to pay the most money for it. For example, an oil company's willingness to pay more for a wilderness tract than the current inhabitants may reflect the relative wealth of the oil company more so than the relative gains the oil company could receive from the area.

We have addressed the efficiency of hiking, chocolate, kissing, landfill sites, clean air, whaling, pizza, T-shirts, tomatoes, orchids, drugs, sex, drinking, recycled paper, rubber bladders, and bottled water. You are now armed with a valuable toolbox of information. The methods described in this chapter hinge on the equation of marginal cost and marginal benefit, and are critical to decisions of all sorts. Of course, real-world solutions aren't as simple as these models suggest. The next chapter builds additional realism into these models.

How much chocolate? As with all things, more resources should be devoted to chocolate production until the marginal cost of another unit would exceed the marginal benefit.

Problems for Review

1. Explain how you could use marginal analysis to determine the optimal amount of time to spend studying environmental economics today. Illustrate your answer with a graph.

2. The marginal utility Hugo receives from planting flowers diminishes as he plants more flowers. On a graph, draw a hypothetical flower demand curve for Hugo. Explain why Hugo should not purchase the quantity of flowers that maximizes his marginal utility.

3. On a graph, show the general shape of the production possibilities frontier for cattle and lumber. Explain why the opportunity cost of each good increases as more is produced.

4. Ally would pay up to $30 for her first umbrella and nothing for any additional umbrellas. Every soccer ball that Ally purchases gives her $9 worth of utility and she could never have too many. Draw Ally's demand curves for umbrellas and soccer balls.

5. Describe some decisions you make on the basis of cost-benefit analysis. Describe some decisions you should make on the basis of cost-benefit analysis but sometimes do not?

6. A tank behind André's service station has leaked a large quantity of heating oil into the soil below. If left uncontained, experts estimate a 5 percent chance that the oil will contaminate local drinking water and cause $1 million worth of illness, and an additional 1 percent chance that the oil will reach both the local aquifer and neighboring waterways, causing an additional $2 million worth of damage. If these are the only risk factors, what is the expected value of damage from André's tank?

7. Suppose you like potted plants in your room, but not so many that they get in the way. Draw a smooth line to show what happens to your marginal utility from potted plants as the quantity increases from zero to 1,000. How would a graph like this explain why some people plant trees in their yards while others with similar preferences have trees removed from their yards?

8. Describe a situation you've learned about in your area or in the news in which a maximization of net financial gain might differ from a maximization of social welfare.

The last two questions draw from information in the appendix.

9. At her current consumption levels, Megan receives 15 utils from an additional cup of tea and 300 utils from an additional pair of sandals. The price of tea is $1 and the price of sandals is $30 per pair. How can you tell whether Megan is allocating her money efficiently? If she is not, what would be a wise first step toward utility maximization?

10. On four separate graphs, draw an indifference curve for each of the following "goods" and "bads":
    a) *Recycling bins and massages (2 goods with free disposal)*
    b) *Toxic waste and headaches (2 bads)*
    c) *Sunshine and economics lectures (2 goods without free disposal, meaning that they become bads when you have too much of them)*
    d) *Beers and drives through the country, consumed at the same time (2 goods with free disposal that are deadly when combined)*

websurfer's challenge

1. Find a description of the "Water-Diamond Paradox" and explain the paradox in your own words.
2. Find an example of economic research that considers *nonmonetary* costs and benefits.
3. Find an online newspaper article that uses the word "efficiency" and compare the meaning of the word in that article to the meaning of the word in this chapter.

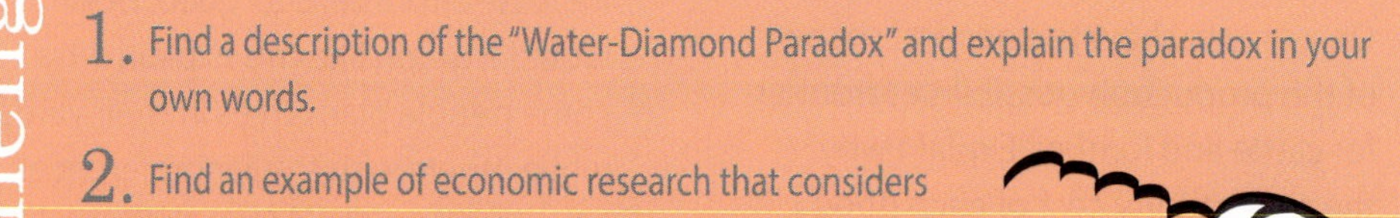

Internet Resources

Advice from Resources for the Future on cost-benefit analysis used for environmental policymaking:
http://www.rff.org/Publications/WPC/Pages/Three-Steps-to-Improving-Cost-Benefit-Analysis-of-Environmental-Regulatory-Rulemaking.aspx

EPA guidelines on cost-benefit analysis:
http://yosemite.epa.gov/ee/epa/eed.nsf/pages/guidelines.html

The International Whaling Commission:
http://iwc.int

Further Reading

Anderson, David A. "The Deterrence Hypothesis and Picking Pockets at the Pickpocket's Hanging." *American Law and Economics Review* 4, no. 2 (2002): 295–313. A study of the capacity of criminals to perform cost-benefit analysis.

Becker, Gary S., and Kevin M. Murphy. "A Theory of Rational Addiction." *Journal of Political Economy* 96, no. 4 (August 1988): 675–700. A theoretical discussion of the possibility that even addiction is rational.

Brenner, Robert D., and Richard D. Morgenstern. "In Response to 'Clearing the Air'." *Regulation* 19, no. 4 (1996). A response by EPA officials to the article condemning Clean Air Act policy assessments by Crandall, Rueter, and Steger. *Regulation* is a Cato Institute periodical.

Crandall, Robert W., Fredrick H. Rueter, and Wilbur A. Steger. "Clearing the Air: EPA's Self-Assessment of Clean-Air Policy." *Regulation* 19, no. 4 (1996). A condemnation of the EPA's assessment of Clean Air Act policies.

Dowie, Mark. "Pinto Madness." *Mother Jones* (September/October 1977): 18–32. An overview of Ford Motor Company's ill-fated cost-benefit analysis of the advisability of additional safety features.

Ryan, Dave. "New Report Shows Benefits of 1990 Clean Air Amendments Outweigh Costs by Four-to-One Margin." *Environmental News* (November 16, 1999): www.epa.gov/airprogm/oar/sect812/r-140.html. A brief summary of cost-benefit findings from an EPA study of the Clean Air Act Amendments.

Wilson, Marshall. "Bart Project Hits Brakes for Snakes." *San Francisco Chronicle* (July 17, 2000). An article about the Bay Area Rapid Transit system's encounter with endangered snakes in the path of construction.

Appendix

Efficiency Criteria in Greater Detail

Allocative Efficiency

Further discussion of the criteria for allocative efficiency provides an opportunity to introduce a few new terms and renew acquaintances with some old ones.[8]

Marginal utility (*MU*) is the additional utility gained by consuming one more unit of a good or service. Suppose consumers purchase food (*F*) and clothing (*C*). The ratio of the marginal utilities of food and clothing is called the **marginal rate of substitution** (*MRS*), and it represents consumers' willingness to pay for one item (food) by giving up another item (clothing):

$$MRS_{FC} = \frac{MU_F}{MU_C}$$

The *FC* subscript indicates that food is being substituted for clothing. Suppose the food units are pizzas and the clothing units are T-shirts. If Jen's marginal utility from pizzas is 4 and her marginal utility from T-shirts is 2, her $MRS_{FC} = 4/2 = 2$, meaning that she would trade at most two T-shirts for another pizza. By giving up two T-shirts for one pizza, she obtains 4 "utils" (**utils** are simply an arbitrary measure of utility) worth of pizza in exchange for 4 utils worth of T-shirts, and her total utility is unchanged. If she paid three T-shirts for a pizza, she would be giving up 3 x 2 = 6 utils worth of clothing for 4 utils worth of food—a net loss.[9] If this is your first exposure to the *MRS* concept, you might want to read the additional explanation provided in the last section of this appendix.

Figure 2.6 illustrates an **indifference curve**, depicting all of the combina-

8 If you have never seen any of these concepts before, you may want to review an introductory economics book in addition to reading this section.

9 These calculations treat the marginal utility from these items as constant, which is reasonable for very small changes in the quantities. In reality, the marginal utility is expected to decrease as more items are acquired.

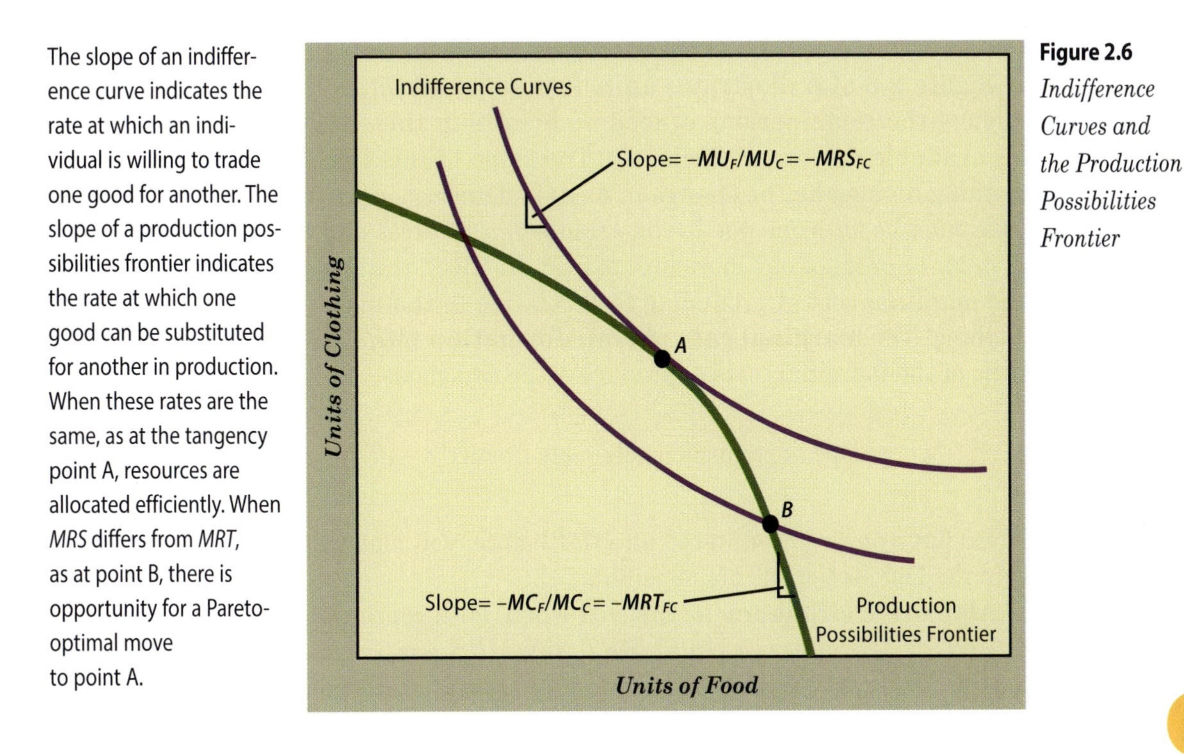

Figure 2.6 *Indifference Curves and the Production Possibilities Frontier*

The slope of an indifference curve indicates the rate at which an individual is willing to trade one good for another. The slope of a production possibilities frontier indicates the rate at which one good can be substituted for another in production. When these rates are the same, as at the tangency point A, resources are allocated efficiently. When *MRS* differs from *MRT*, as at point B, there is opportunity for a Pareto-optimal move to point A.

tions of food and clothing that make the representative consumer equally well off. Since the *MRS* represents the consumer's willingness to exchange clothing for food at a constant level of utility, the slope of the line (the change in clothing divided by the change in food) is equivalent to the negative of the *MRS*:

$$\text{Slope of indifference curve} = -MRS_{FC} = -\frac{MU_F}{MU_C}$$

The indifference curve in Figure 2.6 is drawn assuming that the consumer can freely dispose of any undesired units of either good. This way, the consumer never has too much of anything. In the absence of free disposal, there would come a point when the consumer would need to be compensated for more of one item with more of another. For example, garbage pickup is a good thing up to a point, and Rondi might be indifferent about a trade of one meatloaf for the second garbage pickup in a month. If the garbage truck visited Rondi's house 40 times per month, it might become more of a noisy nuisance than a beneficial service. Rather than being willing to give up some meatloaf in exchange for additional pickups, she would have to receive more meatloaf to compensate her for a forty-first garbage truck visit, assuming she doesn't have too much meatloaf, too. Under the more common assumption of free disposal, Rondi could just say "stop" after the last beneficial pickup and the truck would stop coming. Indifference curves between a good, like the number of scenic views from one's home, and a bad, like the number of miles from one's home to the nearest hospital, have a positive slope to reflect the need to receive more of the good in exchange for enduring more of the bad.

Figure 2.6 also illustrates a production possibilities frontier (*PPF*), which depicts the combinations of food and clothing that could be produced using all available resources efficiently. The slope of this line (again, the change in clothing divided by the change in food) is determined by the amount of clothing that must be foregone due to constraints on resources and production technology in order to produce one more unit of food. In effect, the slope of the *PPF* measures the marginal cost of producing food relative to the marginal cost of producing clothing. The **marginal rate of transformation** (*MRT*) is another name for the ratio of the marginal costs of producing the two goods:

$$\text{Slope of production possibility frontier} = -MRT_{FC} = -\frac{MC_F}{MC_C}$$

If you have never encountered an *MRT* before, you may want to read more about it in the last section of this appendix.

Allocative efficiency is achieved when, for a representative consumer, *MRS* = *MRT*. If *MRS* doesn't equal *MRT*, say $MRS_{FC} = 3$ and $MRT_{FC} = 1$, then the typical consumer would be willing to exchange up to three T-shirts for one pizza, whereas one more pizza could be produced at the cost of just one T-shirt. A net gain in utility could be realized if resources were reallocated to produce more pizza and fewer T-shirts, because a new pizza would generate three times as many utils as would be lost due to a one-unit decrease in T-shirts. In this case, more pizza and fewer T-shirts should be made until *MRS* = *MRT*. If, for example, *MRS* = *MRT* = 2, a new pizza would generate twice as much utility as one T-shirt, but the production of a new pizza would require the loss of two T-shirts, thus providing no net gain in utility.

The determination that allocative efficiency for society follows from the equation of *MRS* and *MRT* may be clear, but individuals and firms generally do not seek efficiency for society. Rather, the decision makers in an economy tend to be more selfish than that. Let us now consider how the self-centered workings of the market might bring about the end result that is best for society.

The benefit from a first meal or article of clothing is tremendous, providing life or decency. The second meal or article of clothing is surely nice to have, but less vital. The fiftieth of either item provides far less marginal utility than earlier units because the most urgent needs and wants are already satisfied. For this reason, the **law of diminishing marginal utility** states that the satisfaction gained from additional units of a good consumed within a given period of time decreases as more units are consumed.

If Alexandra gains 12 utils per additional dollar spent on food and 9 utils per additional dollar spent on clothing, taking a dollar away from clothing and spending it on food would create a net increase in total utility of 12 – 9 = 3. More money should be spent on food and less should be spent on clothing until, as the marginal utility from food decreases with increased consumption (according to the law of diminishing marginal utility) and the marginal utility from clothing increases with decreased consumption, the marginal utility per dollar is the same for food and clothing. *Consumers get the most utility from any given amount of money by equating the marginal utility per dollar spent on each good purchased.* For a consumer who purchases food and clothing for the prices of P_F and P_C per unit respectively, utility is maximized when

$$\frac{MU_F}{P_F} = \frac{MU_C}{P_C}$$

By multiplying both sides by P_C and dividing both sides by MU_F, this equation becomes

$$\frac{P_C}{P_F} = \frac{MU_C}{MU_F}$$

Recall that in a competitive market, price equals marginal cost. Firms have no incentive to produce and sell a product for a price below marginal cost, and they maximize their profit by producing more until their marginal cost rises to equal the price (which is their marginal benefit from selling). If $P_C = MC_C$ and $P_F = MC_F$, then the ratios of these equalities will also be equal:

$$\frac{P_C}{P_F} = \frac{MC_C}{MC_F}$$

From these two equations, it is clear that the price ratio equals both the marginal cost ratio (*MRT*) and the marginal utility ratio (*MRS*):

$$\frac{MU_C}{MU_F} = \frac{P_C}{P_F} = \frac{MC_C}{MC_F}$$

thus satisfying the criterion for allocative efficiency.

As with every application of the efficiency criterion, the challenge when seeking allocative efficiency is to find accurate measures of marginal benefits and marginal costs that include, for example, the opportunity costs of allocating natural resources to production rather than preservation. If either the marginal costs or the marginal benefits are exaggerated, resources will be misallocated to an inefficient set of goods and services. Potential pitfalls that can cause price to differ from marginal cost, or cause perceived costs and benefits to differ from reality, are detailed in Chapter 3.

Productive Efficiency

The tomatoes and orchids story earlier in this chapter illustrates how it is sometimes possible to produce more of one good without producing less of any other good. This is the case if the rate at which one input can be substituted for another—the **rate of technical substitution** (*RTS*)—differs among producers. The RTS between two inputs is equal to the ratio of the *marginal products* of the inputs. For example, the **marginal product of labor** (MP_L) is the additional output produced by one more unit of labor and the **marginal product of capital** (MP_K) is the additional output produced by one more unit of capital. If labor (*L*) and capital (*K*) are the two inputs, then

$$RTS_{LK} = \frac{MP_L}{MP_K}$$

If this is your first introduction to the *RTS*, you may want to read the more in-depth explanation of this concept that begins on the next page. Productive efficiency requires the *RTS* to be equal across all products. Our task now is to determine whether profit-maximizing behavior by firms will lead to this equality.

According to the **law of diminishing marginal returns**, as the quantity of one input increases, holding other input levels constant, the marginal product will eventually decrease. Consider the classic example of growing flowers in a flowerpot. Holding the size of the flowerpot and the amount of sunlight, water, soil, and seeds constant, the marginal product of fertilizer will eventually decrease. The first application of fertilizer in a week is likely to increase growth by more than the second and the third, and the twentieth application of fertilizer may do more harm than good, meaning that the marginal product of fertilizer becomes negative. Conversely, given diminishing marginal returns, as less fertilizer is used, its marginal product will increase. The same story of diminishing returns could be told in regard to increases in a different input such as seeds or water.

Figure 2.7 illustrates diminishing marginal returns for workers and bulldozers. To minimize the cost of producing a given quantity of output, a firm adjusts the quantity of each input to equate the marginal product per dollar spent on each resource. If more roadway is produced per additional dollar spent on workers than per additional dollar spent on bulldozers, workers should be substituted for bulldozers until another dollar spent on workers would no longer increase production more than another dollar spent on bulldozers. If labor and capital (such as bulldozers) are the only two inputs, the cost-minimizing production condition is that the "bang per buck," meaning the marginal product per dollar spent, is the same for both inputs. Letting *w* represent the price of labor and *r* represent the price of capital, the cost-minimizing condition is:

$$\frac{MP_K}{r} = \frac{MP_L}{w}$$

The law of diminishing marginal returns holds that as the amount of one input increases, holding other input levels constant, the marginal product will eventually decrease. For example, as the quantity of labor increases, the marginal product of labor decreases. If the marginal product curve is downward sloping and the quantity of an input decreases, the marginal product increases, as shown here for capital.

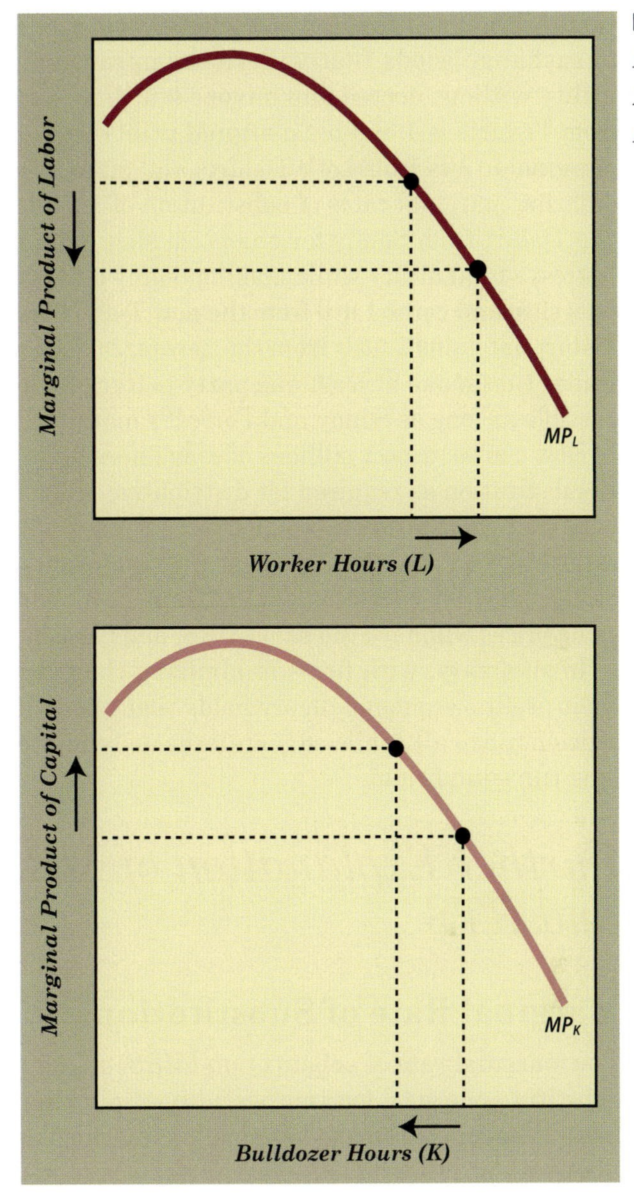

Figure 2.7 *Diminishing Marginal Returns*

Multiplying both sides by w and dividing both sides by the MP_K yields

$$\frac{w}{r} = \frac{MP_L}{MP_K}$$

If each firm minimizes costs by equating its ratio of marginal products with the ratio of input costs, under the assumption that wage and rental rates are constant across firms, the ratio of marginal products will be the same for all firms regardless of what they produce. That means that the marginal product of labor divided by the marginal product of capital will be the same for the production of clothing and roadways and tomatoes and orchids and so on. Hence, this condition for productive efficiency is met as the result of profit-maximizing behavior by firms.

Distributive Efficiency

Just as productive efficiency results from firms maximizing their "bang per buck" in terms of inputs, distributive efficiency follows from consumers making purchases that maximize their utility subject to budgetary constraints. The formal condition for distributive efficiency is that every consumer must have the same MRS. If marginal rates of substitution are not equal, there are opportunities to exchange goods that will yield improvements in at least one consumer's utility without decreasing anyone's utility. Suppose Sonny's marginal utility from T-shirts is 1 and his marginal utility from pizza slices is 2, while Forrest's marginal utility from both T-shirts and pizza slices is 1. Sonny and Forrest have differing marginal rates of substitution of 1/2 and 1 respectively. An exchange of one T-shirt from Sonny for one pizza slice from Forrest would have no effect on Forrest's total utility while making Sonny better off. Forrest loses 1 util by giving up a slice and gains 1 util from the new T-shirt; Sonny loses 1 util by giving up the T-shirt but gains 2 utils from the new pizza slice. Similar Pareto improvements—trades that make at least one party better off without harming anyone—will be possible as long as Sonny and Forrest's marginal rates of substitution differ.

How can we expect millions of consumers to converge on similar marginal rates of substitution as required for distributive efficiency? Remember that consumers maximize their utility by equating their marginal rate of substitution to the price ratio: $MRS = P_C/P_F$. To the extent that consumers face the same prices, P_C/P_F will be the same for every consumer. Thus, profit-maximizing consumers facing the same prices will have the same MRS, and distributive efficiency will be achieved.

In summary, with firms minimizing their costs and consumers maximizing their profits, economic theory holds that allocative, productive, and distributive efficiency are all achieved simultaneously in a perfectly competitive market in long-run equilibrium.

Further Explanation of MRS, MRT, and RTS

Marginal Rate of Substitution

The marginal rate of substitution (*MRS*) is the rate at which an individual can substitute one good for another without altering the individual's level of happiness. Economists refer to happiness as "utility" and units of happiness as "utils." Suppose you are stranded on a deserted island with a lot of matches but only a few pieces of firewood. You are good at catching fish but you don't like sushi. Thus, the ability to build fires is a good thing. A man named Friday, your coinhabitant of the island, also has firewood and offers you the opportunity to exchange matches for firewood. The determination of your *MRS* between firewood and matches is a matter of determining the largest number of matches you would trade for a piece of firewood.

Suppose that one more piece of firewood would give you 20 utils, and that the first match you give up is worth 5 utils to you. This is another way of saying that for you, the marginal utility of firewood (MU_F) is 20 and the marginal utility of matches (MU_M) is 5. What is the largest number of matches you would trade for a piece of firewood assuming these MU levels hold? Four. How is this number determined? By dividing the utils gained from a piece of firewood by the utils lost per match. In exchange for the 20 utils from a log, you would exchange at most 20/5 = 4 matches worth 5 utils each. If you traded fewer than four matches, say three, you would gain 20 utils from the log and only give up 3 x 5 = 15, for a net gain of 20 – 15 = 5 utils. If you traded more than four matches, say five, you would gain 20 utils from the log and give up 5 x 5 = 25 utils from the matches, for a net loss of 5 utils. Of course, you would like to give up as few matches as possible in exchange for firewood, but the most you would give up is four, so that is your MRS_{FM}. This explains why the marginal rate of substitution is found as

$$MRS_{FM} = \frac{MU_F}{MU_M}$$

As more firewood is gained and more matches are traded away, the law of diminishing marginal utility suggests that the marginal utility of firewood declines and the marginal utility of matches increases. The more firewood obtained, the less valuable is one more piece, and the fewer matches held, the more valuable is the next match to be parted with. As MU_F decreases and MU_M increases for these reasons, the value of their ratio, MRS_{FM}, will decrease. Since $-MRS$ is the slope of an indifference curve, this explains why the slopes of indifference curves decrease (the curves become flatter) as one obtains more of the x-axis good (firewood) and less of the y-axis good (matches).

Marginal Rate of Transformation

The marginal rate of transformation (MRT) is the rate at which one good can be produced in place of another. Economists (always liking to make things as simple as possible!) examine such trade-offs in models that assume only two goods can be produced. Suppose that an economy makes only jeans and granola, and at the current production levels, it takes $30 worth of resources to make another pair of jeans and $10 worth of resources to make another pound of granola. In other words, the marginal cost of jeans (MC_J) is $30 and the marginal cost of granola (MC_G) is $10. We will examine the trade-off between these two goods within such a small range of the production possibilities frontier that the marginal costs can be considered constant.

If one fewer pair of jeans is produced, that frees up $30 worth of resources, with which $30/$10 = 3 pounds of granola can be made at a cost of $10 worth of resources per pound. Thus, at this point on the production possibilities frontier, granola can be produced instead of jeans at a rate of three additional pounds of granola for every one pair of jeans foregone:

$$\text{Trade-off} = \frac{\text{Change in granola}}{\text{Change in jeans}} = -\frac{MC_J}{MC_G} = -\frac{\$30}{\$10} = -MRT_{JG} = -3$$

On a graph with the quantity of granola measured on the vertical axis and the quantity of jeans measured on the horizontal axis, $-MRT_{JG}$ is the slope of the production possibilities frontier. If jeans are measured on the vertical axis, the slope is found by simply flipping these terms over to find the inverse of $-MRT_{JG}$, which in this case is –1/3. The negative sign reflects the fact that either the change in granola or the change in jeans is always negative and the other change is positive. This makes sense because when the amount of granola increases, the number of pairs of jeans decreases, and with more jeans must come less granola.

If there is some specialization of resources, as is generally the case, the marginal cost of producing each product will increase as more of it is made. For example, if some workers are better at mixing granola and others are better at weaving cotton for jeans, the workers most skilled at making jeans will make the first pairs of jeans. Slower weavers will make the later pairs, so it will take relatively more labor hours and correspondingly higher payments to workers to make each additional pair of jeans. As the marginal costs change, the ratio of the marginal costs—the marginal rate of transformation—will also change along a production possibilities frontier (*PPF*). If the inputs are exactly the same for the two goods, the *MRT* will be constant and the *PPF* will be a straight line.

Marginal Rate of Technical Substitution

The marginal rate of technical substitution (*RTS*) is the rate at which one input can be substituted for another without changing the output level of the good being produced. Consider the planting of seedlings. Seedlings can be planted with various combinations of capital and labor. For example, 100 seedlings could be planted in an hour by a team of ten workers, each using only a small shovel, or by a single worker operating a properly equipped tractor. Suppose that with a given combination of capital and labor, 1 additional unit of capital (perhaps a shovel or a tractor component) would increase the number of seedlings planted per hour by 2, assuming that the amount of labor did not change. Alternatively, an additional worker would increase the number of seedlings planted per hour by 8 if the amount of capital did not change. This is another way of saying that the marginal product of capital (MP_K) is 2 and the marginal product of labor (MP_L) is 8.

To find the rate at which capital could replace labor without changing the quantity of output, notice that the loss of a worker's contribution of 8 seedlings would require the addition of $8/2 = MP_L/MP_K = 4$ units of capital. Four units of capital adding 2 seedlings each would contribute a total of $4 \times 2 = 8$ seedlings, just equal to the loss from the departing worker. This confirms that the marginal rate of technical substitution (*RTS*) is

$$RTS_{LK} = \frac{MP_L}{MP_K} = \frac{8}{2} = 4$$

A curve that includes all of the combinations of two inputs that create the

An isoquant curve shows all of the combinations of two inputs (here capital and labor) that can be used to produce the same level of output, say the planting of 100 tree seedlings. The slope of any line is "rise over run." In this case a run of -1 represents the loss of one worker, and a rise of *RTS* represents the number of units of capital required to replace the loss of one worker and reach another point on the isoquant with output unchanged. Thus, the slope of the isoquant is equal to rise/run = *RTS*/–1 = –RTS.

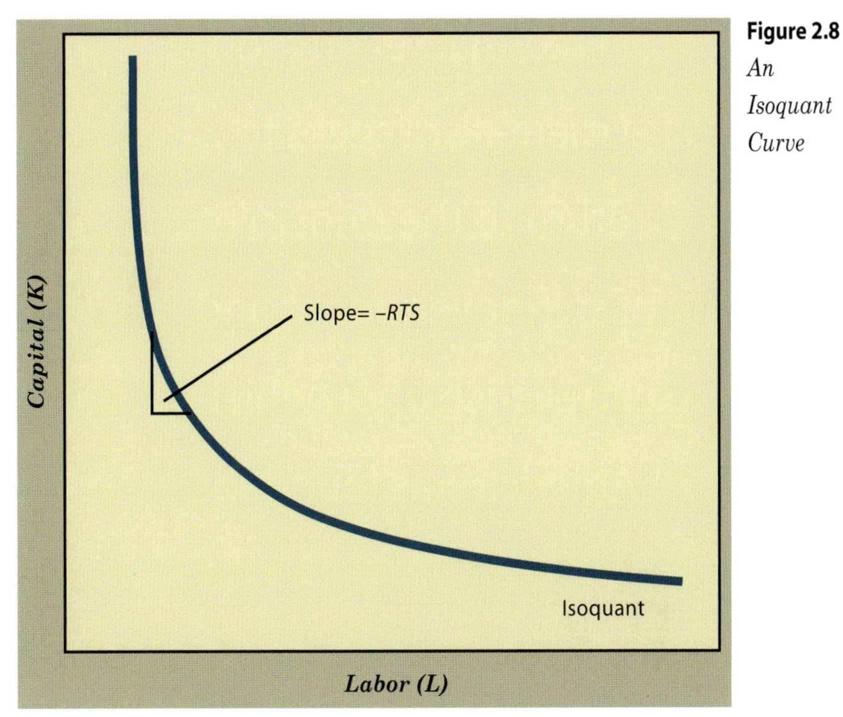

Figure 2.8 *An Isoquant Curve*

same quantity of output is called an **isoquant**. If capital is on the vertical axis and labor is on the horizontal axis, as in Figure 2.8, the slope of the isoquant is the change in capital necessary to compensate for a loss of one worker, which is exactly what the *RTS* tells us (with a negative sign in front to indicate the loss of the marginal productivity of a worker). The *RTS* at a particular point on the isoquant curve is calculated for infinitely small changes in labor and capital, for which the marginal products of the inputs can be treated as constants. As was shown in Figure 2.7, the marginal product of an input eventually decreases as more of the input is employed. Thus, the *RTS* changes along the isoquant curve, decreasing as more labor and less capital is employed, and increasing as less labor and more capital is employed. For example, when seedlings are planted using relatively more labor and less capital than at the point analyzed here, the MP_L might equal 6 and the MP_K might equal 3, making the $RTS = 6/3 = 2$.

"Free-market environmentalism seeks to ... return to the principles of self-government and self-reliance upon which America was founded."

—FRED L. SMITH, JR. AND KENT JEFFREYS

"I can state categorically that the idea that the consumer on his own, by referring to a label, can assess all the possible aftereffects of a new chemical, pharmaceutical or biotechnological product, is nonsense and must be rejected."

—SIR JAMES GOLDSMITH

A classic source of market failure, for reasons explained in this chapter.

3 Market Failure

If Charles Dickens had written about the free market, he might have put it this way: It is the best of forces, it is the worst of forces, it is the embodiment of wisdom, it is the embodiment of foolishness, it is the source of wealth, it is the source of poverty, it is the root of progress, it is the root of destruction, it is the answer to resource allocation, it is the bane of all resources, in short—it is everything we need and less.

In theory, the market is miraculous. Individual consumers and firms, all acting in their own self-interest in the market, can bring about an efficient allocation of goods and services with no more than the worthwhile levels of stress on the environment and natural resources. The logic behind market efficiency follows from the underpinnings of supply and demand. As explained in Chapter 2, the supply curve reflects the marginal cost of production and the demand curve reflects the marginal benefit of consumption. When market forces establish the price and quantity of a good at the intersection of the supply and demand curves, the coveted efficiency criterion is achieved: marginal cost equals marginal benefit. This is the result Adam Smith reveled about in his discussion of the "unseen hand" that seems to guide the economy to efficiency. Unfortunately, the invisible hand can be misguided by unseen environmental costs and benefits, unfettered market power, unrealized information, and unwillingness to pay for goods whose benefits cannot be withheld.

Why Markets Fail

Market failure is the failure of the free market to allocate resources efficiently. Market failure can result from

- *Imperfect competition*
- *Imperfect information*
- *Externalities*
- *Public goods*

This section explains these culprits of inefficiency and their influence on the market's unseen hand.

Imperfect Competition

Imperfect competition occurs when sellers have sufficient market power to charge prices above marginal cost, limit the quantity produced, or produce goods of inferior quality. These practices can lead to an inefficient allocation of resources that does not equate marginal cost and marginal benefit—one of the essential criteria for efficiency. Imperfect competition is particularly relevant to environmental economics because major polluters such as electricity and fuel providers tend to have considerable market power.

Like perfectly competitive firms, monopolies maximize profit or minimize loss by producing the quantity that equates marginal cost and marginal revenue. Facing the entire downward-sloping market demand curve, a monopoly must lower its price on all units in order to sell another unit of output. As the result of this price decrease, the marginal revenue gained from the additional unit of output is the price received for that unit minus the lost revenue from all of the units that would otherwise have sold for a higher price. For example, suppose a monopoly could sell ten birdhouses for $100 each, and a price cut to $95 would allow an eleventh to be sold. The marginal revenue from the eleventh birdhouse would not be the $95 price a customer pays for it. Instead, the marginal revenue would be the $95 price minus the $5 lost on each of the ten birdhouses that would otherwise have sold for $100 and now sell for $95 each. So the marginal revenue is $95 − ($5 × 10) = $45.

Figure 3.1 shows the demand, marginal revenue, and marginal cost for a typical monopoly. The profit-maximizing quantity, Q_m, is found on the quantity axis directly below the intersection of the marginal cost curve and the marginal revenue curve. The monopoly's price, P_m, is found as the height of the demand curve above the profit-maximizing quantity of Q_m. Although the monopoly stops producing at Q_m, additional units up to Q_c would provide a marginal benefit to consumers that exceeds the marginal cost of producing them. We know this

Relative to a competitive industry with the same cost structure, a monopoly will charge more and produce less. Because *MB* > *MC* for a monopoly, the output level is inefficient and there is a deadweight loss, represented by the shaded triangle.

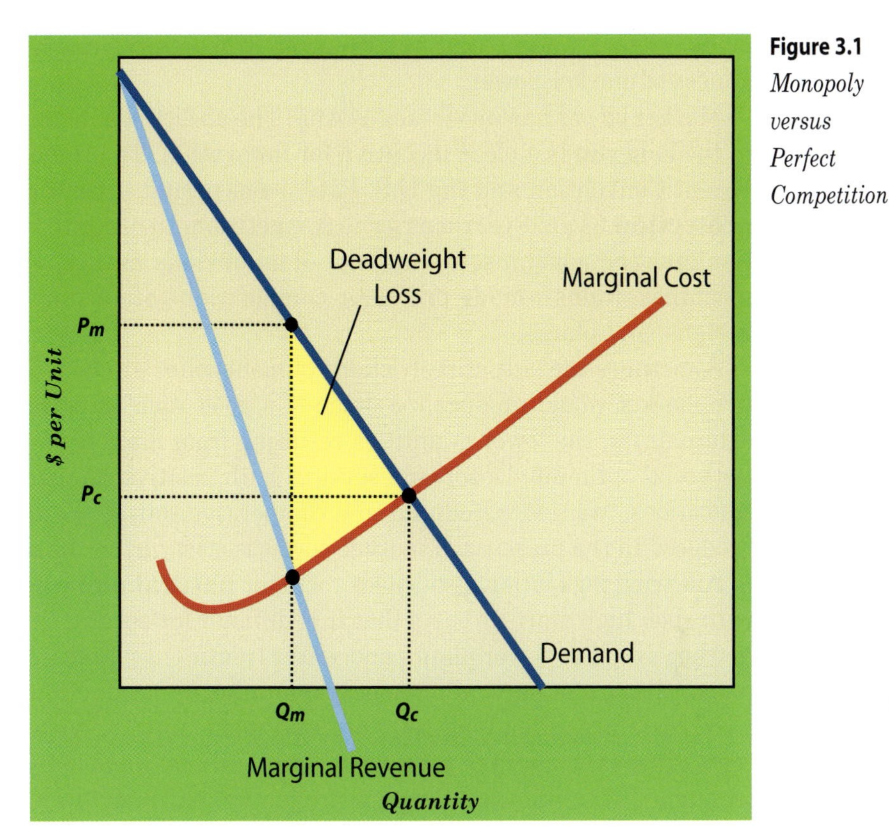

Figure 3.1 *Monopoly versus Perfect Competition*

because the demand curve—an indication of marginal benefit—is above the marginal cost curve for the first Q_c units. The result of not producing the units between Q_m and Q_c is **deadweight loss,** a loss of producer and consumer surplus caused by an inefficient allocation of resources. The yellow deadweight loss area on the graph represents the net loss to society due to the monopoly's restriction of output to only Q_m units.

Chapter 2 explained that in a competitive market, marginal cost determines the supply, and the equilibrium of supply and demand determines the price and quantity. If the market depicted in Figure 3.1 were perfectly competitive and the production costs remained the same, market equilibrium would occur at the intersection of the demand curve and the marginal cost curve. Production would *increase* from Q_m to Q_c and the price would *fall* from P_m to P_c. Competition also encourages quality enhancements, whereas firmly entrenched monopolists have little reason to improve existing products.

The U.S. Congress responded to the problems of imperfect competition in 1890 with the enactment of the first U.S. federal antitrust legislation, the Sherman Act. This was followed in 1914 with the Clayton Act and the Federal Trade Commission Act. With the Federal Trade Commission (FTC) as chief enforcer, these laws and subsequent enhancements punish unfair methods of competition and unfair or deceptive business practices. Although the FTC is effective in many circumstances, legal and financial constraints prevent it from deterring all abuses of market power.

Market power has its virtues as well. The ability of a monopoly to sustain profits in the long run is a clear incentive for innovation. To promote this, the European Patent Convention and the U.S. Patent Act permit inventors to apply for **patent protection** as a 20-year barrier to competition. In order to be patented, an invention must be novel, useful, and not of an obvious nature. Patents are issued for machines, human-made products, compositions of matter, processing methods, designs, and plants.

Sometimes the output restrictions of monopolies are beneficial. When a competitive market would produce too much of a good such as petroleum due to negative externalities, the lower quantities resulting from market power might be closer to the social optimum. Goods and services with positive externalities, such as college educations, are underproduced in a competitive setting. So the restricted quantity produced in the presence of market power is *even further* from the social optimum.

Antitrust legislation also leaves room for **natural monopolies**, which are firms with such high start-up costs that it is difficult for several firms to share the same market. Nuclear power plants and water treatment plants are examples of natural monopolies. As a natural monopoly increases its production, the high start-up or *fixed* costs are spread across more and more units of output. This spreading of costs causes the **average total cost**—the total cost divided by the quantity—to fall throughout the relevant range of production as shown in Figure 3.2. If one such

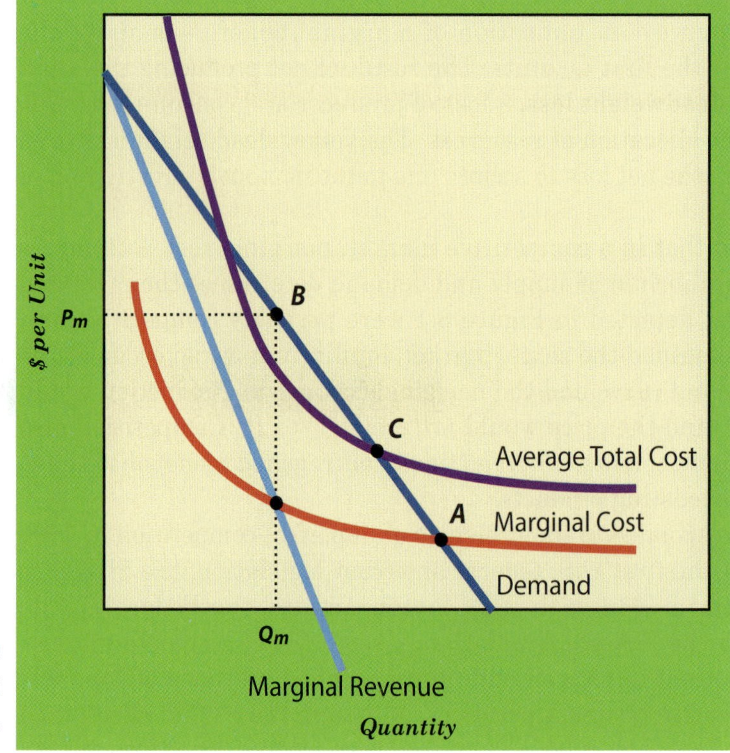

Figure 3.2 *Natural Monopoly*

The average total cost of a natural monopoly falls as output rises, because large fixed costs are spread across a growing quantity of output. This means one firm can serve the market at a lower cost than multiple firms.

firm serves the entire market, its average and marginal costs will be lower than if there were multiple firms. If the natural monopoly acted like a competitive firm and charged the price at which marginal cost equals demand, as shown by point A in Figure 3.2, the average total cost would exceed the price and the firm would experience losses. As a monopoly, the firm would like to operate at point B, charging P_m and producing Q_m. To prevent such high prices and low quantities, regulatory boards typically control prices and output levels for natural monopolies so that they operate at a point like C, where the price equals the average total cost and output is as large as possible without causing losses.

Whenever competition is thwarted, inefficiency and deadweight loss are likely to result. This explains why cartels are forbidden by the antitrust laws of most nations. A **cartel** is a group of firms that has entered into a collusive agreement to restrict output and increase prices in order to obtain monopoly profits. The Organization of the Petroleum Exporting Countries (OPEC) and Colombia's Cali drug cartel are examples. Cartels wish to act like a single supplier and divide the resulting profits among the members. Fortunately for the sake of efficiency, cartel members have an incentive to cheat. When a cartel acts like a monopoly, its price exceeds marginal cost. So an individual member of OPEC, for example, can add to its profit by selling a few thousand gallons of oil secretly on the side. As members of the cartel follow the incentive to cheat, supply increases, price falls, and the cartel's attempts to operate like a monopoly fail. Cartels typically experience periods of great "success" in restricting output and periods when internal monitoring efforts fail and temptations to cheat bring prices and quantities closer to their efficient levels.

Imperfect Information

Did you know that computer components like the ones held by the children in the photo contain heavy metals including arsenic, lead, and mercury?[1] Or that cotton farming is one of the most chemically dependent forms of agriculture?[2] Did you know that common coffee cups, opaque plastic cutlery, and to-go containers made of polystyrene can leach a colorless, sweet-smelling chemical called styrene into food and beverages?[3] The Environmental Protection Agency classifies styrene as a possible human carcinogen, and styrene exposure may

Unaware of the dangers involved, children in India play with computer parts containing heavy metals.

1 See http://cedb.asce.org/cgi/WWWdisplay.cgi?0601832.

2 See www.panna.org/resources/cotton.

3 See www.epa.gov/safewater/dwh/c-voc/styrene.html.

increase the risk of leukemia and lymphoma,[4] not to mention liver and nerve damage, nausea, depression, and weakness.[5]

Imperfect information exists when buyers or sellers have inadequate knowledge about relevant products, prices, markets, customers, suppliers, safety hazards, or environmental concerns to appropriately weigh all of the options. Consumers who do not grasp a product's dangers will purchase too much of it. In the past, incomplete information about the environmental and health effects of products such as tobacco, asbestos, lead, solvents, dioxins and furans may have resulted in inefficient consumption levels. Inefficiencies also stem from consumers paying too much for products because they don't know about lower-priced alternatives, and from producers making too much of one product and not enough of another because they hold inadequate information about consumer demand.

Solutions to imperfect information include requirements for product testing, truth-in-advertising regulations, consumer information services, and market surveys by firms. For better or worse, new trends in civil litigation have also permitted lawsuits over a growing assortment of information problems. Historically, product-related lawsuits have focused on design defects, such as insulation made with asbestos, and manufacturing defects, such as cooling systems that leak Freon. The domain of product liability litigation has expanded to include inadequate hazard warning labels, and civil suits have grown in popularity, length, and award size. Chapter 15 discusses environmental lawsuits.

Information problems also plague decision makers trying to coordinate their strategies. The classic example is the **prisoner's dilemma**: Two crooks are apprehended with limited evidence linking them to a robbery they did commit. Placed in separate rooms for interrogation, they must decide whether to confess to the crime or deny involvement. Table 3.1 illustrates the possible strategies and outcomes for Crook A and Crook B. The numbers indicate the resulting years spent in prison. The number on the left is for Crook A and the number on the right is for Crook B. The best outcome for the crooks occurs if each crook denies involvement in the crime. Then the sentence is a light two years in prison due to a lack of compelling evidence. If one crook confesses and the other denies, the confessor will receive an even lighter one-year sentence in exchange for the confession, and the liar will get a heavy five-year sentence for robbing someone and then lying about it. If they both confess, each will go to prison for four years.

What should the two crooks do? Each sees that if the other denies, it is better to confess in order to receive one year in prison rather than two. If the

Table 3.1

		Crook B	
		Confess	**Deny**
Crook A	**Confess**	4,4	1,5
	Deny	5,1	2,2

4 See www.epa.gov/ttn/atw/hlthef/styrene.html.

5 Agency for Toxic Substances and Disease Registry, *Toxicological Profile for Styrene*, Atlanta, GA: U.S. Public Health Service, U.S. Department of Health and Human Services, 1992; and U.S. Department of Health and Human Services, *Registry of Toxic Effects of Chemical Substances*, Bethesda, MD: National Toxicology Information Program, National Library of Medicine, 1993.

other confesses, it is better to confess in order to avoid the heavy sentence for being a known liar (four years is better than five). Confession is a **dominant strategy** because it is better than the alternative of denial regardless of the other crook's strategy. Given their inability to cooperate, we can expect the two crooks to confess and spend four years in prison. Yet if each knew the other would cooperate by denying, they could spend only two years in prison.

The prisoner's dilemma causes inefficiency in other instances as well. Warring nations may be safer if neither side has atomic weaponry than if both do, but the downside risk of unilateral disarmament leads each side to maintain arms. From the standpoint of stockholders in a firm, it can be similarly undesirable for the firm to unilaterally reduce pollution when the clean-up costs are substantial. Consider a dilemma facing competing tire manufacturers about whether to invest in a more environmentally friendly manufacturing process. The money could go towards cleaner fuels, recycled materials, or advanced filtration systems for emissions. Some, but not all, of the clean-up cost could be passed on to consumers in the form of higher prices. If consumers worry mostly about price when they pick a tire supplier, the payoffs will resemble those in Table 3.2. The numbers represent the firms' profits in thousands of dollars. In each box, the number on the left is Firm 1's profit and the number on the right is Firm 2's profit.

Table 3.2

		Firm 2	
		Clean	**Dirty**
Firm 1	**Clean**	10,10	8,14
	Dirty	14,8	12,12

Due to the clean-up costs borne by the firms and the decrease in the quantity demanded resulting from higher prices, the profit is $10,000 each if both firms run clean and $12,000 each if both firms run dirty. To be the only clean firm when prices are the primary determinant of demand would be even worse. The clean firm would experience higher costs and earn a profit of only $8,000 from loyal customers, while the dirty firm with lower costs and lower prices would earn a profit of $14,000. The dominant strategy in this case is to run dirty, and the best outcome from the firms' point of view requires no cooperation.

Pollution is not always a dominant strategy. If customers exhibit a preference to buy from clean firms despite sharing some of the added expense, the payoff matrix might resemble that in Table 3.3. If both firms are clean or both firms are dirty, and there are no alternatives to purchasing from these two firms, then the outcomes are no different than before.[6] Customers have no opportunity to

Table 3.3

		Firm 2	
		Clean	**Dirty**
Firm 1	**Clean**	10,10	14,8
	Dirty	8,14	12,12

6 If more tires are purchased when firms are clean than when firms are dirty, profits can be higher when both firms clean up.

choose between clean and dirty firms, and profits are higher in the dirty firms because costs are lower. But if one firm stays dirty and the other goes clean, the clean firm enjoys greater popularity and earns a profit of $14,000 while the dirty firm earns $8,000. This presents a prisoner's dilemma. If the firms could cooperate and both run dirty, they would each receive $12,000 in profit, but the risk that the other firm will clean up and lure customers away causes each firm to clean up. Cleaning up in this case is a dominant strategy because it yields the highest profit regardless of what the other firm does. With customers seeking clean production and firms unable to trust each other to cooperate, firms are motivated to clean up even when they would earn more profit with everyone running dirty. Have you noticed that fast-food restaurants use very little non-biodegradable Styrofoam packaging these days? If so, you've seen the motivating effect of consumer preferences.

reality check

Cooperative Games at Sea

The bottlenose dolphin is second only to humans in the ratio of brain size to body size, and dolphins apparently outdo humans in some cooperative games. The discussions of cartels and the prisoner's dilemma convey the value and difficulty of cooperation among players when there is an incentive to cheat. Individual cartel members undermine cooperative strategies by selling more than they should, hoping nobody will notice. Firms that can't cooperate on pricing or environmental strategies end up taking actions with inferior outcomes. Dolphins face similar dilemmas. When eating from a school of fish, dolphins encircle the fish and take turns eating, one dolphin at a time. There is an incentive for the circling dolphins to cheat by eating while on duty. However, if a significant number of dolphins followed that incentive, the fish would disperse and the benefits from coordination would be lost. In reality, the trustworthiness of on-duty dolphins prevails to benefit all of dolphin society.

Marine Biologist Pieter A. Folkens shares this anecdote about dolphin economics: Trash is dangerous to dolphins if they ingest it, so dolphins at Marine World were trained to remove trash from their tank and bring it to their trainer for a reward of fish. One dolphin kept appearing with trash even when the tank appeared clean. An underwater view revealed the dolphin's strategy. The dolphin had established an underwater savings account. He collected all of the available trash and deposited it in a bag at the bottom of the tank. When he made a withdrawal, he did not bring up a whole piece of trash; rather, he tore off a small bit of what remained to increase and prolong his return. With this behavior, the dolphin exhibited a capacity for delayed gratification and the ability to plan for the future.

Perhaps dolphins could teach humans a few tricks.

Marginal external benefit drives a wedge between private marginal benefit and social marginal benefit. Disregarding the marginal external benefit, the apiarist will purchase hives until her private marginal benefit equals her private marginal cost at the quantity of Q_p. If the apiarist internalizes the externalities due to subsidies or side payments, she will produce the socially optimal quantity, Q_s, that equates the social marginal benefit and the social marginal cost.

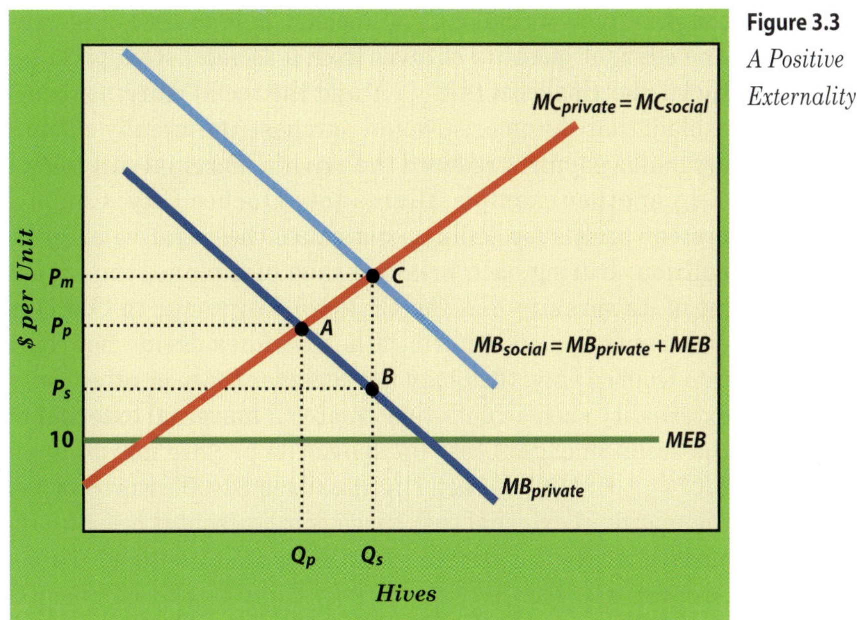

Figure 3.3
A Positive Externality

Externalities

A third source of market failure, externalities, consist of the costs or benefits felt beyond or "external to" those causing the effects. Do you weigh the health and safety costs imposed on others when you decide how many miles to drive in your car? Inefficiencies arise from such spillover effects when decision makers do not consider all of the repercussions of their behavior. Developers may not consider the detriments of habitat loss when deciding where to locate homes. Manufacturers may overlook the costs of pollution when deciding how many gadgets to produce. And consumers may consider only their own gratification as they decide how many flowers and trees to plant on their property, ignoring the value of beauty and clean air provided to others. If these external costs and benefits are neglected during the decision-making process, from a societal standpoint, too many developments crop up in sensitive wilderness areas, too many gadgets are produced, and too few flowers and trees are planted.

For example, honeybees create honey for apiarists (beekeepers), but they also pollinate fruit trees for agriculturalists (farmers) within about a 7-mile radius of the hive. The apiarists may not consider the external benefit of their hives when they decide how many hives to purchase. Figure 3.3 illustrates the divergence of **social marginal benefit** (MB_{social}) and **private marginal benefit** ($MB_{private}$) caused by this positive externality. The private marginal benefit is decreasing due to diminishing marginal returns. The **marginal external benefit** (MEB) is constant at \$10 per hive. The social marginal benefit in this case is the private marginal benefit plus \$10, because $MB_{social} = MB_{private} + MEB$. Private incentives guide the apiarist to point A, the intersection of the private marginal benefit and the **private marginal cost** ($MC_{private}$), and an output of Q_p. Beyond Q_p, the private marginal cost of another hive exceeds the private marginal benefit. The efficient quantity of hives from a societal standpoint is Q_s, which equates the **social marginal cost** (MC_{social}) and the social marginal benefit. Upcoming sections explain that the apiarist would purchase the socially efficient quantity if a subsidy or similar payment reduced the private marginal cost to P_s, as shown at point B.

In another example, flights into Quebec City, Canada, serve travelers and provide profits for airlines, but cause the negative externalities of noise and air polltion. During each brief passage of a plane, the St. Lawrence River loses a bit of its serenity and the Château Frontenac in Old Quebec loses some of its eighteenth-century charm. When airlines decide how many flights to schedule into Quebec City, they may not consider these or other pollution costs. A negative externality such as pollution creates a **marginal external cost** (*MEC*) that brings the social marginal cost up above the private marginal cost, because $MC_{social} = MC_{private} + MEC$. If each flight causes $1,000 worth of noise and air pollution, the marginal external cost curve is a horizontal line and the social marginal cost curve is above the private marginal cost curve by $1,000 as shown in Figure 3.4. Airlines will choose to operate Q_p flights—the number that brings the private marginal cost and the private marginal benefit into equilibrium at point A. (The private marginal benefit for the airline is its marginal revenue.) For goods and services such as flights that impose negative externalities, the privately optimal quantity, Q_p, exceeds the socially optimal quantity, Q_s. One solution is for the

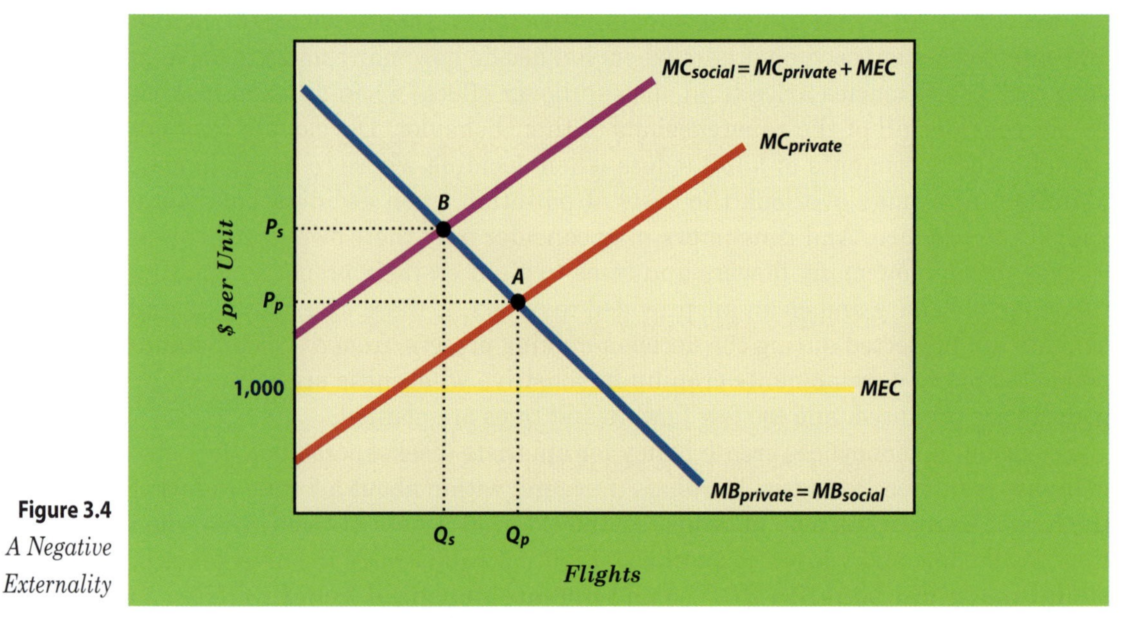

Figure 3.4
A Negative Externality

Marginal external cost separates private marginal cost and social marginal cost. Airlines will add flights until the private marginal benefit equals the private marginal cost at quantity Q_p. The socially optimal quantity of flights, Q_s, equates the social marginal cost and the social marginal benefit. Airlines would choose the socially optimal quantity if they internalized the marginal external cost of their decisions, as would occur if they paid a tax equal to the marginal external cost.

government to limit the quantity to Q_s. Many city governments impose flight restrictions and most prohibited the even louder supersonic Concorde aircraft which are no longer used. An alternative to quantity restrictions is to bring the decision makers to bear the social marginal cost of their behavior. A private marginal cost of P_s would lead the airlines to point B and provision of the socially efficient quantity of flights. Sometimes the assignment of property rights, Pigou taxes, or private negotiations can achieve that end, as discussed next.

Property Rights Inefficiency resulting from externalities is often avoidable. The socially efficient resource allocation can be achieved if decision makers internalize, or feel themselves, the costs and benefits they bring to society. Biologist Garrett Hardin (1968) prescribed the privatization of assets as one route toward internalization. He referred to externalities produced on publicly held property, such as open grazing lands, the seas, the air, and national parks, as the **tragedy of the commons**, and held that abuses of open-access areas could be curtailed if the areas were privately held. Consider a household that dumps sewage into a public lake rather than purchasing a septic system to process and store the waste. Although the social cost of dumping sewage is larger than the cost of a septic system, the household's private cost of dumping is not, because the household bears only a small share of the overall damage of dumping. If the lake area belonged to the household dumping the sewage, that household would internalize the full social cost of dumping and invest in a septic system. If the lake area belonged to someone else, that person would have an incentive to prohibit and carefully monitor dumping. Hardin felt that by assigning property rights to land, water, and air, society could avoid externalities caused by everything from factories to obnoxious music. As evidence of his point, poaching is a far greater problem in countries where property rights are weak than in countries where they are well defined and strictly enforced.

Pigou Taxes Cambridge Economist Arthur C. Pigou (1932) suggested taxes and subsidies to bring private and social costs into line. A **Pigou tax** is intended to equal the marginal external cost of the behavior being taxed. If developers paid a tax equal to the marginal external cost of resulting habitat loss and pollution, they would feel or "internalize" this cost and expand their development only if the social marginal benefit exceeded the social marginal cost. In the airline example, a tax of $1,000 per flight would cause the airlines to internalize the full cost of their behavior and operate at point B in Figure 3.4. Likewise, activities that provide positive externalities, such as education, the raising of bees, and the planting of seedlings, can be subsidized by the value of the marginal external benefit so that the private marginal benefits to students, apiarists, and seedling planters equal the marginal benefits to society. In the beehive example above, a subsidy of $10 per hive would bring the private marginal benefit up to the value of the social marginal benefit. The subsidized apiarist would purchase hives until the now-internalized social marginal benefit equaled the social marginal cost. This outcome is illustrated by point C in Figure 3.3, with an efficient quantity of Q_s and a market price of P_m. Likewise, Pigou has inspired efficiency-seeking governments around the world to tax gasoline and other sources of negative externalities, and subsidize solar panels and other sources of positive externalities.

Coasian Solutions As an extension to the property rights solution, the work of English economist Ronald Coase (1960) suggests that market failure will not result from externalities if the affected parties can bargain to an efficient solution. According to the **Coase Theorem**, *if property rights are clearly defined and transaction costs are zero, the efficient outcome will occur regardless of the legal rules affecting entitlements and their enforcement.*

Transaction costs are the costs of identifying and contacting the relevant parties, assessing costs and benefits, and creating and enforcing contracts. An issue involving two parties requires only one line of communication, perhaps a visit, a letter, or a phone call, for the sharing of ideas. With ten parties involved, 45 lines of communication are needed in order for each party to share ideas with each of the other parties. With 100 parties, 4,950 lines of communication are required. It is evident that the transaction costs associated with negotiations increase exponentially as the number of interested parties increases. This means that efficient private solutions to problems involving many parties or complex issues are less likely.

Suppose that the Good Idea Lightbulb Company releases lead into the air during its production process.[7] You should be familiar with several possible legal rules as we explore the likely outcomes of Coasian bargaining.[8] In terms of entitlement, the law could entitle the lighting factory to the gains from polluting or entitle the nearby citizens to the benefits from clean air. The enforcement of these entitlements could come from an injunctive remedy or a damages remedy. If the citizens are entitled under an **injunctive remedy**, they can prohibit the factory from polluting, and the polluter can only cause damage if it buys off

Table 3.4 *Costs and Benefits of Lightbulb Production*

Production Level (Truckloads)	*Total Profit*	*Total Damage*	*Total Profit Minus Total Damage*	*Marginal Benefit (Additional Profit)*	*Marginal Cost (Additional Damage)*
0	0	0	0	—	—
1	4,000	500	3,500	4,000	500
2	7,000	1,500	5,500	3,000	1,000
3	9,000	4,500	4,500	2,000	3,000
4	10,000	9,500	500	1,000	5,000

7 Lead (Pb) is a recognized carcinogen and a developmental and reproductive toxicant.

8 See Calabresi and Melamed (1972) for further discussion of these solutions to nuisance disputes.

Some lighting companies really do emit lead into the air. Do you think citizens really bargain with them about production levels as Coase suggested would happen?

(bribes) the citizens who are entitled to clean air. If the factory is entitled under an injunctive remedy, the citizens must buy off the factory if they want to reduce pollution damages.

Notice that the entitlements are explained in terms of the *gains* from pollution and the *benefits* from clean air. Under the damages remedy, this is different from having the right to pollute or breathe clean air. If the citizens are entitled under a **damages remedy**, the factory can pollute all that it wants, but it must compensate the citizens for pollution damages, thus giving them the same benefits as if they had clean air.[9] Likewise, if the factory is entitled under the damages remedy, the citizens can restrict the factory's production to any level, but they must compensate the factory for any lost profits.[10]

Table 3.4 describes the benefit (profit) received by the lighting company and the external health and environmental damage imposed on neighboring areas at each production level. For simplicity, assume that the company has no interest in producing more than four truckloads of lightbulbs. The net benefit to society is maximized with the production of two truckloads of lightbulbs, as you can see from the fourth column, which lists the total profit minus the total damage. You can also find this socially optimal production level by comparing the marginal benefit and the marginal cost of each unit and seeing that the second truckload is that last unit for which the marginal benefit exceeds the marginal cost.

9 A classic case illustrating this type of damages remedy is *Boomer v. Atlantic Cement Co.*, 26 N.Y.2d 219, 257 N.E.2d 870, 309 N.Y.S.2d 312 (1970).

10 Entitling the injurer to damages is rare, but there are examples. See *Spur Industries, Inc. v. Del E. Webb Development Co.*, 108 Ariz. 178, 494 P.2d 700 (1972).

Figure 3.5
Marginal Cost and Marginal Benefit

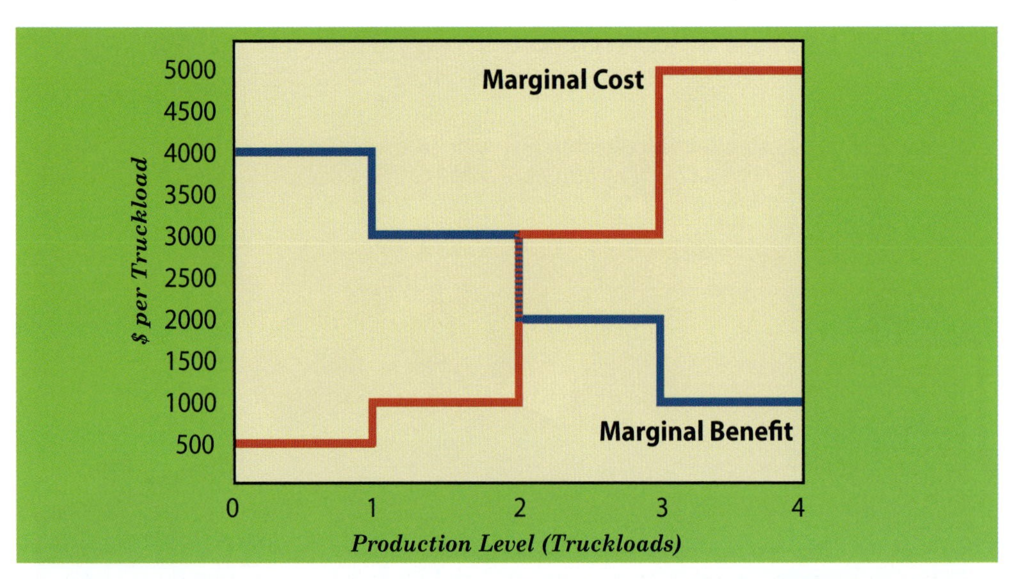

As with the manufacture of most goods, the marginal cost and the marginal benefit of lightbulb production rise and fall respectively. The area between the two lines represents the net gain to society when marginal benefit exceeds marginal cost, and the net loss to society when marginal cost exceeds marginal benefit. The efficient quantity is two truckloads because the marginal cost exceeds the marginal benefit for each truckload beyond two. Coase argues that the gains from the first two truckloads will be realized and the losses from the last two will be avoided through a process of bargaining, and that under the right circumstances, the efficient outcome will occur regardless of the legal rule.

Figure 3.5 provides a model of the lightbulb-production story. The blue line shows the diminishing marginal benefit received from each truckload of lightbulbs and the red line shows the increasing marginal cost. For the first two truckloads the marginal benefit exceeds the marginal cost, creating a net gain for society represented by the area between the red and blue lines. The next two truckloads create a net loss for society because the marginal cost of those truckloads is higher than the marginal benefit. Social welfare is maximized with the production of two truckloads of lightbulbs, at which point marginal cost and marginal benefit intersect.

Now the question is, in the absence of transaction costs, can private bargaining lead to the socially optimal production level? The answer, at least in theory, is yes. The theorized outcomes under two scenarios are described here; two other scenarios are included for your enjoyment among the problems for review.

Suppose the citizens are entitled under the injunctive remedy. This means that the lighting company must negotiate payments to the citizens in exchange for any permission to pollute. The first truckload provides $4,000 in profit to the company and only causes $500 in damage to the citizens. Thus, any payment from the company to the citizens between $500 and $4,000 for permission to produce one truckload will make both sides better off than with no production. For example, if the company pays the citizens $1,500 for permission to produce the first truckload, the citizens receive $1,500 for $500 worth of damage, making them better off by $1,000. At the same time, the company pays $1,500 to earn $4,000 in profit, making the company better off by $2,500 relative to their no-production profit of zero. Whether the company's payment to the citizens is closer to $501 or $3,999 depends on the relative negotiation skills and bargaining positions of the two parties.

Having negotiated to produce the first truckload of lightbulbs, Good Idea Lightbulb Company will naturally seek more profit from increased production. The last two columns of Table 3.4 indicate that the production of a second truckload of bulbs would provide $3,000 in additional profit and cause $1,000 in additional damage. Any payment from the company to the citizens between $1,000 and $3,000 for permission to produce a second truckload would make both sides better off than they were with one truckload, and thus Coase would anticipate an agreement somewhere in that range. After the second unit, there are no further opportunities for mutually beneficial bargaining because the third and fourth units create more damage than profit. The citizens would require at least $3,000 to compensate them for the damage from the third truckload, which the company would be unwilling to pay in order to earn $2,000 in profit. Likewise, the company would not pay $5,000 to earn $1,000 from the fourth truckload.

Notice that this discussion revolves around the additional (marginal) profit and damage from incremental units. Looking just at the total profit and damage, it might appear that even the fourth truckload is negotiable because total profit still exceeds the total damage at that production level. However, since the citizens would accept up to $5,000 less if the fourth unit were not produced, and it is worth only $1,000 to the company, both sides would prefer a lower production level. The same argument can be made against the third truckload. *The trick to Coasian bargaining is to start with the ideal for the entitled party (no production if the victims are entitled, the profit-maximizing quantity if the injurers are entitled) and consider changes from that position, one unit at a time.*

As another example, suppose the factory is entitled under the damages remedy. The citizens again have the right to restrict pollution, but for every unit of production they forbid, they must compensate the lighting company for lost profit. The citizens will gladly pay the $1,000 in lost profit to prevent the fourth truckload and its $5,000 worth of damage. They are also willing to pay the $2,000 to prevent the third truckload and its $3,000 worth of damage. They will not, however, pay $3,000 to avoid $1,000 in damage from the second unit, or $4,000 to avoid $500 in damage from the first unit. Thus, they will restrict production to two truckloads—*the efficient level*—and compensate the lighting company for its total of $3,000 in lost profit from not producing the third and fourth units.

There are a number of complications that could arise to foil the beauty of the Coase Theorem. For instance, strategic behavior could rear its ugly head. Consider an example like the one in which the citizens are entitled under the injunctive remedy. The two sides might enter into a dispute over the gains from bargaining. Although any payment between $500 and $4,000 for the first unit would make both sides better off than no production, the citizens might demand no less than $3,500 and the company might stubbornly refuse to pay more than $1,000. In such situations it can be difficult to settle on a payment that is agreeable to all parties. Other complications arise when the group of victims is too large to gather and organize, the sources of injury are difficult to identify, or social customs allow no such negotiation between injurers and victims. Despite the deadly nature of externalities like secondhand cigarette smoke, social norms alone can prevent fruitful negotiations and payoffs. There is also the problem that if payoffs to deter smokers, noisemakers, polluters, and other creators of externalities became commonplace, people might create more externalities simply to collect the payments for ceasing the troublesome behavior. Director Penny Marshall tells a story of a fellow to whom, in true Coasian form, she paid $100 to stop using his chainsaw while Marshall was filming her movie *A League of Their Own* nearby. Unfortunately, the fellow created his noise pollution repeatedly over several days to receive additional payments. All of these complications represent transaction costs, the size of which determine whether the prospects for Coasian bargaining are mildly fettered or far-fetched.

As final applications of the Coase Theorem, consider the apiarist and airline examples. In the absence of transaction costs, the agriculturalists who benefit from beehives would be willing to pay the apiarists at most the agriculturalists' marginal external benefit for each additional hive. So long as the payment to the apiarists, ρ, equaled or exceeded the difference between the private marginal cost and the private marginal benefit,

$$\rho \geq MC_{private} - MB_{private}$$

the apiarists would be willing to add more hives. As is clear from Figure 3.3 above, the agriculturalists would be willing to pay an amount in excess of $MC_{private} - MB_{private}$ for beehives up to the socially optimal quantity Q_s, at which point the divergence of private marginal cost and private marginal benefit exceeds the agriculturalists' marginal external benefit. After reaching Q_s, the agriculturalists would be unwilling to pay the apiarists enough to justify another hive.

In the flight scenario, those harmed by flights would be willing to pay up to their marginal external cost to reduce the number of flights below Q_p in Figure 3.4. Payments of

$$\rho \geq MB_{private} - MC_{private}$$

from the citizens would at least compensate the airline for its losses from restricting output. Such payments would be possible for restrictions down to Q_s, below which the difference between private marginal benefit and private marginal cost exceeds the marginal external cost, and the citizens would be unwilling to pay the airline enough to compensate for the loss of another flight.

Public Goods

Public goods invoke sharing because we have no choice but to share them. It is human nature to hold possessions closely. Indeed, most of us share little of value with friends, not to mention strangers. Yet sometimes many people can share the benefits of the same good, and sometimes we cannot control the use of a good. Both of these descriptions apply to public goods.

Public goods are characterized as being nonrival in consumption and nonexcludable. A good is **nonrival** if one person's consumption of it does not detract from other peoples' consumption of the good. This is common for animal species that are appreciated for their mere existence. Your pleasure in knowing that polar bears still frolic in the Arctic does not affect your neighbor's appreciation for the same bears. Multiple users, on the other hand, cannot consume the same rival good, such as a fried chicken leg or a housing site.

A good is **nonexcludable** if it is not possible to prevent people from benefitting from it. If environmental protection efforts stabilize or reverse global climate change, it will be impossible to prevent particular individuals from benefiting from that accomplishment. On the other hand, one can, with few exceptions, exclude others from consuming one's lunch or entering one's home.

Other examples of public goods include streetlights, military protection, pollution abatement, airborne radio and television signals, fireworks displays, and disease control. Rivalry and excludability do not always go hand in hand. Satellite television and scenic views from private lands are examples of **quasi-public goods** or **club goods**, which are nonrival but excludable. **Open-access goods** or **common resources** such as timber on public lands and fish in the sea are rival but nonexcludable. Goods that are rival and excludable are called **private goods**.

	Excludable	Nonexcludable
Rival	Private Goods	Open-Access Goods
Nonrival	Quasi-Public Goods	Public Goods

Because multiple users can benefit from a public good at the same time without affecting the consumption of others, the value to society of each additional unit of the public good is found by summing the values to each of the individuals. If 30 million people each place a $10 value on the existence of the last sperm whale herd, the existence value of these sperm whales to society is 30 million times $10, or $300 million. Society would be willing to pay at least $300 million to preserve the sperm whale. This is different from calculating the value of a private good. If there are 30 million people each of whom places a $10 value on the last bucket of chicken at Friendly Fried Food, the total value of that bucket to society is still just $10 because only one of those people will be able to enjoy the chicken.

The market demand curve for a public good is *not* found by adding the

Figure 3.6 *Demand for a Public Good*

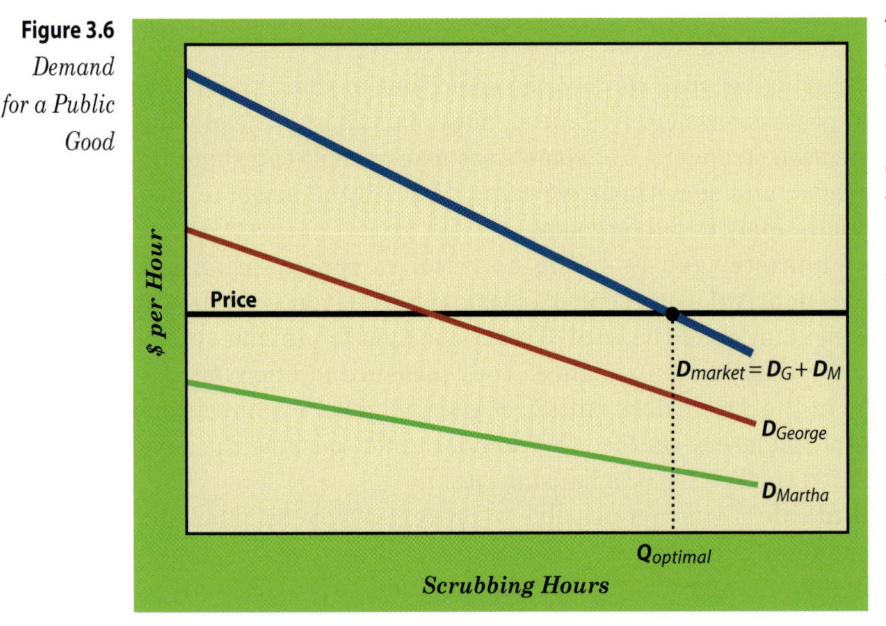

The market demand curve for a public good is found by adding the individual demand curves for everyone in the market vertically, rather than horizontally, as would be the case for a private good.

quantities demanded by each consumer at each price, as with private goods. Suppose that George and Martha are the only two people who care about the appearance of the Washington Monument, a public good.[11] The monument has become darkened by decades of exposure to city air, and society must decide how many person-hours to devote to scrubbing the filth off the monument. Martha and George's demand curves for scrubbing hours appear in Figure 3.6. Since the benefits of monument scrubbing are nonrival and nonexcludable, both Martha and George benefit from each hour of scrubbing. The marginal benefit to society from each hour of scrubbing is thus the sum of Martha's marginal benefit and George's marginal benefit, as indicated by the height of their demand curves. The market demand curve for a public good is therefore the *vertical* sum of each of the individual demand curves.

The problem with public goods is that individuals know they can benefit from the existence of these goods whether or not they pay for them. A door-to-door collection to pay for sperm whale preservation or monument scrubbing would most likely come up short due to the number of **free riders** who attempt to benefit from a public good without paying for it. Given the nonrival and nonexcludable nature of many natural resources, individuals have little incentive to reveal their true preferences. Instead, they may feign disinterest, only to benefit from the preservation efforts and expenditures of others. A solution to the free rider problem is to have the government provide public goods and pay for them with taxes collected from everyone who stands to benefit. This is how many parks and wildlife preservation efforts are funded today.

11 The Washington Monument was erected in Washington, D.C. in memory of the first U.S. President, George Washington.

Summary

Market incentives aren't always what they should be. The efficiency of a free market can be marred by externalities, imperfect information, imperfect competition, and public goods. A manufacturing firm that does not fully internalize the burden of its emissions is unlikely to take the efficient level of precaution against harm to society. The firm may not purchase filters for its smokestacks even if their benefit to society exceeds their cost. If consumers have incomplete information about the health or environmental benefits of the good produced by the firm, they may purchase too few. If the firm is a monopoly, it will charge a relatively high price that leads to an inefficiently low level of production and consumption. And if the good provides benefits that everyone can enjoy regardless of whether they buy the good, consumers will prefer to free ride on the expenditures of others, and purchase an inefficiently small quantity of the good.

Great minds have grappled with solutions to market failure with some success. Arthur C. Pigou suggested taxes and subsidies that would cause decision makers to internalize the full costs and benefits of their behavior. Ronald Coase saw private bargaining between polluters and victims as a path to efficiency. Garrett Hardin advocated the assignment of private property rights as a solution to the tragedy of the commons. And many have called for various forms of government to provide public goods with tax dollars, to enact and enforce antitrust legislation against monopoly power, and to summon greater information sharing with inspections, regulations, and threats of litigation. Market failure persists, as evidenced by existing monopolies, uninformed consumers, underfunded public goods, and mispriced sources of externalities. In light of these problems, the benefit of studying environmental economics far exceeds the cost.

Markets fail when we don't pay the full price of our behavior. Would you ride a bicycle more often if you had to pay the full price of the externalities caused by driving a car?

Problems for Review

1. Draw a graph with "miles driven" on the horizontal axis and "$ per mile "on the vertical axis. Draw curves to represent the marginal social cost, the marginal private cost, and the marginal benefit of driving. Label the socially optimal quantity Q_s and the quantity drivers will actually choose Q_p. Show how the graph would change as the result of a new, cleaner-burning fuel. Between the solutions suggested by Pigou, Hardin, and Coase, which one is most likely to be successful in this context? Why?

2. Consider the situation described in Table 3.4 under the legal rule that the injurer, Good Idea Lightbulb Co., is entitled under the injunctive remedy. Describe how the Coasian bargaining process would proceed and discuss the efficiency of the expected final outcome.

3. Advertising agencies have looked into projecting logos on the moon, which is a public good. Oscar and Craig both prefer a logo-free moon. Oscar's demand curve for logo-free days each year is a straight line starting at $365 with a slope of –1. Craig's demand curve is a straight line starting at $182.50 with a slope of –1/2. Draw Oscar and Craig's demand curves and the market demand curve, assuming they are the only two moon-lovers in the market. Suppose that through Coasian bargaining, logo-free days can be purchased for $200 each. Draw the price line and indicate the socially optimal quantity. How many days would be purchased if Craig were a free rider?

4. The text discusses several applications of the prisoner's dilemma. Explain a different situation in which your own self-interest has led to a noncooperative result that was inferior to the cooperative outcome.

5. Describe a situation in which you could be a free rider. Then, try to come up with a policy or procedure that would remove this temptation to free ride.

6. Consider the situation described in Table 3.4 under the legal rule that the victims (the citizens) are entitled under the damages remedy. Describe how the Coasian bargaining process would proceed and discuss the efficiency of the expected final outcome.

7. Drawing from what you learned in this chapter, briefly explain a major strength and a major weakness of a free market.

8. For each of the following externalities, explain the underlying source of inefficiency (what effects are felt beyond the decision maker) and suggest a solution that could bring the activity to its efficient level:

   a) Billboards along the highway detract from natural beauty.
   b) Vaccinations received by domestic animals help wild animals avoid disease because they won't catch the disease from those vaccinated.
   c) The use of e-mail communications as a substitute for letters reduces the number of trees harvested for paper production.

9. Explain two barriers to successful Coasian bargaining in the real world.

10. List four things you do that could cause externalities. For each, indicate whether you consider the effects on others when you make your decisions, and whether any policies are in place to help you internalize the effects of your behavior.

1. Find a website that describes legislation designed to curtail one of the sources of market failure.
2. Find a website that speaks in favor of free-market policies.
3. Find a website that speaks against free-market policies.

Internet Resources

The International Society on Individual Liberty (a libertarian view):
www.isil.org

Steve Kangas's Free-Market Failures:
www.huppi.com/kangaroo/Marketfailures.htm

Tax-Based Solutions to Market Failure:
www.tutor2u.net/economics/content/topics/marketfail/environmental_taxation.htm

Further Reading

Calabresi, Guido, and A. Douglas Melamed. "Property Rules, Liability Rules and Inalienability: One View of the Cathedral." *Harvard Law Review* 85 (1972): 1089. An overview of rules and remedies applicable in nuisance disputes.

Coase, Ronald H. "The Problem of Social Cost." *Journal of Law and Economics* 3 (October 1960): 1–44. An influential defense of private remedies.

Hardin, Garrett. "The Tragedy of the Commons." *Science* 162 (1968): 1243–1248. A brief article outlining Hardin's famous concept.

Pigou, Arthur C. *The Economics of Welfare*. London: Macmillan, 1932. Pigou's insightful argument for the use of taxes and subsidies to equate private and social costs and benefits.

Smith, Fred L., and Kent Jeffreys. "A Free-Market Environmental Vision." In *Market Liberalism: A Paradigm for the 21st Century*, edited by Ed Crane and David Boaz, Washington, D.C.: Cato Institute, 1993. A pro-free-market perspective from a conservative think tank.

The Ultimate Guide: Dolphins. The Discovery Channel, 2002. Available at www.tursiops.org/dolfin/guide/smart.html. An overview of dolphin intelligence with an environmental economics anecdote or two.

A "free rider" problem? Without government, who would provide the bike lanes and roads?

4 The Role of Government

The movies typically portray government, like romance, as being either idyllic or disastrous. In life, both tend to be a blend of the essential and the absurd. Government's role in the efficient allocation of environmental resources, and its taxonomy as essential or absurd, depend on the effectiveness of the "free market" alternative. When successful, free-market mechanisms can allocate resources to those who value them the most, invite the production of goods until the marginal benefit equals the marginal cost, and price goods to reflect a combination of value and scarcity. As a particular resource becomes relatively scarce, its price will rise, inducing greater efforts to supply the product or find viable replacements. This pricing mechanism goes on display every time rising gas prices motivate research into alternative energy, energy conservation, and new discoveries of oil. Chapter 3 explained why free markets have difficulty allocating resources efficiently in the presence of imperfect information, imperfect competition, externalities, or free riders. Further, some goods, like air and river water, have no formal markets to address their allocation. When markets are inefficient or non-existent, government can provide needed remedies. If mismanaged, government can also come with excessive bureaucracy, ineptitude, misguidance, and corruption.

Being the product of human will, government is potent and pliable. When those in power lose support, the fates of entire nations can shift dramatically. The Arab Spring protests have ousted a handful of leaders since 2011. History has seen some of the most malevolent, domineering

The U.S. Capital Building in Washington, D.C.

regimes replaced by relatively benign assemblages of authority. This was the case in many Eastern European nations during the 1990s and in several African nations in the 2000s. The message is that citizens with courage and insight can indeed shape government. In a democracy, if voters and leaders understand the potential virtues and blunders of government, they are better prepared to exercise collective authority and promote efficient environmental policy. For these reasons, this chapter is devoted to the role of government. The chapters that follow address related issues of policy and procedure.

The Meaning and Purpose of Government

What Is Government?

Saint Augustine quotes a captured pirate as saying to Alexander the Great, "Because I [keep hostile possession of the sea] with a petty ship, I am called a robber, whilst thou who dost it with a great fleet art styled emperor." In perilous times, the primary distinction between a government and a gang can be size. Strength and acceptance also convey authority, and a **government** is a body with the authority to govern. Any type of government can go astray of environmental and social goals, although democratic elections provide incentives for even the most selfish leaders to address their constituents' needs. In modern times, environmentalism has become a political ideology in itself, embraced by political parties such as the Green Parties of Britain, Canada, and the United States.

Political-economic systems parade in myriad forms. What follows is a thumbnail sketch of several of the most prominent models.

An **autocracy** is governed by one individual with unlimited power. Dictatorships such as Iraq under Saddam Hussein and Pakistan under Pervez Musharraf resembled autocracies, although these leaders lacked the absolute power of a true autocrat like King Louis XIV of France. A **theocracy** is a government run by priests or clergy, such as Iran under Ayotollah Khomeini. Theocracies have become more common with the growth of Islamic fundamentalism, and more relevant to the West since the terrorist attacks of September 11, 2001.

A **monarchy** is ruled by a king, queen, emperor, or empress. In this century most European monarchies, such as the British monarchy, have limited power. Some monarchies in Africa, the Middle East, and Asia continue to hold absolute, usually inherited, power. A **plutocracy** is governed by the wealthy, or by those primarily influenced by the wealthy. Legislators in the United States formed the Disclose, Amend, Reform, and Empower task force in 2013 to temper the political influence of the rich. Their campaign finance reform proposals include limits on large political donations, and for small donations, matching funds and tax credits.

Communism is a system designed to eliminate material inequities via collective ownership of property. Legislators from a single political party—the Communist Party—divide wealth for equal advantage among citizens. The pitfalls of communism include a lack of incentives for risk taking and innovation. The critical role of the central government in allocating wealth and setting production quotas makes this scheme particularly vulnerable to corruption.

Socialism shares with communism the goal of fair distribution and the stumbling block of inadequate incentives. However, instead of the wages being controlled by the government as under a communist system, under a socialist system wages are determined by negotiations between trade unions and management, and a single political party does not rule the economy. Quasi-socialist systems exist in Britain, Canada, Sweden, and elsewhere.

Under **pluralism**, governmental decisions are based on negotiations among leaders from business, government, labor groups, and other constituencies. Power is in a state of flux, with no one group retaining a dominant position for long. **Imperialism** is a policy of expansion and domination by a nation's authority. The European imperialism of the fifteenth to nineteenth centuries involved notable territorial acquisition, which was largely dismantled in the twentieth century.

Classical liberalism is a political philosophy espousing freedom from church and state authority, free-enterprise economics, and individual freedoms. It was the foundation of parliamentary democracy in Britain and the philosophy of choice among many founding fathers of the United States. Unlike classical liberals, **modern liberals** are sometimes characterized as favoring more government rather than less, and as advocating a weak form of socialism.

While communism places individuals second to society, **fascism** (also known as **national socialism** or **Nazism**) places individuals second to the state or race. In a rejection of democracy, **fascists** emphasize loyalty to a strong leader (Mussolini or Hitler, for example), national pride, and a collective view of society. The absence of checks and balances in fascist states and the incentives for leaders to abuse their power for national and personal gain are among the reasons why such forms of government have infamous legacies. The relevant catchphrase may be: "Power corrupts, and absolute power corrupts absolutely."

In a **capitalist** society, private individuals own land and businesses, and operate them in the pursuit of profit. Markets determine prices and quantities for goods and services. Wages are set by negotiations between employees or their unions and management. The government may regulate businesses and provide tax-supported social benefits. A **democracy** is governed by the people or their elected representatives. Decisions are made by majority rule, which does not prevent social injustices, but may make them less likely. The United Kingdom, the United States, and Japan are among the many successful democracies.

Is Government Necessary?

Philosophers Thomas Hobbes and John Locke argued that government is essential. Hobbes (1946, Ch. 13) wrote that "during the time men live without a common power to keep them all in awe, they are in that condition which is called war. ... In such a condition there is no place for industry; ... no arts; no letters; no society; and which is worst of all, continual fear, and danger of violent death; and the life of man, solitary, poor, nasty, brutish, short." Karl Marx argued that government is simply an instrument of class domination and would "wither away" with the abolition of distinct classes under communism. **Authoritarians** question the practicality of self-government, and look to centralized government for the advancement of society. **Conservatives** express concern about government's efficiency in the role of environmental steward, as stated by Jerry Taylor of the Cato Institute: "It is not 'market failure' that leads to pollution, but government failure to recognize property rights and to hold polluters fully liable for their activities ... ."[1] Conservatives sometimes advocate privatized or decentralized decision making, arguing that government officials are out of touch or that the process of government is unwieldy.[2] **Libertarians** call for self-government, believing that government's role should be limited to protecting citizens from coercion and violence. **Anarchists** feel that all forms of government

1 See www.cato.org/research/natur-st.html.

2 For a conservative rebuke of U.S. government environmental policies, see Stroup and Meiners (2000).

are oppressive and should be abolished. Anarchists have played a significant role in recent anti-globalization protests, which also focus on environmental issues.[3]

In the context of environmental economics, the call for government involvement ranges from a whisper to a shout, depending on the state of the nation in question. Factors that influence the need for government involvement in environmental protection include:

- *Population density*
- *Religious and social culture*
- *Education*
- *Wealth*
- *Degree of industrialization*
- *Sensitivity of the existing ecosystem*

In the early eighteenth century, 3 million people lived on the North American continent. With no industrialization, the collective environmental impact was negligible and there was little need for government to resolve externalities. The same is true today in a decreasing number of isolated regions in the Arctic, Central America, and Africa.

French philosopher Jean Jacques Rousseau argued that humans are essentially good, but corrupted by society. A society's religious and cultural stance toward the environment can obviate or escalate the need for government intervention. For example, the teachings of Buddhism prohibit harm to all sentient (conscious) beings whether human or animal. As a result, there is little need for the likes of the Endangered Species Act among devout Buddhists. In other situations, government can play a critical role in shaping society. Through education and exemplary leaders, government itself can help foster the type of moral climate that makes its role as forceful defender less necessary.

The environmental concerns associated with sensitive ecosystems and industrialization are clear. The influences of education and wealth are less certain. Education systems can disseminate information about environmental concerns and conservation methods, or pass on a more materialistic focus. Wealth is a double-edged sword. Having more money facilitates waste because wealthy individuals and firms can overindulge in resources in ways the poor cannot. Yet having more money makes expenditures on environmental protection relatively painless. For a typical family in Bangladesh, the price of an emissions-reducing catalytic fireplace represents a full year's income. For a wealthy family, the

3 For an anarchist's view of the link between environmentalism and anarchy, see www.spunk.org/library/intro/sp001695.html.

opportunity cost might be one evening at the Ritz Hotel. Clean air and water are classified as *normal goods*, meaning that people with higher incomes are willing to spend more on them. A study that sorted out the effects of income and education on waste found that resource expenditures decreased with education but increased with income.[4] So support of education, and environmental curricula in particular, may be among the solutions for governments in countries facing rapid industrialization, population growth, or soaring incomes.

The Role of Government: Bit Part? Supporting Actor? Lead?

Historical Ideologies

Advocates of a laissez-faire or free-market approach have long trumpeted the virtues of a market unfettered by government intervention. In the words of the third U.S. president, Thomas Jefferson, "That government is best that governs least." A contemporary of Jefferson's and a fellow classical liberal, Adam Smith, thought that a free market driven by the actions of self-interested individuals would regulate and self-correct itself. Classical conservatives including Edmund Burke felt that classical liberals placed too much faith in human rationality. They argued that people are prone to bouts of unreasonable behavior, irrational passions, and immorality. The classical conservatives favored adherence to the institutions of government and the church as well as to societal traditions and standards in order to avoid the chaotic results of freewheeling human impulses.

The nineteenth century brought with it monopolies, deception of consumers, gross economic inequities, and abuse of the environment. Modern liberals, like classical conservatives, became leery of the laissez-faire approach. They felt that without the influence of regulations and liability, firms did not perform adequate testing to determine the health and environmental safety of their products. Under these conditions, pertinent information held by firms was less likely to be passed on to customers. Led by Englishman Thomas Hill Green in the late nineteenth century, and the likes of Woodrow Wilson and Franklin D. Roosevelt in the early twentieth century, modern liberals championed the causes of labor, education, the environment, and the freedoms of speech and press. With these efforts, the U.S. government received significant new roles in tempering market power, promoting transparency, and combating externalities and free-rider problems.

The role of government progressed similarly in other industrialized nations during the nineteenth and twentieth centuries. For example, Britain passed the Smoke Nuisance Abatement Act in 1853, the Rivers Pollution Prevention Act in 1876, the Protection of Birds Act in 1954, and the Clean Air Act in 1956.

4 See Anderson (2005). Although waste levels appear to increase with income levels, as discussed in Chapter 9, the environmental Kuznets curve suggests that pollution might decrease with GDP when per capita income exceeds about $13,000.

Thomas Jefferson, the third president of the United States, stated: "that government is best that governs least." But abuses of market power in the nineteenth century led to calls for greater government involvement in the marketplace.

Modern Problems with Private Solutions

In Chapter 3 you learned Ronald Coase's theory that private negotiations can lead to efficient outcomes if property rights are clearly defined and the affected parties can bargain with few or no transaction costs. If Coasian bargaining could indeed resolve a broad range of externalities, there would be little need for government taxes, subsidies, and restrictions conceived for the same purpose. However, efficient private solutions like those proposed by Coase are less likely in the presence of complicating factors that include:

- ***Multiple sources of an externality,*** *making it hard to know with whom to bargain*
- ***Multiple victims,*** *making it difficult to organize the affected parties*
- ***Incomplete information*** *about the costs or benefits of the externality*
- ***Strategic behavior*** *involving aggressive attempts to gain larger portions of the benefits from negotiation*
- ***Time lags*** *between the cause and the effect of the externality, making it difficult to identify the externality and its source*
- ***Asymmetric information,*** *which can mean that those creating a negative externality are aware of its danger, but those affected by it are not*
- ***Transaction costs,*** *due to the location, availability, and opportunity costs of those involved, making it difficult to assemble the parties for negotiations*
- ***Social mores,*** *making it uncomfortable for the victims to confront those causing the externalities*

While many of these complicating factors are common, existing social mores may make the other factors moot. Modern society has developed few efficient approaches to financial negotiation over the behavior of others. It is uncomfortable enough to ask those living nearby in the residence hall to stop playing music during study periods, much less offering them money not to do so. Have you ever offered someone a bribe to stop smoking in a restaurant or to stop smacking their gum in the library? Neighbors complains about the unsightly house across the street, but do the complainers ever knock on their neighbor's door with an offer of $1,000 in exchange for a less neon color of house paint? When development or industry threatens natural habitat, the transaction costs of organizing everyone involved and negotiating an agreement make a private solution even less likely.

Government can provide other solutions to such externalities. In the residence hall example, you and others with similar views might be more inclined to communicate with your resident advisor or student government representative—the local government authority—to set out new hall policies about when and where loud music can be played. The resident advisor would also provide authority with which to enforce these policies. Similarly, larger forms of government tax or restrict noise pollution, unleashed pets, overgrown lawns, and hazardous waste, while subsidizing geothermal heating systems, reforestation, wildflower plantings, and education. The next section explains these and other public approaches to market failure.

Governmental Solutions to Market Failure

Enforcement of Property Rights

In the selfishness that is human nature, and with notable exceptions, humans tend to take better care of what they own than what they do not own. People are unlikely to litter in their own yards, dump toxins in their own ponds, or overhunt their own forests. Of course, all of the above occur with open-access resources such as publicly held lands. This is the **tragedy of the commons** problem cited by Garrett Hardin after he observed herdsmen allowing their cattle to overgraze common pastures because the burden is shared by many.

To understand the tragedy of the commons more clearly, consider harvesters of wild blackberry leaves for tea. For simplicity, suppose each blackberry plant has two leaves, one of which must remain on the plant in order for it to survive and grow a second leaf in the following season. Figure 4.1 illustrates a publicly owned tract with four herbal tea collectors and four blackberry plants. If the pickers want to maximize their harvests over the foreseeable future, how many leaves should the tea collec-

With no property rights, tea-leaf harvesters might not internalize the effects of leaving plants without enough leaves to live for another season. If a picker will not be returning to the same patch again, or if other pickers are likely to pick leaves that are left behind, the picker has no incentive to conserve the resource. The excessive leaf collection that results is one example of what Hardin called the tragedy of the commons.

Figure 4.1
Harvesting on Open-Access Property

tors pick upon reaching the blackberry patch? If they are subsequently moving on to another region and will never pick in this region again, they should pick everything they can get their hands on, because the loss of plants is felt only by others. If it is likely that at least one of the other pickers will pick the remaining second leaves off of the plants, it is in each picker's best interest to pick as many leaves as possible. The loss of the plants is inevitable, and leaves that are left by one picker merely end up in the harvest of another picker. Only if all of the leaf pickers want to return to that location to receive benefits from future harvests, *and* if each party can trust each of the other parties to pursue a plan of leaving one leaf per plant, are they wise to leave some leaves alone.

When open access prevents users from internalizing, or feeling for themselves, the full costs of their behavior, one solution is the extension and enforcement of private property rights. Figure 4.2 presents the blackberry leaf scenario with the modification that property lines have been established to divide the land among the herbal tea harvesters. With each picker owning a blackberry plant, the entire loss from picking both leaves is felt by the owner. Even if the picker will be moving on before the next harvest, the value of the resources left behind will be reflected in the selling price the picker can obtain for the property, and thus the losses will be internalized. Ocean fisheries, stocks of hunted game, and subsurface pools of oil owned by multiple parties provide similar opportunities for exploitation when property rights are not well defined and enforced.

The transferability of property rights is critical to efficiency because it allows property to be owned by those who can make the best use of it. In the absence

Figure 4.2 *Harvesting on Private Property*

If each harvester owns a particular plant (or patch), the effects of harvest behavior are internalized. To over-pick a plant is to decrease the value of the picker's own resource. Harvesters thus have an incentive to pick only the efficient quantity of leaves. Similarly, property rights convey incentives for the efficient treatment of fisheries, forests, oil pools, and dumpsites, among other resources.

reality check

Where the Buffalo Roamed

Property rights change behavior, sometimes in favor of wildlife living on the property. Few people would treat their own property the way they treat open-access areas. Trees accessible to loggers in national parks are more likely to become lumber than trees in our own backyards. Animals, too, can benefit from property rights that apply to them and the soil they tread upon. Before property rights were clearly defined in the western United States, buffalo were open-access resources, and they were slaughtered by the thousands—sometimes purely for sport, as with those killed by riflemen riding passenger trains. The U.S. government privatized much of the land west of the Mississippi River with the Homestead Act of 1862. This act divided the land into 160-acre tracts that any citizen could claim. If the homesteaders "improved" the property with a dwelling, grew crops, and remained for at least five years, the tract became their property free and clear. The government then proceeded to support private property ownership with the provision of courts to help resolve land disputes, laws to protect property values, and police to deter trespassers and enforce the findings of the courts. With the enforcement of property rights came private (and public) pollution cleanups, reforestation, and a resurgence of buffalo in the West. Today it would be difficult to hunt buffalo without violating property rights to land and to the animals themselves. Fences prevent buffalo from migrating the way they used to, but the fences also assure protection by the private ranchers who have a personal stake in the natural assets on their property. The ranchers may still turn their stakes into steaks, but only at a sustainable rate.

For a thorough examination of the relationship between buffalo (bison) and property rights, see Lueck (2002).

of market failure and its miscues, the market will allocate property to those who value it the most, be they farmers, developers, or conservation groups such as the Nature Conservancy. Efficient transfers are impeded by incomplete information about ownership, boundaries, and value, and by all sources of transaction costs. Government can facilitate the transfer of property rights by keeping accurate records of exactly what is owned by whom and how much was paid for it. Government also provides courts for the civilized resolution of boundary disputes and other conflicts that arise.

Provision of Public Goods

Beyond defining and protecting property rights, government can allocate goods and services that would be over- or underproduced by private markets. Chapter 3 explained that public goods such as national defense and streetlights would be underprovided without government assistance because "free riders" would misrepresent their interests and seek benefits from the purchases of others. There are many public goods in the realm of the environment and natural resources. When hazardous waste sites are cleaned up, when government-sponsored research findings are disseminated, and when an animal species is protected, society benefits. These benefits are nonrival and nonexcludable in that one's enjoyment of a healthy and biologically diverse environment does not preclude the enjoyment of others, nor can one exclude another from this enjoyment. Without intervention, the protection of wilderness areas, the supply of clean air and water, and the funding of research on environmental issues would be inadequate as individuals feign disinterest. Government's role includes the provision of these environmental public goods, the collection of taxes to pay for them, and the enactment and enforcement of regulations designed to protect them.

Taxes and Subsidies

You have already learned that externalities can be a source of market failure. Figure 4.3 depicts the market for gasoline, in which there are marginal external costs to health and the environment in addition to the private marginal costs of producing and consuming gasoline. For simplicity, assume that the marginal external cost is constant at $1 per gallon of gasoline. (In reality, estimates of the external cost of gasoline exceed $2 per gallon.[5]) In the absence of government intervention, equilibrium occurs at point A, with 1,000 gallons of gasoline consumed at a price of $3.75 per gallon. Note that the social marginal cost (MC_{social}) exceeds the marginal benefit (*MB*) for every gallon in excess of 850, and that consumption exceeds the social optimum by 150 gallons.

One remedy for this case of overindulgence would be a tax equal to the marginal external cost of $1 per gallon. This is effectively a Pigou tax as discussed in Chapter 3. A $1 excise tax on the sellers of gasoline would cause sellers to pay the external cost of gasoline and equate the social marginal cost with the private marginal cost. In Figure 4.3, this means that the private marginal cost curve ($MC_{private}$) would shift up by $1 to coincide with the social marginal cost curve (MC_{social}). The equilibrium between the new private marginal cost and the marginal benefit would occur at point B, and output would be at the efficient level of 850 gallons.

The same result would occur if a Pigovian sales tax were imposed on the consumers of gasoline. In this event consumers would internalize the external

5 For example, see Resources for the Future's 2007 report, "Automobile Externalities and Policies," downloadable at http://www.rff.org/Documents/RFF-DP-06-26-REV.pdf.

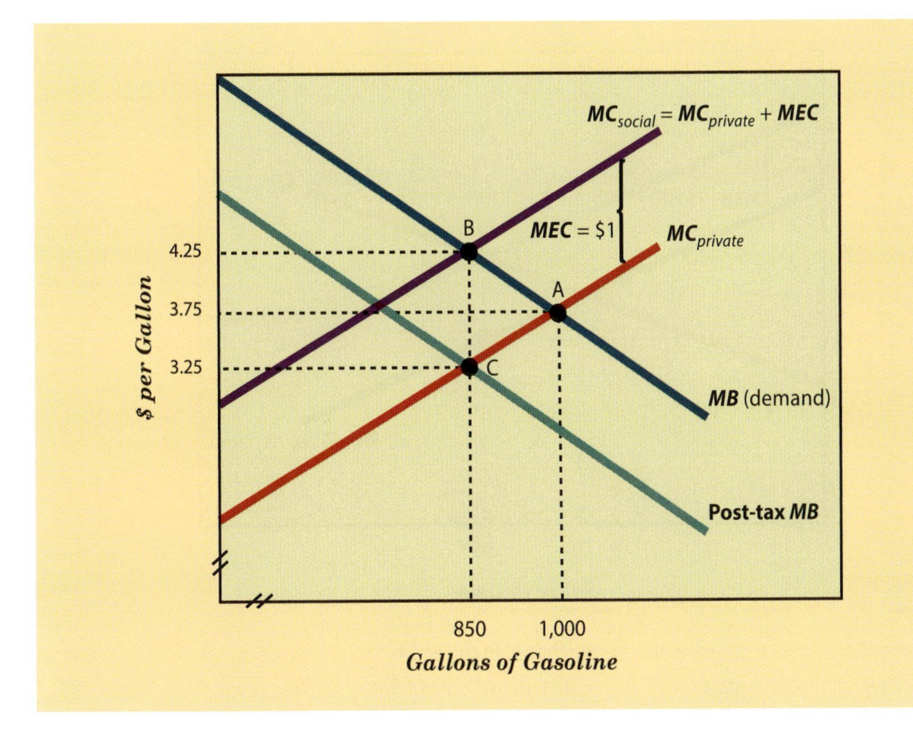

Figure 4.3
Negative Externalities and Pigovian Taxes

The pre-tax equilibrium in this market occurs at point A, with 1,000 gallons of gasoline selling for \$3.75 per gallon. Due to a negative externality of \$1 per gallon, the social marginal cost (MC_{social}) of the last 250 gallons sold exceeds the marginal benefit. To correct for this inefficiency, a Pigovian tax equal to the \$1 marginal external cost (*MEC*) could be imposed on gasoline sales. This would lead consumers to internalize the full cost of their behavior and choose the efficient level of consumption—850 gallons per period. The post-tax price to consumers would be \$4.25; sellers would receive \$3.25 per gallon.

costs, and the market demand curve (reflecting consumers' marginal benefit minus the tax) would shift *down* by \$1, as illustrated by the downward-sloping light blue line. The new equilibrium between the private marginal cost and the post-tax marginal benefit would occur at point C. Regardless of whether the tax is imposed on the buyers or on the sellers, the equilibrium quantity is 850, the buyers' total payment is \$4.25 per gallon, and the sellers' post-tax revenue is \$3.25 per gallon. The division of the tax burden depends on the shapes of the supply and demand curves, and not on the party that actually pays the tax. If the demand curve were less elastic (steeper), for example, the buyers would bear a greater portion of the tax burden.

Government can also address positive externalities. Consider the market for solar panels. In addition to the private benefits from solar panels in terms of energy provision, they provide positive environmental externalities by decreasing the need for fossil fuel extraction and combustion. These benefits go largely to society and are not fully internalized by those deciding how many solar panels

Figure 4.4
Positive Externalities and Government Subsidies

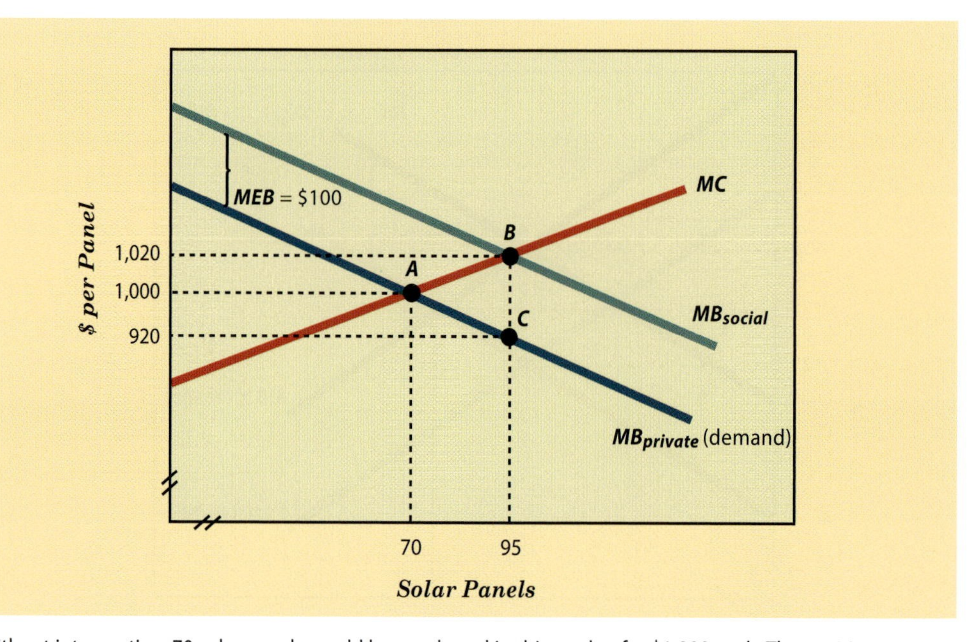

Without intervention, 70 solar panels would be purchased in this market for $1,000 each. The positive externalities associated with solar panels cause the social marginal benefit (MB_{social}) to exceed the private marginal benefit ($MB_{private}$) by $100 per panel. As a result, consumers purchase fewer than the socially efficient quantity of 95 panels. A government subsidy equal to the marginal external benefit (*MEB*) would bring consumers to internalize all of the benefits of their purchases and consume at the efficient level.

to purchase. The free-market equilibrium occurs at point A in Figure 4.4, with 70 panels purchased for $1,000 each. At this level of consumption the cost of providing another panel is below the social marginal benefit (MB_{social}), and society would be better off if more panels were installed. If consumers received a subsidy for each panel equal to the $100 value of the positive externality, the consumers would internalize the benefits they provide to society. The private marginal benefit curve ($MB_{private}$) would shift up to coincide with the social marginal benefit curve, and equilibrium would occur at point B. With the subsidy in place, consumers would purchase the socially optimal quantity of 95 panels. The same outcome would result if producers received a $100 subsidy for each panel. The production subsidy would shift the marginal cost curve down by $100, causing the marginal cost curve to intersect the demand curve at point C, again at the efficient quantity of 95 panels.

The governments of many industrialized nations including Germany and the United States subsidize solar panels, as well as research on alternative fuels, public transportation, and related sources of positive environmental externalities. Coming chapters discuss various mechanisms by which governments can implement taxes and subsidies, including emission charges for pollution, deposit-refund systems for bottles, tax credits for electric vehicles, and equipment subsidies for emission-abatement equipment.

Solar panels and other products that provide positive externalities are under-consumed in a free market. Properly conceived government subsidies can help remedy the resulting misallocation of resources.

Liability

Government provides the systems that create, interpret, and enforce the law. With roughly 18 million new civil cases filed each year in the United States, the litigious tendencies of American society make it more risky and expensive to cause harm to others and the environment. Lawsuits over how the costs will be shared have added more than $10 billion to expenditures on hazardous waste cleanups administered by the federal government's *Superfund* program.[6] At issue is the optimal level of litigation. The open-access nature of the court system may invite overuse. Does the current threat of litigation cause more harm than good? Critics claim that excessive litigation destroys international competitiveness, hinders innovation, and creeps into the prices we pay for most goods and services. Others argue that there is no litigation crisis, and that the threat and cost of litigation are the prices we must pay to promote responsible behavior.

There is no question that the volume of litigation generated by what are called "mass toxic torts" (a tort is a private wrong such as polluting a neighbor's pond) can be tremendous. Mesothelioma[7] and related health problems associated with

6 See http://www.epa.gov/superfund/.

7 Mesothelioma is a type of cancer caused by asbestos. See www.mesotheliomainfocenter.com/.

asbestos exposure generated litigation from an estimated 340,000 claimants. Revelations about the toxicity of Agent Orange, used during the Vietnam War, generated an estimated 125,000 claims over the following two decades. Since the Valdez oil spill in Alaska, Exxon has paid over $3.4 billion for cleanup, compensation, settlements, and fines, and stands to pay another $507 million in punitive damages. And cancer deaths among U.S. veterans following exposure to toxic smoke from garbage incineration pits in Iraq and Afghanistan led to class action lawsuits against military contractor KBR, the pit operator.

Litigation is intended to inhibit behavior that unduly harms humans and the environment. A downside risk is that excessive litigation will inhibit innovation. Developers of new products and processes, including medicinal cures and alternate energies, may not want to bear the risk of costly lawsuits in order to introduce new products with uncertain dangers and rewards. Consider a firm pondering a $2 million project to develop improved lithium-ion batteries for electric cars. The firm estimates a 1-in-3 chance that the new battery will provide $6.9 million worth of benefits to society, which for simplicity we will assume are internalized via revenues or subsidies. There is a 2-in-3 chance that the battery will not produce any benefits, and there is a 1-in-10,000 chance that several years after its introduction, the battery will be found to have caused environmental damage on the scale of the Exxon oil spill. In that case the firm will have to pay $2 billion for cleanup and $4 billion for punitive damages. The firm's **expected cost and benefit**[8] from the new venture are found by multiplying the probability of each possible outcome by the value of that outcome:

$$\text{Expected cost} = \$2{,}000{,}000 + \frac{1}{10{,}000}(\$6{,}000{,}000{,}000) = \$2.6 \text{ million}$$

$$\text{Expected benefit} = \frac{1}{3}(\$6{,}900{,}000) + \frac{2}{3}(0) = \$2.3 \text{ million}$$

It would be unwise for this firm to proceed with development due to the small risk of large punitive damages.

A firm is *risk neutral* if it cares only about the expected value of its cost, and not about the range of possible costs. A firm is *risk averse* if the mere uncertainty involved with damage awards imposes a burden on the firm beyond the expected litigation cost. A risk-averse firm is troubled by facing some probability of paying a large amount and some probability of paying a small amount, and would willingly pay extra to know for sure that the actual cost would equal the expected cost. The largest amount the firm would be willing to pay, in addition to the expected cost, to avoid uncertainty is called the **risk burden**. For example, a firm with a 90 percent chance of avoiding costly litigation and a 10 percent chance of paying $1 million in damage awards faces an expected cost of $(0.9 \times \$0) + (0.1 \times \$1{,}000{,}000) = \$100{,}000$. If the firm would be willing to pay $110,000, $10,000 more than the

8 See Chapter 2 for a review of expected-value calculations.

expected cost, with certainty to avoid the 10 percent chance of having to pay $1 million, the risk burden for the firm is $10,000. The firm would be willing to pay up to $110,000 for insurance that paid the damage award of either zero or $1,000,000, thereby removing all uncertainty for the firm. If you think about it, it's clear that companies selling fire, theft, health, and other types of insurance can earn profits only because risk-averse customers are willing to pay more than the expected cost to avoid uncertainty about the relevant outcomes.

The tool of litigation can deter inappropriate environmental threats if the cost of carrying out potentially damaging activities, including the expected litigation cost and the risk burden, equals the cost of those activities to society. Unfortunately, the determination of appropriate damage awards requires estimates of the likelihood of harm, the likelihood of identifying the offending firms and successfully litigating against them, the dollar value of the damages, the firms' attitudes toward risk-taking, and their associated risk burdens.

Since a firm will not engage in an activity unless the expected benefits exceed the expected costs plus the risk burden, firms with higher risk burdens require relatively low expected damage awards to dissuade them from wrongful behavior. The possibilities for frivolous litigation and litigation against the wrong parties further cloud the quest for effective litigation. For those firms whose levels of precaution would be appropriate *without* the added incentives that litigation provides, the threat of litigation causes excessive levels of precaution. The difficulty of calculating and administering appropriate damage awards has led economists and legal scholars to pursue legal rules that encourage reasonable out-of-court settlements of disputes and alternative forms of dispute resolution. Chapter 15 provides additional discussions on environmental dispute resolution.

Regulations

Some experts advocate regulations as an alternative to liability. Economist W. Kip Viscusi (1991, 173) suggests that "the solution to mass toxic torts and related problems of environmental disease is to eliminate the involvement of the products liability system. Deterrence for previous actions is irrelevant, and deterrence for current and future risk is best provided through effective government regulation of risk exposure levels." Regulations could set standards for environmental safety that are *exculpatory*, meaning that those who comply with a designated level of safety testing, or who maintain their emissions below a particular level, could not subsequently be held liable for those actions. There is no limit to the standard of precaution that could be required under such a policy, and by meeting that standard, firms could avoid the risk of paying highly uncertain jury awards.

Garrett Hardin (1968) of tragedy-of-the-commons fame had his own ideas about how regulations could handle problems of resource scarcity. Like Thomas Malthus, Hardin felt that overpopulation would lead to starvation and environmental degradation. He dismissed technical and scientific solutions as essentially too little too late, and said that governments must regulate population size. According to Hardin, "To couple the concept of freedom to breed with the belief that everyone born has an equal right to the commons is to lock the world into a tragic course of action" (1246). Late in the twentieth century, the Chinese government tried Hardin's solution, admonishing couples to have only one child, with some "success." The United Nations Universal Declaration of Human Rights proclaimed this degree of regulation to be extreme. In any case, less invasive regulations can provide meaningful limits and guidelines to address environmental concerns.

Looking again at the example of fuel consumption, instead of taxing gasoline, a number of different regulations could bring gasoline consumption closer to an efficient level. Norway has the lowest highway speed limit in Europe, 90 kilometers per hour, in part to reduce fuel consumption. The U.S. Congress has debated energy bills that would reduce the externality itself by requiring cleaner-burning fuels, alternative energy sources, and lower-emission engines. Regulations could also set limits on the amount of gasoline consumption or the amount of emissions per firm or household. Another regulatory option is to pursue efficiency by promoting alternative forms of transportation. For example, requirements for bike lanes or sidewalks along short commuter routes would encourage biking and walking and thereby reduce the level of gasoline consumption.

Education and Moral Leadership

Education and moral leadership can elicit environmental consciousness and improve decision making even in the absence of taxes, laws, and more coercive remedies. A nation's leaders set influential examples with their actions. It sends a signal when

- *leaders establish the first wildlife conservation area for a nation, as the government of Papua New Guinea did recently;*
- *an administration triples the renewable energy sources of a country, as Greek Prime Minister Costas Karamanlis's did;*
- *a first lady plants an organic garden at the presidential residence, as Michelle Obama did at the White House; or*
- *a leader implores every citizen to actively promote sustainable development, as Singapore's Prime Minister Lee Hsien Loong did.*

When officials call for their own thermostats be set at a moderate level, their cars to be electric, or their paper to be recycled, this sets a tone for the country, and invigorates efforts on the environmental front.

Government is also the principal provider of schooling. Education is a means of affecting the skills and attitudes of society and of promoting the efficient use

Whitehouse Photo by Joyce N. Boghosian

Role models make a difference. First Lady Michelle Obama and children from a nearby school plant an organic garden at the White House.

of environmental resources. *Together India* reports that out of concern for India's troubled environment, "environment education has been introduced into every self-respecting secondary school's curriculum."[9] Since the energy crises of the 1970s, public school curricula in the United States have included units on how to conserve fossil fuels. More generally, education can teach students to be aware of the costs and benefits of their actions and think creatively about solutions to environmental threats and resource scarcity.

Dispute Resolution

When there is disagreement over the use of a forest, the interpretation of environmental regulations, or the liability of a company for hazardous waste cleanup, government can work to limit the expense and uncertainty of dispute resolution. In the absence of a strong government, civilized dispute resolution is less likely. Even if courts can be set up in such a situation, they have little influence without the backing of a stalwart government.

International conflicts reveal the dangers of limited authority. With no planetwide authority to support them, decisions made by international courts involving, for example, whaling in the oceans, are often ignored with few repercussions. As discussed in Chapter 11, the relative impotence of international law is unfortunate given the global scale of many environmental problems. Chapter 15 explains more of the sources and repercussions of environmental dispute resolution, as well as a variety of solutions.

9 See www.indiatogether.org/2003/aug/edu-envteach.htm.

The EPA and Environmental Legislation

The Environmental Protection Agency (EPA) is the backbone of the U.S. government's efforts to protect the environment. The EPA was established in 1970, a year that also gave birth to Earth Day and an unprecedented decade of environment legislation summarized in the Reality Check below. The environmental initiatives of that period included restrictions on lead-based paint, a ban on the pesticide DDT, phaseouts of leaded gasoline and the persistent organic pollutant PCB, and a phase-in of fuel economy standards for cars.

The momentum for these breakthroughs began mounting in 1962 after the publication of Rachel Carson's best-selling book *Silent Spring*. The book warned of the demise of songbirds due to organic phosphate insecticides, which also contaminate the human food supply. Calls for new environmental policy were rekindled by uproar over the use of a defoliant called Agent Orange during the Vietnam War. The product contained deadly dioxin, and was sprayed over jungles in Southeast Asia to destroy ground cover where opposing forces could hide. Intense public interest in the environment took President Richard Nixon's attention away from the war long enough for him to sign the National Environmental Policy Act on the first day of 1970. Later that year, he called for a strong, independent agency to establish and enforce environmental protection standards, conduct

reality check

Major U.S. Environmental Laws

Freedom of Information Act *5 U.S.C. s/s 552 (1966)*
This act allows any citizen to request government information that is not classified, confidential, a work in progress, or important for national security. Amendments in the law require that all federal agencies make data that will serve the public interest available in electronic form. For example, the National Response Center makes all oil and chemical spill data available online at www.nrt.org.

National Environmental Policy Act *42 U.S.C. s/s 4321 et seq. (1969)*
The National Environmental Policy Act requires all branches of government to file environmental assessments and environmental impact statements prior to taking actions that could significantly affect the environment. For example, these reports precede the construction of highways, airports, and military bases.

Occupational Safety and Health Act *29 U.S.C. 651 et seq. (1970)*
The Occupational Safety and Health Act is intended to secure workplace safety for employees. The act's standards limit exposures to toxic materials, excessive noise levels, extreme temperatures, unsanitary conditions, and mechanical dangers. OSHA also created the National Institute for Occupational Safety and Health to conduct research on employment hazards.

(continued)

Clean Air Act *42 U.S.C. s/s 7401 et seq. (1970)*
The Clean Air Act authorizes the EPA to establish national ambient air quality standards (NAAQS) for every state and direct the states to develop state implementation plans applicable to industrial pollution sources within each state. The act was amended in 1990 to better address associated problems, including acid rain, airborne toxins, ground-level ozone, and stratospheric ozone depletion.

Federal Insecticide, Fungicide, and Rodenticide Act *7 U.S.C. s/s 136 et seq. (1972)*
FIFRA gives the EPA authority to license pesticides, register major users (farmers, exterminators, and others), and study the effects of pesticides on health and the environment. Major users must take certification exams, and products must carry sufficient hazard warning labels. If used properly, the products cannot cause unreasonable harm to the environment.

Endangered Species Act *7 U.S.C. 136; 16 U.S.C. 460 et seq. (1973)*
The Endangered Species Act protects threatened and endangered plants and animals by prohibiting their elimination, import, export, or interstate sale. The law prohibits any action that results in the loss of a listed species or its habitat.

Safe Drinking Water Act *42 U.S.C. s/s 300f et seq. (1974)*
This act authorizes the EPA to establish purity standards for water that is potentially designed for human consumption, regardless of the source.

Resource Conservation and Recovery Act *42 U.S.C. s/s 6901 et seq. (1976)*
RCRA ("rick-rah") authorizes the EPA to oversee hazardous waste generation, transportation, treatment, storage, and disposal. This act does not cover abandoned hazardous waste, which is addressed by the Superfund under CERCLA (see below).

Toxic Substances Control Act *15 U.S.C. s/s 2601 et seq. (1976)*
The TSCA enables the EPA to track and require testing of some 75,000 industrial chemicals currently in use. The EPA can prohibit the manufacture and import of chemicals that pose an unreasonable risk to health or the environment.

Clean Water Act *33 U.S.C. s/s 1251 et seq. (1977)*
The CWA is a 1977 amendment to the Federal Water Pollution Control Act, originated in 1948. Under the CWA, the EPA can set effluent standards for industries on the basis of available technology and set surface-water quality standards for all contaminants. The act makes it illegal to discharge any pollutant into navigable waters without a permit.

Comprehensive Environmental Response, Compensation, and Liability Act *42 U.S.C. s/s 9601 et seq. (1980)*, reauthorized by the **Superfund Amendments and Reauthorization Act** *42 U.S.C. 9601 et seq. (1986)*. CERCLA ("Sir-cla") created the federal Superfund, intended for the cleanup of abandoned, uncontrolled, and (continued) emergency releases of hazardous materials into the environment. The acts also empower the EPA to seek those responsible for the releases and elicit their cooperation in the cleanup.

Emergency Planning and Community Right-to-Know Act *42 U.S.C. 11001 et seq. (1986)*
With Title III of the Superfund Amendments and Reauthorization Act, Congress enacted this legislation to help protect communities from chemical hazards. The act requires each state to name a state emergency response commission that divides the state into emergency planning districts and names a local emergency planning committee for each district.

Marine Protection, Research, and Sanctuaries Act (Ocean Dumping Act)
16 USC § 1431 et seq. and 33 USC §1401 et seq. (1988)
This act prohibits ocean dumping (1) in the U.S. territorial sea by anyone; (2) of material from the United States anywhere; and (3) of material from anywhere by U.S. agencies or vessels, without a permit. The decision standard for permit requests is whether the dumping will "unreasonably degrade or endanger" human health, welfare, or the marine environment.

Oil Pollution Act of 1990 *33 U.S.C. 2702 to 2761*
As the first line of defense against oil spills, this act requires operators of oil storage facilities and vessels to submit oil-spill response plans to the federal government. Oil-spill contingency plans are required for vulnerable areas. The EPA publishes guidelines for above-ground oil storage facilities, and the Coast Guard does the same for tankers. The act also provides that a tax on oil will finance a fund available to clean up spills when the responsible party will not or cannot do so.

Pollution Prevention Act *42 U.S.C. 13101 and 13102, s/s et seq. (1990)*
This act addresses concern that industries lack the information, technology, or focus to reduce pollution at the source, where it may be more easily addressed than at the stages of treatment and disposal. In an effort to promote cost-effective changes in production, operation, and raw materials use, the EPA is authorized to establish a source-reduction program that collects and disseminates information, and provides financial assistance to the states.

Energy Policy Act *42 USC §13201 et seq. (2005)*
This act addresses energy efficiency, renewable energy, oil and gas, coal, tribal energy, nuclear issues, vehicles and motor fuels, hydrogen, electricity, energy tax incentives, hydropower, geothermal energy, and climate change technology. The Act provides loan guarantees for entities that develop or adopt new technologies that reduce greenhouse gases emissions. The Act also increases the amount of biofuel that must be mixed with gasoline sold in the United States.

environmental research, and provide assistance to those working to improve the environment. On December 1, 1970, William "The Enforcer" Ruckelshaus received Senate confirmation as the first EPA administrator.

The U.S. government pooled most of the responsibility for protecting the environment under the auspices of the EPA. This included programs previously controlled by the Department of Health, Education and Welfare, the Department of the Interior, and the Food and Drug Administration. The EPA works to support the approaches to environmental inefficiencies explained in the previous section. The EPA establishes and enforces regulations that protect the environment and our health. The EPA participates in litigation, including lawsuits to establish liability for hazardous cleanup. And the EPA sponsors research and consumer education, thus providing information that is critical to the free-market approach.

Similar agencies enjoy varying degrees of success in most developed nations. These include the aptly named Environment Canada, Environmental Agency of England and Wales, Abu Dhabi Environmental Agency, and Environment Australia. The emergence of these agencies over the past four decades is symbolic of government's growing role in the protection and allocation of natural resources.

In the United States, several cabinet-level agencies share responsibility for policies and research on the environment:

- *The* ***Department of Energy*** *operates the Office of Energy Efficiency and Renewable Energy, which funds research into alternative fuels.*[10]

- *The* ***Department of the Interior*** *oversees the Office of Surface Mining, the Bureau of Land Management, the U.S. Fish and Wildlife Service, and the National Park Service among other agencies concerned with the environment.*[11]

- *The* ***Department of Agriculture*** *operates the Forest Service and the Natural Resource Conservation Service, which in turn oversees the Wetland Reserve programs, the National Resources Inventory, and Backyard Conservation programs.*[12]

- *The* ***Department of Health and Human Services*** *oversees the Agency for Toxic Substances and Disease Registry and the National Institute of Environmental Health Sciences, which studies the effects of pollution.*[13]

- *The* ***Department of Commerce*** *houses the Office of Environmental Technologies Industries and the National Oceanic and Atmospheric Administration, a sponsor of research on oceans, fisheries, and climate change.*[14]

10 See www.energy.gov/.

11 See www.doi.gov/.

12 See www.usda.gov/.

13 See www.dhhs.gov/.

14 See www.noaa.gov/.

- *The* ***Department of Housing and Urban Development*** *handles brownfield cleanup and recovery.*[15]

This broad oversight of the environmental agenda creates similarly broad opportunities for the government to apply economic tools to environmental problems.

Summary

Modern conservatives would like a smaller government. Modern liberals would like it refocused. Communists think it will wither away. Anarchists want to do away with it. But government seems to be here to stay. Laissez-faire approaches have their time and place, but market failure is a persistent nemesis in modern times, particularly in developed places. Government brings tools to the table with which to restrain market failure, including opportunities for

- *Pigovian taxes and subsidies*
- *A tort system*
- *Regulations*
- *Education*
- *Moral leadership*
- *Dispute-resolution mechanisms*
- *The provision of property rights*
- *The provision of public goods*

Government is a malleable human construct. By popular vote, brute force, or tidal changes in public sentiment, the governments of the world are molded for better or worse by human desires. We the people can influence government, and government can influence the environment. So to contemplate the appropriate role of government is to prepare for some of our greatest opportunities to effect environmental change.

15 See www.hud.gov/library/bookshelf07/bfields.cfm.

Problems for Review

1. One morning I received the following memo from the dean regarding noise pollution: "I have been asked to request that faculty members not play music in their offices. Our office walls are paper-thin and allow our neighbors no rest from our loud activities." Why do you suppose Coasian bargaining did not reconcile this problem before it went to the dean? How does this relate to the role of government?

2. What are the strengths and weaknesses of litigation and regulation as deterrents to environmental wrongdoing? Why do you suppose some politicians are outspoken against both litigation *and* regulations?

3. Under capitalism, socialism, and communism, most productive resources are owned respectively by private individuals, the government, and a single political party. Which of these political-economic systems would you expect to experience the fewest problems with the tragedy of the commons? Explain.

4. Present and defend your own favored approach to solving market failure in the case of a firm polluting the surrounding wilderness areas.

5. If you are unaware of the general views and initiatives of your nation's leader, study his or her website to see what the leader is up to. Make a list of what you perceive as the leader's top five priorities for government intervention, starting with the most important. These might include military strength, ending poverty, supporting businesses, protecting the environment, and so on. In your opinion, would an alternative prioritization increase social welfare? List the top five priorities that you would choose if you were the nation's leader and explain your answer.

6. Suppose the president of the Nature Conservancy, the leader of the country where you live, and the president of the He-Man Tree Haters Club are the only inhabitants of an island. They expect to be there for a long time, and they have the opportunity to plant more palm trees, the shade and view of which are public goods they all can enjoy.
   a) On a single graph, draw hypothetical palm tree demand curves as you would estimate them for each of these inhabitants, and a market demand curve for these public goods.
   b) Suppose that the opportunity cost of planting each palm tree equals the Nature Conservancy president's marginal benefit from the first tree according to the demand curve you have drawn. Draw a horizontal price line at that level.
   c) Indicate the quantity of trees that will be planted
      i. If the inhabitants experience free-rider problems and are unable to cooperate.
      ii. If a benevolent dictator could tax each inhabitant and provide the optimal quantity of trees.

7. In the 1978 Tellico Dam decision (*TVA v. Hill, 437 U.S. 187*), the U.S. Supreme Court declared that the Endangered Species Act (ESA) defines the value of endangered species as "incalculable," and that endangered species are to be saved "whatever the cost."
   a) *Would it be economically efficient to treat the value of endangered species as infinite? Explain.*
   b) *In your opinion, does the ESA cause endangered species to be treated as if they had infinite value in practice? Why or why not?*

8. There is current debate in many nations over the private use of public lands. How do you think classical liberals and modern liberals would differ over the issue of logging in the national parks?

9. In the country where you live, what aspects of the government resemble capitalism? What aspects resemble socialism? Are there aspects of other systems of government?

10. Of the factors that complicate private solutions listed in this chapter, which two present the largest problems where you live? What types of government policies could address these specific issues?

More Challenging:

11. A lumber company would cause $10 million worth of health costs by secretly substituting arsenic (a carcinogen) for safer, more expensive preservatives in its pressure-treated lumber. The estimated probability that victims will discover the use of arsenic and successfully litigate against the firm is 20 percent. If arsenic is used, the litigation risk burden for the firm is $1 million. Liability is the only threat to the firm because no enforceable regulation is in place. What is the size of the damage award that, if known in advance, would lead the firm to make the socially efficient choice?

websurfer's challenge

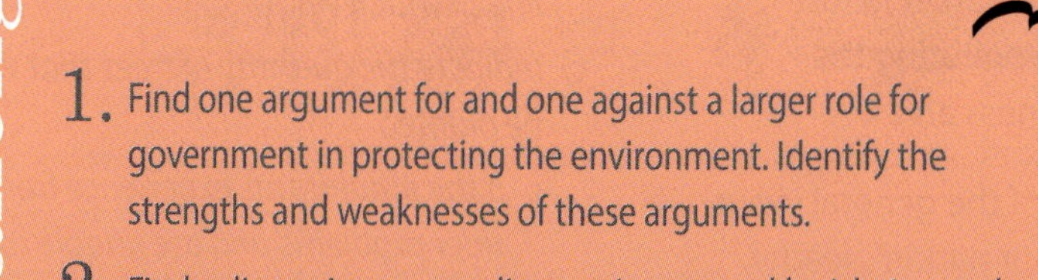

1. Find one argument for and one against a larger role for government in protecting the environment. Identify the strengths and weaknesses of these arguments.
2. Find a discussion on pending environmental legislation and analyze the legislation from an efficiency standpoint.

Internet Resources

Australian Department of the Environment, Water, Heritage and the Arts:
www.environment.gov.au

Economic Policy Institute:
www.epinet.org

Environment Canada:
www.ec.gc.ca

European Environment Agency:
www.eea.europa.eu

Indian Ministry of Environment and Forests:
www.envfor.nic.in

League of Conservation Voters:
www.lcv.org/

New Zealand Ministry for the Environment:
www.mfe.govt.nz

Singapore Ministry of the Environment and Water Resources:
app.mewr.gov.sg

South African Department of Environmental Affairs and Tourism:
www.environment.gov.za/

United Nations:
www.un.org

U.S. Code, including current environmental legislation:
www.law.cornell.edu/uscode/

U.S. House of Representatives:
www.house.gov

U.S. Senate:
www.senate.gov

White House:
www.whitehouse.gov

World Bank:
www.worldbank.org

The government regulates fishing to avoid a tragedy of the commons.

Further Reading

Anderson, D. A. "Government's Role in Property Ownership." In *The Fundamental Interrelationships Between Government and Property*. Edited by N. Mercuro and W. J. Samuels. Stamford, CT.: JAI Press, 1999. A discussion of the benefits and costs of collective authority.

Anderson, D. A. "The Determinants of Municipal Solid Waste." *Journal of Applied Economics and Policy* 24, no. 2 (2005): 23–29. An empirical study of the determinants of municipal solid waste levels.

Augustine, St. *The City of God*. Translated by M. Dods. New York: Charles Scribner's Sons, 1924. A self-proclaimed "giant of a book," this is a work of philosophy, history, and religion that contrasts Roman and Christian cultures.

Carson, R. *Silent Spring*. New York: Houghton-Mifflin, 1962. An influential book about the trade-offs between agricultural chemicals and the environment.

Coase, R. "The Problem with Social Cost." *Journal of Law and Economics* 3 (1960): 1–44. A seminal work suggesting that bargaining may suffice to eradicate externalities without government intervention.

Green, T. H. *The Political Theory of T. H. Green*. Edited by J. R. Rodman. New York: Meredith, 1964. Readings about the influential nineteenth-century "modern liberal" Thomas Hill Green.

Hardin, G. "The Tragedy of the Commons." *Science* 162 (1968): 1243–1248. An often-cited article about the abuse of open-access property.

Hobbes, T. *Leviathan*. Edited by M. Oakeshott. Oxford: Blackwell, 1946. A classic work of political philosophy.

International Center for Technology Assessment. "The Real Price of Gasoline." Washington, D.C.: Center for Technology Assessment, 1998. Available at www.icta.org/projects/ trans/index.htm. A comprehensive study of the external cost of a gallon of gasoline.

Locke, J. *Two Treatises of Government*. New York: Hafner, 1947. Locke's foundation for classical liberalism, including his conception of natural laws and natural rights.

Lueck, D. "The Extermination and Conservation of the American Bison." *Journal of Legal Studies* 31, no. 2 (2002): S609–S652. This article examines the dramatic near extinction and subsequent recovery of the American bison during the nineteenth century using a property-rights model of renewable resource production.

Lueck, D., and J. Michael. "Preemptive Habitat Destruction under the Endangered Species Act." *Journal of Law & Economics* 46, no. 27 (2003): 27–60. Provides evidence that landowners destroy wildlife out of a fear that governmental restrictions may be imposed if endangered species are found on their property.

Marx, K., and F. Engels. *The Communist Manifesto.* New York: International, 1948. A critique of capitalism, and a call for a new political and economic system in response to the inequities of the industrial revolution.

Menger, C. *Problems of Economics and Sociology.* Edited by F. J. Nock. Urbana: University of Illinois Press, 1963. The thoughts of an influential economist and founder of the Austrian school of thought.

Ricardo, D. *The Principles of Political Economy and Taxation.* New York: E. P. Dutton, 1911. The chief work of a principal founder of classical economics who influenced Karl Marx, John Stuart Mill, and Alfred Marshall, among others.

Rousseau, J. J. "The Social Contract." In *Famous Utopias.* New York: Tudor, 1901. A prominent discussion of various forms of government, social engineering, and the general will of mankind.

Smith, A. *The Wealth of Nations.* New York: Penguin, 1970. First published in 1776, this is arguably the most important account of the principles and practice of modern capitalism.

Stroup, Richard L., and Roger E. Meiners (eds). *Cutting Green Tape.* Oakland, CA: Independent Institute, 2000. Volume of essays on the inefficiencies of U.S. environmental policy.

Viscusi, W. Kip. *Reforming Products Liability.* Cambridge, MA: Harvard University Press, 1991. Proposes solutions to the overlapping influence of liability risks and regulation.

Weber, M. *Economy and Society.* Edited by G. Roth and C. Wittich. Berkeley: University of California Press, 1978. A study of the institutional foundations of the modern economy.

TICK TOCK TICK TOCK
NO DUMPING
P SIRIMONGKHON

5 Trade-offs and the Economy

There is no such thing as a free lunch. Every decision is complicated by trade-offs between benefits and costs that can include direct expenditures, externalities, and opportunity costs. Many of the greatest dilemmas in environmental economics involve choices between long-run and short-run benefits, and between financial and environmental gains. To harvest a tree today is to forego its future growth. To replace a meadow with a shopping mall is to forego the meadow's natural beauty and wildlife habitat. And to consume nonrenewable resources today is to forego their benefits for the rest of time.

The formation of environmental policy raises questions as challenging as they are important. How sustainable should our practices be? What values should policymakers place on benefits that will be received by future inhabitants of the Earth? This chapter explains approaches to contemplated trade-offs that go beyond basic cost-benefit analysis. You will learn about dynamic efficiency, present-value calculations, and the discounting of future costs and benefits. The final section clarifies the differences between measures of economic growth and measures of well-being, and explores prospects for economic growth that are consistent with environmental goals.

If we harvest too many fish today, there will be too few fish to catch tomorrow.

Trade-offs Between Present and Future

Why Discount Future Benefits?

You can deposit money in a savings account and earn interest on your deposit. Given any such opportunity to earn a positive rate of return, the earlier money is available to invest, the larger are the returns in the future. People also feel impatience, fear uncertainty and inflation, and have finite lifetimes, all of which makes it preferable to receive money and other benefits sooner rather than later. Consider the option to receive $1,000 today or in 10 years. When would you rather have the money? The rational response is today, in part because:

- *Money received now can be invested to obtain even more money in the future.*
- *It is discomforting to delay gratification from money and expenditures.*
- *The later a benefit comes, the more likely it is that you will not live to receive it, or that it will come when you are less able to enjoy it due to poor health.*

Because people prefer to receive benefits soon, 80 to 90 percent of lottery winners decide to receive a lump-sum payment of around half of their earnings immediately rather than annual payments over several decades. If the carbon dioxide build-up in the oceans were curbed, annual revenues for the mollusk fishing industry alone would increase by between $75 million and $187 million over the coming decades, but the delay of benefits dampens interest in policies that would reduce carbon emissions. To prefer benefits now and place a lower value on benefits received later is to "discount" future benefits.

Why Discount Future Costs?

Costs to be paid later are preferable to costs paid up front. People appreciate the luxury of time when trying to assemble payments. On a global scale, the desire to pay for purchases later explains the accumulation of several trillion dollars of credit card debt. Wouldn't you prefer to pay $1,000 in 10 years rather than today? The option to put things off has several advantages:

- *It gives you more time to acquire the money needed.*
- *You could invest the money now and earn even more before the payment is due.*
- *Anything can happen in 10 years. You might die before the payment must be made.*

Non-monetary costs are also more tolerable when delayed. Consider whether alcohol consumption would be moderated if hangovers hit with the first sip. Because the health and environmental costs of pollution come some time after the activities that cause pollution, the costs weigh more lightly on the decisions to pollute than if the costs were immediate. To pay less attention to costs that come later rather than sooner, or to favor costs that come later, is to discount the value of future costs.

Our discounting of the future means that the timing of costs and benefits matters. The loss of a forest today is not justified by the gain of an equivalent forest in 1,000 years. It would therefore be inappropriate to evaluate policies by simply comparing amounts paid or received at different times, even if the amounts were adjusted for inflation. To make a valid comparison, future costs and benefits can be discounted to reflect their values in the present. The following sections explain how this discounting is performed and how policymakers approach the determination of discount rates.

Dynamic Efficiency

A **static** model depicts a situation in one time period. The analysis of static models is sufficient when decisions are independent across time periods. For example, individuals can decide to recycle today whether or not they recycled yesterday, and with no effect on tomorrow's decision to recycle. So recycling decisions over the period of a year can be seen as a series of static analyses of one-day situations. It may be that every day the individual weighs the costs and benefits of recycling and makes an independent decision one way or the other. In contrast, individuals cannot choose to tap rubber trees today on a plot of land that was burned yesterday for cattle grazing. *When today's decisions affect the* *choices available in the future, dynamic analysis is appropriate.*

Dynamic efficiency is achieved when the present value of net benefits is maximized. When deciding the fate of a plot of land in Brazil, for example, the owner would want to determine the net present value of each possible use of the land: cattle grazing, rubber tapping, commercial development, rental, sale, and so on. The timing of the stream of net benefits from these options matters a great deal. To simplify the story, assume there are only two periods: this year and next year. Suppose that immediate sale of the land would bring net benefits of $1,000 this year, rubber tapping would bring net benefits of $500 each year, and cattle grazing would yield $1,000 in profits upon the sale of the cattle next year. Despite the equality of the total payoffs, the preferred option of immediate sale is unambiguous. As we have seen, and as summarized by the principle of the **time value of money**, it is preferable to receive a given amount of money sooner rather than later. Monetary benefits of $1,000 received this year could be invested at any positive rate of return to yield more than $1,000 next year, making immediate sale the clear choice. If the choices were $950 this year, $500 each year, or $1,040 next year, the best choice would be unclear. In this case, satisfaction of the dynamic efficiency criterion requires present-value calculations and the selection of a discount rate.

Present-Value Calculations

Amid technologically advanced cities, South America's Amazon basin holds barter economies where goods and services are exchanged for the likes of 20-pound balls of smoked rubber and bushels of cocoa beans. This can lead to confusion when a canoe seller receives alternative offers of 5 balls of rubber, 150 pounds of cocoa beans, or 6 machetes. The relative value of differing options is uncertain in the absence of a common metric for comparison. The same is true when comparing monetary costs or benefits that come at different points in time, such as receiving $950 this year or $1,040 next year. In the case of international markets for goods, prices stated in a common currency simplify comparisons among the prices charged in different countries. Likewise, to simplify comparisons among streams of costs and benefits that differ in their timing, **present-value calculations** determine the value today of amounts paid or received in the future.

Present-value calculations are motived by the natural desire to receive benefits earlier rather than later. Retail stores still compete with relatively inexpensive Internet e-tailers in part because consumers prefer to have their products today rather than tomorrow. The **rate of time preference** is the discount rate applied to benefits received in the future to determine their present value. If you would be indifferent between receiving 10 music downloads this year or 11 next year, your rate of time preference is 10 percent; you would require 10 percent more benefits next year to be just as happy as if you received the benefits today.

For easier analysis, we can summarize the relationship between present values and future values with an equation. According to your preferences, 11 downloads in the future are equivalent in value to 10 downloads in the present. In addition to the 10 downloads you would receive now, to accept a delay, you would require compensation of 10 percent of the present value of 10. So your future value of 11 equals your present value of 10 plus 10 percent of 10. We can write this as 11 = 10 + 0.10(10), or equivalently,

$$11 = 10(1 + 0.10)$$

More generally, with a future value of *FV*, a present value of *PV*, and a rate of time preference of *R*, the future value that compensates for a one-period delay is

$$FV = PV(1 + R)$$

Solving the equation for *PV* yields

$$PV = \frac{FV}{(1 + R)}$$

Knowing any two of these variables, we can solve the present value equation to determine the third.

Let's compare the three options presented to the Amazon landowner under the assumption that the rate of time preference is 10 percent. As a reminder, the options were to receive $950 in the first period, $500 each period, or $1,040 in the second period. The present value of the $950 from an immediate sale would simply be $950. There is no need to discount money received in the present. The $500 received in the second period from rubber production would have a present value of

$$PV = \frac{\$500}{(1 + 0.10)} = \$454.50$$

Combined with the $500 received for rubber in the first period, rubber tapping would yield a total of $500 + $454.50 = $954.50 in present value. The cattle grazing option would bring in a net value of $1,040 in the second period, which has a present value of

$$PV = \frac{\$1{,}040}{(1 + 0.10)} = \$945.40$$

So the harvest of rubber from the plot of land would yield the greatest present value ($954.50) and provide the dynamically efficient outcome.

It is no problem that reality involves more than two periods. The present value of a net benefit *t* periods in the future is

$$PV = \frac{FV}{(1 + R)^t}$$

where t can be any value from zero to infinity. Solving for the future value yields

$$FV = PV(1 + R)^t$$

A similar apparatus can handle more complicated situations with little difficulty. To find the net present value of a stream of benefits, B, and costs, C, received once per period for n periods, sum the discounted net benefits for each period:[1]

$$PV = \sum_{t=0}^{n} \frac{(B_t - C_t)}{(1+R)^t}$$

When a net-present-value calculation accurately reflects all benefits and costs including external benefits, external costs, and opportunity costs, a positive net present value indicates that the project should be carried out. A negative net present value indicates that the project should not be pursued.

Discount Rates—Who's Got the Number?

The previous numerical examples applied a 10 percent rate of time preference to discount net benefits received in the future. Policymakers use estimates of the rate of time preference, referred to simply as **discount rates**, to adjust anticipated future payments and receipts to reflect present values. The federal Office of Management and Budget (OMB) in the United States previously used a 10 percent discount rate to calculate the present value of future regulatory costs and benefits; now it uses a 7 percent discount rate. The selection of discount rates can make or break decisions based on present-value calculations. Table 5.1 illustrates the present values of each option for the Amazon land given the two discount rates used by the OMB and a third rate of 12 percent. With a discount rate of 7 percent, the greatest net present value is achieved by clearing the land for cattle. With a discount rate of 10 percent, the trees should stand for rubber tapping. With a discount rate of 12 percent, the land should be sold. The importance of discount rate selection is clear.

Table 5.1

		Discount Rate		
		0.07	**0.10**	**0.12**
Land Use	**Sell**	950.00	950.00	950.00
	Rubber	967.29	954.55	946.43
	Cattle	971.96	945.45	928.57

1 In case you have not seen this type of notation, the large Greek letter *sigma* (Σ) with a zero below it and an n above it indicates the summation for each period from period zero to period n. The term $(B_t - C_t)$ represents the net benefits in period t, and the term $(1 + R)^{-t}$ discounts the benefits to reflect present values.

As low as zero percent

10 percent

Between 2 and 8 percent

3, 7, and 10 percent

Between 2 and 7 percent

Unfortunately, discount rate selection is not straightforward. Past and present members of the President's Council of Economic Advisers report that a wide variety of discount rates have been applied to the future costs and benefits of environmental policies being considered by their respective administrations.[2] William Nordhaus said that when Jimmy Carter was in office, discount rates as low as zero were proposed. William Niskanen said that when Ronald Reagan was in office, the Council favored a discount rate of 10 percent. Nobel Laureate Joseph Stiglitz said that under Bill Clinton's administration, they discussed discount rates as low as 2 to 3 percent and sometimes as high as 7 to 8 percent. John List recalled that the administration of George W. Bush used rates of 3, 7, and 10 percent, depending on the situation. And Michael Greenstone said that the administration of Barack Obama would go with rates between 2 and 7 percent. The wide range of applicable discount rates and their dramatic influence on policy decisions indicate the importance of selecting these rates carefully.

There is a connection between discount rates and the rates of return on investments that provides clues about appropriate discount rates. Suppose an investor discounts the future at an annual rate of 2 percent. She will forego alternative uses of her money to make a risk-free investment only if the investment offers a rate of return of 2 percent or more. So by observing the risk-free rate of return that motivates large numbers of investors to forego the use of their money, we have a good starting point for discount-rate approximations. Bonds issued by stable governments are an example of nearly risk-free investments, and typically offer returns in the vicinity of 1–2 percent. However, there is more to consider. Four normative questions are central to discount-rate debates:

1. **How self-serving should discount rates be?**

   Impatient individuals naturally discount future benefits and costs, preferring to receive benefits now and pay later. Time preference is rational at a personal level because one might not be alive in the future to enjoy delayed benefits or pay delayed costs. It is also rational to desire money now rather than later because dollars obtained in the present

2 Personal communication, American Economic Association meetings, January 6, 2001, and e-mail, June 30, 2005 and June 6, 2009.

can be invested to gain even more dollars in the future. Selfish concerns for immediate gratification lead to relatively high discount rates.

Political theorist John Rawls argues against the influence of self-interest and feels that decisions about discounting should be made as if policymakers did not know the period in which they would live. This approach removes discounting based on impatience and time preference. However, this does not mean that a $1,000 investment today would be justified by a $1,000 benefit (after adjusting for inflation) in 50 years. The real (inflation-adjusted) returns society could receive from alternative investments represent opportunity costs, with or without impatience and time preference. The Rawlsian approach would thus retain discounting of the benefits from an investment to reflect the social opportunity cost of the best foregone alternative investment.

In the process of policy evaluation, the returns from a policy can be compared directly with the returns available from alternative investments *if* the alternative returns would accrue with the same timing as the policy's benefits. If the alternative returns would not last as long or would fluctuate over time, the *shadow price* provides a more accurate measure of the opportunity cost of the policy. To find the **shadow price**, calculate the present value of the returns from the best alternative investment. Then compare this shadow price with the present value of the policy's benefits.

An example for you if you're up to a little math: Suppose an environmental policy would have a firm spend $1 million on smokestack filters for the benefit of avoiding $70,000 worth of health and environmental damage each year for the next 40 years. Because $70,000 is 7 percent of $1 million, the avoided damage represents a 7 percent annual return. Suppose the best alternative investment would yield a 10 percent return for 5 years, at which time the higher return would be unavailable, but the funds could be reinvested to earn a 6 percent return for the next 35 years. It would be inappropriate to argue for the alternative investment on the basis of the higher initial rate of return that would only last for 5 years. If we discount the benefits of each option at the social discount rate of 2 percent as advocated in the next section, the shadow price of the environmental policy—the present value of the best alternative—is $1,829,867.[3] This is equivalent to the present value of a consistent $66,892 (6.69 percent) annual return for 40 years on a $1,000,000 investment.[4] The smokestack filters provide a higher present value of $1,914,884, making them the socially efficient choice.

2. Should environmental benefits receive special treatment?

The costs of environmental regulation generally come sooner than the benefits,

3 The present value of an annual benefit of *A* received for *n* years with a discount rate of *i* can be found using the equation

$$\text{Present Value} = A\left[\frac{1-(1+i)^{-n}}{i}\right]$$

The shadow price is found by applying this formula to the 5 years of receiving 10 percent ($100,000) per year and the 35 years of receiving 6 percent ($60,000) per year. Since the application of the formula to the returns of the last 35 years produces the present value at the time of reinvestment, before the two sets of returns are added together, the return for the later years must be discounted an additional 5 years to find the present value in the very beginning.

4 The $66,892 figure is found by plugging the present value of $1,829,867, $n = 40$, and $i = 0.02$ into the equation in footnote 3 and solving for the annual return, A.

meaning that the application of a single discount rate to costs and benefits diminishes the present value of the benefits more so than the costs. For this reason, the number of regulations deemed appropriate by cost-benefit analysis decreases as the discount rate increases. If the benefit itself is unchanged between the present and the future, some economists argue that there is good reason to apply different discount rates for benefits and costs. A dollar spent now causes the spender to forego the after-tax return she could receive each year if, instead, she were able to invest that dollar. The risk-free real rate of return on capital is around 1 percent.[5] On the other hand, a life saved now does not increase to 1.01 lives next year, nor does a life in the future grow out of a partial life today. Daniel Farber and Paul Hemmersbaugh[6] are among the scholars who advocate assessment of the opportunity costs of regulatory compliance on the basis of shadow prices, while discounting environmental benefits at a lower social discount rate of 1 percent or so to reflect the fact that current lives don't increase in value.[7] The opposing view, upheld by the Fifth Circuit Court and (at times) *The Economist* magazine,[8] is that environmental benefits should not receive special treatment. They argue that relatively low discount rates will encourage excessive investment in environmental benefits.

3. **How should we treat benefits and costs that extend to future generations?**

When future costs and benefits will accrue to another generation, self-interested discount rates may rationally be higher than when they accrue to the generation making the decisions. This depends on the extent to which the people involved feel a responsibility to future generations or derive utility from providing benefits to others. The more responsibility felt, or utility gained, the lower are appropriate discount rates for future benefits and costs. There are also arguments in favor of applying higher discount rates. Given the trend for each generation to be wealthier than the one before it, the law of diminishing marginal utility implies that the additional benefit that tomorrow's wealthier generations will receive from a dollar will be smaller than the benefit received today. Under this assumption, relatively large discount rates would satisfy desires for intergenerational equality.

There is risk in reliance on time preference because preferences are likely to change. Policies made on the basis of discounting for time preference may be lamented in the future. Although research subjects have expressed a preference to save 1 human life today rather than 8 people in 25 years,[9] if given the same option 25 years later, the same respondents would likely prefer to save the 8 lives. Economist Arthur C. Pigou (1932) called this type of inconsistency a perversion of the human "telescopic faculty."

5 Accommodations for risk and uncertainty are discussed under question 4.

6 See www.ciesin.org/docs/010-291/010-291.html.

7 See Farber and Hemmersbaugh (1993).

8 The opinion of the Fifth Circuit Court is explained in the Reality Check section. *The Economist* made this argument in its March 23, 1991 article entitled, "What Price Posterity?"

9 See Cropper and Portney (1990).

4. **What is the appropriate treatment of uncertainty?**

As discussed earlier in this section, if the benefits from a contemplated policy are clear and certain, the risk-free rate of return may be an appropriate guideline for estimating the discount rate. In the case of risky investments, relatively high expected rates of return are needed to attract investors who dislike uncertainty and the possibility of losses. For example, if stock market investments provided average returns no higher than the return on low-risk government bonds, there would be little incentive to purchase stocks. People invest in stocks despite the risk of low or negative returns because, on average, stock investments yield a higher return than low-risk bonds. The difference between the risk-free rate of return and the average rate of return on risky investments is called the **risk premium**. The risk premium provides an incentive for investors to bear risk. For example, if a risk-free investment offers a 2 percent rate of return and the average rate of return on stock investments is 8 percent, there is an 8 - 2 = 6 percent risk premium that attracts investors to the stock market.

It is argued that investments in environmental policies with uncertain returns warrant the addition of a risk premium to the discount rate. This lowers the assessed present value of an investment to reflect disfavor in having a range of possible outcomes. For example, suppose a 2 percent discount rate would be appropriate for a risk-free project, but the project being assessed involves risks of failure similar in scale to the risks of stock market investments. Policymakers could add a risk premium of 6 percent to the discount rate when estimating the present value of the project. The appropriate size of the risk premium depends on both the risks involved and the investors' attitude toward risk. There are three categories of risk preference among investors:

Risk-neutral investors care only about the expected value of the outcome. So they have no preference between receiving \$1 with certainty and a fair coin flip that will determine whether they receive \$0 or \$2, each with equal probability.[10]

Risk-averse investors care not only about the expected value of the outcome but also about the range of possible outcomes. They would pay a premium to receive a certain \$1 rather than being subjected to the uncertainty of the coin flip. Most people who purchase insurance pay a premium in excess of the expected value of their losses from a house fire or an auto accident in exchange for the certainty that they will have a house and a car at the end of the day regardless of their luck.

Risk-loving investors prefer a range of possible outcomes to a certain outcome with the same expected value. They would pay a premium to receive the outcome of the coin flip rather than a certain \$1. Similarly, gamblers typically pay more than the expected value of a lottery ticket for the small chance of winning big.

Risk-neutral investors need not attach a risk premium to their discount rate because risk doesn't bother them. Risk-loving investors would actually decrease their discount rate for uncertain future benefits, meaning that their risk premium would be negative. The more risk averse the investor is, the larger the risk premium she should add to the discount rate in the face of uncertainty. Individual investors, including individual car owners and homeowners, are likely to be risk averse because they cannot bear the

10 As explained in Chapter 2, the expected value of the coin flip outcome is (0.5)(\$0) + (0.5)(\$2) = \$1.

reality check

Corrosion Proof Fittings v. EPA

The case of *Corrosion Proof Fittings v. EPA (*947 F.2d 1201) highlights the complexity and controversy behind discounting future costs and benefits, and describes how the debate played out in a U.S. Circuit Court.

Asbestos is a naturally occurring fibrous material used in heat-resistant insulation, cements, building materials, clothing, and brake linings. Exposure to asbestos dust can result in mesothelioma, asbestosis, and lung cancer. The EPA issued a final rule under Section 6 of the Toxic Substances Control Act to ban asbestos in almost all products by August 26, 1996. They estimated this rule would save either 202 or 148 lives, depending on whether future lives were discounted, and cost between $450 million and $800 million, depending on the prices of substitute goods. A number of petitioners, including Corrosion Proof Fittings, contended that the EPA rule-making relied on flawed analyses of the necessary trade-offs between the environment and the economy. The U.S. Court of Appeals for the Fifth Circuit asked the EPA to reconsider the matter.

In the eyes of the Court, the EPA may have demonstrated that a complete ban of asbestos was preferable to the status quo, but "failed to show that there is not some intermediate state of regulation that would be superior to both the currently-regulated and the completely-banned world." In other words, the EPA compared the total costs and benefits of a ban without conducting sufficient marginal analysis of incremental policies, as described in Chapter 2.

While discounting the future monetary *costs* of an asbestos ban, the EPA presented alternative cost-benefit analyses that did and did not discount future *benefits*. Recognizing the ongoing dispute over discounting benefits measured in terms of human lives, the Court stated a preference for discounting everything, monetary or otherwise. The EPA chose to use a real discount rate of 3 percent. Citing historical real (inflation-adjusted) interest rates in the range of 2 to 4 percent, the Court found the 3 percent figure to be "not inaccurate."

The Court criticized the EPA for discounting health losses from the time of exposure to asbestos, rather than from the time when injury would result. If, without the ban, some individuals would be exposed to asbestos in five years and feel the adverse health effects in ten years, the Court held that the health losses should be discounted by ten years rather than five. The Court also reprimanded the EPA for including only the lives saved over the next 13 years, and counting lives saved after that time as simply "unquantified benefits." The EPA's mistakes came at an early stage in the application of cost-benefit analyses to human lives. More carefully crafted studies followed this valuable scrutiny.

burden of a large loss even if the risk is small. In their classic 1970 article, economists Kenneth Arrow and Robert Lind (1970) suggest that society at large should be relatively risk neutral when evaluating public investments because society can spread any losses far and wide. So the assignment of a risk premium to environmental policies is less appropriate when large segments of society pay the costs and receive the benefits.

Kenneth Arrow and Anthony C. Fisher (1974) and Claude Henry (1974) argue for special treatment for policies that might cause irreversible environmental losses. The loss of $1 million can be divided among 100 million taxpayers for an average burden of 1 cent. In contrast, the burden of losing an animal species to extinction is augmented, not diminished, when the loss is felt by all of society for all time. According to Arrow and Fisher, "even where it is not appropriate to postulate risk aversion in evaluating an activity, something of the 'feel' of risk aversion is produced by a restriction on reversibility." When weighing the costs and benefits of development projects, for instance, policymakers who ignore the potential for irreversible damage will overestimate the net benefits and permit inefficiently high levels of development. Henry points out that policymakers may not even know what is at stake when making an irreversible decision. For example, no one knows what species of wildlife or medicinal cures might be discovered in a wilderness area in the future if it is preserved. For these reasons, Arrow, Fisher, and Henry suggest additional discounting of the net benefits of decisions that carry the risk of permanent losses.

What's Your Number?

The subjectivity of discount rate selection and the complexities involved explain the broad range of chosen values. Studies find significant numbers of individuals favoring discount rates in every range, including negative and infinite values.[11] Low and negative discount rates may be signs of altruism. Indeed, parental expenditures on education would seem to indicate negative discount rates, as they involve people effectively placing their children before themselves. Rational, selfish individuals should adopt a discount rate of at least the probability that they will not live until the next period—around 1 percent for most age groups—a rate that, interestingly, approximates the risk-free real rate of interest.

From a societal standpoint there are again rational discount rate guidelines. The social opportunity cost is an appropriate lower bound for discount rates. For example, if society can receive a 1 to 2 percent risk-free real rate of return on investments in government bonds, it would make no sense to discount future returns by less than that amount. To adopt a 0 or ½ percent discount rate would be to advocate expenditures on projects with lower net returns to society than an investment in bonds.

A thought experiment will provide perspective on the relatively subjective upper bound for social discount rates. Policies that curtail pollution save "statistical lives," meaning it is unknown who will be saved. Assume that a statistical (unidentified) life is worth $6 million today—a figure close to the estimates of

11 In a study by Horowitz and Carson (1990), one-third of the respondents used zero or negative discount rates.

many economists.[12] What amount would you say is the most society should spend on an environmental regulation that, with certainty, would save 1,000 lives 300 years from now? Read on after you have decided on a maximum expenditure.

Table 5.2 indicates the maximum expenditure implied by several discount rates. If the discount rate is 9 or 10 percent, society would only be willing to spend a fraction of a cent on an environmental regulation that would certainly save 1,000 lives with a combined value of $6 billion in 300 years. If it were appropriate for society to forego 56 cents or more—less than the price of a can of soda—to save 1,000 lives in 300 years, then discount rates would have an upper bound of 8 percent and the appropriate discount rate range would be from 0 to 8 percent. Find the maximum expenditure in Table 5.2 that is the closest to your own. The corresponding discount rate is an approximation of your own discount rate.

There is some appeal to the application of a single social discount rate when analyzing environmental regulations because it would prevent self-serving manipulations of the rate. Flexibility opens the door for rate selection that ushers particular programs in or out, depending on the agenda of the rate selector. Among economists, the broadest agreement on rates lies in the 2 to 3 percent range. For example, British economists David Pearce and David Ulph favor a social discount rate of 2.4 percent. Rates in the 2–3 percent range have been adopted in the United States by the General Accounting Office, the Environmental Protection Agency, and the Congressional Budget Office, among other prominent agencies. Discount rate selection in other contexts should hinge on the particular goals of the project. In general, low-risk projects intended to benefit society should receive lower rates, while riskier projects and those meant to satisfy private goals should receive relatively high rates.

Discount Rate (%)	*Maximum Expenditure ($)*
10	0.0023
9	0.035
8	0.56
7	9.18
6	153.60
5	2,638.53
4	46,574.63
3	845,247.39
2	15,779,735.59
1	303,206,924.70
0	6,000,000,000.00

Table 5.2 *Discounting the Value of Future Lives*

12 See Viscusi (2004) for a discussion of value-of-life studies.

Trade-offs Between Growth and the Environment

Every decision involves trade-offs. Economic growth offers a path to new goods and services, employment, and development. But depending on its make-up, growth can also leave a trail of environment degradation and trample on health, natural resources, free time, and other contributors to the quality of life. What is the net effect on social welfare? After defining relevant terms, this section explains how the virtues of growth can be measured apart from associated problems, and how some of the perceived problems need not be associated with growth at all.

Growth versus Welfare

By the curious standard of the GDP, the nation's economic hero is a terminal cancer patient who is going through a costly divorce. . . . The most desirable habitat is a multibillion-dollar Superfund site.

—Clifford Cobb, Ted Halstead, and Jonathan Rowe

Gross domestic product (GDP) is the final value of goods and services produced within a country in one year. It is a common measure of growth in the economy, and the media often herald GDP growth as a uniformly splendid event. In reality, increases in GDP may or may not reflect welfare improvements. A better measure of social welfare would exclude expenditures that make no net contribution to welfare, and add components of welfare not captured in GDP.

Defensive goods and services are purchased in response to pollution, congestion, work-related anxiety, and other unfortunate side effects of economic growth, and to recover from unwelcome events such as crime. Expenditures to remedy environmental degradation indicate that society has suffered losses. Counselors and physical therapists are paid to help workers cope with the stress and strain of fast-paced jobs, but those payments reflect recovery and not advancement in social welfare. The same is true of expenditures on disease, war, natural disasters, and crime. Spending on what some call *regrettables* should be subtracted from GDP to form a better measure of social welfare.

Buildings, machines, and equipment are examples of **capital**—goods used to make other goods. **Capital depreciation** occurs whenever the value of capital erodes during the production process. Suppose $25 worth of metal stamping equipment must be replaced due to wear and tear after the production of $1,000 worth of filing cabinets. GDP would increase by $1,025 with the production of the filing cabinets and new stamping equipment, whereas the net gain for society would only be $1,000 because the $25 worth of stamping equipment simply replaces worn-out machinery. The U.S. government publishes net national product (NNP) figures that adjust GDP for the depreciation of human-made) capital. The NNP does not account for losses of natural capital such as forests, coal seams, and environmental sinks (bodies of water and other components of the environment able to absorb pollution). A true measure of social welfare would include depreciation in natural capital.

National income is all of the income earned by factors of production owned by a nation's citizens. It is equal to GDP plus subsidies, minus depreciation, indirect taxes, and the net income of foreigners. Improvements in national income do not necessarily correspond with improvements in income distribution. That is, an overall increase in national income does not guarantee that most people are earning higher incomes; it may be that a small percentage of citizens are earning more while the incomes of others are stagnating. An ideal measure of social welfare would incorporate changes in income distribution.

Nonmarket production provides benefits to society in the absence of explicit prices and purchases. Work performed for the benefit of the worker and the worker's family—child care, yard work, housework, chores—is not counted in GDP, although the same duties are counted in GDP when performed by a paid professional. Unreported production in the illegal *underground* or *cash economy* is not reported to the government and is not counted in GDP. Volunteer work goes uncounted as well. It is important to include these goods and services to the extent possible in a true measure of social welfare.

Scholars have proposed numerous indicators of welfare and progress as alternatives to GDP. These include:

- *Net National Welfare (NNW)*
- *Economic Aspects of Welfare (EAW)*
- *Green GDP*
- *Canadian Index of Wellbeing (CIW)*
- *Measure of Economic Welfare (MEW)*
- *Human Development Index (HDI)*
- *Happy Planet Index (HPI)*
- *Index of Leading Cultural Indicators (ILCI)*
- *Index of Social Health (ISH)*
- *Genuine Progress Indicator (GPI)*
- *Index of Sustainable Economic Welfare (ISEW)*

Many of these are considered *enlarged GDP indicators* because they begin with GDP and make adjustments to correct for items that do not promote social welfare. For example, the formula for Net National Welfare is:

NNW = GDP + Nonmarket Output

– Externality Costs – Pollution Abatement and Cleanup Costs

– Depreciation of Created Capital – Depreciation of Natural Capital

Some of the measures start from scratch. For example, the basic Index of Sustainable Economic Welfare[13] equation is

ISEW = Personal Consumption / Distribution Inequality[14]

+ Household Labor + Value of Services from Consumer Durables

+ Streets and Highways + Public Expenditures on Health and Education

– Consumer Durables – Defensive Private Spending on Health and Education

– National Advertising – Commuting Costs – Cost of Urbanization

– Cost of Auto Accidents – Cost of Water, Air, and Noise Pollution

– Loss of Wetlands and Farmlands – Depletion of Nonrenewable Resources

– Long-term Environmental Damage

+ Net Capital Growth + Change in Net Intergenerational Position

The Genuine Progress Indicator equation is very similar to the ISEW equation.[15]

Several of the measures emphasize particular sources of welfare, as with the Index of Leading Cultural Indicators, which allows disaggregated comparisons of crime rates, family values, educational attainment, youth behavior, popular culture, and civic participation over time. Calculations of the Canadian Index of Wellbeing incorporate eight "domains": leisure and culture, democratic engagement, community vitality, education, environment, healthy populations, living standards, and time use.[16] The Human Development Index is based on life expectancy at birth, literacy, school enrollment, and standard of living as measured by GDP per capita.

Most of the alternative index values differ significantly from GDP, particularly since 1980. Figure 5.1 illustrates the divergence of GDP per capita and the GPI for the United States. Figure 5.2 shows the difference between changes in GDP per capita, the overall Canadian Index of Wellbeing, and the CIW for the environment. All of the alternative measures provide a broader target for dynamic efficiency: maximize the present value of net national welfare. Because GDP figures alone can be misleading, it is important for policymakers and the media

13 See Daly and Cobb (1989), pp. 418–419.

14 An index similar to the Gini Coefficient, which is a measure of income inequality explained in most economics textbooks.

15 See http://rprogress.org/sustainability_indicators/genuine_progress_indicator.htm.

16 See www.ciw.ca/.

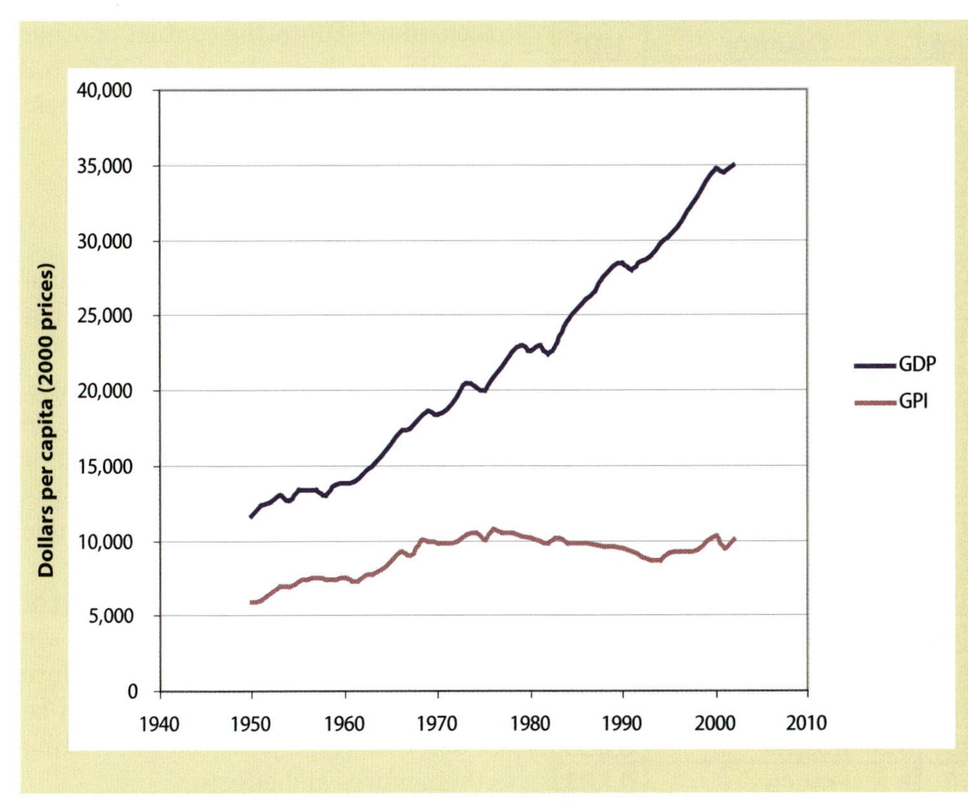

Figure 5.1
GDP and the Genuine Progress Indicator for the United States

Data from www.rprogress.org/publications/2007/GPI2006_ExecSumm.pdf.

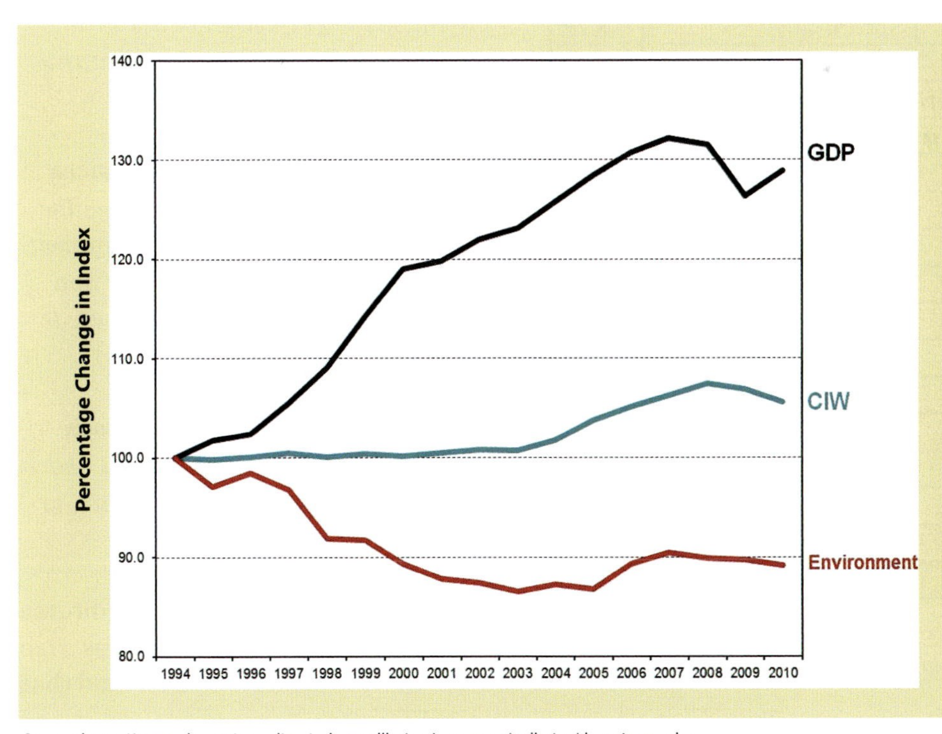

Figure 5.2
Changes in Per Capita GDP, the Overall CIW, and the CIW for the Environment

Source: https://uwaterloo.ca/canadian-index-wellbeing/resources/galleries/domain-graphs.

Table 5.3 *The 38 Countries with the Highest Human Development Index Values*

Rank	Country	HDI
1	Norway	0.943
2	Australia	0.929
3	Netherlands	0.910
4	United States	0.910
5	New Zealand	0.908
6	Canada	0.908
7	Ireland	0.908
8	Liechtenstein	0.905
9	Germany	0.908
10	Sweden	0.904
11	Switzerland	0.903
12	Japan	0.901
13	Hong Kong (SAR)	0.898
14	Iceland	0.898
15	South Korea	0.897
16	Denmark	0.895
17	Israel	0.888
18	Belgium	0.886
19	Austria	0.885
20	France	0.884
21	Slovenia	0.884
22	Finland	0.882
23	Spain	0.878
24	Italy	0.874
25	Luxembourg	0.867
26	Singapore	0.866
27	Czech Republic	0.865
28	United Kingdom	0.863
29	Greece	0.861
30	United Arab Em.	0.846
31	Cyprus	0.840
32	Andorra	0.838
33	Brunei	0.838
34	Estonia	0.835
35	Slovakia	0.834
36	Malta	0.832
37	Qatar	0.831
38	Hungary	0.816

The Human Development Index measures health, education, and standard of living.

to consider GDP in the context of other measures such as the HDI. Table 5.3 shows the 38 countries with the highest HDI values.

"Green" Growth

Alfred Marshall, the father of neoclassical economics, described utility, not material accumulation, as the true standard of production and wealth. Utility and economic growth can be derived from a host of activities that tread lightly on the environment. It is therefore a fallacy to present economic growth as the antithesis of environmental goals. Some types of growth, particularly in the service industries, are not at odds with the environment. More broadly, the components of GDP can be divided into three categories according to their causes and effects:

- ***Defensive goods and services*** *are purchased in response to undesirable occurrences, including crime, natural disasters, and pollution*

- ***Utility-justified goods and services*** *involve subjective trade-offs between the benefits of consumption and employment, and the costs of resource depletion and environmental degradation (most goods and services fall into this category)*

- ***Environmentally beneficial goods and services*** *provide employment and utility with no net loss, or a net gain, to the environment*

You've already read that expenditures on defensive goods and services rise when society becomes worse off, and that these expenditures are subtracted from GDP in the calculation of net national welfare. The tools of discounting and the criteria for sustainable development can be applied to potentially utility-justified goods to determine whether the trade-offs are indeed in the best interest of society. People who see growth and the environment as adversarial interests overlook the subset of goods and services with minimal environmental impact, and those that benefit the environment, such as safer pesticides, more efficient appliances, and toxic waste cleanups. A balanced perspective on growth must recognize opportunities to improve the standard of living without large resource costs. The next section highlights more goods and services that require few environmental trade-offs.

Treading Lightly

The service occupations in Table 5.4 represent relatively low-impact sources of jobs and satisfaction. Of course, there are examples of some sort of resource use associated with virtually all industries. Workers in the service industries typically need motorized transportation to get to work and perform their jobs in heated or cooled buildings. But in other industries these same needs are compounded with additional resource demands associated with production, processing, packaging, delivery, and use. Society can look to myriad service-oriented industries for economic expansion with fewer externalities.

To improve sustainability within the manufacturing sector, consumers and policymakers can support high-quality, multi-use products rather than inferior and single-use products. Ceramic mugs can last for centuries, unlike single-use Styrofoam cups. And a well-made bike that lasts 20 years is preferable to a series of five low-quality bikes that last four years each. Environmentally beneficial goods provide win-win opportunities for employment and sustainability.

Is There Employment Outside of Manufacturing?		
Author	Therapist	Guard
Mechanic	Teacher	Entertainer
Dietician	Doctor	Firefighter
Police Officer	Masseur	Lawyer
Actor	Politician	Chef
Programmer	Athlete	Professor
Repairperson	Farmer	Secretary
Analyst	Scientist	Historian
Banker	Nurse	Coach
Economist	Ranger	Clergy
Insurance Agent	Broadcast Producer	Artist
Sociologist	Curator	Musician

Table 5.4 *Service Occupations*

President Barack Obama's plan to build wind-energy capacity to satisfy 20 percent of U.S. electricity needs by 2030 will create 250,000 new jobs and reduce the environmental degradation caused by coal extraction and combustion. Producers of alternative fuels such as biodiesel, high-efficiency batteries, geothermal heating systems, and solar panels, all of which can substitute for relatively damaging production, provide employment and a net environmental gain. The standard of living increases with improvements in education, health care, communications, entertainment, and food service without substantial adverse consequences. With more focus on the efficient use of recycled materials, insulation, alternative energy sources, and water conservation, architects and builders can take great strides toward sustainable development.

A critical mass of consumers purchasing low-impact goods and services will support mass production and permit economies of scale, thereby reducing the cost of goods, including recycled paper, photovoltaic cells, wind turbines, and plug-in hybrid automobiles. For these reasons many environmental economists see the current tension between the economy and the environment as a problem of information and attitude, rather than of opportunity.

Summary

Why put off until tomorrow what you can do today? Impatience, opportunity cost, selfishness, and mortality cause decision makers to prefer benefits sooner and costs later. Dilemmas arise when the choice is between a benefit now and a slightly larger benefit later. Environmental policy often entails choices between expenditures that provide immediate benefits, and expenditures that provide larger benefits in the future. Discount rates recast future benefits and costs in present-value terms. Although there is no consensus on a particular social discount rate for environmental benefits, most of the defensible rates are in the 1 to 8 percent range, and many economists agree that rates should fall between 2 and 3 percent.

Economic growth sometimes creates externalities that work against social and environmental goals. GDP, a common measure of economic growth, is not a valid measure of social welfare. GDP does not account for some good things such as leisure, and increases with expenditures on some "regrettables" including pollution and crime. Economists have developed alternative measures such as the ISEW and the GPI that are designed to increase if and only if society is better off.

In the process of allocating scarce resources among competing ends, we encounter compelling reasons to make trade-offs between the environment and growth. The good news is that some of the imagined trade-offs are avoidable, and others can be minimized with the appropriate efforts. Satisfying architectural, employment, and consumption practices can occur within the guidelines of sustainability and dynamic efficiency. Even so, free lunches are rare. Decision makers at every level must struggle with the difficult trade-offs between the present and the future and between growth and the environment. Economic tools can guide those endeavors.

Problems for Review

1. What criterion determines whether it is appropriate to apply static or dynamic analysis?
2. Donna is trying to decide whether to pick the 60 tulips growing in her yard today or let them grow for another 2 years, in which case they will multiply and more will be available to pick. If Donna's discount rate is 10 percent, at least how many tulips must be available in 2 years in order to justify her waiting until then to pick them?
3. Suppose that a $150,000 expenditure today on insulating layers to prevent toxic landfill seepage would eliminate $1 million worth of healthcare costs 20 years from now. If the social discount rate were 10 percent, would society be willing to spend the $150,000 today?
4. How would your answer to Problem 3 change if the discount rate were 5 percent? What is the most that society would spend to avoid the $1 million loss in 20 years with a 5 percent discount rate?
5. What discount rate would (will) you recommend if (when) you sit on the President's Council of Economic Advisors? Write one paragraph to defend your answer and its implications on the environment.
6. Provide one example (not given in this chapter) of each of the following:
   a) A defensive good or service
   b) A utility-justified good or service
   c) An environmentally beneficial good or service
7. Explain why GDP is not a good measure of social welfare.
8. What is the difference between GDP and NNW?
9. Explain two reasons why environmental degradation need not accompany growth.
10. In the opinion of the Fifth Circuit Court, what was one thing the EPA did right and one thing the EPA did wrong in their analysis of asbestos policies?

websurfer's challenge

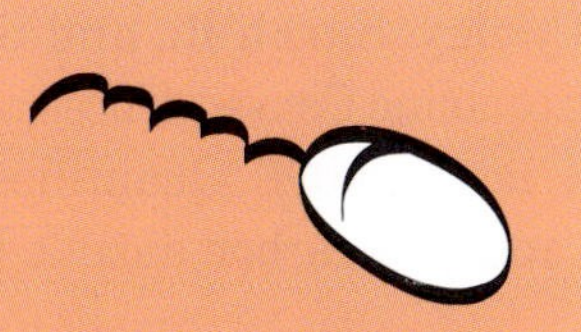

1. Find detailed descriptions of at least two alternatives to GDP that may provide more accurate measures of national welfare.
2. Find a website that discusses trade-offs between economic growth and the environment. Do you agree with the arguments made on this site?
3. Find a website that describes the application of discount rates to a specific environmental cost or benefit in the future. Do you agree with the rate they have applied?

Internet Resources

Friends of the Earth page on measuring progress:
www.foe.co.uk/campaigns/sustainable_development/progress/

Institute of Wellbeing:
www.ciw.ca

Office for Management and the Budget: Guidance on Discount Rates:
www.whitehouse.gov/omb/circulars/a094/a094.html#8

Resources for the Future:
www.rff.org/

Further Reading

Arrow, Kenneth J., and Robert C. Lind. "Uncertainty and the Evaluation of Public Investment Decisions." *American Economic Review* 60, no. 3 (1970): 364–378. Suggests that public investments should be evaluated from the perspective of a risk-neutral party.

Arrow, Kenneth J., and Anthony C. Fisher. "Preservation, Uncertainty, and Irreversibility." *Quarterly Journal of Economics* 87 (1974): 312–319. Demonstrates that decisions involving a risk of irrecoverable loss should receive special cautionary treatment.

Baumol, William J. "On the Social Rate of Discount." *American Economic Review* 58 (1968): 788. Argues for a discount rate that equals or exceeds the market rate of interest.

Cobb, Clifford, Ted Halstead, and Jonathan Rowe. "If the GDP Is Up, Why Is America Down?" *The Atlantic Online* (October 1995): www.theatlantic.com/ politics/ecbig/gdp.htm. As the subtitle says, "why we need new measures of progress, why we do not have them, and how they would change the social and political landscape."

Cooley, Sarah R., and Scott C. Doney. "Anticipating Ocean Acidification's Economic Consequences on Commercial Fisheries." *Environmental Research Letters* 4, no. 2 (2009). Quantifies the damage to the U.S. fishing industry from acidification caused by carbon dioxide build-up.

Cropper, Maureen L., and Paul R. Portney. "Discounting and the Evaluation of Lifesaving Programs." *Journal of Risk and Uncertainty* 3 (1990): 369–379. Reports survey results about time preferences for saving human lives.

Daly, Herman E., and John B. Cobb, Jr. *For the Common Good: Redirecting the Economy Toward Community, the Environment, and a Sustainable Future.* Boston: Beacon Press, 1989. Introduces the index of sustainable economic welfare and presents comparisons between it and the gross national product.

Farber, Daniel A., and Paul A. Hemmersbaugh. "The Shadow of the Future: Discount Rates, Later Generations, and the Environment." *Vanderbilt Law Review* 46 (1993): 267–304. A thoughtful and accessible discussion of discount rates, admittedly leaning toward "future-mindedness."

Henry, Claude. "Investment Decisions Under Uncertainty: The Irreversibility Effect." *American Economic Review* 64 (1974): 1006–1012. Finds that developers who overlook the opportunity to learn more about the effects of their behavior over time will be biased toward overdevelopment.

Horowitz, John K., and Richard T. Carson. "Discounting Statistical Lives." *Journal of Risk and Uncertainty* 3 (1990): 403–410. A study in which one-third of the respondents assigned greater weight to future lives than to present lives.

Howe, Charles W. "The Social Discount Rate." *Journal of Environmental Economics and Management* 18 (March 1990): S1–2. This edition of *JEEM* includes a collection of articles focusing on social/environmental discount rates.

Lind, Robert C., Kenneth J. Arrow, Gordon R. Corey, et al. *Discounting for Time and Risk in Energy Policy*. Washington, D.C.: Resources for the Future, 1982. A classic collection of essays on discount rates and their influence on policy.

Nordhaus, William, and James Tobin. "Is Growth Obsolete?" *Economic Growth Economic Research: Retrospect and Prospect* 5 (1972). Presents the authors' measure of economic welfare.

Pigou, Arthur C. *The Economics of Welfare*. London: Macmillan, 1932. A classic in which Pigou questions human foresight.

Portney, Paul R., and John P. Weyant (eds). *Discounting and Intergenerational Equity*. Washington, D.C.: Resources for the Future, 1999. An updated collection of papers on discounting written by many of the foremost environmental economists, including Lind, who was behind the first such collection.

Rawls, John. *A Theory of Justice*. Cambridge, MA: Belknap Press, 1999. In this classic, Rawls explains his "veil of ignorance" from which to consider fair procedure.

Taylor, Jerry. "Energy Conservation and Efficiency: The Case Against Coercion." *Policy Analysis* 189 (1993), available at http://www.cato.org/pub_display.php?pub_id=1049. An article suggesting relaxed standards and higher discount rates for conservation efforts.

Viscusi, W. Kip. "The Value of Life: Estimates with Risks by Occupation and Industry." *Economic Inquiry* 42, no. 1 (2004): 29–48. An overview of techniques and outcomes of empirical value-of-life studies.

"What Price Posterity." *The Economist* (March 23, 1991): 73. A lucid overview of the discounting of environmental benefits.

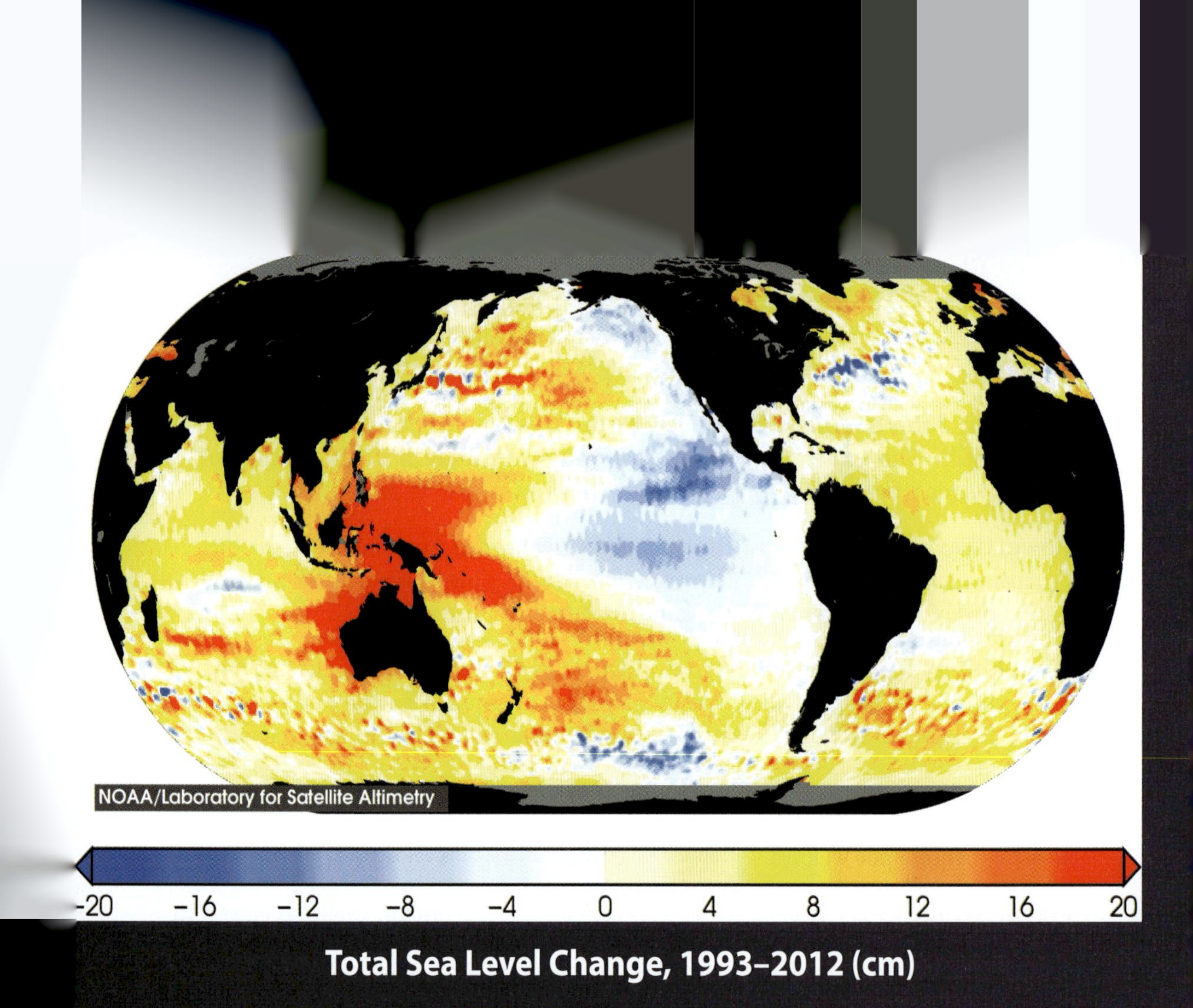

Total Sea Level Change, 1993–2012 (cm)

Global climate change has warmed the oceans and melted land ice, raising the mean sea level by 5.6 centimeters (2.2 inches) between 1993 and 2012. As shown above, the rise is not uniform—the warmer the water, the higher the sea level. Ocean heat and its movement across the globe are pivotal to the Earth's climate. A rising sea level can also destroy developments and ecosystems in coastal areas.

6 Environmental Quality

More than 1,300 hazardous waste sites threatened environmental quality in the United States in 2013, and industries released about 2 million tons of toxic chemicals.[1] Every individual, firm, and government faces decisions that affect environmental quality. Many of these decisions could be improved. The efficient size and scope of environmental initiatives depends on the enormity of impending problems. Regrettably, views of environmental quality are clouded by information constraints and biased by personal agendas. Fervor for votes, profits, or environmental concerns may blind some politicians, manufacturers, and environmentalists from moderate (and more accurate?) standpoints. Such distractions from efficiency criteria are a global problem with global repercussions.

The United Nations Environment Program[2] tracks countries' pledges to cut greenhouse gas emissions. The goal is to limit global warming to 2 degrees Celsius in this century. The Program reports the ***emissions gap*** *between the projected level of emissions in 2020 and the 44-gigaton level needed to remain on target. In 2012, the reported gap was 8 gigatons, 2 gigatons more than in 2011. Progress is hampered by differing perspectives and competing interests among the world's policymakers. Amid alarm and apathy, dispassionate research and objective quality measures offer a basis for convergence. This chapter summarizes foundations for common understanding and case studies about possible solutions.*

1 See the EPA's Toxic Release Inventory, available online at www.epa.gov/tri/index.htm.

2 See www.unep.org/.

What Is the Quality of the Environment?

Terms of the Trade

A few key terms are useful in discussions of environmental quality. They are presented here in one place to help you compare and contrast terms, and for convenience when you need to locate them again.

An **environmental sink** is a repository for potentially damaging by-products of human activity. As with a kitchen sink, we can send a certain amount of "gunk" into an environmental sink before problems occur. Limited amounts of some pollutants can be transformed, diluted, dispersed, or absorbed into the environment without causing any damage. Animals can store small traces of DDT pesticide in their fat tissues with little or no ill effects. Soil can receive controlled amounts of organic waste before harm is done. And by a process called **carbon sequestration**, the oceans and vegetation absorb carbon dioxide (CO_2), release oxygen (O), and store carbon (C).

Carbon sequestration is part of a set of reactions known as photosynthesis, in which solar energy, carbon dioxide from the atmosphere, and water combine to form carbohydrates (sugars) that are the building blocks of **biomass** (plant matter). In light of this, possible solutions to excessive carbon dioxide levels include reforestation and the placement of iron in the oceans to generate more carbon-dioxide-absorbing phytoplankton.[3] When biomass or fossil fuels (which were previously biomass) are burned, the process is reversed. Oxygen from the atmosphere combines with released carbon to produce carbon dioxide once again.

Americans discard some 240 million tires annually, many of which contribute to environmental degradation as in this unsightly confluence of nature and neglect.

Natural capital includes natural resources (forests, oceans, mineral deposits) and ecosystems that provide clean air and water. Natural capital is susceptible to resource degradation from the overharvesting of natural resources and **pollution** that results from the exhaustion of environmental sinks. The environment has little or no absorptive capacity for **stock pollutants**, which

3 Researchers are studying numerous related sequestration concepts, including the injection of carbon dioxide into geologic formations or deep into the ocean, and chemically transforming it into various products. The U.S. Department of Energy is progressing with a process that pumps carbon dioxide gas into slurry made of water, salt, and magnesium silicate. The slurry is heated and then compressed into solid rock. The CO_2 is thereby transformed chemically into a mineral that will remain stable over millions of years. See www.fe.doe.gov/techline/tl_arc_sequestration.shtml.

For practical reasons, environmental regulations typically apply to the output *of stationary pollution sources like refineries and to the* inputs *into mobile pollution sources such as automobiles.*

quickly overwhelm environmental sinks and accumulate in the environment over time. Examples of stock pollutants include polychlorinated biphenyls (PCBs), dioxin, DDT, and heavy metals. Pollutants for which the environment has some absorptive capacity are called **fund pollutants**. Examples of fund pollutants include carbon dioxide and organic waste. **Flow pollutants** can be initially damaging, but are dissipated into environmental sinks with relative ease. Examples include light, noise, and heat pollution, biodegradable litter, and smog.

Natural pollutants include harmful emissions from the Earth and its creatures. Volcanoes and bubbling springs emit large amounts of carbon dioxide. Decaying plants emit methane (CH_4). Oceans and bacteria in soil release a third "greenhouse gas," nitrous oxide (N_2O). Animals, including humans, emit hydrogen methane (H_2), hydrogen sulfide (H_2S), nitrogen (N_2), and carbon dioxide in the processes of breathing, eating, and digestion. **Anthropogenic pollutants** are the undesired products of human activity. When humans manufacture goods, transport themselves and their possessions, heat and cool their homes, and turn on their lights and other electronics, they generate pollution. After goods are manufactured, transported, and consumed, their disposal creates further pollution. Garbage in landfills and sewage in treatment plants emit methane and nitrous oxide, among other pollutants, into the air, water, and soil.

Whether pollution comes from a **stationary source** like a power plant, or a **mobile source** like a motor boat, has implications for pollution-control efforts. It is relatively easy to monitor the *output* of stationary sources. Regulators always know where smokestakes and other stationary source are, and the sources tend to be quite large. Mobile sources such as motor vehicles are much harder to keep track of. A solution is to regulate the types of fuel that go *into* the mobile sources. For example, policies in many countries restrict the *output* of sulfur dioxide (SO_2) from manufacturing plants and prohibit the use of lead (Pb) as an *input* into gasoline.

This pipe in India flows directly into the Arabian Sea. Point sources of pollution like this are identifiable and can be targeted for cleanup.

Any identifiable source of pollution is considered a **point source**. Smokestacks, effluent pipes, and leaking oil tankers are all examples. Stationary point sources whose emissions are diffuse, such as wildfires, and those too small to track individually, such as homes, are called **area sources**.

Nonpoint source (NPS) pollution comes from many diffuse sources that are not identified. The degradation of water quality is generally associated with NPS pollution. The runoff of rain and melted snow picks up pollutants, including fertilizers, herbicides, insecticides, oil, road salt, and bacteria from human and livestock waste. The runoff then flows into waterways, wetlands, and underground sources of drinking water. Because of its unidentified sources, NPS pollution presents real challenges for policymakers. The U.S. Environmental Protection Agency tells the public, "*You* are the solution to NPS pollution."

Figure 6.1 illustrates how pollutants are categorized on the basis of their range and density. A **uniformly distributed pollutant** (also called *uniformly mixed*) causes the same environmental damage regardless of where it is released. Examples include **greenhouse gases**, which include carbon dioxide, methane, nitrous oxide, and hydrofluorocarbons. When released anywhere on Earth, these gases cause the **greenhouse effect** by trapping heat in the atmosphere. Similarly, chlorofluorocarbons erode the protective ozone layer and allow more solar radiation to penetrate the atmosphere.

A **concentrated pollutant** causes damage primarily within a local area. For example, the activity within a city creates noise, light, and smog that are unlikely to cause much damage beyond the urban boundaries. Radiation levels from normally functioning nuclear power plants, X-ray equipment, and radon releases become insignificant outside the immediate areas of the sources. **Hotspots** in the context of pollution are areas with high levels of concentrated pollutants.

A **nonuniformly distributed pollutant** (also called nonuniformly mixed) causes some harm elsewhere, but has a relatively large effect on the local area. For example, nitrogen from fertilizers and other sources runs off into the

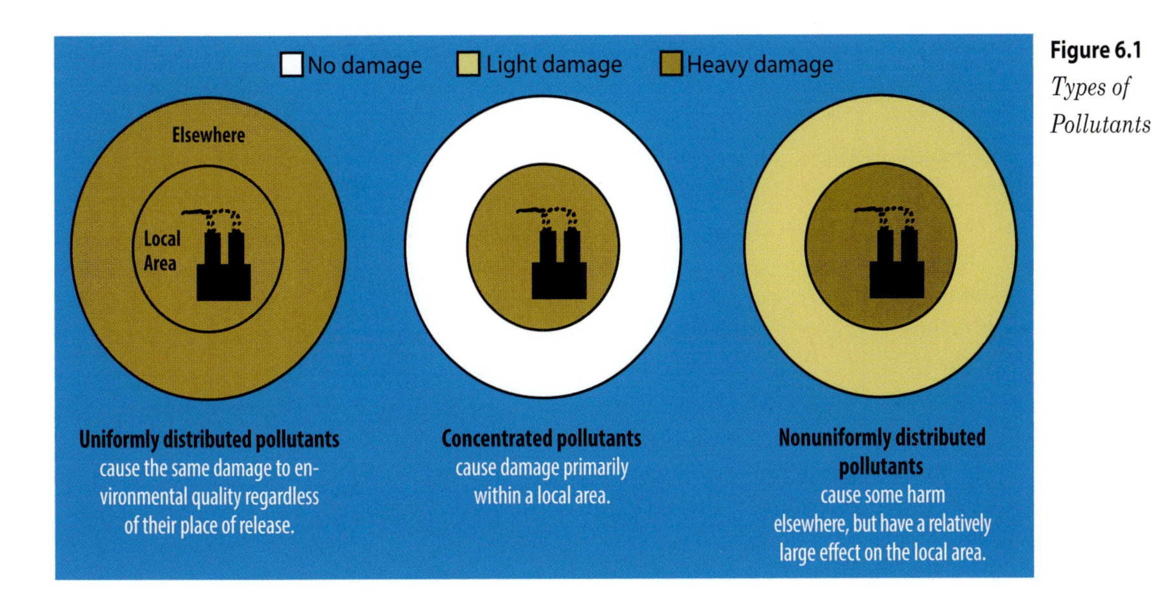

Figure 6.1 *Types of Pollutants*

Mississippi River and draws oxygen from the water. The resulting *hypoxia* is deadly to aquaculture and has created a *dead zone* covering over 7,000 square miles in the Mississippi Delta. The worst effects are felt at the mouth of the river, but decreases in marine life extend into the coastal waters of Texas.[4]

Air Quality

Air quality is subject to both natural and anthropogenic influences. Natural air pollutants include gaseous emissions from the Earth, volcanic ash, pollen, and methane emitted by termites among other living creatures. Sources of anthropogenic air pollution include motor vehicles, power plants, and factories. Although there is controversy over the relative importance of natural air pollutants, it is clear that anthropogenic sources are more readily controllable by existing technologies.[5] For that reason, anthropogenic pollution is the focus of this section.

Standards **Ambient air** is the air that surrounds us. There were days in 2013 when the ambient air quality in Beijing, China, was so poor that school children and the elderly were forced to stay indoors. The record-high pollution levels had the Chinese media speaking of an "air-pocalypse." Problems with air quality are not limited to developing countries. In 1952, smog killed roughly 4,000 people in London, England, within only four days and led to passage of the U.K. Clean Air Act of 1956. In keeping with the U.S. Clean Air Act of 1970, the EPA establishes the National Ambient Air Quality Standards (NAAQS) for six **criteria air pollutants** considered harmful to public health, welfare, or the environment. Table 6.1 on the following page provides summary information for each pollutant.

Primary standards are designed to protect public health, including that

4 For more on the dead zone, visit www.epa.gov/gmpo/gmnet.qut005.htm.

5 This may change in the future, as scientists develop improved methods for controlling earthquakes and volcanoes, the weather, and other natural occurrences.

Table 6.1 *Criteria Air Pollutants*

Pollutant	*Anthropogenic Sources*	*Health and Welfare Effects*	*Control Methods*
Particulate Matter (PM_{10}, $PM_{2.5}$) Airborne particles less than 10 microns in diameter (PM_{10}) or less than 2.5 microns ($PM_{2.5}$) in diameter	• Power-plant boilers • Steel mills • Chemical plants • Unpaved roads and parking lots • Wood-burning stoves and fireplaces • Motor vehicles	• Aggravates respiratory diseases • May cause lung and heart problems • May carry toxic materials deep into the respiratory system • Impairs visibility	• Filters • Scrubbers • Reduction in fuel combustion
Sulfur Dioxide (SO_2) Colorless, nonflammable gas	• Power-plant boilers • Sulfuric acid plants • Petroleum refineries • Smelters • Paper mills • Fuel combustion in diesel engines	• Respiratory irritant • Aggravates lung and heart problems • Can damage marble, iron, steel, crops, and vegetation • Impairs visibility • Precursor to acid rain	• Use of low-sulfur fuel • Energy conservation (reduces power plant emissions) • Pollution control equipment
Carbon Monoxide (CO) Odorless, colorless gas	• Incomplete combustion of carbon-based fuels in motor vehicle and industrial boilers	• Impairs the delivery of oxygen to vital tissues • Impairs vision • Can cause dizziness, unconsciousness or death	• Transportation planning • Vehicle emissions testing • Efficient combustion techniques • Energy conservation

(*continued*)

Adapted from information compiled by Ken Larson (www.co.broward.fl.us/aqi02700.htm) and the EPA (www.epa.gov/reg5oair/emission/critpllt.htm).

Table 6.1 *(continued)*

Pollutant	*Anthropogenic Sources*	*Health and Welfare Effects*	*Control Methods*
Ozone (O_3) Colorless or bluish gas (smog) formed from volatile organic compounds (VOC) and nitrogen oxides	• Fuel combustion in motor vehicles • Gasoline storage and transport • Solvents and paints • Landfills	• Irritates mucous membranes • Aggravates lung and heart problems • Damages rubber, some textiles and dyes • Damages plants • Reduces crop yield	• Use of low-VOC solvents • Evaporative controls • Vehicle emissions testing • Pollution control equipment
Nitrogen Dioxide (NO_2) Reddish-brown gas	• Fuel combustion in motor vehicles and industrial sources	• Respiratory irritant • Aggravates lung and heart problems • Precursor to ozone and acid rain • Causes brown discoloration of atmosphere	• Exhaust gas recirculation • Reduction of combustion temperatures • Energy conservation • Pollution control equipment
Lead (P_b) Toxic heavy metal	• Smelters • Lead-acid battery manufacturing • Electric-arc furnaces • Incineration of garbage containing lead • Use of leaded gasoline	• Toxic to the nervous system, organs, and most levels of body function	• Phase-out of leaded gasoline • Use of pollution control equipment in industrial plants

Table 6.2 *National Ambient Air Quality Standards*

Pollutant	*Standard Value*	*Standard Type*
Carbon Monoxide (CO)		
8-hour average	9 ppm	Primary
1-hour average	35 ppm	Primary
Nitrogen Dioxide (NO_2)		
1-hour average	100 ppb	
Annual arithmetic mean	53 ppb	Primary and secondary
Ozone (O_3)		
8-hour average	0.075 ppm	Primary and secondary
Lead (Pb)		
Rolling 3-month average	0.15 $\mu g/m^3$	Primary and secondary
Particulate (PM_{10}) *Particles with diameters of 10 micrometers or less*		
24-hour average	150 $\mu g/m^3$	Primary and secondary
Particulate ($PM_{2.5}$) *Particles with diameters of 2.5 micrometers or less*		
Annual arithmetic mean	12 $\mu g/m^3$	Primary
Annual arithmetic mean	15 $\mu g/m^3$	Secondary
24-hour average	35 $\mu g/m^3$	Primary and secondary
Sulfur Dioxide (SO_2)		
1-hour average	75 ppb	Primary
3-hour average	0.50 ppm	Secondary

Source: www.epa.gov/air/criteria.html

of children, the elderly, asthmatics, and other particularly sensitive groups. **Secondary standards** are designed to protect public welfare, which is diminished by damage to plants, animals, buildings, and agriculture, and by reduced visibility. Table 6.2 indicates the National Ambient Air Quality Standards for each of the criteria air pollutants.

In addition to the criteria air pollutants, the Clean Air Act amendments of 1990 added 189 **hazardous air pollutants** (HAPs), also called **toxic air pollutants** or **air toxics**.[6] These pollutants are known or suspected to cause serious health problems as well.

Actual Levels Over 4,000 air quality monitoring stations across the United States measure pollutant concentrations on an hourly or daily basis. States submit their air monitoring data monthly for inclusion in the EPA's Aerometric Information Reporting System (AIRS) database. Table 6.3 indicates the number

6 A list of HAPs from Section 112(b)(1) of the Clean Air Act is available at www.epa.gov/ttn/atw/188polls.html.

Criteria Pollutant	*People Living in Noncompliant Counties*
CO	75,810,917
Pb	9,669,000
O_3	123,004,000
PM_{10}	29,202,000
$PM_{2.5}$	74,316,000
SO_2	1,217,000

Table 6.3 *Population Exposed to Noncompliant Pollution Levels in the United States.*

Source: *EPA Green Book*, 2012, http://www.epa.gov/oar/oaqps/greenbk/popexp.html.

of people living in counties with criteria air pollutant concentrations in excess of the National Ambient Air Quality Standards in 2010. In that year, 232 counties failed to meet the standards for ozone, 270 failed for particulate matter-10, 123 failed for particulate matter-2.5, 131 failed for carbon monoxide, 9 failed for sulfur dioxide, and 23 failed for lead.

Typical punishments for nonattainment counties include *offset sanctions* and the withholding of federal highway funds. When expansion or new development causes a firm in a nonattainment county to increase its emissions by some amount, a **2:1 offset sanction** requires the firm to reduce existing emissions by twice the amount of the increase. This reduction can be accomplished with pollution control equipment or by purchasing tradable pollution permits as described below. For example, suppose a factory expansion causes a firm to emit 10 additional tons of lead per year. The firm would have to reduce lead emissions from another part of its operations by 20 tons. The idea is that nonattainment counties must decrease their emissions to reach the acceptable standard, and a 1:1 offset (meaning each additional ton of emissions in the new facilities would be offset by one fewer ton of emissions elsewhere) would simply maintain the current level of pollution. If firms must reduce their emissions by twice the amount created by the new facilities, total emissions will fall to a level closer to the desired standard. Over the past two decades the EPA has sent out hundreds of formal notifications of intent to apply sanctions. Most counties remedy the problem within the 18-month period between formal notification and the imposition of sanctions. Actual sanctions have been imposed fewer than 20 times in as many years.

Acid Deposition Acidity is measured on a pH scale, with lower numbers meaning higher acidity. Wet **acid deposition**,[7] commonly referred to as acid rain, occurs when rainwater, fog, or snow has a pH level lower than 5. Pure water has a pH of 7.0. Rain has a slight natural acidity caused by atmospheric carbon dioxide, giving it a pH of about 5.5. Rain falling in the United States has measured pH levels as low as 4.3. Acid rain is deadly to forests, aquaculture, and humans, and damaging to automobiles and buildings. The ability for trees

7 Nearly half of atmospheric acidity falls back to the earth as dry gases and particles. Wind and fallen rain carry these dry acidic deposits to buildings, wildlife, and waterways.

to absorb nutrients is dependent on soil acidity, and increases in acidity can starve trees and other vegetation. Beyond its direct toxicity, acid releases copper, aluminum, and mercury stored in rocks and pipes. The primary cause of acid rain is sulfur dioxide (SO_2), which dissolves in water to form sulfuric acid (H_2SO_4). Various oxides of nitrogen (mostly NO_2 and NO_3), collectively called NO_x, and hydrochloric acid are contributing causes. Coal-fired power plants are the largest controllable source of SO_2 and NO_x, followed by industry and road transportation.

The effects of acid deposition can occur great distances from the causal sources of air pollution. Lifeless trees and lakes in Canada and Norway have been attributed to sulfur dioxide emissions in the United States and central Europe. Environment Canada reports that the United States emits six times as much SO_2 as Canada, and that 95,000 lakes remained damaged by acid rain even after control programs were fully implemented in 2010.[8] Norway's defensive expenditures on acid rain amount to an estimated $360 million each year.[9] The EPA reports that as of 2010, decreases in mortality, hospital admissions, and emergency room visits in the United States brought the annual health benefits from the Acid Rain Program to $50 billion.[10]

As the most accessible supplies of low-sulfur coal are depleted, power companies turn to coal with sulfur levels up to ten times higher. Scrubbers that remove SO_2 and NO_x from power-plant emissions have price tags in the hundreds of millions of dollars. On the bright side, an innovative approach to acid rain involving tradable pollution allowances has reduced annual sulfur dioxide emissions in the United States by about 10 million tons. The economics of scrubbers and emissions trading is mentioned in greater detail in the last section of this chapter and in Chapter 12.

Global Climate Change Among the myriad repercussions of air pollution, global climate change is the most prominent of the twenty-first century. Pollution contributes to collections of greenhouse gases that hold heat within Earth's atmosphere and keep it about 33 °C (59 °F) warmer than it would otherwise be. Atmospheric concentrations of the most prevalent greenhouse gas, carbon dioxide, have risen by nearly 30 percent since the industrial revolution. Methane concentrations have more than doubled, and nitrous oxide concentrations have risen by about 15 percent. These increases, among other human and natural trends, may be to blame for the reported 0.5°C to 1.0 °C increase in global temperatures over

Warmer oceans fuel hurricanes likes Sandy (left), which caused more than $60 billion worth of damage in 2012, and Katrina (right), which caused more than $100 billion worth of damage in 2005.

Photos courtesy of NASA/SVS

8 See www.ec.gc.ca/acidrain/acidfact.html.

9 See www.grida.no/soeno97/acidrain/state.htm.

10 See www.epa.gov/airmarkets/acidrain/effects/health.html.

reality check

Global Climate Change

According to the Intergovernmental Panel on Climate Change:*

- Warming of the climate system is unequivocal, as is now evident from observed increases in the global average air and ocean temperatures, widespread melting of snow and ice, and the rising global average sea level.
- Global atmospheric concentrations of carbon dioxide, methane, and nitrous oxide have increased markedly as a result of human activities since 1750 and now far exceed pre-industrial values determined from ice cores spanning many thousands of years.
- The global increases in carbon dioxide concentration are due primarily to fossil fuel use and land use change, while those of methane and nitrous oxide are primarily due to agriculture.
- Improvements in the understanding of anthropogenic warming and cooling influences on climate have led to very high confidence that the global average net effect of human activities since 1750 has been one of warming.
- Palaeoclimatic information supports the interpretation that the warmth of the last half century is unusual considering at least the previous 1,300 years.
- The last time the polar regions were significantly warmer than they are now for an extended period—about 125,000 years ago—reductions in polar ice volume led to a 4 to 6 meter rise in the global sea level.
- For the next two decades, a warming of about 0.2°C per decade is projected for a range of emission scenarios.
- Most of the observed increase in global average temperatures since the mid-twentieth century is very likely due to the observed increase in anthropogenic greenhouse gas concentrations.
- Discernible human influences now extend to other aspects of climate, including ocean warming, continental-average temperatures, temperature extremes, and wind patterns.
- It is very likely that hot extremes, heat waves and heavy precipitation events will continue to become more frequent.

*See www.ipcc.ch/.

Table 6.4 *Indications of Climate Change*

Indicators
Greenhouse Gases
• U.S. Emissions
• Global Emissions
• Atmospheric Concentrations
• Climate Forcing
Weather and Climate
• U.S. and Global Temperature
• High and Low Temperatures
• U.S. and Global Precipitation
• Heavy Precipitation
• Drought
• Tropical Cyclone Activity
Oceans
• Ocean Heat
• Sea Surface Temperature
• Sea Level
• Ocean Acidity
Snow and Ice
• Arctic Sea Ice
• Glaciers
• Lake Ice
• Snowfall
• Snow Cover
• Snowpack
Society and Ecosystems
• Streamflow
• Ragweed Pollen Season
• Length of Growing Season
• Leaf and Bloom Dates
• Bird Wintering Ranges
• Heat-Related Deaths

On the basis of these indicators, the EPA concludes that climate change already affects ecosystems and society, and that it is linked to fossil fuel combustion.

the past century. The ten warmest years since record keeping began in 1850 have all occurred since 1997, and the warmest year was 2012. The warming trend has already caused more powerful hurricanes (also called cyclones),[11] a thinning of ice over the Arctic Ocean, more frequent extreme rainfall, and a 4–8 inch increase in the sea level over the past century.[12]

The EPA tracks the 26 indicators of global climate change shown in Table 6.4. The indicators are selected on the basis of the quality of available data. Results for each indicator are linked to the EPA website provided in footnote 13 below. The conclusion is that climate change is already affecting society and ecosystems. The EPA reports that, "Scientists are confident that many of the observed changes in the climate can be linked to the increase in greenhouse gases in the atmosphere, caused largely by people burning fossil fuels to generate electricity, heat and cool buildings, and power vehicles."[13]

Figure 6.2 shows estimates from the Intergovernmental Panel on Climate Change (IPCC) of global temperature change over the next century. The range of estimates results from varying assumptions about future trends in greenhouse gas emissions and sulfate aerosol use. Scientists working for the United Nations Environment Program report that with current trends in emissions and emission-reduction efforts, we are on track for temperature increases in excess of 2°C by the end of this century. Continuing changes in climate, soil moisture, sea level, and weather patterns threaten vital ecosystems and agricultural production. According to research by Dasgupta et al.,[14] hundreds of millions of

11 See www.pewclimate.org/hurricanes.cfm.

12 See http://yosemite.epa.gov/oar/globalwarming.nsf/content/Climate.html.

13 See www.epa.gov/climatechange/science/indicators/index.html.

14 See www-wds.worldbank.org/servlet/WDSContentServer/WDSP/IB/2007/02/09/000016406_20070209161430/Rendered/PDF/wps4136.pdf.

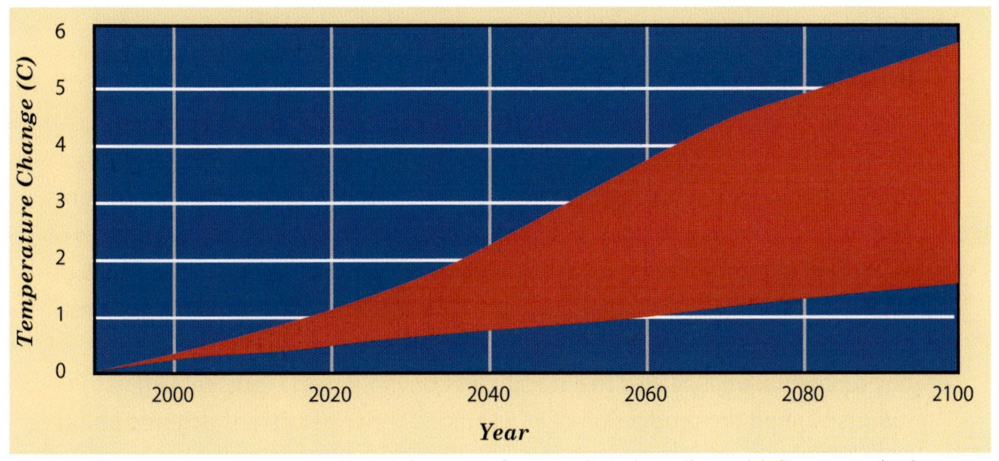

Source: EPA/IPCC, http://yosemite.epa.gov/OAR/globalwarming.nsf/content/ClimateFutureClimateGlobalTemperature.html.

Figure 6.2 *Projected Global Temperature Change*

people in East Asia, the Middle East, and North Africa are likely to be displaced by sea level change in this century.

Water Quality

> *"In Louisiana's 'Cancer Alley,' over a hundred heavy industrial facilities 'provide jobs and pay taxes' in the area, but they also release poison into the air, land, and water at a rate of almost half a billion pounds per year. The common sense of the local people tells them that the petrochemical industry is about more than jobs and taxes; it also brings sickness and death."*
>
> —Witness to the Future[15]

Surface water is water that is open to the Earth's atmosphere. It includes the rivers, lakes, oceans, and streams that cover 70 percent of the planet. **Groundwater** is fresh water located primarily in large aquifers beneath the Earth's surface. Over 95 percent of the world's water supply is salt water in oceans and inland seas. Groundwater, ice caps, and glaciers make up almost all of the fresh water. Fresh surface water makes up only 0.01 percent of the total water supply.[16] None of these sources is impervious to pollution.

Unlike today's youth, their parents remember when bottled water was not commonplace. People no longer have the same trust in their water supplies. In the distant past, those canoeing the great rivers could push a paddle into the water and then lift the paddle above their heads to drink water as it ran off the handle. Don't try this on your next canoe trip. Like air, water is vulnerable as a common-property resource for which few property rights exist. As detailed in the next Reality Check, pollutants are found in virtually every corner of the world. In 1969, the surface of the badly polluted Cuyahoga River in Ohio caught fire and burned for several days. Still today there are thousands of advisories warning consumers about high levels of mercury, PCBs, or dioxin in certain types of fish

15 See www.witnesstothefuture.com/meet/cancer.html.

16 See Speidel and Agnew (1988), p. 28.

reality check

Even in the Arctic: PCBs and Hermaphrodite Polar Bears

PCBs are a group of synthetic industrial chemicals used in everything from coolants and casting wax to pesticides and plastics. There are no known natural sources of PCBs. Due to their extreme toxicity, the Toxic Substances Control Act of 1976 directed the EPA to ban the manufacture of PCBs and regulate their use and disposal, which the EPA did in 1978. Most industrialized nations followed suit. In 2004, an environmental treaty called the Stockholm Convention on Persistent Organic Pollutants banned the production of PCBs among other **persistent organic pollutants** (POPs) throughout the world. Nonetheless, they are still present in and around many waterways, landfills, and industrial spills in the United States and elsewhere.

How far does pollution travel? Scientists know only too well. PCBs and other POPs including dichlorodiphenyltrichloroethane (DDT) are showing up at dangerous concentration levels in the most remote regions of the Earth. On the Arctic island of Svalbard, PCBs are thought to be the cause of hermaphrodite polar bears with both male and female reproductive organs. Analysis of the DDT components found in the Arctic indicates that some of the culprit chemicals are only weeks old when they arrive. This is evidence that the banned substances are still in production, and that their damage spans the globe.

Polar bears aren't the only ones exposed to PCBs. The PCB levels Bytingsvik et al. (2012) found in polar bear cubs were 100 times the levels known to affect thyroid hormones in human babies. PCBs can also cause reproductive disorders, skin ailments, liver disease, and cancer in humans. PCBs accumulate in body fat and are passed through the food chain. The U.S. Food and Drug Administration has issued an advisory against eating fish with more than 2 parts per million of PCBs, and the EPA has established a maximum PCB contamination level of 0.5 parts per billion in drinking water. Sport anglers, human and otherwise, take heed.

from waterways in Ohio among many other states.[17] Swimming also poses health risks in many waterways. It is no longer appealing for rafters to dangle their legs in the Mississippi River as described by Mark Twain. The abuse of river resources is particularly tempting because effluents released into flowing water are "water under the bridge," immediately becoming the problem of someone else downstream. Of course, that is the short-run story. What goes around comes around. Rivers flow into oceans, which provide food for the masses and support critical ecosystems for the planet as a whole.[18]

17 See www.michigan.gov/documents/FishAdvisory03_67354_7.pdf and www.epa.ohio.gov/dsw/fishadvisory/questions.aspx.

18 A sobering anecdote: In 2001, an economist from Wisconsin (one of the northernmost tributaries to the Mississippi River) passed away after eating toxic seafood from Louisiana (where the Mississippi flows into the sea).

Study	Quality Issue	Group Studied	Estimated Value
Viscusi, Huber, and Bell (2008)	A one-percent increase in waterways with "good" water quality	U.S. residents	$32 per person (for regional improvements)
Legget and Bockstael (1999)	A 100-count change in fecal coliform bacteria in Chesapeake Bay	Homeowners in Maryland	$5,115–$9,842 per home
Guha (2007)	Availability of drinkable water	435,000 in Calcutta, India	$4.5 million per year
Phaneuf, Kling, and Herriges (1998)	A 20 percent reduction in toxins in the Great Lakes	Anglers in Wisconsin	$35.85/angler per year
Georgiou et al. (1998)	Clean water at bathing beaches	Bathers in England	$8.17/bather per year
Greenley, Walsh, and Young (1981)	Lower heavy metal concentrations in rivers	Homeowners in Colorado River Basin	$1 billion in discounted present value
Michael, Boyle, and Bouchard (2000)	Lake water clarity	Homeowners in Maine	$5,000–$10,000 per home

Table 6.5
The Value of Clean Water

The Value of Water Quality Astronomers are ever alert for evidence of water on other planets because it is a precursor for all life forms. Life on Earth is no exception. Some amount of non-toxic water must pass through all living things during the **hydrological cycle** that takes water down from the clouds as precipitation, to (and below) the Earth's surface, up through evaporation, and back down as precipitation again. About 350 billion gallons of fresh water are used in the United States every day.[19] The human body is about 60 percent water. Beyond that, we rely on varying degrees of water quality for hygiene, aquatic life support, recreation, agriculture, many facets of production, and sustenance of the natural environment more broadly.

There are many available estimates of the value of water quality to humans. According to the EPA's Office of Water, in the United States, $44 billion is spent making 910 million annual trips to coastal areas, and 35 million adults pursue the sport of fishing. Table 6.5 provides an assortment of additional examples. Notice that most of these studies estimate the value of clean water to specific groups

19 See http://pubs.usgs.gov/circ/1344/.

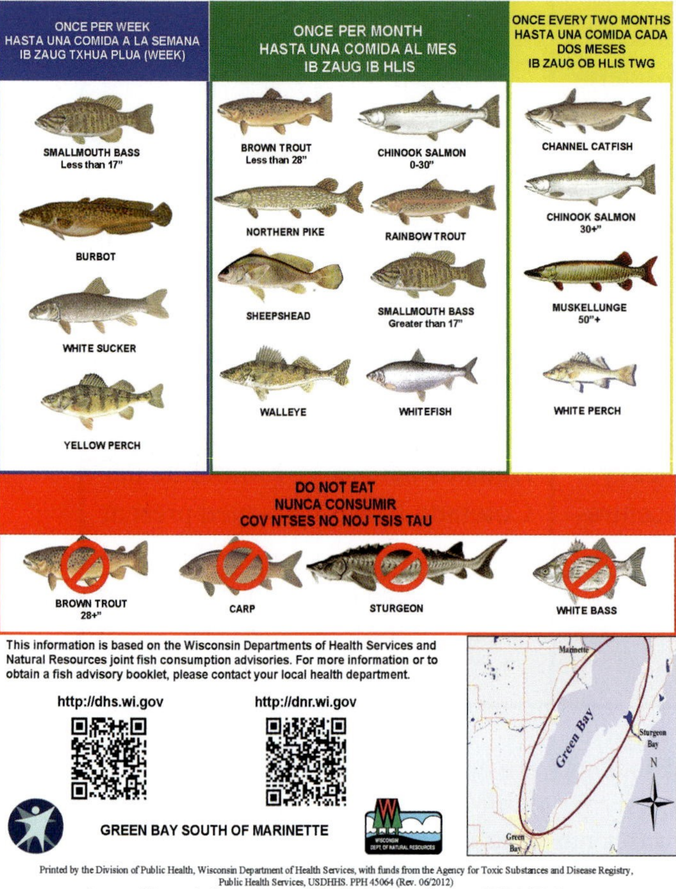

Source: Wisconsin Department of Health Services, Accessed 3/29/2013.

like homeowners or anglers. Many other individuals value clean water for its existence and availability, now and in the future, for humans and wildlife. Chapter 10 discusses the specific methods of placing value on natural capital, and provides additional examples of estimated values placed on wildlife.

Losses from oil spills provide striking examples of the costs of polluted water. A 2010 spill at an offshore drilling rig called the *Deepwater Horizon* released 210 million gallons of oil into the Gulf of Mexico. Payments for resulting lost earnings in the seafood industry, medical costs, and property damage are expected to exceed $7.8 billion. Loss estimates for the 1989 *Exxon Valdez* spill that spread 10.8 million gallons of oil across 1,300 miles of Alaskan coastline exceed $9 billion.[20] In 2007, the South Korea-bound *Cosco Busan* hit the San Francisco Bay Bridge and spilled 58,000 gallons of oil, killing fish and roughly 20,000 birds.

Polluted water causes death and disease among humans and wildlife alike. Well-publicized examples include the California cancer cases portrayed in the film *Erin Brockovich,* the Massachusetts leukemia cases behind the film *A Civil Action,* the so-called cancer alleys in Louisiana and New Jersey, and the Love Canal landfill contamination that caused 950 families to be permanently evacuated from their homes in New York.[21] Globally, consumers purchase nearly 200 billion liters of bottled water each year for roughly $1 per liter—yet another

20 The estimate is adjusted to 2013 dollars. See http://are.berkeley.edu/~gh082644/Exxon%20Valdez%20Oil%20Spill.pdf.

21 The Love Canal incident led to federal legislation governing landfills and nearby development. See www.epa.gov/Region2/superfund/npl/0201290c.htm.

Source of Discharge	*Incidents*
Stationary Sources (refinery, plant, machinery)	10,004
Land Vehicles (trucks, cars, trains)	5,043
Watercraft (ships, barges, private vessels)	4,696
Unknown Sources of Material on Water	4,437
Storage Tanks	2,069
Drilling / Exercise Locations	2,333
Pipelines	1,043
Offshore Platforms	1,140
Aircraft	154
Continuous Releases above Federal Limits	76
TOTAL	**30,995**

Table 6.6 *Pollution Incidents Reported to the U.S. National Response Center, 2012*

Source: www.nrc.uscg.mil/incident_type_2000up.html.

indication of the value of clean water to humans.[22] Indeed, as an essential ingredient to life, the value of potable (fit to drink) water can be no less than the value of life.[23]

Threats to Water Quality The United Kingdom's Environmental Agency reported 120 "serious" pollution incidents involving the water and sewage industry in 2011, up from 65 in 2010. Spills that are not considered serious are far more common. Table 6.6 indicates the sources of 30,995 releases reported to the U.S. National Response Center in 2012. Among the policy responses to past oil spills, the Oil Pollution Act of 1990 requires vessels operating in U.S. waters to have protective double hulls by 2015.[24] The International Convention for the Prevention of Pollution from Ships (MARPOL) requires new tankers to be double-hulled and that single-hulled tankers be modified or replaced within 30 years of construction.[25]

Unlike the air, almost anything can be spilled or dumped into water. Despite the thousands of identified oil spills and effluent releases ever year, nonpoint source pollution is the leading cause of water pollution. The U.S. Clean Water Act requires states to conduct biennial water quality inventories. In 2013, the EPA's Office of Water reported that 55 percent of U.S. rivers are in "poor" condition.[26] About 40 percent of all U.S. lakes, rivers, and estuaries are too polluted to support basic uses such as swimming and fishing.[27] Excessive nutrients, metals

22 See www.cbc.ca/news/background/consumers/bottled-water.html.

23 Specific estimates of the values of human and animal lives are discussed in Chapter 10.

24 See Brown and Savage (1996) for a cost-benefit analysis of the double hull requirement.

25 See www.imo.org/environment/mainframe.asp?topic_id=231.

26 See http://water.epa.gov/type/rsl/monitoring/riverssurvey/upload/NRSA0809_Report_Final_508Compliant_130228.pdf.

27 See http://water.epa.gov/polwaste/nps/outreach/point1.cfm.

Figure 6.3 *Impaired U.S. Waters*

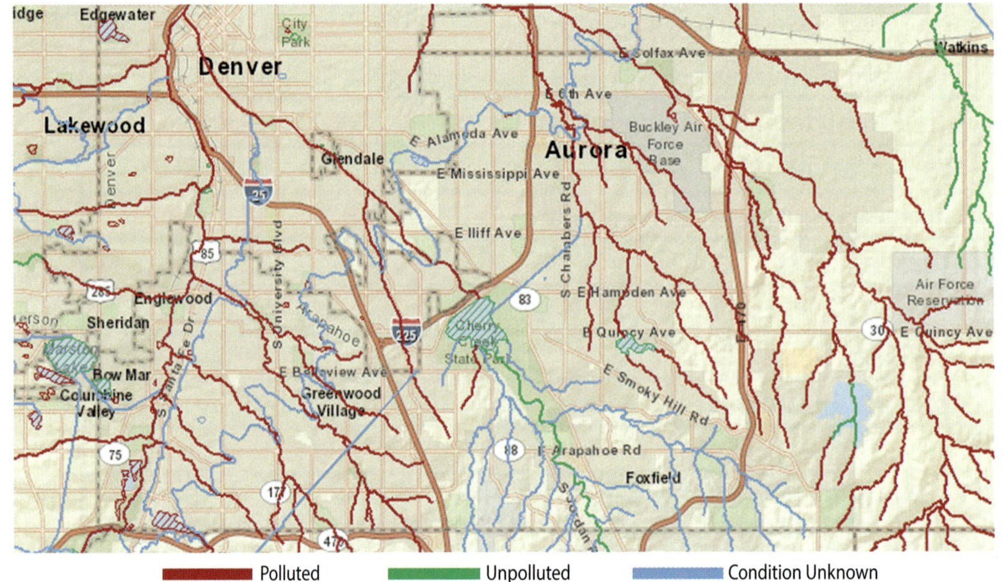

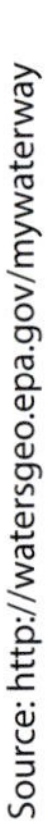

Pollution threatens waterways around the world. Even places like Colorado, which is famous for its natural beauty, struggle with water impairments that limit acquatic life and recreational opportunities.

(primarily mercury), bacteria, siltation, oxygen-depleting substances, and pesticides are among the leading pollutants. Figure 6.3 provides an example of waterways designated as polluted in the state of Colorado. According to China's water authority, up to 40 percent of Chinese rivers are seriously polluted, and 20 percent are too polluted to come into contact with.[28]

Standards The EPA sets standards for more than 100 water pollutants.[29] It measures the condition and vulnerability of the water supply with the Index of Watershed Indicators (IWI). A **watershed** is a land area that catches rain and snow, and sheds or drains it into surface water or groundwater. It is watersheds that carry nonpoint pollutants into the flow of consumable water. If you live in the United States, you can learn the specifics of your own watershed at http://cfpub.epa.gov/surf/locate/index.cfm. The IWI consists of 18 indicators of the "pulse" of water quality. Examples include ambient water quality, fish and wildlife consumption advisories, and wetland loss.[30] On the basis of these indicators, the EPA assigns a score to each watershed and places it into a descriptive category. Fifteen percent of U.S. watersheds have "relatively good" water quality; 36 percent have "moderate problems"; 22 percent have "more serious water quality"; and 27 percent do not have enough information to be characterized.

Under the Clean Water Act, states face federal sanctions if they fail to restore impaired bodies of water. States often delegate standard setting, implementation, and enforcement duties to branches of local government or designated conservation districts. Standards are applied by an overlapping set of general discharge prohibitions, agriculture laws, forestry laws, fish and game

28 See www.upi.com/Business_News/Energy-Resources/2013/03/11/Dead-pigs-contaminating-Chinese-river/UPI-27121363028366/.

29 For a complete list of drinking water standards, see www.epa.gov/safewater/mcl.html.

30 See www.epa.gov/iwi/help/help_e.html.

laws, nuisance prohibitions, land-use planning and regulatory laws, and criminal laws. The **general discharge prohibitions** either require a permit for the release of designated substances, or prohibit emissions that cause (or help cause) water quality levels to violate established standards. Although clear-cut cases exist, the difficulty of proving a direct link between specific releases and water quality weakens the efficacy of such prohibitions.

The requirement of a **discharge permit** removes the need to demonstrate any causal link between pollution and the violator's behavior, and thereby lessens the burden of enforcement. The polluters are asked to file for a permit, identifying themselves and in some cases subjecting themselves to inspection. Polluters who do not obtain a permit face sanctions upon discovery, regardless of any demonstrable association between their releases and subsequent damage. Many of the more targeted laws are enforced as petty criminal offenses. These include laws that limit the percentage of vegetation that may be removed near a waterway, special rules for timber operations near wetlands, and sediment control laws.

Noise and Light Pollution

Problems on Terra Firma[31] Noise and light are good examples of flow pollutants because they do not build up in the environment. Even so, they can cause considerable damage. The World Medical Association Statement on Noise Pollution[32] says that "excessive sound levels produced by industrial sources, transportation systems, audio systems and other means, may lead to permanent hearing loss, other pathophysiologic effects, and emotional disturbances."

The detrimental effects are not limited to humans. Dune-buggy noise causes temporary deafness for the desert kangaroo rat, making it easy prey for rattlesnakes until several days later.[33] Aircraft flying over the national parks can cause extreme panic in animals and hinder their growth and reproductive fitness.[34] Research indicates that the heart rates of mule deer and bighorn sheep are significantly elevated for two to three minutes each time a plane passes overhead.[35] The repercussions of associated stress on animals can include reduced food intake, poor digestion, and subsequent weight loss. Overflights cause a startle reflex (an activation of the sympathetic nervous system) in caribou and a tendency to bolt. These behaviors are thought to threaten injuries to calves, cow and calf separations, stillbirths, reduced milk production, and reduced thyroid function (which inhibits growth and increases the probability of death by predation).[36]

Problems Under the Sea Noise pollution is also a problem underwater, where sources include supertankers and ships of all sizes, oil exploration equipment, military sonar, pingers, explosives, and dredgers. According to the Natural

31 Latin for solid ground.

32 See www.wma.net/e/policy/17-g-1_e.html.

33 See Immel (1995).

34 See Fletcher (1980, 1990).

35 See Weisenberger et al. (1996).

36 See Harrington and Veitch (1991).

Resources Defense Council,

At close range, a powerful sound can cause tissue in the lungs, ears, or other parts of the body to rupture and hemorrhage. Further away, the same sound can induce temporary or permanent hearing loss. And at even greater distances, it can affect behavior, leading animals to swim off course, or abandon habitat, or stop vocalizing, or turn aggressive. In addition, any loud noise has the potential to drown out other sounds—calves, mates, predators—around the same frequency, a phenomenon known as "masking".[37]

The European Parliament and the U.S. Congress are among many legislatures that have considered noise restrictions. Examples include John McCain's proposed National Overflights Act, which would create no-fly zones over some national parks.[38] A related proposal by the Natural Resources Defense Council would create noise-free marine reserves.[39] While good ideas abound, it is challenging to enact and enforce noise pollution standards. The common property aspects of the oceans and skies are further complicated by the international scope of polluters and the many mobile, nonpoint sources.

Problems In the Sky Noise pollution isn't much to look at, but the NASA photograph on the next page sheds light on another flow pollutant. Excess light that spills into the atmosphere represents wasted energy. Note the uneven distribution of this waste across densely populated areas with differing levels of wealth and development. For example, India has four times the population of the United States but wastes less light. As discussed in the next chapter, the production of energy is a primary source of environmental damage worldwide. Light pollution also causes stress for wildlife just as noise pollution does, and its mere existence can render otherwise suitable wildlife habitat uninhabitable.

Contemporary light fixtures tend to spread light outward and upward where it is not needed. Some scientists estimate that in the United States, skyward light emissions expend $2 billion worth of energy annually, which amounts to 17 billion kWh.[40] Solutions include:

- *The use of "fully shielded" or "full-cutoff" outdoor lighting that points light downward and inward on the subject to be illuminated rather than outward and upward*
- *The elimination of unnecessary light fixtures*
- *The transition from all-night illumination to illumination only when facilities are in use (with the exception of security lighting)*
- *The reduction of bulb wattages*
- *The replacement of incandescent bulbs with fluorescent bulbs*

37 Reprinted with permission. See www.nrdc.org/wildlife/marine/sound/exec.asp.

38 See the National Overflights Act of 1997, S268, 105th Congress, 1st Session, at www.netvista.net/~hpb/s268.html.

39 See Natural Resources Defense Council (1999).

40 See www.noao.edu/news/2011/pr1101.php.

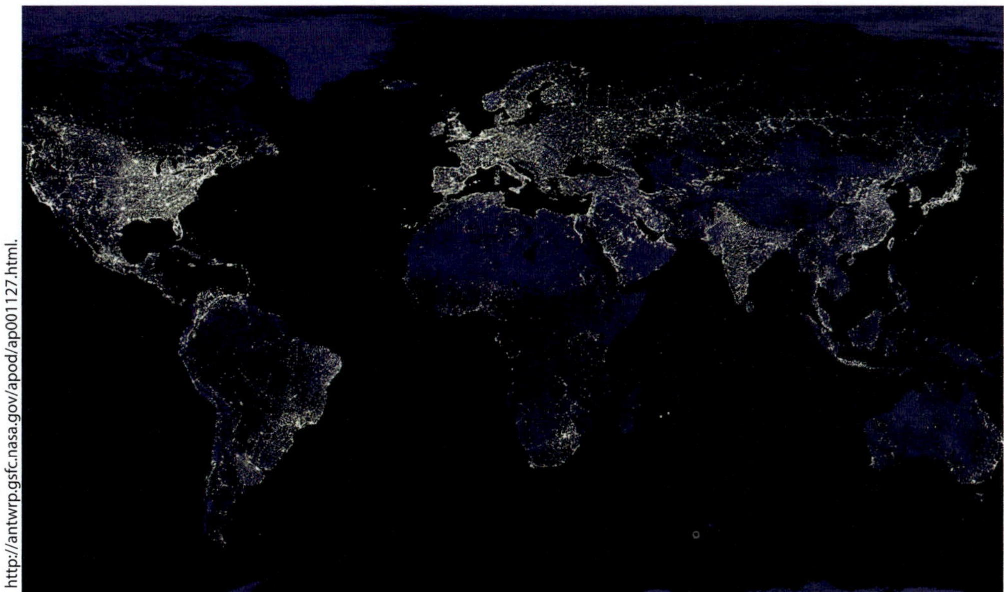

Source: C. Mayhew and R. Simmon (NASA/GSFC). More information available at http://antwrp.gsfc.nasa.gov/apod/ap001127.html.

Excess light that spills into the atmosphere represents wasted energy and light pollution that can disrupt wildlife and disturb humans.

No place knows light bulbs like Las Vegas, where several hotels boast multimillion bulb light displays that shine all night long. The MGM Grand recently replaced old incandescent bulbs that used 560 watts with fluorescent bulbs that use 214 watts in its 5,005 guest rooms and suites. By what kind of light do you read?

Standards The Noise Control Act of 1972 requires the EPA to regulate major sources of noise. The Federal Highway Administration enforces EPA noise emission standards for motor vehicles used in interstate commerce; the Occupational Safety and Health Administration regulates workplace noise; the Federal Aviation Administration regulates aircraft noise emissions; and the National Environmental Policy Act requires agencies to assess noise impact as part of environmental impact statements. Although noise regulations are in place,[41] and many are effectively enforced, noise regulation has run into some muddy water itself. The Noise Control Act created the Office of Noise Abatement and Control (ONAC) within the EPA. In a unique move, the Office of Management and Budget (OMB) under President Ronald Reagan informed the director of ONAC early in 1981 that the OMB intended to end ONAC funding. Congress complied with the removal of funding, although it did not repeal the Noise Control Act itself. Thus, the EPA still has responsibility for enforcing regulations issued under the Noise Control Act, but it has no funding legislated for that intent. In many circumstances the Noise Control Act preempts state and local noise regulations, making it difficult for local governments to fulfill the goals of unfunded federal programs.[42]

To accommodate the differing needs and interests of diverse communities, light

41 For example, the Boeing Corporation operates a website about airport noise regulations around the world. See www.boeing.com/commercial/noise/index.html.

42 See www.acus.gov/recommendation/implementation-noise-control-act..

Homes in Sedona, Arizona, where local policies restrict light and sound pollution and require buildings to be painted colors that blend in with the natural environment.

pollution is generally regulated at the local level. As an example, the Keep Sedona Beautiful Dark Skies committee in Sedona, Arizona, helps the city establish and enforce its lighting ordinances. Targets include accident-causing glare, light trespass from neighboring homes and businesses, energy waste, and sky glow. The committee works explicitly to balance commercial needs for signage and safety lighting with community needs for public health, safety, and welfare. Careful attention to the environmental issues of lighting, noise, water quality, and low-impact development has also been a boon to local tourism and property values.[43]

Where Do We Go From Here? A Brief Look

Efficiency dictates that the optimal quantity of pollution is not zero. Chapter 2 explained the desirability of continuing all activities until the marginal benefits no longer exceed the marginal costs. The marginal benefits from the first few tons of SO_2 emissions might be that ambulances can rush accident victims to hospitals. At the same time, a few tons of SO_2 spread around the atmosphere might not have any appreciable marginal cost. Given that the marginal benefits of activities that cause pollution start out high and the marginal costs start out low, some positive level of pollution is efficient and permissible in the name of human welfare, as illustrated in Figure 6.4. The marginal benefits decrease after the most valuable polluting activities are carried out, and marginal costs increase as environmental sinks are exhausted and contamination levels become unsafe.

When pollution levels exceed the efficient level, the task is to identify which incremental clean-up efforts provide benefits that exceed costs. There are ongoing debates over the efficiency of measures to thwart global warming, regulations on nuclear power, and emissions standards for automobiles. The advisability of other measures is more clear-cut. Low-wattage light bulbs, low-volume-flush toilets,

43 For more photos of Sedona's eco-friendly environment, see web.centre.edu/enviro/sedona.htm.

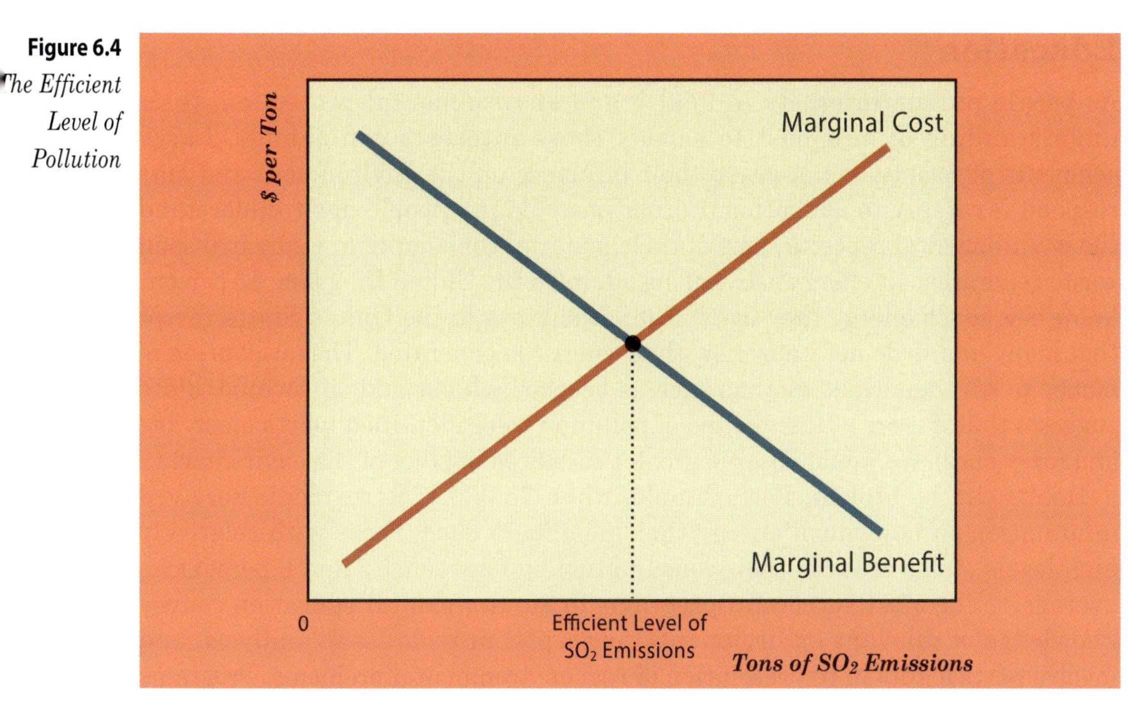

The efficient level of pollution is not zero. It is the level that equates the marginal cost and the marginal benefit.

and improved home insulation can all cut costs and pollution at the same time, as can turning out the lights when leaving a room. Similarly, Chapter 7 discusses alternative energy sources with few environmental costs. This section begins the conversation about how to progress towards efficient levels of pollution.

Policy

Point sources of pollution are easier to monitor than nonpoint sources, making emissions standards easier to enforce and emissions charges easier to collect. For example, planes landing at the Bern-Belp Airport in Switzerland pay a landing fee based on the level of NO_x emissions and the noise level generated by the particular type of aircraft.[44] Nonpoint sources, although harder to monitor, can be influenced by environmental policy when the manufacturers of products that cause nonpoint pollution (for example, aerosol cans and asbestos), rather than the polluters themselves, can be effectively regulated.

Unlike flow pollutants, stock pollutants affect present and future generations, and necessitate the selection of discount rates with which to analyze future costs and benefits. Paradoxically, the most damaging pollutants are often the most difficult to regulate. While concentrated pollutants are more likely to be internalized and controlled locally, distributed pollutants can extend beyond national jurisdictions. The control of uniformly distributed pollutants such as greenhouse gases and nonuniformly distributed pollutants such as SO_2 may require multinational accords established at meetings like the UN Climate Change Conference in Germany.

44 See www.boeing.com/commercial/noise/bern.html.

Education

As people pursue interests in health and environmental protection, their understanding of how best to satisfy those interests can change. Large segments of society do not grasp their influence on the environment and may respond favorably to educational programs.[45] Many people don't understand the environmental repercussions of their material consumption, municipal solid waste generation, or energy use. Among adults in the United Kingdom, 13 percent know how much energy they use.[46] Similar surveys in the United States reveal that many adults do not know how their energy is generated. The outpouring of money to save identified victims such as beached whales and oil-covered otters suggests that if more of the victims of pollution were identified (particularly big and fuzzy ones), we would observe greater sacrifices in favor of the environment.

Habits can be broken. For example, when 75,000 U.S. residents received information on how much energy their neighbors used, those with relatively high levels of use reduced their consumption by between 1.2 and 6 percent on average.[47] The most successful programs in environmental education convey knowledge of relevant environmental concepts, provide issue analysis, and involve participants in the resolution of real environmental problems. Programs that last several months or longer are more effective than brief or one-time activities.[48] Education also fuels wealth, which can lead to more consumption of material goods, but also to more spending on environmental concerns. Many wealthy nations achieve relatively high air and water standards and spend more on environmental regulations and the agencies that enforce them.

New Technology

Led by Honda with the Insight and Toyota with the Prius, automobile manufacturers have introduced **hybrid electric vehicles** (HEVs) with gas-and-electric engines that reduce pollution by nearly doubling the gas mileage of their all-gasoline counterparts. A hybrid engine operates using electricity at low speeds when gasoline engines are the least efficient, and reverts to gasoline at higher speeds for improved power and range. These technologies are changing gas guzzlers into sippers. In 2010, Nissan introduced the all-electric Leaf automobile and GM introduced the Chevy Volt, which travels 40 miles on lithium-ion batteries before reverting to gasoline. The 2014 Honda Accord Plug-In Hybrid gets the equivalent of 115 miles per gallon of gasoline. And Phinergy hopes to market aluminum-air batteries that extend the range of electric cars beyond 1,000 miles by 2017. Other energy-saving technology for cars includes **integrated starter-generator** (ISG) systems that prevent idling by automatically shutting the engine down at stoplights and restarting it when the brake is released. A

45 Smith (1997) evaluates the role of education and wealth in spurring environmentally friendly behavior.

46 See www.telegraph.co.uk/finance/personalfinance/consumertips/household-bills/9459578/Brits-do-not-know-how-much-they-spend-on-energy.html.

47 See www.nber.org/digest/feb10/w15386.html.

48 See www.ed.gov/databases/ERIC_Digests/ed320761.html.

regenerative braking system captures energy from braking to help recharge the battery. With growing acceptance, economies of scale will make these innovations more affordable.

Elaborate scrubbing systems are effective in removing large amounts of SO_2 and other pollutants from the emissions of coal-powered electric utilities. With price tags in the hundreds of millions, however, they are not an easy sell. The Clean Coal Technology (CCT) Demonstration Program is a $5.2 billion collaboration of government and industry whose mission is to "foster a secure and reliable energy system that is environmentally and economically sustainable."[49] The CCT program has already spawned a variety of new technologies. For example, fluidized-bed combustion systems send flue gas and fly ash through a hot "cyclone" and a hot gas particulate filter system to remove about 90 percent of the SO_2 and NO_x released. Advanced combustion systems like the coal diesel engine emit 25 percent less CO_2 than conventional coal-fired plants and have SO_2 and NO_x emissions 50 to 70 percent below current performance standards.[50] The next section describes one successful means of encouraging the use of clean coal technology.

Market-Based Incentives

Tradable emissions permits and other incentives for pollution control are discussed in great detail in Chapter 12, but receive an introduction here as an important item in any list of policy options.

Market-based mechanisms for environmental protection include tax credits, emissions fees, and the relatively new and innovative emissions trading programs. Beginning in 1995, one type of emissions trading, allowance trading, or cap and trade, was adopted in the United States to address the acid rain problem. Similar programs are in place at the regional level to control NO_x in the northeast United States and both SO_2 and NO_x in the Los Angeles, California, area. Like most **cap-and-trade programs**, the U.S. Acid Rain Program sets a limit or "cap" on the volume of a particular pollutant (SO_2) that can be released from regulated sources. Each existing source then receives **allowances** to emit a set amount of a pollutant. When the cap is set below existing emissions levels, the total volume of emissions is reduced.

Command-and-control programs require uniform reductions or specific technology applications for all sources. For example, a rule that all power plants must employ a cement kiln flue gas recovery scrubber[51] to limit emissions would be easy for some plants to obey and difficult for others, depending on their age and the adaptability of their equipment. Emissions trading programs allow room for flexibility and creativity. Permissible emissions levels can be achieved via conservation, new technology, alternative energy sources, lower-sulfur coal, or the purchase of allowances—whichever is the most feasible and affordable to a particular pollution source. Older sources that could only reduce emissions

49 See www.lanl.gov/projects/cctc/index.html.

50 See www.lanl.gov/projects/cctc/factsheets/disel/ccddemo.html.

51 This is simply one type of system that cleans pollutants out of the emissions of coal plants..

at great expense can purchase allowances from newer sources that achieve reductions relatively inexpensively.

Under a cap-and-trade program, firms have incentives to keep reducing emissions even after falling below the level of the emissions cap as long as the reductions cost less than the going price of allowances. That way the firms can earn extra allowances that can be sold to other firms for a profit. The applications of this approach are without limit. For example, tradable permits are used to allocate fish in New Zealand among other countries, and tradable fuel economy credits have been proposed for automakers.[52]

Summary

During the early stages of child development, infants watch objects while they are visible, but do not pursue them behind a blanket, as if they did not exist when they cannot be seen. In some contexts, this out-of-sight, out-of-mind mentality continues into adulthood. Some people litter as if the trash did not exist when they cannot see it. Worldwide, consumption decisions lead to the release of more than 32 billion metric tons of carbon dioxide, as if what goes around did not come around.[53] Are we polluting too much? And if so, how important is the problem? The answers to these questions determine the extent to which individuals and policymakers should press private and public environmental efforts. This chapter assesses environmental quality as affected by anthropogenic pollution, and explains some of the terminology, measurements, and problems that are relevant to economic decisions.

Air pollution can impair the heart, lungs, and nervous system of humans, and threatens wildlife, buildings, and the global climate. Rising ocean temperatures due to global climate change intensify hurricanes such as Paul, Rafael, and Sandy. Water pollution contaminates drinking water, laps at the habitat of endangered species, and causes mutations even in the farthest reaches of the planet. It also threatens food supplies, not to mention the world's most popular participation sport: fishing. Noise pollution causes hearing loss, injurious stress, and mammalian deaths. Beyond being a nuisance to humans, light pollution causes exorbitant energy consumption, animal fright, habitat loss, and the erosion of property values. The accumulation of stock pollutants, the loss of animal species, and global climate change can force the problems from today's pollution onto future generations.

The crossroad of marginal cost and marginal benefit occurs at a positive level of pollution. Reaching this efficient level is easier said than done, and it is a moving target. Innovative products and processes are lowering the marginal benefit from pollution while the exhaustion of environmental sinks increases the marginal cost. There are a variety of possible solutions. Some members of society respond to educational programs that raise awareness of problems and alternative paths. Even decision makers who are entirely self-interested respond to market-based incentives, and emissions trading programs have decreased pollution at the regional and national levels. Above all, cognizance of the state of our environment is the first step toward larger successes in the optimization of environmental practices and policies.

52 See http://cta.ornl.gov/cta/Publications/Reports/Tradable_Fuel_Economy_Credits_2009.pdf.

53 See http://cdiac.ornl.gov/ftp/ndp030/global.1751_2008.ems.

Problems for Review

1. Classify the following pollutants as uniformly distributed, concentrated, or nonuniformly distributed:
   a) Belching (and other CO_2 emissions) from cattle
   b) Noise pollution from rock band rehearsals
   c) Emissions from a paper-cup factory
2. Among animal manure, excessively loud bands, and factories, which would you consider to be point sources of pollution?
3. Of the types of policies that are appropriate for the control of point sources of pollution, which would you choose to control emissions from a paper-cup factory. Explain your choice.
4. Explain one type of policy that you would suggest for the control of automobile emissions. Would the policy you recommended for manufacturing plants be as effective for automobiles? Why or why not?
5. Given conflicting information about the severity of an environmental problem such as global warming, answer the following questions.
   a) Why do you suppose that some people argue ardently that there is no problem?
   b) Why do you suppose that some people argue ardently that the problem is alarming?
   c) How often do people on each side argue against their own short-term financial interests?
6. Ask five friends if they know which chemicals cause acid rain, and the major controllable sources of those chemicals. Record your results and comment on how well informed your survey respondents are.
7. In your carefully considered opinion, what is the role of education in bringing about the efficient treatment of natural resources and the environment? Briefly describe the type of education programs you would recommend.
8. What do you see as the role for policy in bringing about the efficient treatment of natural resources and the environment? Provide a specific example of a policy you would create or abolish.
9. If each adult angler in the United States would value a 20 percent reduction in toxins at the same rate as anglers in Wisconsin, what annual value would a nationwide 20 percent reduction provide to U.S. anglers? *Hint: You will find the numbers you need for this calculation in the chapter.*
10. Suppose that in order to reduce the amount of smog, the city where you live is contemplating either (1) requiring everyone to ride a moped to work, or (2) providing each family with 10 gallons of gas per week, which can be bought or sold among families.
    a) Which broad category of policies does each of these policies fall into?
    b) Explain which policy would be more efficient and why.

1. Use the scorecard.org site listed under Internet Resources to find the five major polluters in your Zip code area, or in Zip code 90210 if you don't live in the U.S. Determine the health hazards of the three major pollutants in that area.

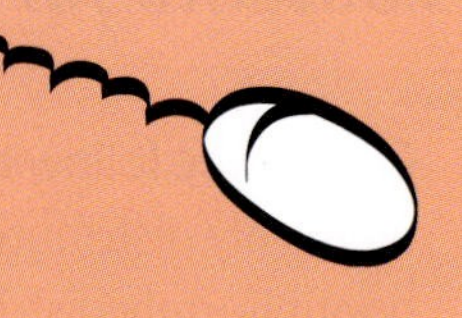

2. Find one map that indicates levels of a particular type of pollution in the area where you live.
3. Find one site that agrees and one site that disagrees that global warming is a serious problem. Evaluate the relative quality of the arguments.

Internet Resources

Toxic chemicals released by industries this year: *www.worldometers.info/view/toxchem/*

The Indoor Air Quality Association: *www.iaqa.org*

The Noise Pollution Clearinghouse: *www.nonoise.org*

The U.S. Environmental Protection Agency: *www.epa.gov*

United Nations Framework Convention on Climate Change: *www.unfccc.int*

World Forum for Acoustic Ecology: *www.wfae.net*

Further Reading

Anderson, H. A., C. Falk, L. Hanrahan, et al. "Profiles of Great Lakes Critical Pollutants: A Sentinel Analysis of Human Blood and Urine—The Great Lakes Consortium." *Environmental Health Perspectives* 106, no. 5 (1998): 279–289. Provides evidence that, despite a ban, at-risk populations continue to be exposed to PCBs in the Great Lakes.

Brown, R. Scott, and Ian Savage. "The Economics of Double-Hulled Tankers." *Maritime Policy and Management* 23, no. 2 (1996): 167–175. A cost-benefit analysis of double-hull requirements for oil tankers.

Bytingsvik, J., E. Lie, J. Aars, A. E. Derocher, O. Wiig, and B. M. Jenssen. "PCBs and OH-PCBs in Polar Bear Mother-Cub Pairs: A Comparative Study based on Plasma Levels in 1998 and 2008." *Science of the Total Environment* 417–418 (2012): 117–128. Research on the lingering effects of illegally produced persistent organic pollutants on polar bears in the Canadian Arctic.

Fletcher, J. L. "Effects of Noise on Wildlife: A Review of Relevant Literature: 1971–78." In *Proceedings, Third International Congress on Noise as a Public Health Problem,* edited by J. V. Tobias, G. Jansen, and W. D. Ward. Rockville, MD: American Speech-Language-Hearing Association, 1980. A summary of 1970s research on noise pollution and the environment.

Fletcher, J. L. "Review of Noise and Terrestrial Species: 1983–1988." In *Noise as a Public Health Problem Vol. 5: New Advances in Noise Research Part II*, edited by B. Berglund and T. Lindvall. Stockholm: Swedish Council for Building Research, 1990. A summary of 1980s research on noise pollution and its effects on the environment.

Georgiou, S., I. H. Langford, I. J. Bateman, and R. K. Turner. "Determinants of Individual's Willingness to Pay for Perceived Reductions in Environmental Health Risks: A Case Study of Bathing Water Quality." *Journal of Environment and Planning* A 30 (1998): 577–594. A "contingent valuation" (CVM) study of the value of clean water to bathers in England.

Greenley, D. A., R. G. Walsh, and R. A. Young. "Option Value: Empirical Evidence from a Case Study of Recreation and Water Quality." *The Quarterly Journal of Economics* 96, no. 4 (1981): 657–673. A CVM study of the value of clean rivers in Colorado.

Guha, Shion. "Valuation of Clean Water Supply by Willingness to Pay Method in a Developing Nation: A Case Study in Calucutta, India." *Journal of Young Investigators* (October, 2007), available online at www.jyi.org/issue/valuation-of-clean-water-supply-by-willingness-to-pay-method-in-a-developing-nation-a-case-study-in-calcutta-india/. A CVM study that finds that the value of providing clean water in Calcutta would exceed the cost.

Harrington, Fred, and Alasandair Veitch. "Short-term Impacts of Low-Level Jet Fighter Training on Caribou in Labrador." *Arctic* 44, no. 4 (1991): 318–327. Discusses the numerous dangers that noise pollution imposes on caribou.

Hunter, T., and D. Crawford. "The Economics of Light Pollution." In *Light Pollution, Radio Interference, and Space Debris*, edited by D. Crawford. Astronomy Society Pacific Conference, Series 17 (1991): 89–96. A discussion of the extent of light pollution and the financial repercussions on humans.

Immel, Richard. "Shhh . . . Those Peculiar People Are Listening." *Smithsonian* 26, no. 1 (1995): 151–160. Reports that kangaroo rats are deafened by dune-buggy noise for several days.

Kemp, Jack. "Warming Diplomacy ... At What Cost?" *The Washington Times* (July 5, 2001): Op-ed page. Conservative commentary on the National Academy of Sciences report on global warming.

Legget, C. G., and N. E. Bockstael. "Evidence of the Effects of Water Quality on Residential Land Prices." *Journal of Environmental Economics and Management* 39 (1999): 121–144. A study of the effect of water quality on home prices in the Chesapeake Bay area.

Michael, H. J., K. J. Boyle, and R. Bouchard. "Does the Measurement of Environmental Quality Affect Implicit Prices Estimated from Hedonic Models?" *Land Economics* 76, no. 2 (2000) 283–298. This study looks at the determinants of housing prices in Maine, including water clarity, which turns out to make a sizable difference.

National Academy of Sciences, Committee on the Science of Climate Change, National Research Council. *Climate Change Science: An Analysis of Some Key Questions.* Washington, D.C.: National Academy Press, 2001. A well-publicized report on global warming requested by George W. Bush, available online at http://books.nap.edu/books/0309075742/html.

Natural Resources Defense Council. *Sounding the Depths: Supertankers, Sonar, and the Rise of Undersea Noise*, 1999, www.nrdc.org/wildlife/marine/sound/sdinx.asp. A comprehensive assessment of noise pollution under the sea.

Pascal, C. *Global Warring: Environmental Change and the Looming Economic, Political and Security Crisis.* Toronto: Key Porter Books, 2010. Discusses the social volatility that could accompany climate change.

Phaneuf, D.J., C. L. Kling, and J. A. Herriges. "Valuing Water Quality Improvements Using Revealed Preference Methods When Corner Solutions Are Present." *American Journal of Agricultural Economics* 5 (1998): 1025–1031. A study of the value of clean lake water to anglers in the Great Lakes, based on their travel cost expenditures.

Shapiro, Sidney A. "The Dormant Noise Control Act and Options to Abate Noise Pollution." Administrative Conference of the United States, http:// www.nonoise.org/library/shapiro/shapiro.htm#INTRODUCTION (1991: accessed July 17, 2001). This report criticizes the lack of action on, and funding for, the Noise Control Act of 1972.

Smith, J. B., et al. "Assessing Dangerous Climate Change Through an Update of the Intergovernmental Panel on Climate Change (IPCC) 'reasons for concern'." *Proceedings of the Nationtal Academy of Sciences USA* 106 (2009): 4133–4137. Evaluates reasons for concern about global climate change.

Smith, V. Kerry. "Social Benefits of Education: Feedback Effects and Environmental Resources." In *The Social Benefits of Education*, edited by Jere R. Behrman and Nevzer Stacey. Ann Arbor: The University of Michigan Press, 1997, 175–218. This chapter examines why wealthier nations with higher levels of educational attainment generally have higher levels of environmental quality.

Speidel, David H., and Allan F. Agnew (eds). *Perspectives on Water: Uses and Abuses*. New York: Oxford University Press, 1988. Thirty-six chapters on water uses, problems, hazards, management, regulation, and economics. If this isn't more than you ever wanted to know about water, consider a career in hydrology!

U.S. Bureau of the Census. *Statistical Abstract of the United States: 2000*. Washington, D.C., 2000. This publication is filled with data on everything from abrasives to zinc. The chapters on the environment and parks are particularly relevant.

Viscusi, W. Kip, Joel Huber, and Jason Bell. "The Economic Value of Water Quality." *Environmental Resource Economics* 41 (2008): 169–187. An assessment of the value of lake and river water quality changes in the U.S. based on stated preference values.

Weisenberger, M. E., P. R. Krausman, M. C. Wallace, D. W. Deyoung, and E. O. Maughan. "Effects of Simulated Jet Aircraft Noise on Heart Rate and Behavior of Desert Ungulates." *Journal of Wildlife Management* 60, no. 1 (1996): 52–61. A study finding that overflights raise the heart rates of mule deer and bighorn sheep for several minutes.

"It takes 26 new cars today to produce the tailpipe pollution of one new car in the 1960s because of cleaner burning gasolines and improved automobile technology."

—AMERICAN PETROLEUM INSTITUTE

"The global business analysts say that solar can be competitive now if it is mass produced, but BP and Shell say they won't mass produce solar panels because they won't be able to sell them. Catch 22."

—GREENPEACE

"Wind power is capable of supplying 10% of the world's electricity within two decades, even if we double our overall electricity use in that time."

—EUROPEAN WIND ENERGY ASSOCIATION

"Coal is cheap, plentiful and dirty—as cheap as dirt, as plentiful as dirt, and as dirty as dirt—since after all, coal is little more than dirt that burns."

—UNION OF CONCERNED SCIENTISTS

A Solar Panel

7 Energy

The confluence of environmental concerns and profit motives creates particularly muddied waters in the realm of energy production. At the core of the problem is the enormity of our reliance on energy from nonrenewable sources. Since Thomas Edison harnessed electricity and Nikolaus A. Otto popularized the internal combustion engine, energy derived from fossil fuels has received a central role in commerce and everyday life. Ripple effects from increases in energy prices disrupt the sectors of manufacturing, transportation, and retail trade. The health and environmental costs of burning fossil fuels appear at every stage of production and consumption. Invasive exploration for new supplies of coal and oil brings noise, roads, and heavy equipment into vulnerable wilderness areas. Mining and drilling operations perpetuate human presence in natural habitat and can involve the stripping off of topsoil and the build-up of silt, among other damaging by-products. The transportation of fossil fuels to their processing and distribution sites necessitates truck, train, and ship emissions, and involves thousands of accidents and spills each year. The refinement of oil into fuel is a source of toxic emissions into the air, wastewater discharges, and hazardous waste. And the combustion of fuels in power plants and engines brings carbon dioxide, carbon monoxide, nitrogen oxide, and volatile organic compounds into communities around the globe.

Let us not forget the benefits side of the equation. The U.S. petroleum and coal industries generate more than $1 trillion in sales annually[1] and leave their customers with handsome amounts of consumer surplus. Oil and

1 U.S. Bureau of the Census (2012), Table 939.

coal provide 60 percent of the marketed energy humans use to attain their current standard of living. And conventional alternatives to fossil-fuel-based heating systems and electric lights, such as wood stoves and candles, are not environmentally friendly either.

Controversy surrounds the availability of "better" alternatives to fossil fuels. What is certain is that the money to be made in the energy industry garners adversarial politics and strong lobbies on each side of debates over energy policy and use. This chapter details the primary energy sources and describes representative policy approaches to energy's environmental and economic quandaries.

A coal-fired power plant like this one creates many benefits and many costs.

Energy Sources

Wise decisions about energy sources hinge on information about available options and necessary trade-offs. The availability of viable substitutes determines the need to endure the side effects of traditional energy sources, prospects for energy independence, appropriate levels of investment in alternative fuels, the need to pursue fossil fuels in environmentally sensitive areas, and the likely consumer response to dramatic changes in fossil fuel prices. This section provides a critical base of information on energy sources and raises pertinent economic issues along the way.

Energy Terminology

Energy is the amount of work a physical system is capable of performing. Strictly speaking, energy cannot be created, consumed, or destroyed. The catch is that **entropy**—the amount of energy not available to perform useful work—increases every time someone mows a lawn or lifts a finger, because energy is dissipated into the universe as heat. Energy can also be converted or transferred into different forms. **Kinetic energy** is the energy of motion. The kinetic energy of moving air molecules can be converted into **rotational energy** by the rotor of a wind turbine, and then converted into **electrical energy** by a wind turbine generator. Since the real use of a wind turbine is to convert one type of energy into another, purists sometimes call them **wind energy converters** (WECs). With each conversion, part of the energy from the source is converted into **heat energy**. The **thermal efficiency** (TE) of an energy source indicates the percentage of its energy that can be used directly in the next link of the energy conversion system, rather than being converted into heat. A coal-fired power plant is about 33 percent efficient, meaning that it uses 3,000 megawatts of energy stored in coal to generate 1,000 megawatts of electricity. The other 2,000 megawatts are lost as heat energy. The TE of a typical car is about 26 percent. Some racing engines have a TE of 34 percent.[2] The photovoltaic cells in solar panels are 7 to 44 percent efficient.

Energy is measured in joules (J) or kilowatt hours (kWh). One **calorie** equals 4.18 joules, the energy needed to raise the temperature of one gram of water by one degree Celsius. A **British thermal unit** (BTU) equals 1,055 joules, the energy needed to raise one pound of water one degree Fahrenheit. **Power** is the rate of energy transfer per unit of time. Power is measured in watts or horsepower. A watt is one joule per second, so a 60-watt light bulb uses 60 joules of energy per second, converting the electric energy into light energy and heat energy. One **horsepower** equals 746 watts. One **kilowatt** (kW) equals 1,000 watts and one **megawatt** (mW) equals one million watts.[3]

Mentions of energy "production" or "generation" refer to the conversion of energy into a more usable form. Energy "loss" means that energy is dissipated as heat, or for some other reason becomes unavailable for useful work. The fundamental task of most commercial electricity production is to make turbines spin and thereby create an electrical current. Both nuclear fission and coal combustion create steam that turns turbines. The kinetic energy from wind and falling water turns turbines directly to generate electricity. You can generate electricity yourself by turning a properly rigged bicycle wheel or the crank on some emergency radios. A photovoltaic cell, in contrast, converts light energy into direct-current electricity with no moving parts and no emissions.

Global energy consumers receive 41 percent of their electricity and 28 percent of all marketed energy from coal. Petroleum and other liquids (including biofuels) are the largest source of marketed energy, followed by coal, natural gas, renewable resources (other than biofuels), and nuclear power, as shown in Figure 7.1 on the next page. The following section explains relevant information about each of these sources of energy.

2 For more about what efficiency means in engine science, see www.auto-ware.com/combust_bytes/eng_sci.htm.

3 For more on the theoretical side of energy, see www.benwiens.com/energy1.html.

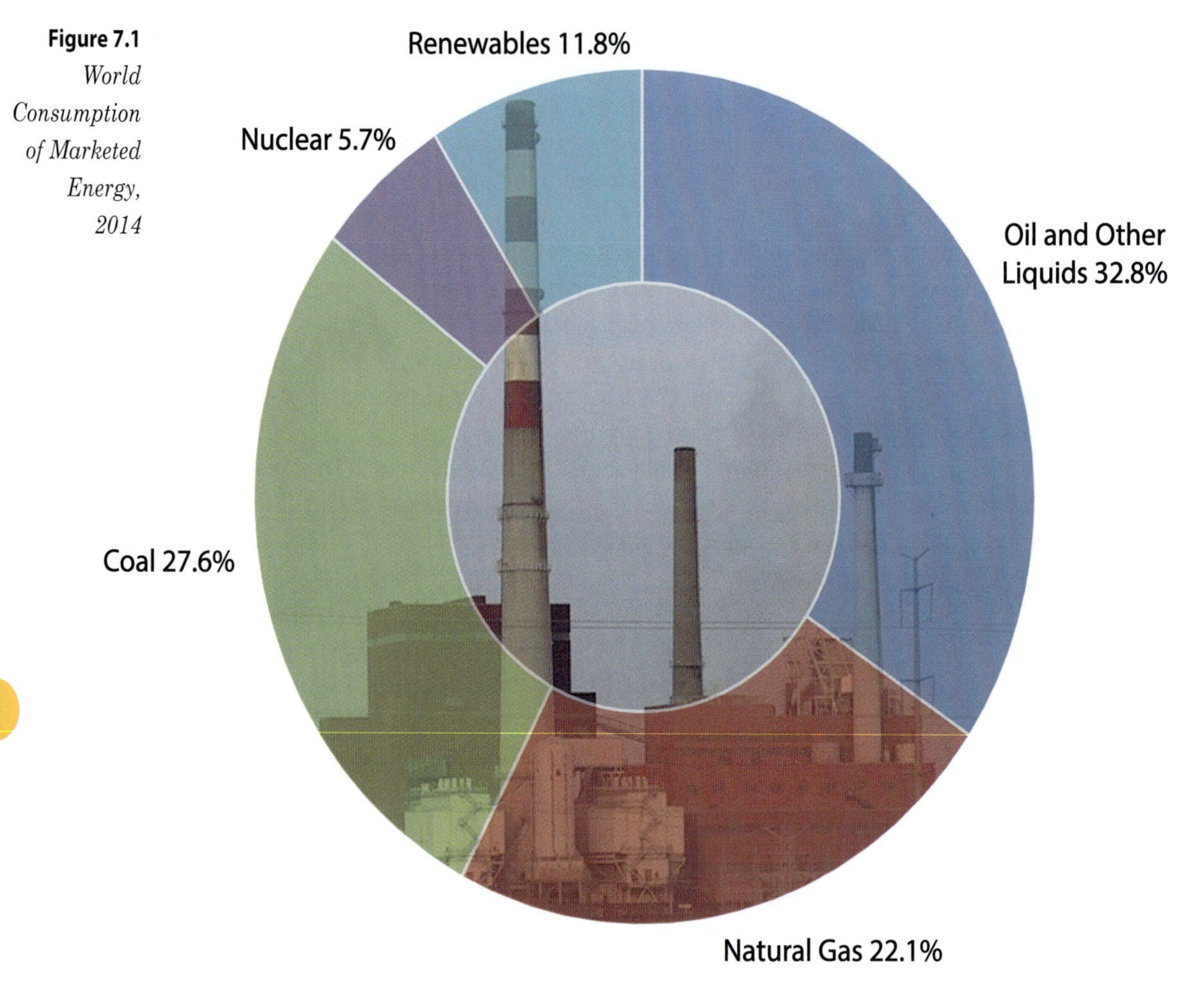

Figure 7.1 *World Consumption of Marketed Energy, 2014*

Source of data: Energy Information Administration (www.eia.doe.gov/oiaf/ieo/world.html)

Fossil Fuels

Coal **Coal** is the compressed remains of tropical and subtropical plants, predominantly from the Carboniferous and Permian periods 225 million to 345 million years ago. Coal includes varying levels of carbon, hydrogen, sulfur, and nitrogen. Coals are classified according to their carbon content, from the lowest to the highest, as lignite, subbituminous, bituminous, and anthracite. Coals with higher concentrations of carbon are harder and hold more energy. North America has the world's largest coal reserves, followed by the former USSR, China, India, and the European Union. Current majors producers of coal also include Australia, Indonesia, and South Africa. Lignite, with the least energy available to burn, is the most abundant in the United States; high-energy anthracite is relatively rare. In general, coals from the eastern and midwestern United States are bituminous, with high heat values but high levels of acid-rain-causing sulfur as well. Coals from the western states are largely subbituminous or lignite, with low heat value and low sulfur content.

The first commercial coal mine in the United States opened in Richmond, Virginia, in 1745. The United States now has almost 2,000 mines producing over 1 billion tons of coal each year.[4] Coal is burned to produce heat and electricity, and is a component in electric stoves, refrigerators, and water heaters. The environmental hazards from coal arise from mining and combustion. Mines scar the Earth and threaten collapse and groundwater contamination. The result of coal dust, black lung disease takes the lives of around 1,500 miners each year.[5] Upon combustion, coal releases sulfur and nitrous oxides, the sources of acid deposition. New clean coal technologies (CCTs) and land reclamation programs are reducing the environmental impact of coal. Critics argue that greater benefits would come from expenditures on emission-free, renewable energy sources.

Oil **Crude oil**, or **petroleum**, is a formation of aliphatic hydrocarbons. Hydrogen and carbon atoms link together to form molecular chains of all lengths. Shorter chains are liquid at room temperature;[6] longer chains form solids. In the refinery, distillation separates the hydrocarbon chains into "fractions" that can be blended to produce fuels with desired characteristics. Hydrocarbons with between 7 and 11 carbon atoms per molecule form gasoline. Related processes form kerosene, diesel fuel, fuel oil, lubricating oil, and asphalt.[7]

The scarcity of oil forces heavy users to rely on a limited number of primary providers. Most of the world's oil is produced in Saudi Arabia, Russia, the United States, Iran, China, Canada, the United Arab Emirates, and Venezuela. Beyond the political and financial risks of oil dependency, the extraction, transportation, refinement, and combustion of petroleum products are major sources of pollution and environmental degradation. Concerns about energy security and environmental health prompt interest in gasoline-ethanol blends among other renewable, domestically produced, and cleaner-burning fuels. World Bank President Robert Zoellick, Barack Obama, George Bush, and Bill Clinton are among supporters of subsidies to help ethanol blends compete with gasoline. However, ethanol production is energy intensive and therefore not a clear choice above oil from an environmental standpoint, as discussed in the section on ethanol below.

As the current source of about one-third of marketed energy, oil conveys power and wealth. Long ago labeled "black gold," oil is still the font of envy and international conflict. The Organization of the Petroleum Exporting Countries (OPEC) oil cartel provides almost half of the world's oil and has a strong influence on oil prices. The private costs in the United States remain low relative to many industrialized nations in Europe and Asia, in part due to relatively low taxes. Critics claim that these low prices are also the result of heavy government

4 For more on the U.S. coal industry, see www.eia.doe.gov/cneaf/coal/special/coalfeat.htm.

5 See www.umwa.org/?q=content/black-lung or www.courier-journal.com/dust/.

6 This applies to chains as large as $C_{18}H_{32}$, meaning that they contain 18 carbon atoms and 32 hydrogen atoms.

7 For more on oil processing, see the U.S. Department of Energy website at www.fossil.energy.gov/programs_oilgas.html.

Figure 7.2 *The Oil Market*

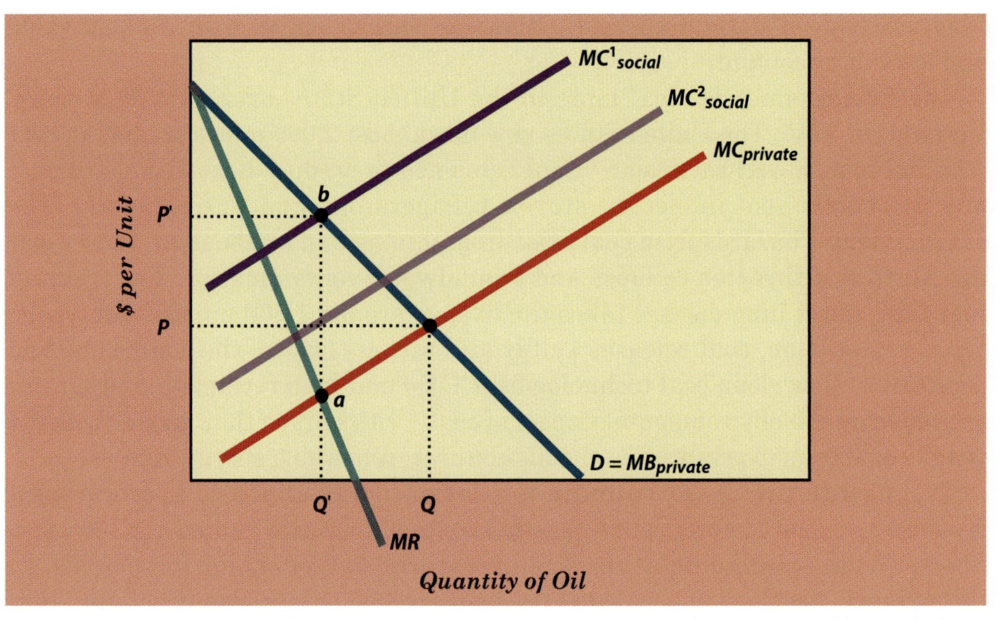

A competitive oil market would produce quantity *Q* at price *P*. A cartel like OPEC would try to behave like a monopoly and maximize profits by restricting quantity to *Q*' and charging *P*'. The same price and quantity, *P*' and *Q*', would also result if competitive sellers paid a tax represented by the vertical distance between points *a* and *b*. For goods such as oil that cause negative externalities, quantity restrictions associated with cartels, monopolies, and taxes can lead to more efficient outcomes. It is also possible for these quantity restrictions to be too great and lead to relatively less efficiency.

subsidization.[8] Where higher prices exist, the silver lining may be that these higher private marginal costs more closely resemble the true social marginal costs. That is, higher prices encourage users to internalize more of the negative externalities of oil use. Inefficiency would also exist if prices were so high that the private marginal cost exceeded the social marginal cost.

Consider the oil market depicted in Figure 7.2 and assume that the marginal cost curves would be the same for competitive, monopolistic, and cartel producers. In a competitive market, economic theory predicts a price equal to private marginal cost, resulting in the production of quantity *Q* at price *P*. This quantity is excessive because it does not take into account the negative externalities of oil use. A monopoly would produce the quantity *Q*' which equates marginal revenue with private marginal cost, and charge the highest price that consumers would pay for that quantity, *P*'. A cartel would try to reap monopoly profits and divide them among the member firms. With success in quelling incentives to cheat, the cartel would produce *Q*' and charge *P*' just like a monopoly.

If the social marginal cost were at the level of the dark purple line labeled MC^1_{social}, the competitive outcome would be excessive and the monopoly/cartel outcome would be efficient. A tax equal to the marginal external cost (the vertical

8 For example, see the Union of Concerned Scientists site at www.ucsusa.org/publication.cfm?publicationID=149.

distance between points *a* and *b*) would be one way to bring a competitive oil market to produce the efficient quantity Q' for price P'. On the other hand, if the social marginal cost were MC^2_{social}, the monopoly/cartel production level would be too low and potentially less efficient than the competitive outcome. The Market Structure and Price Controls section discusses further implications of differing market structures. For a review of graphs involving externalities, see Chapter 3.

Natural Gas Like coal and oil, **natural gas** has its origins in the swamps of past geologic periods. Natural gas is primarily methane (CH_4) with a mixture of other hydrocarbons. It is obtained from gas wells and as a by-product of crude oil extraction. Although it is a fossil fuel, it is also considered an "alternative" fuel because of its clean-burning qualities and relative abundance. Unlike most alternative fuels, natural gas has a broad infrastructure available to transport it, making it relatively accessible and affordable. In 2014, natural gas provided 22 percent of the marketed energy consumed worldwide. In 2013, natural gas powered about 14.8 million vehicles worldwide.[9]

The world's major natural gas producers include Russia, the United States, Canada, Qatar, and Iran. Natural gas is produced in most regions of North America and transported through pipelines in liquid or gaseous form to every mainland state. Pure methane is a highly flammable, odorless gas with high marks for safety and limited emissions. Although leaks of unburned gas can ignite and explode, gas companies have inserted foul-smelling additives into natural gas to make leaks detectable ever since a natural gas explosion killed 293 people in a New London, Texas, school in 1937.

Oil and natural gas is sometimes trapped within shale rock. A procedure called **hydraulic fracturing** or *fracking* releases the fuel by forcing various combinations of sand, water, and chemicals into the rock. The fracking process was implemented a half century ago. New applications that involve drilling horizontally into shallower rock are increasingly controversial. Among potential threats to health and the environment, fracking requires large volumes of water, it can release methane—a greenhouse gas—into the air, and the chemicals injected into the ground may contaminate groundwater supplies. The EPA is currently studying the potential dangers of fracking and will release its findings in 2014.

Nuclear Energy

Fission is the splitting of atoms to release energy. **Fusion** is the combination of atoms, again with the release of energy. Nuclear power can come from the fission of uranium, plutonium, or thorium, or from the fusion of hydrogen into helium. Convenience and accessibility make uranium the fuel of choice in today's reactors. Nuclear power has appeal because the fission of a uranium atom produces 10 million times the energy produced by the combustion of a carbon atom in coal. Excluding naval power reactors, there are 103 active nuclear reactors in the

9 For more on natural gas vehicles, see the Natural Gas Vehicle Coalition site: www.ngvc.org/ngv/ngvc.nsf.

United States and about 400 in the world. These reactors satisfy 20 percent of U.S. electricity consumption and 6 percent of global energy use.

The greatest environmental threats from nuclear power involve the storage of spent radioactive fuel from reactors and the possibility of accidents. The worst accident in a commercial reactor occurred on April 26, 1986, when a reactor in Chernobyl, Ukraine, melted down and released at least 3 percent of its core radiation.[10] The incident killed 32 local workers immediately and thousands more in the following years. The plume of radiation reached Asia, Europe, and parts of the United States. Radioiodine and radiocaesium contaminated food supplies, increasing the incidence of thyroid cancer, mutations, and associated health effects.[11] As of 2005, there were around 100 threatened species living in the evacuation area, including deformed fish living in the reactor's cooling ponds. Victor Dolin of the Ukrainian National Academy of Sciences estimates that it will be many hundreds of millennia before humans can live there again.[12] In the United States there are currently over 40,000 metric tons of depleted uranium fuel stored in 34 states. Plans to open a nuclear waste repository under Yucca Mountain, Nevada, were halted in 2009 due to potential health and environmental risks. Both the storage of radiated waste and its transportation across the country have met with violent opposition.[13] Proponents of nuclear energy assert that nuclear power plants cause less than 1 percent of U.S. radiation exposure.[14]

Alternative Fuels

Alternative fuels are generally renewable, available domestically, and less toxic than their mainstream counterparts. The U.S. Department of Energy promotes alternative fuels not only for their environmental benefits, but also because they provide energy security by reducing reliance on foreign sources of fossil fuels.[15] One trade-off is that many alternative fuels are not cheap. The direct costs of ethanol and liquefied natural gas are higher than those of gasoline, although improved technology and economies of scale via mass production could make any of the alternative fuels economically viable, even from a private perspective.

Biodiesel **Biodiesel** is a cleaner-burning diesel fuel made from renewable plant oils or animal fats. It can run in current diesel engines, either blended with petroleum diesel fuel or straight. B20 is a common biodiesel blend of 20 percent biodiesel and 80 percent petroleum diesel. Biodiesel emissions are sulfur-dioxide-free and contain 75 to 90 percent lower levels of unburned hydrocarbons,

10 There are some claims that as much as 80 percent of the core was released. See www.ratical.com/radiation/inetSeries/ChernyThyrd.html.

11 See library.thinkquest.org/3426/?tqskip1=1&tqtime=1010 for more on the Chernobyl disaster.

12 See www.physorg.com/news5774.html.

13 See Piore (2001) for a provocative discussion of plans to transport nuclear waste by train.

14 For more, see the U.S. Department of Energy's Nuclear Q and A: www.nuc.umr.edu/nuclear_facts/answers/answers.html/.

15 The U.S. Department of Energy provides an "Alternative Fuels Data Center" at www.afdc.doe.gov/.

aromatic hydrocarbons, and carbon dioxide than diesel emissions. Biodiesel is also less flammable than petroleum diesel, reducing the risk of vehicular fires. But biodiesel has a relatively high private cost. Soy-based biodiesel currently costs about three times as much as petroleum diesel. Researchers hope to increase the oil content of soybeans as one way of lowering the overall biodiesel cost.

Electric Fuel **Electric vehicles** (EVs), a subset of **zero emission vehicles** or ZEVs, require no tailpipe and provide no opportunity for fuel evaporation. Their electric power can come from solar panels, or be transported from power plants to homes and industries through the same power grids that provide electricity for your computer. Of course, unless the power source itself uses an alternative fuel, the problem of pollution from the power plant remains. Some EVs are expensive, although high start-up costs can be balanced by low fuel costs if the electricity is cheap. Tax incentives and manufacturers' promotions also serve to ameliorate initial pricing concerns.[16] The Tesla Roadster EV will travel 244 miles on a single charge of its rechargeable battery pack and the packs last seven years. The Department of Energy and the major U.S. automakers have spent $260 million on research to develop more efficient batteries, the results of which are forthcoming.[17] As added encouragement, California law requires at least 12 percent of the cars made by major manufacturers to be ZEVs, rising to 14 percent in 2015.

Ethanol **Ethanol** (CH_3CH_2OH), also called ethyl alcohol or grain alcohol, is a clear, colorless liquid with an agreeable odor and a sweet taste when properly diluted.[18] This biofuel is distilled from a mash of renewable sources that can include corn, barley, wheat, and waste accumulated from wood and paper processing. Ethanol and animal feed can be produced simultaneously from the same corn. Scholars debate whether ethanol production from corn and related inputs creates more energy than is required to grow the crops and produce the fuel. According to Pimental and Patzek (2005), ethanol production from corn requires 29 percent more fossil fuel than the amount of ethanol fuel produced. The same study reports a net energy loss when switchgrass and wood are used to make ethanol. Hill et al. (2006) find a net energy gain of 25 percent from corn-based ethanol production, mostly attributable to the energy value of the animal feed produced at the same time. Weighing in its favor, ethanol combustion releases lower levels of greenhouse gases than gasoline combustion, and the growth of ethanol feedstocks draws carbon dioxide from the atmosphere. Ethanol is already popular as a fuel in Brazil, and serves as a common octane-enhancing additive to gasoline in Canada, Europe, Thailand, and the United States. The most common mixture, containing 5 to 10 percent ethanol, is called **gasohol**. Gasoline-ethanol blends made up of 85 percent and 95 percent ethanol, called E-85 and E-95 respectively, are currently available for specially modified "flexible-fuel" vehicles.

16 In the case of hybrid cars, Toyota introduced its Prius model at a price close to the production cost, hoping to encourage experimentation. The Nissan Leaf electric car is expected to be relatively inexpensive as well.

17 See the Department of Energy's electric fuel site: www.epa.gov/OMS/10-elec.htm.

18 Don't try this at home! The ethanol component of these fuels is denatured to make it unfit for consumption.

Of the 178,000 service stations in the United States in 2009, 2,200 sold E-85.

Hydrogen **Hydrogen gas** (H_2) can power combustion engines and fuel-cell electric vehicles. Electricity generated from the reaction of hydrogen fuel and oxygen from the air provides fuel cells with clean, quiet power. The only emissions are pure water and heat. A steam reformation process splits hydrogen atoms from carbon atoms in natural gas (primarily methane, CH_4). Electrolysis or extreme heat (2,800°C) can also split hydrogen atoms from the oxygen atoms in water. Fuel cells and hydrogen-fueled internal combustion engines already power cars and buses; trains and submarines are in the works.[19]

Hydrogen is the primary propellant used in space flight. Hydrogen fuel cells on the space shuttle powered life-support systems and computers, returning drinkable water as a by-product. Back on Earth, most major automakers are experimenting with hydrogen fuel cell vehicles. The challenge at this point is to safely distribute and store the hydrogen. Hydrogen is an explosive gas at room temperature. Scientists are exploring more manageable forms, including compressed hydrogen, liquid hydrogen, and chemical bonding between hydrogen and metal hydrides. Little infrastructure is in place to transport hydrogen. If fuel cells become popular, as proponents predict, pipelines may replace the current canister and tanker truck distribution systems in the near future.[20]

Methanol **Methanol** (CH_3OH) serves as a gasoline additive, a replacement for gasoline and diesel fuels, and a source of hydrogen for fuel cells. Methanol sources include natural gas and many renewable resources containing carbon, including seaweed, waste wood, and garbage. Relative to gasoline, methanol offers lower emissions of hydrocarbons, nitrogen oxides, and particulate matter. Methanol's fuel efficiency is currently half that of gasoline, although that may improve with ongoing research. Methanol's high-octane performance and low flammability make it the only fuel used in Indianapolis 500 race cars.

Propane **Liquefied petroleum gas** (LPG) is primarily propane and contains a mixture of hydrocarbons, including butane, butylene, and propylene. LPG is a by-product of petroleum refinement and natural gas processing. While it is gaseous at room temperature, propane can be delivered to vehicles as a gas or liquid. As a liquid, propane is 270 times more compact than as a gas. Propane fuels cause less carbon build-up than gasoline or diesel, allowing spark plugs and engines to outlast their counterparts in gasoline and diesel engines. Propane has been in use worldwide for over 60 years. More than 350,000 propane-powered vehicles are driven today.[21] The Ford Motor Company offers a propane-powered F-Series truck that is eligible for California's Alternative Fuel Vehicle tax incentive. Propane vehicles are popular for corporate fleets, offering lower emissions

19 The military is particularly interested in fuel-cell vehicles because their relatively cool and quiet engines are more difficult to detect. For more on hydrogen, see the National Hydrogen Association site: www.hydrogenus.org/index.asp.

20 Among plans in the works, Shell Oil has teamed up with fuel-cell maker Xcellsis to develop hydrogen infrastructure.

21 Propane-fueled vehicles include many sheriff and police cars, school buses in Kansas and Oregon, and the Las Vegas taxi fleet. For more information, see the Department of Energy's propane site: www.afdc.doe.gov/altfuel/propane.html/.

Photo by Stefano Paltera / North American Solar Challenge, used with permission

The winner of a 2,500-mile solar-powered car race. The sun is an abundant source of energy.

and fuel prices 5 to 30 percent below those for gasoline-fueled vehicles.

P-Series and D-Series Stephen Paul of Princeton University developed **P-Series**, a combination of ethanol, natural gas liquids, and biomass-derived methyltetrahydrofurans (MTHF). The ethanol and MTHF come from renewable resources such as agricultural and wood waste. Relative to gasoline, the virtues of P-Series include fewer toxins and faster biodegradability. P-Series is designed for use in flexible fuel vehicles (FFVs), which can use any combination of ethanol or methanol and gasoline. Chrysler, Ford, and Mazda have all introduced FFVs. **D-Series**, a product of the Pure Energy Corporation, is another complex mixture of renewable and fossil fuels that provides a cleaner alternative to gasoline.[22]

Solar Fuel The sun emits energy at a rate of 1.56×10^{18} kWh per year. All humans combined require less than 0.1 percent of this amount of energy. Collecting solar energy is the hard part, but it's not that hard. Solar thermal applications use the sun's energy directly to heat air or liquid, primarily for residential use. Photoelectric methods use semiconductors and photovoltaic cells to convert solar energy into electricity. A photovoltaic cell can convert 7 to 17 percent of light energy into electrical energy.[23] Once thermal or photoelectric

22 For more on D-Series and a new diesel-ethanol fuel mixture called E-Diesel, see the Pure Energy Corporation website: www.pure-energy.com/pureindex.html.

23 For more, see the Department of Energy's photovoltaic site: www.eren.doe.gov/pv/.

These wind turbines in Hawaii provide enough electricity for more than 10,000 homes.

applications are in place, the use of solar energy creates no emissions and no noise. Worthwhile amounts of solar energy can be collected even under cloudy conditions, although energy is not produced at night, and more energy is collected in sunny places than in cloudy places.

As indicated in the Greenpeace quote at the beginning of this chapter, a chicken-and-egg problem exists for solar energy among other alternative fuels. It will not become popular until the price comes down, and the price may not come down until popularity provides for economies of scale. The good news is that operational and maintenance costs are negligible, and use is already flourishing in places like Germany and Japan. A photovoltaic power plant in California powers 660 homes. Despite Ronald Reagan's removal of the solar panels Jimmy Carter placed on the White House roof, the U.S. government is getting in on the act as well. The Energy Policy Act of 1992 provided an income tax credit for firms that invested in solar technology, and consumers receive a tax credit for installing solar panels.

Wind Wind whips some regions of the Earth at speeds exceeding 200 mph. Small wind turbines can create energy using a minimum of 8 mph winds; large turbines require 13 mph winds to achieve efficiency. Wind turbines use long blades called rotors that spin by the force of the wind and create electricity. Wind turbines offer an infinite source of kinetic energy and create no emissions. A disadvantage is that the turbines are currently expensive. A field of turbines, sometimes called a wind farm, is needed to power a town of significant size, and sufficient wind energy is only available in certain areas. The capital cost of wind turbines has fallen from about $2,500 per kW to below $1,000 over the past 15 years. Further price decreases may make them competitive with traditional fuels in the near future.

While there are environmental concerns about birds being swept into the rotors, collisions are uncommon, and the Danish Ministry of the Environment reports that power lines from any source are a far greater threat to birds than wind turbines.[24] The majority of U.S. wind turbines are located in California, with sizable operations in 17 states. Wind turbines are a sustainable source of clean energy. In light of their ability to supplant negative externalities from fossil fuels, the Energy Policy Act of 1992 provided a 1.5 cent per kWh tax credit for wind energy facilities brought online by July of 1999.[25]

Geothermal **Geothermal energy** is heat held beneath the Earth's crust. This energy can be brought up to the surface to heat buildings or icy sidewalks, or converted into electricity for broader applications. Chevron, the world's largest private producer of geothermal energy, plans to double its geothermal capacity in Indonesia and the Philippines by 2020. Geothermal power plants in the western United States have a combined generating capacity of 2,700 mW, enough electricity for more than 3.5 million people.[26] Even in areas with no hydrothermal reservoirs, liquid antifreeze can be cycled underground to pick up the Earth's relatively constant ground temperature. In the winter, **geothermal heat pumps** (GHPs) transfer heat from the ground into homes and buildings. In the summer, GHPs transfer indoor heat into the ground and draw up the relatively cool temperatures from below. Approximately 50,000 GHPs are installed in the United States each year, including one in the home of this author. The Galt House East Hotel and waterfront office buildings in Louisville, Kentucky share the world's largest GHP. The owners estimate they will save $2,250,000 relative to the cost of normal heating and cooling systems.[27] **Direct-use geothermal systems** in Iceland pump hot water from underground directly into buildings and greenhouses for heating, and below city streets for effortless snow removal. Likewise, residents of Klamath, Oregon, cherish the safety of their snow-free streets and sidewalks, all cleared by naturally hot water piped beneath them.

Energy Policy

Efficient Source Selection

Energy sources are largely interchangeable. Electricity can be derived from any of the alternative fuels described in the preceding section. Petroleum products, electricity (from any source), and natural gas are among the many fuel options for heating systems and cars. The challenge, then, is to determine the appropriate

24 For more on the compatibility of birds and windmills, see www.windpower.dk/tour/env/birds.htm.

25 See the Environmental Protection Agency's wind energy site: yosemite.epa.gov/oar/globalwarming.nsf/uniqueKeyLookup/SHSU5BWK54/$file/windenergy.pdf.

26 For more on this, see the National Renewable Energy Lab's geothermal site: www.nrel.gov/lab/pao/geothermal_energy.html/.

27 See the International Ground Source Heat Pump Association's Galt House site: www.igshpa.okstate.edu/Publications/CaseStudy/Galt_House/Galt.html/.

Figure 7.3 *The Energy Market and Representative Components*

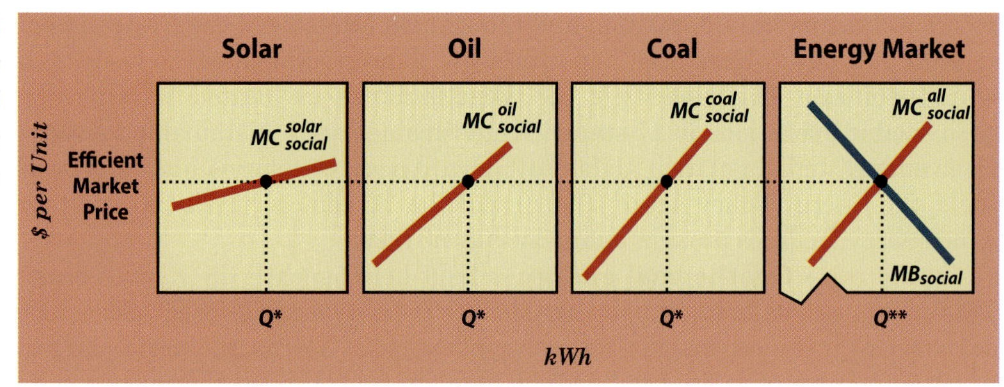

The market social marginal cost (MC_{social}) curve for energy is found by summing the MC_{social} curves for each energy source horizontally. At each cost level, the horizontal distance between the vertical axis and the MC_{social} curve for each source is added up to obtain the total number of kWh the energy market could produce at or below that social marginal cost. The efficient level of energy use equates MB_{social} and MC_{social}.

level of use for each energy source. Figure 7.3 illustrates the approach to this task for a representative set of sources. The first three graphs indicate the social marginal cost of producing electricity from solar energy, oil, and coal. The last graph shows the social marginal benefit of each level of electricity production and the *market* social marginal cost curve, found as the "horizontal sum" of the social marginal cost curves for all available sources. To find the horizontal sum at any particular cost level, simply add up the distance from the vertical axis to the social marginal cost curve for each energy source. For example, if 20 cents were the MC_{social} for the 2 billionth kWh of electricity from solar energy, the 1 billionth kWh from oil, and the 0.5 billionth kWh from coal, then the horizontal sum would be 2 + 1 + 0.5 = 3.5 billion kWh. This number of kWh could be produced in the combined energy market at a social marginal cost of 20 cents or less.

As you might expect, energy should be produced until the social marginal cost equals the social marginal benefit. A market price determined by the equilibrium of MC_{social} and MB_{social} yields production and consumption at the efficient level, Q^{**}. Remember that the private marginal benefit curve is equivalent to the demand curve, and that the private marginal cost curve above average variable cost is equivalent to the supply curve in a competitive industry. Thus, in a competitive market with externalities either absent or internalized (meaning that $MC_{private} = MC_{social}$ and $MB_{private} = MB_{social}$), the market equilibrium between supply and demand is efficient. These are pipe dreams, although targeted policies can lead toward these goals. The next section describes how price controls can bring monopolies to behave more like competitive firms, and Chapter 3 explained how taxes and subsidies can cause externalities to be internalized.

The efficient levels of solar-, oil-, and coal-sourced electricity are found at the intersections of the efficient market price (the price that equates MC_{social} and MB_{social}) and the social marginal cost of each source. The Q^*s in Figure 7.3

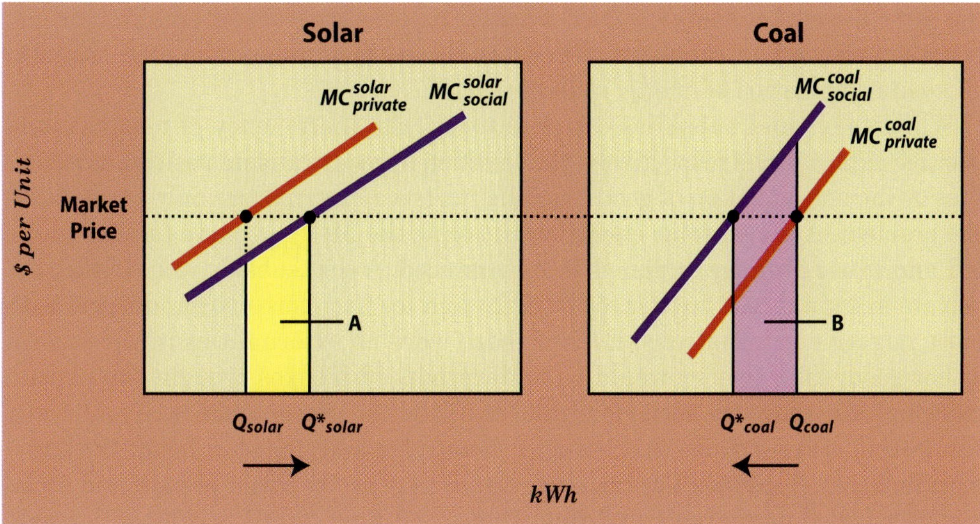

Figure 7.4
The Gains from Switching

When the social marginal cost of producing each type of energy source is not equal, society can benefit from producing less energy with the relatively expensive source and more with the relatively inexpensive source. In this example, area A represents the added cost of increasing solar energy production from Q_{solar} to Q^*_{solar}, and B represents the savings from reducing coal energy production by the same amount. The net benefit to society of equating the dollars per kWh of solar and coal energy is B - A.

indicate the efficient levels. Just as the goal was to equate the dollars per unit of marginal benefit in the efficiency discussions of Chapter 2, here we want to equate the dollars per kWh, which is just another type of marginal benefit. Figure 7.4 illustrates the opportunity for a net gain if the social marginal cost of energy from coal exceeds the social marginal cost of energy from solar. The area under an MC_{social} curve along any section of the quantity axis indicates the additional cost to society of producing the quantity represented by that section. Area A represents the additional cost of increasing solar-sourced electricity production from Q_{solar} to Q^*_{solar}. Area B represents the cost savings from reducing coal-sourced electricity production from Q_{coal} to Q^*_{coal}. By switching that amount of energy production from coal to solar sources, the net benefit to society is B minus A.

Inefficient levels of production such as Q_{solar} and Q_{coal} can result from externalities or market power, among other sources of market failure as discussed in Chapter 3. With consumers not feeling the positive externalities from solar power[28] or the negative externalities from coal, the red private marginal cost curves bring about production levels Q_{solar} and Q_{coal} at the market price. Note that as drawn, the sum of the two $MC_{private}$ curves in Figure 7.4 would yield the same market MC curve as the sum of the two MC_{social} curves. In this situation,

28 Beyond replacing fuels that create pollution as they generate energy, the use of solar energy reduces the dependence most countries have on foreign oil. According to the National Energy Laboratory (www.nrel.gov/lab/pao/concentrating.html), solar power plants create 2.5 times as many skilled jobs as fossil-fuel power plants. The use of photovoltaic cells may also serve to inspire and educate others about the availability of alternative fuels.

the same amount of energy is used whether externalities are internalized or not, but when they are internalized, the cost to society is minimized because the most efficient combination of energy sources is used.

While taxes and subsidies can counteract the inefficiency of negative and positive externalities respectively, the taxation of goods causing positive externalities or the subsidization of goods causing negative externalities only exacerbates the problem. A tax on solar energy would shift the $MC_{private}$ curve further to the left and cause even fewer panels to be produced. A coal subsidy would bring the private marginal cost further to the right and lead to more overproduction with more negative externalities. Even if there were no externalities involved with either good, solar energy would be underproduced if taxes brought the private marginal cost above the social marginal cost, and the overproduction of coal would result from coal subsidies that brought the private marginal cost below the social marginal cost. Subsidies that increase the divergence between private and social costs are called **perverse subsidies**. Myers and Kent (2001) document perverse subsidies for fossil fuel, nuclear energy, and road construction. They estimate that direct and indirect perverse subsidies worldwide approach $2 trillion annually.

The social marginal cost of using nonrenewable resources such as oil and coal includes the opportunity cost of future generations not being able to use the resources. As more nonrenewable resources are depleted, future uses of greater importance are foregone, and the social marginal cost of their use rises. The social marginal cost of renewable energy sources such as solar and wind can be small and constant, making their social marginal cost curves horizontal, and rendering obsolete those energy sources with a higher social marginal cost.

Market Structure and Price Controls

The structure of energy markets, determined by the number of firms and the distribution of market power, is varied and in a state of flux. Large-scale power plants are sometimes natural monopolies, although there is considerable heterogeneity in the efficient scale of power generation.[29] A global wave of deregulation is shaking up current market structures, eliminating some local monopolies, and, with luck, spurring competition. In the context of negative externalities, the restricted output of monopolies can actually yield a more efficient outcome than competition. This section describes the implications of these market structures.

Competition, one of the conditions for free-market efficiency in the absence of externalities, is not out of the question in the energy market. It is conceivable that most homes could have solar panels on their roofs and wind turbines could sit on most farms, representing millions of small energy production facilities. Indeed, the 1978 Public Utilities Regulatory Policies Act (PURPA) established the right of independent power producers to sell electricity to regulated utilities when they create more energy than they need for their own purposes. Note also

29 See, for example, Atkinson and Halvorsen (1984).

that, just as a penny saved is a penny earned, a kWh saved is effectively a kWh produced. In that sense, the ability of each individual to "produce" (save) energy can help in some ways to keep producers in check. Since the 1970s, energy made available via savings has exceeded energy made available by new energy sources.

Rocky Mountain Institute founder Amory Lovins (1976) described two paths for energy dependence: a **soft path** of many renewable energy sources as described in the previous paragraph, and a **hard path** of centralized fossil fuel production. Currently, large, centralized producers generate about 90 percent of energy in the United States; we are still largely on the hard path. Path-dependence theory suggests that once a particular path is taken, it becomes increasingly difficult to change course. Investments in research and development, infrastructure, training, and end-use systems create commitments to stay the course. The enormous fixed costs of entry into the traditional energy market create monopolies. In some cases, monopolies can be required to produce at relatively efficient levels and charge prices that approximate competitive market prices. This section discusses the use of price controls for this purpose.

Figure 7.5 on the next page illustrates three possible structures for the energy market. The first graph depicts a competitive market, as would result from millions of rooftop solar power sources. The second is a typical monopoly graph. This approximates the market structure for energy sources with barriers to entry and moderate fixed costs, including P-Series, which has a single producer.[30] The last graph depicts a **natural monopoly**, characterized by high fixed costs and decreasing average costs over the relevant range of output levels. Natural monopolies would operate at a loss under the competitive condition that price equals marginal cost. Coal-fired electric utilities and nuclear power plants can be natural monopolies because they necessitate fixed costs of several hundred million dollars and enjoy tremendous economies of scale.[31] With increased production, the average cost falls because the large fixed cost can be spread over more units of output. Natural monopolies preclude competition because a single firm can supply the entire market at a lower cost than could two or more firms.

In the absence of externalities and imperfect information, the equilibrium of supply and demand will yield the efficient price and quantity ($P_{competition}$ and $Q_{competition}$) in a competitive market. The imposition of a price ceiling in such a market would reduce the quantity supplied and increase the quantity demanded, causing a shortage. Production would occur at level Q^* in the top panel of Figure 7.5, which is below the efficient quantity. In the presence of negative externalities, the competitive quantity would be excessive. A price ceiling that intersected the private supply curve at the socially efficient quantity (where $MC_{social} = MB_{social}$)

30 See www.iags.org/pseries.htm. For information on the latest mergers and acquisitions in the energy market, see www.energyinfosource.com/.

31 Baumol, Panzar, and Willig (1982) argue that it is not economies of scale or scope that create natural monopolies. Rather, it is sunk costs (expenditures on facilities and equipment that have no alternative use or opportunity cost) that create insurmountable barriers to entry. In the context of their argument, it is likely that an operating nuclear reactor could be considered a sunk cost.

Figure 7.5
Price Ceilings

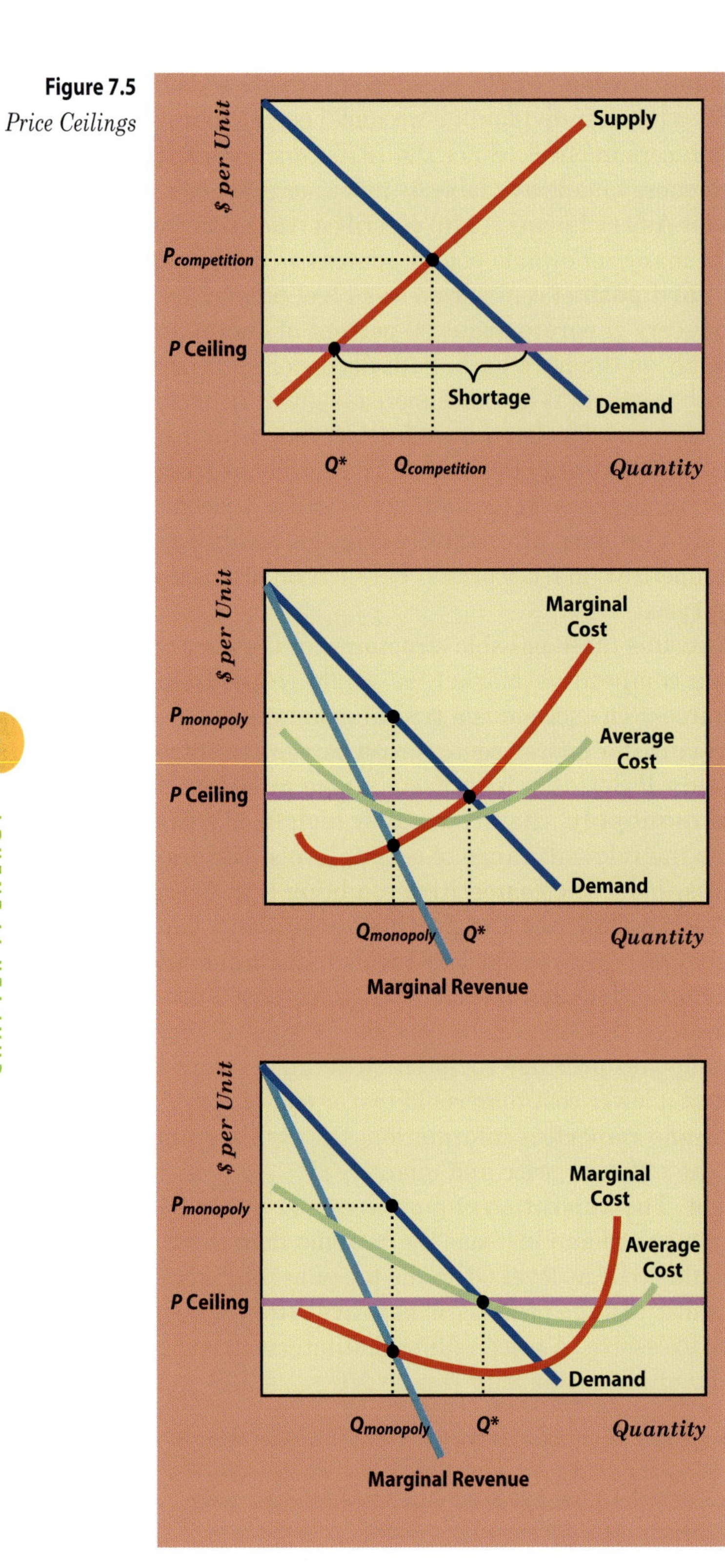

Perfect Competition
A price ceiling in a competitive market causes a decrease in the quantity supplied and a shortage.

Monopoly
A price ceiling on a monopoly market can increase the quantity supplied while lowering the price and eliminating deadweight loss.

Natural Monopoly
A natural monopoly cannot operate under competitive conditions, but average-cost pricing can lead to reasonable prices for consumers and "normal" returns for the firm.

could then bring about the efficient level of output. (This variation on the graph is left as an exercise for you.) Particular care must be taken when applying price ceilings. The resulting shortage will necessitate energy rationing and may cause a decline in the quality of energy services provided.

A profit-maximizing monopoly chooses the quantity that corresponds with the intersection of marginal revenue and marginal cost ($Q_{monopoly}$ in the middle panel of Figure 7.5), and finds the highest price consumers are willing to pay on the demand curve above that quantity ($P_{monopoly}$). The monopoly charges more and produces less than would a competitive firm with similar costs. If the market depicted on the middle graph were competitive, price and quantity would be determined by the intersection of marginal cost and demand. Remember that the marginal revenue curve is below the demand curve for a monopoly because it must lower its price to sell more units. If a price ceiling is imposed at the competitive price ($P_{ceiling}$), the firm will be able to sell up to Q^* units at that price, and the line representing the price ceiling becomes the firm's marginal revenue curve for quantities up to Q^*.[32] If the price ceiling is set correctly, the monopoly's new marginal revenue will equal its marginal cost at the competitive (and efficient) price and quantity, $P_{ceiling}$ and Q^*. Such a price ceiling provides one solution to the overly restrictive monopoly/cartel scenario described in the section on oil.

The natural monopoly in the bottom graph of Figure 7.5 will select its price and quantity just as the monopoly did. A price ceiling at the intersection of demand and marginal cost would fall below the average cost curve. And with its price below average cost, the firm would take a loss. On the other hand, a price ceiling set where demand equals average cost, as shown, would cover all costs, and the quantity would be as large as is feasible if energy is to be sold at a single price. This makes such a price ceiling inviting to price-setting authorities. Note that for quantities above Q*, the average cost curve is above the demand curve, indicating that the average cost would exceed the price consumers are willing to pay for those quantities.

A second policy option is to permit **price discrimination**, whereby different customers pay different prices. Business customers and wealthy individuals are generally willing to pay relatively more for electricity. Under **perfect price discrimination**, each customer pays the most he or she is willing to pay. Although the consumers receive no consumer surplus, this outcome is efficient if externalities are absent or internalized. Because the height of the demand curve at any given quantity represents both the marginal customer's willingness to pay and the additional revenue gained by serving that customer under price discrimination, the demand curve and the marginal revenue curve become one

32 Marginal revenue is the additional revenue received from selling one more unit. If a firm must lower its price from $1.00 per gallon of P-series to $0.90 per gallon in order to increase its sales from 5 gallons to 6 gallons, its total revenue increases from $\$1 \times 5 = \$5.00$ to $\$0.90 \times 6 = \$5.40$ and its marginal (additional) revenue from the sixth gallon is $0.40. On the other hand, if it can sell up to 10 gallons at a price ceiling of $0.70, then it can sell 5 gallons for $0.70 per gallon and it can sell 6 gallons for $0.70 per gallon. Total revenue is $\$0.70 \times 5 = \$3.50$ for 5 gallons and $\$0.70 \times 6 = \$4.20$ for 6 gallons and the marginal revenue from the sixth gallon equals the price ceiling of $0.70.

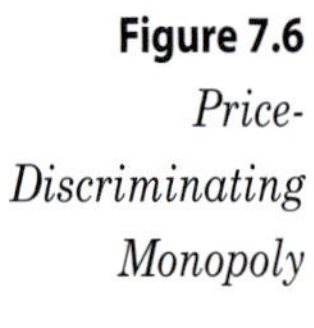
Figure 7.6 *Price-Discriminating Monopoly*

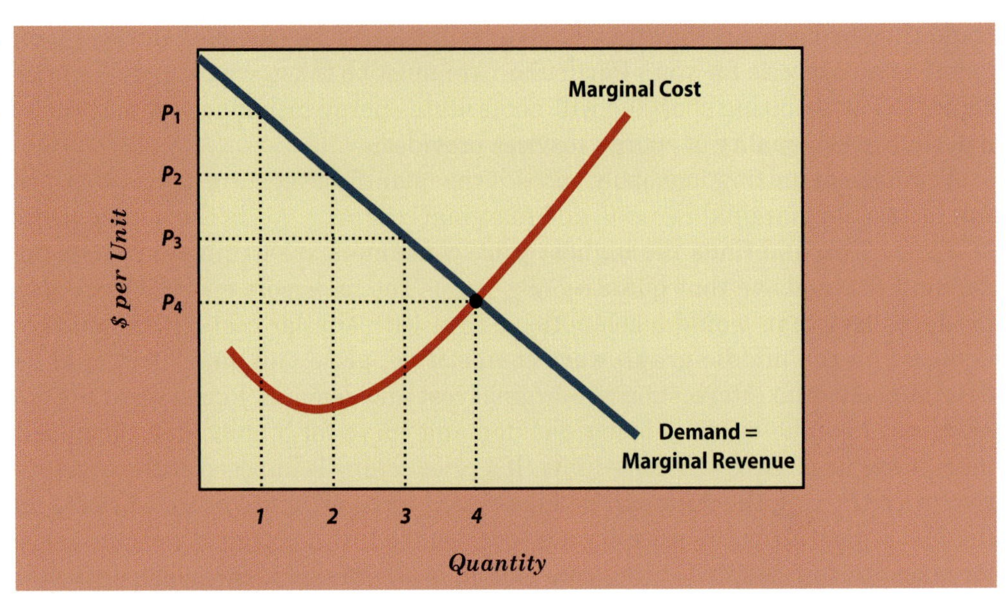

A price-discriminating monopolist charges each customer the most he or she would be willing to pay as indicated by the height of the demand curve. Since the monopolist does not have to lower its price in order to sell additional units, its marginal revenue curve corresponds with the demand curve. The monopolist maximizes profits by producing until marginal cost equals marginal revenue at *4* units. This production level is efficient in the absence of externalities.

and the same. For example, in Figure 7.6, the consumer of the first unit would pay at most P_1 for that unit, and is charged P_1. The second unit is valued at, and sells for, P_2, and so forth. Perfect price discriminating utilities maximize profits by producing where the demand/marginal revenue curve intersects the marginal cost curve. The utilities' profits can be diminished using a lump-sum tax and redistributed as desired.

Although *perfect* price discrimination as described here is seldom possible, multi-tiered pricing plans that charge different consumers different prices are common. As advocated by economist William S. Vickrey,[33] pricing mechanisms also provide useful incentives for off-peak energy use. Power companies struggle to meet demands during hot summer days and cold winter nights. Peak-load pricing systems that charge more during the day than at night successfully motivate people with flexible needs to use more energy during off-peak periods.

Deregulation

"The U.S. is steadily moving toward a functioning deregulated energy marketplace and more than half the country's population is scheduled to be able to choose their electricity supplier by 2004."

—Enron[34]

33 For more on Vickrey, see pw1.netcom.com/~masonc/vickrey.html.

34 See www.ees.enron.com/enrondirectus/deregulation.html. Accessed January 2002.

"Enron exploited the deregulation mania to the max, and the result has been economic ruin for thousands of hard-working families."

—Bob Herbert, *New York Times* Columnist[35]

Beyond price controls, government policy often influences the very structure of the electricity industry. As a means of deterring national conglomerates from dominating the electricity market, the 1935 Public Utility Holding Company Act (PUHCA) effectively gave U.S. electric utilities a monopoly in their geographic area, but prevented them from expanding into other regions. The 2005 Energy Act repealed PUHCA, although the long-term effects of deregulation are uncertain. Current technology allows electricity produced in one region to be sold in another, meaning that deregulation could introduce competition from other areas. It could also spawn dominant conglomerates. Suppose major power utilities A and B operate in Region 1 and Region 2, respectively. Regulation prevents Utility A from selling its power to Region 2 and Utility B from selling to Region 1. A stated intent of deregulation is to reduce rates for consumers by allowing utilities like A and B to compete as service providers in both Region 1 and Region 2. Earlier legislation already allowed for some competition. The 1992 National Energy Policy Act allowed power producers to compete for the sale of electricity to utilities, and the 1996 Federal Energy Regulatory Commission (FERC) Order 888 required utilities to open their electricity "grids" (transmission lines) to small-scale producers.[36]

The wisdom of energy deregulation is hotly contested. Some worry that rather than fostering competition, deregulation will defeat the purpose of PUHCA by allowing Utility A and Utility B to be replaced by deregulated Electric Company C, which will dominate the energy market in both regions. The American Public Power Association represents utilities owned by government agencies and municipalities. They argued that the repeal of PUHCA would threaten consumer access and fair pricing, and that without government monitoring there would not be an even playing field between these utilities and large investor-owned electric companies.[37] The Edison Electric Institute (EEI), a trade association of investor-owned electric companies and utility holding companies, favors deregulation free from government oversight.[38] The EEI advocates consumer choice among electricity providers and argues that deregulation allows consumers to choose among providers A, B, and C, among others, and to pay competitive rates. The National Rural Electric Cooperative Association, representing consumer-owned energy cooperatives, feels that deregulation could have negative effects on small-scale

35 *New York Times*, January 17, 2002, Sec. A, p. 29, Col. 6.

36 This policy is expected to save between $3.8 billion and $5.4 billion per year. For more information, visit www.converger.com/fercnopr/888_889.htm.

37 See www.appanet.org.

38 See www.eei.org.

reality check

Reality Check: California's Energy Woes

California brought us the hula-hoop, the skateboard, the cable car, and the Frisbee. But we would not want to follow all the past trends of the Golden state. In 2001, California experienced rolling **brownouts** (periods of low voltage in power lines that cause lights to dim and equipment to malfunction) and **blackouts** (complete power failures due to storms or, in California's case, overburdened power grids). Stores were closed, traffic lights went out, cable cars halted, and elevators jammed. Energy prices in the state increased by anywhere from 12 to 55 percent.

Behind this calamity were natural and human errors, and political and economic motives. Wholesale energy production in California was deregulated in 1996. The state's power utilities sold power plants to a handful of private energy wholesalers. The utilities purchased power from the deregulated wholesalers and sold it to customers at regulated retail prices. Increased energy demand and decreased supply caused the wholesale prices to exceed the fixed retail prices, leading to energy shortages and multibillion-dollar debt among the utilities. Compounding these problems were increasing temperatures that caused more precipitation to fall as rain rather than snow, leaving less snowmelt to fuel hydroelectric power stations. Cold snaps in the winter and excessive heat in the summer increased energy demands. During the same period, a number of power plants were under maintenance and could not produce at full power.

Some have pointed their fingers at the power companies, which may have restricted supply to force prices and profits upward. In the long run, the higher prices may have served the opposite purpose. Californians, already leaders in the use of alternative-fuel vehicles, have embraced solar and wind power among other means of gaining independence from the electricity grid. The number of energy-efficient homes made of used tires and straw bales is on the rise. Perhaps those trends will fly east like the Frisbee.

electricity providers and consumers.[39] They favor regulatory authority at the state level. Consumers themselves have varied perspectives. For example, those in states where energy is relatively abundant and inexpensive worry that with deregulation, energy produced in their states will be sold at higher prices elsewhere, and that local rates will increase.[40]

The economics of deregulation cannot be divorced from the politics involved. Parties on all sides of the energy deregulation debate have funded political contributions, lobbyists, and advertisements in publications aimed at Congress. Before becoming embroiled in controversy for allegedly concealing over $1 billion in debt, large-scale energy trading pioneer Enron was a major contributor to pro-deregulation members of Congress and presidential candidates. Although the true impact of deregulation is not yet clear, the story in the Reality Check exemplifies the mixed results of partial deregulation.

Politics Rears Its Ugly Head Again: Oil and Automobiles

> *"I get pork-barrel politics. I understand senators from oil states protecting the windfall profits of oil companies. What I don't get is empty-barrel politics — Michigan lawmakers year after year shielding Detroit from pressure to innovate on higher mileage standards, even though Detroit's failure to sell more energy-efficient vehicles has clearly contributed to its brush with bankruptcy."*
>
> —Thomas L. Friedman, *New York Times*, October 3, 2007

The quote above refers to one of the perennial battles between "big business" and environmental concerns. Of concern is the possibility that political and financial forces may impede efficiency within the markets for fuel, automobiles, and other goods that affect the environment. Worldwide, biofuel subsidies amount to more than $22 billion annually.[41] It would be naïve to suppose that the economics of fuel subsidies have only to do with the internalization of external benefits. Ethanol producer Archer Daniel Midland Co. spent $1.4 million on lobbying in 2012, and three oil and gas companies spent more than $10 million each on lobbying in the same year. London-based petroleum giant BP announced it would end political contributions in 2002 because the legitimacy of the political process is "crucial both for society and for us as a company working in that society."[42] Nonetheless, BP spent $8.6 million on lobbying in 2012.[43]

Influence may also be found in political ties. The father of former Vice President Al Gore, the late Senator Albert Gore, Sr., served on the board of Occidental

39 See www.nreca.org.

40 For a summary of deregulation considerations in each state, see www.eia.doe.gov/cneaf/electricity/chg_str/regmap.html.

41 See www.iisd.org/gsi/sites/default/files/bf_stateplay_2012.pdf.

42 See www.globalpolicy.org/component/content/article/172/30219.html.

43 See www.opensecrets.org.

Petroleum Corporation, and the Gore family inherited a large number of shares. After serving as Secretary of Defense under the first President George Bush, Dick Cheney went on to earn $5.1 million as the CEO of Halliburton Company, a diversified energy services company. He then returned to Washington to serve as Vice President under the second President George Bush. Cheney pushed for drilling in the Arctic National Wildlife Refuge unsuccessfully during both terms in Washington. Pro-deregulation Senator Phil Gramm's wife was a board member for pro-deregulation energy company Enron.

The discussion of Figure 7.4 explained that misplaced subsidies could result in the excessive use of an energy source that creates negative externalities. Governments worldwide paid $409 billion to subsidize oil, gas, and coal in 2010, and $60 billion to subsidize renewable energy.[44] Renewable energy proponents can only wonder where the solar and wind energy industries would stand today if the subsidies were allocated to renewable sources instead.

Is environmental and natural resource economics in a political quagmire? Read on. The plight of emissions and corporate average fuel economy (CAFE) standards in the United States further exemplifies the struggle between short-run political interests and the long-run interests of society.

CAFE Standards and Emissions Caps

Most modern automobiles receive their power from fuel combustion within their engines. Efficient combustion would turn the fuel's hydrogen and carbon atoms into water and carbon dioxide.[45] In reality, combustion is less than efficient, and by-products include unburned hydrocarbons, nitrogen oxides, and carbon monoxide. **Hydrocarbons** (HC) are the result of partially burned fuel molecules. They react with sunlight and nitrogen oxides (NO_x) to create ground-level ozone, a major component of smog. **Carbon monoxide** (CO) is created when fuel is only partially oxidized in the engine. When breathed, CO limits the flow of oxygen to the bloodstream and can cause severe illness or death. Fuel evaporation adds to the vehicle emissions problem. **Running losses** occur when a vehicle's operating temperature causes fuel to vaporize. **Hot soak** is the vaporization of fuel when a car has been turned off but is still hot. **Refueling losses** occur when fuel is being transferred from a stationary tank into a vehicle. **Diurnal evaporation** occurs as the temperature rises, causing fuel tanks to heat and vent vapors.

What follows is a brief history of U.S. public policy in response to emissions problems. The government regulates emissions by controlling both what goes into the fuel and what comes out of the average tailpipe. Some states also require each automobile to pass emissions tests to monitor exhaust problems that come about as some cars age. The events listed in the following time line illustrate the political struggle between corporate and environmental interests. Similar power games are played in the arenas of development, waste disposal, deregulation, and myriad regulatory fronts.

44 See www.businessweek.com/articles/2012-10-21/when-it-comes-to-government-subsidies-dirty-energy-still-cleans-up.

45 For a discussion of why this isn't the case, see www.howstuffworks.com/question407.htm.

Time Line

1955 Congress passes the Air Pollution Research Act after deadly smog engulfs New York City and shuts down industries and schools in Los Angeles.

1959 California becomes the first state to impose automotive emissions standards, requiring a blow-by valve to recycle crankcase emissions in tailpipes. Automobile companies protest the mandatory use of the $7 device, which leads to an anti-trust lawsuit by the Justice Department.

1960 The Schenk Act funds a two-year study on air pollution from cars.

1965 The U.S. Senate holds hearings on leaded gasoline, during which several scientists testify that high lead levels are man-made and endemic. The Motor Vehicle Air Pollution Control Act creates the first federal emissions standards, which apply to 1968 model cars.

1968 & 1969 Over half the cars produced in these model years do not meet the Motor Vehicle Air Pollution Control Act requirements.

1970 The Clean Air Act is introduced, declaring that by 1975, HC and CO emissions must
decrease by 90 percent relative to 1970 levels. NO_x emissions must decrease by 90 percent relative to 1971 levels by 1976. The newly formed EPA is asked to oversee vehicle emissions standards.

1973 The EPA extends deadlines for HC, CO, and NO_x standards by one year (to 1976 for HC and CO and 1977 for NO_x).

1974 The EPA approves another one-year extension for HC, CO, and NO_x.

1975 The EPA approves another one-year extension for HC and CO, setting 1978 as the deadline for automakers to reduce all three pollutants by 90 percent.

1977 The Clean Air Act is amended to push the HC and CO deadlines back to 1980. The NO_x standard is lowered and its deadline is extended until 1981. The EPA sets lead standards at 0.8 grams of lead per gallon of gasoline (g/gal) for large refineries, effective immediately. Small refineries can add up to 2.65 g/gal until October of 1982, at which time they must comply with the 0.8 g/gal standard.

1980 The EPA reduces the lead standard to 0.5 g/gal, effective for large refineries immediately. The EPA also limits diesel particulate emissions for the 1982–1984 truck model years. The EPA calls for a 90 percent reduction in CO emissions for heavy-duty trucks effective in the 1984 model year.

1981 Emission standards are weakened and extended until the 1990s. The EPA anticipates diesel particles standards for heavy-duty trucks, hoping to have them resolved by 1982. Regulations never materialize.

1982 The October 1981 deadline for small refineries is extended indefinitely. The EPA pushes back limits for diesel particulates until the 1987 model year and postpones CO reduction for heavy-duty trucks for one year.

1983–1985 The CAFE standard for cars is raised gradually from 26.0 to 27.5 miles per gallon.

1986 The CAFE standard for cars is lowered from 27.5 back to 26 mpg.

1990 The CAFE standard for cars is raised to 27.5 mpg. The Clean Air Act is revised to limit tailpipe emissions and promote low-emissions vehicles. The EPA proposes 40 percent and 60 percent reductions in automobile HC and NO_x emissions by the year 2000.

1992 Oxygenated gasoline is introduced in cities with high CO levels.

1994 The EPA sets emission standards for benzene and formaldehyde. New standards for urban buses become effective for the 1994 model year. Bus systems in noncompliant cities would be forced to run on alternative fuels.

1995 General Motors recalls 500,000 Cadillacs and pays $45 million in penalty and repair costs for excessive CO emissions.

1999 The EPA releases Tier 2 vehicle emission standards focused on reducing ozone. Vehicles meeting Tier 2 standards will be 99 percent cleaner than those in the 1960s. The EPA issues more rigid NO_x standards for new passenger cars and light trucks effective in the 2004–2007 model years. All pickup trucks, vans, and SUVs are required to meet more rigid NO_x standards by 2009.

2001 President George W. Bush considers weakened requirements for vehicles from 2004 to 2009, citing concern that reducing emissions could also reduce fuel efficiency. Environmentalists cry foul.

2003 The National Highway Traffic Safety Administration increases CAFE standards for light trucks from 20.7 mpg to 21.0 mpg by 2005, 21.6 mpg by 2006, and 22.2 mpg by 2007, the first increase in 10 years.

2005 President Bush proposes a reduction in CAFE standards for larger light trucks to 21.3 mpg by 2011. Smaller light trucks would have the higher standard of 28.4 mpg and models weighing between 8,500 and 10,000 lbs would remain exempt from CAFE standards.

2007 President Bush signs the Energy Independence and Security Act targeting CAFE standards of 35 mpg for cars and light trucks by 2020. CAFE standards for cars remain at 27.5 mpg until 2011.

2009 President Barack Obama announces that CAFE standards for cars will be 30.2 in 2011 and increase to 39 mpg by 2016.

2011 CAFE standards are modified so that bigger cars have lower standards.

2012 The formula for size-specific CAFE standards is simplified, but lower standards remain for larger cars.

Politics and environmental economics are irrevocably intermeshed. When seeking progress on the environmental front, politicians and economists who look only within their own field, and disregard the importance of the other, run the risk of accomplishing little of value in either area.

Summary

As economic efficiency requires, we tolerate the climate-changing, health-degrading, environment-impairing costs imposed by the fossil fuels that turn the wheels of industry and agriculture. The question is: Are we tolerating too much? A host of renewable fuels are poised to provide far more clean energy than they do today. Solar and wind energy draw from virtually infinite sources and generate emissions-free electricity. Fuel cells create only pure water and heat but lack supporting research into low-cost hydrogen sources. Biofuel mixtures reduce the emissions from gasoline and come from carbon-sequestering vegetation. Nonetheless, we have not yet embraced a substitute for fossil fuels, largely for want of economies of scale. We face the puzzle of needing popularity for mass production and needing mass production for the low prices required for popularity.

Political, economic, and scientific hurdles barricade the status quo in energy production. Strife in oil-exporting countries and the vulnerability of centralized energy producers to blackouts and hurricanes may motivate fresh approaches. Only with an understanding of our energy alternatives can society allocate resources efficiently between fossil fuels, renewable sources, and the research and development needed for the next generation of options. This chapter is intended to foster such an understanding and to explain the implications of various market structures that can be created or controlled with energy policy.

Problems for Review

1. Identify a strength and a weakness of each of the following fuels:
   a) Coal
   b) Hydrogen
   c) Natural Gas
   d) Solar Fuel

2. If all of the energy from the sun were captured by solar cells with efficiency levels in the middle of the range of solar cell efficiency, how much energy could be converted to useful work each year?

3. Suppose that solar energy were made available at a constant MC_{social} just below the preexisting market price in Figure 7.3. Draw a set of graphs similar to those in Figure 7.3 with the appropriate adjustments in the solar energy graph and the market MC_{social} curve. Indicate the appropriate level of energy production from each source. Repeat these steps under the new assumption that the constant MC_{social} for solar energy is almost zero, which is less than the MC_{social} for the first unit of oil or coal.

4. The introduction to this chapter discusses the environmental costs of fossil fuel consumption. Omitted are the environmental costs of manufacturing the trucks, oil rigs, bulldozers, and other equipment used in fossil fuel production. Choose one of those items and list at least five stages of its creation that cause pollution. (*Hint*: Think about the components of the item. How is steel made? Where does iron ore come from? and so on.)

5. Suppose the solar and coal industries were producing at the levels Q_{solar} and Q_{coal} as determined by the $MC_{private}$ curves in Figure 7.4. Describe two specific policies that could correct for these inefficiencies.

6. Suppose that the supply curve in the top panel of Figure 7.5 represents $MC_{private}$, and that the demand curve represents MB_{social}. Draw an MC_{social} curve such that Q^* is the efficient level of output. Besides a price ceiling, what other policy could reduce output to Q^*?

7. Draw a monopoly graph and include a price ceiling that would *decrease* the quantity of output to a level below the monopoly level of output.

8. If you had $10,000 to invest in an alternative fuel, which one would you pick? Explain your answer.

9. Some alternative fuels and energy-saving devices would save more money than their own cost of implementation. Examples include water-saving showerheads and toilets, energy-saving lightbulbs and furnaces, and low-emissions vehicles. From your own experience, provide two or three reasons why more people do not adopt these seemingly negative-cost items.

10. Draw hypothetical *marginal cost*, *marginal revenue*, *average cost*, *demand*, *quantity*, and *price* lines for:
    a) A nuclear power plant
    b) One of the energy providers in a country that has taken the "soft" energy path

1. Find a website that provides an update on the plight of corporate average fuel economy (CAFE) standards.
2. Find the website of a major newspaper that includes a story about energy, and read it.
3. Find a picture of a wind farm.

Internet Resources

American Petroleum Institute:
http://*.api-ec.api.org/newsplashpage/index.cfm*

American Solar Energy Society:
www.ases.org

Energy Information Agency:
www.eia.doe.gov

Geothermal Education Office:
http://*geothermal.marin.org*

International Energy Agency:
www.iea.org

International Energy Policy Institute:
www.ucl.ac.uk/australia/research#tabs-4

International Renewable Energy Agency:
www.irena.org

National Renewable Energy Lab:
www.nrel.gov

PV (photovoltaic) Power Resource Site:
www.pvpower.com

Real Goods Renewable Energy Information:
www.solareco.com/index.cfm

Renewable Energy International:
www.solarenergy.org

Renewable Resource Data Center:
http://*rredc.nrel.gov*

Rocky Mountain Institute:
www.rmi.org

U.S. Department of Energy
Radioactive Waste Disposal Information:
www.em.doe.gov/Pages/wmdi.aspx

Further Reading

Atkinson, Scott E., and Robert Halvorsen. "Parametric Efficiency Tests, Economies of Scale, and Input Demand in U.S. Electric Power Generation." *International Economic Review* 25, no. 3 (1984): 647–662. An empirical study finding considerable heterogeneity in the efficient scale of power plants.

Baumol, William J., John C. Panzar, and Robert D. Willig. *Contestable Markets and the Theory of Market Structure.* New York: Harcourt Brace Jovanovich, 1982. A seminal work that argues that natural monopolies cannot result from fixed costs alone.

Hill, Jason, Erik Nelson, David Tilman, Stephan Polasky, and Douglas Tiffany. "Environmental, Economic, and Energetic Costs and Benefits of Biodiesel and Ethanol Biofuels." *Proceedings of the National Academy of Sciences* 103, no. 30 (2006): 11206–11210. A report on the net energy and pollution created by corn-based ethanol and soybean-based biodiesel, with comparisons to the fossil fuels they displace.

Hubbard, Harold M. "The Real Cost of Energy." *Scientific American* 264 (April 1991): 36–40. A commentary on the costs of energy that are not paid by consumers at the pump.

Koplow, Douglas. *Federal Energy Subsidies: Energy, Environmental and Fiscal Impacts.* Washington, D.C.: Alliance to Save Energy, 1993. An enumeration of government subsidies for the energy industry.

Koplow, Douglas. *A Boon to Bad Biofuels.* Cambridge, MA, and Washington, D.C.: Earth Track and Friends of the Earth, 2009. A report on federal tax credits and mandates for biofuels that create negative externalities.

Koplow, Douglas, and Aaron Martin. "Global Warming: Federal Subsidies to Oil in the United States, Industrial Economics Incorporated, a Report for Greenpeace." 2001, www.greenpeace.org/~climate/oil/fdsub.html. A thorough report breaking down direct and indirect subsidies, and credits that benefit oil production.

Lovins, Amory. "Energy Strategy: The Road Not Taken?" *Foreign Affairs* 55, no. 1 (1976): 65–96. Sets forth the concepts of "hard" and "soft" paths for energy production.

Myers, Norman, and Jennifer Kent. *Perverse Subsidies: How Misused Tax Dollars Harm the Environment and the Economy.* Washington, D.C.: Island Press, 2001. A perspective on how government subsidies can create inefficiencies.

Pimental, David, and Tad W. Patzek. "Ethanol Production Using Corn, Switchgrass, and Wood; Biodiesel Production Using Soybean and Sunflower." *National Resources Research* 14, no. 1 (2005): 65–76. Research suggesting that ethanol and biodiesel production typically takes more energy than the fuels provide.

Piore, Adam. "A Nuke Train Gets Ready to Roll." *Newsweek* (July 30, 2001): 26–28. A story of policy and protest relating to the transport and storage of spent uranium fuel.

U.S. Bureau of the Census. *Statistical Abstract of the United States: 2012.* Washington, D.C., 2012. A favorite for data-grubbing of all sorts. The chapter on energy is particularly relevant.

Watkiss, Jeffrey P., and Douglas W. Smith "The Energy Policy Act of 1992—A Watershed for Competition in the Wholesale Power Market." *Yale Journal of Regulation* 10, no. 2 (Summer 1993): 447–482. Discusses avenues for small-scale competitors in the market for electricity.

Yergin, Daniel. *The Prize: The Epic Quest for Oil, Money, and Power.* New York: Simon & Schuster, 1993. A colorful history of the world petroleum industry.

Your author at the helm of a power plant. The next Homer Simpson?

"At the beginning of this Summit, the children of the world spoke to us in a simple yet clear voice that the future belongs to them, and accordingly challenged all of us to ensure that through our actions they will inherit a world free of the indignity and indecency occasioned by poverty, environmental degradation and patterns of unsustainable development."

—FROM THE JOHANNESBURG DECLARATION ON SUSTAINABLE DEVELOPMENT
WWW.JOHANNESBURGSUMMIT.ORG

8 Sustainability

In the small coastal town of Arcata, California, the Marsh Commons Cohousing Community adjoins a state wildlife refuge. The 13 housing units are built largely of recycled lumber, environmentally friendly SmartWood, Trex brand recycled-material decking, recycled paint, and carpets made from recycled plastic bottles. The inhabitants share a common garden, laundry room, shop, guest room, meeting and dining area, children's play area, workroom, and craft area. Among the primary goals of this and many similar cohousing communities worldwide is sustainability. By sharing common spaces and avoiding the use of virgin, depletable materials, the communities have a relatively small effect on the environment and on the options available to future generations.

Individuals, organizations, and governments share the goal of sustainability for differing reasons. People who wish to leave a legacy of health and environmental wealth for future generations seek to use resources in ways that can continue indefinitely. Ecological ethics bring many to tread lightly. Members of organizations that espouse sustainability, like the National Wildlife Federation and participants in the Student Summit for Sustainability in Zurich, see sustainability as a vital component of long-term social welfare. Elements of sustainability—energy conservation, recycling, and the sustainable use of raw materials—appeal to the profit motives of firms as well. When the National Cancer Institute gave Bristol-Myers Squibb the rights to produce the anticancer drug Taxol, the drug was made from the bark of a yew tree found in the U.S. Pacific Northwest. These forests are home to endangered species including the spotted owl.

Bristol-Myers Squibb found that twigs and needles served as a sustainable substitute for bark as their essential ingredient, without harming the trees and with minimal impact on the ecosystem at large.

Sustainability *is a nebulous but attractive concept with a guiding question for every activity: Can this go on? An activity with an unlimited time horizon is sustainable. This general concept of sustainability can be applied to everything from production and consumption to the flows of natural, physical, and human capital. The Bruntland Report issued by the World Commission on Environment and Development (1987) described* ***sustainable development*** *as "development that meets the needs of the present without compromising the ability of the future to meet their own." In the context of economics, the terms "sustainability" and "sustainable development" are often used interchangeably.*

As a prescription for the allocation of scarce resources, sustainable development is closely tied to the world of economics. Like many environmental and resource economics issues, decisions about sustainable development force normative judgments about the welfare of present and future generations that encroach into ethics, as discussed in Chapter 16. This chapter explains differing interpretations of the sustainability criterion, explores their implications, and discusses policies that support sustainability.

Sustainability Criteria

The concept of sustainability complements the human instincts to endure and leave a legacy. However, economists disagree over the appropriate target. Aside from debates over discount rates and the treatment of future generations as discussed in Chapter 5, there is controversy over the appropriate substitutability criterion. That is, if we do favor nondecreasing welfare over time, how is that best achieved and how can we measure our level of achievement?

Weak Sustainability

At the heart of long-lived controversies over sustainability is the substitutability of natural capital (fossil fuels, biomass, the ozone layer, and so on) and physical capital (man-made capital such as machines, buildings, and roads). Advocates for **weak sustainability** argue that physical and natural capital are *substitutes,* making the relevant question: Is our accumulation of physical capital sufficient to make up for our loss of natural capital? The criterion for weak sustainability

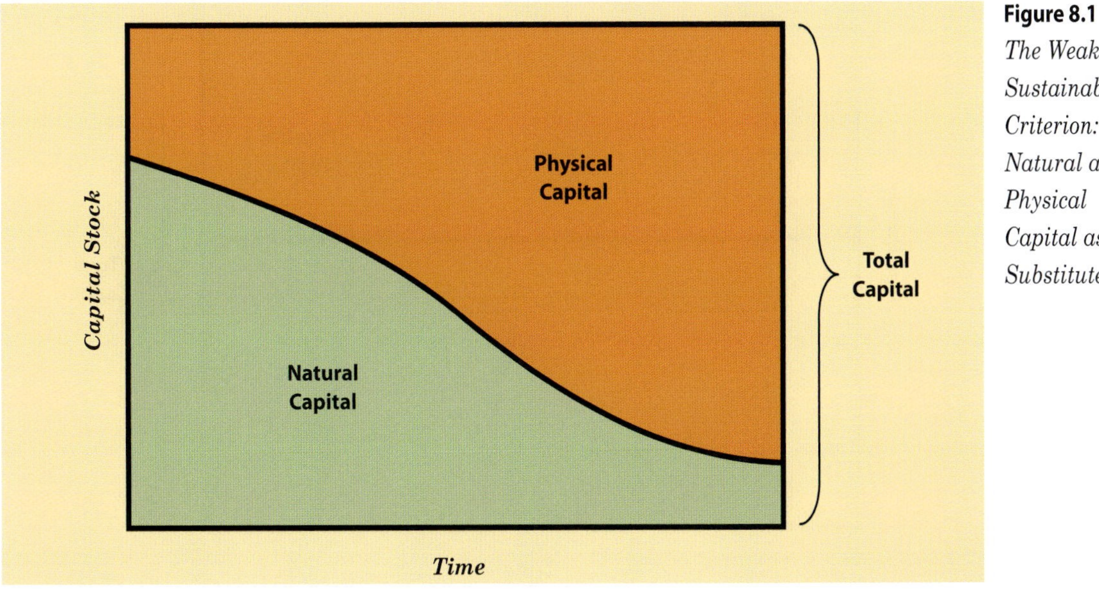

Figure 8.1 *The Weak Sustainability Criterion: Natural and Physical Capital as Substitutes*

Advocates of weak sustainability argue that physical and natural capital are substitutes. As levels of natural capital decline, they believe that technological innovations will allow physical capital to take its place. Thus, the key to sustained welfare is maintenance of the *total* capital stock.

is the maintenance of the total capital stock, represented by the horizontal line going across the top of Figure 8.1.

Neoclassical economists John Hartwick and Robert Solow are among those who have argued that decreases in natural capital over time will not be problematic if balanced by increases in physical capital. According to **Hartwick's Rule** (Hartwick, 1977), with no population growth and no depreciation of physical capital, consumption levels can remain constant from one generation to the next. The stipulation is that exhaustible natural resources are never consumed, but rather are turned into physical capital. The total stock of productive capital is thus sustained because the current generation converts natural capital into physical capital and "lives off" the output of physical and human capital.

David Pearce and Giles Atkinson (1995) present an index of weak sustainability. They begin with the assumption that human capital will not depreciate because it has public-good aspects and can be passed from one generation to another. Fitting with the assumptions of weak sustainability, they also assume that savings are invested in physical capital, which they treat as a perfect substitute for natural capital. The maintenance of the total capital stock, then, depends on a national savings rate that is at least as great as the combined depreciation rate of natural and physical capital. The relevant condition for sustainability is thus:

$$Z = \frac{\text{Savings}}{\text{GDP}} - \frac{(\text{Depreciation of Natural Capital} + \text{Depreciation of Physical Capital})}{\text{GDP}} \geq 0$$

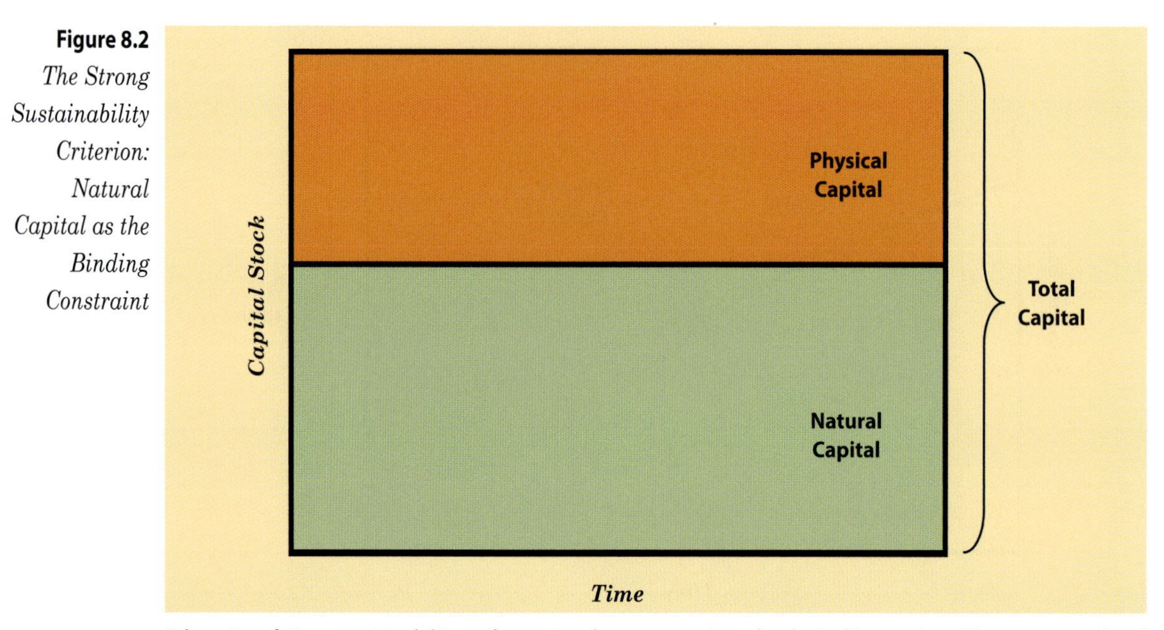

Figure 8.2 *The Strong Sustainability Criterion: Natural Capital as the Binding Constraint*

Advocates of strong sustainability prefer not to rely on uncertain technological innovations. They see natural and physical capital as complements, and expect limited amounts of natural capital to form the binding constraint on future welfare. The strong sustainability criterion is the maintenance of sustainable levels of natural capital.

Pearce and Atkinson suggest the value of Z as an index of sustainability. They calculated index values for 22 countries, finding that countries including Brazil, Japan, and the United States have sustainable economies. Mexico, the Philippines, and the United Kingdom are marginally sustainable, and Ethiopia, Mali, and Nigeria are among countries with unsustainable economies.

Strong Sustainability

On the other side are ecological economists championed by Herman Daly. Their **strong sustainability** criterion calls for the maintenance of natural capital as shown in Figure 8.2. They see natural and physical capital as complements, not substitutes, with natural capital being an essential ingredient in production, consumption, and welfare. They perceive too many uncertainties and feel it is too dangerous to assume that physical capital can take the place of biodiversity or the life-sustaining cycles of oxygen, carbon, nitrogen, and water, for example. In their view, neoclassical economists give inadequate attention to environmental degradation and pollution, which can curtail social welfare regardless of the maintenance of total capital levels.

Several available measures of strong sustainability reflect the emphases of this criterion. Daly and Cobb's index of sustainable economic welfare, as detailed in Chapter 5, explicitly adjusts GDP for pollution and losses in natural capital. Others have discussed net domestic product (NDP) as an indicator of sustainability. The strong sustainability version of the Pearce–Atkinson sustainability rule is

$$\frac{\text{Natural Capital Depreciation}}{\text{GDP}} \leq 0$$

This requires natural capital depreciation to be zero, or negative, which would cause an appreciation in natural capital. None of the 22 countries Pearce and Atkinson examined meet this criterion, although the Netherlands, Japan, and Finland come the closest, with values of 1, 2, and 2, respectively.

Given that natural capital is indeed decreasing as in Figure 8.1, the achievement of strong sustainability would require changes that end the net loss of natural capital. This might mean fewer cars per household, smaller homes, and greater recycling efforts, among other sacrifices. Figure 8.3 illustrates this story as it relates to social welfare. If the goal is a sustainable level of welfare as indicated by the horizontal purple line, ecological economists advise a gradual adjustment of resource use to achieve a sustainable level of welfare starting now, as illustrated by the green line. If we continue to deplete natural resources at current rates, they say, we could sustain or improve welfare in the short run as shown by the red line, but cause irreversible environmental damage and a corresponding loss of welfare in the future.

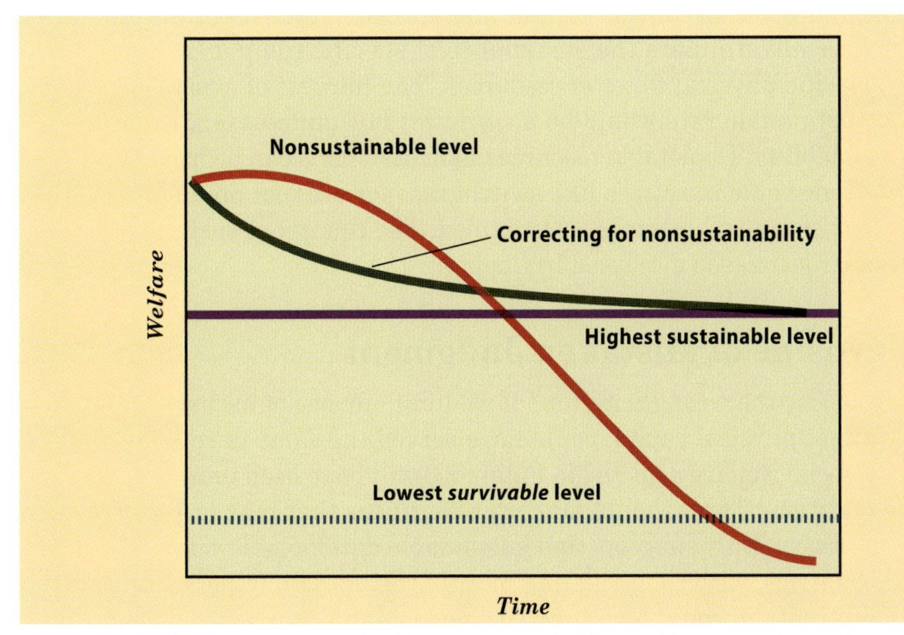

Figure 8.3
The Course of Intergenerational Welfare

If our current levels of resource use and welfare are not sustainable, we will have to make sacrifices now to reach the highest sustainable level of welfare. Delays in this correction may lead to decreases in the highest level that can be sustained. As indicated by the red line that starts upward and then falls to the horizontal axis, some economists believe that continued consumption at current levels could cause severe environmental losses and bring welfare below the survivable level in the future.

Sign at the Columbus Zoo.

Strong sustainability requires the maintenance of aggregate levels of natural capital. It does *not* stipulate the sustenance of specific components of natural capital or specific physical flows of resources. The harvest of every fishery and forest at a sustainable rate would be a *sufficient* but unnecessary condition for strong sustainability. Depletable resources like fossil fuels can be used if they are replaced by renewable resources like switchgrass for ethanol production so that the total stock of natural capital is maintained. The concept of sustainable yields from particular sources is discussed in Chapters 13 and 14.

The Downside of Mistaken Judgment

What if we choose the wrong criterion? If we limit our use of natural capital and it turns out that physical capital could have served the same purposes, then the reduction in social welfare depicted in Figure 8.3 will have been unnecessary. This raises the question of who should make the sacrifices that may or may not turn out to be necessary. Daly suggests that sustainable development begin within the developed countries, with them bearing most of the burden. Others fear that the brunt of conservation would be felt by the developing countries, which could be denied the luxuries of their rich neighbors.

Sustainable practices are a deliberate attempt to improve intergenerational equity. If this interest in equity across time carried over to equity across individuals, policymakers would allocate the sustainability burden by placing constraints on rich nations, while allowing poor nations to improve their conditions. In practice, any actual decrease in resource use would most likely occur in developed countries; developing nations have relatively little to sacrifice. A policy of holding resource use steady without mechanisms for redistribution would be a more direct threat to developing countries, which would have to compete with stronger economies for now-scarcer resources. In the end, policy and ethics will guide who sacrifices what.

If natural capital turns out to be the binding constraint on output and we allow the stock of natural capital to decrease substantially, social welfare may be irreversibly diminished. If disruptions in food chains, environmental sinks, and broader ecosystems cannot be repaired with physical capital, the repercussions will be severe. If laboratories can't synthesize the medicinal cures that lost species would have provided, more human lives will be lost.

The potential irreversibility of losses in natural capital has led some economists to call for **safe minimum standards**. These standards could include the maintenance of viable populations of unique species and limits on the damage that can be done to the air, water, and climate. Safe minimum standards would guide public policies affecting the distant future, for which estimates of costs and benefits may be too tenuous to compare.

Other Types of Sustainability

Although the strong and weak sustainability criteria have received considerable attention among economists, a number of other criteria have been proposed. One that has already been mentioned is a target of sustenance for every specific component of natural capital and every flow of particular natural resources. This concept has been called "very strong" sustainability and **environmental sustainability**, and is associated with the deep ecology movement discussed in Chapter 16. Strictly interpreted, this criterion would seem impossible to meet, given the natural changes in biodiversity and other natural capital. In practice, deep ecologists equate their brand of sustainability with respect for the environment and prioritization of ecological concerns over economic development, recognizing the natural course of change.

The term *environmental sustainability* shows up in many contexts with somewhat differing interpretations, as does the term *ecological sustainability*. In 1999, a group of scientists commissioned by the U.S. Department of Agriculture advanced the meaning of **ecological sustainability** as "maintaining the composition, structure, and processes of an ecological system." The *composition* of an ecological system refers to its biodiversity, including the diversity of its genetics, species, and landscape. The *structure* refers to characteristics with biogenic origin, such as fallen trees, bog, and coral reefs, as well as physical attributes, including navigable rivers, mountains, valleys, and wetlands. Natural *processes* include hydrologic and nutrient cycles, photosynthesis, disturbances like floods and fires, and the stages of succession within forests, prairies, ponds, and other wilderness areas.

Implicit in the goal of intergenerational equity are at least two other forms of sustainability: human sustainability and social sustainability. **Human sustainability** entails sustenance of the human capital needed to maintain levels of health, wealth, production, and therefore welfare. Social welfare is also dependent on citizens' ethics, discipline, tolerance, and trust, among other elements of social capital maintained under **social sustainability**. John Pezzey (1992) discusses the less ambitious bottom line of **survivability**, which would allow social welfare to fall as long as consumption remains above the subsistence level. In Figure 8.3, a light blue dotted line represents the lowest survivable level of welfare. As discussed in Chapter 9, some economists expect current trends in population and consumption to take us on a welfare path below the highest sustainable level but above the collapse of human civilization, permitting survivability at an inferior level of welfare.

Sustainability and Efficiency

Economists generally focus on efficiency, leaving equity concerns aside. The issue of sustainability provides an exception, for it involves vital resource allocation questions wrapped up in human values and equity concerns. The general goal of sustainability is welfare equity over time. This meets popular standards for fairness, including the Rawlsian *veil of ignorance*, under which decisions are made as if the decision makers did not know in which period they would live. But welfare equity over time does not coincide with dynamic efficiency. Sustainability does not imply efficiency, nor does efficiency imply sustainability. The following example illustrates the distinction and the special case of compatibility between efficiency and the equity goal of sustainability.

We will examine the problem with a two-period model. The simplification of life into two periods permits a useful perspective on activities in the present (Period 1) and the future (Period 2). The implications carry over to relatively complex models with a more realistic number of periods. Consumers in each period are assumed to have the same preferences and receive diminishing marginal benefits, net of any associated costs, from a depletable resource. This resource might be coal, oil, clean water, or a combination of resources. The "consumption" described in this example refers to resource expenditures for the sake of utility in the period of consumption, not investments in the first period that would provide utility in the second period.

Figure 8.4 models the two-period allocation dilemma. Consumption in Period 1 starts at zero on the left side of the graph and increases to the right. Consumption in Period 2 starts at zero on the right side and increases to the left. The sustainable level of use is 50 percent, meaning that half of the resource is used in Period 1 and the other half in Period 2. The red arrows below the graph represent Period 1 consumption, and the blue arrows below the graph represent

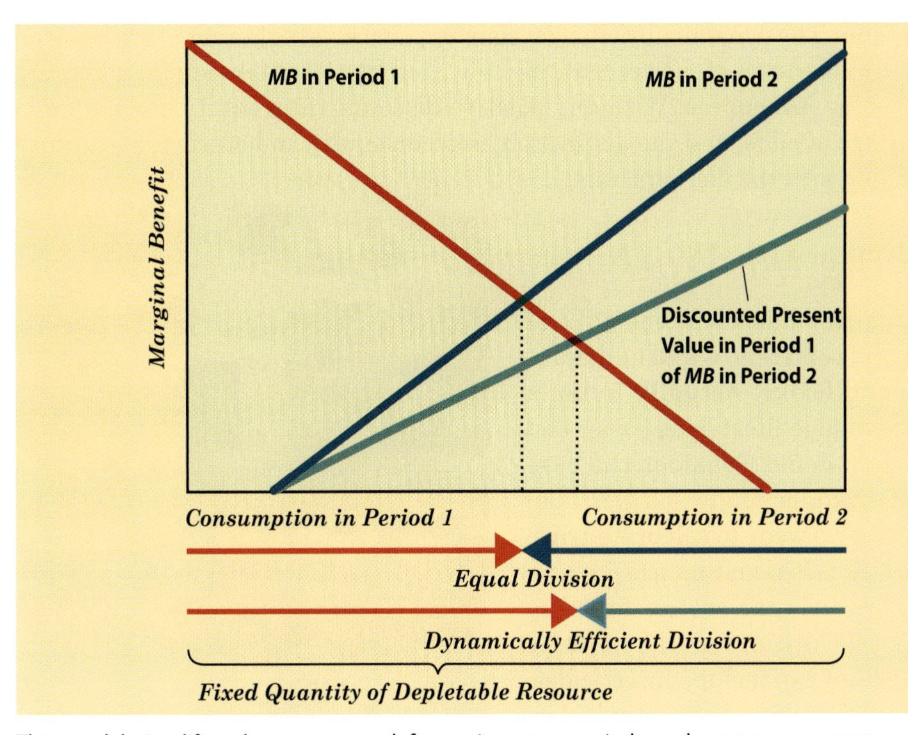

Figure 8.4 *Equity versus Efficiency in a Two-Period Model*

This model simplifies the present and future into two periods and assumes constant preferences. Consumers in each period receive diminishing (net) marginal benefits from a depletable resource. Consumption in Period 1 starts at zero on the left side of the graph and increases to the right. Consumption in Period 2 starts at zero on the right side and increases to the left. The sustainable level of use is 50 percent, meaning that half of the resource is used in Period 1 and the other half in Period 2. A dynamically efficient allocation maximizes the present value of benefits by dividing the resource at the intersection point of the red and light blue curves that measure the present value of marginal benefits in each period. An equal division would only be dynamically efficient if the discount rate were zero. A positive discount rate decreases the present value of marginal benefits in Period 2, as from the dark blue line to the light blue line, and the dynamically efficient consumption level in Period 1 exceeds the sustainable level of 50 percent.

Period 2 consumption. Similarly, the red *MB* curve represents marginal benefit in Period 1, and the blue *MB* curve represents marginal benefit in Period 2.

To achieve dynamic efficiency, each unit of the resource would be allocated to the period in which it provides the largest present value of its marginal benefit. In terms of the graph, that allocation occurs at the intersection of the marginal benefit curves, with the marginal benefit in Period 2 discounted as desired. With any other allocation, the last units received in one period would be worth more in the other period, and therefore should be reallocated to the other period.

An equal division is dynamically efficient only if the discount rate placed on benefits in the second period is zero. In that case, the appropriate allocation occurs at the intersection of the red and dark blue *MB* curves, which are mirror images of each other and cross in the middle of the graph. A positive discount rate decreases the present value of marginal benefits in Period 2, as from the dark blue line to the light blue line. The dynamically efficient consumption level in Period 1 then exceeds the sustainable level of 50 percent, as indicated by the intersection of the red and light blue *MB* curves. With any positive discount rate, equity and dynamic efficiency are at odds, and the distinction between equity and efficiency outcomes grows larger with the discount rate.

Walking the Walk

Sustainability has been the talk of recent world conferences and numerous articles and books. Actually living a more sustainable lifestyle is easier discussed than done. Consider the case of cotton, the pleasingly soft fabric in the T-shirts we wear to celebrate trips, colleges, 5K races, and political statements. Traditional cotton farming involves the intensive use of toxic chemicals that can include insecticides, herbicides, fertilizers, and fungicides. And it takes up to 2,700 liters of water to grow the cotton for one T-shirt. Patagonia is among several companies selling clothing made with organically grown cotton, but it isn't cheap. Walking the walk of sustainability means making efforts at the individual, corporate, and government levels to moderate the use of products made in unsustainable ways. The necessary sacrifices are often reduced by the availability of more sustainable substitutes. In the case of cotton, and depending on the production process employed, these include fabrics made of recycled fibers, bamboo, flax, or hemp.

Efforts toward sustainability require moderation in the use of products with a large environmental footprint. This includes the traditional cotton T-shirts bought to celebrate trips, colleges, and sports teams.

Efforts toward sustainability are nothing new. Noting the "profound impact of man's activity" on the environment, the National Environmental Policy Act of 1969 made it the policy of every level of the U.S. government to "use all practicable means and measures ... to create and maintain conditions under which man and nature can exist in productive harmony, and fulfill the social, economic, and other requirements of present and future generations of Americans." This nod to sustainability was followed by the National Forest Management Act of 1976 (NFMA), which requires the U.S. Secretary of Agriculture to provide for, among other things, sustainable timber harvests and diversity of plant and animal communities. A committee of scientists, asked by the U.S. Department of Agriculture to recommend management practices for national forests and grasslands in the new century, stated that the NFMA standards should be interpreted to mean ecological sustainability as defined earlier in this chapter.

At the international level, Agenda 21 of the 1992 U.N. Conference on Environment and Development asked all participating countries to introduce national strategies for sustainable development (NSSDs). Participants in the 2012 U.N. Conference on Sustainable Development acknowledged "the need to further mainstream sustainable development at all levels, integrating economic, social and environmental aspects and recognizing their interlinkages, so as to achieve sustainable development in all its dimensions."

Specific policies and practices that support sustainability include advancements in renewable energy, tradable emissions permits, CAFE standards, brownfield (abandoned commercial site) reclamation, product substitution (hybrid cars for combustion engines, services for goods), municipal solid waste reduction, scrubbers and other "clean" technology, and "green" architecture. The remainder of this section discusses recycling, which can help make resource use sustainable.

Recycling

Historically, those who salvaged trash have been looked down upon. In order to thwart trash pickers, late-nineteenth-century Parisian prefect Eugene Poubelle required residents to set their trash out only minutes before collection time. Colonel George E. Waring, New York City's commissioner of streets during the same period, despised the many poor immigrants who picked garbage from the

A variety of scavengers collect plastic, metal, and food scraps from a dump in Mumbai (Bombay), India. Such recycling efforts are credited for alleviating the tremendous municipal solid waste burden in this city of 18 million people.

streets and saw them as a threat to sanitation. Still today, at dumpsites and trash receptacles, informal recyclers are often considered a nuisance.

To **recycle** is to take used goods and make them into new goods. For example, 36 used PolyEthylene Terephtalate (PET) water bottles can be recycled into one square yard of carpet. Most of the plastic, metal, glass, and paper removed from the waste stream will be recycled into new goods. Some items can simply be reused as *alternatives* to newly manufactured goods. Thrift stores, flea markets, garage sales, and eBay visitors share the mission of making one person's junk another's treasure. Recognition of the private and public benefits of reusing and recycling has swayed some opinions. Poubelle gained greater appreciation for the benefits side of the equation and relaxed his Parisian policy after 30,000 beneficiaries of recycling rioted in the streets. In Hanoi, Vietnam, not unlike other developing urban areas, scavengers reuse or recycle about 30 percent of the city's refuse.[1] Recycling's reputed contributions to environmental, natural resource, and sustainable development goals have made it the in-vogue practice of soccer moms and ragpickers alike.

Current Trends

Table 8.1 illustrates the dramatic growth in recycling over the past several decades. About 34 percent of U.S. waste is recycled, a rate that has more than tripled since 1980. Recycling and composting now avert more than 85 million tons of material from U.S. landfills and incinerators each year. In 2010 that included 72 percent of newspapers, 29 percent of plastic bottles and jars, 69 percent of steel packaging, and 65 percent of major appliances. Fifty percent of aluminum beverage cans are recycled in the United States, as are 94 percent in Brazil, 91

Table 8.1 *U.S. Recycling Rates*

Material	*1980*	*1990*	*2010*
Paper/Paperboard	21.3%	27.8%	62.5%
Ferrous metal (steel)	2.9	17.6	33.8
Aluminum	17.9	35.9	19.9
Other nonferrous metals	46.6	66.4	70.5
Glass	5.0	20.1	27.1
Plastics	0.3	2.2	8.2
Yard waste	0	12.0	57.5
Food, other wastes	1.9	3.6	2.8
Total	**9.6**	**16.0**	**34.1**

Source: www.epa.gov/epawaste/nonhaz/municipal/pubs/2010_MSW_Tables_and_Figures_508.pdf

1 See, for example, Hiebert (1993).

percent in Japan, 85 percent in Singapore, and 58 percent in Western Europe. The recycling of metals is notable because metal mining produces in excess of 3 billion pounds of toxic chemical releases annually—three times the amount produced by electric utilities. The recycling of aluminum cans also saves about 95 percent of the energy used to make them.

Curbside recycling programs were virtually nonexistent 30 years ago. In 2013, about 9,000 programs served over half of the U.S. population, and 12,000 drop-off centers make recycling an option for most of the remainder. Economists have studied the effects of recycling programs and demographics on recycling rates. Callan and Thomas (1997) examined recycling in Massachusetts, finding that curbside recycling and per-unit waste disposal fees caused recycling to increase significantly, as did higher education and income levels. Sterner and Bartelings (1999) found similar results in a study of households in southwest Sweden. These studies demonstrate that the growing trend of recycling responds to economic policy. The following sections discuss whether these trends are advisable from an efficiency standpoint and highlight two policies that influence recycling rates.

Is It Efficient?

Naturally, the efficiency of recycling is case specific and changes with societal needs and technology. It is efficient to water plants with recycled dishwater rather than new water drawn from the tap—the distance the waterer must travel is the same either way and the dishwater is even easier to use because it is already dispensed. It would be inefficient to recycle chalk dust—there is no shortage of the raw material and the used resource is widely dispersed and unthreatening. The challenge is to decide where to draw the line between items to recycle and items to compost or send to the landfill. Fluctuations in the supply and demand of recyclable materials, and for the products made from them, make it impossible to create a durable list of materials that should or should not be recycled. However, there are relevant approaches and points that are important to address.

Some economists advocate free-market solutions. Mike Munger (2007) wrote, "If recycling were efficient, someone would pay you to do it." Jesse Walker and Pierre Desrochers (1999) stated, "The American ritual of separating trash into various categories of glass, paper, etc., would not survive without public coercion and private compulsion." Others feel the recycling ritual is beneficial and worry that the amount of free-market recycling might fall below efficient levels due to market failure. These economists argue that externalities are prevalent in the environmentally sensitive contexts of resource extraction and waste disposal.

A study by Frank Ackerman (1997) found that market prices provide inadequate incentives for recycling. When the private market determines the price for recycled paper, for instance, the price may be formed without regard for the external benefits from avoided pollution, protected human health and wildlife, and averted landfill disposal. Thomas Kinnaman (2006) lists the external costs of landfill disposal as the loss in property values near the landfill, the threat to groundwater from possible leakage, the release of carbon dioxide and methane, and the congestion and air pollution created when transporting waste to the landfill. So that potential recyclers will bear more of the burden of waste disposal that is placed on society at large, Kinnaman suggests a landfill tax set equal to the marginal external cost of solid waste disposal, which he estimates to be between $5.38 and $8.76 per ton, minus any "host fees" already paid to the local area by the landfill operators.

Imperfect information compounds problems with externalities. Even when they care about the harm they cause to the environment and society, some market participants lack the knowledge that, for example, a ton of paper made from recycled pulp saves approximately 17 trees, 4,200 kWh of electricity, 7,000 gallons of water, and 3 cubic yards of landfill space, while avoiding the emission of 60 pounds of airborne effluents. A synthesis of 67 empirical studies on recycling behavior performed by Hornik et al. (1995) found that consumer knowledge was one of the strongest predictors of recycling. Recycling rates in Pensacola, Florida, tripled between 2010 and 2012 after an ambitious education campaign. This suggests that market failure in recycling could result from imperfect information as well as externalities.

Figure 8.5 applies the social efficiency analysis introduced in Chapter 3 to the case of recycled paper. The market demand reflects private marginal benefit, which is derived from the market for products made of recycled paper. The market supply reflects the private marginal cost of recycling. We will assume that the private and social costs of recycling are the same, while the private and social benefits differ due to externalities, as discussed in the previous paragraph. In the presence of marginal external benefits, private incentives result in recycling at the inefficient level Q_p.

There are a number of available remedies for this inefficiency. The socially efficient level, Q_s, can be attained if the marginal external benefits are internalized or the marginal cost is reduced, either of which could result from subsidies or Coasian side payments. Many communities lower the marginal cost of recycling by subsidizing curbside pickup and drop-off sites. If estimated correctly, Q_s can also be attained via mandated recycling, as occurs in Japan for specified home appliances, and in the United States for oil and tires, among many other examples. Remedies also include per-unit waste fees, moral suasion, advertising, and the promotion of markets for products made from recycled materials.

The penultimate economic message is that only when the *social* marginal benefits and costs are considered can the efficient decision be made. Improvements could be made over extremist positions for or against recycling by reverting to the correct efficiency criterion—the equality of social marginal cost and social marginal benefit—and applying it on the basis of unbiased estimates. Cost estimates must include the time and energy required to sort and transport recycled materials, and expenditures on recycling equipment, containers, and labor. In 2013, New York City paid about $72 per ton to recycle glass and metal.

The benefits from recycling include revenues from the resale of some recycled

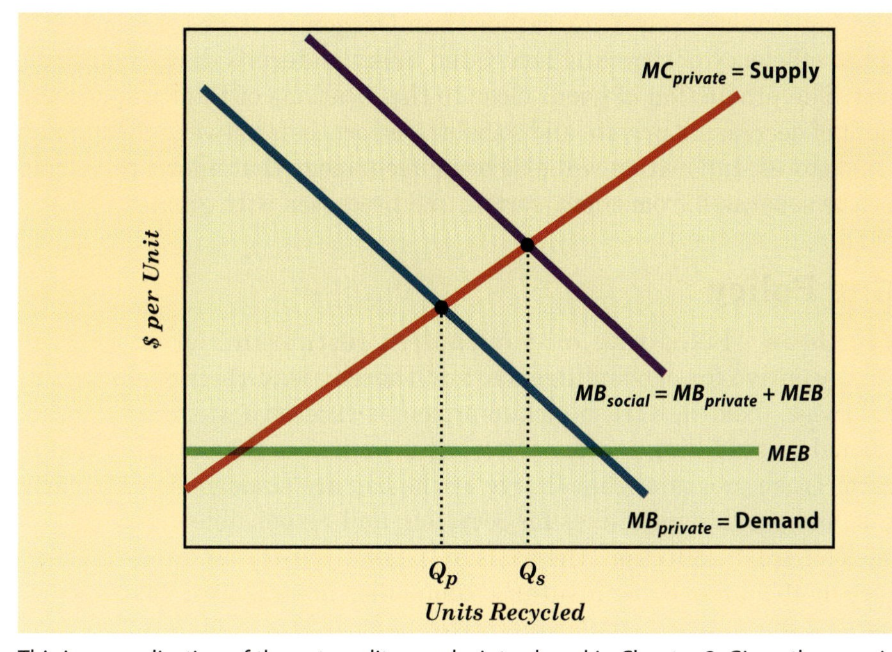

Figure 8.5 *The Market for Recycled Paper*

This is an application of the externality graphs introduced in Chapter 3. Given the marginal external benefit from recycling, the social marginal benefit exceeds the private marginal benefit ($MB_{private}$). The privately optimal quantity of recycling is Q_p, which falls short of the socially efficient quantity Q_s. Policies intended to bring recycling efforts to the efficient level include legislated recycling, per-unit waste fees, moral suasion, advertising, curbside pickup, Coasian side payments, and subsidies.

materials and an array of gains from cost-avoidance. For example, recycling corresponds with decreased municipal solid waste production. With a waste disposal cost of $86 per ton in New York City, a ton of paper sent for recycling represents $86 in savings on landfill or incineration costs beyond the roughly $10 per ton received for the recycled material. Overall, recycling and composting could save New York City $60 million per year by diverting 30 percent of its waste away from landfills.

Beyond missing the health and environmental benefits, the market value of recyclables also does not reflect the value of education, habit formation, symbolic gestures, and what Walker and Desrochers (1999) call the rituals of recycling. Exposure to the recycling process teaches children about resource scarcity. The exercise of recycling engages participants in environmental stewardship that might be the precursor for broader investments in volunteerism and environmentalism. Involvement in recycling makes people more aware of the level of waste they generate and may promote conservation. And recyclers derive good feelings or a "warm glow" from doing what they feel is the right thing.

As technology improves and recycling trends continue, so will the efficiency of recycling. In the past, manufacturing plants have logically been located close to the source of virgin materials, which is often not so close to the source of recycled materials. In the future, manufacturing plants can be built closer to the source of recovered materials—New York rather than Oregon in the case of paper—improving the efficiency of recycling heavy and bulky materials that are difficult to transport. The production of goods close to the locations of their use has the added benefit of decreasing private and social transport costs between the production sites and stores. Innovation will also bring technology that allows recyclable materials to be separated from trash, sorted, and processed with greater ease.

Recycling Policy

Pay as You Throw Fixed-rate all-you-can-eat restaurants eliminate the financial disincentive for overindulgence, and thereby lead their customers to overeat. Likewise, fixed-rate trash pickup promotes excessive waste generation, as the marginal cost of filling another trash bag is limited to the trouble of taking it to the curb. Trash programs that charge by the bag are analogous to à la carte restaurants, and provide incentives for recycling and responsible consumption. Per-unit fees for trash collection, the basis of "pay-as-you-throw" programs, are now in place in 46 states. Some insurance companies are adopting "pay-as-you-drive" programs that provide similar incentives to drive less. And in Australia, a program aimed to decrease the water consumed by flushing toilets among other uses has humorously been dubbed "pay-as-you-go."

The incentives of pay-as-you-throw programs appear to matter. Miranda et al. (1994) studied market-based incentives to reduce municipal solid waste with survey data from 21 U.S. cities. They found that pay-as-you-throw programs reduced solid waste disposal by 18.5 to 47.5 percent. Likewise, Folz and Giles (2002) found that recycling rates increased significantly due to the incentives provided by pay-as-you-throw fees.

Bottle Bills Bottle bills are laws that require a deposit on recyclable cans and bottles. Deposits of five to ten cents apply to standard glass, plastic, and aluminum beverage containers. Consumers pay the deposit at the time of purchase, and receive the same amount back upon returning the containers to any participating store for recycling. If a consumer is not sufficiently swayed by the incentive to recycle and throws a bottle on the ground, the incentive remains for passersby to return the bottle and obtain the deposit. Bottle bills are in place in 11 U.S. states, Canada, and 9 European nations.

The incentives of these policies seem to matter as well. A study of 7 states found that, after passage of a bottle bill, there was a 70 to 83 percent reduction of beverage container litter and a 30 to 47 percent reduction in total litter. Michigan policymakers attribute a 6 to 8 percent reduction in overall waste flow to their bottle bill, and residents of New York saw aluminum can recycling increase by 64 percent and glass bottle recycling increase by 74 percent after the passage of a bottle bill. A study by Franklin Associates, Ltd, estimated that the New York bottle bill saves the energy equivalent of 2 million barrels of oil each year.

On the negative side, the patchwork of states with bottle bills presents perverse incentives for those living near the border between a state with a bottle

reality check

Charting the Course to Sustainability

Any meaningful change in the sustainability of human behavior would likely come as the result of long-term, concerted efforts. Several international initiatives seek to lay the foundation for critical progress on this front.

In earlier groundwork, the Oslo Ministerial Roundtable of 1995 defined the goal of sustainable production and consumption (SP&C) as "the production and use of goods and services that respond to basic human needs and bring a better quality of life, while minimizing the use of natural resources, toxic materials, and emissions of waste and pollutants over the life cycle, so as not to jeopardize the needs of future generations."

The World Business Council for Sustainable Development (WBCSD) is currently preparing a sustainable development agenda for 2015 to succeed the Millennium Development Goals established by the United Nations. The WBCSD and the United Nations Development Program (UNDP) joined forces to promote their own brand of sustainability, eco-efficiency. As defined at the Antwerp Workshop on Eco-efficiency, eco-efficiency is "reached by the delivery of competitively priced goods and services that satisfy human needs and bring quality of life while progressively reducing ecological impacts and resource intensity throughout the life cycle to a level at least in line with the earth's estimated carrying capacity." The WBCSD identified the following paths to eco-efficiency:

- Reduce the material intensity of goods and services
- Reduce the energy intensity of goods and services
- Reduce toxic dispersion
- Enhance material recyclability
- Maximize sustainable use of renewable resources
- Increase material durability
- Increase the service intensity of goods and services

The UNDP and the WBCSD hope to demonstrate the profitability of eco-efficiency and clean production, catalyze sustainable-development partnerships between industries and governments, and promote sustainability at a global level. In the quest for sustainability, these efforts are among the first steps, which the ancient Chinese proverb reminds us are the beginning of every long journey.

bill and a state without one. Retailers in states with bills worry that customers will purchase their beverages in neighboring states where no deposit is required. Although border crossing is not a problem in Hawaii, space is. Shopkeepers there and elsewhere point out that the storage of increasing numbers of recycled containers places a strain on space constraints. Major beverage producers oppose bottle bills because they necessitate more staffing and accounting to track the bottles and deposits. The slow adoption of bottle bills within the United States reflects this contention. At the same time, no existing bottle bill has been repealed, so apparently to know one is to like one.

Broader Policies Toward Sustainability

More ambitious initiatives are needed to meet sustainability goals, and the strong sustainability criterion in particular. Many of the environmental policies discussed in this text would contribute to sustainability. The three proposals featured in this section have appeared in many contexts, and were synthesized by Robert Costanza as a possible foundation for policy consensus.

Natural Capital Depletion Tax

A substantial national capital depletion (NCD) tax on consumers could constrain natural capital exploitation to sustainable levels while serving interests on both sides of the sustainability issue. An NCD tax would safeguard natural capital in the event that ample substitutes were not forthcoming and promote the development of substitutes to the extent that they are available. In that way, Costanza (1994b) suggests that an NCD tax should appeal to weak- and strong-sustainability advocates alike.

The size of the tax would be a source of debate, as is the size of any tax. The tax would fall heavily on fossil fuels. As mentioned in Chapter 7, economists have estimated the social marginal cost of gasoline, for example, although a compromise among the various estimates would be necessary. Acquiescing in a ballpark figure, Costanza writes, "It would be helpful to have better quantitative measures of these perceived costs, just as it would be helpful to carry along an altimeter when we jump out of an airplane. But we would all prefer to have a parachute than an altimeter if we could only take one thing."

Other details would need to be addressed as well. This tax would fall largely on consumers of energy and energy-intensive products. Because the poor spend a larger fraction of their income on energy than the rich, the tax would be regressive. As a remedy, the revenues from the NCD tax could be used to decrease income taxes and perhaps even provide a negative income tax, so as to make the overall tax effect neutral or progressive (placing a higher burden on the rich). The issue of unfair competition from abroad is addressed below.

Precautionary Polluter Pays Principle

Environmental policy strategists struggle with the uncertainty of the future. Maybe depletion of the ozone layer will cause the ice caps to melt. Maybe pollution will choke the food chain or cause cancer rates to skyrocket. Maybe we will not find physical capital to replace depleted natural capital. Rather than taking a stance on one side or the other, the precautionary polluter pays principle (4P) takes the bottle bill concept and makes a safety net out of it.

The idea is that those who take risks with natural resources would post a bond large enough to cover the best estimate of the worst-case scenario for future environmental damages. For example, those building a landfill would have to post an assurance bond sufficient to pay for cleanup costs in the event of groundwater contamination. This causes the resource users to internalize the risk burden associated with their behavior. If subsequent damages are not forthcoming, or it can be demonstrated that the worst-case scenario is not as bad as originally thought, the users receives the portion of the bond (plus interest) corresponding with the absolved risk.

If damage does occur, the deposited funds are used to repair and compensate for those damages. If there is no damage, the entire deposit plus interest is returned to the resource user. In that way, activities that cause no harm end up with no loss from the deposit, unless they could have invested the funds elsewhere for a higher rate of return.

Ecological Tariffs

On their own, NCD tax and 4P policies do not motivate sustainability outside their jurisdictions, and present problems with unfair competition from firms in countries with lower environmental standards. If Country A adopts an NCD tax and Country B does not, firms in Country A will have higher costs and thus difficulty competing with imports from Country B. Ecological tariffs could prevent the short-run competitive advantages of low standards and provide incentives for improved environmental policies among exporting countries. In effect, the imposition of tariffs can bring the cost of unsustainable production on par with that of sustainable practices.

Countries with comparable NCD taxes and 4P policies could engage in free trade on fair terms and with common safeguards for natural capital. Ecological tariffs would be collected on exports from countries without such policies. Since the tariffs should reflect the burden of uncertainty and the value of natural capital lost in the exporting countries, investment of the revenues into natural capital in those countries would help remedy the underlying environmental neglect.

Whether or not these policies are implemented as stated, they represent prototypes for available policy directions. They are starting points and options to build on. And they exemplify the ways in which economic incentives can be managed to achieve sustainability targets.

Summary

With the goal of providing intergenerational equity in opportunity, sustainability can be seen as a constraint on growth in deference to the future. Sustained intergenerational welfare would require the maintenance of capital levels, including physical capital, natural capital, human capital, and social capital. This goal can be achieved by harvesting renewable resources only at the rate of replacement, exploiting depletable resources only as fast as renewable substitutes are found, and creating wastes only at the rate of assimilation.

The appropriate criterion for sustainability is under debate. Advocates of weak sustainability feel that natural and physical capital are substitutes, and that the maintenance of the total capital stock would provide nondecreasing welfare. They believe that short-run investments of natural capital will be rewarded with sustainable long-run payoffs from physical capital. Supporters of strong sustainability argue that natural and physical capital are complements. They feel that neoclassical economists place too much faith in the unrealized substitutability of natural and physical capital, and too little emphasis on pollution and other externalities. In their view, welfare can only be maintained by a nondecreasing stock of natural capital.

Policies that promote sustainable practices include pay-as-you-throw trash programs and bottle bills, both of which have increased recycling rates. The efficiency of recycling particular materials depends on fluctuating markets for end products, technology, and the cost of disposal alternatives. Those conducting efficiency analyses must be careful to consider all of the social costs and benefits of recycling. Costs include the value of time spent sorting materials, and the expense of collection and processing operations. Benefits include the avoided externalities from energy use, pollution, and resource use associated with waste disposal and the processing of virgin materials.

More ambitious policy options would help decision makers internalize the costs of their actions. A natural capital depletion tax would steer manufacturers toward conservation. A precautionary polluter pays principle would require deposits as security against potential environmental tragedies. And ecological tariffs would prevent unfair price competition from producers whose practices are unsustainable.

The debates over reasons and methods for sustainability rage on, but the concept has become a fixture within and beyond the fields of environmental and natural resource economics. Armed with an awareness of the relevant issues and approaches, you will be better equipped to contribute to the ongoing discussions that may alter daily life.

Problems for Review

1. For this problem you'll make use of a two-period model like the one in Figure 8.4. Suppose each period's net marginal benefit curve for oil is a straight line with a vertical intercept of $100 and a horizontal intercept of 50 barrels. Assume the discount rate is zero. What is the dynamically efficient allocation in each period if the total quantity of oil is 120 barrels? What is the dynamically efficient allocation in each period if the total quantity of oil is 60 barrels? Illustrate your answers with graphs.

2. *This problem requires the use of algebra.* Consider the scenario given in the previous problem with a total quantity of 60 barrels of oil. Note that in each period, $MB = 100 - 2Q$. What is the dynamically efficient allocation if the discount rate is 10 percent per period?

3. Choose one policy from the chapter that you could implement locally. What do you think would be the biggest challenge to implementation and how would you overcome it?

4. Identify a particular group that is likely to object to an NCD tax and explain the basis for their objection.

5. Identify two groups that are likely to benefit from ecological tariffs and explain how they would benefit.

6. The world population is growing by about 80 million people per year. The growth in population and the depreciation of physical capital violate the assumptions of which "rule" as described in the chapter? Draw a modification of the total capital line in Figure 8.1 that would satisfy a desire for constant per-capita welfare, given increasing population growth.

7. Take a moment to reflect on the sustainability of your activities in the past week. Consider, for example, your acquisitions and your modes of travel.
   a) *What was your least-sustainable activity over the last week?*
   b) *What costs and benefits did you consider when deciding to carry out that activity?*
   c) *Was your decision socially efficient?*
   d) *If natural capital was involved, do you think that physical capital could become a substitute for the natural capital you used?*

8. Some claim that fervent recycling is the result of a "religion" of conservation that makes people feel good despite a lack of concrete reason. Suppose that the curves in Figure 8.5 exclude the value of such good feelings. Suppose further that when the value of good feelings is added to the private marginal benefit curve in Figure 8.5, the combined *MB* curve (monetary benefit plus good feelings benefit) is above the MB_{social} curve that excludes the value of these feelings. Re-create Figure 8.5 and add the combined *MB* curve as described. Would the quantity of recycling at the intersection of the combined *MB* curve and the *MC* curve be excessive from the standpoint of social efficiency?

9. The popularity of sustainability has flourished over the past decade. In your own opinion, how can this popularity be explained, given sustainability's likely betrayal of dynamic efficiency?

10. *(For those who have studied budget constraint/indifference curve diagrams and want a challenge.)* Draw a graph with trash pickup services on the horizontal axis and "other goods/services" on the vertical axis. Draw two budget constraints, one reflecting a fixed fee for unlimited trash pickup and one reflecting a pay-as-you-throw program. Use indifference curves to explain the likely effects of these two policies on the amount of trash individuals generate.

websurfer's challenge

1. Find a website that describes cutting-edge sustainable living. This might involve cohousing, green architecture, freeganism, or sustainable architecture.
2. Find a policy proposal relating to sustainable development put forth by an ecological economist and evaluate its message.
3. Find a website that speaks against some aspect of sustainable development and evaluate its message.
4. Find a website that discusses recycling policies or levels in your state and summarize your findings.

Internet Resources

Bottle Bill Resource Guide:
www.bottlebill.org

Example of Architects Focusing on Sustainability:
www.krausfitch.com

Fostering Sustainable Behavior:
www.cbsm.com

International Institute for Sustainable Development:
www.iisd.org/default.asp

List of Sustainable Development Organizations:
www.webdirectory.com/Sustainable_Development/

Marsh Commons Cohousing site:
www.northcoast.com/~startrak/

Towards Sustainability (UK):
www.towards-sustainability.co.uk

Further Reading

Ackerman, Frank. *Why Do We Recycle? Markets, Values, and Public Policy.* Washington, D.C.: Island Press, 1997. A report on the costs and merits of recycling, and an analysis of the effectiveness of market incentives as a motivator for efficient behavior.

Anderson, David A. *Treading Lightly: The Joy of Conservation, Moderation, and Simple Living*. Danville, KY: Pensive Press, 2009. A collection of information and ideas about sustainable living.

Arrow, Kenneth. "Rawls' Principle of Just Saving." *Swedish Journal of Economics* 75, no. 4 (1973): 323–335. A discussion of intergenerational equity.

Callan, Scott J., and Janet M. Thomas. "The Impact of State and Local Policies on the Recycling Effort." *Eastern Economic Journal* 23, no. 4 (1997): 411–423.

Castle, E. N., and R. P. Berrens. "Endangered Species, Economic Analysis, and the Safe Minimum Standard." *Northwest Environmental Journal* 9 (1993): 108–130. Explains the distinction between cost-benefit analysis and the safe minimum standard.

Ciriacy-Wantrup, S. V. *Resource Conservation.* Berkeley: University of California Press, 1952. An early discussion of safe minimum standards.

Costanza, Robert (ed.). *Ecological Economics: The Science and Management of Sustainability.* New York: Columbia University Press, 1994a. Provides an overview of the school of thought behind the strong sustainability criterion.

Costanza, Robert. "Three General Policies to Achieve Sustainability." In *Investing in Natural Capital: The Ecological Economics Approach to Sustainability*, edited by A. M. Jansson, M. Hammer, C. Folke, and R. Costanza, Washington, D.C.: Island Press, 1994b, 392–407. Describes policies meant to maintain the level of natural capital.

Daly, Herman E. "Sustainable Growth: An Impossibility Theorem." *Development* 40, no. 1 (1997): 121–125. Argues that the constraints of natural capital would prevent any sustained level of growth.

Daly, Herman E., and John B. Cobb, Jr. *For the Common Good: Redirecting the Economy Toward Community, the Environment, and a Sustainable Future.* Boston: Beacon Press, 1989. Introduces the index of sustainable economic welfare and presents comparisons between it and the gross national product.

Folz, David H., and Jacqueline N. Giles. "Municipal Experience with 'Pay-as-You-Throw' Policies: Findings from a National Survey." *State and Local Government Review* 34, no. 2 (2002): 105–115. Provides evidence that pay-as-you-throw programs cause recycling rates to increase significantly.

Hartwick, J. M. "Intergenerational Equity and the Investing of Rents from Exhaustible Resources." *American Economic Review* 67 (1977): 972–974. An important note that demonstrates the Hartwick rule.

Hicks, John R. *Value and Capital.* Oxford: Oxford University Press, 1975. An overview of economic theory by a Nobel Laureate.

Hiebert, Murray. "Recycling: A Fortune in Waste: Scarcity Forces Vietnam to Reuse Its Resources." *Far Eastern Economic Review* 156, no. 51, 23 (1993): 36. Estimates the resources conserved by scavengers in Hanoi.

Hornik, Jacob, Joseph Cherian, Michelle Madansky, and Chem Narayana. "Determinants of Recycling Behavior: A Synthesis of Research Results." *Journal of Socio-Economics* 24, no. 1 (1995): 105–127. Classifies variables affecting recycling from 67 empirical studies and proposes a model of consumer motivation.

Kinnaman, Thomas C. "Policy Watch: Examining the Justification for Residential Recycling." *Journal of Economic Perspectives* 20, no. 4 (2006): 219–232. An overview of recycling issues including cost, benefits, and landfill fees.

Miranda, Marie Lynn, Jess W. Everett, Daniel Blume, and Barbeau A. Roy, Jr. "Market-Based Incentives and Residential Municipal Solid Waste." *Journal of Policy Analysis and Management* 13, no. 4 (1994): 681–698. Survey research finding that pay-per-throw programs reduce waste levels.

Munger, Michael. "Think Globally, Act Irrationally: Recycling." *Library of Economics and Liberty* (July 2, 2007), available at http://econlib.org/library/Columns/y2007/Mungerrecycling.html. An argument that recycling often takes more energy than it saves.

Pearce, David, and Giles Atkinson. "Measuring Sustainable Development." In *Handbook of Environmental Economics*, edited by Daniel W. Bromley. Cambridge, MA: Blackwell, 1995, 166–181. A useful overview of weak and strong sustainability and international trade issues.

Pezzey, John C. V. *Sustainable Development Concepts: An Economic Analysis.* World Bank Environmental Paper No. 2, Washington, D.C., 1992. An overview of sustainability concepts, including sustainable development and survivability.

Solow, Robert. "On the Intergenerational Allocation of Natural Resources." *Scandinavian Journal of Economics* 88 (1986): 141–149. A classic discussion of sustainability across generations.

Sterner, Thomas, and Heleen Bartelings. "Household Waste Management in a Swedish Municipality: Determinants of Waste Disposal, Recycling and Composting." *Environmental and Resource Economics* 13 (1999): 473–491. An empirical study of the influence of policy and demographics on waste.

Tiller, Kelly H., Paul M. Jakus, and William M. Park. "Household Willingness to Pay for Drop-off Recycling." *Journal of Agricultural and Resource Economics* 22, no. 2 (1997): 310–320. A CVM study of the value of recycling opportunities in rural/suburban areas.

Toman, Michael A. "Economics and 'Sustainability': Balancing Trade-offs and Imperatives." *Land Economics* 70, no. 4 (1994): 399–413. Seeks to clarify the meaning of economic sustainability.

U.S. Census Bureau. *Statistical Abstract of the U.S.* Washington, D.C., 2010.

Vitousek, Peter M., Paul R. Ehrlich, Anne H. Ehrlich, and Pamela A. Matson. "Human Appropriation of the Products of Photosynthesis." *Bioscience* 36, no. 6 (1986): 368–373. Estimates a specific range for the proportion of solar energy that is appropriated by humans.

Walker, Jesse, and Pierre Desrochers. "Recycling Is an Economic Activity, Not a Moral Imperative." *The American Enterprise Online*, www.theamerican-enterprise.org/taejf99d.htm, Jan. 1999. Argues that some types of recycling are not efficient.

Wenger, R. B., C. R. Rhyner, and E. E. Wagoner. "Relating Disposal-Based Solid Waste Reduction Rates to Recycling Rates." *Resources, Conservation, and Recycling* 20, no. 4 (1997): 267–276. Estimates the correlation between recycling activity and the demand for municipal solid waste disposal.

World Commission on Environment and Development. *Our Common Future*. Oxford: Oxford University Press, 1987. A standard-setting document on sustainability.

Permaculture, a form of sustainable living, gets its name from contractions of permanent and culture as well as permanent and agriculture. Crystal Waters Permaculture Village is part of the Global Ecovillage Network. Learn more at http://gen.ecovillage.org/ or http://www.ecologicalsolutions.com.au/crystalwaters/.

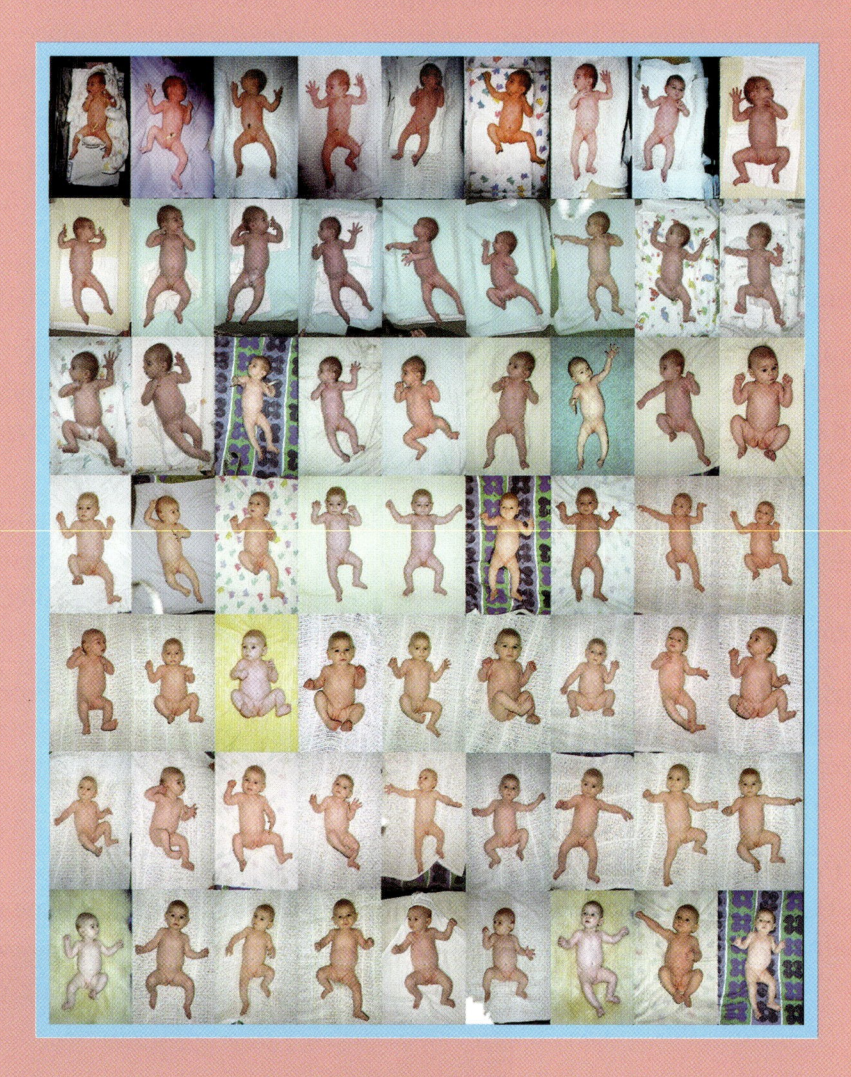

IMAGE BY BETSY SCHNEIDER

9 Population, Poverty, and Economic Growth

After exploring wilderness areas around the world and producing more than 115 films about the planet and its creatures, Jacques-Yves Cousteau called population growth "the primary source of environmental damage." For millennia the world population was nearly constant. Over the past century growth has become exponential, doubling every 30 to 40 years. Some of today's elderly have watched the world population quadruple.

A rising population means more mouths to feed, more homes to build, and more goods to manufacture. As population growth rates in developing countries march upward, and those in developed countries decline, the economic growth behind development can be seen as a panacea for population problems. But as a vehicle for many changes good and bad, economic growth is a double-edged sword. When properly conceived, it can eradicate poverty and rampant population growth; when haphazard, it can assault biodiversity with equal force.

Simon Kuznets (1955) found that as income per capita grew, income inequality first increased and then decreased. More recently, economists studying pollution have observed the same increasing and then decreasing pattern in response to income growth. Unfortunately, like population growth, growing income levels worsen the mounting international problem of waste generation, which appears to buck the Kuznets up-and-down scenario and just keep increasing.

Thomas Malthus (1798) feared that a lack of self-discipline would put population growth on a collision course with limited resources in the nineteenth century. He was wrong about the timing, but the logic of his argument—that a growing population must at some point outstrip the resources of the planet—has kept the concern alive and well. This chapter introduces the economics of population growth, the effects of income growth, and some reasons for optimism about economic growth in regard to the environment.

Population Growth and Resource Scarcity

Thomas Malthus

Even in the eighteenth century, the concept that the human population might outgrow its resources was not novel. In the preface to his 1798 *Essay on the Principle of Population*, Malthus himself wrote, "It is an obvious truth, which has been taken notice of by many writers, that population must always be kept down to the level of the means of subsistence." But for his eloquence and sway, Thomas Malthus has become the most famous of population theorists. The crux of Malthus's argument was that the insatiable human appetites for sex and food would lead to a disaster of resource inadequacy. He wrote, "towards the extinction of the passion between the sexes, no observable progress has hitherto been made."[1] Malthus argued that unchecked human reproduction would increase populations *geometrically*, causing them to double every so many years, while food supplies could only increase *arithmetically* by a constant amount per period due to diminishing marginal returns from land.

Malthus came to this conclusion after noting that in the United States, where resources were not a binding constraint, the population reportedly doubled every 25 years. As for food, Malthus reasoned that nowhere on Earth could food supplies double every 25 years, and at best they could grow by the amount of the 1798 food supply every 25 years. Starting with a food supply that would feed the 7 million people in his home of England, he felt the best-case scenario was that there would be enough food for 14 million people in 25 years, 21 million people in 50 years, 28 million people in 75 years, and so on. At the same time, if the population were unchecked and doubled over each 25-year period, there would be 14, 28, and 56 million people in 25, 50, and 75 years. Figure 9.1 illustrates the dreary conclusion that the food supply would fall short of consumptive needs after 25 years.

The **population growth rate** is the birth rate minus the death rate plus immigration minus emigration. Malthus warned that population growth rates that exceeded growth rates for food supplies would lead society into a **Malthusian population trap**, in which the subsistence level of food per capita limited the population. In the absence of deliberate restraints on population growth, natural checks would be inevitable. Malthus first described the checks on population as the misery of war, famine, and disease, along with havoc, hatred, and vice. In the

1 See Malthus (1798), p. 50.

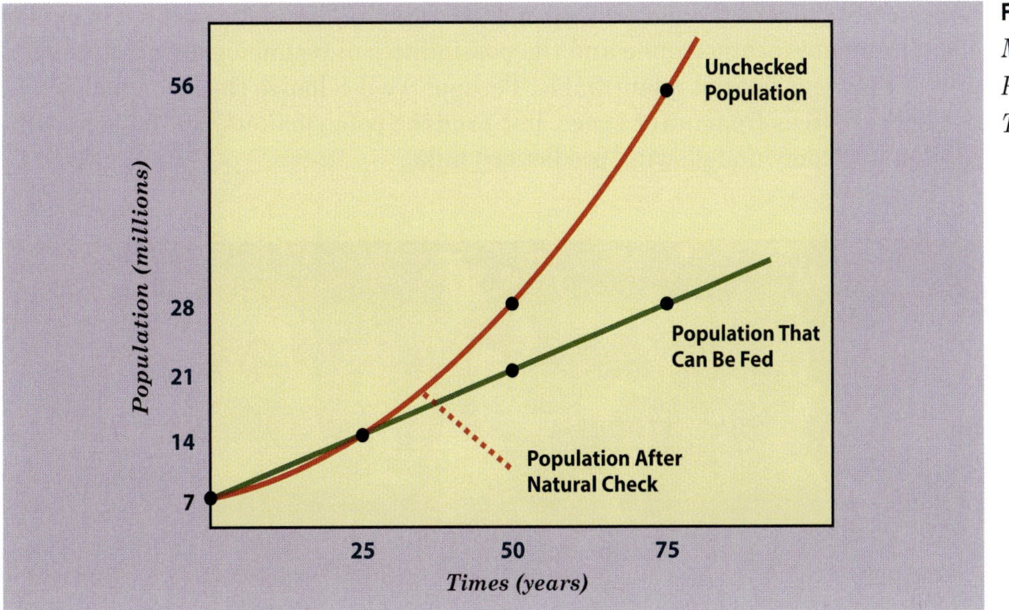

Figure 9.1 *Malthusian Population Trap*

Malthus reasoned that with the population doubling every 25 years and the means of subsistence increasing by a constant quantity each period, the population would inevitably exceed the available supplies of food and other resources. After that point, rather than being able to continue unchecked as on the solid curved line, the population would be brought back below the level for which there is food by the natural checks of famine, disease, and war, as indicated by the dotted line.

second edition of his essay, he added the check of moral restraint, explained as "delaying the gratification of passion from a sense of duty."

Malthus's theory of stagnating output per capita is consistent with the human experience over most of history.[2] However, the **agricultural revolution** of farming advances in the nineteenth and late eighteenth centuries, such as crop rotation and plows drawn by domesticated animals, resulted in rapid increases in food production. Then, the **green revolution** of chemical and technological advances in the twentieth century brought hybrid grains, chemical fertilizers, pesticides, mechanized harvesters, and irrigation equipment. These changes allowed food production to grow geometrically over most of the twentieth century and allayed the Malthusian fear of famine in many regions. England now has a population of 53 million and ample food to serve them.

The next section describes decreases in the birth rates of developed countries that have dealt a further blow to Malthusian predictions. Although increases in food production and decreases in population growth have dispelled past forecasts of doom, uncertainty remains. Global climate change, drought, and environmental toxicity could hinder food supplies, while most estimates project another doubling of the world population before stability becomes a reality. As explained in Chapters 8 and 10, the carrying capacity of the Earth and the

2 For a summary of related findings, see Galor and Weil (2000), p. 807.

terrestrial products of solar energy may become binding constraints.[3] The risks of environmental catastrophe and the possibilities of technological advancement are ever-present but not quantifiable. Perhaps we'll colonize the moon and obtain needed resources from outer space, but prudent policymakers will respond with caution to gloomy and glowing predictions alike.

The Economics of Population Growth

Since the time of Malthus, unforeseen advances in birth control have served as a partial substitute for moral restraint from sexual behavior. In many areas, population growth has been further curbed by improved opportunities for education, employment, and health care. These changes reflect new cultural attitudes toward women and their rights, as well as advancements in transportation, communication, and education systems.

Children have costs and benefits just like goods and services, placing the decision to have children under the purview of microeconomic analysis. It costs money to feed, clothe, and educate children, but the benefits can be great. Children become workers in the home, earners in the workforce, and caregivers as their parents grow old. As women gain access to better educational opportunities and higher wages, the opportunity cost of their time spent raising children increases. Career women tend to put off marriage and children until later in life when their childbearing years are limited. As incomes, sanitation, and health care improve, it is no longer necessary to conceive as many children in order to assure that some will survive. And as care for the elderly improves and labor-intensive jobs are replaced by mechanization, the value of children for labor and old-age security decreases.

The theory of demographic transition defines four stages of population growth for developing nations according to the relative frequency of births and deaths. As

3 For an accessible discussion of carrying capacity issues, see dieoff.org/page110.htm.

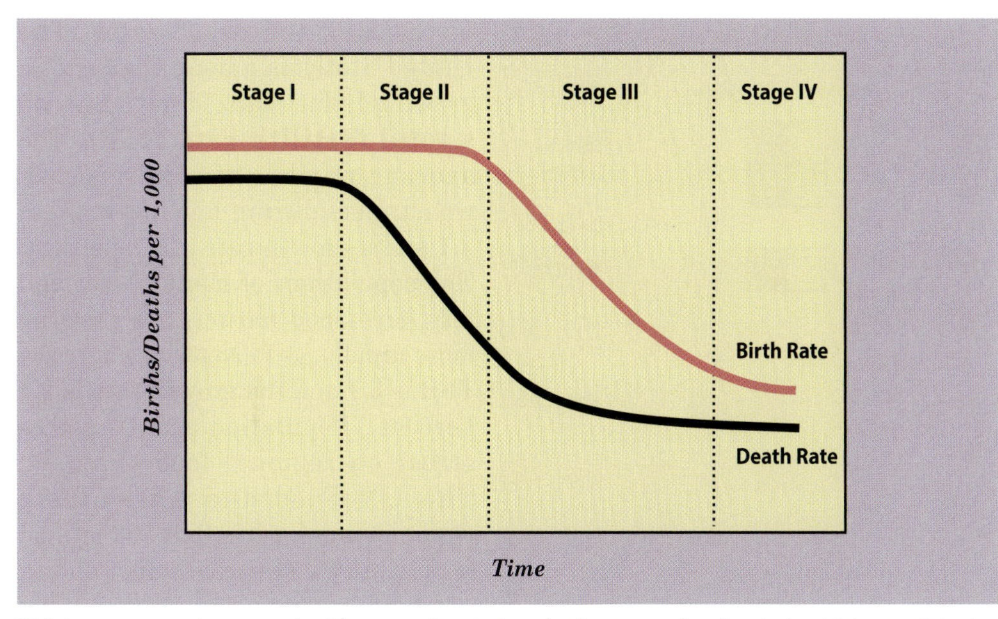

Figure 9.2 *Stages of Demographic Transition*

With improvements in income, health care, and sanitation, death rates tend to drop before birth rates, bringing a period of rapid population growth before birth rates drop as well.

illustrated in Figure 9.2, these stages are:

1. **High birth rates and high death rates.**
   Early in the development process, a paucity of educational opportunities, jobs, and family planning resources keeps birth rates high. Poverty, unsanitary conditions, and health service limitations cause high and fluctuating death rates. The net result is relatively low rates of population growth.

2. **High birth rates and declining death rates.**
   As development progresses, improvements in pubic health services, better nutrition, and safer living conditions increase life expectancy and decrease death rates. These changes are not immediately accompanied by a change in birth rates.

3. **Low death rates and declining birth rates.**
   Birth rates eventually fall as well, influenced by changing cultural attitudes and the availability of education, employment, and birth control.

4. **Low birth rates and low death rates.**
   After both birth rates and death rates have fallen, the nations experience relatively low population growth rates once again.

Western Europe developed roughly according to this theory, reaching Stage III at the beginning of the twentieth century, and is now experiencing nearly identical

Figure 9.3
Growth and Total Fertility

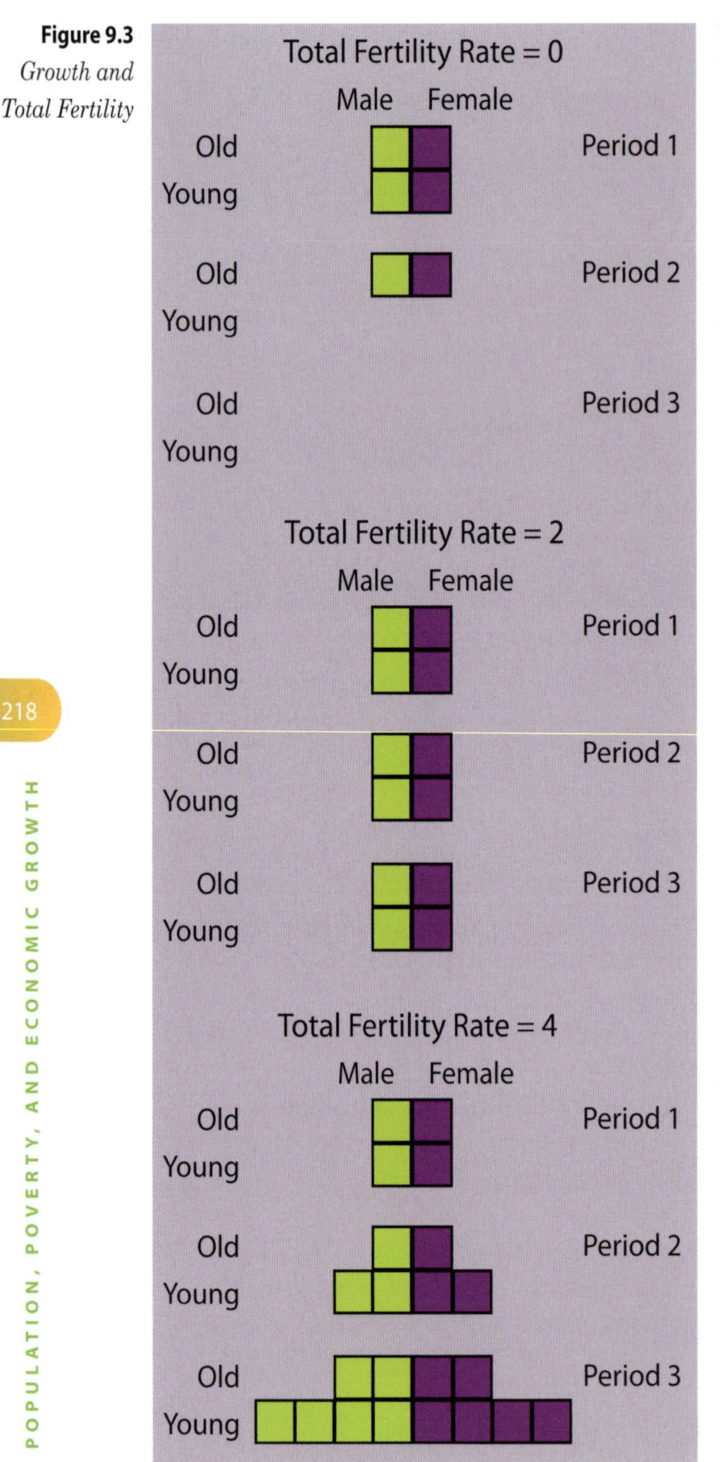

Total fertility rate matters. Beginning with two males and two females living two periods each and reproducing only when young, the population in Period 3 is 0, 4, or 12, depending on whether the total fertility rate is 0, 2, or 4.

birth rates and death rates. The United States is among the fastest-growing industrialized nations with a **total fertility rate** (TFR)—the average number of children each woman has during her lifetime—of 2.1 and a growth rate of 0.9 percent. The populations of many poorer and less developed nations are growing more rapidly, as in Nigeria, where the TFR is 5.7 and the growth rate is 2.7 percent.[4] Population growth places stress on regional food supplies. The UN Food and Agriculture Organization reports that 792 million people in 98 countries cannot obtain adequate nutrition,[5] and according to the World Food Program, 24,000 people die each day from starvation and related causes.[6]

Figure 9.3 illustrates the influence of the total fertility rate in a simplified situation in which people are either young or old. After each period the young are able to reproduce, the young become old, and the old die. Each green square represents a male, each purple square represents a female, and half of each age group is assumed to be female. In period 1 there is one male and one female in each age group.

A total fertility rate of zero as in the top scenario of Figure 9.3 means there is no reproduction. In period 2, those who were old in period 1 die, those who were young in period 2 become old, and there are no new young people because there were no births. In period 3 the old from period 2 are dead and there is no one left.

4 For this type of data on any country, see www.census.gov/ipc/www/idbsum.html.

5 See www.fao.org/docrep/x8200e/x8200e02.htm.

6 See www.wfp.org/aboutwfp/introduction/overview.html.

Strict celibacy and the resulting TFR of 0 led to the demise of the Shaker religion that began in England and spread to America in the nineteenth century. The regional TFR of 0.41 in Heilongjiang, China, is the lowest on record.

A total fertility rate of 2, as in the middle scenario, allows the young generation to exactly replace itself before turning old. In each new period there are two new young people to replace the two people who grew old. In reality, a TFR of 2 will lead to a slight decrease in population over time because, unlike in this model, some people die early in life.

With a total fertility rate of 4, each young pair is replaced by two young pairs in the next period. The population triples from 4 to 12 between period 1 and period 3. In period 4 the population would be 24 and in period 5 the population would be 48. In 2013 there were 40 countries with TFRs above 4, including Afghanistan (5.54), Angola (5.49), Ethiopia (5.31), and Mali (6.25).

The mathematics of population growth are complicated by the age and gender structure of the population. For a given population size and total fertility rate, a population can have zero, negative, or positive population growth, depending on its age structure. A population that is disproportionately beyond childbearing age or of a single gender carries less reproductive momentum than younger, more gender-balanced populations. The average age in many developed nations is increasing, while shorter life expectancies and rapid growth contribute to younger populations in many developing countries. Figure 9.4 illustrates the age structure in Canada and Uganda. Although each country has approximately 33 million citizens, the large number of Ugandans of childbearing age give the country tremendous population momentum. The population growth rate is 3.6

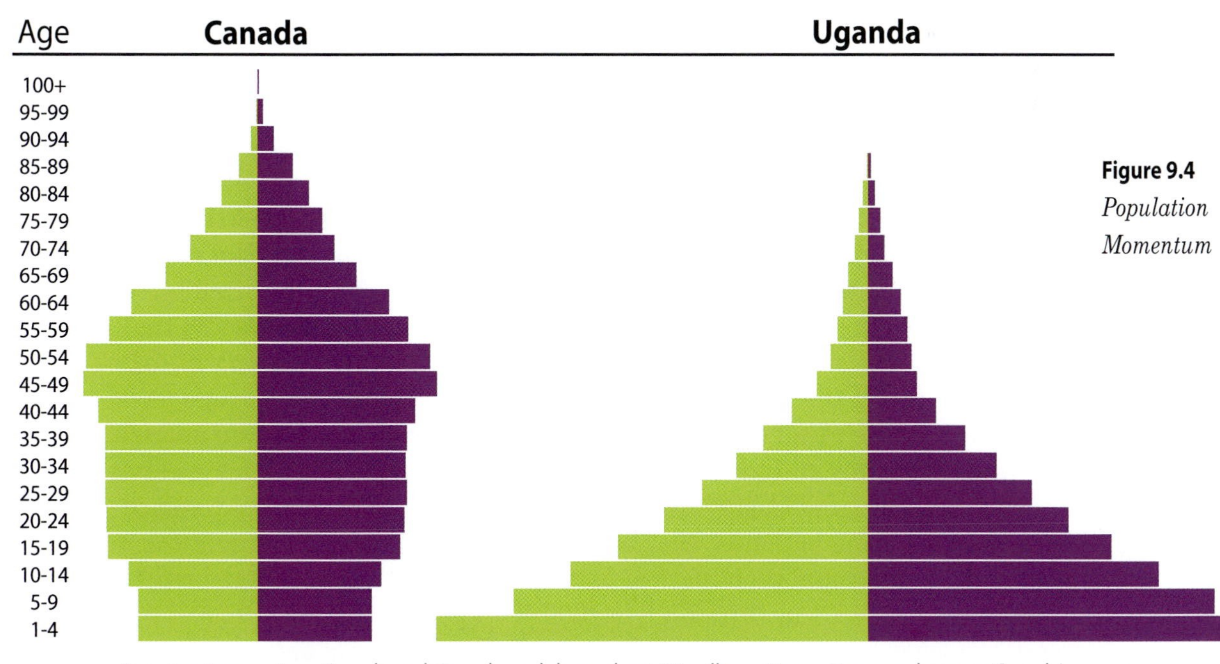

Figure 9.4 *Population Momentum*

Age structure matters. Canada and Uganda each have about 33 million citizens. However, because Canada's population is concentrated at non-childbearing ages and most of Uganda's population is of childbearing age, the growth rate is 0.9 percent (0.3 percent without immigration) in Canada and 3.6 percent in Uganda.

Figure 9.5 *World Population Growth*

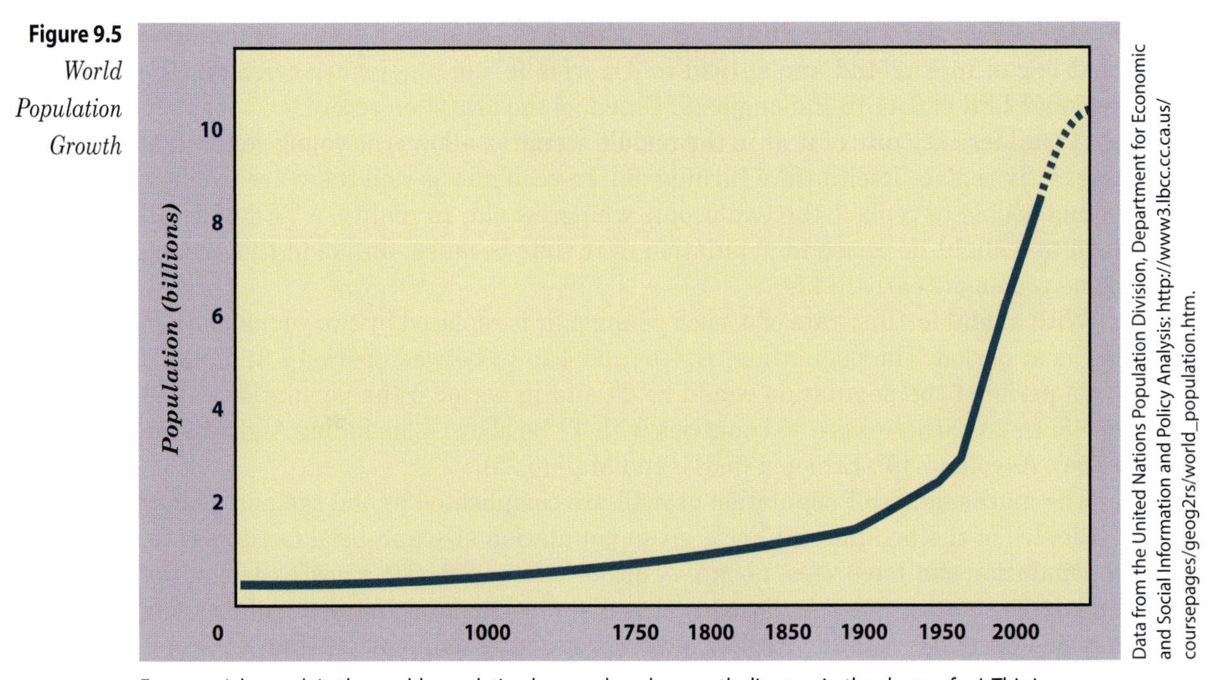

Exponential growth in the world population has produced a growth diagram in the shape of a J. This is expected to level off to form an S at a population of around 10 billion people.

percent in Uganda and only 0.9 percent (0.3 percent without immigration) in Canada. When a high proportion of the population is young, even when the total fertility rate falls below the replacement rate of just over two infants per woman, the population can continue to grow for several decades as larger, younger generations replace themselves while smaller, older generations pass away.

In terms of policy, some efforts to reduce population growth have addressed determinants of the demand for children with opportunities for education, employment, and care for the elderly. For example, Grameen banks in Bangladesh make loans to help women start small businesses. The subsequent employment increases the opportunity cost of bearing children, and the loan workshops include the provision of family planning information. The cost of avoiding unwanted pregnancies is sometimes decreased with subsidized birth control. In 2009, efforts in India included expanded energy availability so that young adults might stay up watching television rather than engaging in sex. Other policies target the marginal cost of children. In 1979, China began a one-child-per-couple policy that imposed fines of as much as half of a couple's annual salary when too many children were delivered. Some couples lost land grants, loans, supplies, jobs, and Communist Party membership, while doctors received bonuses for sterilizing patients. The goal was to limit China's population to 1.2 billion in 2000. The population reached 1.3 billion in 2000, but the total fertility rate decreased from 5.01 in 1970 to 1.8 in 2000. This partial "success" came at the expense of alleged human rights violations and large numbers of abortions.[7]

7 See, for example, www.cnn.com/2002/WORLD/asiapcf/east/07/23/china.abortion/.

Figure 9.5 illustrates the creeping world population growth until around 1900 and the exponential growth since that time. The J-shaped population expansion—some have called it an explosion—is expected to level off to form a logistic S-curve at a world population of around 10 billion.

Population, Poverty, and Other Determinants of Waste

The Growing Problem of Municipal Solid Waste

Economic theory suggests that aggregate demand grows with populations and incomes, resulting in increased production and consumption. Consumption begets waste. Residents of Europe, the United States, and Japan—a relatively wealthy 16 percent of the world population—are responsible for about 80 percent of natural resource consumption on an annual basis. The annual purchasing habits of the average U.S. citizen require the use of 25 tons of raw materials, and the 4.6 percent of the world population living in the United States operate about one-third of the world's automobiles and consume one-quarter of the global energy supply.[8]

Municipal solid waste (MSW) comes from households, small industrial enterprises, and municipalities. It is made up of paper (28.5%), food scraps (13.9%), yard trimmings (13.4%), plastics (12.4%), metals (9.0%), rubber, leather, and textiles (8.4%), wood (6.4%), glass (4.6%), and miscellaneous other materials (3.4%). U.S. residents generate about 4.4 pounds of municipal solid waste per person per day, more than any other Organization for Economic Cooperation and

After decades of municipal solid waste dumping nearby, "Glass Beach" in Hawaii is made up almost entirely of crushed bits of glass and pottery that have washed up on shore.

8 See www.cnn.com/US/9910/12/population.cosumption/.

reality check

Trash on Vacation: Barges of Garbage

As the population's waste generation exceeds the carrying capacity of domestic landfills, urban garbage goes on some amazing adventures. On March 22, 1987, Captain Duffy St. Pierre departed New York with 3,186 tons of trash aboard the *Mobro 4000*. New York's landfills were full, and the intent was to ferry the trash to Morehead City, North Carolina, where it could be turned into methane fuel. North Carolina officials turned the trash away after hearing that it might contain medical waste. The *Mobro* was then rejected by Louisiana and thwarted by the Mexican Navy in the Yucatán Channel. Belize and the Bahamas were among the six states and three countries that refused the trash. Returning to New York, the *Mobro* was prevented from docking in Queens by a court order, but it was allowed to anchor in New Jersey before a final trip to Brooklyn, where the cargo was incinerated. The 430 tons of ash were laid to rest where the journey began, in Islip, New York, after traveling for three months and 6,000 miles.

July of 2002 marked the end of another famous refuse cruise that went off and on for 16 years. In that case the garbage had already been incinerated, and there were 15,500 tons of ash with no place to go. Starting in Pennsylvania, the ash was hauled onto a barge called the *Khian Sea*, which found no takers in Bermuda, Honduras, or Chile. A load of 2,500 tons of the ash was dumped on a beach in Haiti, while the remaining 13,000 tons went "deep sea diving." Haiti did not want any of the ash, and sent it on the barge *Santa Lucia* to Florida. Florida spent $614,000 shipping the ash by rail to Hagerstown, Maryland, and from there it was trucked to the Mountain View landfill in Franklin County, Pennsylvania.

As the Pennsylvania ash was finding its way home in 2002, New York Sanitation Commissioner John Doherty was recycling the idea of sending trash to the Caribbean, saying, "could we find an island and do something?" (see www.mindfully.org/Plastic/Recycling/Response-NYC-Garbage1jul02.htm). In support of this type of practice, in December of 1991, Lawrence Summers, then World Bank chief economist and current director of the National Economic Council, wrote in an internal memo:

> *The measurements of the costs of health-impairing pollution depends on the foregone earnings from increased morbidity and mortality. From this point of view a given amount of health-impairing pollution should be done in the country with the lowest cost, which will be the country with the lowest wages. I think the economic logic behind dumping a load of toxic waste in the lowest-wage country is impeccable and we should face up to that. (See www.whirledbank.org/ourwords/summers.html.)*

Summers apologized for the memo the next day. He seems to have forgotten that there are many types of costs beyond foregone earnings; environmental costs are among them. It follows from better economic logic that countries with low wages often have large populations, and thus large labor supplies that suppress wage rates. To dump toxic waste in those places would be to cause inefficiently large losses in human life.

As growing urban populations produce mounting volumes of municipal solid waste, we can send it on vacation, but what goes around has a tendency to come around. Ditto for memos.

Development (OECD) country. The residents of Mexico, Turkey, and the Czech Republic, for example, produce less than half as much waste per capita.[9]

Figure 9.6 indicates the growth in MSW generation in the United States. The waste per person started to drop after 2000, although population growth caused the total amount of waste to continue its ascent. The volume of our waste may reflect broader societal attitudes. Per-capita waste generation increased by only 12 percent during the decade of the 1970s, which spawned the EPA and Earth Day, and then by 24 percent during the "me" decade of the 1980s. Increases of 2 percent and –6 percent in the 1990s and 2000s coincide with renewed environmentalism spurred by famous garbage barge fiascoes (see the Reality Check on page 222), scientific acknowledgement of global climate change, visible effects of pollution, gas shortages, information sharing via the Internet, and educational efforts such as former Vice President Al Gore's documentary, *An Inconvenient Truth*.

The previous section explained that development can help to stabilize population growth, and the section that follows describes evidence that development can lead to higher standards for environmental quality. In those respects there are reasons for developing countries to emulate the performance

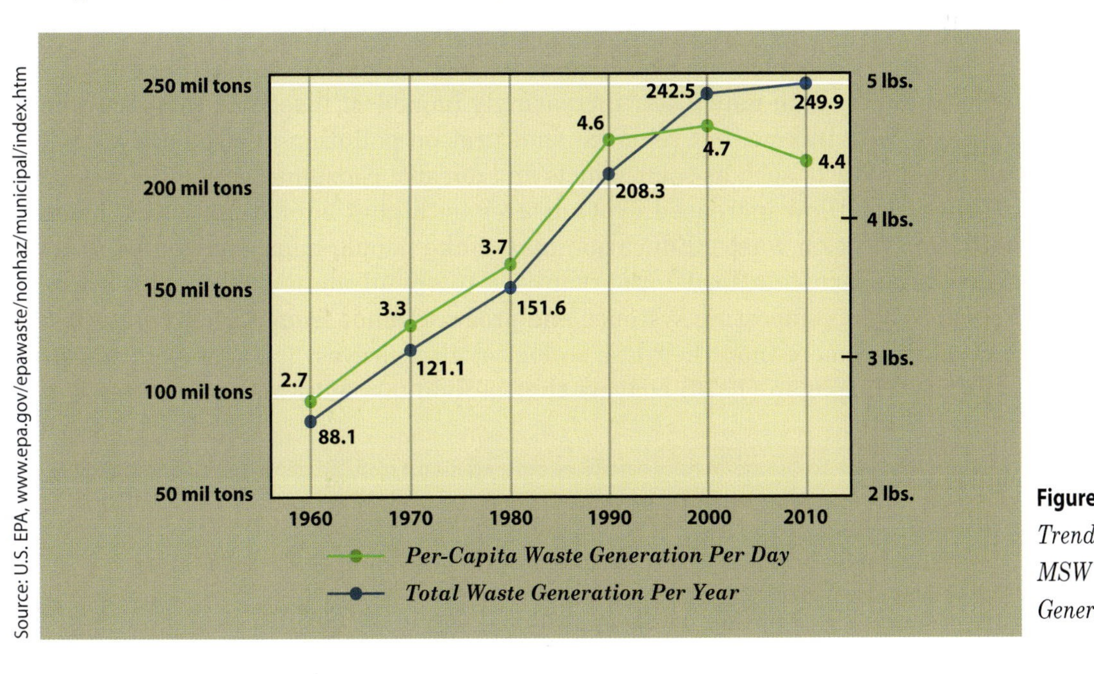

Figure 9.6 *Trends in MSW Generation*

9 See U.S. Bureau of the Census (2004), table 1332.

of developed countries, but in terms of waste generation, the opposite is true. The growing scarcity of landfill sites will require policymakers in developed countries to bring their levels of waste generation closer to the levels of their poorer neighbors.

Belgium, Britain, Germany, Luxemburg, and the Netherlands reportedly have less than ten years of landfill capacity left.[10] The same is true for many U.S. states.[11] Pennsylvania and Virginia, which currently have excess landfill space, receive waste from dozens of other states.[12] The number of U.S. landfills has declined from 7,924 in 1988 to less than 2,000 today, although the average size of landfills has risen.[13] As existing dumpsites are filled and urban sprawl pushes new sites further from urban centers, the direct and external costs of transporting and land-filling MSW increase. Beyond transportation issues, potential external costs include groundwater contamination at landfills and toxic ash emissions from the 17 percent of U.S. MSW that is incinerated.[14]

Demographic Trends and the Determinants of Waste[15]

The demographic determinants of waste become relevant as the characteristics of the world population change, and as we have opportunities to slow or accelerate these changes. Income, education, agrarian populations, population density, age structure, and ethnic makeup are all slated for widespread change. In the United States, real median incomes are increasing in every region of the country, and mean incomes are on the rise for each income quintile. Education levels are also on the rise. Since 1970 the percentage of the adult population with less than a high school diploma has decreased from 44 percent to 17 percent, while the percentage with at least some college education has more than doubled, from 22 percent to 58 percent.

The effects of education and income on MSW generation are theoretically indeterminate. Both may foster increasingly immodest lifestyles. Consumption increases with income, but so do expenditures on pollution-abating and waste-reducing products such as solar panels and durable consumer goods. Increasing incomes also allow increased expenditures on higher education, which has a negative effect on waste. Education may make people more environmentally aware, and income affords opportunities to spend money on conservation. Recycling bins, composting systems, and products made from recycled materials generally cost more than their less ecological alternatives. The economic models of Conway Lackman (1976) suggest that individuals with higher incomes will

10 See www.independent.co.uk/news/uk/home-news/uk-warned-it-will-run-out-of-landfill-sites-in-eight-years-2021136.html.

11 See https://apps.asce.org/reportcard/2005/page.cfm?id=33.

12 See www.actionpa.org/waste/.

13 See http://www.environmentalistseveryday.org/docs/research-bulletin/Municipal-Solid-Waste-Landfill-Facts.pdf.

14 See www.epa.gov/wastes/nonhaz/municipal/wte/basic.htm and Denison and Ruston (1990).

15 Data on trends were obtained from the U.S. Census Bureau (www.census.gov) and the Population Reference Bureau (www.ameristat.org). Unless otherwise noted, findings on the determinants of waste are from Anderson (2005).

generate relatively more solid waste.[16] Given the higher opportunity cost of their time, Lackman reasons that high-income groups will prefer to spend money on disposable items rather than spending time on repairable or returnable goods. Subsequent empirical research supports these findings.

Education may teach alternatives to resource exploitation and convey the repercussions of waste. Some secondary school curricula require students to construct solar water heaters and learn conservation techniques. Some college-level courses provide exposure to more advanced conservation methods. And some college campuses bring students into contact with recycling bins and environmentalists. For such reasons, college-level education is found to have a negative effect on waste-generation levels.

Rural areas offer improved opportunities for composting and on-site disposal. They also offer inferior access to retail shopping venues, perhaps reducing the temptation to dispose of assets that are maintainable or reusable. Anecdotal evidence includes quilts made from old clothing and tractors built from old parts. The stereotypes of frugality among farmers and rural communities are borne out in research findings that waste increases as the number of farmers and the land per capita decrease. Scott J. Callan and Janet M. Thomas (1997) also find that population density has a negative and significant effect on recycling levels.

Attitudes and culture also matter. Modern Eskimo and Aleutian cultures carry remnants of historical reverence for the animals that sustained their communities,[17] and the mentality that no piece of flesh or bone should go to waste. These groups are found to produce less waste. Over the next 25 years, the Asian, American Indian, Eskimo, Aleutian, and Pacific Islander population is expected to increase from 4.5 percent to 7 percent of the U.S. population.

A crowded Florida theme park. The U.S. population growth rate is low, but our consumption per person is high. It would take over five planets identical to the Earth to provide enough resources for everyone to consume at the rate of the average North American. For details, see www.myfootprint.org.

16 See Lackman (1976).

17 For example, whaling ship captain Burton "Atqann" Rexford wrote: "The bowhead [whale] is our brother. Our elders tell us that the whales present themselves to us so that we may continue to live. If we dishonor our brother or disturb his home, he will not come to us anymore." See the *World Council of Whalers News*, www.worldcouncilofwhalers.com/Newsletter/NL93.html.

Figure 9.7 *Environmental Kuznets Curve*

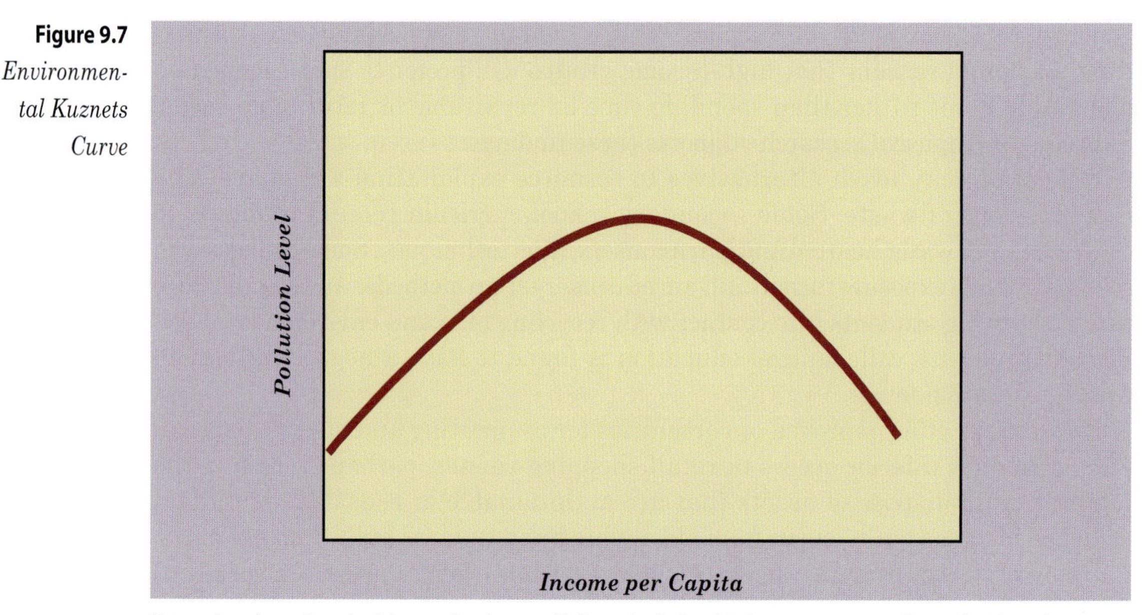

Researchers have found evidence of an inverse-U-shaped relationship between some pollution levels and income per capita. This suggests that with the right approach, economic growth need not be accompanied by environmental degradation.

Age may play an important role in resource management. Today's seniors, who lived through the imposed frugality of the depression (or were closer to the generation that did), generate less waste than younger adults or children. Over the next 25 years, the under-20 and 20-to-64 populations are projected to decrease by 1 to 2 percent, and the over-65 population is projected to increase by 40 to 56 percent. It remains to be seen whether future generations of elderly citizens will be as frugal as those with closer proximity to the depression era.

Economic Growth and the Environment

Economic growth can help the poor by providing more jobs and higher incomes. Simon Kuznets (1955) reported an inverted-U-shaped relationship between income and income inequality, suggesting that growth influences the distribution of income as well. The **Gini coefficient** is a measure of income inequality that equals 0 when everyone in an economy earns the same income and 1 when the richest person in an economy earns all of the money. Very poor countries have a low Gini coefficient because almost everyone is poor. Bangladesh has an estimated Gini coefficient of 0.283. Moderately wealthy countries have a larger proportion of people in each income class, and the moderate levels of income place constraints on the ability to make income transfers to the poor. For example, Chile has an estimated Gini coefficient of 0.566. In wealthy countries, it is relatively easy for the many who are well off to provide transfers to the few who are poor. The estimated Gini coefficient for Canada is 0.286.[18] The Gini coefficient for the

18 See www.worldbank.org/research/growth/dddeisqu.htm.

United States is about 0.430.[19]

Gene Grossman and Alan Krueger (1995) found similar inverted-U-shaped relationships between per-capita income and pollution. Figure 9.7 illustrates this relationship with what is known as the **environmental Kuznets curve** (EKC). Looking at fecal contamination, oxygen depletion, heavy metals in rivers, and urban air pollution, Grossman and Krueger found in most cases that pollution levels initially increased with income levels, but then began to decrease when income per capita reached around $15,000 to $17,500.[20] Related studies have found Kuznets relationships between income and sulfur dioxide, deforestation, particulates, nitrogen oxides, carbon monoxide, and automotive lead emissions.[21] Grossman and Krueger conclude that, "contrary to the alarmist cries of some environmental groups, we find no evidence that economic growth does unavoidable harm to the natural habitat."

This line of research is relatively new, having begun in the 1990s, and some of the results are currently under debate. Harbaugh, Levinson, and Wilson (2002), for example, find varying relationships between sulfur dioxide emissions and per-capita income depending on the assumptions made and the areas and years studied. Many of their curves begin as an inverted U and then spring back up at incomes above $17,500 per year. For other substances, including municipal solid waste and carbon dioxide, the existing studies consistently find a positive relationship between income and pollution.

It is conceptually clear that higher incomes could lead to higher environmental standards and an increased ability to pay for pollution abatement. Findings in support of the environmental Kuznets curve are evidence that nothing about economic growth destroys those possibilities, at least in regard to some pollutants. Findings to the contrary remind us that pollution abatement requires more deliberate efforts than are taking place. Chapter 5 described many ways in which economic growth could occur in concert with environmental goals. This relationship between economic growth and pollution rests in part on decisions by the population about how to exercise their affluence and shape their technology.

Paul Ehrlich and John Holdren (1971) modeled the relationship between environmental impact and growth with the equation

$$\text{environmental impact} = \text{population} \times \text{affluence} \times \text{technology}^{22}$$

Using the first letters in impact, population, affluence, and technology, this is abbreviated as $I = P \times A \times T$ or *IPAT*. Defining *affluence* as output per person and

19 See www.census.gov/hhes/income/incineq/p60204/fig7.html.

20 These figures have been adjusted to reflect 2010 dollars using the consumer price index.

21 See, for example, Hilton and Levinson (1998). Andreoni and Levinson (2001) present a model that explains the environmental Kuznets relationship on the basis of increasing returns to pollution abatement technology.

22 This is a modern adaptation of the original equation that appeared in Ehrlich and Holdren (1971). Dietz and Rosa (1994) provide a history of the concept and an overview of empirical research on the relationship.

technology as pollution per unit of output, this equation forms the identity

$$\text{environmental impact} = \text{population} \times \frac{\text{output}}{\text{person}} \times \frac{\text{pollution}}{\text{output}} = \text{population} \times \frac{\text{pollution}}{\text{person}}$$

This equation suggests that we could cut the environmental "footprint" of human behavior by the same proportion, say 10 percent, by cutting the population *or* the output per person *or* the pollution per unit of output by 10 percent, or with some combination of the three reductions. Efficient policies should target the area out of these three that can be decreased at the lowest cost.

Ehrlich and Holdren used the *IPAT* relationship to show that technological progress that reduces the amount of pollution per person will offer no improvement if accompanied by a proportional increase in the population. Some scholars feel that market pressures will avert environmental problems by increasing the prices of goods that become scarce, and that the market mechanism will prevent a simultaneous escalation of population, output, and pollution. Ehrlich's stance is: "If I'm right, we will save the world. If I'm wrong, people will still be better fed, better housed, and happier thanks to our efforts."[23]

Summary

Over the next half-century, the population of the 48 least-developed countries will nearly triple. There is a net gain of 2.37 people per second in the world and one person every ten seconds in the United States, where the population is becoming older, wealthier, more diverse, and better educated. Some of these trends are favorable to the environment. Education, age, and ethnic diversity can bring environmental sensitivity that is otherwise difficult to convey.

Increases in income have a positive influence on the generation of waste. Evidence of an environmental Kuznets curve, however, shows that growth in income per capita can have a moderating effect on some types of pollution. Accompanied by the right attitude, affluence can elevate environmental standards and the willingness to pay for conservation measures.

Rapid population growth in less developed countries, like rampant materialism in developed countries, creates incessant policy challenges. Without adequate policy responses, these and related trends will increase the anthropogenic footprint on the environment by hastening resource depletion and expanding municipal solid waste production. Even with stable per-capita waste and pollution levels, increasing populations result in growing environmental burdens. Concurrent decreases in the number of available landfills place added pressure on existing wilderness areas and environmental sinks. The resource and disposal needs of growing populations also lead to heated disputes, which are the topic of Chapter 15.

23 See Ehrlich (1971), p. 179.

Problems for Review

1. Draw a downward-sloping demand curve and a downward-then-upward -sloping marginal cost curve for having children. Indicate how each of the following influences affects the graph. In each case, explain the resulting effect on the quantity of children.
   a) *An economy that was primarily agricultural becomes primarily industrial, and child labor is prohibited in the industrial sector.*
   b) *Employment rates and wages increase for women.*
   c) *Infant mortality rates decrease.*
   d) *The country adopts a system of support for the elderly.*
2. "Doubling time" is the number of years it takes a population to double in size. The doubling time is found by dividing 69.3 by the population growth rate. Calculate the doubling time for the following countries:
   a) *Afghanistan: growth rate 3.5 percent*
   b) *Belgium: growth rate 0.2 percent*
   c) *Canada: growth rate 1.0 percent*
   d) *Bangladesh: growth rate 1.6 percent*
3. If you presided over an international organization and wanted to increase the population doubling time in Bangladesh, what specific policy would you suggest? Explain your choice.
4. Panama's annual birth rate has fallen from 32 to 19 per 1,000 since 1975 and its death rate is steady at 5 per 1,000. In which stage of demographic transition is Panama? Belgium is in Stage IV of demographic transition. Describe the characteristics of that stage.
5. Suppose that fruit flies on Kiwi Island live for three days. On their first day they are considered young and reproduce with a TFR of 2. Half of their offspring are female. On the second day the flies are middle-aged and cannot reproduce. On the third day they are considered old and they cannot reproduce. All fruit flies live to old age. Indicate the number of fruit flies on Kiwi Island on days 2, 3, and 4 under each of the following scenarios:
   a) *On day 1 there are equal numbers of males and females in each age category, including six old flies, four middle-aged flies, and two young flies.*
   b) *On day 1 there are two males and two females in each age category.*
   c) *On day 1 there are 100 young male flies and 100 middle-aged female flies.*
   d) *On day 1 there are equal numbers of males and females in each category, and there are six young flies, four middle-aged flies, and two old flies.*
6. Starting with the situation in Part (d) of Problem 5, on what day would the population stabilize, in the sense that it would be the same as the day before, in each of the following situations:
   a) *With no change from the scenario in Problem 5.*
   b) *Fruit flies increase their life span by one day, but can still only reproduce on their first day.*
   c) *One young male and one young female fruit fly die each day before reproducing.*

7. Income and education levels are on the rise in many parts of the world.
   a) How do you think your own post-college boost in income (after you land your first "real" job) will affect your consumption behavior?
   b) How do you think your decision to attend college will affect the timing of any children you might have relative to if you ended your schooling after high school?
   c) Do you think most people would provide similar answers? What does this suggest about policy and preparation for related demographic changes?
8. Using economic reasoning, explain why it might be appropriate for a rich suburb to dump its trash in a poorer area.
9. Using economic reasoning, explain why it might *not* be appropriate for a rich suburb to dump its trash in a poorer area.
10. If the environmental Kuznets curve held for individual households, what would the pollution-minimizing Gini coefficient be? Interpret this outcome and explain some of its drawbacks.

websurfer's challenge

1. Find one website with modern arguments against population growth and one that argues that population growth is not a problem. Evaluate the primary arguments on each side.
2. Find a website that indicates the growth rate for your state or region. Calculate the population doubling time for that area using the formula provided in Problem 2. Discuss whether this rate of growth is problematic in regard to the environment.

Internet Resources

EPA Office of Solid Waste:
www.epa.gov/osw/

Joint Center for Poverty Research:
www.jcpr.org

Population Connection:
www.populationconnection.org

Population Reference Bureau:
www.prb.org

United Nations Population Fund:
www.unfpa.org

U.S. Census Bureau Population Clocks:
www.census.gov/main/www/popclock.html

Further Reading

Anderson, David A. "The Determinants of Municipal Solid Waste." *Journal of Applied Economics and Policy* 24, no. 2 (2005): 23–29. An empirical study of the determinants of municipal solid waste levels.

Andreoni, James, and Arik Levinson. "The Simple Analytics of the Environmental Kuznets Curve." *Journal of Public Economics* 80, no. 2 (2001): 269–286. Presents a model in support of the environmental Kuznets curve on the basis of increasing returns to pollution abatement technology.

Callan, Scott J., and Janet M. Thomas. "The Impact of State and Local Policies on the Recycling Effort." *Eastern Economic Journal* 23, no. 4 (1997): 411–423. Estimates the determinants of recycling rates.

Dasgupta, Parth. *Human Well Being and the Natural Environment.* New York: Oxford University Press, 2001. A discussion of population, poverty, and the environment as influences on the state of human affairs.

Denison, Richard A., and John Ruston. *Recycling and Incineration: Evaluating the Choices.* Washington, D.C.: Island Press, 1990. Describes the externalities associated with landfills and waste incineration facilities.

Dietz, Thomas, and Eugene A. Rosa. "Rethinking the Environmental Impacts of Population, Affluence and Technology." *Human Ecology Review* 1, no. 2 (1994): 277–300. An update on the IPAT relationship, including an overview of past developments.

Ehrlich, Paul R. *The Population Bomb.* Cutchogue, NY: Buccaneer Books, 1971. A provocative discussion of population dynamics and the environment.

Ehrlich, Paul R., and John P. Holdren. "Impact of Population Growth." *Science* 171 (1971): 1212–1217. The initial presentation of the IPAT concept, and influential arguments for greater attention to population growth issues.

Environmental Protection Agency. *Municipal Solid Waste Generation, Recycling and Disposal in the U.S.: 1999 Facts and Figures.* EPA530-R-01-014, July 2001. Quantifies the declining availability of landfills in the United States.

Galor, Oded, and David N. Weil. "Population, Technology, and Growth: From Malthusian Stagnation to the Demographic Transition and Beyond." *American Economic Review* 90, no. 4 (2000): 806–828. Explores the dynamics of population and growth at three levels of economic development.

Grossman, Gene M., and Alan B. Krueger. "Economic Growth and the Environment." *Quarterly Journal of Economics* 110, no. 2 (1995): 353–377. Finds an inverted-U-shaped Kuznets relationship between per-capita income and several categories of pollution.

Harbaugh, William T., Arik Levinson, and David Molloy Wilson. "Reexamining the Empirical Evidence for an Environmental Kuznets Curve." *Review of Economics and Statistics* 84, no. 3 (2002): 541–551. Questions the inverted-U-shaped income–pollution relationship after looking at data from different locations and years.

Hilton, Hank, and Arik Levinson. "Factoring the Environmental Kuznets Curve: Evidence from Automobile Lead Emissions." *Journal of Environmental Economics and Management* 35, no. 2 (1998): 126–141. Finds empirical support for the Kuznets relationship between income and automobile emissions.

Kuznets, Simon. "Economic Growth and Income Inequality." *American Economic Review* 45, no. 1 (1955): 1–28. Finds an inverted-U-shaped relationship between income and income inequality, much like the possible relationship between income and pollution that was later named after Kuznets.

Lackman, Conway L. "A Household Consumption Model of Solid Waste." *Journal of Economic Theory* 13 (1976): 478–483. Suggests that wealthier people choose disposable items due to a relatively high opportunity cost of time.

Malthus, Thomas R. *An Essay on the Principle of Population.* London: Printed for J. Johnson, 1798, available at: www.ac.wwu.edu/~stephan/malthus/malthus.0.html. The famous progenitor of many modern discussions of population growth and resource scarcity.

U.S. Bureau of the Census. *Statistical Abstract of the United States: 2004.* Washington, D.C., 2004. Includes tables on municipal solid waste, poverty, and pollution.

World Bank. *World Development Report 1992: Development and the Environment.* Washington, D.C.: World Bank, 1991. An examination of how economic growth might affect the environment by what is reportedly, and for better or worse, the world's single largest employer of economists.

World Bank. *World Development Report 2003: Sustainable Development in a Dynamic Economy.* Washington, D.C.: World Bank, 2002. Available online at econ.worldbank.org/wdr/wdr2003/. A data-laden manuscript discussing policy-related facets of poverty, economic growth, and the environment.

Guatemala is the most populous country in Central America. Among indigenous families there, the total fertility rate is 6.2. Several factors contribute to rapid population growth in Guatemala. The median age is 20, so most women are of childbearing age. The large services and agricultural sectors offer many opportunities for children to contribute labor. Children are the primary source of retirement care. And the limited opportunities for education and employment for women lower the opportunity cost of having children early in life.

"There's so much we don't know about the natural world, and we're destroying large parts of it before we even appreciate our ignorance."

—MICHAEL ZASLOFF

"In nature's infinite book of secrecy, a little I can read."

—WILLIAM SHAKESPEARE
ANTHONY AND CLEOPATRA

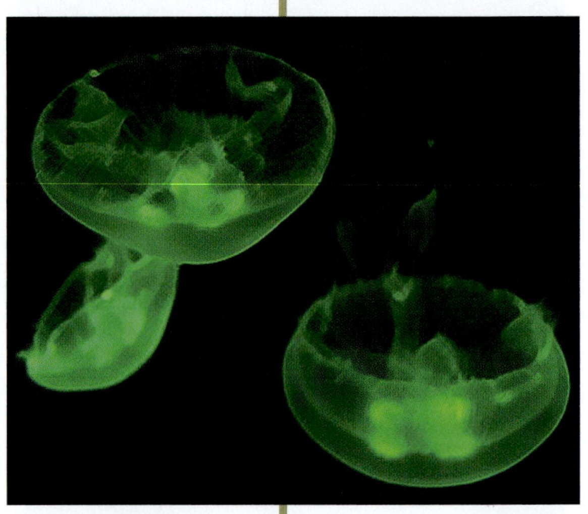

"The Forest Service now works to restore national forests to the ecological condition they had prior to European westward expansion. ... This philosophy implies a negative moral judgment on much of modern industrial society."

—ROBERT H. NELSON

"I think that I shall never see a poem lovely as a tree."

—JOYCE KILMER

10 Biodiversity and Valuation

The virtues of diversity are among the basic tenets of economics. We derive more utility from relatively balanced amounts of two goods, like sunshine and rain or food and clothing, than from just one or the other. This lesson applies to biological diversity as well. **Biological diversity**, *or* **biodiversity**, *refers to the variety of ecosystems, species, and genetic differences within species. From an ecocentric standpoint, biodiversity is critical to life. Decomposers like bacteria eat high-level carnivores or omnivores like humans, which eat lower-level carnivores like wild boars,*[1] *which eat herbivores like rats, which eat primary producers like corn plants. With this complex interdependence among wildlife, the loss of a family or species can threaten the sustenance of the food chain. The domino effect of losses resulting from extinction does not just extend* up *the food chain. Take the example that frogs eat insects, snakes eat frogs, birds eat snakes, and so on. The loss of the Suriname redtail boa (*Boa c. constrictor*) might threaten not only the laughing falcon (*Herpetotheres cachinnans*) and other species above it in the food chain, but also the dark rice-field mosquito (*Psorophora columbiae*) and other members of the Insecta class because snakes keep frog populations in check and thus help insect populations to survive. Table 10.1 summarizes the classification system for plants and animals.*

From an anthropocentric viewpoint, biodiversity is important not only for the sustenance of the food chain atop which we sit, but for medicinal cures, fibers, petroleum substitutes, agents for the restoration of soil and water, natural beauty, tourism, pride, and education. Aspirin, penicillin, steroids, digitalis, and morphine are among the many medicines that have

1 For wild boar recipes, see www.bowhunting.net/susieq/boar.htm.

already come from nature. Tourism, the purpose of which is often to enjoy biodiversity, is among the largest industries in the world.

Economists have developed primarily anthropocentric techniques for estimating the value of biodiversity. These techniques allow for informed, although imperfect, decisions about the advisability of production and development at the expense of wildlife. This chapter identifies the many facets of biodiversity's value, reviews common valuation techniques, and reports findings from the application of these methods.

Deforestation threatens the habitat of the kinkajou (Potos flavus) *in South and Central America.*

Biodiversity Loss

Like Shakespeare, we have some windows into nature's infinite secrecy. Fossil remains provide information about the number of plant and animal species that existed at approximate points in time going back hundreds of millions of years. Estimates of the numbers of *living* species in various locations and classifications come from biological inventories. For example, in remote Ecuadorian rainforests, Terry Irwin of the Smithsonian Institution sprays a fog of biodegradable insecticide into the jungle, sending insects onto collection sheets below for cataloging and enumeration.[2] Most estimates place the total number of living species at between 7 million and 100 million. About 1.75 million species have been classified with Latin names.

Biodiversity is naturally in a mild state of flux, with some species becoming extinct and new species emerging. Table 10.2 details five mass extinctions over the past 500 million years. The causes of these extinctions are under debate, but may have included cosmic impacts, glaciations, volcanic eruptions, and associated

2 See Morell (1999).

Scientific Names, from the Most to the Least Inclusive	*The Human*	*The Tickseed Sunflower*
Kingdom	**Animalia**	**Plantae**
Phylum	Chordata	Spermatophyta
Class	Mammalia	Angiospermae
Order	Primates	Asterales
Family	Hominidae	Asteraceae
Genus	*Homo*	*Bidens*
Species	*Homo sapiens*	*Bidens aristosa*

Table 10.1 *The Hierarchical System of Scientific Names*

climate changes. Volcanic eruptions send large doses of sulphates into the atmosphere and eject ash clouds that could lower global temperatures. Dust clouds from meteorite impacts have a similar effect. Glaciers lower temperatures, and their accumulation of ice causes sea levels to fall, threatening marine life. Glacial melting has the opposite effect of raising sea levels and threatening land species.

The ongoing quaternary extinction is the direct result of human behavior. Ecosystems around the world are undergoing changes in composition, structure, and function caused by human activity. Like the other causes of mass extinctions, we too have sent sulphates into the atmosphere, contributed to global climate change, and directly impinged on biodiversity. Deforestation, agricultural practices, urban sprawl, overhunting and fishing, and pollution take their toll. Scientists estimate that present extinction rates of between 10 and 1,000 species per year are 100 to 10,000 times higher than the prehuman rates of extinction.[3] Among the hardest hit so far are large mammals, birds, beetles, and amphibians.

Funding limitations and opportunity costs constrain policy measures that would protect endangered species and force the prioritization of conservation efforts. The selection of species to preserve is influenced by their value, as

Extinction	*Approximate Number of Years Ago*	*Families Lost*
Ordovician	438 million	25%
Devonian	360 million	19%
Permian	248 million	54%
Triassic	208 million	23%
Cretaceous	65 million	17%
Quaternary	0 (ongoing)	To be determined

Table 10.2 *The Great Extinctions*

3 See www.guardian.co.uk/environment/2010/mar/07/extinction-species-evolve, Pimm et al. (1995).

Figure 10.1 *Global Biodiversity Hotspots*

The richest biology on Earth, and the largest number of species living nowhere else, is found in the "biodiversity hotspots" marked in red. These locations include the Atlantic Forest, the California Floristic Province, the Cape Floristic Region, the Caribbean Islands, Caucasus, Cerrado, the Chilean Winter Rainfall-Valdivian Forests, the Coastal Forests of Eastern Africa, the East Melanesian Islands, Eastern Afromontane, the Guinean Forests of West Africa, Himalaya, the Horn of Africa, Indo-Burma, Irano-Anatolian, Japan, Madagascar and the Indian Ocean Islands, the Madrean Pine-Oak Woodlands, Maputaland-Pondoland-Albany, the Mediterranean Basin, Mesoamerica, the mountains of Central Asia, the mountains of Southwest China, New Caledonia, New Zealand, the Philippines, Polynesia-Micronesia, Southwest Australia, Succulent Karoo, Sundaland, Tropical Andes, Tumbes-Choco-Magdalena, Wallacea, Western Ghats, and Sri Lanka.

discussed later in this chapter. Environmental policies can also target specific regions that provide habitat for large numbers of species. Figure 10.1 indicates such biodiversity "hotspots." According to environmental analyst Norman Myers and his colleagues, "25 hotspots contain the sole remaining habitats of 44% of the Earth's plant species and 35% of its vertebrate species, and these habitats face a high risk of elimination."[4] The "hottest of the hotspots" are Madagascar, the Philippines, Sundaland, Brazil's Atlantic Forest, and the Caribbean. Behavior in North America and elsewhere affects the biodiversity in these regions. The United States produces a quarter of the human-made greenhouse gases that threaten to overheat sensitive species in the hotspots, and many of the hotspots are sources of lumber, seafood, agricultural goods, and manufactured products for the developed countries.[5]

As policymakers prioritize areas for preservation, land values must be

4 See Myers et al. (2000), p. 853.

5 For example, Wendy's, McDonald's, and Burger King obtain beef from hotspots like Australia and New Zealand. See www.usatoday.com/money/retail/2002-04-03-mcdonalds-beef.htm.

considered alongside biological data to establish cost-effective strategies.[6] In areas of similar size, Brazil's Atlantic Forest contains about 20,000 plant species and 1,361 vertebrate species, while central Chile contains 3,429 plant species and 335 vertebrate species.[7] However, if land costs ten times as much in the Atlantic Forest as in central Chile, more species can be saved with a given expenditure by purchasing land for conservation in central Chile and in similar locations. With the money it would take to protect the Atlantic Forest, ten areas similar to central Chile could be protected for the benefit of some 34,290 plant species and 3,350 vertebrate species. If all species were valued equally, an efficient policy would shift dollars to the location where the largest fraction of a species could be saved per dollar,[8] until the savings per dollar was equalized across locations. The logic is that if more benefit is achieved per dollar in one location than in another, more dollars should be spent in that location to take advantage of its greater "bang per buck." With diminishing marginal returns, the marginal benefit per dollar spent in the funded location will eventually fall in line with the marginal benefit of spending elsewhere.[9] When species have differing values, efficiency is achieved in the same way, except that the marginal benefit is measured in terms of the *value* of the particular species saved, rather than simply the *number* of species saved. Methods of distinguishing between species of greater or lesser value are discussed next.

Models of Biodiversity Loss

Humans are at the helm during this sixth surge of extinctions. We have the prerogative to make difficult choices about rates and locations of growth and pollution. We control the acceleration of biodiversity loss with the degree to which our policies

- *Fragment wilderness areas with roads*
- *Drain wetlands*
- *Introduce non-native species that become pests to wildlife*[10]
- *Clear forests*
- *Convert grasslands for agriculture or development*

6 See Polasky, Camm, and Garber-Yonts (2001).

7 See Myers et al. (2000), p. 854.

8 For example, if a species could be saved for $1 million, we could say that one one-millionth of a species is saved per dollar.

9 See Chapter 2 for a discussion of diminishing marginal returns and an in-depth explanation of the efficiency of equalizing the marginal benefit per dollar spent on inputs or outputs.

10 For example, the zebra mussel (*Dreissena polymorpha*) is native to the Caspian Sea region of Asia. It was found in Lake Erie in 1988, probably carried there by transoceanic ships. These mussels now live in all of the Great Lakes, the Mississippi River, and inland lakes as well. Beyond clogging water intake pipes for industries, zebra mussels filter plankton out of the water, removing an important food source for larval fish and breaking a link in the food chain. See www.state.ia.us/fish/news/exotics/zebra.htm.

- *Alter the global climate*
- *Extract natural resources*
- *Emit air, water, light, and noise pollution*
- *Otherwise encroach on natural habitat*

This global exercise in the allocation of scarce resources among the competing ends of agriculture, development, production, recreation, and wilderness areas helps to determine the variety of species that coexist on the planet. Economic analysis can assist with the daunting decisions of which species to preserve and what values to place on living things. This section describes two useful approaches.

Cost-Benefit Applications

> *"At the end of the day, all the brave talk about 'win-win' situations, which simultaneously produce sustainable development and conserve biodiversity, will not help us sort out how many children's hospitals should be sacrificed in the name of preserving natural habitats."*
>
> —Andrew Metrick and Martin L. Weitzman (1998)

Reining in the quaternary extinction would mean substantial changes for humans. The housing, transportation, diet, and material possessions common in developed countries all come at a high environmental price. In some cases, biodiversity loss results from a conscious decision to substitute a set of material assets (like a subdivision) for a set of natural assets (like a forest and its inhabitants). How much biodiversity loss is too much? Cost-benefit analysis provides one answer to this question. It should be clear that the costs and benefits referred to in this type of economic analysis do not necessarily involve the transfer of money. Maintenance expenditures and user fees represent a small portion of the economic costs and benefits of natural areas. The preservation of plant and animal species generates commerce by way of ecotourism and medical cures, but it also creates warm feelings in the hearts of humans and the joy of being able to introduce new generations to these living things. Economists are able to estimate the monetary value that individuals place on warm feelings and joy. For the benefit of making the associated trade-offs explicit, it is common to convert all of the costs and benefits into monetary values. Emotional and other nonmonetary concerns are not neglected; they are simply measured in terms of a standard unit for comparison.

Biodiversity can be quantified in terms of genetic variation, types of ecosystems, or the number of families or species. This chapter refers to the number of species preserved. Similar conclusions would apply to investigations using most alternative measures of biodiversity as well. Other things being equal, it is prudent to begin with those efforts that preserve species at the lowest cost.

*Industrial pollution-runoff threatens the weedy sea dragon (*Phyllopteryx taeniolatus*), found only in Tasmania and along the southern coastline of Australia.*

Photo by Donna Anderson

Property for a new farm may cost only a few hundred dollars more per acre in an area with no endangered species than in an environmentally sensitive area, providing a relatively inexpensive opportunity for preservation. On the other hand, it might cost several million dollars more to build a multistory parking structure as a substitute for paving two or three acres of forest near a production facility.

The preservation of different species also necessitates different levels of expenditure. Many species of rodents, grasses, and cockroaches may well outlive humans even if we spend nothing to preserve them. On the other hand, in recent history, commercial interests in fishing, logging, and transportation have been held at bay by the preservation of species of whales, woodpeckers, and snakes, respectively. As more and more species are preserved, more and more expensive steps must be taken in the name of biodiversity. While the costs of preserving additional species increase with the number preserved, the corresponding benefits are likely to decrease. The species with the top priority for preservation, presumably *Homo sapiens*, is valued quite highly. Additional species provide large benefits, but the more species that exist, the less of a contribution each additional species makes to available diversity. This is especially true within particular taxonomic groups. The first species within the phylum of (sea) sponges[11] contributes to diversity in a way that the ten-thousandth species does not.

One could line up all species in ascending order of their marginal cost of preservation, starting, say, with the brown-banded cockroach (*Supella longipalpa)* and the brown rat (*Rattus norvegicus*),[12] and ending with *Homo sapiens* for whom most expenditures are made.[13] It is also possible to line up species in descending order of their marginal benefit, starting with *Homo sapiens* and ending, perhaps, with the ten-thousandth species of sponge, the brown-banded cockroach, and the brown rat. As illustrated by these examples, there is no reason to think that the species with the largest marginal benefit of preservation is also the species with the smallest marginal cost of preservation. Some species are arguably more important than others, which can justify the preservation of species that are not necessarily the least expensive to preserve.[14] Thus, it would be overly simplistic to construct a graph with increasing marginal costs and decreasing marginal

11 Sponges are a phylum with many families and about 10,000 species.

12 All rats are not so enduring. The Stephens' kangaroo rat (*Dipodomys stephensi*) is an endangered species.

13 For example, Americans spend $2.5 trillion on human health annually. See www.census.gov/compendia/statab/2012/tables/12s0134.pdf.

14 See Naeem et al. (1995) for discussions of the importance of biodiversity to ecosystem functioning.

benefits for the same list of species to determine the efficient degree of preservation. Instead, the net marginal benefit (marginal benefit minus marginal cost) could be estimated for each species. For efficiency, those species with a positive net marginal benefit should be saved, and priority should be given to those species with the largest net marginal benefit. The prioritization of species for preservation according to their net marginal benefit is easier said than done. The next section describes a specific approach for doing so.

The Noah's Ark Model

Two recent studies view the decision of which species to preserve as the "Noah's Ark Problem."[15] Like Noah, we have some control over what species can survive on the "ark" we call Earth. There is a cost associated with efforts to preserve species, exemplified by the expense of conservation projects and the foregone profits that could be earned if the species' habitats were not preserved. The value of a species in the Noah's Ark model is measured in terms of direct benefits (commercial, recreational, and emotional) and contributions to diversity (distinctiveness in comparison to the closest relative). The task of prioritizing species to board the ark given limits of space, time, and money involves a fourth variable: the increased likelihood of survival attributable to protection. Some species will persist regardless of intervention; others are vulnerable but can survive with assistance.

For notation, D represents the value of a species' distinctiveness, B is the value of its direct benefits, S is the percentage increase in survivability resulting from protection, and C is the cost of preservation efforts. The societal gain per dollar of expenditure on preservation is thus

$$\frac{(D+B)S}{C}$$

According to this model, social welfare is maximized when assistance is prioritized for species that provide the greatest additional benefit per dollar spent on protection. Species' welcome onto the ark should be positively correlated with greater distinctiveness, higher direct benefits, larger survivability gains from protection, and lower protection costs. Conservation efforts should continue until the marginal benefit from additional effort is less than or equal to the marginal cost. To the extent that the values of D, B, S, and C can be estimated, the Noah's Ark model can guide the prioritization of conservation efforts. Even if the numbers cannot be closely estimated, the model is useful in highlighting the variables and formula policymakers should consider to the extent possible. The Reality Check that follows demonstrates the applicability of this model.

15 See Weitzman (1998) and Metrick and Weitzman (1998).

reality check

Are We Loading the Right Species onto the Ark?

Andrew Metrick and Martin L. Weitzman collected data on the four criteria of the Noah's Ark model—direct benefits, distinctiveness, survivability, and cost—and examined whether actual rankings correspond with the logic of the model. For measures of society's rankings of species, they looked to the nomination process for protection under the Endangered Species Act. This included counts of positive comments made about species, the decision whether or not to include species on the protected list, and public expenditures to protect species.

Direct benefits were measured in terms of species' size and taxonomic class. As a measure of distinctiveness, Metrick and Weitzman determined whether a species was the sole representative of its genus and whether it was a subspecies. For survivability they used a 1 to 5 ranking of endangerment created by the Nature Conservancy. For cost they used a variable indicating whether or not recovery of the species conflicts with public or private development plans.

The findings indicate that humans place a high priority on large, cuddly "charismatic megafauna" such as bears and cats. More surprisingly, they suggest that society spends more money on less endangered species than on more endangered species, and expenditures do not increase significantly for more unique species. Further, society is more likely to spend money on an animal whose preservation conflicts with development plans than on those that could be saved at a lower cost. In other words, according to this study, our current strategies for environmental protection do not coincide with what most economists would recommend in terms of maximizing social welfare.

Valuing Costs and Benefits

Cost-benefit analysis is central to the determination of appropriate levels of biodiversity. Policies that affect biodiversity are available at every expense level, and decision makers must decide which efforts are worthwhile. This warrants a further breakdown of the types of values and their measures. To miss, or discount, costs or benefits might lead society to neglect worthwhile species or load too many onto the ark. Values can come from hands-on use, the option to use a resource, the ability to leave a resource for other humans to enjoy, or simply the knowledge that certain animals and plants are able to survive. In some cases economists can estimate these values on the basis of market prices for associated goods. As described next, "contingent valuation surveys" and "hedonic pricing models" provide estimates for the many environmental goods not sold in markets. Although these valuation methods are discussed in the context of species biodiversity, many of the same techniques can be applied to any asset, natural or not, be it a mountain, a river, clean air, or Hollywood Boulevard.

Types of Values

Both the existence of a species and the alternatives foregone to preserve it have values to users and nonusers alike. **Use values** come from the firsthand enjoyment of resources and their by-products. While users of forests, for example, benefit from hiking trails and natural beauty, there are others who never enter a forest or see a particular animal species but who nonetheless place a **nonuse** or **passive-use value** on them. Passive-use values can be divided into the **option values** people place on the option to use a resource in the future, and **existence values** that are unrelated to any possibility of ever using the resource or its by-products. Existence values include the **bequest value** of knowing that preservation allows others to use a resource and the **sympathy value** of knowing that a resource is alive and well. Bequest values are evident in the efforts of recyclers, conservationists, and environmentalists, and are epitomized by the work of Johnny Appleseed, who planted trees to benefit another generation.[16] Sympathy values drive the establishment of nature preserves with no human access, and protests against the cutting of trees in remote areas. Perhaps symbolic of sympathy values, a young woman named Julia Butterfly Hill lived in a 1,000-year-old Redwood tree deep in the woods for two years to protect it from loggers.[17] In policymaking, our motives for preservation are typically a combination of the many sources of value.

Values are often measured in terms of people's stated or implied willingness to pay or willingness to accept payment for a resource. An individual's **willingness to pay** (WTP) is the largest amount of money she or he would be willing to pay in exchange for the resource. An individual's **willingness to accept** (WTA) is the smallest amount of money she or he would accept to forego the resource. Note that WTA is determined from the standpoint of already having the resource, and WTP is determined from the standpoint of lacking the resource. Because positions of greater wealth (having versus not having the resource) lead individuals to place higher valuations on goods they desire, the WTA is generally higher than the WTP. As an example, media mogul and environmentalist Ted Turner owns over 1.7 million acres of land in the United States. It is unlikely that someone without such holdings would be willing to pay a price that Ted, from his position of relative wealth, would accept for some of this property.

16 Johnny Appleseed, whose real name was John Chapman (1774–1845), traveled through what are now the states of Ohio, Indiana, and Illinois, planting apple seeds and tending hundreds of square miles of apple seedling nurseries.

17 Read more about Ms. Hill's protective action at www.circleoflifefoundation.org/home.html.

Metrick and Weitzman found that humans place the highest priority on saving large, cuddly looking "charismatic megafauna" such as the kangaroo (Macropus canguru)*.*

Measures of Value

Direct valuation methods estimate monetary values either on the basis of prices paid in markets for the environmental assets to be valued or using "contingent valuation" survey techniques that ask respondents what they would pay for assets in hypothetical scenarios. **Indirect valuation** methods use observable behavior to infer the monetary value of assets that are not sold in markets. Consider, for example, expenditures on substitute goods purchased to avoid the effects of lost environmental assets. The $5.2 billion spent on bottled water each year in the United States and the roughly $2 billion annual expenditure on household water filters suggest that a policy that made tap water satisfactorily clean would be worth *at least* $7.2 billion. This is called the **avoidance expenditure** method of valuation. Other indirect methods of placing values on environmental assets look at expenditures on complementary goods such as travel, or try to tease the importance of the assets out of property values and wages, as explained next.

Market Prices Some forms of biodiversity are traded in the marketplace; many others have associated market products. Exotic orchids, birds, fish, and reptiles, among many plants and animals, are bought and sold like televisions. The market prices of health products, food, and clothing attributable to biodiversity indicate the minimum valuation current users place on the sources of those products and services. We can learn about the use value of national parks by considering the travel costs paid in order to see them, and the prices people pay for medicines, dyes, and fruits taken from them. The existence of consumer surplus means that actual expenditures are conservative estimates of value and invites the estimation of demand curves that indicate benefits in excess of costs.

Economic theory also predicts that price will reflect marginal cost in a competitive market with complete information and no externalities. So a product's price approximates both the costs and the benefits associated with the last unit sold. Chapter 3 explains exceptions caused by market failure. When there is no market for a species, preferences are sometimes revealed by expenditures on trips to see it, spending to defend it, and participation rates in efforts to preserve it.

First proposed by economist Harold Hotelling in a letter to the National Parks Service in 1947, the **travel cost method** (TCM) looks at expenditures in the market for travel, which serves as a complement to environmental goods. Consumers' willingness to pay for travel to experience biodiversity and other environmental assets is an indirect indication of the use value of these assets. Since consumer surplus plays an important role in this type of analysis, this discussion begins with a review of the relationship between consumer surplus, demand curves, and marginal anthropocentric value.

Consumers typically receive diminishing marginal utility from their purchases and will buy more of a good or service until its price surpasses the value of the marginal utility it provides. This behavior is illustrated in Figure 10.2. Suppose trips to Madagascar cost $1,300. George values the first trip at $1,355 because

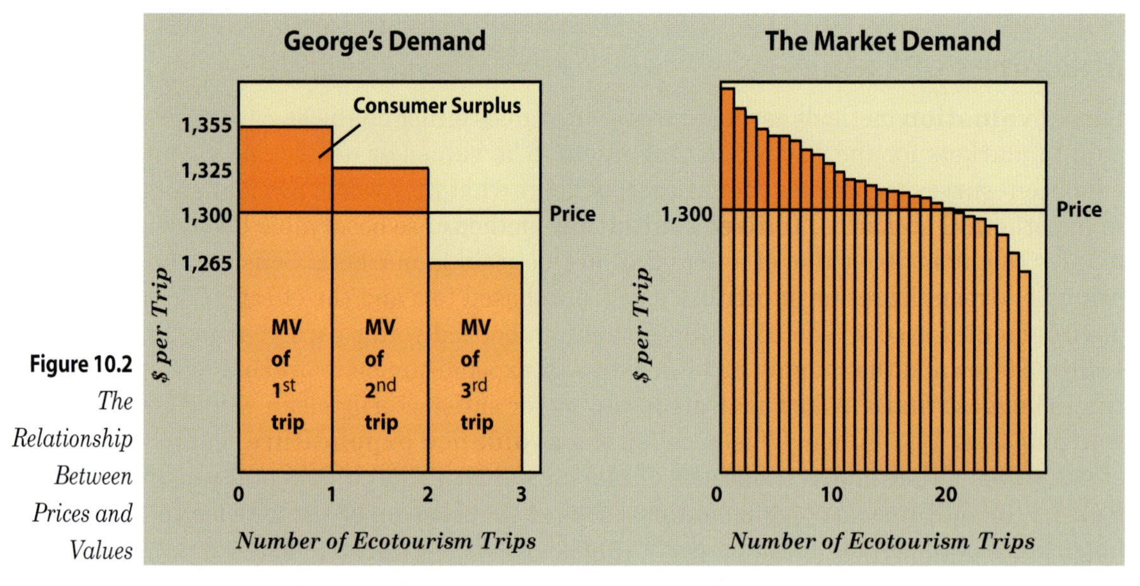

Figure 10.2 *The Relationship Between Prices and Values*

Consumers purchase goods and services until the marginal value of one more unit no longer exceeds the price. George will take two ecotourism trips but not a third, because a third is worth $1,265 to him and would cost $1,300. In a market with many consumers, it is likely that the price will closely resemble the marginal value to the consumer of the last unit, as illustrated in the second panel.

it allows him to visit a new location and see lemurs in their natural habitat for the first time. The second trip is worth $1,325 to him because it's a great place, but having been there before, he finds some of the novelty has worn off. Tired of traveling and having seen it twice before, George values the third trip at $1,265. George will take the first and second trip but not the third, because the first two are worth more to him than their cost and the third is not.

As shown in the right panel of Figure 10.2, in a market with many consumers, the observed market price of a good provides a close approximation of the value of the last unit of that good that is purchased. A great deal of consumer surplus—value in excess of payments—may be gained from units prior to the last unit sold. George gained $1,355 – $1,300 = $55 worth of consumer surplus from the first trip to Madagascar and $1,325 – $1,300 = $25 from the second trip.

Figure 10.3 demonstrates how, for a given equilibrium price and quantity, consumer surplus increases with the steepness of a straight-line demand curve. When the market demand curve is horizontal as shown by D_A, there is no consumer surplus, and the market price indicates the value to consumers of each unit of the product. If the demand curve for travel to Madagascar were flat, the total expenditure on travel to go there, $1,300 × 20 = $26,000, would indicate the total value received by the travelers. If the demand curve resembles D_B, the market price indicates the value of the last unit purchased, but consumers

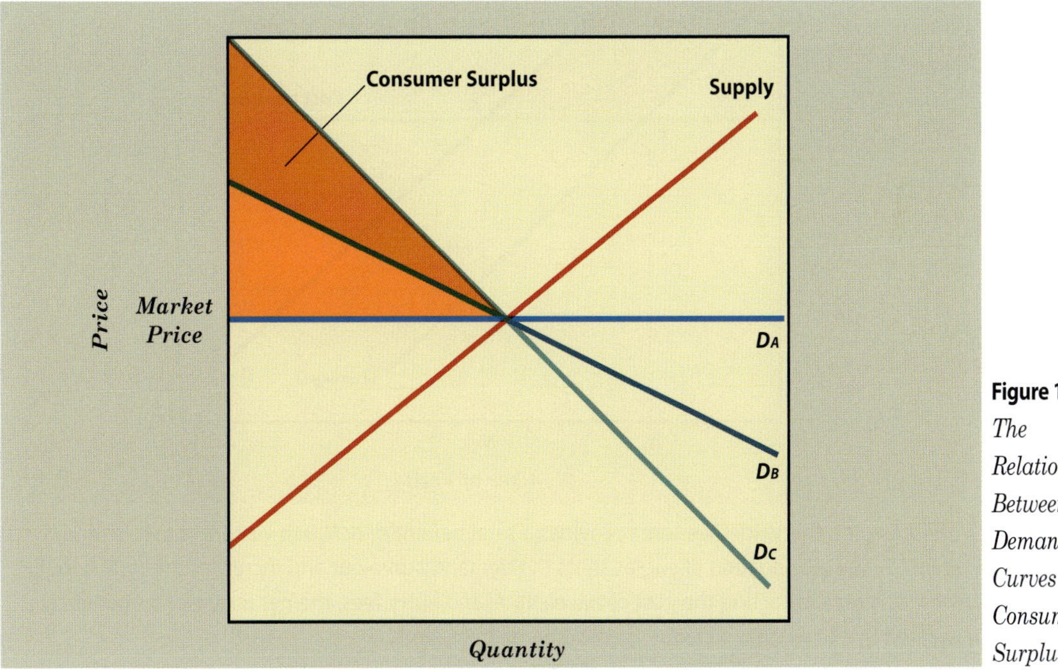

Figure 10.3 *The Relationship Between Demand Curves and Consumer Surplus*

If the market demand curve resembles D_A, the market price is equal to the value of the product to *each* consumer in the market. If the demand curve resembles D_B, the market price indicates the value of the *last* unit, but earlier units have larger values to consumers. The difference between the value to consumers and the actual payment is consumer surplus. If the slope of the demand curve is even steeper, like that of D_C, the price is an even more conservative estimate of the product's value.

place values on the other units that exceed the price, so they receive consumer surplus. If the demand curve is even steeper, like D_C, consumers gain even more value from the product than the market price and receive a correspondingly high consumer surplus. In that case, the price is an even more conservative estimate of the product's value

The travel cost method has evolved to include means of capturing values that are part of consumer surplus.[18] Travel expenditures, visitation rates, and demographic data can be used to estimate demand curves.[19] The area under the demand curve and out to the actual number of visits made measures the per-period use value of biodiversity and other amenities at a site. Figure 10.4 illustrates demand curves for visits to a wilderness area before and after the introduction of bald eagles (*Haliaeetus leucocephalus*). Before the introduction, the total benefit to visitors is area dcN_00, which they enjoy at the cost of PcN_00, including travel costs, time, and entry fees. The incremental value of an environmental change can be measured by changes in the demand curve. If the introduction of bald

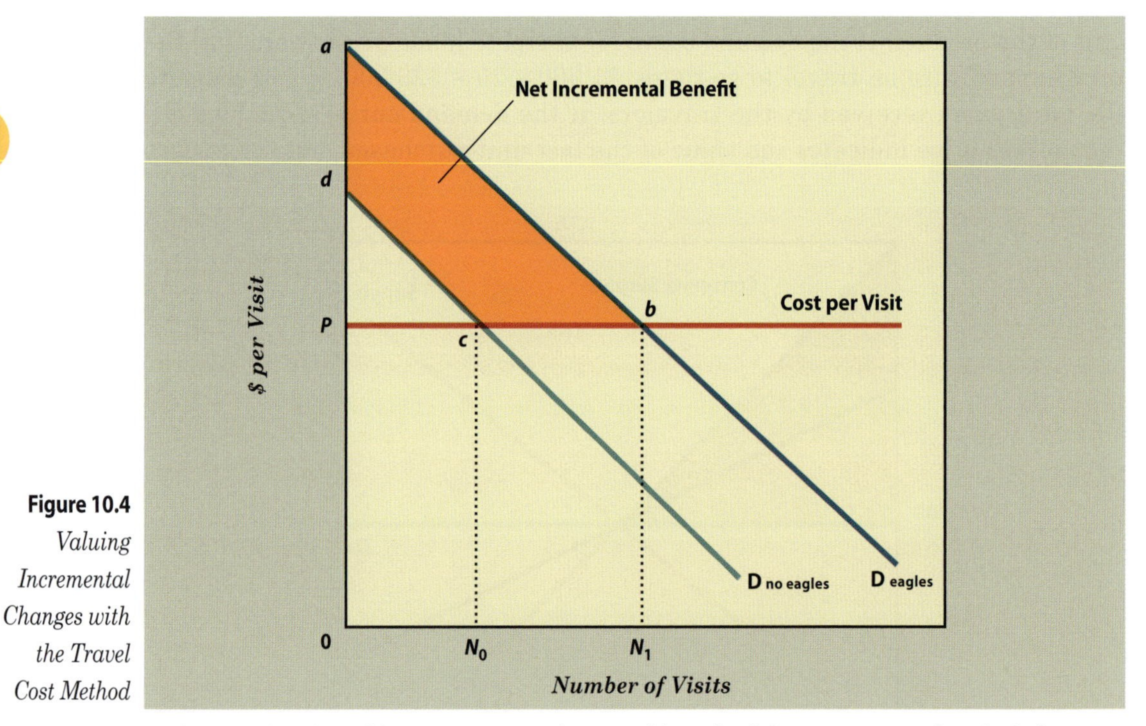

Figure 10.4 *Valuing Incremental Changes with the Travel Cost Method*

Without eagles, this wilderness area provides a total benefit of dcN_00 to visitors, for which they pay PcN_00. The introduction of eagles shifts the demand curve out and increases the total benefit to abN_10. After subtracting the cost of travel, time, and entry fees, the net incremental benefit is measured by the shaded increase in consumer surplus, *abcd*.

18 For a history of travel cost methods, see Smith and Desvousges (1996).

19 The traditional TCM derives demand curves by considering visitation levels among many visitors located various distances from a site and therefore incurring differing travel costs to get there. The hedonic TCM looks at users facing various costs and choices among sites with varying attributes. For technical information on the derivation of recreational demand curves, see Van Kooten and Bulte (2000), pp. 113–120.

eagles would increase demand as indicated in Figure 10.4, the total benefit would become $abN_1 0$, and the net incremental benefit would be the orange area *abcd*.

Sohrabi et al. (2009) used the travel cost method to evaluate the recreational value of a natural forest in Iran. They found the recreational value of the forest to be 25 times its value for timber production, which informed relevant policy decisions about whether or not to preserve, expand, and equip the site for recreational use.

There are several limitations to the travel cost method. Although it is appealing to analyze actual travel costs rather than values drawn from hypothetical scenarios, some economists argue that travel costs themselves can be subjective and unobservable.[20] The TCM generates estimates of use values but not option or existence values. The TCM is appropriate for estimating values to recreational users but not to commercial users and others who reside near a resource. And there is a real risk that embedded into travelers' willingness to pay to visit natural areas are the values of such extraneous benefits as the beauty of the trip to get there. (The embedding effect is discussed further in the next section.) When travelers choose among a variety of alternative natural areas with differing characteristics, the related **random utility recreation model** (RURM) approach becomes more suitable. The RURM technique involves sophisticated regression analysis to determine the value of distinguishing site attributes such as particular types of biodiversity.[21]

Contingent Valuation The contingent valuation method (CVM) gets around the absence of markets for some environmental goods by analyzing responses to hypothetical survey questions. Contingent valuation methods can assist in the estimation of both use and passive-use values. To estimate the values humans place on forests, clean air, or particular animal species, this approach is simply to ask them. It is called "contingent" valuation because people are asked to state their willingness to pay, contingent on a hypothetical scenario involving environmental assets. CVM surveys can collect data on wildlife like worms and mosses for which there are few associated expenditures that would reveal their value.

CVM studies have employed four primary question formats. **Open-ended questions** simply ask the participant for his or her maximum willingness to pay for the environmental improvement being studied. **Dichotomous choice methods** provide a single value that can either be accepted or rejected. The sample question below about river preservation is an example of the dichotomous choice method. **Payment cards** with several values printed on them are sometimes shown to participants, who are asked if any of those values are close to their maximum willingness to pay. And in **bidding games,** participants receive values sequentially, either in ascending order until a value is rejected, or in descending order until a value is accepted. Some empirical research suggests that the question format does not have a statistically significant effect on the estimated willingness to pay, although the payment card method seems to

20 See Randall (1994).

21 For more on the RURM, and for a comparison of TCM and RURM methods, see Pendleton and Mendelsohn (2000).

reality check

Findings: Some Interpretations of Prices

John Loomis, Shizuka Yorizane, and Douglas Larson (2000) used TCM methods to estimate a willingness to pay of $43 per person per day for whale-watching trips. Gamini Herath (1999) studied the consumer surplus derived from Lake Mokoan in Australia using the TCM, finding a value of about $30,000 per year. As a reminder that the TCM is strictly anthropocentric, note that unwatched whales and unvisited lakes would receive no value under this approach, despite their ecocentric, existence, and option values.

Adrian Phillips (1998) of the World Commission on Protected Areas provides the following valuation estimates from case studies. Forests in Kenya are worth $323 per household per year for medicines, wild foods, hunting, building materials, and related uses. The total present value of Borivli National Park to residents of Mumbai (Bombay) is $35 million. The introduction of lions into the Pilanesberg Protected Area in South Africa cost between $74,000 and $784,000 for purchase and maintenance, but increased tourism revenues by between $6.2 million and $14 million. And in Nepal, broadleaf forests have a net present value between $2,877 and $3,807 per hectare (a hectare equals 2.47 acres), while evergreen forests in the same region are valued at $2,282 per hectare.

In 1998, $495 million in state and federal funds were spent to purchase and protect the 7,500-acre Headwaters Forest Preserve, which was the largest privately owned stand of old-growth redwoods (*Sequoiadendron gigantium*) left in the world. This suggests a lower bound for the value society places on the ancient redwoods and other endangered wildlife that live there, including the marbled murrelet (*Brachyramphus marmoratus*) and the northern spotted owl (*Strix occidentalis caurina*).

Many U.S. states including Kentucky offer environmental license plates with a $10 premium, some of which goes to protect endangered species. Similarly, power companies such as the Lansing Board of Water and Light offer energy from environmentally friendly sources for an additional charge of $7.50 per 250 kWh block (see www.lbwl.com). Although free-riding is a temptation whenever public goods are involved, participation rates and expenditures on these programs are another indication of the value individuals place on endangered species and the environment. In 2012, the Kentucky Heritage Land Conservation Fund earned $571,970 from environmental license plate sales. The important point is that we are not in the dark when it comes to the valuation of environmental assets, whether or not the assets are sold in the market. The prices of substitutes and complements hold considerable information, and increasingly accurate indicators of value are appearing in the environmental economics literature to guide policymaking.

improve response rates.[22]

Several other pitfalls can bias CVM results if not handled adequately. **Hypothetical bias** results from respondents who do not take the hypothetical situation seriously or provide unrealistic responses because they do not actually have to pay the amounts of money they assign to resources. Saying that you would pay $10 to save the manatee is easier than reaching into your pocket and handing over the money. For this reason, survey designers word questions to encourage a mindset similar to that which would exist if the money discussed were real. The following example comes from a CVM study of rivers in the "Four Corners" region of the western United States that provide habitat for nine species of threatened or endangered fish:[23]

> *Suppose a proposal to establish a Four Corners Region Threatened and Endangered Fish Trust Fund was on the ballot in the next nationwide election. How would you vote on this proposal? Remember, by law, the funds could only be used to improve habitat for fish. If the Four Corners Region Threatened and Endangered Fish Trust Fund was the only issue on the next ballot and it would cost your household $______ every year, would you vote in favor of it? (Please circle one.)*
> *YES / NO*

The researchers filled in the blank beforehand with a randomly selected amount between $1 and $350. They concluded that a typical household was willing to pay about $195.

If it is apparent from the survey design that the purpose of a study is to determine whether or not to go forward with a policy to save the manatee, respondents might exaggerate their WTP if they favor the policy, or understate their WTP if they oppose the policy. This is called **strategic bias**. Because survey results are suspect if the intent is transparent and vulnerable to strategic bias, studies often conceal or disguise their intent.

Embedding effects are a concern when many benefits are associated with a particular action, because expressed values might apply to more than the benefit being evaluated. Svedsater (2000) found that respondents were willing to pay more to limit global warming alone than when asked to attach values to global warming and three other environmental concerns. This suggests that the values for the other three concerns might have been embedded into the value assigned to global warming alone. Similarly, if people are asked what they would pay for a decrease in paper production involving chlorine,[24] their stated values might incorporate the benefits from reductions in broader categories of air and water pollution that would accompany a general decrease in paper production. In

22 See Reaves, Kramer, and Holmes (1999).

23 See Ekstrand and Loomis (1998). A similar study was conducted in New Mexico by Berrens, Ganderton, and Silva (1996), finding a mean willingness to pay of $90.

24 For a discussion of paper bleaching supported by the Wild Rockies Information Network, see www.wildrockies.org/cmcr/Pulp/TCFvsECF.html. For a discussion supported by the chemical industry, see www.ecfpaper.org/epp/guidelines.html.

reality check

Findings: Examples of CVM Valuations for Animal Species

Despite the necessary caveats, CVM studies are popular for their versatility in valuing the reintroduction or preservation of environmental assets. In a summary of past CVM estimates, Richardson and Loomis (2009) reported average per-person, per-year WTP values of $39, $13, and $81 for bald eagles, wild turkey, and salmon/steelhead, respectively.

Stevens et al. (1991) found that although 80 percent of CVM respondents attributed importance to animal species, the majority indicated no willingness to pay to reintroduce them into the wild. The reasons for these apparently irrational WTP values of zero included payment vehicle bias (they were opposed to the donation payment vehicle), information bias (they were uncertain about their valuation), and the belief that nature should not be valued in dollar terms. The authors concluded, "the CVM may not provide a valid measure of existence value and we therefore argue that benefit-cost analysis should generally not be used to make decisions about the existence of wildlife."

Reaves, Kramer, and Holmes (1999) asked U.S. residents what they would pay per year to increase the probability of survival of the red cockaded woodpecker from 50 percent to 99 percent. The average willingness to pay was about $14, which suggests a preservation value of $3.8 billion per year for the 274 million U.S. residents. Discounting future benefits at 3 percent per year, the present value of the benefits over all time would be $127 billion. Each of the estimated values in this section is for the protection of a single species. As explained, as more and more species are eliminated, the value of protecting subsequent species is expected to increase.

Rubin, Helfand, and Loomis (1991) used contingent valuation methods to estimate a value for the spotted owl of about $43 per resident of Washington State. They went on to calculate the cost of preservation in terms of logging jobs and effects on the price of timber. The long-term gain from preservation was estimated to be $1.84 million, while the estimated long-term cost was $0.62 million. Given that the benefit exceeds the cost, these findings suggest that the appropriate policy would be to reduce logging enough to preserve the species. In the absence of a policy to reduce logging, Ronald Coase would point out that both groups—those benefiting from preservation and those harmed by it—would be better off if those harmed were compensated with some amount between $0.62 million and $1.84 million in exchange for preservation. If those in the timber market were compensated with exactly their $0.62 loss, society at large would gain $1.84 – $0.62 = $1.22 million relative to its position with logging.

anticipation of this, CVM studies must carefully clarify the change to be valued and/or include follow-up questions to discern what benefits respondents have associated with their stated willingness to pay.

Respondents are also subject to the following types of bias:

Information bias: They have insufficient information about the asset being valued.

Interviewer bias: They are influenced by the person who is conducting the survey.

Payment vehicle bias: They are influenced by the type of payment mentioned in the survey, such as taxes or donations.

Sampling bias: Those selected as respondents do not represent the larger population.

Self-selection bias: Those with strong opinions may be more likely to respond.

Starting point bias: Respondents are influenced by the values listed in the survey.

These and related sources of bias make the survey design of utmost importance and necessitate careful scrutiny of survey-based conclusions.

Hedonic Pricing The **hedonic pricing** approach evaluates differences in the prices of goods or services caused by (in this context) environmental assets or liabilities. If workers are willing to accept a lower wage for planting trees in a forest than for planting seeds on a farm, other things being equal, the difference in wages reflects the workers' valuation of being in the forest. Likewise, if the price of hotel rooms is higher in areas with more biodiversity than in areas with less, other things being equal, this difference reflects a use value for biodiversity. Regression analysis allows economists to study the hedonic (quality adjusted) effects of chosen variables like pollution or biodiversity levels on prices while holding the effects of other measurable price determinants constant. Hedonic methods have also become dominant in economic research into the value of our own species, as discussed in the upcoming Reality Check.

A downside of hedonic pricing methods, as with other price-based valuations, is that there are often passive-use values that do not enter into the prices of products associated with biodiversity. For example, the effect of the Cockscomb Basin Wildlife Sanctuary on room rates at the nearby Jaguar Reef Lodge in Belize does not indicate the existence or option values of the sanctuary's sensitive biodiversity to citizens of, say, Sweden. Another drawback is that large datasets are typically needed to establish statistically significant relationships between prices and environmental variables while holding other price determinants constant. While demographic and employment variables are readily available, environmental variables are harder to come by in large collections of data.

Findings: The Hedonic Value of Homo Sapiens

Economists often seek values for natural assets to inform policy decisions about what expenditure level is warranted in order to preserve those assets. The same is true for *Homo sapiens*, whom myriad environmental policies are designed to save. Kaiser (2003) writes that EPA regulations on drinking water save lives for between zero and $6.8 million each, while Occupational Safety & Health Administration regulations on industrial exposure to methylene chloride save lives at a cost of $12.7 million each. Some asbestos regulations are said to save lives at over $100 million each. As with owls and woodpeckers, we must decide where to draw the line in terms of expenditures per life saved.

Over and above the value we place on other animals, one might think that we consider ourselves priceless. This is not the case. If human life were invaluable, every risky activity would involve an infinite expected value of loss (the risk of death times the infinite value of life), and every policy that might save a life would warrant whatever expenses it entails. The fact that people leave the safety of their homes, drive in cars, and walk across streets demonstrates that we place finite values on human life.

Hedonic pricing studies have estimated the values of species including *Homo sapiens*. Viscusi and Aldy (2003) review 60 studies of the value of a "statistical life" and report a median value for *Homo sapiens* of around $7 million. A **statistical life** is not the life of a particular individual, but the expected value of one life made up of a small chance of losing many different people's lives, such as a 1 in 10,000 chance of death faced by 10,000 people. Economists can measure the value of a small risk of death by examining the trade-offs between wages and risks of occupational fatalities, adjusting for other determinants of wages. Additional observable trade-offs between death risks and either money or time (which has monetary value) involve driving speeds, the purchase of safety equipment, and safety belt use. If the average worker will accept an extra $700 per year in exchange for a 1 in 10,000 annual risk of death, that worker implicitly values 1/10,000th of his or her life at $700, and an entire statistical life would be worth 10,000 × $700 = $7,000,000. We may not be priceless, but we are certainly our own favorite contribution to biodiversity.

Making Use of the Numbers

Armed with estimates of the value of animals, we are now better prepared to evaluate policy proposals. The estimated value of the human animal suggests drinking water regulations that saved lives for $500,000 each were a bargain, but the particular uranium and asbestos regulations that saved lives for $30 million to $100 million exceeded our own willingness to pay for a statistical life.

As another example, annual road-kill losses in Florida's Paynes Prairie State Preserve amounted to an estimated 100,000 animals per year.[25] Floridians were faced with the decision of whether to build a barrier to prevent animals from entering the road that passes through Paynes Prairie. The barrier would cost $3.6 million, which we will initially assume is an all-or-nothing proposition.[26] Knowing the number of animals lost each year, the cost of the barrier, and an appropriate discount rate, some straightforward mathematics will guide us to the cost of preserving each animal.

The present discounted value of a **perpetuity** (an unending series of benefits or costs), such as the lives saved by the barrier, equals the value per period divided by the discount rate per period. With an annual discount rate of 0.03 as discussed in Chapter 5, the present discounted value of the barrier would be

$$\frac{100{,}000 \times \text{monetary value per animal}}{0.03}$$

Setting this perpetuity value equal to $3.6 million and solving for the monetary value per animal yields a value of $1.08. If a valuation method determined that the actual value per animal was $1.08 or higher, as has been the case in past research on various animal species as discussed in the Realigy Check, the expense of the barrier would be justified.

If there are a variety of options regarding the length (or height or material quality) of the wildlife barrier, the fact that the total benefit would exceed the total cost for a particular length does not imply that building a wall of that length would be efficient. As explained in Chapter 2, there are often a number of policies under which the total benefit would exceed the total cost, but only one policy that would achieve efficiency by equating the marginal benefit and the marginal cost, and thereby maximizing the difference between the total benefit and the total cost. Floridians will receive the largest net benefit by extending the wildlife barrier until the marginal benefit of another unit of length would no longer exceed the marginal cost.

25 See Associated Press (2000).

26 Due to the various expenses of tax collection and administration, it costs more than $1 for the government to spend $1 on a project. For the purposes of this example, assume that the $3.6 million includes all associated expenses.

Uncertainty

"Whether the species offers immediate advantage or not, no means exists to measure what benefits it will offer during future centuries of study, what scientific knowledge, or what service to the human spirit."

—Edward O. Wilson[27]

Biodiversity loss involves the complicating factors of uncertainty and irreversibility. We never know what benefits would have come from a lost species, or how many species are eliminated before being discovered. The benefits gained from existing species and the measured decline in known species give us some indication. Over 120 prescription drugs are currently derived from plants, and a quarter of all Western pharmaceuticals are derived from rainforest ingredients. At the same time, only 1 in 100 plants has been tested for medicinal value.[28]

The discount rates discussed in Chapter 5 influence the value we place on future discoveries. If we valued future benefits the same as today's, any annual benefits to begin in the future would have an infinite value when multiplied by the infinite number of years ahead. Economic models generally presume that we discount the value of future benefits in some way. The subjectivity of discount rates and uncertainty about the number of undiscovered benefits cloud estimates and open the door for assumptions that yield desired conclusions for or against conservation efforts. Recent discoveries that the skin of the African clawed frog secretes a previously unknown family of antibiotics, and that the liver of the dogfish shark contains a cancer-fighting steroid called squalamine,[29] are reminders that biodiversity may speak to many unanswered questions.

The prospect of irreversible species loss and uncertainty surrounding the value of biodiversity has led some scholars to advocate a **safe minimum standard** (SMS) of conservation as an alternative or adjunct to cost-benefit analysis.[30] As first conceived, the SMS strategy aims to maintain at least the minimum viable population of a species unless the cost of doing so is intolerably high. Given uncertainty about valuation techniques, undiscovered benefits, and the requirements for species viability, proponents argue that it is advisable to err on the safe side. This strategy de-emphasizes the benefit side of cost-benefit analysis in regard to conservation efforts. In practice, it may be difficult to divorce our tolerance level for preservation costs from our perception of the associated benefits. Nonetheless, the point is well taken that estimated benefit levels for biodiversity are often tentative at best, and that we should preserve species when it is realistic to do so.

27 Kellert and Wilson (1993), p. 37.

28 See Taylor (1998).

29 See Swerdlow (1999). Squalamine is a natural steroid that fights cancer by cutting off blood flow to tumors. A chemical structure similar to that of squalamine is found in the bark of the Holarrhena tree and in *Chonemorpha macrophylla*, a climbing plant that grows in the Himalayan foothills.

30 The SMS concept was originated by Ciriacy-Wantrup (1963), first published in 1952. More recent discussions include Seidl and Tisdell (2001) and Berrens et al. (1998).

Summary

Economic analysis can inform the choice and design of policy instruments to achieve biodiversity goals. Although none of the valuation methods is as accurate as we would like, given the wide array of policy options and their varying costs, it is often better to have some idea of the value of wildlife than no idea. Cost-benefit analysis is a useful tool for allocating natural resources when costs and benefits are carefully considered; otherwise it can be misleading. Among the categories of values that should not be overlooked, *option values* are associated with the ability to use a resource in the future. *Use values* are derived from the actual use of resources and their by-products. *Nonuse* or *passive-use values* are not associated with the hands-on use of a resource, but are derived from its mere existence and the ability of others to benefit from it. *Existence values* come from knowledge that a resource exists, unrelated to present or future use of the resource. *Sympathy values* come from knowing that a species has survived, and not from the ability to come into contact with the species. One's *willingness to accept* is the smallest amount of money one would willingly accept to forego a resource. One's *willingness to pay* is the largest amount of money one would be willing to pay in exchange for a resource.

Do you have a sympathy value for this caterpillar species?

The tools of economics lend themselves to the valuation and management of biodiversity, at least from an anthropocentric viewpoint. Prices indicate the marginal value users receive from marketed natural resources. Expenditures on wilderness views, forest products, and medicinal cures indicate the lower bound for the use values of their sources. *Hedonic pricing* methods evaluate the effect of biodiversity on market prices such as room rates at hotels, home prices, and wages. With that information, economists can extrapolate to estimate the value of biodiversity itself. The *contingent valuation method* uses sophisticated surveys to summon revealing responses about the value of resources to society. By these means, economists gain critical estimates of values for comparison with preservation costs as society addresses the prudence of production and development projects. The appropriate management of biodiversity must rest on carefully considered values that are direct and indirect, present and future, financial and emotional, and well informed. Only then can we make wise trade-offs between natural resources and the competing fruits of civilization.

Problems for Review

1. Write out a food chain that starts with plankton and ends with humans. Why is an understanding of the food chain important to the economic analysis of plant and animal species?

2. What is the most you would be willing to contribute in a one-time payment for the return of the passenger pigeon (*Ectopistes migratorius*)? What is the least you would accept in a one-time payment for the loss of the white-crowned pigeon (*Columba leucocephala*)? Explain why these values are different, or why they are the same.

3. If everyone in your country responded to a survey about the white-crowned pigeon by stating the same willingness to pay that you did, what is the CVM valuation of the white-crowned pigeon? What components of value would this estimate omit?

4. Room rates in rural Bland, Virginia, are $34 per night. Rates in suburban Plainville, Connecticut, are $77 per night. Comparable accommodations cost $89 per night in rural West Yellowstone and $96 per night in suburban Everglades City, Florida. Interpret these findings.

5. A value of what type is revealed by your answer to Question 4? Which valuation method does this information lend itself to?

6. Do you feel it is appropriate to make decisions about species preservation on the basis of anthropocentric values? Why or why not?

7. If you were Noah and you could preserve half of the species on the planet, how would you decide which species to provide with boarding passes? Be specific. Your method does not need to be one of those described in this chapter.

8. Provide a specific example that is not found in this textbook of each of the following:

    a) An option value

    b) A bequest value

    c) A sympathy value

9. Suppose there is a 1 in 1,000 chance that a snake will bite you while you are walking to class, and if you are bitten, you will certainly die unless you are carrying antivenin with you at the time. What is the most you would be willing to pay for a dose of antivenin? What does that tell you about your valuation of a statistical life?

10. Describe a weakness of the CVM method. What makes this method attractive despite potential flaws?

1. Find a list of currently endangered species and a list of extinct species.
2. Find a website that discusses the monetary value of an animal or plant species.
3. Find a website that challenges the validity of the contingent valuation method.

Internet Resources

Conservation International, a site dedicated to biodiversity:
www.conservation.org

Ecotourism Explorer:
www.ecotourism.org

Environment Canada information on Nature and Biodiversity:
http://www.ec.gc.ca/nature/

United Kingdom Joint Nature Conservation Committee:
http://jncc.defra.gov.uk

The U.S. Fish and Wildlife Service's Endangered Species Program:
endangered.fws.gov

Further Reading

Anderson, David A. "Evaluating Policies for Sustainability: The Neglected Influence of Visual Images." *International Journal of Environmental, Cultural, Economic and Social Sustainability* 1, no. 5 (2006): 1–8. Finds that the value humans place on environmental assets depends critically on the level of personal exposure to those assets.

Associated Press. "Building Begins on U.S. 441 'Wildlife Wall' Through Paynes Prairie." *The Orlando Sentinel* (January 7, 2000). Discusses the physical barrier between a highway and a wilderness area that saves 100,000 animals each year.

Berrens, Robert, Davis S. Brookshire, Michael McKee, and Christian Schmidt. "Implementing the Safe Minimum Standard Approach: Two Case Studies from the U.S. Endangered Species Act." *Land Economics* 74, no. 2 (1998): 147–161. Provides examples of SMS applications to the threat of irreversible losses of at-risk species.

Berrens, Robert, Philip Ganderton, and Carol Silva. "Valuing the Protection of Minimum Instream Flows in New Mexico." *Journal of Agricultural and Resource Economics* 21, no. 2 (1996): 294–309. A CVM study of the value of river habitat.

Bowker, J. M., and J. R. Stoll. "Use of Dichotomous Choice Nonmarket Methods to Value the Whooping Crane Resource." *American Journal of Agricultural Economics* 70 (1988): 372–381. An example of nonmarket research on the value of animal species.

Ciriacy-Wantrup, S. *Resource Conservation: Economics and Policies.* Berkeley: Division of Agricultural Sciences, University of California, 1963. The seminal work on the safe minimum standard conservation strategy.

Ekstrand, Earl R., and John Loomis. "Incorporating Respondent Uncertainty When Estimating Willingness to Pay for Protecting Critical Habitat for Threatened and Endangered Fish." *Water Resources Research* 34, no. 11 (November 1998): 3149–3155. A CVM study of the value of river habitat in the Four Corners region, where water is in high demand for multiple uses.

Herath, Gamini. "Estimation of Community Values of Lakes: A Study of Lake Mokoan in Victoria, Australia." *Economic Analysis and Policy* 29, no. 1 (1999): 31–44. Uses the CVM and TCM to assess the value of a small lake.

Kaiser, Jocelyn. "How Much Are Human Lives and Health Worth?" *Science* 299 (2003): 1836–1837. A discussion of the application of value-of-life estimates to policy decisions.

Kellert, Stephen R., and Edward O. Wilson. *The Biophilia Hypothesis.* Washington D.C.: Island Press, 1993. An edited volume of essays by various authors about the human dependence on nature.

Loomis, John, Shizuka Yorizane, and Douglas Larson. "Testing Significance of Multi-destination and Multi-purpose Trip Effects in a Travel Cost Method Demand Model for Whale Watching Trips." *Agricultural and Resource Economics Review* 29, no. 2 (2000): 183–191. Compares alternative TCM models and associated estimates of willingness to pay to view biodiversity.

Metrick, Andrew, and Martin L. Weitzman. "Conflicts and Choices in Biodiversity." *Journal of Economic Perspectives* 12, no. 3 (1998): 21–34. A discussion of the Noah's Ark method and how its implications compare to reality.

Morell, Virginia. "The Variety of Life." *National Geographic* (February 1999): 6–18. A rich and accessible article on biodiversity and its proponents.

Myers, Norman, Russell A. Mittermeier, Cristina G. Mittermeier, Gustavo A. B. da Fonseca, and Jennifer Kent. "Biodiversity Hotspots for Conservation Priorities." *Nature* 403 (2000): 853–858. Describes the analytic methods and findings of research into hotspots that harbor the greatest concentration of plant and vertebrate species.

Naeem, S., L. J. Thompson, S. P. Lawler, J. H. Lawton, and R. M. Woodfin. "Empirical Evidence That Declining Species Diversity May Alter the Performance of Terrestrial Ecosystems." *Philosophical Transactions of the Royal Society* (London, B.) 347 (1995): 249–262. A fascinating examination of the relationship between species "richness" and function.

Nelson, Robert H. "The Forest Service's Tinderbox." *Today's Commentary.* Cato Institute (February 2, 2001): www.cato.org/dailys/02-02-01.html. A call to release national forests to the states and otherwise increase human access to forested lands.

Pendleton, Linwood, and Robert Mendelsohn. "Estimating Recreation Preferences Using Hedonic Travel Cost and Random Utility Models." *Environmental and Resource Economics* 17, no. 1 (2000): 89–108. Compares the underlying assumptions and outcomes from the TCM and RURM approaches to valuing recreational sites.

Phillips, Adrian. *Economic Values of Protected Areas: Guidelines for Protected Area Managers*. Cambridge: IUCN Publications Services Unit, 1998. An overview of values for nonmarket goods.

Pimm, Stuart L., G. J. Russell, J. L. Gittleman, and T. M. Brooks. "The Future of Biodiversity." *Science* 269 (1995): 347–350. A collection of forecasts and estimates relating to biodiversity's "big picture."

Polasky, Stephen, Jeffrey D. Camm, and Brian Garber-Yonts. "Selecting Biological Reserves Cost-Effectively: An Application to Terrestrial Vertebrate Conservation in Oregon." *Land Economics* 77, no. 1 (2001): 68–78. Describes cost-effective conservation efforts that consider differential land costs in addition to biodiversity.

Randall, Alan. "A Difficulty with the Travel Cost Method." *Land Economics* 70 (1994): 88–96. Argues against the use of the TCM to derive value estimates for cost-benefit analysis, saying that travel costs are unobservable.

Randall, Alan, and John P. Hoehn. "Embedding in Market Demand Systems." *Journal of Environmental Economics and Management* 30, no. 3 (1996): 369–380.

Reaves, D. W., R. A. Kramer, and T. P. Holmes. "Does Question Format Matter? Valuing an Endangered Species." *Environmental and Resource Economics* 14, no. 3 (1999): 365–383. Compares the results of three different formats for CVM questions.

Richardson, L. and J. Loomis. "The Total Economic Value of Threatened, Endangered and Rare Species: An Updated Meta-analysis." *Ecological Economics* 68, no. 5 (2009): 1535–1548. An overview of contingent valuation studies that finds that newer studies estimate higher willingness to pay values for wildlife than older studies.

Rubin, Jonathan, Gloria Helfand, and John Loomis. "A Benefit-Cost Analysis of the Northern Spotted Owl." *Journal of Forestry Research* 89 (1991): 25–30. A CVM study conducted in Washington State.

Seidl, Irmi, and Clem A. Tisdell. "Neglected Features of the Same Minimum Standard: Socio-economic and Institutional Dimensions." *Review of Social Economy* 59, no. 4 (2001): 417–442. A worthwhile discussion of SMS interpretations and applications.

Smith, V. Kerry, and William H. Desvousges. "Averting Behavior: Does It Exist?" In *Estimating Values for Nature: Methods for Non-Market Valuation,* edited by V. K. Smith. Cheltenham: Elgar, 1996, 426–431. Reviews the evolution of methods to estimate the demand for natural assets.

Sohrabi, Saraj B., A. Yachkaschi, D. Oladi, Teimouri S. Fard, and H. Latifi. "The Recreational Valuation of a Natural Forest Park using the Travel Cost Method in Iran." *iForest* 2 (2009): 85–92. Available at www.sisef.it/iforest/show.php?id=497. A travel cost study of the Abbas Abad Forest with policy implications for harvest decisions.

Stevens, T. H., J. Echeverria, R. J. Glass, T. Hager, and T. A. Moore. "Measuring the Existence Value of Wildlife: What Do CVM Estimates Really Show?" *Land Economics* 67 (1991): 390–400. A CVM study of bald eagles.

Svedsater, Henrik. "Contingent Valuation of Global Environmental Resources: Test of Perfect and Regular Embedding." *Journal of Economic Psychology* 21, no. 6 (2000): 605–623.

Swerdlow, Joel L. "Biodiversity." *National Geographic* (February 1999): 6–8. A colorful narrative on biodiversity, its virtues, and efforts to study it.

Taylor, Leslie. *Herbal Secrets of the Rainforest.* Roseville, CA: Prima Communications, Inc., 1998. A discussion of some of the many discoveries that biodiversity may hold.

Van Kooten, G. Cornelis, and Erwin H. Bulte. *The Economics of Nature.* Malden, MA: Blackwell Publishers, 2000. A rigorous overview of natural resource management, including valuation techniques.

Viscusi, W. Kip, and Joseph E. Aldy. "The Value of a Statistical Life: A Critical Review of Market Estimates Throughout the World." *Journal of Risk and Uncertainty* 27, no. 1 (2003): 5–76. A literature review of attempts to place a value on human life.

Weitzman, Martin L. "The Noah's Ark Problem." *Econometrica* 66, no. 6 (1998): 1279–1298. Discusses the theory and practice of the Noah's Ark method.

P.SIRIMONGKHÖN

11 International and Global Issues

Before his plane disappeared in the Nevada desert, Steve Fossett circled the globe on a sailboat, and floating under a balloon, and in an airplane without refueling. Our planet is small enough for solo circumnavigation, and many of the planet's environmental problems likewise transcend national borders. Greenhouse gases and other uniformly distributed pollutants float like Fossett and his balloon across the globe. Many nonuniformly distributed pollutants pose international risks as well, including sulfur dioxide and nitrogen oxides as sources of acid deposition. On the ground are the similarly intricate international issues of deforestation, endangered species, and polluted seas, to name a few.

Consider complications in the market for ivory. Among those favoring the legal trade of ivory are residents of Japan, Taiwan, and China, who treasure it, and hunters in Botswana, Namibia, South Africa, and Zimbabwe, who would like to supply it. Proponents of a complete ban on the trade of ivory include many residents of Kenya, Zambia, Mali, and Liberia, who value elephants as part of their natural heritage, and residents of the United States, India, and European nations, who place a high existence value on charismatic megafauna. Without a ban, the elephant population fell steeply from 1.3 million in 1979 to below 750,000 in 1988. With a complete ban starting in 1989, affluent buyers could not obtain their treasures, and impoverished hunters lost their incomes. Compounding this international dilemma are debates over the size of existing elephant populations and the herd size necessary for viability.

While many environmental and natural resource issues can be addressed unilaterally, large and complex threats exemplified by global climate change and species endangerment require cooperation. Globalization may foster communication and mutual understanding among nations, though not without posing environmental threats of its own. This chapter focuses on environmental and natural resource problems with remedies that involve international cooperation, and discusses the organizations, policies, and agreements that govern resource allocation and the environment.

Globalization and the Environment

The Good, the Bad, and the Ugly

The term "globalization" itself is seemingly innocuous and straightforward, meaning that something—in our context commerce—takes on a global scope. In terms of its implications, however, globalization means different things to different people. Globalization is both feared and revered for the exports and influences that extend across regional boundaries. The exchange of ideas and information can foster education and promote the understanding of other cultures. Cooperation can lead to important medicinal cures and technological leaps. And it is economically efficient to allow regions to specialize according to their comparative advantages and then trade to achieve a desired balance of goods and services.

Why, then, are some groups fervently opposed to globalization? Critics voice several concerns. They worry that the influence of multinational corporations rivals that of democratically elected representatives and represents an unsettling concentration of power among those driven by profit motives. Intensified globalization might lead to a relatively homogeneous world market, causing cultures to lose their identities. And without ecological tariffs or similar policies as discussed in Chapter 8, production might easily be shifted to countries with low environmental and humanitarian standards, increasing the exploitation of human and natural resources. This section explores the contentious paths of cooperation, homogenization, and exploitation that stem from the growing trend of globalization.

Cooperation International cooperation is economically prudent in several contexts. Specialization and trade provide the benefits of comparative advantage and economies of scale. Shared information, about clean energy technology for example, can provide a public good for those who would otherwise have to reinvent products or processes on their own. International cooperation to assemble financial and human capital can contribute to the success of environmental research, as with efforts to track and propagate endangered species, and the work of the Center for International Forestry Research.[1] Increased legal cooperation improves the ability to enforce regional environmental policies.

Cooperation also permits the sharing of risk. Much like the purchase of

1 See www.cifor.cgiar.org/.

health insurance, with sick individuals receiving funds from the collective pool of premiums, international organizations can pool funds and disburse them for relief from environmental disasters, including oil spills, droughts, storms, and floods. When Hurricane Sandy devastated Haiti in 2012, UNICEF[2] provided clean water and sanitation equipment, and the Red Cross stepped up its efforts to provide food and shelter that had continued since the earthquake there in 2010.

Cooperative educational efforts include the work of UNESCO, the United Nations Educational, Scientific, and Cultural Organization. UNESCO sponsors educational programs on climate change, sustainability, biodiversity, and conservation, among other topics, across nearly 200 member nations.[3] In 2012, the World Bank helped 145,420,000 people gain access to improved water supplies.[4] Cooperative efforts to address five other types of environmental problems are discussed later in the chapter.

Homogenization While understanding and information are benefits of cultural exchange, homogenization can be an associated cost. Signs of change include lost languages and dialects, and new eating habits in the 121 countries now served by McDonald's. Fast food restaurants themselves are of concern to some environmentalists,[5] who eschew excessive packaging, the clearing of forest for cattle and their feed, and the inefficiency of eating high on the food chain.[6] To critics of globalization, the fast food franchises are symbolic of a more general dissemination of unsustainable practices and lifestyles. These environmental issues are aside from the inevitable conclusion that homogeneous cultures would be dull.

Spices on display in India. Homogenization can result in the loss of cultural diversity. For better or worse, McDonald's, KFC and Domino's already compete with traditional Indian fare.

Some worry that seductive corporate advertising and contagious materialistic values could create a world of people with insatiable appetites for consumption. If the world population consumed at the rate of those in the United Arab Emirates, the United States, Kuwait, Denmark, and Australia, for example, it would take four to five planets like Earth to supply the resources. Even with current global

2 UNICEF is the United Nations Children's Fund, with offices in 126 countries. The acronym comes from the organization's original name, the United Nations International Children's Emergency Fund.

3 See www.unesco.org.

4 See www.worldbank.org

5 See www.mcspotlight.org/issues/environment/index.html.

6 It takes more than ten times as much acreage and water to produce a pound of meat as it does to produce a pound of wheat. For related discussions, see Ehrlich and Ehrlich (1979).

lifestyle standards, the average human is consuming 30 percent more resources than the Earth can sustain.[7] Other things being equal, one might expect a cultural give-and-take in which citizens from high-consumption countries gained ideas about how to live simply from countries with more sustainable economies. Yet with an imbalance in marketing savvy, a balance in influence is unlikely.

Of course, international trade has been going on for millennia, and its influences are nothing new. America has adopted plant and animal species, fashions, and cuisine from its trading partners since Asian and European visitors first arrived. Newer, however, are the marketing mechanisms by which firms persuade other cultures to sidestep tradition and adopt their products. If major sportswear, restaurant, electronics, and chemical companies, among others, are becoming increasingly adroit at changing the customs of international customers, the assertions of globalization critics may be noteworthy—there may indeed be new problems stemming from the old practice of global trade.

Exploitation In theory, global trade could permit a spreading of wealth. That has not yet been the case in practice. The share of global income received by the poorest 20 percent of people remains at or below 1 percent. It is increasingly convenient for profit-maximizing firms to shop across countries for production sites where labor or environment standards are low. When the goal is production at the lowest possible cost, both workers and the environment can suffer. For example, Gills (2002) found that globalization has led to the exploitation of female workers in Asia, and Dasgupta, Mamingi, and Meisner (2001) found that globalization promoted pesticide use in Brazil, particularly on export crops.

Modern trade policies often include provisions to protect the environment. For example, the North American Free Trade Agreement (NAFTA) includes language that prevents strict environmental standards from being challenged as non-tariff trade barriers. NAFTA also discourages countries from lowering their environmental standards as an incentive for firms to relocate. Even so, the difficulties of funding, monitoring, and enforcing environmental protection policies across international borders mean the provisions are often inadequate.[8] Improved systems of ecological tariffs are one solution advocated by some economists;[9] advancements in monitoring technology may provide another. At this point, however, the possibility of environmental and labor exploitation should be considered among the costs of global trade.

Organizations

The elements of successful policy initiatives are somewhat different at the international and global level than at the national or local level. Cultural and governmental influences are muted at borderlines. Even the strongest armies have difficulty enforcing policy among rogue nations. And international law

7 See www.panda.org/lpr/08/.

8 See www.foreignpolicy-infocus.org/briefs/vol4/v4n26nafta.html.

9 See Ederington (2001).

is only as binding as the multinational commitments that back it up. At the same time, humans share sources of oxygen, environmental sinks, habitat for endangered species, and the repercussions of environmental degradation. Our vital interests in international oversight have spawned several organizations of considerable strength and controversy. Given their awesome responsibilities, it is of value to be familiar with them. It will add meaning to your daily perusal of environmental economics in the media, and given your interests, you may well work for or lead one of them in the future.

The United Nations The United Nations (UN) began in 1945 with 51 countries seeking to "maintain international peace and security; to develop friendly relations among nations; to cooperate in solving international economic, social, cultural and humanitarian problems and in promoting respect for human rights and fundamental freedoms; and to be a centre for harmonizing the actions of nations in attaining these ends."[10] The organization now boasts 193 member countries, 40 agencies and organizations, and an extensive array of programs and bodies. On the environmental front, the UN "family of organizations" includes the Global Program on Globalization, Liberalization and Sustainable Human Development, the Inter-Agency Committee on Sustainable Development, the International Seabed Authority, the UN Food and Agriculture Organization, and the UN Environment Program. The latest activities of these organizations are summarized online at www.unsystem.org.

The United Nations has focused global attention on the environment with major conferences, including the 1992 Rio de Janeiro Conference on Environment and Development (UNCED), the 2002 World Summit on Sustainable Development in Johannesburg, South Africa, and the 2013 UN Climate Change Conference in Bonn, Germany. These gatherings set forth a plethora of initiatives and commissions, including the Rio Declaration on Environment and Development (Agenda 21)[11] and the Statement of Principles for the Sustainable Management of Forests. The Commission on Sustainable Development (CSD) was created in 1992 to follow up on the goals of UNCED and monitor the implementation of environmental agreements.

At the 1999 World Economic Forum in Switzerland, UN Secretary-General Kofi Annan challenged world business leaders to "embrace and enact" the principles of the UN Global Compact.[12] Covering human rights, labor, and the environment, the compact's principles include the development and use of environmentally friendly technologies, initiatives to promote greater environmental responsibility, and support for a "precautionary principle" of erring on the safe side of environmental risks (discussed later in this chapter). These principles are representative of the UN's stance on the environment.

The World Trade Organization In 1995, the World Trade Organization (WTO) succeeded the World-War-II-era General Agreement on Tariffs and Trade (GATT)

10 See www.un.org/aboutun/basicfacts/unorg.htm.

11 See www.un.org/esa/sustdev/agenda21chapter11.htm.

12 See 65.214.34.30/un/gc/unweb.nsf/.

as the global authority on rules of international trade. WTO policies are the result of negotiations among its 144 member nations. Among these, the General Agreement on Trade in Services (GATS) is the services equivalent to GATT, which covers merchandise. Merchandise represents 40 percent of global production but 80 percent of global trade. These trade agreements seek to create "a credible and reliable system of international trade rules; ensuring fair and equitable treatment of all participants (principle of non-discrimination); stimulating economic activity through guaranteed policy bindings; and promoting trade and development through progressive liberalization."[13]

The Trade-Related Aspects of Intellectual Property Rights (TRIPS)[14] agreement covers copyrights, undisclosed information, patents (as for new varieties of plants), and related intellectual property issues. Article 27 of TRIPS allows members to exclude from patentability those products or processes the "commercial exploitation" of which is necessary to protect plants, animals, or the environment.[15] The International Council of Chemical Associations supports patent protection under TRIPS, saying that enforceable patents encourage inventions to preserve the ozone layer, reduce energy consumption, decrease the toxicity of pesticides, grow carbon-sequestering plants, and upgrade products and processes that currently harm the environment.[16]

The WTO has come under fire for allegedly placing commercial interests ahead of environmental protection.[17] The Working Group on the WTO/MAI claims, for example, that WTO rulings have relaxed the environmental standards for Venezuelan (among other) oil refineries, undercut United States requirements that shrimp must be caught using specific turtle-safe excluding devices, and neglected precautionary policies that call for the WTO to err on the safe side of environmental concerns.[18]

Neither the intent nor the result of WTO actions is easily pigeonholed. It is clear, however, that environmental economics was on the minds of the architects of the WTO. The preamble to the 1994 Marrakech Agreement establishing the WTO states that

> *relations in the field of trade and economic endeavor should be conducted ... while allowing for the optimal use of the world's resources in accordance with the objective of sustainable development, seeking both to protect and preserve the environment and to enhance the means for doing so in a manner consistent with their respective needs and concerns at different levels of economic development.*[19]

In support of this, umbrella clauses such as Article 20 of the GATT permit

13 See www.wto.org/wto/english/tratop_e/serv_e/gatsqa_e.htm.

14 See www.wto.org/wto/english/tratop_e/trips_e/intel2_e.htm.

15 See www.cptech.org/ip/health/cl/cl-art27.html.

16 See www.cefic.be/position/icca/pp_ic019.htm.

17 See www.ifg.org/wto.html.

18 See www.citizen.org/documents/wto-book.pdf.

19 See www.econ.iastate.edu/classes/econ355/choi/wtomara.htm.

countries to act in the defense of human, animal, or plant life or health, and to conserve exhaustible natural resources. The trade rules allow subsidies for environmental protection. Whether or not efficient environmental stewardship has been a reality in WTO policies of the past, the tone the organization chooses in the present will have considerable influence on environmental economics and natural resource management in the future.

The World Bank and the International Monetary Fund Financial ministers from 45 governments gathered in Bretton Woods, New Hampshire, in 1944 as architects of the modern international economy. With fresh wounds from the Great Depression and World War II, they sought economic stability and revitalization. One result was the creation of the World Bank to assist with rebuilding war-torn Europe. With that task completed, the World Bank turned to less-developed countries, aiming to envelop them into the global economy and reduce poverty. The World Bank is now the "world's largest financier of biodiversity," with 226 projects that encourage protected areas, sustainable use of biodiversity, the eradication of alien species, and conservation through improved management of natural resources in production.[20]

Like the World Bank, the International Monetary Fund (IMF) was conceived as part of the Bretton Woods agreement. It serves as a stabilizing force for the currencies and economies of its 188 member countries by overseeing exchange-rate policies, lending to countries with balance-of-payment problems, and assisting with the development of monetary and fiscal policy.[21] The IMF does not target environmental concerns directly, although it notes an overlap between the environment and its agenda to promote economic growth. As discussed in Chapter 9, development results in increased resource use, but if environmental standards are a normal good, the correspondingly higher incomes will result in improved environmental protection. The IMF sees this as a reason to "embrace policy changes to build strong economies and a stronger world financial system that will produce more rapid growth and ensure that poverty is reduced."[22]

There are some who believe that the World Bank and the IMF are not allocating resources in a socially efficient manner, and that the costs of their policies outweigh the benefits. The Friends of the Earth organization, for example, claims that the IMF is responsible for an 80 percent cut in Thailand's budget for pollution control since 1997 and a 50 percent cut in Brazil's funding to enforce environmental programs in 1999.[23] In 1997 the World Bank approved a $310 million loan to support a Bolivia–Brazil natural gas pipeline, allegedly granted without addressing the impacts of oil and gas exploration and infrastructure on the Amazon basin.[24]

As with criticisms of the other international organizations, these charges are

20 See www.worldbank.org.

21 See www.imf.org.

22 See www.imf.org/external/np/exr/2000/041200.htm,p.1.

23 See www.foe.org/camps/intl/imf/selling/asia.html and www.foe.org/camps/intl/imf/selling/latin_america2html.

24 See www.ems.org/banks/bolivia_brazil_gas.html.

difficult to assess. These organizations have come to symbolize desired order for some, and the imposition of selfish ideals for others. It is nonetheless possible to identify several important questions that should be applied to policy proposals:

- *Are the proposed policies appropriate to the cultures and environments where they are being imposed, and not just where they were conceived?*
- *Have all of the social costs and benefits been considered with the appropriate degree of precaution?*
- *Are developing countries receiving a fair share of the benefits derived from their human and natural resources?*
- *Have the desired standards of sustainability been applied?*
- *Are incentives aligned with the desired behavior?*
- *Are there opportunities for monitoring and enforcement?*
- *Are we learning from past mistakes?*

Special interest groups would have their own additions to this list. Most importantly, social efficiency cannot be achieved without asking many questions.

Approaches to Specific Global Environmental Threats

Preceding chapters have detailed causes and repercussions of the following maladies. This section focuses on international efforts to limit or solve the associated problems.

Acid Deposition

Atmospheric releases of sulfur dioxide (SO_2), nitrogen oxides (NO_x), and hydrochloric acid cause "acid rain," or **wet acid deposition**, that returns to the earth as acidic rainwater, fog, or snow. The same gases and particles are also blown in the wind and deposited on land surfaces and trees as **dry acid deposition**. Both threaten the health of flora and fauna, and damage cars and buildings. Coal-fired power plants, manufacturing processes, and road transportation in industrialized nations are the primary anthropogenic causes; lifeless trees and lakes in formerly pristine areas of North America and Europe are among the effects.

While some of the most significant reductions in acid deposition will follow from unilateral measures such as Title IV of the U.S. Clean Air Act and tradable emissions permits, efforts at international teamwork have also been notable.

Twenty-five countries signed the Protocol to Abate Acidification, Eutrophication and Ground-Level Ozone (AEGLO) in Sweden during a 1999 meeting of the United Nations Economic Commission for Europe (UN ECE). The same gathering marked the twentieth anniversary of the UN ECE Convention on Long-Range Transboundary Air Pollution (LRTAP). AEGLO covers Canada, the United States, and much of Europe, and requires participants to reduce emissions of sulfur dioxide, nitrogen oxides, volatile organic compounds (VOCs), and, in Europe only, ammonia.[25] Prior to that, the 1991 Canada-United States Air Quality Agreement restricted SO_2 and NO_x emissions in Canada and the United States.[26]

Deforestation

To slow the melting of glaciers like this one in Alaska, we may need to slow deforestation in places like Brazil.

Forests provide essential habitat, food, building supplies, and medicine. They also absorb the greenhouse gas carbon dioxide (CO_2), sequestering the carbon (C) and releasing the oxygen (O) that we breathe. Tree products, including rubber, fruit, lumber, and tropical oils, are prominent in global trade. The benefits of climate control and breathable air are public goods, generated on continents far from many of their recipients. Trees in South America, for example, are important to the global air supply and moderate climate. With localized benefits and global costs, deforestation presents a classic externalities problem.

The size of the Earth's tropical forests has fallen from 7.1 billion acres to 3.5 billion acres since 1800, and an estimated 80,000 acres are cleared every day.[27] The World Resources Institute estimates that a species becomes extinct every 15 minutes due to deforestation.[28] And forest degradation and deforestation account for almost 20 percent of greenhouse gas emissions—more than all global transportation.[29] Myriad efforts aim to stave off excessive deforestation.

- *The* **Tropical Forestry Action Program** *(TFAP)[30] was launched in 1985 as a joint effort of the UN Food and Agriculture Organization (FAO), the UN Development Program (UNDP), the World Bank, and the World Resources Institute. The goal was to promote international donor coordination in the development of National Forestry Action Plans (NFAPs), and stimulate related policy initiatives and data collection.*

25 See www.ec.gc.ca/press/acidrn_b_e.htm.

26 See www.epa.gov/airmarkets/usca/uscan96.html.

27 See www.scientificamerican.com/article.cfm?id=earth-talks-daily-destruction.

28 See www.wri.org/biodiv/tropical.html.

29 See http://www.un-redd.org/aboutredd/tabid/582/default.aspx.

30 See www.ciesin.org/docs/002-162/002-162.html.

- *The* **International Tropical Timber Agreement** *(ITTA)*[31] *is a binding commodity agreement between consumers and producers of tropical timber, each of whom hold half of the votes. The ITTA was signed in 1983 at the United Nations Conference on Tropical Timber. A 2006 renegotiation of the ITTA came into force in 2011. The objective of the agreement is to promote research, collaboration, and information sharing in the interest of sustainable timber management. The ITTA governs the work of the International Tropical Timber Organization (ITTO).*

- *The* **Convention on International Trade in Endangered Species of Wild Fauna and Flora** *(CITES) is a binding international treaty established to regulate the trade of endangered species, as discussed in the next section.*

- *The* **G7 Pilot Program** *(G7-PP) is an effort by the Group of Seven nations*[32] *to collaborate with Brazil on the preservation of the Amazon rainforest. The World Bank and Brazilian governmental agencies are responsible for G7-PP implementation. Participants have pledged $250 million for such projects as the demarcation of Indian reserves to prohibit encroachment by commercial interests and the protection of fishing communities from large competitors.*

- *The* **United Nations Forum on Forests** *(UNFF), the current torchbearer for UN oversight, was asked to "promote the management, conservation, and sustainable development of all types of forests, and to strengthen long-term political commitment to this end."*[33] *The UNFF is the current incarnation of work energized by the 1992 United Nations Conference on Environment and Development (UNCED).*

- *The* **United Nations Reducing Emissions from Deforestation and Forest Degradation** *(REDD+) effort creates financial incentives for developing countries to reduce emissions from forested lands. The "+" represents incentives for conservation and sustainable forest management.*[34] *REDD+ addresses tensions between desires in developed countries for a stable climate and desires in developing countries to generate income by harvesting forests and turning them into sites for agriculture, housing, or industry. REDD+ policies resemble Coasian-style "bribes" to countries like Brazil for not felling trees.*

The importance of forestation issues has prompted a large collection of initiatives. A few of the more significant efforts are mentioned here. The

31 See http://sedac.ciesin.org/entri/texts/ITTA.1994.txt.html.

32 The G7 is made up of Germany, the United States, Japan, Italy, the Netherlands, Great Britain, and Canada.

33 See www.iisd.ca/linkages/download/asc/enb1383e.txt, p. 7.

34 See www.unredd.net/index.php?option=com_docman&task=doc_download&gid=4200&Itemid=53.

Montreal Process[35] and the Helsinki Process[36] seek consensus on criteria and indicators for sustainable forest management. The Forest Stewardship Council[37] is working on certification systems that would identify wood that comes from sustainable sources. The Intergovernmental Working Group on Forests[38] hopes to bridge regional differences in forest policies. And the Center for International Forestry Research[39] has identified policy-relevant research priorities in support of sustainable forest management.

The limited progress of international efforts in curtailing deforestation may result from the initiatives' lack of teeth. The initiatives are difficult to implement, monitor, and enforce. As much as incentives matter, it is difficult to supersede the incentive in developing regions to clear forests for roads, pasture, and construction projects. Market-based solutions promoting ecotourism and the products of living forests (fruits and nuts) have been successful, but are limited in scope.

Threatened Species

A rhino-foot ashtray.

Photo by the Author
© The Field Museum, #57683.

High prices motivate producers to produce more. If the price of corn increases relative to the prices of other goods, farmers plant more corn. The difference in the context of many wildlife species is that domestic propagation is difficult, or it yields inferior products. Farm-raised ginseng is a poor substitute for wild ginseng, and many wild animals resist breeding in captivity. In such cases, high prices lead to excessive harvests in open-access areas, without the likelihood of an increase in cultivation or breeding. The result is that many species are brought to the brink of extinction.

Unfortunately, scarcity and temptation go hand-in-hand in the context of endangered species. Scarcity and restricted trade cause leftward shifts in the supply curve, raising the price further and providing all the more temptation for poaching and illegal trade in these species. This has been true for precious materials like ivory, traditional medicines like rhino horn and ginseng, and delicacies like shark fin.

In response to these problems, the Convention on International Trade in Endangered Species of Wild Fauna and Flora treaty was established in 1975 as the only global treaty for the protection of plant and animal species from unregulated international trade. Membership includes 178 countries and continues to grow. New additions in 2013 included Maldives and Lebanon. Among the species receiving protection under the CITES treaty are the African and Asian elephant, American ginseng, giant pandas, and several types of rhinos and tigers.

In 2000, Russia and the United States signed an agreement to conserve polar

35 See www.iisd.ca/linkages/forestry/mont.html.

36 See www.iisd.ca/linkages/forestry/hel.html.

37 See www.fscoax.org/.

38 See www.iisd.ca/linkages/forestry/iwgf.html.

39 See www.cifor.cgiar.org/.

Figure 11.1 *A Ban on Ivory*

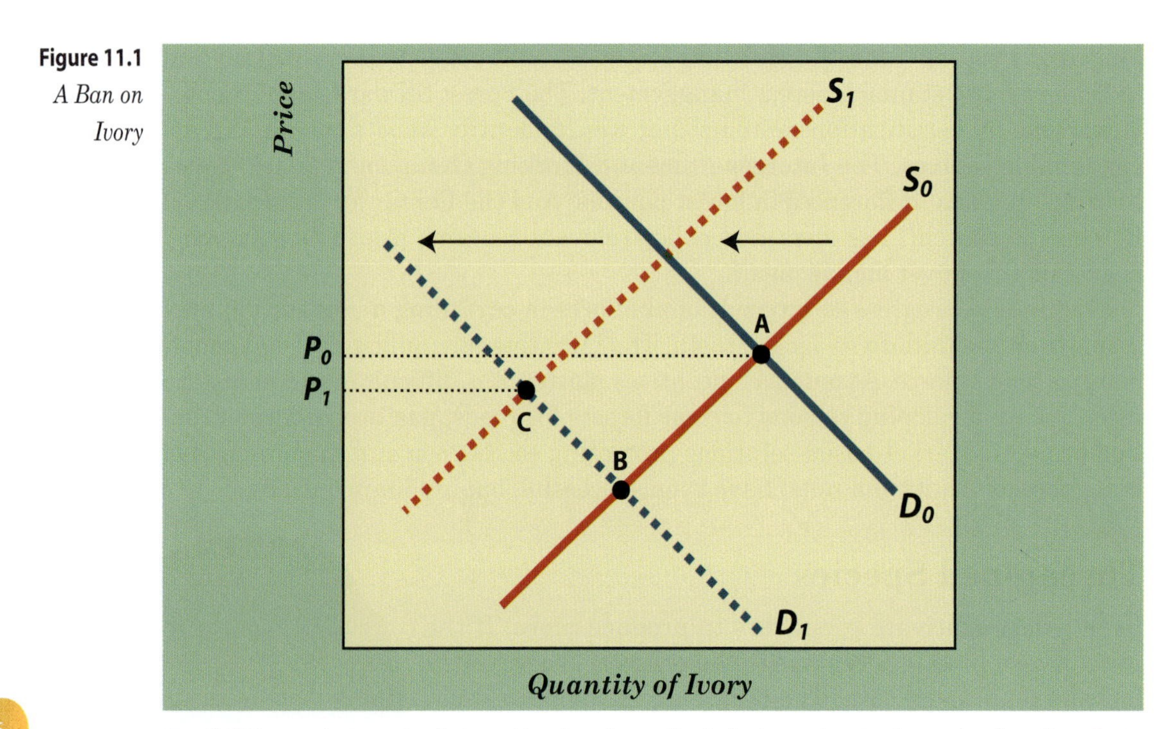

The CITES ban on ivory trade eliminated legal markets, effectively decreasing the demand as from D_0 to D_1. It also eliminated the legal supply of ivory, reducing the supply curve to the black-market supply, S_1. Both the decrease in demand and the decrease in supply caused the quantity of ivory bought and sold to decrease. In theory, the net effect on price is indeterminate. In reality, the price fell, meaning that the price-lowering influence of the decrease in demand dominated the price-raising influence of the decrease in supply.

bears, enhancing the 1973 Multilateral Agreement on the Conservation of Polar Bears between the United States, Russia, Norway, Denmark (for Greenland), and Canada. The agreement allows for a sustainable harvest by Alaska and Chukotka natives, but prohibits the harvest of females with cubs less than one year old.[40]

The protection of a species is aided by policies that decrease the demand for products made with that species. A decrease in demand lowers the equilibrium quantity—the overall objective. The corresponding decrease in price suppresses interest in poaching and black-market activities. A decrease in quantity can also be achieved with a decrease in supply, although the resulting increase in price may encourage illegal trade, as is the case with illegal drugs.[41] The 1989 CITES ban on the trade of ivory seems to have accomplished both. The ban eliminated legal markets for ivory, effectively decreasing the demand, as from D_0 to D_1 in Figure 11.1. This alone would bring the equilibrium from point A to point B, lowering the equilibrium price and the quantity supplied. At the same time, the supply curve shifted to the left, as from S_0 to S_1 in Figure 11.1. This occurred because legal sales were eliminated, and because poachers could no longer mix their ivory in with legal ivory. A complete ban simplifies monitoring because

40 See international.fws.gov/pdf/pbearagmt.pdf.

41 The high street price of illegal drugs motivates sellers to take great risks in selling on the black market, and encourages "pushers" to stimulate demand with free samples, loans of cash, and other aggressive marketing practices.

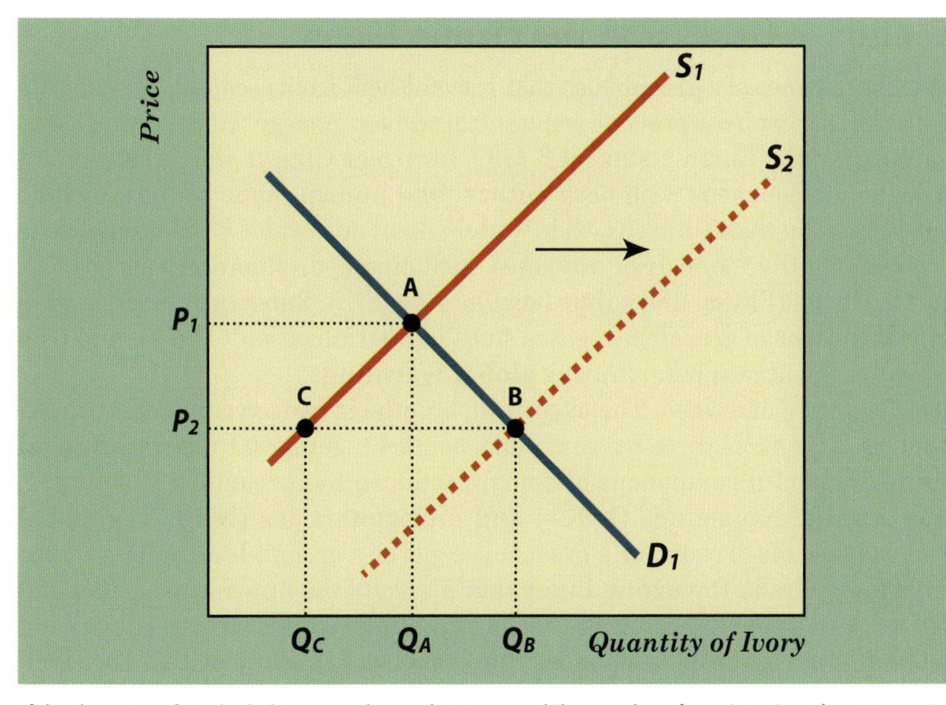

Figure 11.2 *Dumping Ivory on the Market*

If the dumping of stockpiled ivory on the market increased the supply as from S_1 to S_2 without increasing demand or black-market supply, the supply from poachers would *decrease* from Q_A to Q_C. The balance of the equilibrium quantity, $Q_B - Q_C$, comes from the released stockpiles. If demand or black-market supply increases, the amount of poaching may increase or decrease, depending on the relative size of the shifts.

any ivory that is discovered is clearly illegal. The end result was an equilibrium represented by point C, with a substantial decrease in the trade of ivory and therefore a decrease in the killing of elephants. Kenya, for example, lost about 3,500 elephants to poachers each year before the ban, but only an estimated 50 elephants in 1993. The reported decrease in the market price of ivory, as from P_0 to P_1, suggests that the decrease in demand had a larger influence on price than the decrease in supply, as indicated in Figure 11.1.

One policy option is to dump large quantities of the animal products on the market. Just as supply restrictions increase the price, dumping increases the supply and decreases the price, lowering the temptation for illegal activities. Indeed, in 1999, the Standing Committee of CITES approved the commercial sale of nearly 60 tons of stockpiled ivory from Zimbabwe, Namibia, and Botswana to Japan. Supplies were closely monitored to prevent a flare-up of poaching.

In an ideal scenario in which the legalized sale came from existing stockpiles and demand did not increase, the equilibrium quantity would increase, but the number of animals killed would actually decrease. Consider the shift from S_1 to S_2 in Figure 11.2, representing the influx of stockpiled ivory. The equilibrium moves from point A to point B. At the new equilibrium price of P_2, Q_B units of ivory are demanded, but only Q_C are supplied by the black market. The quantity $(Q_B - Q_A)$ comes from the legal stockpiles, and the quantity of ivory coming from illegal kills is *reduced* by $Q_A - Q_C$.

Greenhouse Gases and the Ozone Layer

Like the glass panes of a greenhouse that prevent heat from escaping, greenhouse gases in the atmosphere prevent some infrared heat energy from escaping into space, keeping the Earth about 59°F (33°C) warmer than it would be without them. Greenhouse gases with both natural and human-made sources include carbon dioxide, methane, nitrous oxide, water vapor, and ozone. Other greenhouse gases come only from industrial processes, including hydrofluorocarbons (HFCs), perfluorocarbons (PFCs), and sulfur hexafluoride (SF_6). Substantial increases in the concentrations of greenhouse gases since industrialization[42] threaten to trap more heat in the atmosphere, causing **global warming**.

Ozone is a form of oxygen. The oxygen we breathe is two oxygen atoms bonded together (O_2). Ozone is three oxygen atoms bonded together (O_3). **Ground-level ozone** is a harmful component of smog, produced by a reaction of sunlight, volatile organic compounds (VOCs) and nitrogen oxides (NO_x). The global concern is not so much ozone as a greenhouse gas or a ground-level pollutant, but thinning and holes in the **ozone layer** that blankets the upper atmosphere and shields the Earth from harmful ultraviolet rays. Chlorofluorocarbons (CFCs) and related industrial gases have damaged the ozone layer in many places. The satellite photo on the previous page shows the seasonal ozone hole over Antarctica. Thinning of the ozone layer increases ultraviolet radiation on Earth and may affect biomass that reduces carbon dioxide, thus causing further climatic changes.

Attempts to measure ozone depletion are a good case study in international environmental cooperation. A British Antarctic survey team discovered the ozone hole in 1985,[43] although it

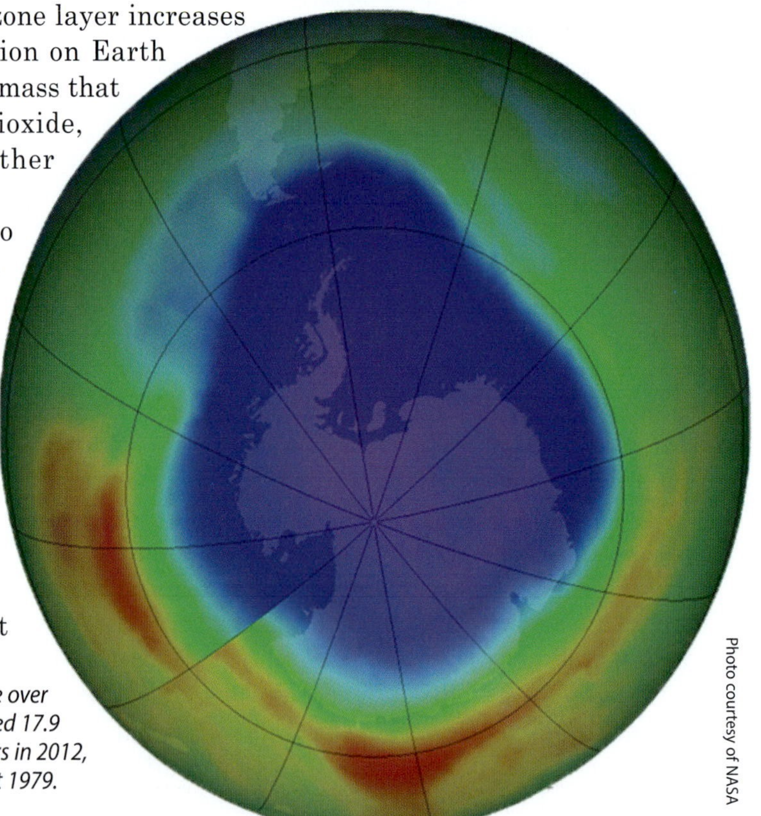

The seasonal ozone hole over Antarctica, which covered 17.9 million square kilometers in 2012, has existed since at least 1979.

Photo courtesy of NASA

42 Since the eighteenth century, for example, carbon dioxide levels have increased by 30 percent and methane levels have increased by 100 percent. See www.doc.mmu.ac.uk/aric/eae/english.html.

43 For a tour of the ozone hole, see www.atm.ch.cam.ac.uk/tour/.

is now known to have existed since at least 1979. NASA studies the ozone using Total Ozone Mapping Spectrometers (TOMS). Ozone-depletion measurements from TOMS are the basis for several international agreements to phase out the use of CFCs and other ozone-depleting chemicals. In 1991, the former Soviet Union launched a Meteor-3 satellite carrying a TOMS instrument provided by NASA. The Japanese Advanced Earth Observations Satellite (ADEOS) carried a TOMS into orbit in 1996. NASA's Earth Observing System-Chem series launched a satellite in 2002 to provide the international community with additional data on atmospheric chemistry and solar radiation important to ozone studies.[44]

Prior to the discovery of ozone thinning, CFCs were commonly used in refrigerators, air conditioners, and spray cans. The Montreal Protocol on Substances that Deplete the Ozone Layer, signed in 1987 and substantially amended in 1990 and 1992, is the landmark agreement on CFC reductions. The Montreal Protocol stipulated a phaseout of CFC production and use by 2000 (2005 for methyl chloroform).[45] The bad news is that CFCs can be difficult to monitor and it takes up to a century for a CFC molecule to break down in the atmosphere.

At the heart of international efforts toward global climate control are a series of Conferences of the Parties (COP) to the UN Framework Convention on Climate Change.[46] In 1997, COP 3 produced the Kyoto Protocol, under which countries were assigned emissions targets for greenhouse gases depending on their environmental circumstances and economic profiles. For example, relative to 1990 levels, the European Union sought to reduce CO_2, CH_4, and N_20 emissions by 15 percent by 2010 and Japan sought a 5 percent cut in the same gases by 2012. Developing nations also received reduction targets. The Kyoto Protocol entered into force on February 16, 2005, with a commitment period ending in 2012. In 2012, representatives from 194 nations met for COP 18 in Doha, Qatar. The outcomes included rules for a second commitment period for the Kyoto Protocol, extending from 2013 to 2020. As of April of 2013, 191 countries had ratified the agreement.[47] The United States is a notable exception.

Innovation and market-based incentives are also on the way for the control of greenhouse gases. The International Emissions Trading Association (IETA) was created in 1999 to establish international emissions trading programs for greenhouse gases. These programs set caps on greenhouse gas emissions and allow those who must emit to buy and sell permits on the open market. If the market works, this process provides incentives for those who can cut back on emissions to do so, while allowing those who most value emissions rights to purchase more when necessary. Similar programs have been successful in the United States and elsewhere, as discussed in Chapter 12.[48]

44 See www.gsfc.nasa.gov/gsfc/service/gallery/fact_sheets/earthsci/ozonestu.htm.

45 Exceptions were granted in 1996 for specific medical devices, space shuttle applications, and research.

46 See http://unfccc.int/.

47 See http://unfccc.int/resource/convkp.html. For those seeking an advanced discussion of global warming policy under uncertainty, see Woodward and Bishop (1997).

48 See www.ieta.org/.

Polluted Seas

What washes ashore—oil, trash, medical waste—is some indication of what is in the world's oceans.

The oceans covering two-thirds of the planet are critical sources of biodiversity, food, and carbon sequestration. They are also largely open-access resources, where those withdrawing marine life, depositing refuse, or transporting oil do not internalize the full cost of these actions. This problem has prompted several international agreements over the past half century.

The spillage of 31 million gallons of oil from the *Torrey Canyon*[49] supertanker between England and France in 1967 prompted the Agreement for Cooperation in Dealing with Pollution of the North Sea by Oil. The agreement was signed in Bonn, Germany, by nine European countries in 1969. Under the Bonn Agreement, participants agreed to share information on contingency plans for spills, alert each other to ongoing emergencies, and provide assistance to each other in the event of environmental disasters at sea.

An attempt by the Dutch ship *Stella Maris* to dump chlorinated water into the North Sea in 1971 led to the 1972 Oslo Convention for the Prevention of Marine Polluting by Dumping from Ships and Aircraft. Signed by 13 countries, the Oslo Convention established a commission to regulate and control the dumping of industrial wastes and sewage sludge into the sea, and the incineration of industrial wastes at sea. These dumping and incineration activities were subsequently phased out in the northeast Atlantic during the 1990s.[50] To regulate the land-based sources of ocean pollution, 13 countries and the European Economic Community ratified the Convention for the Prevention of Marine Pollution from Land-based Sources—the Paris Convention—in 1974.

The Paris and Oslo commissions gathered in London in 1992 to form a single entity under the Convention for the Protection of the Marine Environment of the North-East Atlantic—the OSPAR Convention. The policies under the Oslo and Paris Conventions continue under OSPAR. These include a precautionary principle described in the Reality Check and a polluter pays principle similar to that in United States Superfund legislation. Participants are also required to adopt the best-available techniques (BAT) and the best environmental practices (BEP), including clean technology.

49 See www.davidaxford.free-online.co.uk/torreycn.htm.

50 See www.ospar.org/eng/html/background.htm.

reality check

The Precautionary Principle

The precautionary principle, introduced as a candidate among sustainability policies in Chapter 8, is a reality among international environmental agreements. Examples include the OSPAR treaty, the CITES treaty, Principle 15 of the Rio Declaration on the Environment and Development, the revised Treaty of Rome, Article 3.3 of the UN Framework Convention on Climate Change, Agenda 21 of the Rio Conference, Amendments to the Montreal Protocol on Substances that Deplete the Ozone Layer, and the UN Convention of Biological Diversity.

The Australian Intergovernmental Agreement on the Environment (IGAE) explains the precautionary principle this way:

> Where there are threats of serious or irreversible environmental damage, lack of full scientific certainty should not be used as a reason for postponing measures to prevent environmental degradation. In the application of the precautionary principle, public and private decisions should be guided by
>
> *(i) careful evaluation to avoid, wherever practicable, serious or irreversible damage to the environment; and*
> *(ii) an assessment of the risk-weighted consequences of various options.*

As with the sustainability principle, some see the precautionary principle as a departure from dynamic economic efficiency. Dickson (1999), for example, contends that sacrifices made by humans receive inadequate consideration under CITES-treaty precautionary measures. Gollier, Jullien, and Treich (2000) and Woodward and Bishop (1997), argue that by taking account of great uncertainty or risk aversion, the precautionary principle can be viewed as a rational criterion for efficient policymaking. A reality check of the popularity of the precautionary principle, not to mention our speed limits, helmet laws, and insurance purchases, suggests that in some situations humans indeed like to err on the safe side.

The Mixed Baggage of Tourism

Tourism is among the largest industries in the world, employing an estimated 220 million workers and generating 9.4 percent of global sales revenues.[51] Tourism can be pro-poor, pro-development, and pro-environment, or quite the opposite, depending on particular practices. Some tourists bike or hike to their

51 See www.wttc.org/eng/About_WTTC/.

destinations and follow the maxim, "take only memories, leave only footprints";[52] others drive mobile homes, take home bulging suitcases, and leave trails of waste. As with other forms of globalization and trade, tourism carries the risks of homogenization and exploitation.

Unlike "staycations"—the recession-era trend of staying near home for vacation—destination tourism requires transportation, which itself has substantial environmental impacts. The 3,105-mile round-trip from Los Angeles to Mexico City creates a carbon dioxide footprint of approximately 1,052 pounds per passenger.[53] Driving the same distance alone in an automobile that travels 25 miles per gallon would create 2,422 pounds of carbon emissions. Making the trip by train would create a carbon footprint of 1,304 pounds per person.

International tourism promotes a sharing of cultures, a transfer of wealth, and an incentive to preserve the drawing card that wildlife represents. Indeed, with tourists attracted to jungle safaris, pristine beaches, and national forests, entrepreneurs and policymakers have reason to keep wilderness areas intact. The associated airports, hotels, restaurants, gift shops, and casinos might erase the environmental gains. The effects of tourism on the local environment are assessed in several ways:

- *Measures of* **tourism carrying capacity**, *such as the tourism environmental bearing capacity (TEBC), involve estimates of the number of tourists that could visit an area before the environment (or the tourism experience, depending on the particular measure) would be substantially degraded. Comparisons can then be made between that capacity and the actual number of tourists, with implications for policies to limit the number of tourists or spread tourists out across locations or time.*

- **Limits of acceptable change** *(LAC) result from a modification of the carrying capacity concept to focus on the level of tourism that best balances interests between tourism and environmental protection,*[54] *rather than the level the area can withstand. The LAC process includes an invitation for users of the area to share their goals, and a consideration of plans to bring the impact of tourism within acceptable limits.*

- **Environmental impact assessments** *(EIAs), also known as environmental impact studies (EISs), are performed to estimate the effects of policies or development. In many countries an EIA is a prerequisite for major projects such as highway construction to encourage the consideration of environmental consequences.*[55]

52 This quote is often attributed to Native American Chief Seattle, who may have said it during a 1854 speech. See www.answers.com/topic/chief-seattle.

53 See www.TerraPass.org.

54 See, for example, www.fs.fed.us/r8/boone/lac/.

55 For an evaluation of EIAs, see http://ec.europa.eu/environment/eia/pdf/eia_study_june_09.pdf.

Can tourism and wilderness areas mix? Environmental impact studies assess the level of damage that would be caused by proposed tourist attractions among other development projects.

Critics advocate more comprehensive measures that capture the global impact of tourism. For example, the **touristic ecological footprint** (TEF) measures the broader demands of tourism on the environment in terms of the area of productive land and water needed to support them. Typical TEF calculations consider travel, lodging, sightseeing, purchases, entertainment, food, and waste. The resulting footprints can be compared across industries, activities, and locations. For example, Peter Johnson calculated the per-person, per-day ecological footprint in hectares (1 hectare = 2.47 acres) for tourists in Ontario, Canada, with various types of lodging.[56] Considering lodging, food, transportation, and activities, he estimated an average TEF of 0.208 for those staying in resort hotels, 0.085 for those in budget hotels, 0.023 for those in eco-lodges, and 0.020 for those camping in the backcountry. In a study of tourists in Shangri-La, China, Li and Yang (2007) found that lodging and food have a substantial TEF, while travel and entertainment activities in that area are relatively efficient.

The World Travel and Tourism Council, an advocacy group for the industry, reports a balanced mission of "generating profit as well as protecting natural, social and cultural environment."[57] In practice, the tourism industry is largely consumer driven, and its impact depends on the interest and awareness of those taking part. The growing trends of ecotourism, culturally and environmentally sensitive tourism, and voluntary payments for green energy offsets for the carbon footprint of tourism bode well for tourism with a smaller footprint than the mass tourism of the past. From a policy perspective, government support for low-impact tourism, as with the creation of new hiking trails everywhere from Dominica to Greenland, show promise for more backcountry camping, fewer mobile homes, and less tourism baggage.

Summary

From some perspectives our planet is small—one-tenth the size of Saturn and circled every 90 minutes by commercial satellites. The close proximity of human populations means no nation is isolated from environmental influences elsewhere on the planet. International environmental policies are for naught if they do not

56 See http://etd.uwaterloo.ca/etd/pa2johns2003.pdf, which includes a useful survey of the TEF literature.

57 See www.wttc.org.

engage multiple parties with adequate incentives and legitimate enforcement mechanisms. The United Nations, the World Trade Organization, the World Bank, and the International Monetary Fund, among other international organizations, pursue the Herculean goal of managing our global economy with appropriate sensitivity to the overarching environment without which there is no demand and no supply. The degree of success in doing so is a matter of debate.

Policy approaches to the specific global environmental problems of acid deposition, deforestation, threatened species, climate change, and pollution in the seas have several common themes. In each case, international committees have been formed, educational efforts have broadened awareness, multilateral agreements have been negotiated, and economic incentives provide a motivating force. The precautionary principle is the prevalent approach to uncertainty. In the face of potentially irreversible environmental degradation, most organizations contend that a lack of absolute scientific certainty should not subvert safety measures.

The social efficiency of common policies to deal with global scarcity is questionable. Depending on its application, the precautionary principle may cause excessive safety. On the other hand, zeal for economic progress among organizations may result in insufficient calculations of the environmental costs of development projects. The policies and organizations you learned about in this chapter appear frequently in the media as humans struggle with global constraints on clean air and water, landfill space, environmental sinks, energy sources, wildlife habitat, and recreation areas. With knowledge of their successes and failures, current approaches will become stepping-stones to better solutions in the future.

Photo by James Morgan, used with permission.

Economic analysis reveals that burning ivory is generally not the best policy approach to the protection of elephants.

Problems for Review

1. Globalization may permit firms to shop across countries to find low environmental standards. Explain the remedy you favor for this practice.

2. List four influences that may prevent international environmental policy from achieving social efficiency and explain a specific solution for any two of them.

3. What incentives do policymakers in international organizations have to prioritize commercial interests? What incentives do they have to prioritize environmental interests? Are these incentives appropriate? If not, how could the incentive structure be changed?

4. In a symbolic gesture against poaching, Kenyan President Daniel arap Moi burned 2,500 elephant tusks. Does this make sense from an economic standpoint? Using a graph, illustrate the effect of this burn on the quantity of tusks supplied illegally by poachers, *assuming that the 2,500 burned tusks would otherwise have been on the market legally, and that the remaining supply comes from poachers*. How would your answer change if worldwide media coverage of the event dissuaded potential consumers of ivory?

5. Consider the scenario represented in Figure 11.2, with S_1 representing the black-market supply of ivory (which we'll assume remains constant). Let the shift from S_1 to S_2 represent an influx of legal ivory due to a partial lifting of the ivory ban. Suppose that the relaxation of the ban increases ivory demand. Draw the largest possible increase in demand that would *not* result in an increase in the quantity of black-market sales relative to the initial level, Q_A.

6. Consider the ivory market once more. Starting from an equilibrium at point A in Figure 11.2, suppose that a partial lifting of the ivory ban lowers the marginal cost of selling on the black-market, but ivory demand is unchanged. Draw a graph that shows both an increase in black-market ivory resulting from lower costs and an influx of legal ivory *such that at the new equilibrium, the quantity of black-market sales remains at* Q_A.

7. What do you see as the greatest *specific* cost and benefit of globalization?

8. As the director of the World Bank, what one question would you add to those listed in the section on the World Bank and the IMF as a consideration prior to the adoption of a policy?

9. Giant pandas live in China. Which of the types of values discussed in the previous chapter make the threat of giant panda extinction an international problem? How might international cooperation lead to a solution?

10. Why is it unlikely that country-level policy would be socially efficient in regard to acid deposition?

1. Find one website that speaks in favor of globalization and one site that speaks against it. Briefly summarize their arguments.
2. Find a website calling for the addition of a species to the CITES preservation list. Do you agree that the species in question deserves special protection? Why or why not?
3. Find a website that describes an act of international environmental cooperation that is not discussed in this chapter. Briefly describe the project.

Internet Resources

EPA global warming site:
www.epa.gov/globalwarming/

International Monetary Fund:
www.imf.org

Living Planet Report:
www.panda.org/lpr/08/

United Nations:
www.un.org

The U.S. Fish and Wildlife Service's CITES treaty site:
http://international.fws.gov/cites/cites.html

World Bank:
www.worldbank.org

World Trade Organization:
www.wto.org

Further Reading

Daly, Herman E., and Kenneth N. Townsend. *Valuing the Earth: Economics, Ecology, Ethics*. Cambridge, MA: MIT Press, 1993. A provocative discussion that argues, among other things, that "sustainable growth" is an oxymoron.

Dasgupta, Susmita, Nlandu Mamingi, and Meisner, Craig. "Pesticide Use in Brazil in the Era of Agroindustrialization and Globalization." *Environment and Development Economics* 6, no. 4 (2001): 459–482. A time-series study of agricultural practices finding a significant influence from globalization.

Dickson, Barnabas. "The Precautionary Principle in CITES: A Critical Assessment." *Natural Resources Journal* 39, no. 2 (1999): 211–228. Relates the prevention of environmental damage to risk aversion and prescribes standards for the application of the precautionary principle.

Ederington, Josh. "Environmental Duties and International Harmonization of Standards." *Southern Economic Journal* 68, no. 2 (2001): 418–432. A game-theoretic investigation of environmental tariffs designed to level the playing field between trading partners with differing standards.

Ehrlich, Paul, and Anne Ehrlich. *Population Resources Environment: Issues in Human Ecology*. Washington, D.C.: Population Reference Bureau, Inc., 1979. A discussion of global demands on food, resources, and the environment.

Gills, Dong-Sook S. "Globalization of Production and Women in Asia." *Annals of the American Academy of Political and Social Science* 581 (2002): 106–20. Discusses adaptations of labor relations in response to increased globalization.

Gollier, Christian, Bruno Jullien, and Nicolas Treich. "Scientific Progress and Irreversibility: An Economic Interpretation of the 'Precautionary Principle.'" *Journal of Public Economics* 75, no. 2 (2000): 229–253. States that the impact of conservation policies on humans must be considered when applying the precautionary principle.

Li, Peng and Guihua Yang. "Ecological Footprint Study on Tourism Itinerary Products in Shangri-La, Yunnan Province, China." *Acta Ecologica Sinica* 27, no. 7 (2007): 2954–2963. A study of the environmental impact of seven components of tourism, including travel, food, lodging, waste disposal, and entertainment.

Schelling, Thomas C. "The Cost of Combating Global Warming: Facing the Tradeoffs." In *Economics of the Environment: Selected Readings (2000)*, edited by Robert N. Stavins. New York: Norton, 2000, 510–516. A thoughtful and provocative piece on the politics of greenhouse gases.

Woodward, Richard T., and Richard C. Bishop. "How to Decide When Experts Disagree: Uncertainty-Based Choice Rules in Environmental Policy." *Land Economics* 73, no. 4 (1997): 492–507. Discusses global warming policy, safe minimum standards, and the precautionary principle.

World Resources Institute, UN Environment Programme, UN Development Program, and the World Bank. *1998–1999 World Resources: A Guide to the Global Environment*. Oxford: Oxford University Press, 1998. A reference book on global environmental statistics and trends.

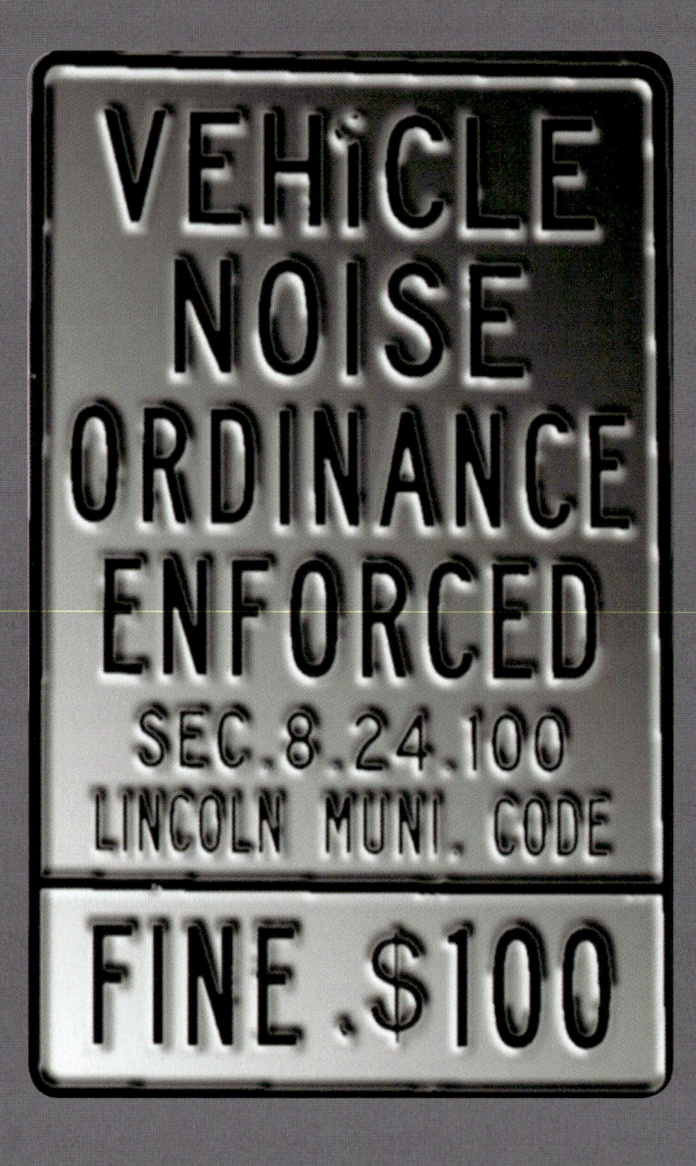
VEHICLE
NOISE
ORDINANCE
ENFORCED
SEC.8.24.100
LINCOLN MUNI. CODE
FINE.$100

12 Perspectives on Environmental Policy

The pigs escaped from my grandfather's farm while my parents held their wedding reception in the farmhouse. There was no question among the revelers that the wayward swine posed a problem, but as they slogged through rain and mud, the men in tuxedos had differing perspectives on how best to remedy the situation. Some pushed pigs, some pulled, some prodded them with sticks. Others pronounced that the pigs would return to the pen if left alone. With a combination of these approaches, the pigs were eventually placed under control, whether by the most efficient means or not. Environmental policy is much the same: there is broad agreement that environmental losses are a problem, but whether it is best to push decision makers with command-and-control policies, pull them with incentives, or prod them with the sticks of litigation and punishment is another issue. Some feel that if left alone, the market will attain efficiency on its own.

Policy itself is pulled and pushed by the political machine, replete with myriad constituents and special interests, and limited by incomplete information and egocentric intent. Out of this melee come efforts to remedy market failure, discover environmental perils, and serve present and future constituencies—both human and otherwise—that have little or no voice in the matters. There is much to be sorted out in filling this tall order.

Mancur Olson (2009) notes that the individual benefit received from many activities is small or negative when few people participate, and large when they are well subscribed. For example, if only a few people drive electric cars, then the recharging stations, repair shops, and development expenditures that make electric cars convenient will not arise. Likewise, the potential benefits of recycling, clean fuels, and organic products aren't realized until a critical mass of customers supports the research and infrastructure expenditures that make them attractive. Another role of policy is to help promote participation levels that benefit all users.

This chapter discusses the two major categories of environmental policy and the optimal deterrence of environmental wrongdoing. **Incentive-based policies** *set an environmental target, such as an amount of carbon dioxide emissions per year, and allow those producing the emissions to decide how to achieve that target.* **Command-and-control regulations** *typically set both a target and a path by which that target shall be met. Examples of these paths include the use of particular fuels, fishing equipment, or pollution-scrubbing devices. From an efficiency standpoint, we will see that incentive-based regulations are sometimes superior due to their flexibility. In other cases, flexibility is less important than the ability to apply and enforce common standards.*

These are among many available types of policies. Support for science and technology initiatives can lead to lower-impact products and machines, including cleaner fuels and better smokestack scrubbers. The dissemination of information about environmental issues can help individuals and firms make more appropriate decisions regarding the environment. For example, the Emergency Planning and Community Right-to-Know Act of 1986 requires facilities to report the use and release of hazardous chemicals so that surrounding communities can make informed responses. A Reality Check in Chapter 14 explains that programs fostering cooperation and trade among individuals, firms, and nations can include environmental standards among the rules of fair play. And the success of pollution-abatement measures can be bolstered by more effective enforcement policies.

Command-and-Control Regulations

Command-and-control policies typically require certain behaviors or forbid others. The inflexibility of such stipulations can cause inefficiencies when there are numerous solutions to the underlying problem. When given the option, for example, municipalities can achieve water quality standards by purchasing infrared lights that sterilize the output of their water treatment plants, rebuilding their sewer system to better manage floodwaters, or adding employees to monitor and reduce the illegal dumping of emissions and waste into nearby water supplies. Different solutions will be cheaper and more productive in different locations, and a rigid mandate that every municipality must purchase infrared sterilization equipment might not be the most efficient solution in many communities. Regional differences in the costs of capital and labor, and facility-specific differences in the severity of problems and the adaptability of existing equipment, make flexibility desirable for the attainment of technical efficiency.

Command-and-control regulations set out the following three types of standards: **Ambient standards** designate targets for pollution concentrations at specified locations of measurement. In accordance with the Clean Air Act, the EPA has established national ambient air quality standards (NAAQS) for six criteria air pollutants. These standards are provided in Table 6.2; further discussion of air quality standards can be found there as well. The Clean Water Act requires every state to set ambient water quality standards with goals including swimmable and fishable waterways. Emissions and technology standards are then set in an effort to achieve these ambient standards.

Technology standards stipulate the use of particular methods or types of pollution-control equipment. Examples include pollution-abating catalytic converters in cars,[1] scrubbers in coal-fired power plants, and minimum heights for chimneys. Under the Clean Air Act, major new or modified sources of pollution in **nonattainment areas**—areas not meeting ambient air quality standards—are required to adopt technology so as to emit at the lowest achievable emission rate (LAER). Major new or modified sources in areas meeting the standards are required to employ the "best available control technology" (BACT).[2] And existing polluters in nonattainment areas must use "reasonably available control technology" (RACT). The exact requirements under these categories are defined for specific processes and types of equipment, and made available by the EPA's RACT/BACT/LAER Clearinghouse.[3]

Emission standards require firms to reduce emissions by a designated percentage or to a set amount. An example is the National Pollutant Discharge Elimination System (NPDES) permit program authorized by the Clean Water Act. NPDES regulates point sources of pollution such as industrial and municipal discharge pipes. Effluent discharge permits are granted on the basis of the available abatement technology and the wasteload capacity of the receiving water that would ensure the maintenance of ambient water quality standards.[4] When technology-based standards are sufficient to meet the needs of the receiving body of water, NPDES permit writers stipulate a minimum level of treatment for discharge while allowing polluters to choose their specific treatment method.

In the United States, the EPA oversees the research and review process for

1 To learn how catalytic converters work, see www.howstuffworks.com/catalytic-converter.htm.

2 The European Union and others employ a similar concept, BATNEC, an acronym for best available technology not entailing excessive costs.

3 See, for example, the BACT Clearinghouse for California: www.arb.ca.gov/bact/bactsearch.htm.

4 See http://cfpub.epa.gov/npdes/generalissues/watertechnology.cfm.

NPDES and other environmental standards. Proposed rules are printed in a government-wide collection of documents called the *Federal Register*. After interested members of the public have the opportunity to comment on a proposal, the EPA makes revisions as appropriate and then publishes the final rule, again in the daily *Federal Register* and in the annual *Code of Federal Regulations*. The EPA is also charged with monitoring and enforcing these standards.

The debates over appropriate standards are compounded by debates over the use of regulations to meet those standards. Regulatory solutions make sense when there is one clear path to solving an environmental problem, and may be justified when the provision of greater flexibility to firms would prohibit effective monitoring. Even in these cases, there is the drawback that once standards are met, there is little incentive for further emissions reductions. The next section discusses alternative approaches that offer improved incentives and flexibility.

Incentive-Based Solutions

As an alternative to traditional command-and-control approaches, policymakers use incentive-based policy instruments to pursue the same efficiency goals from a different angle. The market's own engine of self-interest is teamed with influences designed to circumvent market failure. The market-based incentive might be a subsidy or tax credit, a Pigovian pollution tax,[5] a deposit/refund program as with bottle bills, or one of the relatively new and innovative emissions trading programs. A virtue of incentive-based solutions is that they allow individuals and firms with differing circumstances to address environmental problems in different ways. Earlier chapters have explained the influences of taxes, subsidies, and deposits; this section provides more specific policy examples and emphasizes the use of tradable emissions rights.

Market Approaches to Automobile Externalities Around the World

Rush hour congestion occurs because an overload of drivers wants to be on the same road at the same time. Some of those people *really* need to be driving then, others *kind of* need to be driving then. Those on the margin have a private marginal benefit that barely exceeds the private marginal cost of bearing the traffic, and if they had to pay the marginal external cost their own car imposes on others, they would instead choose an alternative time or mode of transportation.

5 Chapter 3 defines a Pigou tax as a tax that equals the marginal external cost of the behavior being taxed. Upon paying such a tax, the decision maker internalizes the full cost of his or her behavior.

The idea of **congestion pricing** or **peak-load pricing** is to spread out resource use by charging higher prices during peak consumption periods. This encourages those with relatively flexible schedules or good alternatives to make adjustments. Movie theaters do it with matinee prices. Hotels do it with low-season discounts. Now roadway congestion pricing has arrived in the United Kingdom. To drive in central London during peak driving times costs an extra $13 per day. If that fee approximates the marginal external cost of such driving, drivers will use busy roads during peak periods only if it is efficient, in that their marginal benefit exceeds the social marginal cost. The controversial program has enjoyed measured success, with a 20 percent reduction in traffic (20,000 fewer vehicles per day), a 37 percent increase in traffic speed, and a 14 percent increase in bus riding.[6] Congestion pricing systems are now in place in cities in Australia, Canada, France, Germany, Italy, South Korea, Singapore, Sweden, Norway, and the United States.

During the transition away from leaded gasoline in the 1980s and 1990s, countries from Mexico to Thailand used higher taxes on leaded gasoline to successfully usher in unleaded varieties. Today's transition to electric and hybrid cars and to alternative fuels is being promoted with similar tax incentives in Japan, the United States, and elsewhere. In 2010, Canada began offering incentives ranging from $3,600 to $8,900 for the purchase of a new plug-in hybrid or electric car. Since 1993, Finland's system of excise taxes has favored low-sulfer diesel fuel.

Rapid improvements in automobile efficiency make it desirable to get older cars off the road. Austria has done that by simultaneously decreasing value-added taxes on new vehicles and lowering registration fees for the most efficient cars. In 2009, the Car Allowance Rebate System (CARS) in the United States allowed consumers to trade in a car that got 18 or fewer miles per gallon and receive $4,500 toward the purchase of a new vehicle that got at least 10 more miles per gallon. The engines of the old cars were destroyed but the parts were reused or the materials were recycled.

Just as cash deposits encourage the return of beverage containers for refunds in several countries, deposit programs in Greece, Norway, and Sweden encourage the return of car bodies for recycling. Deposit-return programs succeed in keeping materials out of the waste stream and placing them into new production. Among broad-ranging uses, deposits are applied to car batteries in Denmark, the Netherlands, and the United States, industrial products in South Korea, disposable cameras in Japan, and computers in Australia.

Tradable Emissions Rights: A Two-Firm Pollution Model

Firms value the right to emit pollution because it conveys the ability to produce goods and earn profits. Restricting emissions levels, dividing the rights to the permitted emissions among firms, and allowing the firms to buy and sell those

6 See www.vtpi.org/london.pdf.

rights will theoretically result in a more efficient distribution of pollution rights. Figure 12.1 illustrates the marginal value of emissions for each of two hypothetical firms. Firm 1 emissions increase from left to right; Firm 2 emissions increase from right to left. The curves indicate that Firm 2 receives less value from any given amount of emissions than Firm 1, perhaps because it is newer and operates with state-of-the-art emissions-control equipment. If each firm is restricted to the same emissions standard of half of the allowable emissions, the total value to Firm 1 is the sum of areas A and B, and the total value to Firm 2 is the sum of areas D, E, and F.

The efficient allocation equates the firms' marginal values from emissions. With the efficient allocation, the total value to Firm 1 is A + B + C + D and the total value to Firm 2 is E + F. Relative to the equal division of emissions rights, Firm 2 loses area D, but Firm 1 gains areas C and D, for a net societal gain of area C.

The efficiency gain in this example is attractive, but achieving it with government controls would require a great deal of information. As discussed previously, it is difficult to establish the optimal total amount of pollution, although meaningful targets are available. The next challenge is to determine the values placed on pollution by the various firms. If asked to report the benefits received from the ability to pollute, each firm would have an incentive to exaggerate its marginal value of emissions in order to increase what appears to be its efficient share of the emissions allotment. It is with this challenge that tradable emissions permits work their magic.

Given a market for emissions permits, each firm faces a per-unit opportunity cost of emissions equal to the market price of emissions permits. Firms that do not have enough permits have an incentive to find ways to reduce their emissions to minimize the need to purchase more permits. Even if a firm has the permits needed to produce at maximum capacity, it has an incentive to pollute less as long as emissions reductions cost less than the market price of permits, so that it can sell the excess permits to someone else.

Consider the situation in Figure 12.1 in which each firm begins with the right to emit half of the allowed pollution. The firm that can reduce its emissions at the lowest cost (Firm 2) will end up selling permits to the firm for whom cleanup is relatively expensive and polluting is relatively valuable (Firm 1). This will occur until the efficient allocation of pollution is achieved, after which point the marginal value of another unit of emissions is higher for Firm 2 than for Firm 1. Then, the *most* Firm 1 would be willing to pay for another permit is less than the *least* Firm 2 would accept for a permit, and trading will cease. During this process, each firm makes decisions based on its true marginal value of emissions—a value critical to the determination of efficient levels of emissions as indicated in Figure 12.1, but difficult to ascertain by any other means.

The initial distribution of permits affects the distribution of funds between the firms. The more permits a firm receives in the beginning, the more it can sell or the fewer it must buy. But this distribution has no influence on the efficiency of

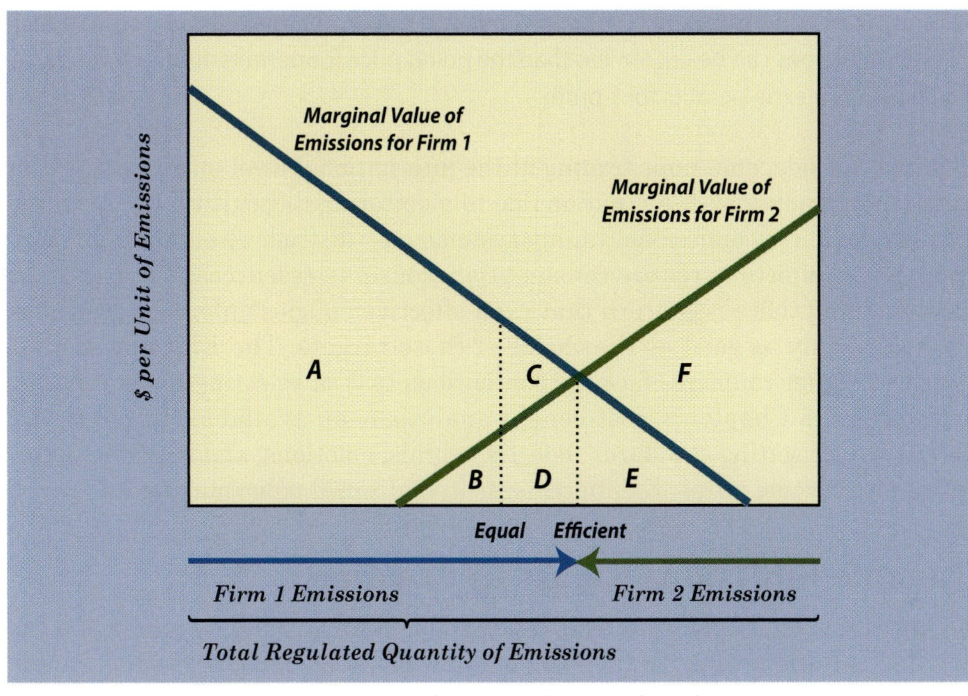

Figure 12.1 *The Efficient Allocation of Pollution Rights*

This diagram illustrates the marginal value of emissions for each of two firms. Firm 1 emissions increase from left to right, and Firm 2 emissions increase from right to left. As indicated by the lower, green marginal value curve, Firm 2 receives less value from any given amount of emissions than Firm 1. If each firm is permitted to emit the same volume of emissions, the total value to Firm 1 is the sum of areas A and B, and the total value to Firm 2 is the sum of areas D, E, and F. The efficient allocation is achieved where the firms' marginal values are equal. With the efficient allocation, the value to Firm 1 is A + B + C + D and the value to Firm 2 is E + F. The net gain from efficient allocation is area C.

the final outcome. Whether permits are all given to Firm 1, or all to Firm 2, or there is some intermediate allotment, trades between the two firms are in each firm's best interest until the marginal value to each firm is the same and the efficient distribution is achieved. The same is true when there are many firms: regardless of the initial allotment of pollution rights, trading will occur until the firms' marginal values of pollution are equal, thus marking the efficient distribution of pollution rights.

There are three primary benefits from emissions trading programs:

1. **They allow flexibility and creativity.**
   Permissible emissions levels can be achieved via conservation, new technology, alternative energy sources, lower-sulfur coal, or the purchase of permits—whichever is the most feasible and affordable to a particular pollution source.

2. **They allocate emissions rights to those who value them the most.**
   Newer, cleaner firms can sell their permits to firms for whom it would be much more difficult to reduce emissions levels.

3. **They provide incentives for reductions beyond the level stipulated by regulations.** When emissions can be cut for less than the going price for permits, firms will do so and sell their extra permits for a profit.

On the con side, emissions trading at the international level might be less successful than trading within a nation due to monitoring difficulties. Focus on the development of new emissions trading systems may distract attention from more fundamental efforts to reduce consumption, conserve resources, and moderate behavior.[7] And there is concern that even effective policies enforcing emissions targets are only as good as the choice of those targets. The EPA and similar agencies in other countries face the contentious task of selecting the standards. As discussed in Chapter 2, cost-benefit analysis is an available but politically volatile tool for setting standards. Politics, morals, emotions, and imperfect information also become influential ingredients in real-world policymaking.[8]

Tradable Emissions Rights in Practice

The practice of emissions trading is being adopted worldwide. Depending on the program, pollution rights in the form of allowances, permits, or credits, can be purchased at auction or obtained via one of the following mechanisms:

Banking *occurs when a firm achieves emissions levels below an established standard and is allowed to save or "bank" pollution permits for future sale or use.*

Bubble provisions *effectively allow trading within a firm or area by aggregating all sources of a specific pollutant within a "bubble" and looking only at the total amount of pollution released from the bubble. Increased emissions from one part of the bubble are acceptable if accompanied by a sufficient decrease in emissions elsewhere in the bubble. This provides the flexibility for some operations to emit particularly large amounts of pollution if others are particularly clean.*

Offsets *allow increased emissions in an area that has not met environmental quality standards if they are offset by even larger reductions elsewhere in the same facility or in another facility. Offsets differ from area bubbles in that offsets apply only to environmental nonattainment areas. The 2:1 offset sanctions discussed in Chapter 6 are an example of this.*

Netting *allows existing firms to expand their operations and avoid the relatively strict emissions standards for new facilities provided that their net increase in emissions falls below a set level. Netting always occurs within a single firm and allows for a net increase in pollution, unlike bubbles and offsets.*

7 See, for example, www.oneworld.org/ips2/Dec98/07_14_005.html.

8 For perspectives on ethical and emotional arguments, see Chapter 16, Ott and Sachs (2000) and http://ecoethics.net/hsev/newscience/200012b-res.htm.

An emissions trading scheme called **cap-and-trade** is among those that set a limit on releases of particular pollutants and allocate allowances for portions of that quantity among existing firms that can then trade them on the open market. A cap-and-trade program began in the United States in 1995 to address the acid deposition problem by controlling SO_2 at the national level and NO_x in some regions. The trading of pollution allowances is similar to that of stocks and commodities. Sulfur dioxide allowances are available from allowance brokers, environmental groups, and an annual EPA auction conducted by the Chicago Board of Trade.[9] Each allowance is for one ton of SO_2 emissions. In the 2013 SO_2 auction, the market-clearing price was $0.17 and 125,000 allowances were sold. Among the buyers were Holy Cross Energy, the Acid Rain Retirement Fund, and the University of Tampa Environmental Protection Coalition.

Articles 6, 12, and 17 of the 1997 Kyoto Protocol on Climate Change set forth greenhouse gas emissions trading on a global scale.[10] To comply with emissions restrictions under the Kyoto Protocol, countries can reduce emissions in their own country, earn emissions credits by assisting with "clean development" projects in developing countries, earn credits on the basis of land use changes such as reforestation, or purchase credits. Unit transfers and acquisitions are tracked by the United Nations Climate Change Secretariat based in Bonn, Germany.

As a component of the Kyoto Protocol trading plan, the European Union Emission Trading System commenced in 2005 as the largest permit trading scheme of its type in the world. The program currently covers CO_2 and NO_x and targets a 20 percent reduction in greenhouse gas emissions relative to 1990 levels by 2020. The American Clean Energy and Security Act proposed in 2009 (also called the Waxman-Markey Bill) would have created an analogous cap-and-trade program in the United States and reduced U.S. carbon emissions to 17 percent below 2005 levels by 2020. The bill was approved by the House of Representatives but was defeated in 2010 by the Senate.

Innovative uses of emissions trading have proliferated. In Australia, where salt pollution by salt and coal mines threatens to make water unsuitable for drinking and irrigation, inter-state salinity credit trading has led to substantial cuts in salinity levels. To limit automobile congestion and pollution, Singapore has a permit system for cars: those wishing to drive can bid on "certificates of entitlement" at twice-monthly auctions. The U.S. Environmental Protection Agency oversees a credit trading program for phosphorus, nitrogen, and sediment releases into waterways as part of the National Pollutant Discharge Elimination System.[11] And members of the British parliament have proposed an individual-level carbon trading program dubbed "pay as you pollute." This program would allocate 1,000 carbon-use points to each person annually, deduct points for flights, gasoline fill-ups, and other carbon use, and further incentivise conservation by allowing excess points to be sold.[12]

9 Links to all of these allowance sources are available at www.epa.gov/airmarkets/trading/buying.html.

10 See http://unfcc.int/resource/docs/convkp/kpeng.html.

11 See www.epa.gov/npdes/pubs/wqtradingtoolkit_fundamentals.pdf.

12 See www.guardian.co.uk/environment/2006/jan/24/business.travelnews.

reality check

Market Incentives and the Endangered Species Act

In 2013 there were 2,057 species listed as *endangered* (in danger of extinction) or *threatened* (likely to become endangered in the foreseeable future) under the Endangered Species Act (ESA) of 1973. The United States Secretary of the Department of the Interior approves domestic plants, wildlife, and inland fish for the list and creates recovery plans for each species without regard to the cost. The Secretary of Commerce does the same for ocean-going fish and marine animals. When a species is listed, the Secretary must designate areas as protected "critical habitat" for the species. Private landowners are not compensated when the use of their land is limited by critical habitat designation.

The inflexibility of command-and-control policy is less of an issue when it comes to protecting endangered species—there aren't a lot of alternative ways to save these plants and creatures. Endangered species are often those that do not adapt well to substitute habitats and do not reproduce readily in captivity. Saving these species may come down to protecting their existing habitat.

This being the case, the influence of incentives remains critically important. Given the threat of land-use restrictions without compensation, the incentive for landowners is to preemptively destroy endangered species in order to avoid the burden of compliance. According to U.S. Representative Richard Pombo (R-California) and supported by economic research by Lueck and Michael (2003), landowners "frequently act to eliminate habitat, for fear of losing use of their property to federal government regulations" (see http://web.outsidemag.com/news/specialreport/esa/pomboedit2.html).

Pombo and his colleague Representative Don Young (R-Alaska) proposed the Endangered Species Conservation and Management Act, ostensibly to remedy problems with poor incentives. The act would have compensated landowners whose property value decreased by more than 20 percent due to protective action, and provided tax incentives for property owners to promote species recovery. As with many bills, however, the fine print elicited detractors. The Sierra Club said the proposed act would "gut" the ESA by permitting the destruction of endangered species habitat, delaying the listing of species, and loosening other standards for protection. The National Wildlife Federation noted that the ESA already has virtually no restrictions on property use for landowners with endangered plants, and proposed its own set of incentives, including a conservation easement program that would provide tax breaks to landowners who preserve endangered species habitat. The general consensus is that even with command-and-control regulations, behavior hinges on incentives, and a policy will fail if the trail of incentives does not lead to the policy goal.

Mixed Approaches to Carbon Emissions in China and the United States

China and the United States are the world's first and second largest emitters of CO_2. Policymakers in both countries are pursuing a mix of market incentives and command-and-control regulations to limit pollution damage. During the 2008 Olympics in Beijing, the Chinese government prohibited owners of private cars from driving in the city on alternate days, depending on whether the last number of their license plate was odd or even. Trucks and cars with relatively high emissions were banned from city driving. The sky-clearing success of these regulations inspired watered-down versions after the Olympics, including requirements that each private car be kept off the road one day out of each week. The Chinese government also mandated a boost in renewable energy capacity that included the construction of seven giant wind farms, each with the capacity of more than 16 coal-fired power plants.

China's market-based solutions include incentive programs for commuters who find alternatives to private automobiles, subsidies for methane reduction and reforestation, and formal training programs in market-based environmentalism. The Environmental Defense Fund reports that the Chinese government has hired their Chief Economist, Daniel Dudek, to develop incentive programs including the sort of cap-and-trade systems explained above.[13]

In the United States, the American Recovery and Reinvestment Act of 2009 included more than $60 billion in clean energy investments such as 3,000 miles of transmission lines to bring renewable energy from sources to cities, weatherization for 2 million homes of low-income residents, energy efficiency upgrades for 75 percent of federal buildings, $600 million for "green job" training programs, and $2.4 billion in federal grants for the development of more efficient, battery-powered vehicles.

President Barack Obama's 2014 budget proposal cut funding for the EPA by almost 5 percent, but increased spending on other environmental programs by the same proportion. Consistent with his spending priorities, Obama's 2013 nominee to lead the Department of Energy described his principle job as to minimize the cost of low-carbon energy technologies. In his first term, Obama supported higher CAFE standards for vehicles, stricter efficiency standards for home appliances, and a program to tap the waters of the outer continental shelf for electricity from wind, waves, and ocean currents. In his second inaugural address, he said, "We will respond to

U.S. Senate Photo

13 See www.edf.org/page.cfm?tagID=28833.

the threat of climate change, knowing that the failure to do so would betray our children and future generations. Some may still deny the overwhelming judgment of science, but none can avoid the devastating impact of raging fires, and crippling drought, and more powerful storms." Advocating an economy-wide cap-and-trade program for greenhouse gasses, he stated during his first campaign, "Businesses don't own the sky, the public does, and if we want them to stop polluting it, we have to put a price on all pollution. It's time to make the cleaner way of doing business the more profitable way of doing business."[14]

Punishment and Deterrence

Deterrence via the Legal System

From ten years, in violation of the Clean Water Act, Chemetco, Inc., allegedly discharged pollutants including zinc, lead, and cadmium into Long Lake, a tributary of the Mississippi River. Investigators say the toxic substances were released through a "secret pipe" from the company's copper smelting plant in southwestern Illinois. The case was investigated by the EPA's Criminal Investigation Division, the FBI, the U.S. Department of Transportation, the State Police, and the Illinois EPA. The U.S. District Court ordered a fine of $3,865,100 and $400,000 in restitution payments by Chemetco. The individuals accused of building or using the secret pipe face up to eight years in prison and up to $500,000 in fines. This case highlights both the risks that some people take to circumvent environmental policy and the many agencies that devote resources to monitoring and enforcement.

Environmental policy loses its influence when enforcement mechanisms are weak. Environmental abuses are difficult to police because toxic releases can happen anywhere at any time. The most vulnerable wilderness areas are often the most remote, meaning that watchful eyes are not upon them. These monitoring difficulties have implications on the best approaches to enforcement. This section outlines the theory of optimal deterrence in the context of environmental policy.

We have seen that socially optimal behavior is expected when decision makers internalize the full costs and benefits of their contemplated actions. When illegal dumping or other misdeeds are considered, the expected value of punishment weighs into the compliance decision. The **expected punishment cost** equals

(the probability of punishment) × (the punishment cost if imposed)

The probability of punishment is itself the product of the probabilities of apprehension, conviction given apprehension, and punishment given conviction. Thus, even if the chance of getting caught is 80 percent, if half of those apprehended are convicted and half of those convicted pay a $10,000 fine while the rest get a warning, the probability of punishment is $0.80 \times 0.50 \times 0.50 = 0.20$

14 See www.marketwatch.com/story/obama-calls-for-pollution-cap-and-trade-program.

Punishment Probability	*Punishment Cost*	*Expected Punishment Cost*
1	$10,000	$10,000
1/10	$100,000	$10,000
1/100	$1,000,000	$10,000
1/10,000	$100,000,000	$10,000
1/1,000,000	$10,000,000,000	$10,000

Table 12.1 *Punishment Alternatives*

and the expected punishment cost is only $0.20 \times \$10,000 = \$2,000$.

As described in Chapter 4, risk-averse people feel a burden from the uncertain outcomes of risky behavior. Environmental crimes constitute risky behavior, and the associated risk burden (or risk enjoyment felt by risk-loving individuals) is an added component of the expected punishment cost.

Socially efficient decisions are made when external marginal costs and benefits are internalized. When a firm or household receives all of the benefits from, say, illegal dumping, efficiency is achieved if the expected punishment cost equals the marginal external cost. This will cause decision makers to internalize the marginal external cost and only deviate from policy when the marginal benefit exceeds the social marginal cost. When monitoring is difficult, as is typically the case for environmental misconduct, the low probability of punishment can be made up for with a high punishment cost. Table 12.1 indicates several combinations of punishment probabilities and costs, all of which yield an expected punishment cost of $10,000 for a risk-neutral decision maker.

If the marginal external cost of dumping is $10,000, any of these combinations will result in the efficient amount of dumping. If monitoring is costly, however, *the solution that minimizes monitoring costs is that which imposes the highest possible punishment cost.* A fine of $10 billion coupled with the minimal monitoring efforts required to catch one in one-million criminals would have the same deterrence effect on risk-neutral criminals as a certain fine of $10,000. The difference is that it would be prohibitively expensive to bring about certain detection. The burden of uncertain punishment for risk-averse criminals means that, with a one in one-million chance of apprehension, there is a fine less than $10 billion (depending on their degree of risk aversion) that would elicit the same behavior as a certain fine of $10,000. Monitoring-cost minimization is one of the reasons why we see large jury awards in environmental crimes, as was the case for Chemetco.

In 1990 the EPA increased the penalties for hazardous waste violations under the Resource Conservation and Recovery Act (RCRA). Some fines were increased by 10 to 20 times their original size by the revised RCRA Civil Penalty Policy. Research by Sarah L. Stafford (2002, 294) found that within three years of this policy change, the number of violations per EPA inspection began a steady though less-than-hoped-for decline. Controlling for other influences, Stafford also found fewer violations in states where more citizens were members of environmental organizations. Apparently while incentives matter, so does attitude.

Excessive Deterrence

While the inability to monitor some types of environmental damage can result in capricious behavior on the part of polluters, policymakers and other detractors must be alert to the possibility of excessive precaution. One problem with combining private and public remedies is that the expected punishment, compounded with the burden of uncertainty, can exceed the marginal external cost of a particular action. There is often uncertainty about the standard for appropriate precaution—how many tests must be run before a jury would find that PondClear Corp. did enough to establish the safety of its new algae killer to fish and swimmers? With the prospect for uncapped damage awards from juries or unchecked ecoterrorism, there is no limit to the costs that might be imposed.

Excessive deterrence can also result from the combination of regulation and liability. When monitoring is effective, an overlap of legal remedies and regulations may provide production disincentives that are too strong. For example, a combination of pollution taxes and the threat of litigation for subsequent environmental risks can bring production below the efficient level. As illustrated in Figure 12.2, if Pigou taxes are set to bring about the efficient level of production, Q^*, the addition of expected litigation costs will lead to the inefficiently low production level Q_L, and any associated risk burden[15] or ecoterrorism threat will result in production levels even further below the efficient level, such as Q_R. The moral of the story is that those who establish policy must consider the entire set of incentives so that the *combined* effect elicits the efficient level of care for the environment.

Some economists advocate regulation as an alternative to litigation. W. Kip Viscusi states:

> *One cannot rely on tort liability in lieu of regulation because products liability incentives are ill-suited to the task. Not all injured parties file claims, and court awards are far below what is required to promote efficient safety incentives.*[16]

Legislation could stipulate tests and approval procedures for a new product that are *exculpatory*, meaning that their successful completion would release the producer from subsequent litigation over the issue of that product's safety. For example, suppose litigation threats make it prohibitively risky for a company to introduce an energy-saving battery for hybrid-electric cars that has a small chance of leaking acid and triggering a multimillion-dollar jury award. The satisfaction of a specified set of safety standards—say a hazard warning program compliant with current regulations, the completion of 25 successful crash tests at highway speeds, and approval by a national product safety commission—could constitute a level of care beyond legal challenge. The trick here is to set an appropriate standard for safety. This may again require cost-benefit analysis and subjugation

15 As explained in Chapter 4, a risk burden is the largest amount one would be willing to pay to avoid uncertainty about the possible outcomes and know for sure that the actual cost will equal the expected cost.

16 See Viscusi (1991), p. 129.

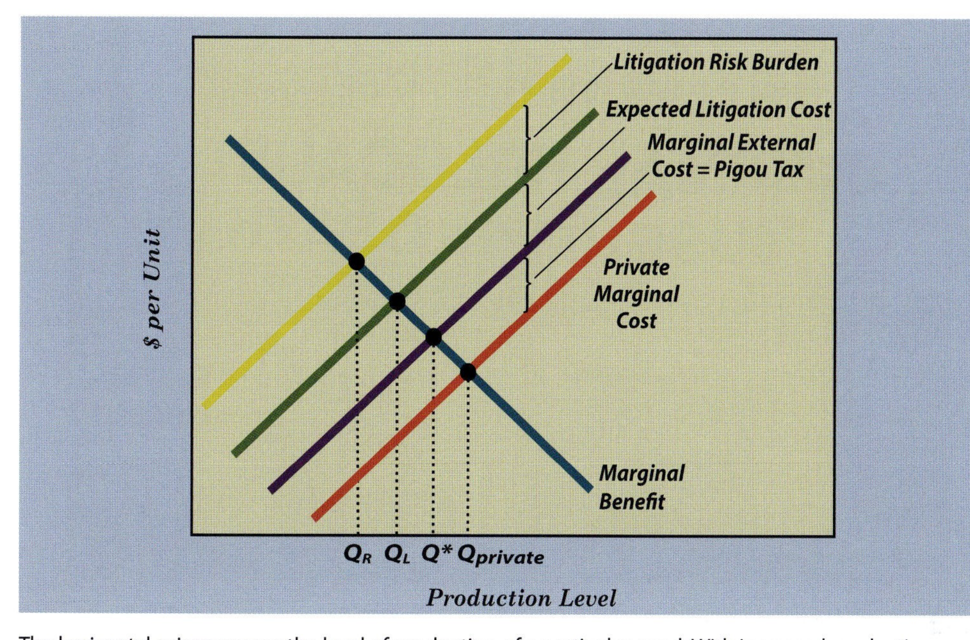

Figure 12.2 *Excessive Deterrence*

The horizontal axis measures the level of production of a particular good. With increased production comes increased pollution and related externalities. In the absence of litigation and taxes, the firm will produce the inefficiently large quantity $Q_{private}$ as indicated by the intersection of the firm's private marginal cost and marginal benefit curves. A Pigou tax equal to the marginal external cost causes the firm to internalize the externalities and produce at the socially efficient level, Q^*. If litigation over the externalities is an added risk, the marginal cost rises again and production will occur at the inefficiently small quantity Q_L. Risk aversion on the part of the firm will result in the added cost of a risk burden and the still smaller quantity Q_R.

to the political process. However, if a panel of jurors can be relied upon *after* a claim has been filed to determine whether safety checks were adequate, a similar panel should be able to make the same determination *before* the product has been released. This would allow companies to innovate and market new products without fear of extraordinary reprisals.

Activism and Vigilante Justice

Frustrated by what they perceive as insufficient policy standards, monitoring efforts, or punishments, some individuals and groups have decided to take matters into their own hands. Private eco-activism ranging from letters to politicians to violent acts of ecoterrorism add to the landscape of incentives for socially responsible behavior. In grassroots efforts, consumers have voted with their pocketbooks against everything from Coke (due to allegedly insufficient recycling initiatives)[17] to U.S. coal (due to U.S. nonadherence to global environmental policy protocols).[18] Some of the more successful efforts have led

17 See www.hotkey.net.au/~gargoyle/CDL/BoycottCocaCola/CokeSurveyResults.htm.

18 See www.spacedaily.com/news/010524134527.208biooq.html.

Activists erected this display at Venice Beach, California, to raise public awareness about animal cruelty.

the fast food industry away from Styrofoam[19] and coaxed fashion retailers away from fur coats.[20] Greenpeace is famous for its peaceful but aggressive campaigns to influence policy on nuclear threats, whaling, toxic releases, deforestation, and global climate change, among their other concerns.[21]

Like litigation and prosecution, the threat of responses from activists poses a small risk of large costs, but with a vigilante twist. For example, in 2001, the anti-urban-sprawl Earth Liberation Front (ELF) allegedly burned new homes using crude explosives, damaged bulldozing equipment, and scrawled "meat is murder" and "if you build it we will burn it" on a restaurant and a home. The *New York Times* quotes a 1997 Internet communiqué from ELF saying, "We take inspiration from the Luddites, Levellers, Diggers, the Autonome squatter movement, ALF, the Zapatistas, and the little people—those mischievous elves of lore."[22] Such groups have placed metal spikes in trees to make logging dangerous, destroyed labs where genetically engineered crops were developed, and released animals being kept to harvest for their fur.[23] While peaceful protests have influenced policy and practice, violent approaches are largely ineffectual. For governments to cater to criminal actions would be to invite more crime, and so the response to ecoterrorism has been limited almost exclusively to actions against the terrorists.

19 See www.mcspotlight.org/campaigns/countries/usa/usa_toxics.html.

20 See, among many examples, www.geocities.com/boycottthebay/.

21 See www.greenpeace.org/campaigns/.

22 See the *New York Times*, January 3, 2001, accessed online at www.nytimes.com/2001/01/03/nyregion/03EART.html.

23 See www.earthliberationfront.com.

Summary

There is more than one way to skin a cat, and likewise to catch a pig and to control pollution. Differing perspectives complicate the formation of environmental policy, although economic theory provides guidelines. There is general consensus among economists that approaches that allow flexibility and provide incentives are critical, as are allocative mechanisms that grant pollution rights to those who value them the most. Back in 1997, 2,509 economists signed a statement on climate change that advocated market-based solutions as a source of each of these criteria.

When a variety of alternative solutions are allowable and enforceable, flexibility permits firms to meet environmental standards using cost-effective methods appropriate to the age of the facility and the options available. In other situations, command-and-control regulations are appropriate, as when there exists a single effective and enforceable solution. Ambient environmental quality standards can be the target for both command-and-control and incentive-based policies. Technical standards, emission standards, and cap-and-trade programs are all among common attempts to meet air- and water-quality standards.

Efficiency requires that the marginal cost of pollution abatement be the same across firms, which can be achieved with cap-and-trade programs that limit the total releases of specific forms of pollution and allocate tradable permits to pollution sources. The expectation is that those who derive the most benefit from polluting will buy permits from those who value the rights the least and those who can reduce their emissions at the lowest cost. Trade will continue as long as one firm can reduce emissions at a lower cost than another, resulting in an efficient outcome. Thanks to their flexibility, efficient allocation mechanism, and incentives for continued abatement, tradable emissions permits have become popular worldwide over the past decade.

Threats of litigation and prosecution serve as added incentives for compliance with environmental policy. The expected punishment cost of environmental misconduct is the product of the probability of punishment and the punishment cost if imposed. When other incentives for compliance are not present, efficient behavior results from an expected punishment cost equal to the marginal external cost. Monitoring costs can be reduced for a given expected punishment cost by maximizing the punishment and thereby minimizing the probability of punishment necessary to achieve the desired expected cost. When legal threats are combined with risk burdens, environmental taxes, and other pollution disincentives, the result can be an inefficiently low level of pollution and production.

Activism, and in the extreme, ecoterrorism, are private approaches to environmental justice. Violent measures generally get nowhere because a favorable response to violence would invite more violence. On the other hand, grassroots efforts demanding corporate responsibility and peaceful protests by environmental organizations have influenced firm behavior and received widespread support.

Problems for Review

1. Environmental policies have not been changed at the behest of ecoterrorists, nor are concessions typically made to other terrorists or kidnappers. What is the logic behind a policy of noncompliance with the demands of terrorists? What would happen if we gave some terrorists what they desired?

2. Consider an electric utility that in 2013 had enough SO_2 allowances to cover its current emissions. If the utility could have reduced its emissions at a cost of \$0.15 per ton, should it have done so? Why or why not?

3. Suppose that rather than regulating the amount of pollution, the government regulated the amount of pollution abatement. Draw a graph similar to Figure 12.1 except with units of pollution *abatement* on the horizontal axis and the increasing marginal cost of *abatement* for two firms (rather than the decreasing marginal value of pollution). The width of the graph now represents the total amount of abatement required. On your graph, shade with horizontal stripes the total cost of abatement if each firm must eliminate the same amount of pollution. Shade with vertical stripes the total cost of abatement if tradable emissions permits allow the firms to reallocate abatement responsibilities as desired.

4. Draw two graphs with identical demand curves for pollution defined by the equation $Q = 100 - P$, with Q being the quantity of pollution and P being the price per unit of pollution. Assuming that all pollution costs are external, label the quantity of pollution in the absence of intervention as Q_0 on each graph. On the first graph, draw a flat-rate Pigou tax of \$25 per unit of pollution and label the resulting quantity of pollution Q^*. On the second graph draw a vertical line at 75 units of pollution representing the total quantity of pollution permits available.
   a) *Compare the relative efficiency of the Pigou tax and the pollution permits approach.*
   b) *Compare the information required under each approach to set policy limiting pollution to the efficient level.*

5. In what situations are command-and-control regulations most appropriate? Provide a specific example that is not from this book.

6. The Endangered Species Act stipulates that recovery plans be established for each listed species *without regard to the cost of recovery*. Using economic reasoning, explain what you perceive as the pros and cons of this approach.

7. Draw a graph as in Figure 12.2 and label the four cost curves W, X, Y, and Z, in that order, from left to right. Assume that firms are risk neutral unless told otherwise, there are no Pigou taxes in place, litigation is always a risk, and the vertical distance between each neighboring set of cost curves is 2. For each of the following firms, indicate the per-unit tax or subsidy that would lead them to the efficient production level.

a) Tree-Huggers Inc., which feels the pain of every environmental cost.

b) Risky-Business Inc., whose love of taking chances gives it a negative risk burden equal to the expected litigation cost.

c) Selfish-Me Inc., which cares only about itself.

d) Sotomayor's-Sis Inc., owned by the sister of a Supreme Court justice who feels immune to litigation risks.

8. The text explains how command-and-control policies, including the Endangered Species Act and the National Pollutant Discharge Elimination System, might be combined with market incentives to yield more desirable results. Describe another possible marriage of incentive-based and command-and-control policies.

9. Describe an environmental problem that might be solved with activism and the type of activism you would recommend. Discuss the combination of incentives the source of this problem will face and how you feel they would respond to the incentives. Be specific.

10. Suppose that ChemsAreUs Corporation is contemplating the production of Agent Yellow, an update of defoliant Agent Orange. Agent Yellow has a 10 percent chance of causing $1 billion worth of unintended environmental damage, and a 90 percent chance of causing no damage beyond the intended defoliation. If Agent Yellow is produced and the damage occurs under existing policies and enforcement levels, there is a 30 percent chance that ChemsAreUs will have to pay a $3 billion fine. Discuss the company's incentives for efficient behavior under the following conditions:

    a) ChemsAreUs is risk neutral and faces no threat from activists.

    b) ChemsAreUs is risk averse and the mere possibility of paying the stated fine imposes a $10 million risk burden on the company.

    c) ChemsAreUs is risk neutral, but in addition to the risk of paying a fine, there is a 50 percent chance that environmental activists will organize a successful boycott that causes the company to lose $40 million.

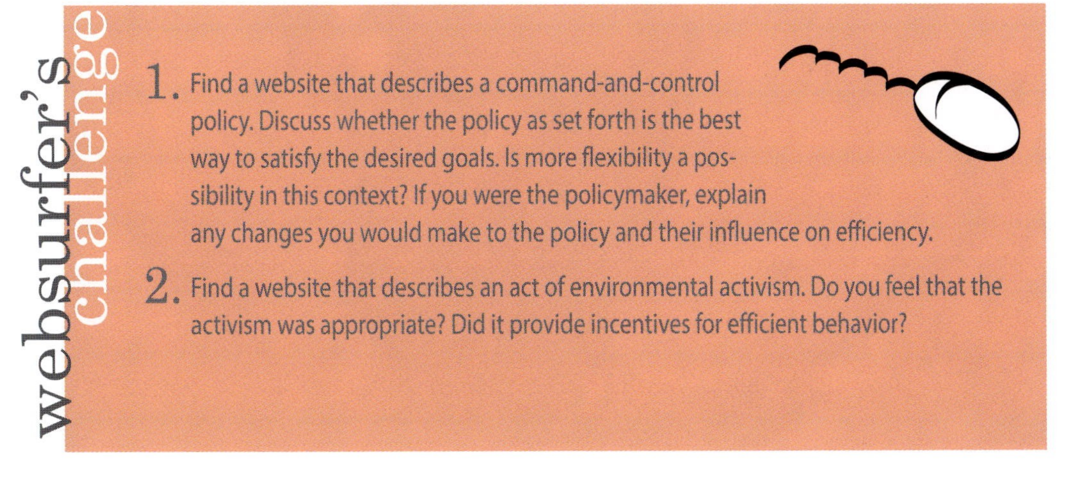

Internet Resources

EPA page on NPDES Regulation:
cfpub.epa.gov/npdes/regs.cfm

EPA page on Policy, Economics, and Innovation:
www.epa.gov/opei/

Global Policy Forum page on United Nations Environmental Policy:
www.globalpolicy.org/socecon/envronmt/indxmain.htm

U.S. Department of Energy, Office of Environmental Policy and Guidance:
tis-nt.eh.doe.gov/oepa/

Further Reading

Arimura, Toshi H. "An Empirical Study of the SO_2 Allowance Market: Effects of PUC Regulations." *Journal of Environmental Economics and Management* 44, no. 2 (2002): 271–289. Discusses the combined influence of tradable SO_2 allowances and public utility regulations on the decision to use lower-sulfur coal.

Brown, Gardner M. Jr., and Jason F. Shogren. "Economics of the Endangered Species Act." *Journal of Economic Perspectives* 12, no. 3 (1998): 3–20. An accessible overview of the act and possible improvements that could be made.

Hansjurgens, Bernd, Ralf Antes, and Marianne Keudel (eds). *Permit Trading in Different Applications*. Oxford: Routledge, 2010. A contemporary outlook on permit trading.

Lueck, D., and J. Michael. "Preemptive Habitat Destruction under the Endangered Species Act." *Journal of Law & Economics* 46, no. 1 (2003): 27–60. An empirical study of the influence of the ESA on timber harvests near known endangered species habitat.

Mott, Joshua A., et al. "National Vehicle Emissions Policies and Practices and Declining U.S. Carbon Monoxide-Related Mortality." *Journal of the American Medical Association* 288, no. 8 (2002): 988–995. Evaluates the influence of national vehicle emissions policies and practices on carbon monoxide-related deaths between 1968 and 1998.

Olson, Mancur. *The Logic of Collective Action*. Cambridge, MA: Harvard University Press, 2009. Develops the theory of group behavior and discusses the optimal provision of public goods.

Ott, Hermann E., and Wolfgang Sachs. "Ethical Aspects of Emissions Trading." In *Equity and Emission Trading—Ethical and Theological Dimensions*, Saskatoon, Canada: World Council of Churches, 2000. Available online at www.wupperinst.org/Publikationen/WP/WP110.pdf. A critique of international tradable emissions permit systems.

Stafford, Sarah L. "The Effect of Punishment on Firm Compliance with Hazardous Waste Regulations." *Journal of Environmental Economics and Management* 44, no. 2 (2002): 290–308. Finds that the EPA's 1991 increase in penalties led to a decrease in hazardous waste violations.

Stavins, Robert N. "What Can We Learn from the Grand Policy Experiment? Lessons from SO_2 Allowance Trading." *Journal of Economic Perspectives* 12, no. 3 (1998): 69–88. Provides a summary of the benefits and challenges of the first three years of allowance trading in the United States.

Viscusi, W. Kip. *Reforming Products Liability*. Cambridge, MA: Harvard University Press, 1991. Proposes solutions to the overlapping influence of liability risks and regulation.

Harvested crayfish near Pensacola, Florida

13 Natural Resource Management: Renewable Resources

Populations of Pacific rockfish—the 60 or so species that include yelloweye, canary rockfish, and bocaccio—are in trouble. Trawling nets dragged across the continental shelf catch these fish and everything else in their paths. About half of the global continental shelf is now trawled, and the repercussions of inefficient fishery management are widespread. Falling fish populations affect those who eat seafood and those who rely on it for income. Fishing and the industries it supports, such as boat manufacturing and canning, generate an estimated $240 billion in annual revenues worldwide.[1] *Disturbances in fish stocks also affect species above and below them in the food chain. For example, populations of the Steller sea lion, which competes for food with commercial fishing operations in the heavily trafficked North Pacific, have dropped by 80 percent since 1960.*[2]

A **fishery** *is an area where fish are caught—a fishing ground—or a firm in the fishing business.* **Bycatch** *is the term used for fish, birds, turtles, and marine mammals caught in a fishery, but discarded because they have little or no commercial value or they do not meet regulatory requirements. Bycatch represents an estimated 60 billion pounds or 25 percent of the overall global catch each year. Under the Sustainable Fisheries Act (SFA) of 1996,*[3] *a fish species that falls below 25 percent of its natural (unfished) population must be rebuilt to 40 percent of its natural population.*[4] *Many*

1 See Dyck and Sumaila (2010).

2 See www.americanoceans.org/ak/steller-pack.htm.

3 The SFA amended the Magnuson Fishery Conservation and Management Act of 1976, which was renamed the Magnuson-Stevens Fishery Conservation and Management Act. See http://ipl.unm.edu/cwl/fedbook/magfish.html.

4 See www.californiafish.org/.

species of rockfish meet this criterion for overfishing. Similarly, 43 percent of measurable U.S. fish stocks are overfished.[5]

Possible solutions include the closure of fisheries, quotas, government buyouts of fishing rights, and regulations that require safer fishing equipment, including excluders, which allow some marine animals to escape. Policymakers must decide what level of fishing effort is ideal and how that goal should be addressed. This chapter introduces a popular model of natural resource management using fisheries and forests as the central examples of renewable resources. The chapter also discusses the pros and cons of available policy options and the policy implications of uncertainty. Chapter 14 follows up with case studies of depletable and replenishable resources.

Fishery Management

A Biological Growth Function

Analyses of fishery economics have so many applications to other common property resources that some economists refer to any common property as a fishery. Our study of fisheries begins with a discussion of growth in the number of fish as it depends on the fish population, or **stock**, in a fishery. Growth rates are relevant to fishing concerns because sustainable fish harvests cannot exceed the growth in fish stocks.

M.D. Schaefer (1957) modeled fishery growth as a function of the fish stock as in Figure 13.1. The horizontal axis measures the size of the fish stock and the vertical axis measures the number of additional fish spawned each period, which we will think of as a year. For example, if Stock_A represents the number of fish, the stock will grow by Growth_A fish over the next year. For simplicity, we will assume that all fish are of the same size and that other variables that affect fish populations, including food sources, water temperature, and pollution levels, are held constant. The small increments of growth at low and high stock levels and the larger growth increments at middling population levels are characteristic of **logistic growth functions**. This type of relationship is commonly used to model biological growth patterns where an initial period of exponential growth is followed by a leveling off as food supplies or other constraints limit further growth.[6]

In the fisheries example the story can be told this way: At very low population levels, food and space are abundant but mates are scarce. As the population grows, opportunities for reproduction increase while food and space remain negligible constraints, allowing for large growth increments. As the stock approaches the

5 See www.pewoceans.org/inquiry/fishing/.

6 The form of a symmetric logistic growth function is $y = K / (1 + \exp(a + b * x))$, where K is the carrying capacity (maximum population size), and a and b are constants that determine the shape and scale of the function.

Forty-three percent of measurable U.S. fish stocks are overfished.

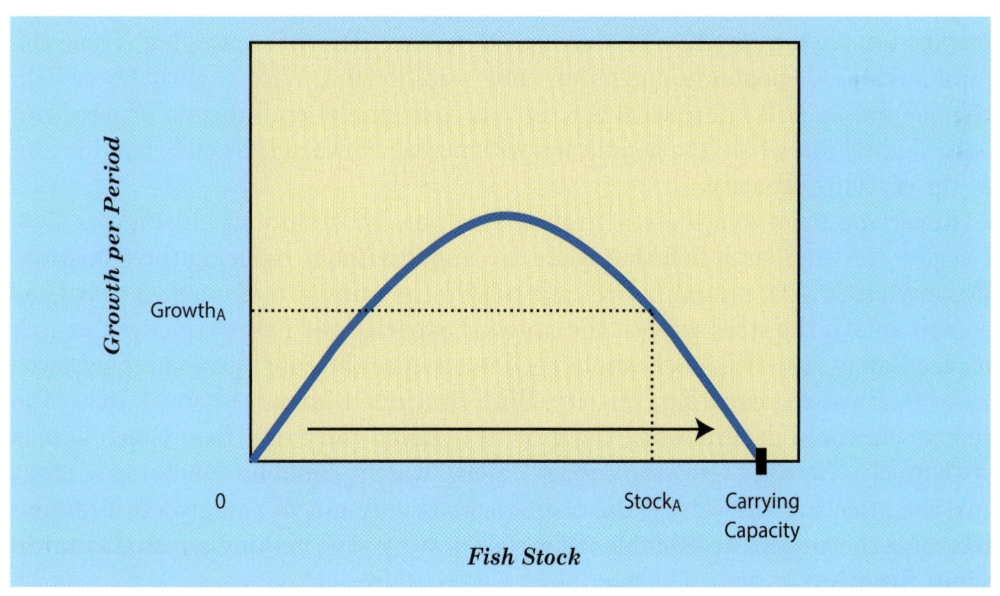

Figure 13.1
The Growth of Fish Stocks

This curve shows the relationship between the size of a fish stock and the growth in that stock per period. Small fish stocks do not propagate rapidly, in part because mates are scarce. With some growth in the fish stock, food and space may still be abundant and propagation accelerates due to the increased availability of mates. As the fish population starts to meet space and food constraints, growth slows until the carrying capacity of the fishery is met.

maximum size supportable by its habitat—its **carrying capacity**—incremental growth declines. Fish must compete for food and places to escape predation. When the carrying capacity is reached, and when the fish stock is zero, there is no growth and the population remains constant.

In the absence of outside influences such as fishing, the carrying capacity is a **stable equilibrium**, meaning that if the fish stock deviates slightly from this number, natural forces of growth or death will bring it back to the equilibrium. The arrow in Figure 13.1 starting to the right of zero and pointing toward the carrying capacity indicates that a fish stock with this growth function has a natural tendency to increase until it reaches the carrying capacity. Each positive quantity of fish results in growth that brings the population size further to the right until capacity is met. A fish stock of zero is an unstable equilibrium. With zero fish there can be no growth in the population, but if a few fish are introduced, the population size (in this example) will grow toward the stable equilibrium rather than tending back to zero.

The slope of a growth function equals the stock's rate of growth.[7] Notice that in Figure 13.1 the slope is always decreasing as the stock increases. In contrast, the slope of a **depensated growth function** increases initially, and then decreases.[8] The graph in Figure 13.2 is a special case of a depensated growth function. A **critically depensated growth function** such as this begins with a negative slope and may be more realistic than the simplified growth function in Figure 13.1. Rather than suggesting that growth will occur with any positive quantity of fish, it allows for a **minimum viable population**, below which there are too few fish to maintain or increase the population. A very small population may be unable to reproduce fast enough to replace fish that are dying. Thus, the minimum viable population is an unstable equilibrium. With slightly fewer fish, the population will fall toward the (in this case stable) equilibrium of zero, and with slightly more fish, the population will increase toward the stable equilibrium at the carrying capacity.

Reverting back to a logistic growth function for simplicity, in Figure 13.3, consider the number of fish that could be caught without reducing the fish stock. For any stock size, an annual catch equal to the annual incremental growth is sustainable. If the stock were at the carrying capacity and fishers removed a catch of size $Catch_A$, the fish stock would decline because the catch exceeds the growth rate of zero at the carrying capacity. With continued catches of size $Catch_A$, the fish stock would decline until the growth equaled the catch size, which occurs with $Stock_A$. Because $Growth_A$ equals $Catch_A$, $Catch_A$ could be sustained without further affecting the size of the fish stock. The height of the growth function indicates the largest sustainable yield at each stock size, making it a **sustainable yield function** as well. The maximum sustainable yield occurs at $Stock_B$. As we will see, the socially efficient yield will fall below the maximum sustainable yield.

7 The growth increment divided by the stock equals the percentage change in the stock, or the growth rate.

8 See Clark (1990).

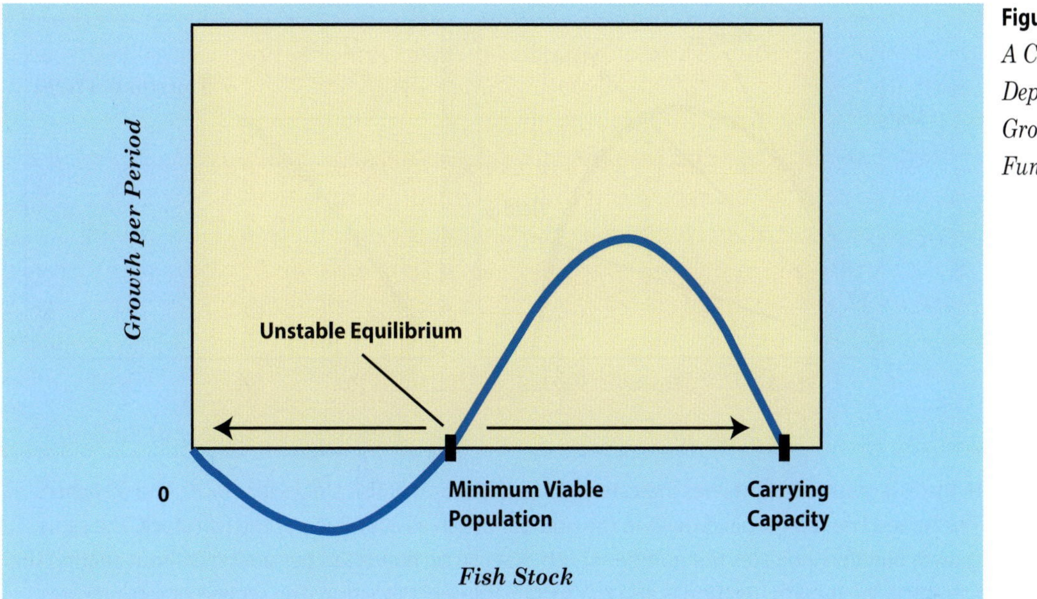

Figure 13.2 *A Critically Depensated Growth Function*

A critically depensated growth function has stable equilibria at each extreme and an unstable equilibrium at the minimum viable population. A fish stock smaller than the minimum viable population cannot reproduce as fast as fish are dying, and eventually collapses. Larger fish stocks continue to grow until the carrying capacity is met.

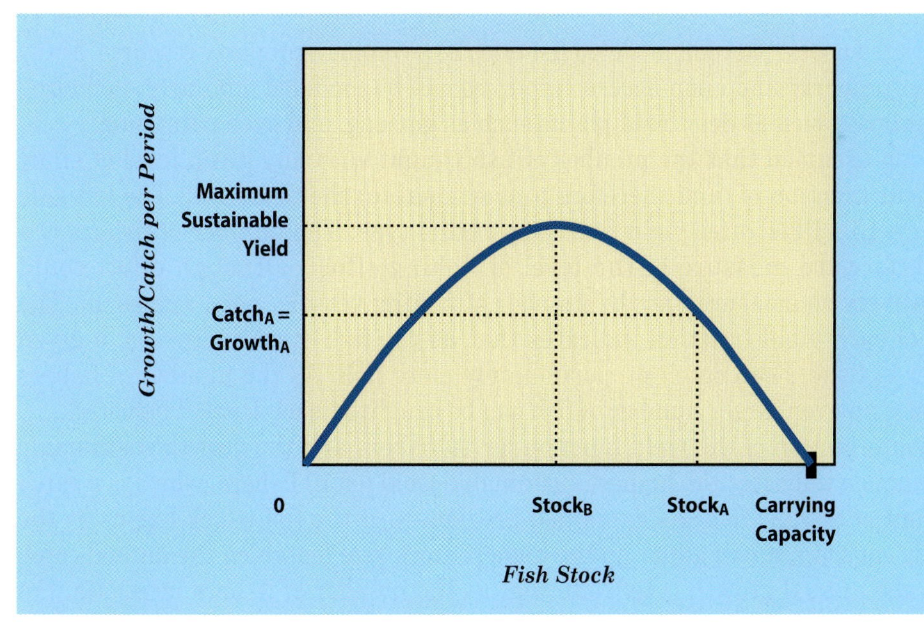

Figure 13.3 *Growth and Sustainable Yield*

For a given stock size, a catch per period that equals the growth per period, such as Catch$_A$ when the stock level is Stock$_A$, can be sustained indefinitely. If the catch per period is smaller than the growth per period, the stock will grow until the catch equals the growth per period. If the catch per period is larger than the growth per period, the stock size will fall until either the growth per period equals the catch per period or the fishery is eliminated, whichever comes first.

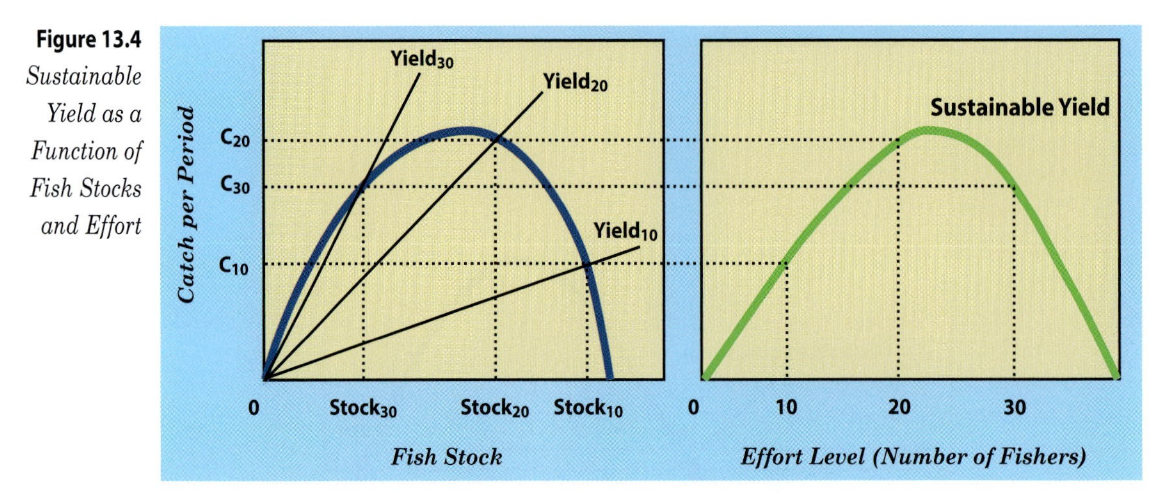

Figure 13.4 *Sustainable Yield as a Function of Fish Stocks and Effort*

In the first graph, straight lines indicate yield as a function of fish stocks for 10, 20, and 30 fishers. The curved line represents growth in the number of fish as a function of the fish stock. The same growth function indicates the number of fish that can be harvested per period without altering the fish stock: the growth function is also the sustainable yield function. The second graph indicates sustainable yield as a function of effort rather than as a function of fish stocks.

Sustainable Yield Functions

H. Scott Gordon's model of fishing effort is useful for explaining why the maximum sustainable yield is not the efficient yield, and why the efficient yield is not chosen by unrestricted users.[9] Gordon modeled fisheries as a common-property resource. Many common-property and open-access resources can be modeled similarly, including game animals such as deer, wild plants such as ginseng, and even petroleum.

Gordon assumed that the number of fish caught with any given level of effort is a linear function of (and therefore proportional to) the fish stock. The left side of Figure 13.4 illustrates yield functions of this type. The number of fishers is a straightforward measure of the level of fishing effort, although effort could alternatively be measured as the number of fishing vessels, nets, and so on. The shape of each yield function indicates that as the fish stock increases, a given number of fishers can catch proportionately more fish. As the number of fishers increases, an even larger number of fish can be caught at each level of fish stock.

The intersection of the yield function for 10 fishers and the growth/sustainable yield function indicates the highest sustainable yield for 10 fishers, which is a catch of C_{10} out of Stock_{10} fish. As explained previously, if the fish stock begins at the carrying capacity, it will adjust to the highest stock size for which the annual catch equals the annual growth rate. Note that as the number of fishers increases, the sustainable yield increases and then decreases as the increasing yield functions intersect higher and then lower sections of the sustainable yield function.

The right side of Figure 13.4 maps out the relationship between the effort level and the sustainable yield. The yield function for 10 fishers reaches its sustainable yield at C_{10}, so the height of the sustainable yield function is C_{10} at an effort level

9 See Gordon (1954), p. 124.

The peak of the total revenue curve corresponds with the maximum sustainable yield, but not the efficient yield. The marginal cost of each unit of effort beyond $Effort_1$ exceeds the social marginal revenue, so those effort levels are inefficient, and economic rent is maximized with $Effort_1$. In the top graph, $Effort_1$ corresponds with the effort level at which total revenue exceeds total cost by the greatest amount, which is at the tangency point between total revenue and the green tangent line.

Individual fishers will enter until $Effort_3$ is reached, at which point their private marginal benefit from fishing—the average revenue received by each fisher—equals the opportunity cost of their time. The entrance of a new fisher causes the catch of every existing fisher to decrease, and the societal marginal revenue curve indicates the new fisher's catch *minus* the losses to the other fishers. The socially efficient effort level is $Effort_1$, at the intersection of social marginal revenue and marginal cost. The shaded rectangle represents the maximized economic rent gained from $Effort_1$.

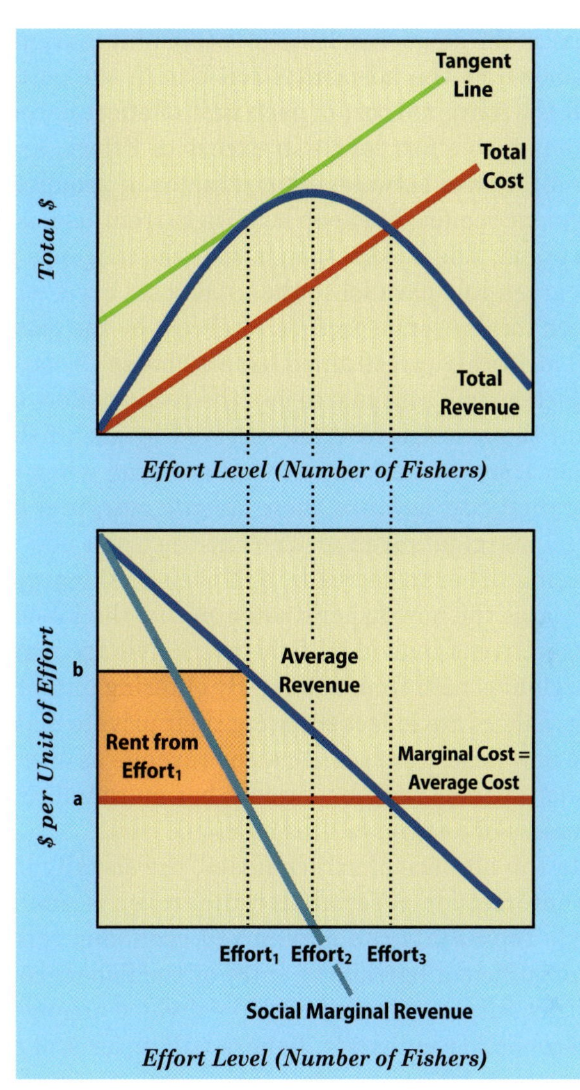

Figure 13.5 *The Gordon Fishery Model*

of 10 fishers, and so on. As effort increases, the sustainable yield increases and then decreases, making for another inverted-U-shaped relationship that is differentiated from the growth function because effort rather than fish stock is on the horizontal axis.

The Choice of Effort Levels

The sustainable yield-effort relationship becomes even more interesting when it is "monetized" by multiplying the sustainable yield for each effort level by the price per fish, which Gordon assumes is constant. The result is a total revenue curve, as illustrated in the top graph of Figure 13.5. For example, if 20 fishers could catch 1 million fish per year and each fish sold for 50 cents, the height of the total revenue curve above an effort level of 20 fishers would be 1 million × \$0.50 = \$500,000.

The peak of the total revenue curve corresponds with the effort level $Effort_2$ that attains the maximum sustainable yield, but this is not the efficient yield in the presence of fishing costs. Gordon assumes that the opportunity cost of each fisher's effort is the same, resulting in a constant marginal cost that equals average cost as shown by the horizontal red line in the bottom graph in Figure 13.5. Note that the marginal cost of each unit of effort beyond $Effort_1$ exceeds the marginal revenue, so effort levels in excess of $Effort_1$ are inefficient. **Economic rent**, the difference between what a factor of production receives and the minimum payment required to keep it in its current use, is maximized with $Effort_1$. In the top graph, $Effort_1$ corresponds with the tangency point between total revenue and the green line parallel to the total cost curve, which indicates the effort level at which total revenue exceeds total cost by the greatest amount. Which effort level will identical, unrestrained fishers choose? None of the above!

Fishers will continue to join the fishing effort until $Effort_3$ is reached, at which point the average revenue received by each fisher equals the opportunity cost of her time. Fishers do not stop entering when social marginal revenue equals marginal cost because their *private* marginal gain from entering exceeds the social marginal revenue. The entrance of a new fisher causes the catch of every existing fisher to decrease, and the social marginal revenue curve in the graph indicates the new fisher's catch *minus* the losses to the other fishers. From the perspective of individual fishers, the average revenue curve reflects their private marginal benefit from fishing. By entering until average revenue equals marginal cost, fishers are in fact equating their private marginal benefit and marginal cost. The new fisher receives the same revenue as everyone else—the average revenue. If that average revenue exceeds her marginal cost, she is content. Such revenue in excess of cost constitutes economic rent.

In the absence of externalities, the socially efficient effort level is $Effort_1$ at the intersection of social marginal revenue and marginal cost. The orange rectangle represents the maximized economic rent gained from $Effort_1$. If there were sufficient barriers to entry or the fishers could form a successful cartel and restrict output, this rent could be divided among them. With open access, as long as economic rent exists, fishers will enter and compete for it. The open access outcome is $Effort_3$, at which point each fisher receives revenue exactly equal to her opportunity cost, and the economic rent is zero. This dissipation of rents exemplifies the tragedy of the commons introduced in Chapter 3.

The Gordon model is forward looking in the sustainability of its outcomes, but static in its lack of discounting. The sustainable yield is dynamically efficient only if the discount rate is zero. Positive discount rates for future costs and benefits imply larger efficient catches today. With substantial discount rates, the opportunity costs of foregone net benefits are diminished, warranting greater effort levels in the short run. Colin Clark (1990) demonstrated that as the discount rate approaches infinity, the socially efficient effort level approaches the zero-rent level $Effort_3$.

Policy Responses

Fisheries, among other common-property and open-access resources, face a difficult challenge in the quest for efficient yields. The success of policy solutions rests initially on the ability to enforce policy at all. Concurrent with the growing popularity of fish, nations have sought jurisdiction over extended territorial waters. Historically, it was the maritime custom for countries including the United States to claim jurisdiction over waters and resources within three miles of shore. The United States, Europe, and Canada, among other countries, then extended fishing restrictions to 12 miles, and now a 200-mile exclusion zone is the norm.

The 1976 Magnuson Act established a 200-mile exclusive economic zone (EEZ) on U.S. coasts in which foreign ships must have a permit and can harvest only highly migratory species or fish in excess supply. The Act stipulated a maximum penalty of $100,000, one year in prison, and forfeiture of the unauthorized fishing vessel. Despite claims of jurisdiction, enforcement remains a problem, particularly at the distant ends of territorial waters. Some economists fear that EEZs may actually worsen overfishing problems by promoting the development of domestic fishing fleets in coastal countries, while foreign fleets continue to harvest a bit farther out in international waters.[10]

To the extent that policy is enforceable, several policy initiatives can address inefficient resource-use decisions. If the marginal cost to fishers is increased to the amount *b* in Figure 13.5, fishers will choose the efficient effort level $Effort_1$, at which their new marginal cost will equal their private marginal benefit (which equals average revenue). This could be accomplished by requiring fishers to fish farther from the shore or to use smaller nets, boats, or motors, among other command-and-control techniques. However, these methods of artificially increasing the cost of fishing cause a loss of the economic rent otherwise gained at the efficient level of effort. Instead, a fee equal to the difference between marginal cost and average revenue at $Effort_1$, represented by segment *ab* on the graph, would bring the fishers' marginal cost up to the level *b* necessary to elicit optimal fishing effort. The revenues from the fee would equal the shaded economic rent otherwise obtained from the efficient effort level, and these revenues could be distributed as the collecting agency sees fit.

Restrictions could also limit the effort level or the size of the catch. Total catch quotas are often called **total allowable catch** limits or TACs. Similar restrictions on effort are achieved by closing fisheries or limiting fishing to certain days or seasons, which is the case for lobster trapping. As with most regulations of common-property and open-access resources, effort and catch limits are difficult to monitor and enforce. The rents earned on the last fish caught leave fishers wanting more, thereby creating temptation and political unrest.[11]

A simple TAC program also elicits a race to catch fish, as individual fishers each want to harvest as much as possible as quickly as possible before the quota is reached. This competition breeds inefficient expenditures on oversized vessels and related fishing capital. A relatively new approach involves **individual transferable quotas** (ITQs). Under this system, total allowable catches are divided into quotas for individual fishers, who may then sell their rights to shares of the TAC, or buy larger shares. Being assured a particular share of the total catch,

10 See McKelvey, Sandal, and Steinshamn (2002).

11 See, for example, news.bbc.co.uk/1/low/uk/northern_ireland/568660.stm and www.enn.com/news/wire-stories/2001/04/04032001/krt_fishing_42864.asp.

reality check

And Overfish We Do

Fish have been an important source of protein since before protein sources set foot on land, but fish consumption by humans has increased dramatically over recent decades. Between 1960 and 2010, annual worldwide fish consumption per-capita increased from 9 kg to 17 kg (19.8 lb to 37.4 lb), an increase of 89 percent. In 2012, the worldwide catch was about 157 million tons, including 67 million tons of fish raised in commercial "aquaculture" farms. Among the countries with the highest annual fish consumption per capita are Iceland with 91.5 kg/201.7 lb, Japan with 66.1 kg/145.7 lb, and Guyana with 51.5 kg/113.5 lb.

Growing fish harvests have strained fishery stocks. One-quarter of the world's commercially viable fish populations are overfished by the Sustainable Fisheries Act standards. The U.S. Fish and Wildlife Service lists 149 threatened and endangered fish species.

The steelhead trout (*Oncorhynchus mykiss*), for example, has had a bad bout with human activity. Beyond commercial, recreational, and tribal harvests, the U.S. Office of Protected Resources lists the following as factors in the steelhead's severe decline: logging, road construction, urban development, grazing, mining, agriculture, hydropower development, flood control, loss of large woody debris in waterways, and artificial propagation (aquaculture). The most surprising of these problems might be aquaculture. In fact, fish "farmed" in aquaculture facilities result in a considerable loss of fish in natural settings. Farmed fish are often fed wild fish for improved health and flavor, and fish that escape from farms threaten wild fish by competing for food, interbreeding, and spreading parasites and diseases. For more on the downside of aquaculture facilities, see www.panda.org/about_our_earth/blue_planet/problems/aquaculture/.

fishers need not use resources inefficiently in a rush to harvest.

The market-based ITQs approach lowers capital expenditures and allows relatively efficient fishers to purchase fishing rights from relatively inefficient fishers, leading to a lower societal cost of catching fish. New Zealand initiated the first major ITQ program in 1986. The United States operates ITQ programs for surf clams and ocean quahog in mid-Atlantic and New England waters, for wreckfish along the south Atlantic coast, and for halibut and sablefish off Alaska. Australia, Canada, Iceland, Italy, the Netherlands, and South Africa have similar programs. Monitoring issues remain, as does controversy over the appropriate TAC.[12]

12 For a detailed overview of ITQs, see Anderson (1995).

Policy Under Uncertainty

> *"We will manage stocks of uncertain status in a precautionary manner in response to the level of uncertainty. In fisheries for which scientific information is especially uncertain or lacking entirely, management will be more conservative to avoid accidental overfishing."*
>
> —National Oceanic and Atmospheric Administration (NOAA)[13]

Variations in fishery conditions make the shape of growth functions difficult to pinpoint. Even if the best available data support an estimated growth function, as in Figure 13.6, changes in the sea temperature, pollution levels, predators, or food supplies can shift the growth function up or down. If a TAC of $Catch_A$ is instituted and the annual growth is $Growth_B$, the fish stock will grow beyond the intended equilibrium level $Stock_A$. If the annual growth rate is $Growth_C$, a TAC of $Catch_A$ cannot be maintained at any stock level. The fish stock will fall, possibly hastened by increasing effort put forth to maintain the allowable catch, until the stock is eliminated or the TAC is modified. Given a fish stock of $Stock_A$, a precautionary approach would be to set the TAC at $Growth_C$, meaning that fish populations will either remain unchanged or grow.

Landing fees, catch quotas, and effort quotas all provide similar incentives for efficient fishery management in a simple model with costless enforcement. The complication of uncertainty makes some policies better than others. Martin Weitzman (2002) argues that when setting fishery management policy in the face of ecological uncertainty, a landing fee is superior to a catch quota. This is because less information is needed to set an optimal landing fee than to set an optimal quota. The quota belongs at the intersection of social marginal revenue

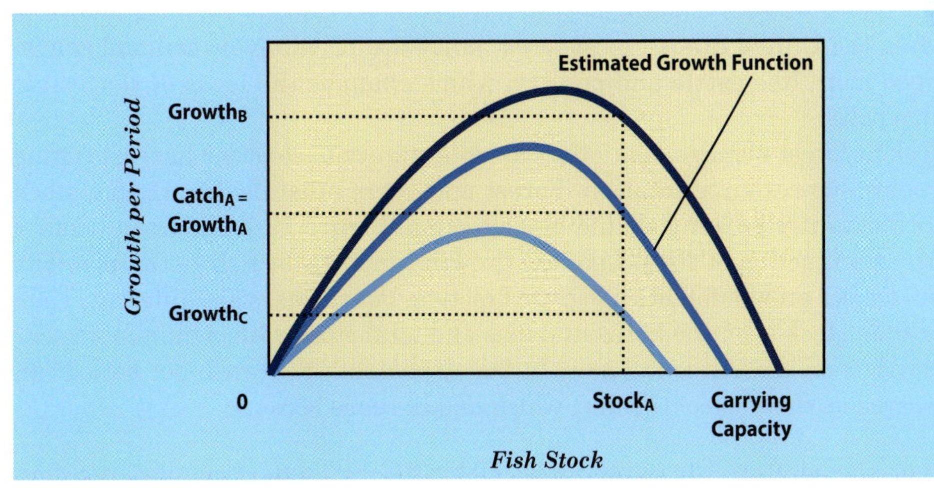

Figure 13.6 *Uncertainty and the Growth Function*

Uncertainty regarding water conditions and the adequacy of food supplies cloud growth function estimates for fisheries. Overly optimistic growth estimates can lead to catch rates that reduce or eliminate fish stocks. Pessimistic estimates can lead to unexpected fishery growth.

13 See www.noaa.gov/nmfs/vision/sustain_vision.html.

and marginal cost, whereas the optimal fee is based only on the marginal external cost of fishing.

Asgeir Danielsson (2002) used mathematical models to compare the efficiency of effort quotas and catch quotas. He concluded that effort quotas are the clear winner when the price sensitivity (or "elasticity") of demand is high and the growth rate is more variable than the catch per unit of effort. When the price elasticity of demand is low and the catch per unit of effort is more variable than the growth rate, catch quotas are more efficient than effort quotas. These studies demonstrate that policymaking with disregard for the effects of uncertainty can lead to suboptimal results.

Forest Management

After deforestation contributed to Yangtze River flooding that killed 3,656 people and caused $31 billion worth of damage, forestry policy in China took a dramatic turn toward reclamation. Logging was banned in 17 provinces as part of a nation-wide Natural Forest Protection Plan. When such policies are enforced, as they were in China, they serve targeted areas well. Without a decrease in forest-product demand, however, logging is simply displaced—China's logging ban led to increased timber imports from Southeast Asia. Complementary policies to decrease demand are needed to reduce deforestation on a broader scale. China addressed demand by promoting wood substitutes including "plybamboo" and bamboo chopsticks, and sought to increase the supply of timer with a Grain-to-Green policy that gave grain subsidies to communities that planted trees.

China, Australia, and Canada are among the countries whose forests are largely controlled by government. Trees on open-access lands are like fish in open-access waters and the endangered elephants and rhinos of Chapter 11: they present problems with monitoring and harvest-effort control. In other countries including the United States, most forest lands are privately owned and can be managed more like cattle and poultry, which changes the focus of renewable resource policy.

A look at forest management offers an opportunity to consider harvest timing and renewable-resource rotation. Forest managers must decide when a stock that is constantly growing should be harvested. Figure 13.7 illustrates timber growth as a function of time. Like the growth function for fish in the previous section, timber growth follows a logistic function, but the axes are different. Time rather than stock is on the horizontal axis and total stock rather than incremental growth is on the horizontal axis. In this depiction, the growth per period can be observed as the slope of the line, which makes sense because

slope = rise / run = change in volume / change in time = growth per period.

Not surprisingly, the decision of when to harvest a tree comes down to marginal

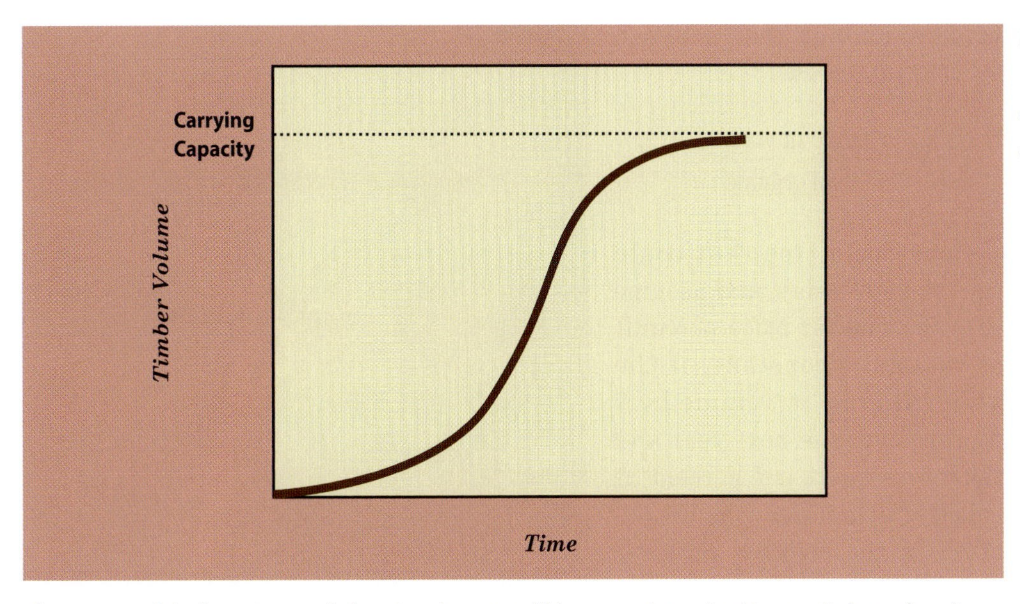

Figure 13.7 *Timber Volume as a Function of Time*

This version of the logistic growth function shows total biomass volume (in this case timber volume) on the vertical axis, rather than the growth in volume as in previous graphs. Also, unlike the graphs for fisheries, the horizontal axis measures time. The starting volume for a particular section of forest can be zero; a global function would need to start at the volume of the minimum viable stand of forest. The slope of this line is the growth of timber volume per period. The growth per period increases at an increasing rate initially, then at a decreasing rate, slowing to zero at the carrying capacity of the forest.

analysis. We know that every activity should continue until the marginal cost equals the marginal benefit. The marginal benefit of maintaining an investment in a tree for another year is that it will grow in volume and be worth more in the next year. The marginal cost is the best alternative return that the money invested in that tree could earn. This might be the amount that could be earned by harvesting the tree and putting the revenue in the bank to earn annual interest rate R.

For the moment, assume that the increase in timber volume and the opportunity cost of lost interest are the only benefits and costs. That is, the tree under consideration can be harvested for free; the land the tree is on will sit idly in your backyard when the tree is gone; no spotted owls have made a home in the tree; and no one is fond of thinking about, looking at, or hugging the tree. Such a tree should become a telephone pole or a textbook at the time when the marginal benefit of increased volume no longer exceeds the marginal cost of lost interest—in other words, when the tree's rate of growth equals the interest rate. The tree's growth rate is found by dividing the change in volume by the total volume, making the condition for optimal harvest:[14]

$$R = \frac{\text{change in volume}}{\text{total volume}}$$

Consider a tree that could sell for $500 today, and assume that the market price per unit of volume is constant. If the tree will grow in volume by 7 percent over the next year and the interest rate is 5 percent, it is better to maintain the investment in the tree for another year. The tree will be worth

$$\$500 + (0.07 \times \$500) = \$535$$

next year, whereas if the tree is sold and the money is deposited in the bank, the value next year will be

$$\$500 + (0.05 \times \$500) = \$525$$

Eucalyptus trees such as these grow relatively quickly and allow for sustainable harvests in managed timberlands. The first page of this chapter includes an illustration of selective cutting, one type of sustainable harvest that limits erosion and habitat destruction. Sustainably managed eucalyptus plantations are the source of paper for many textbooks.

The decreasing slope of the latter part of the growth function indicates that the growth rate will eventually fall toward zero. At the point when the growth rate equals 5 percent, the money will earn as much in the bank as it will invested in the tree for another year. In subsequent years, it will earn relatively more in the bank.

Trees will grow for many years before harvest, and the simplified harvest decision is effectively a series of comparisons between the growth rate and the rate of return on alternative investments. The optimal year for harvest is the first year in which the tree's growth rate falls to equal the annual rate of return from

14 This equation can be derived using calculus. Let t represent time, $V(t)$ represent the volume of the tree as a function of time, and P represent the market price for a unit of tree volume. The present discounted value (PDV) of the tree is $e^{-Rt}V(t)P$. The optimal harvest condition is found by setting the derivative of this equal to zero: $dPDV(t)/dt = e^{-Rt}V'(t)P - Re^{-Rt}V(t)P = 0$. Dividing both sides by $e^{-Rt}P$ and solving for R yields the equation given, where $V'(t)$ is the change in volume and $V(t)$ is the total volume. Note that the price drops out of the equation, as would a term for the initial cost of planting the tree, which has become a "sunk cost" that should be ignored after it is incurred.

the next-best investment. Now let's remove some of the simplifying assumptions and see how the harvest condition changes.

We will incorporate the harvest cost, the land value, and the standing value of the forest. The harvest cost is the cost of felling trees and bringing them to market. This cost should be subtracted from the timber value when comparing the returns from maintaining a tree stock with the returns from selling the timber.

Trees generally stand on land that will provide a stream of net benefits from continued tree harvests or other uses. If trees are left to grow for another year, the land cannot be sold, used as pasture for cattle, or replanted with the next generation of trees. It is appropriate to assess the value of land as the present value of the future net benefits achievable from the land. This land value is foregone for another year if the existing trees are not harvested, and the lost annual return on the land value should be included in the cost of not harvesting in a particular year.

The last consideration is the standing value of the forest itself. As China learned through tragedy along the Yangtze River, the standing value of a forest includes flood and erosion control. It also includes the ability to use the forest to sequester carbon, look at, recreate in, and promote biodiversity. If the forest provides some of the last viable habitat for the endangered black-footed ferret,[15] for example, the standing value is substantial.

To grasp the effects of these considerations, begin by rewriting the simplified condition for optimal harvest in terms of dollars. The total volume of the trees can be expressed in monetary terms as the timber value, which is simply the total volume multiplied by the market price per unit of volume. Likewise the change in timber value is the change in volume multiplied by the market price per unit of volume. With these changes, the harvest condition becomes

$$R = \frac{\text{change in timber value}}{\text{timber value}}$$

Multiplying both sides by the timber value gives us

$$R(\text{timber value}) = \text{change in timber value}$$

The left side is the interest to be gained by harvesting the trees now and putting the money in the bank (assumed for simplicity to be the best alternative investment) for a year. The right side is the gain from waiting another year to harvest.

Now we can add the new items. The sum of money on which interest could be earned if the trees were cut now is decreased by the harvest cost and increased by the land value. The interest rate times the resulting amount indicates the

15 The black-footed ferret was thought to be extinct in the late 1970s, but a small colony was discovered in 1981. Several hundred now live in captivity and some have been released into the wild.

Figure 13.8
Optimal Forest Rotation

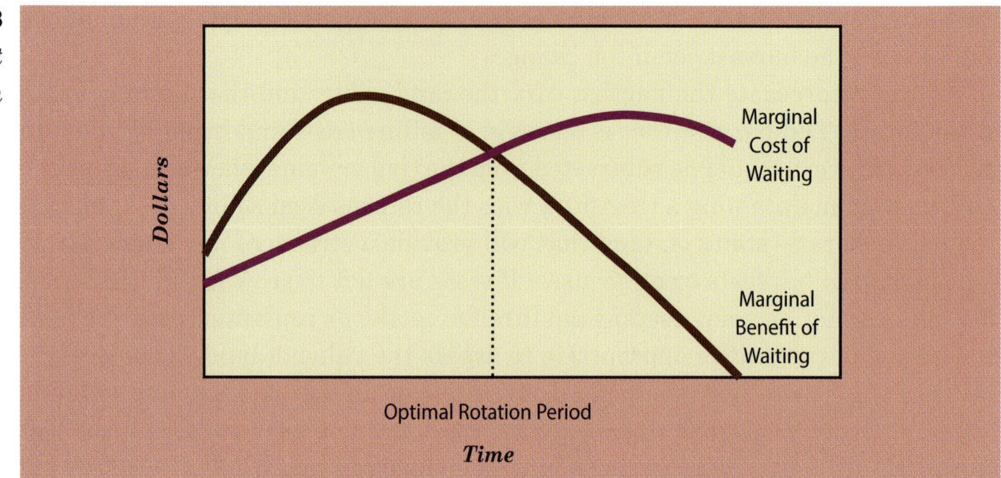

The marginal cost of waiting another year to harvest is the interest that could be earned on the timber value and the land value minus the cost of harvest. The timber value and therefore the marginal cost is initially low, but increases to a maximum as the trees grow, and eventually decreases as the trees stop growing and are subject to disease, death, and forest fires. The marginal benefit of waiting another year to harvest is the change in the timber value plus the annual standing value for recreation, animal habitat, scenery, carbon sequestration, and the like. This marginal benefit will increase and decrease with the growth rate. The optimal rotation period extends to the intersection of these two lines, after which time the marginal cost of waiting another year exceeds the marginal benefit.

marginal cost of waiting to harvest. The marginal benefit of waiting another year is increased by the annual standing value. With these adjustments, the harvest condition becomes

$$R(\text{timber value} - \text{harvest cost} + \text{land value}) = \\ \text{change in timber value} + \text{annual standing value}$$

where the top line is the marginal cost of waiting and the bottom line is the marginal benefit.

Figure 13.8 shows the time-dependent relationship between the marginal cost and marginal benefit of waiting another year to harvest. The marginal cost of waiting moves with the timber value on which interest is foregone, starting low, increasing to a maximum as the trees grow, and then decreasing as the trees stop growing and are subject to disease, forest fires, and death.

The marginal benefit of waiting another year to harvest increases initially and then decreases, driven by the increasing and decreasing growth rate of timber. (The benefit of waiting another year is higher when the tree is growing more quickly.) The optimal rotation period, after which the existing trees are harvested and new trees are planted, extends to the intersection of these two lines. After that time, the marginal cost of waiting another year exceeds the marginal benefit.

Figure 13.8 and the equation above offer insights into the harvest decision. An increase in the standing value of a forest, as might occur if pollution levels make carbon sequestration more important, will shift the marginal-benefit-of-waiting curve upward to intersect the marginal cost curve at a longer rotation length. An increase in land value or a decrease in harvest cost will shift the marginal cost of waiting curve upward and decrease the optimal rotation length. Only if the interest rate—and therefore the marginal cost of waiting—were zero would harvest occur at or beyond the time when trees stop growing.

The management of a forest may involve hundreds or thousands of acres of trees. In a planned forest with an optimal rotation length of t years, a steady flow of timber can be acquired by harvesting $1/t^{th}$ of the forest each year. For example, if the optimal rotation is 20 years, $1/20^{th}$ of the forest can be harvested and replanted each year. That method provides an unchanging annual harvest even though each tree will stand for t years.

Summary

Although fisheries and forests have the ability to rejuvenate themselves, these and other renewable resources require careful management. When there is open access to fisheries, economic rents are dissipated by fishers who disregard the lost yield their entrance imposes on others. The Gordon fishery model determines the optimal effort level and the entrance fee that would bring fishers to internalize the full cost of their behavior. In addition to entrance fees, policy options include total allowable catch limits, individual transferable quotas, and limits based on seasons, locations, and equipment.

The Magnuson Act established exclusive economic zones and limits on overfishing in the United States; similar policies exist elsewhere. Fishery policy is complicated by enforcement difficulties and uncertainty about stocks, growth rates, and yields. As fishing technology has improved and seafood has grown in popularity, the fish stocks of many major fisheries have fallen to dangerously low levels that necessitate a phase of rebuilding.

The decision of how often to harvest forests depends on a comparison of the benefit from another year's growth and the opportunity cost of the money that could otherwise be invested elsewhere. Trees should be harvested when the growth rate of timber volume falls to the level of the best alternative rate of return. Forests will be harvested more frequently given a relatively high opportunity cost of money or land, or a relatively low harvest cost or standing value. The benefits provided by standing trees include carbon sequestration, watershed protection, recreation, and wildlife habitat.

Problems for Review

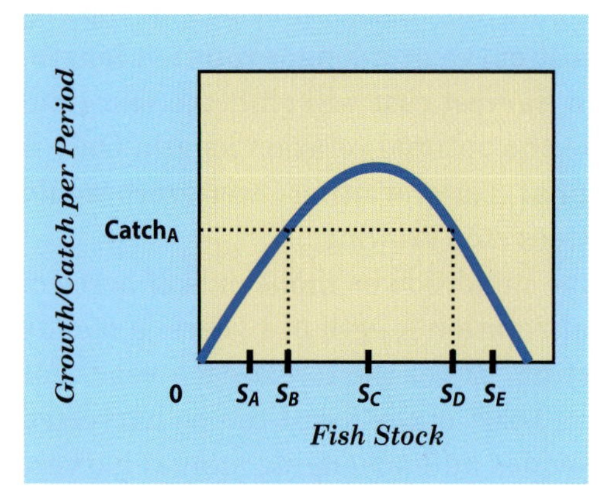

Figure 13.9 *Growth Function for Problem 1*

1. Consider a fishery with annual growth as shown in Figure 13.9. Explain what would happen if there were a continued annual catch of Catch$_A$ with a beginning stock of each of the following:

   a) S_A
   b) S_B
   c) S_C
   d) S_D
   e) S_E

2. Draw a depensated growth function that is not critically depensated. Label any stable or unstable equilibria. Discuss whether this function might apply to the growth of some animal stocks.

3. Wild morel mushrooms are a delicacy in soups and salads. The following table shows the number of mushrooms that can be harvested per picker per hour in a fictional forest, depending on the number of pickers.

Pickers	Mushrooms per Picker per Hour
1	70
2	60
3	50
4	40
5	30
6	20
7	10

   a) Assuming that each mushroom sells for $1, graph the average and marginal revenue for society at each level of effort (number of pickers).

   b) Given that the opportunity cost of each picker's time is $10 per hour, label the socially optimal number of pickers and the number of pickers that will enter if the forest is an open-access resource. Explain why the pickers will dissipate the economic rent.

4. Considering the data provided in Problem 3, what is the economic rent with the socially optimal number of pickers? What economic rent results from entry based on private incentives? What entry fee would result in the socially optimal number of pickers?

5. Consider once more the situation in Problem 3. Explain two policies that do not involve a fee that could result in the optimal level of effort. What complications might arise in the administration of these policies?

6. List three common-property resources not discussed in this chapter to which the models explained in the chapter could be applied.

7. Discuss the implications on fishery policy decisions of each of the following:

   a) An increase in certainty about the catch per unit of effort

   b) An increase in certainty about growth rates

   c) An increase in monitoring technology

8. Draw a graph with growth per year on the vertical axis and time on the horizontal axis that corresponds with the total growth function in Figure 13.7. Explain why the optimal harvest is unlikely to occur at the highest point of either of these graphs.

9. Policymakers sometimes consider relaxing access to national forests for logging purposes. Relative to harvest decisions made for trees on private land as discussed in this chapter, how would you expect decisions and the associated graph (Figure 13.8) to differ when the harvests occur on government-owned, open-access property?

10. How would each of the following affect the socially optimal rotation intervals for trees?

    a) An increase in the demand for real estate

    b) An increase in soil erosion on deforested land due to global warming

    c) Engineers perfect the harvest-cost-saving Super-Axe-Hacker (conceived by Dr. Seuss in The Lorax*)*

"At the current rate of decline, the last tropical rain forest tree will fall in 2045."

—THE COLUMBUS ZOO

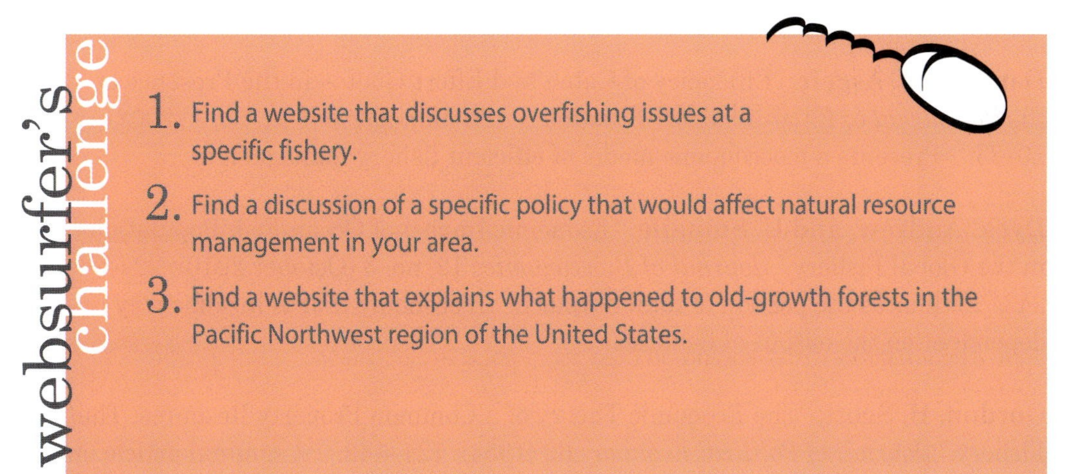

Internet Resources

American Tree Farm System:
www.treefarmsystem.org

Canadian Forest Service:
www.nrcan.gc.ca/cfs-scf/

Fisheries and Oceans Canada:
www.dfo-mpo.gc.ca/index.htm

National Fish Hatchery System:
fisheries.fws.gov/FWSFH/NFHSmain.htm

National Marine Fisheries Service:
www.nmfs.noaa.gov

Sustainable Fisheries Act site:
www.nmfs.noaa.gov/sfa/

U.S. Fish and Wildlife Service:
www.fws.gov

USDA Forest Service:
www.fs.fed.us/land/fm/index.php

Further Reading

Anderson, Lee G. "Privatizing Open Access Fisheries: Individual Transferable Quotas." In *Handbook of Environmental Economics*, edited by Daniel W. Bromley. Cambridge, MA: Blackwell, 1995. An in-depth overview of the theory of ITQs.

Clark, Colin W. "Profit Maximization and the Extinction of Animal Species." *Journal of Political Economy* 81 (1973): 950–960. Identifies the importance of dynamic optimization elements, including discount rates and harvest costs, to the risk of species extinction.

Clark, Colin W. *Mathematical Bioeconomics*. 2nd ed. New York: Wiley, 1990. An introduction to the theory of biological conservation.

Danielsson, Asgeir. "Efficiency of Catch and Effort Quotas in the Presence of Risk." *Journal of Environmental Economics and Management* 14, no. 1 (2002): 20–33. Presents a bioeconomic model of efficient fishery management.

Dyck, Andrew, and U. Sumaila. "Economic Impact of Ocean Fish Populations in the Global Fishery." *Journal of Bioeconomics* 12, no. 3 (October 2010): 227–243. Estimates the portion of total output in an economy that is in some way dependent on the output of fisheries.

Gordon, H. Scott. "The Economic Theory of a Common Property Resource: The Fishery." *Journal of Political Economy* 62 (1954): 124–142. A seminal article on the modeling of fishery resources.

Hartman, Richard. "The Harvesting Decision When a Standing Forest Has Value." *Economic Inquiry* 14 (1976): 52–58. A classic discussion of the timing of tree harvests.

Klemperer, W. David. *Forest Resource Economics and Finance.* New York: McGraw-Hill, 1996. A textbook devoted to forest economics.

McKelvey, Robert W., Leif K. Sandal, and Stein I. Steinshamn. "Fish Wars on the High Seas: A Straddling Stock Competition Model." *International Game Theory Review* 4, no. 1 (2002): 53–69. Models the conflict between foreign distant-water fishing fleets and domestic fleets on either side of EEZ boundaries.

Repetto, Robert, and Malcolm Gillis (eds). *Public Policy and the Misuse of Forest Resources.* Cambridge: Cambridge University Press, 1988. A useful guide to the pros and cons of forest policy options.

Schaefer, M. D. "Some Considerations of Population Dynamics and Economics in Relation to the Management of Marine Fisheries." *Journal of the Fisheries Research Board of Canada* (now called the *Canadian Journal of Fisheries and Aquatic Sciences*) 14 (1957): 669–681. A seminal article on growth functions for fisheries.

Weitzman, Martin L. "Landing Fees vs. Harvest Quotas with Uncertain Fish Stocks." *Journal of Environmental Economics and Management* 43, no. 2 (2002): 325–338. A theoretical comparison between fishing fees and harvest quotas with and without uncertainty about fish stocks.

"And at that very moment, we heard a loud whack!
From outside in the fields came a sickening smack
of an axe on a tree. Then we heard the tree fall.
The very last Truffula Tree of them all!"

—THEODORE GEISEL (DR. SEUSS), *THE LORAX*

"When the well's dry, we know the worth of water."

—BENJAMIN FRANKLIN, *POOR RICHARD'S ALMANACK*

"[Water] is the most widely used resource by industry; it is used to produce energy; it provides the basis for much of our outdoor recreation; it is an important part of our transportation network; it serves as a vehicle for disposing of wastes; and it provides important cultural and amenity values."

—KENNETH D. FREDERICK, *RESOURCES FOR THE FUTURE*

"It is difficult for people living now, who have become accustomed to the steady exponential growth in the consumption of energy from fossil fuels, to realize how transitory the fossil-fuel epoch will eventually prove to be when it is viewed over a longer span of human history."

—M. KING HUBBERT, "THE ENERGY RESOURCES OF THE EARTH"

14 Natural Resource Management: Depletable and Replenishable Resources

From the great oceans and swamps of prehistoric time came the most popular energy sources of our time. Plants and animals store solar energy from the sun and retain some of that energy when they die. Accumulations of biomass were entombed by layers of mud and silt for hundreds of millions of years, where pressure and heat transformed them into the simpler chains of carbon and hydrogen that make up the fossil fuels we burn today. These resources provide a different type of challenge than deciding when to harvest a tree. With oil, it is no longer a question of whether to wait for the next incremental growth in the resource—any realistic discount rate makes the present value of supplies that may be created in thousands or million of years virtually zero.

After discussing the oil that fuels our motors, this chapter covers the water that fuels the cells in our bodies. As with motor fuel, wars over water may be ahead. Citing human populations that are increasing without corresponding increases in water, Klaus Toepfer, Director-General of the United Nations Environment Program, wrote that he is "completely convinced" that wars over water are in our future.[1] On a regional scale, water disputes have already raged between residents of the western United States,[2] Pakistan and India,[3] Bechtel Corporation and Bolivia,[4] and others. A worthwhile movie directed by Robert Redford, the Milagro Beanfield War, *is based on a true story about water disputes. Dispute*

1 See www.abc.net.au/science/news/stories/s18191.htm.

2 See Naeser and Smith (1995) and www.findarticles.com/cf_dls/m1272/2658_128/60868317/p1/article.jhtml.

3 See www.guardian.co.uk/leaders/story/0%2C3604%2C726675%2C00.html.

4 See www.unesco.org/courier/2000_12/uk/planet2.htm.

resolution is the topic of Chapter 15; the underlying scarcity of water and ways to allocate it are discussed here.

To be precise, we call fossil fuels **depletable resources** *because their time frame for renewal is beyond the scope of practical consideration. Supplies of* **renewable resources**, *such as the fish and forests of Chapter 13, can increase over a reasonable period of time. Some stocks of nonliving resources, including water, can be replenished within a reasonable period of time, and we differentiate them from resources that increase via biological growth by calling them* **replenishable resources**.[5] *Air and water are among the life-sustaining replenishable resources. This chapter provides case studies of oil as an example of a depletable resource and water as an example of a replenishable resource.*

Oil

Like the sources of other fossil fuels, and of metals, gems, and water, oil is in relatively fixed supply. We don't know precisely what the supplies of any of these resources are, although in some cases we can make reasonable approximations.[6] In 1956, M. King Hubbert correctly predicted that U.S. oil production would resemble a bell-shaped curve, reaching what became known as **Hubbert's Peak** in the 1970s and then declining.[7] Oil companies will discover additional resources over time, and supplies that are not economically viable today—as with oceans for drinking water—will become viable with improved technologies and increas-

5 Elsewhere, the terms "renewable" and "replenishable" are sometimes used interchangeably to mean any resource, biological or not, that can increase over time.

6 A collection of forecasts of future oil production appears at www.oilcrisis.net/curves.htm.

7 For a detailed page on Hubbert, see www.hubbertpeak.com/hubbert/. For a graph of U.S. oil production in the lower 48 states, see www.hubbertpeak.com/blanchard/.

ing resource prices. But we do know that these resources don't grow like trees in the forest, and this knowledge must be reflected in our decisions. With no growth, the incremental and total growth functions are flat, and the sustainable yield is zero. Factoring in discount rates and increasing costs, economic models can suggest the efficient distribution of these resources over time.

Hotelling's Rule

Harold Hotelling (1931) studied the specific relationship between the discount rate and the stream of economic rent (price minus extraction cost) over time. He modeled the extraction of a homogeneous, nondurable resource with a fixed supply, not unlike oil. His famous conclusion, known as **Hotelling's rule**, was that in competitive equilibrium, the marginal rent (rent from the last unit) must rise at a rate equal to the discount rate. With constant extraction costs, the rent from every unit within a period will be the same, and the present value of rent from all periods will be the same, according to Hotelling's rule. Given this, Merton Miller and Charles Upton proposed **Hotelling's valuation principle**—that the value of mineral reserves can be estimated as the current price minus the marginal cost, multiplied by the estimated volume of extractable reserves.[8]

Empirical tests of Hotelling's rule provide mixed results. As exemplified by the erratic price of crude oil shown in Figure 14.1, the prices of depletable resources do not necessarily increase consistently over time. Marginal rent can increase

Figure 14.1 *U.S. Crude Oil Prices*

Data Source: U.S. Energy Information Administration: www.eia.doe.gov.

8 See Miller and Upton (1985), and Davis and Cairns (1999).

even when prices are decreasing if marginal extraction costs are falling faster than prices. Nonetheless, marginal rents themselves appear not to adhere to steady growth.[9] There are several likely reasons for this. *Known* supplies are not rigidly fixed and some resources are not homogeneous as Hotelling assumed. Extraction industries are also capital intensive, making it difficult for them to respond quickly to anticipated price changes. To the extent that supply is insensitive to price ("inelastic"), changes in demand will cause prices and rents to fluctuate relatively widely, resulting in price and rent volatility.

The Appendix for this chapter explains Hotelling's rule in greater detail and provides a model of oil allocation between two periods.

Transitions

The largest amount consumers are willing to pay for the first unit of a resource per period is called the **choke price**. This is represented graphically as the vertical intercept of the demand curve. The availability of substitutes can reduce the demand and choke price for a resource. Consider the market for gasoline, in which ethanol and hydrogen are among the potential substitutes.[10] Remember that externalities are an important part of energy costs and that policies can help users internalize these costs. For example, ethanol and hydrogen are relatively clean-burning fuels and their use is subsidized, whereas per-unit extraction charges called **severance fees** often apply to oil and other fossil fuels.[11] For simplicity, assume that decision makers internalize the cost of their behavior.

Gasoline is currently the fuel of choice for automobiles, but with biofuels and electric cars on the market and hydrogen fuel cells in development, gasoline is not a necessary input for trips to distant work, school, health care, or recreation. Relative to a situation with no alternatives, the gasoline substitutes waiting in the wings can cause our willingness to pay for gasoline to fall to the price of the lowest-cost alternative. As the cost of gasoline comes to exceed the cost of one or more substitutes, drivers will hasten their transition to alternative-fuel vehicles.

Decreased reliance on gasoline will result in a lower net marginal benefit of using gasoline in the future and thus a lower marginal opportunity cost of gasoline use today. When the opportunity cost of using something decreases, current consumption increases. The exhaustion of depletable resources thereby accelerates with the promise of affordable substitutes. In the extreme, if it were known that a renewable perfect substitute for gasoline with the same or lower marginal cost would be available next period, the opportunity cost of consuming gasoline this period would fall to zero, and all economically viable stocks of gasoline would be tapped.

If other resources are close substitutes, the transition from one resource to the next is straightforward. Figure 14.2 illustrates hypothetical per-mile marginal

9 For recent inquiry into the empirical relevance of depletable resource theory, see Chermak and Patrick (2001).

10 These and other energy alternatives are discussed in detail in Chapter 7.

11 For example, in Texas there is an oilfield cleanup severance tax of 0.625 cents per standard barrel of crude oil extracted. See Osmundsen (1998) and www.window.state.tx.us/taxinfo/taxpubs/tx96_251.html.

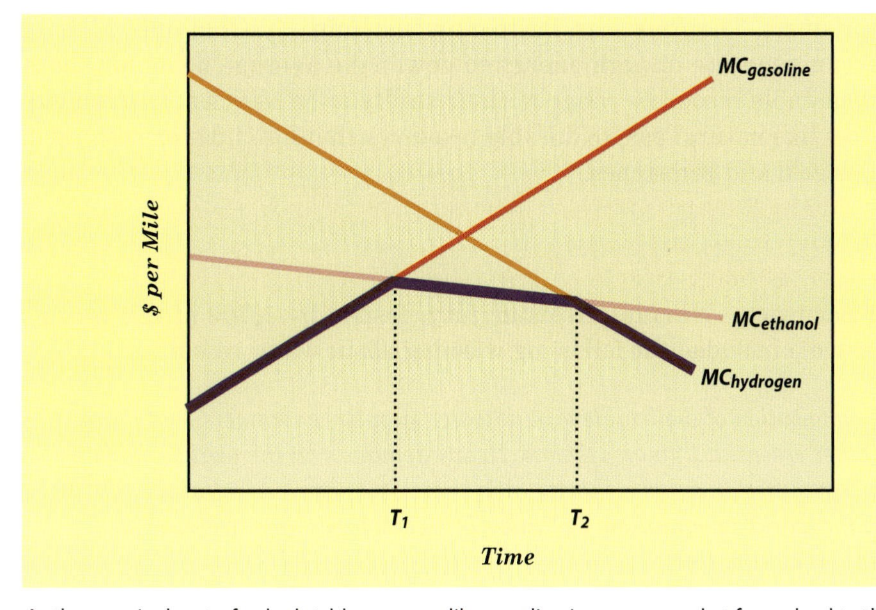

Figure 14.2
Switch Points for Automobile Fuels

As the marginal cost of a depletable resource like gasoline increases, market forces lead to the development and use of less expensive alternatives. At T_1, ethanol becomes less expensive per mile and drivers switch fuels. There is no spike in fuel costs, because at the switch point, the marginal cost of the two fuels is the same. Yet there may be costs associated with converting vehicles and changing habits that prevent an immediate or complete transition. Likewise, T_2 is the switch point between ethanol and hydrogen.

cost curves (including extraction costs and opportunity costs) and the switch from gasoline to ethanol to hydrogen over time. Of course, the curves and fuel choices are simplified for the purposes of exposition. In this story, an increase in the marginal cost of gasoline eventually makes renewable ethanol and hydrogen fuels relatively inexpensive. Technological advancements, including the development of cost-effective ways to separate hydrogen atoms from oxygen atoms in water, make hydrogen the least expensive of these fuels in the long run. When the marginal cost of gasoline increases to the marginal cost of ethanol at T_1, drivers switch to ethanol. In terms of fuel costs, the transition will be smooth because the marginal costs of the two fuels will be equivalent at the switch point. In reality, the switch will not be immediate or costless, due in part to changes that may be necessary in the automobiles we drive.[12] At T_2, hydrogen has become relatively economical, and drivers can be expected to switch fuels once again.

As the marginal cost of a resource increases, market forces lead to the development and use of relatively less expensive alternative resources. In the case of oil, depending on the type of use, substitutes might include any of the alternative energy sources discussed in Chapter 7. Another alternative to virgin resource use is recycled forms of the resource. Although the oil burned in combustion engines cannot be recycled, motor oil is readily recycled,[13] as are plastics and related

12 Several automobile manufacturers have now developed flex-fuel and bifuel vehicles, which can operate on multiple fuels. See www.fueleconomy.gov/feg/flextech.shtml.

13 See www.api.org/pasp/recycleoil/.

petroleum products. The American Petroleum Institute says that one gallon of recycled oil can generate enough energy to power the average home for about 24 hours. Depletable resources range in their ability to be recycled, from single-cycle resources like natural gas, to durable resources that lose little or nothing in reuse, such as gold and gemstones.

Water

The World Scientists' Warning to Humanity, issued by 1,700 of the world's leading scientists, included the following warning about water resources:

> *Heedless exploitation of depletable groundwater supplies endangers food production and other essential human systems. Heavy demands on the world's surface waters have resulted in serious shortages in some 80 countries, containing 40 percent of the world's population. Pollution of rivers, lakes, and groundwater further limits the supply.*[14]

Chapter 6 discusses the value of water and water pollution levels. This section focuses on issues of water availability and allocation.

The major cities were built around waterways when water was critical to transportation; it is still essential to industry, recreation, and the environment. Unlike most resources, for which substitutes are a possibility, switching to an alternative resource is not an option when it comes to water's role in sustaining life. There will be no switch points for this common-property resource. Management issues involve the efficient allocation of surface water, the sustainable extraction of replenishable groundwater, and the prudent mining of nonreplenishable groundwater.

Water is the most abundant of the Earth's resources, but having it where it is needed, when it is needed, with tolerable levels of pollution and salt, is a growing problem. Freshwater withdrawals for all purposes average over 1,300 gallons per U.S. resident per day, while almost half of the world lacks adequate water for sanitation purposes.[15] Ninety-seven percent of the Earth's water contains too much salt for drinking or irrigation. At

Many water distributors employ pricing structures that provide no incentive for water conservation.

14 This warning was written by Henry Kendall. See www.worldtrans.org/whole/warning.html.

15 See www.waterindustry.org/frame-1.htm and www.gcrio.org/CONSEQUENCES/spring95/Water.html.

present it is not economically viable to remove salt from water for most purposes, although the U.S. Water Desalinization Act of 1996 and similar efforts are promoting new technology to reduce desalinization costs.[16] Most of the freshwater is in the ice caps or in inaccessible underground aquifers.

The **hydrologic cycle**, in which moisture falls to the Earth as precipitation and returns to the atmosphere via evaporation and transpiration (from plants), replenishes some of our water supplies. **Surface water** in lakes, rivers, and oceans receives runoff from watersheds. **Groundwater** has accumulated over millennia in underground aquifers of sand, gravel, and fractured rock. About 2.5 percent of the extractable groundwater in the United States is replenishable by percolation (seepage) into aquifers. The remainder is depletable in the sense that after it is "mined," water will no longer be available from that groundwater source. After the water serves its purpose in agriculture, industry, or household use, the hydrologic cycle will distribute the withdrawn water across the mostly inaccessible havens for moisture on the Earth and in the atmosphere. Groundwater can be used sustainably if extraction rates do not exceed the rate of recharge. The efficient allocation of depletable groundwater resources can be analyzed similarly to that of oil resources.

Surface Water Allocation

The 100,000 cubic kilometers of surface water in rivers and lakes would be more than adequate to serve our current demands if it were all in the right places. The great variation in precipitation and freshwater storage volume across locations results in ample supplies in some parts of the world and shortages elsewhere. For example, in the United States, the city of Columbia, South Carolina, enjoys an average of 49.9 inches of annual rainfall, while Phoenix, Arizona, receives 7.7 inches. As is sometimes the case with food supplies, the high cost of transporting large volumes of water makes more equal distribution a challenge aside from issues of ownership. Ambitious ideas include the movement of icebergs,[17] and the seeding of clouds with silver iodide crystals or dry ice to stimulate precipitation over relatively dry areas—at the expense of having less rain downwind.[18] With the technology for such heroic water transportation efforts still in its infancy, prayer and animal sacrifices are still in use.[19]

The replenishable nature of surface water makes its management largely an issue of who has the right to what part of the annual flow. The efficient allocation of water between two groups can be studied with a static model similar to the dynamic model used for allocations between two periods. Consider the recent drought in Taiwan that forced officials to allocate water between farmers for their rice paddies and high-tech computer chip makers for washing chips after they are etched. The width of Figure 14.3 represents the water supply available for

16 See www.usbr.gov/water/desal.html.

17 See www.theage.com.au/news/national/2001/11/20/FFXIZCD47UC.html.

18 Cloud seeding has enjoyed limited success. See www.xmission.com/~nawc/wmfaq.html.

19 For an example of animal sacrifices in the quest for rain, see news.bbc.co.uk/1/hi/business/1871039.stm.

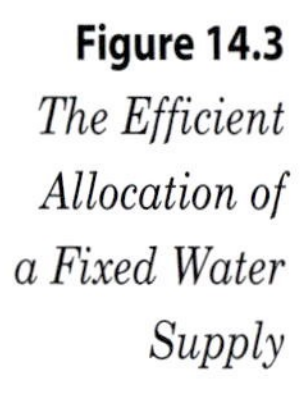

Figure 14.3 *The Efficient Allocation of a Fixed Water Supply*

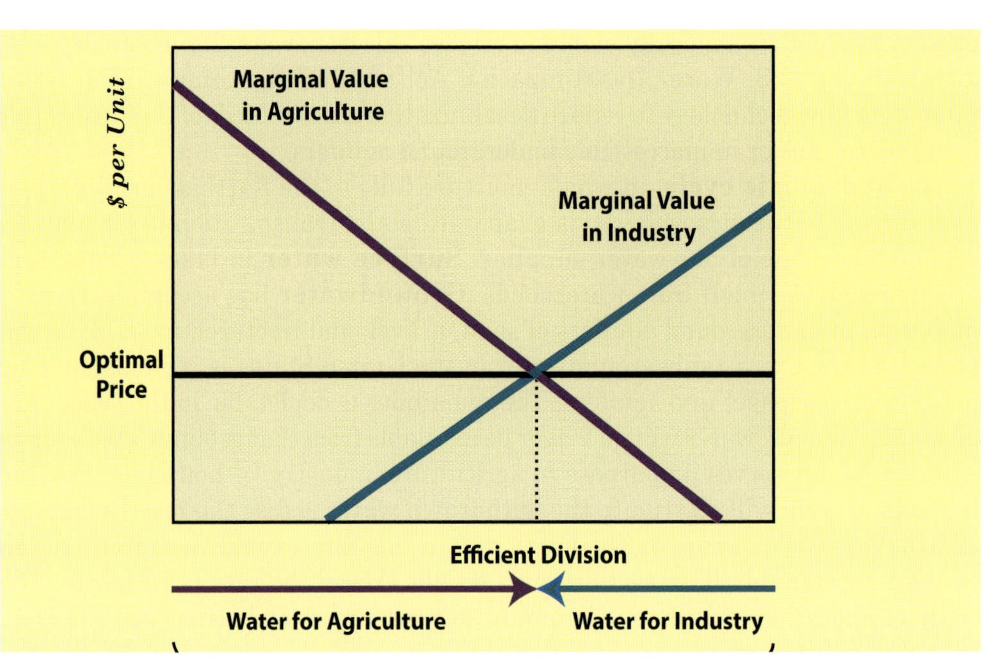

A recent drought in Taiwan forced difficult water-allocation decisions between the computer chip industry and rice farmers. The graph illustrates hypothetical marginal value (demand) curves for each sector. The efficient division occurs where the marginal value is equal for agriculture and industry. At any other allocation, the movement of one unit of water from the sector with the lower marginal value to the sector with the higher marginal value would yield a net gain to society.

allocation within a given period. The thick solid line represents the hypothetical marginal value curve (or equivalently, the demand curve) for rice farmers. The double line represents the marginal value of water to the chip industry. Because the quantity of water for industry begins at zero on the far right and increases to the left, the industry marginal value curve is correspondingly reversed to indicate decreasing marginal value as the quantity of water increases from right to left. The marginal extraction cost of water in this case is assumed to be zero.

The efficient division equates the marginal value of water for agriculture and industry. This occurs at the optimal price level as shown in Figure 14.3. If the price were lower, the demand for water would exceed the fixed supply. Higher prices would result in a surplus of water despite the drought. Thus, the market should settle into equilibrium at the optimal price. In reality, a free market for water would also involve private consumers, many of whom could not pay substantial prices for the water they need to survive. Thus, nonprice rationing is a consideration, as was the case in Taiwan. The government took 34,580 acres of rice paddies out of production, set aside sufficient water supplies for household use, and reallocated the remainder to industry.[20] Notice that if this were not the efficient division of water, the movement of one unit of water from the sector with the lower marginal value to the sector with the higher marginal value would have yielded a net gain to society.

20 See news.bbc.co.uk/1/hi/business/1871039.stm.

Water Rights

Competing interests in water for agriculture, industry, cities, wildlife, and indigenous groups has intensified scrutiny of water rights. Systems of water rights vary across countries and even within countries such as England and the United States. A complex set of laws covers *use* rights, not ownership rights, and the diversion of water from its natural flow. **Riparian laws**, common in the eastern United States, protect the water use rights of landowners on riverbanks and lakeshores. These rights are generally retained regardless of whether the landowners make use of the water. Riparian water use is limited to reasonable, beneficial use. The water cannot be diverted for use elsewhere, and it cannot be stored for later use. When water supplies are inadequate for the demands of riparian users, it is typical for household use to take priority over commercial use, and for riparian use to take precedence over use by appropriators as described next.

Prior appropriation laws, common in the western United States, grant rights to those who first used the resource, provided that they are still using it. One such "first in time, first in right" law was upheld by the California State Supreme Court in 2000 after cities in San Bernardino County tried to divert water away from farming operations for city use.[21] These laws generally permit the trading or sale of use rights, and the diversion of unclaimed water for beneficial use.

There is no particular reason to expect either riparian laws or prior appropriation laws to allocate water efficiently. Those whose property abuts water and those who used the water first may value the rights to use marginal units of water less than someone else. Consider Figure 14.3 once more. With prior appropriation rights and a negligible marginal cost, the farmers (in San Bernardino County or Taiwan or elsewhere) will use water until the marginal value in agriculture (MVA) curve meets the horizontal axis—exceeding the efficient division between agriculture and industry. At that point, the marginal value in agriculture is zero and the marginal value in industry is positive, so a reallocation of some water to industry would benefit industry more than it would hurt farmers. Requirements of continued use under prior appropriation laws might encourage water use even by those who place little or no current value on it, so as not to lose the right to future use.

Alternatives to rights-based allocation methods are available, for better or worse. The loss of overall benefits to society that occurs in the opposite extreme when many people have unrestricted access to a resource such as fish—or the water they swim in—was the topic of Chapter 13. In some countries the government oversees water allocation, the efficiency of which rests on the government's information, skills, and intentions. Canada, the United States, New Zealand, and more recently Australia, have granted special water rights to indigenous populations. The salability of appropriation rights makes market-based solutions another possible solution. There is an online "water rights market" that helps to bring together buyers, sellers, and traders of water rights

21 See wwwghcc.msfc.nasa.gov/forums/regional/msg/217.html.

in the western United States.[22] Like the markets for fishing rights and pollution rights discussed elsewhere in this book, the market for water rights could serve efficiency goals in at least two ways: it provides an incentive for efficient water use by those holding water rights, because they can sell the rights they don't use, and it allocates rights to those who value them the most, because those with a lower use value will sell their rights to others with a higher use value.

Domestic Water Use

Over 42 million users in the United States tap directly into groundwater sources with private wells. Even so, households are the largest users of public water supplies.[23] Household use accounts for 8 percent of all freshwater withdrawals and 26 percent of household use is *consumptive*, meaning that the water is not returned to its source. This is compared with about 2 percent consumption for thermoelectric use, 15 percent for commercial and industrial use, and 61 percent for agricultural use. Figure 14.4 provides detailed information on water use.

Households receive priority in water allocation, which does not mean that they enjoy unrestricted use. Municipalities often impose constraints during dry periods, including limits on watering lawns and washing cars. While these restrictions may limit some unnecessary use, they do not allocate water to those who value it the most or otherwise lead to the distributive efficiency economists seek. Water use will be efficient if the price that users pay equals the marginal cost to society. Users will then withdraw water only as long as their marginal benefit exceeds the societal marginal cost. Pricing mechanisms can be more effective in achieving efficiency, yet the most common pricing structures are not the most efficient. Here are several price structure options:

Flat rate: A fixed amount paid per unit of water used

Flat fee: A fixed amount paid per period regardless of water use

Decreasing block: A per-unit price that decreases as water use increases

Increasing block: A per-unit price that increases with water use

Average cost: A flat rate equal to the average cost of providing water

Peak-load: The price increases at times of shortage

Marginal cost: The price reflects the marginal cost of providing water

As examples, residents of Reno, Nevada, pay a flat monthly fee of $49.19 for service limited only by the 3/4-inch connection. In New Castle, Delaware, consumers pay a flat fee of $10 per month plus a flat rate of 0.027 cents per cubic foot of water. A flat fee does not encourage efficient use because the marginal

22 See www.uswaternews.com/ads/waterrights2.html.

23 See water.usgs.gov/watuse/.

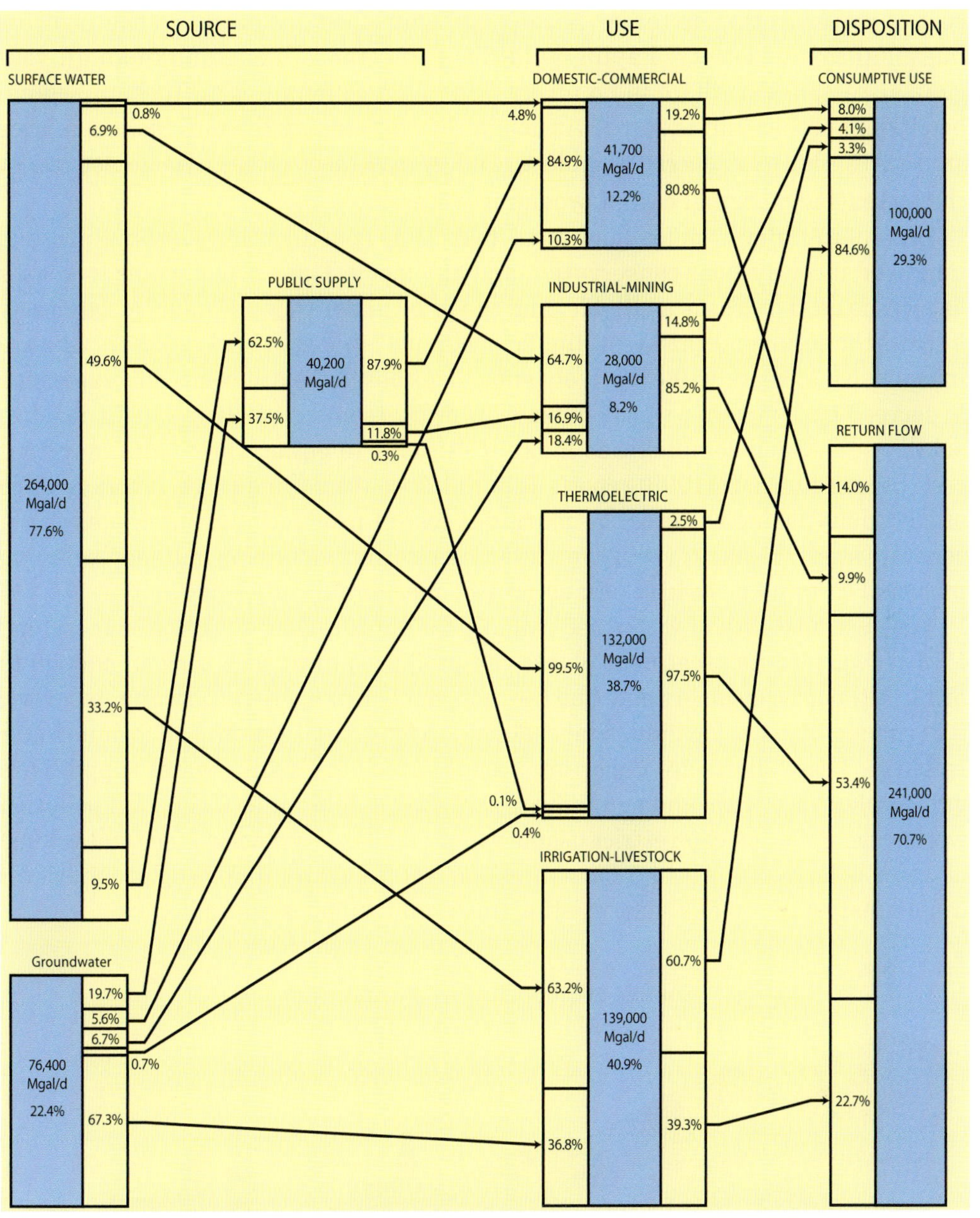

Figure 14.4
Water Sources and Uses

Source, use, and disposition of freshwater in the United States. For each water-use category, this diagram shows the distribution of water from source to disposition. For example, surface water was 77.6 percent of total freshwater withdrawn, and going from the "Source" column to the "Use" column, the line from the surface-water block to the domestic and commercial block indicates that 0.8 percent of all surface water withdrawn was the source for 4.8 percent of the total water supply for domestic and commercial purposes. Going from the "Use" column to the "Disposition" column, the line from the domestic and commercial block to the consumptive use block indicates that 19.2 percent of the water for domestic and commercial purposes was for consumptive use; this represents 8.0 percent of total consumptive use by all water-use categories.

Source: U.S. Geological Survey, http://water.usgs.gov/watuse/pdf1995/pdf/summary.pdf, used with permission.

cost of water to the customer is zero and therefore not equal to the positive marginal cost to society. Paying a flat fee for water is like going to an all-you-can-eat restaurant: there is no incentive to stop consuming until the marginal benefit of another unit is zero.[24] Although they are among the most common price structures, flat rate, decreasing block, and average cost prices also do not reflect the increasing marginal cost of providing water.

Increasing block, peak-load, and marginal cost pricing systems provide improved incentives for conservation and efficiency. The price of water increases as more is used or less is available, and the price under these systems more closely mirrors the social marginal cost. Inefficiencies will still exist because users who are inexpensive to serve will effectively subsidize those who are relatively expensive to serve: Nearby users will subsidize distant users and large users will subsidize small users. Such complexities make it difficult to equate price and marginal cost. Steven Renzetti (1999) reports that in Vancouver, Canada, the average price of electricity is one-third of the marginal cost of production. Nonetheless, in a separate study, Renzetti (1992) verified that alternative pricing systems including marginal cost and peak-load pricing provide measurable efficiency gains.

The sustainability of water use can also be improved through water recycling. Modern wastewater treatment plants can produce output that is clean enough to drink. Although consumers may find the thought of drinking recycled water unsavory, it is commonly used for industrial cooling, landscape irrigation, and groundwater recharge. These efforts are important because even our existing water supplies are vulnerable. Waterways and aquifers are threatened by point and nonpoint pollution worldwide. Pollution can restrict usable water supplies even where the total volume of water is large. Figure 14.5 illustrates some of the many sources of groundwater contamination that make some existing freshwater supplies unusable.

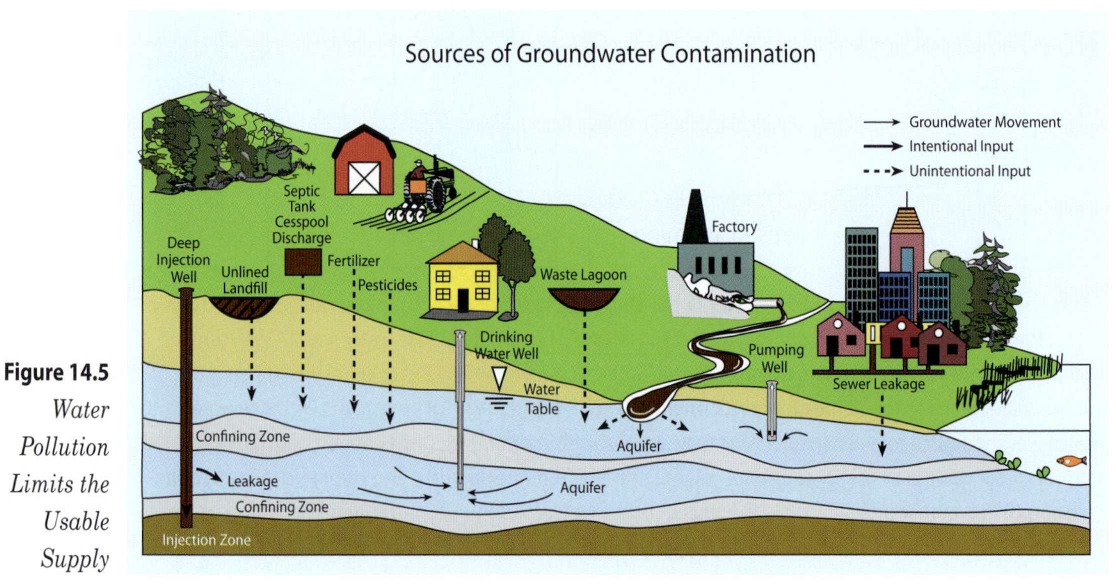

Figure 14.5 *Water Pollution Limits the Usable Supply*

Source: EPA, www.epa.gov/safewater/protect/98_305b_gwqchap.pdf. Used with permission.

24 Flat fees are sometimes justified by the cost of installing meters to measure household water use.

reality check

Draining an Oasis

In October of 2000, President Bill Clinton and King Abdullah II of Jordan witnessed the signing of a historic free trade agreement between the United States and Jordan. The goals included improved prospects for economic growth, stability, and peace in the Middle East. According to U.S. trade representative Charlene Barshefsky, the trade agreement was also groundbreaking with its "key provisions that reconfirm that free trade and the protection of the environment ... can go hand in hand" (see www.ustr.gov/releases/2000/10/00-75.html). More generally, 1999 U.S. Executive Order 13141 (64 *Fed. Reg.* 63169) requires a review of the environmental effects of all proposed free trade agreements, and that trade agreements contribute to the "broader goal of sustainable development." These environmental provisions are prudent given the many environmental effects of global trade, as discussed in Chapter 10. They are also important given the ongoing water resource management issues in Jordan.

In the Syrian Desert, 60 miles east of Amman, lies Jordan's Azraq Oasis and Wetland Reserve. From at least the early Stone Age until the early 1990s, two abundant artesian springs attracted human development to the Oasis. Reeds were used for basket-making, pools of water served as fish farms, and marshes grew forage plants for livestock. As the only perennial water source within 7,500 square miles, it was also a wildlife hotspot, with hippos, 21 species of waterbirds, and unique plants and fish, including the Azraq killifish (*Aphanius sirhani*). All of this brought ecotourism dollars as well. And then came the demands for water elsewhere.

By the early 1980s the cities of Amman and Zarqa, along with regional farmers, were pumping tens of millions of cubic meters of water out of Azraq every year. Extraction from the aquifer has exceeded its natural recharge rate in every year since 1983, and water tables (the level of underground seeping moisture) declined rapidly after that time. Discharge from the springs that fed the wetlands fell, and both springs had completely dried up by 1992 . As a result, the ecosystem collapsed. Tourism collapsed. Farming collapsed. The peaty soil became so dry that fires spread through the site. As has occured in Florida and elsewhere, the declining water table allowed saline (salt) insurgence and the salinity of the groundwater nearly tripled. The only good news was that the salt industry of Azraq flourished.

The question became one of priorities between meeting the short-run water demands of growth and trade and rehabilitating one of the world's most important wetlands. The 1991 National Environment Strategy for Jordan made the revival of the Azraq oasis one of the nation's highest priorities in wildlife conservation. Environmental stipulations like those of Executive Order 13141 and the U.S.–Jordan Free Trade Agreement support the continued prioritization of long-term environmental goals.

Beginning in 1994, the former wetlands were fenced and a staff of five patrolled the area to control illegal grazing and fires. Water was pumped in from a government well north of the oasis, and the two spring pools were dredged and enlarged. A visitor's center opened in 1998 to promote ecotourism, educational programs highlighted the importance of wise conservation, and wildlife habitats were restored. The wetlands managers are now looking into new water supplies from recycled domestic water or nearby seasonal lakes and rivers. Even so, the wetlands may never be what they once were, and appropriate resource management would have prevented the oasis from becoming a mirage.

Summary

Oil, among other fossil fuels and mineral resources, is classified as depletable because its time frame for renewal is beyond the scope of practical consideration. There is no positive sustainable yield for depletable resources, making their management a matter of when to exhaust economically viable supplies. A two-period model shows that the dynamically efficient use of these resources is accelerated by higher current net benefits, higher discount rates, lower future net benefits, and the availability of reasonable alternatives. Harold Hotelling predicted that producers would extract stocks so that the marginal rent from a depletable resource increases over time at a rate equal to the discount rate. This implies that the value of a mineral reserve is equal to the current net price multiplied by the volume of extractable reserves.

Water is a life-sustaining replenishable resource, meaning that although stocks do not grow over time, some can be replenished within a reasonable length of time. Water for consumptive uses is not returned directly to its accessible source, but returns to the Earth through the hydrologic cycle in largely inaccessible forms—primarily as seawater. Fresh surface water is replenishable, but it is often not where it is needed, it is vulnerable to pollution, and it is a small fraction of the total water supply. Only 2.5 percent of the extractable groundwater is replenishable; the remainder accumulates in aquifers created over millions of years and is depletable.

The efficient allocation of water occurs when the net marginal value of water is equivalent across users. Some water division is under the purview of governments. Some regions, including the eastern United States, have riparian laws that protect the water use rights of landowners along waterways. In other regions, prior appropriation laws dominate, such that those who first used water from a source and continue to do so will maintain the right to that use. Appropriation rights are now marketable in the western United States and elsewhere, which allows existing users who place a relatively low value on the rights to sell them to those who would gain the most from them. Efficiency in domestic water use can be encouraged with pricing schedules that resemble the marginal cost of use, and peak-load pricing that discourages use during periods of excess demand.

Problems for Review

1. Given Hotelling's valuation principle and constant extraction costs, what is the total value of a stock of 1 million "dry long ton units" of extractable iron ore if the current price is 40 cents per dry long ton unit and the extraction cost is 25 cents per dry long ton unit?
2. Some investigators have concluded that Hotelling's rule does not apply. List two of Hotelling's assumptions that are inconsistent with the real-world oil situation.
3. Do you agree with Klaus Toepfer that wars over water are inevitable? What do you see as the most realistic policy approach to minimizing future conflicts over water? Would you be in favor of water rationing in your area? Why or why not?
4. Indicate whether the following statement is true, false, or uncertain, and explain your answer: Riparian water rights are more efficient than prior appropriation rights.
5. The section on water allocation discusses the division of water between industry and agriculture in Taiwan. Using a graph similar to Figure 14.3, explain how this analysis would change in the following circumstances:
   a) There is a positive marginal extraction cost of water.
   b) The demand for computer chips increases.
   c) The local supply of water increases.
6. Draw a graph with the price per unit on the vertical axis and the number of units purchased on the horizontal axis. Draw the relationship between per-unit price and quantity for each of the following plans on the same graph:
   a) A flat fee
   b) A flat rate
7. Draw another graph with the price per unit on the vertical axis and the number of units purchased on the horizontal axis. Draw the relationship between price and quantity for each of the following plans on the same graph:
   a) A decreasing block plan under which the price decreases after each 10-unit increase in usage.
   b) An increasing block plan under which the price increases after each 10-unit increase in usage.
8. Of the plans you graphed in Problems 6 and 7, rank them in order from best to worst in their ability to promote efficient resource use. Which of these plans most closely resembles the pricing plan you face for water? Which most closely resembles the pricing plan you face for oil? Discuss why these pricing plans might be in place.
9. Indicate whether the following statement is true, false, or uncertain, and explain your answer: If every type of water use were 100 percent nonconsumptive, the only major problems regarding the world water supply would involve allocation and distribution.

The last problem draws on information from the Appendix.

10. Indicate whether the following statement is true, false, or uncertain, and illustrate your answer using a set of graphs similar to those in Figure 14.6: If the marginal cost of extraction increases over time and the marginal benefit curve is the same for each period, then the undiscounted net marginal benefit decreases over time and the resource price must rise in order for marginal rents to rise.

websurfer's challenge

1. Find a website for a firm or association in a depletable resource industry that has some mention of the scarcity of its resource. Evaluate the even-handedness of the statement.
2. Find a website that provides water resource data for your state or country. Summarize the condition of the water supply in a few sentences.

Photo by Jeff Vanuga, USDA Natural Resources Conservation Service

Handline sprinkler irrigation helps crops germinate in Yuma, Arizona.

The Lucky Peak Power Plant in Idaho collects energy from the Boise River as it flows through a dam.

Internet Resources

American Water Resources Association:
www.awra.org

American Water Works Association:
www.awwa.org

Canadian Water Resources Association:
www.cwra.org

Chartered Institution of Water and Environmental Management, London:
www.ciwem.org

Energy Information Administration
www.eia.doe.gov

Ministry of the Environment and Water Resources, Singapore:
http://app.mewr.gov.sg

Ministry of Water Resources, India:
http://wrmin.nic.in

Ministry of Water Resources, P.R. China:
www.mwr.gov.cn/english/

National State of the Environment Report, South Africa, Freshwater Systems and Resources:
www.ngo.grida.no/soesa/nsoer/issues/water/

The Oil Depletion Resource Page:
www.gulland.ca/depletion/depletion.htm

U.S. Environmental Protection Agency site on water supply and demand:
www.epa.gov/seahome/groundwater_dis-claim/html

U.S. Geological Survey Water Resources Division:
http://water.usgs.gov

Further Reading

Chermak, Janie M., and Robert H. Patrick. "A Microeconometric Test of the Theory of Exhaustible Resources." *Journal of Environmental Economics and Management* 42, no. 1 (2001): 82–103. A recent examination of depletable resource theory which finds, contrary to many studies, that the theory may apply to reality.

Davis, Graham A., and Robert D. Cairns. "Valuing Petroleum Reserves Using Current Net Price." *Economic Inquiry* 37, no. 2 (1999): 295–311. Considers the controversy over whether Hotelling's valuation principle provides an upper or lower bound for the value of oil reserves.

Frederick, Kenneth D., and Gregory E. Schwarz. "Socioeconomic Impacts of Climate Change on U.S. Water Supplies." *Journal of the American Water Resources Association* 35, no. 6 (1999): 1563–1584. Combines the issues of climate change, the valuation of water resources, and efficient resource allocation.

Hotelling, Harold. "The Economics of Exhaustible Resources." *Journal of Political Economy* 39, no. 2 (1931): 137–175. The seminal article on resource depletion that sets forth Hotelling's rule.

Howe, Charles W., Mark Griffin Smith, Lynne Bennett, Charles M. Brendecke, J. Ernest Flack, Robert M. Hamm, Roger Mann, Lee Rozaklis, and Karl Wunderlich. "The Value of Water Supply Reliability in Urban Water Systems." *Journal of Environmental Economics and Management* 26, no. 1 (1994): 19–30. A contingent valuation study of the value of reliable water supplies.

Hubbert, M. King. "The Energy Resources of the Earth." In *Energy and Power*, New York: Scientific American, 1971, 31–40. Available online at www.hubbertpeak.com/hubbert/energypower/. A discussion of Hubbert's Peak, with forecasts of the depletion rates of oil, coal, and other energy sources.

Krautkraemer, Jeffrey A. "Nonrenewable Resource Scarcity." *Journal of Economic Literature* 36, no. 4 (1998): 2065–2107. An excellent overview of Hotelling's rule and more recent adaptations.

Miller, Merton H., and Charles W. Upton. "A Test of the Hotelling Valuation Principle." *Journal of Political Economy* 93, no. 1 (1985): 1–25. Introduces a method of valuing depletable resource stocks based on Hotelling's rule and studies the method's empirical validity.

Naeser, Robert B., and Mark G. Smith. "Playing with Borrowed Water: Conflicts of Instream Flows on the Upper Arkansas River." *The Natural Resources Journal* 35, no. 1 (1995): 93–110. Illustrates the competition for water resources in the American Southwest.

Osmundsen, Petter. "Dynamic Taxation of Non-renewable Natural Resources under Asymmetric Information about Reserves." *Canadian Journal of Economics* 31, no. 4 (1998): 933–951. A rigorous analysis of optimal regulation of resource extraction that considers more complexities than the simpler model in the text.

Renzetti, Steven. "Evaluating the Welfare Effects of Reforming Municipal Water Prices." *Journal of Environmental Economics and Management* 22, no. 2 (1992): 147–163. Uses a simulation to estimate aggregate consumer surplus under various water-pricing plans.

Renzetti, Steven. "Municipal Water Supply and Sewage Treatment: Costs, Prices, and Distortions." *Canadian Journal of Economics* 32, no. 3 (1999): 688–704. Compares average prices with marginal cost as a measure of efficiency, and estimates the welfare loss from overconsumption.

Appendix

Intertemporal Allocation and Hotelling's Rule

Allocation Between Periods

The model introduced in Chapter 8 to describe the efficient allocation of depletable resources between two periods can be applied to the allocation of oil supplies between the present and the future. The object is to decide how much oil to use in the first period and how much to conserve for use in the second period. With reality necessitating a series of decisions between use now and use later, the two-period model is a reasonable simplification of dynamic allocation.

The solid lines in the top graph of Figure 14.6 represent the marginal extraction cost and marginal benefit in a hypothetical oil market. The vertical distance between these two lines is the net marginal benefit for period 1, shown in the bottom graph decreasing from left to right as consumption increases. If the first period were the only period as in a static model, or the last period that anyone cared about (implying an infinite discount rate and discounted period 2 benefits equal to zero), then consumption would continue up to Q_A, at which point the net marginal benefit (*NMB*) in period 1 is zero. In a static model, Q_A is the competitive equilibrium quantity at which marginal extraction cost equals marginal benefit and period 1 welfare is maximized.

The bottom graph depicts the two-period model. The width of the horizontal axis represents the fixed supply of oil. Consumption in period 1 starts at zero on the left and increases to the right; consumption in period 2 starts at zero on the right and increases to the left. The *NMB* curves for periods 1 and 2 represent the decreasing net marginal benefit of consuming oil. NMB_1 is the difference between marginal benefit and marginal extraction cost from the top graph, and NMB_2 is the difference between period 2 marginal benefit and marginal extraction cost.

The two-period model incorporates the opportunity cost of using resources now, which is that they can't be used later. The discounted NMB_2 is the present value *in period 1* of period 2 benefits, calculated at each consumption level as $(NMB_2)/(1 + r)$, with r being the discount rate. The solid discounted NMB_2 line ascending from left to right is sometimes called the **in situ value**, meaning the value of the resource if left in its original place. As the value foregone by consumption in period 1, the in situ value of each incremental unit is the marginal opportunity cost of present use. After the intersection of NMB_1 and discounted NMB_2 at quantity Q_B, the opportunity cost

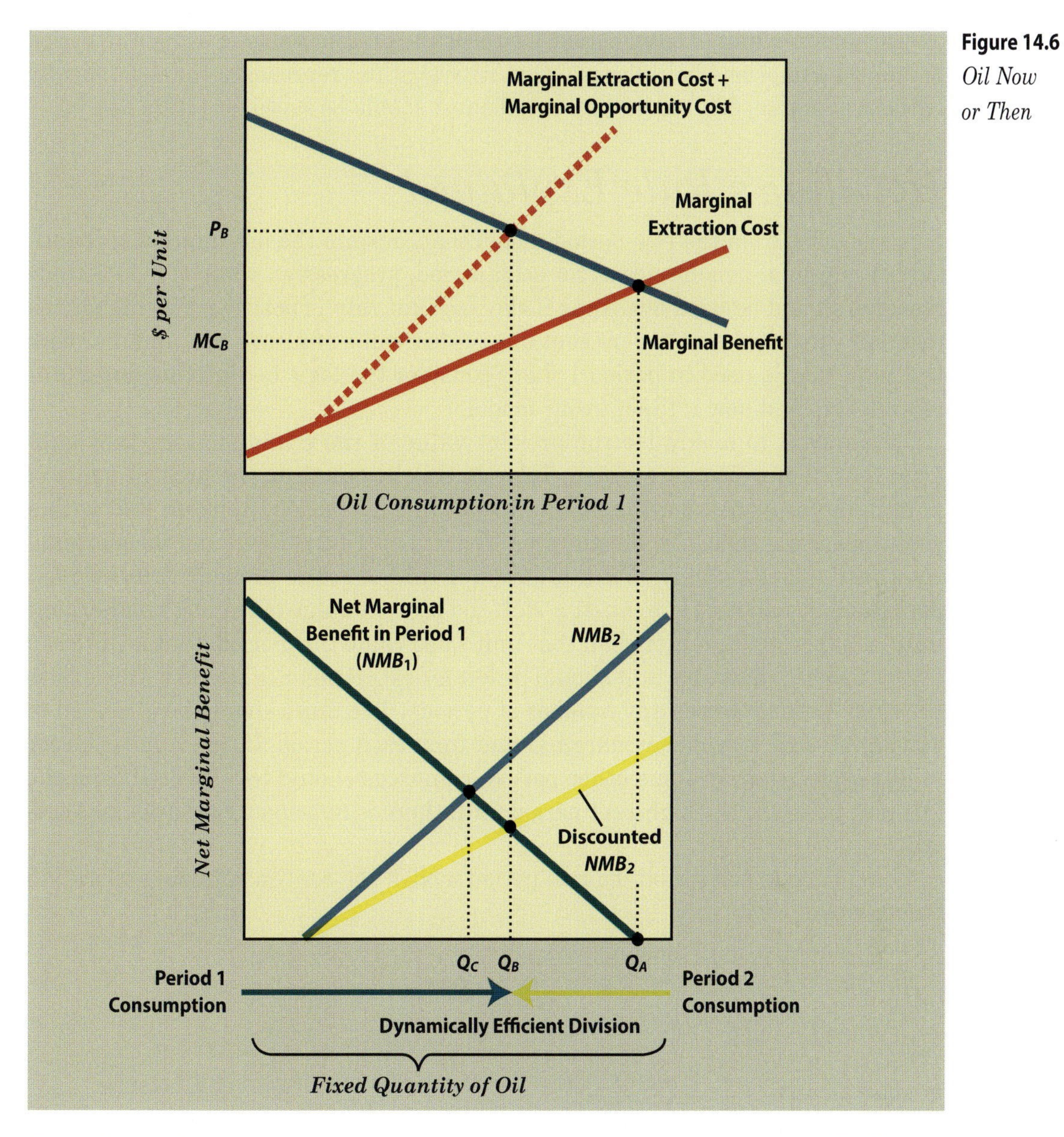

Figure 14.6
Oil Now or Then

The solid lines in the top graph show the period 1 marginal benefit and marginal extraction cost. The difference between these two values is the net marginal benefit in period 1, as shown in the bottom graph. In a static model with perfect competition, the equilibrium would occur at the intersection of marginal extraction cost and marginal benefit. The corresponding quantity Q_A maximizes the net marginal benefit in period 1. When two periods are considered, every unit consumed in period 1 represents a unit that cannot be consumed in period 2. Period 2 consumption increases from right to left on the bottom graph as period 1 consumption decreases. The present value of the opportunity cost of period 1 consumption is the discounted net marginal benefit in period 2. The dynamically efficient outcome equates the present value of net marginal benefits in each period, which occurs when Q_B is consumed in period 1 and the remainder in period 2. This corresponds with the intersection of marginal benefit and marginal extraction cost plus marginal opportunity cost, as shown by the dotted red line in the top graph.

of using another unit of oil in period 1 exceeds the present value of using it in period 2, and consumption should cease. Quantity Q_B thus represents the dynamically efficient allocation of oil to the present; the rest should be saved for future use.

Hotelling's Rule Explained

It is apparent from the two-period model that, despite the assumption of identical net marginal benefit curves for each period, progressively less of a depletable resource should be used over time if the discount rate is positive. The higher the discount rate, the lower the present discounted value of future use, and therefore the more that is used in period 1. Let's consider the logic behind this important relationship and how it fits into our model.

Firms want to maximize the present value of the economic rent they gain from control of a scarce resource. They do this by equating the present value of marginal rent (rent from the last unit sold) in each period. Suppose that with a given extraction schedule, the marginal rent this period is $Rent_1$ and the marginal rent next period is $Rent_2$. With a discount rate of r, the present value of next period's marginal rent is $Rent_2/(1 + r)$. If the present value of leaving another unit until next period is greater than that unit's use value this period, that is, if $Rent_2/(1 + r) > Rent_1$, then that unit should be left for extraction next period. The logic is the same looking across any number of periods: The units should be allocated to equate the present value of marginal rent from each period. If this value is larger in one period than in some other period, resources should be allocated from the low-rent period to the high-rent period until there is no longer gain from reallocation.

Going back to the simplified two-period model, the rent-maximizing allocation occurs when

$$Rent_1 = \frac{Rent_2}{1+r}$$

or equivalently,

$$Rent_1(1 + r) = Rent_2$$

This is Hotelling's result—that marginal rent in each subsequent period (in this case $Rent_2$) should equal marginal rent in the previous period ($Rent_1$) plus growth at the discount rate. This condition holds in the model in Figure 14.6.

Looking at the top graph, we know that, despite the assumption of competition in this market, firms extracting scarce oil will produce less than the quantity that equates the marginal extraction cost and the marginal benefit because of the added opportunity cost of foregone period 2 sales. The competitive industry supply curve is the vertical sum of marginal extraction cost and marginal opportunity cost, represented by the thick dotted line. The equilibrium quantity is found where this aggregation of marginal costs equals marginal benefit, at Q_B.

At equilibrium, period 1 marginal rent, $Rent_1$, equals the difference between P_B and MC_B, as shown in the top graph. These levels of price and marginal cost differ by the discounted *NMB* for period 2, which defines the marginal opportunity cost of use in period 1. In other words, in equilibrium, $Rent_1 = NMB_2 /(1 + r)$. Note also that in each period, $NMB = MB - MC_{extraction}$ and $Rent = P - MC_{extraction}$, and because $MB = P$ at equilibrium, *NMB* will equal *Rent* at equilibrium as well. Thus, $NMB_2 /(1 + r)$ is equivalent to $Rent_2/(1 + r)$, and at equilibrium, the equality of $Rent_1$ and $NMB_2 /(1 + r)$ corresponds with the equality of $Rent_1$ and $Rent_2/(1 + r)$ as theorized by Hotelling.

With constant extraction costs, the rent from every unit within a period will be the same, and the present value of rent from all periods will be the same, according to Hotelling's rule. A useful application is that the value of a resource is simply the current net price multiplied by the total extractable volume.

For a resource with no extraction cost, the marginal rent equals the price, and Hotelling's rule implies that price will increase at the discount rate. Positive extraction costs imply price increases at less than the discount rate. For example, with an initial price of $30, an extraction cost of $10, and a discount rate of 5 percent, marginal rent in the first period is $20 and we would expect a 5 percent ($1) increase in marginal rent in the second period. With stable extraction costs, this $1 marginal rent increase represents a $1/$30 = 3.33 percent price increase. If the demand curve does not change over time, increasing prices are achieved only by decreasing supply (extraction) over time.

The dynamically efficient decrease in exploitation described in the two-period model and implied by Hotelling's rule is accelerated by increases in extraction costs or interest rates. Higher extraction costs in period 2 decrease NMB_2, and higher interest rates decrease $NMB_2 /(1 + r)$, thereby lowering the opportunity cost of consumption in period 1. It is reasonable to expect extraction costs to rise over time as the most readily available supplies are tapped, and smaller, deeper, more remote sources must be sought. For coal, ores, and similarly heterogeneous resources, materials of the highest quality will be removed first, followed by materials that are more costly to remove and refine. On the other hand, new discoveries and improved extraction technology may cause costs to decrease. In the long run if not sooner, however, easily accessible supplies will be consumed and costs can be expected to rise.

"The way the law worked, people were afraid to go in and clean up a brownfield site for the fear that they would be liable if a suit was ever brought for cleanup of that site."

—VANCE

MCMAHON

"Brownfields and alternative dispute resolutions can work together to encourage sustainable, community-driven efforts."

—DEBRA L. NUDELMAN, SENIOR MEDIATOR, *RESOLVE*

15 Environmental Dispute Resolution

As socially efficient as environmental initiatives may be, they often face inertia, in part because progress isn't cheap. It is costly to clean up dumpsites, limit commercial fishing, forego development, and purchase emissions reduction equipment. To complicate matters, these efforts benefit many at the expense of a few, and the few have a financial incentive to resist the burden. When the few cry foul, environmental disputes are born. More broadly, disputes arise over

- *What should or should not be done*
- *Who should pay for it*
- *Who owns or controls what resources*
- *What constitutes compensable environmental damage*
- *How quickly progress should be made*
- *What steps are necessary to ensure endangered species viability*

and the list goes on. It is common for disputes to arise over compliance with the environmental legislation discussed in this text, including the Clean Air Act, the Clean Water Act, CERCLA, and the Endangered Species Act. The importance of environmental dispute resolution is clear from the large expenditures made to resolve related disputes, the law firms and institutes devoted to environmental and natural resource disputes, and the vast literature on the topic.[1]

Recent responses to the burgeoning cost of environmental dispute resolution include legislation and heightened interest in alternative dispute resolution (ADR). For example, President George W. Bush signed the Small Business Liability Relief and Brownfields Revitalization Act in 2002 to limit corporate liability for abandoned commercial sites that threaten environmental and human health.[2] *On the ADR side, RESOLVE, Inc. exemplifies the nonprofit organizations specializing in environmental dispute resolution. RESOLVE has used alternative dispute resolution techniques to mediate disputes over environmental cleanup costs, facilitate agreements over incentives for sustainable fishing, build consensus on estuary protection, assist conflict resolution over endangered salmon, and promote policy dialogue about wind energy.*[3] *New and improved methods of dispute resolution may offer faster and cheaper remedies. In this chapter you will learn more about these and related techniques for the dispute resolution that is critical to the advancement of environmental goals.*

Litigation

Litigation is the civilized remedy of last resort for environmental disputes. The litigation process is often costly, slow, and potentially injurious to the reputations of individuals and firms. Litigation over the 1989 *Exxon Valdez* oil spill is a case in point. In 2009, 20 years after the incident, litigation continued over such things as interest payments on the $507 million in yet-to-be-paid punitive damages. As of 2013, litigation over the 2010 Deepwater Horizon oil spill had generated roughly 90 million pages of documents.[4]

The U.S. Comprehensive Environmental Response, Compensation, and Liability Act (CERCLA) spawned a wave of litigation over liability for hazardous waste cleanup. Global environmental concerns over acid deposition, deforestation, and global warming threaten international conflict, with fewer formal avenues of last resort. Regional examples include a suit filed by the U.S. Department of Justice over emissions from a Japanese garbage incinerator near the Atsugi naval air base, and a $251 million lawsuit filed by Ethyl Corporation of the United States against the Canadian government for imposing a ban on the toxic gasoline additive MMT.

1 Examples of the literature appear in the Further Reading section. The Diepenbrock Law Firm is among the many specializing in environmental and natural resources law (www.diepenbrock.com). Institutes include the U.S. Institute for Environmental Conflict Resolution (www.ecr.gov). Expenditures on Superfund litigation alone exceed $10 billion. Schools like Brown University teach entire courses on environmental conflict resolution.

2 See www.epa.gov/swerosps/bf/sblrbra.htm.

3 See www.resolv.org/.

4 See www.huffingtonpost.com/2013/02/25/bp-spill-trial_n_2758057.html.

In another case, Ecuadorian tribes have sued Texaco Petroleum for its alleged involvement in dumping 4.3 million gallons of toxic waste in Ecuador each day during operations that ended over a decade ago. Highlighting the limited avenues in international cases, plaintiff's lawyer Cristobal Bonifaz stated, "Texaco can't be brought before international human rights tribunals and there is no chance of finding justice in Ecuador, so we filed a suit in its own backyard."[5] In 1999, a Manhattan federal court declared the case should be heard in Ecuadorian courts.

Roughly 25,000 U.S. environmental lawyers represent manufacturers, farmers, real estate developers, waste disposal companies, municipalities, and federal agencies, among others.[6] Environmental law flourished as a direct result of a series of environmental statutes adopted in the 1970s and 1980s, including the National Environmental Policy Act, the Resource Conservation and Recovery Act, the Clean Water Act, the Clean Air Act, the Toxic Substances Control Act, and CERCLA. CERCLA gave rise to the Superfund trust fund used to clean up hazardous waste sites. When the trust fund is used, the EPA attempts to recoup cleanup costs by taking legal action, when necessary, against past polluters as explained further in the Reality Check.

Superfund litigation spurred the problem of "brownfields." **Brownfields** are abandoned commercial sites that are generally not as dangerous as Superfund sites, but nonetheless make developers wary because of the potential for environmental lawsuits by individuals claiming to be victims of pollution from the sites. **Greenfields** are fields and forests that provide attractive alternatives to the potential for costly environmental conflict over brownfields. Risk-averse manufacturers are especially dissuaded by the threat of trial by jury due to the large variation in potential liability levels. If improved dispute resolution techniques—the focus of this chapter— make solutions less costly and outcomes more predictable, the expected liability cost of using brownfields will decrease, and their use for manufacturing will increase relative to the use of environmentally sensitive greenfields.

A Simple Bargaining Model

Pretrial settlement can limit the losses of money, time, and reputation resulting from litigation. Settlement occurs often, but not often enough. This section presents a simple bargaining model and defines some sufficient conditions for settlement. The **plaintiff (p)** is the party filing the claim, and the **defendant (d)** is the party accused of wrongdoing:

J_d, J_p = Defendant's and plaintiff's respective expected jury awards.

F_d, F_p = Expected future attorney fees and other unrecoverable litigation costs for each side.

5 See *Texaco vs. Ecuadorian Tribes* (1999).

6 See Sablatura (1995).

T_d, T_p = The **threat points** of the defendant and plaintiff, meaning espectively the lowest and highest offer that the parties cannot independently improve upon. The **settlement range** is the set of settlement values between the two parties' threat points that make both parties better off settling than going to trial.

BR = The **bargaining rent**—the amount of money represented by the settlement range ($BR = T_d - T_p$).

Beyond what the defendant has already paid in legal costs at any given time—her sunk costs—the defendant expects that if she proceeds to trial she will have to pay the expected jury award (J_d) plus expected future attorney fees (F_d). Her threat point is thus $J_d + F_d$, because an offer to settle for more than that would be inferior to going to trial. Likewise, excluding sunk costs, the plaintiff expects to receive an award of J_p at trial less attorney fees of F_p. The plaintiff's threat point is therefore $J_p - F_p$.

A litigant whose goal is to maximize financial gain (or minimize financial loss) from the case should not consider settlement offers inferior to her threat point. A litigant will also refuse offers preferable to her threat point if she believes she can negotiate an even better settlement. Self-perceived bargaining positions depend on subjective assessments of relative experience levels, optimism, persuasive ability, and monetary resources, as well as the political, precedential, and emotional repercussions of trial. These assessments can change as learning occurs during the bargaining process. If the parties feel evenly matched, each will expect to acquire half of the bargaining rent, and settlement will occur for the amount of the expected jury award with no need for added inducement. Unequal bargaining skills or finances can result in unequal expected gains from bargaining. For example, both sides might expect the defendant to gain one-third of the bargaining rent and the plaintiff to gain two-thirds. Differing levels of information or optimism can lead to overlapping expectations, as if both sides expected to gain two-thirds of the bargaining rent.

Figure 15.1 illustrates the simple bargaining situation. On the first number line, the plaintiff and the defendant expect the same jury award ($J_d = J_p$). There is no overlap between the two parties' expectations, and the bargaining rent is equal to the sum of the two parties' attorney fees ($BR = F_d + F_p$). The plaintiff would receive more from the net trial outcome than from an offer to the left of her threat point. Likewise, the defendant would pay less at trial than in a settlement to the right of her threat point. Both parties would prefer to settle for any value in the settlement range over going to trial.

On the second line, the two parties have differing expectations for the trial outcome. The parties' optimistic expectations for the jury award translate into a lower threat point for the defendant than if J_d equaled J_p, meaning she is willing to pay less in a settlement, and a higher threat point for the plaintiff, meaning she will demand more in a settlement. The settlement range is smaller than in the case of

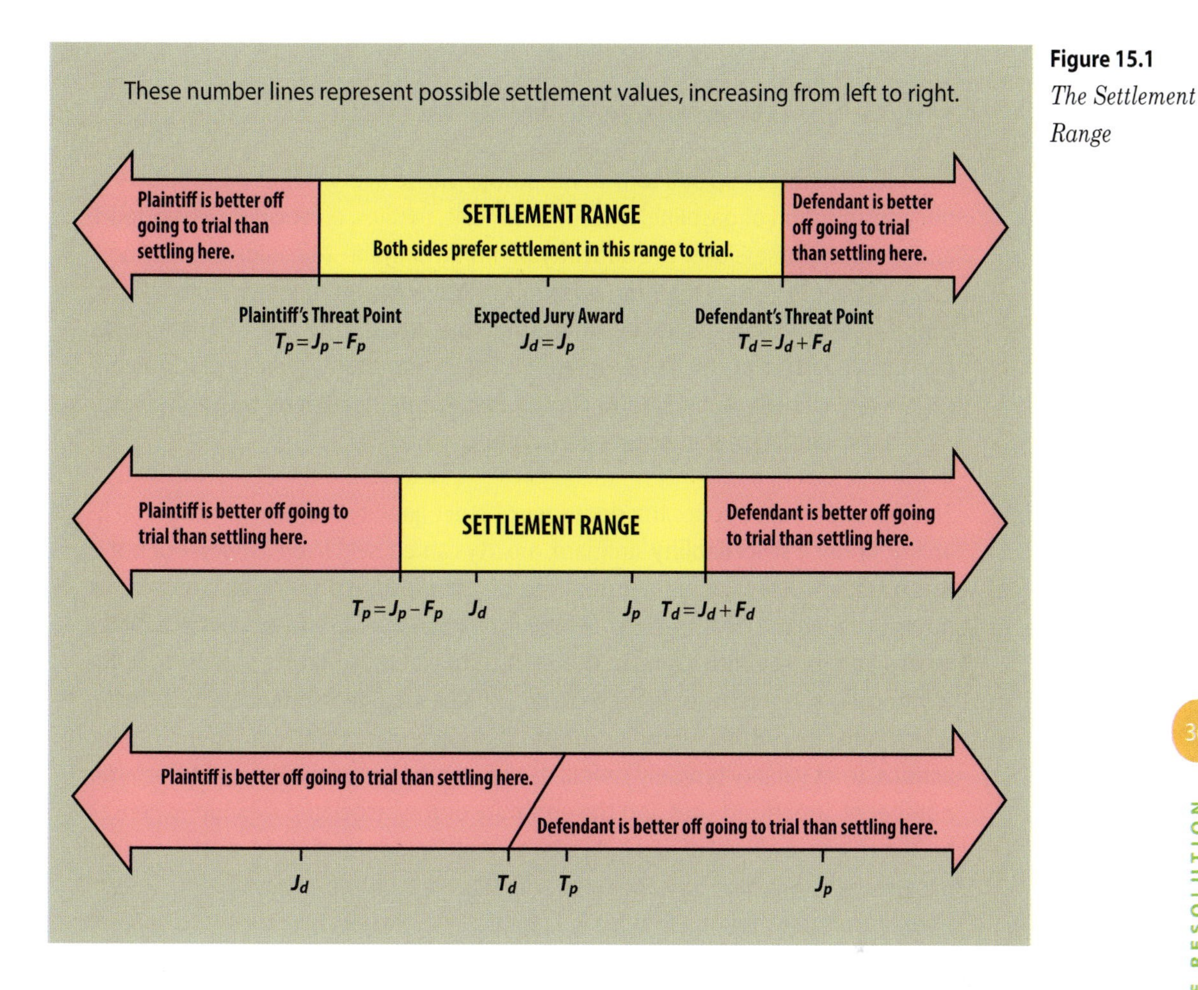

Figure 15.1 *The Settlement Range*

equal expectations. If the parties were relatively pessimistic rather than optimistic, the settlement range would increase relative to the case of equal expectations. Can you illustrate a scenario with relative pessimism on a number line like those in Figure 15.1?

The last line represents an extreme case in which very different and relatively optimistic expectations result in the absence of a settlement range. Because the plaintiff expects more from going to trial than the defendant expects to pay, there is no out-of-court settlement that both sides would prefer over trial. The plaintiff will reject offers less than T_p, the defendant will reject demands greater than T_d, and neither party will settle for an amount between T_p and T_p.

Beyond formal legal disputes, this model applies to everyday disputes and negotiations. For example, large purchases often involve bargaining over price, employment involves wage negotiations, and international relations involve disagreements over property. In negotiations with someone you might hire to install solar panels on your roof, the installer's threat point will be the opportunity cost of her time—perhaps the $12,000 she could earn installing panels for someone down the road. Your threat point is what you could pay someone else to do the job,

reality check

Superfund Dispute Resolution

The U.S. generates 700,000 tons of hazardous waste every day as by-products of our consumption of gasoline, metals, chemicals, textiles, electronics, wood, food, and material possessions. The difficulty of monitoring the 24 million U.S. business establishments, not to mention all levels of government, military installations, hospitals, and universities, means that dangerous amounts of waste find their way into unsafe resting places. The Comprehensive Environmental Response, Compensation, and Liability Act (CERCLA) set out to clean up hazardous waste sites with Superfund legislation that applies a "polluter pays" policy.

The Superfund act applies the doctrines of strict liability and joint and several liability. Under a **strict liability** standard, a party can be held liable whether or not it was negligent. For example, a firm can be responsible for cleaning up a hazardous dumpsite even if the firm's disposal practices were legal. **Joint and several liability** means that those contributing to the hazards of a dumpsite can be sued individually or collectively for the cleanup costs. Unlike a **negligence standard** of liability, which requires plaintiffs to demonstrate that defendants were negligent in their actions, strict liability typically simplifies the litigation process. However, the large number of Superfund sites and the enormity of the associated cleanup expenses have resulted in a level of expenditures on environmental dispute resolution that irks everyone involved, save perhaps some lawyers on the receiving end. Potentially responsible parties (PRPs) are in litigation with the EPA over their involvement and appropriate contribution levels. PRPs are also suing each other in attempts to collect payment for "orphan shares"—portions of cleanup costs attributable to unidentified, defunct, or insolvent parties.

The EPA spends more that $200 million a year on its own legal staff, for whom the Superfund is the largest single project. Total legal costs on Superfund litigation have exceeded $10 billion, and about $15 billion in private spending has gone to site cleanups. Eight hundred and four sites were cleaned up in the first 21 years of the Superfund program. With over 527 official sites left to clean up as of 2009, and more problems being created and discovered every year, environmental dispute resolution will continue to be of great importance for some time to come.

or the benefit you would receive from the panels, whichever is less. Suppose that your benefit is $20,000 and no one else is available to install the panels. Because the installer's threat point is below yours ($12,000 < $20,000), a settlement range exists and the bargaining rent is the $8,000 difference between your threat point and hers. Both sides would prefer any price between $12,000 and $20,000 to no deal. Disputes over prices are unlikely to find their way to trial, but the task is still one of deciding how the bargaining rent will be divided between the two parties. To settle on a price of $15,000, for instance, would be to give the installer $3,000 of the bargaining rent and you $5,000 of the bargaining rent.

Deadlock and trial can be averted by any one of the following:

- ***Brute force***. *For better or worse, the successful application of force can supersede interests in negotiation or litigation.*
- *A **decision rule**. One of the disputants or a third party can put forth an acceptable or enforceable means of deciding the outcome.*
- ***Agreement***. *There might be agreement over the settlement range and the appropriate division of the bargaining rent. Alternatively, the parties may be relatively optimistic about the settlement range but relatively pessimistic about the share of the bargaining rent they can obtain, making for compatible differences.*
- *Ability to make a **take-it-or-leave-it offer**. One party may be capable and willing to make a credible final offer within an existing settlement range, forcing the other party to take the offer, or leave it and receive an inferior outcome at trial.*

Efforts to avert or resolve environmental conflicts should, as a minimum requirement, seek to satisfy one of these four conditions. Past efforts have not always taken aim at the correct targets, the result being civil rules, such as Federal Rule of Civil Procedure 68, which appear to have settlement-inducing characteristics but turn out to be disappointing because they do not satisfy any of the conditions for settlement. The remainder of this chapter describes attempts to achieve one of these conditions with varying trade-offs between ease of application, fairness, speed, and success.

Dispute Remedies

Brute Force

Various world powers, environmentalists, and industrialists have adopted brute force as a remedy of last resort. Too often, destructive force is applied out of frustration with the perceived ineffectiveness of alternative dispute remedies. *The Oregonian* reports, "Arsons, bombings and sabotage in the name of saving the environment and its creatures have swept the American West over the last two decades."[7] The reality television show *Whale Wars* is about activists using butyric acid, blockades, and other physical means to disrupt whale harvests. A disgruntled environmental activist is allegedly responsible for the 2002

7 See www.landrights.org/ALRA.oregonian.eco-terrorism.htm.

Photo by Matthew Acosta, Courtesy of U.S. Army

Brute force is a primitive yet common form of dispute resolution.

assassination of Dutch politician Pim Fortuyn, who had told an environmental group that he was "sick to death" of their movement.[8] And ecoterrorism became a negotiating tactic in France, where workers laid off from a chemical plant won a severance package after dumping 790 gallons of sulfuric acid into a tributary of the Meuse River in 2000.[9]

War is the most primitive and costly means of dividing natural capital, and continues to be prominent in international land disputes when no authority can enforce the results of civilized dispute resolution processes. Over 566,000 American lives were lost in the five largest U.S. conflicts, and worldwide military expenditures exceed $1 trillion annually. Beyond the financial losses shared by violent and litigious solutions, and the human casualties of violence, war has the unfortunate effect of destroying the sought-after natural capital. During the Vietnam War, forests and wildlife were destroyed by over 11 million gallons of dioxin-laden Agent Orange.[10] Nuclear proliferation increases the environmental stakes for violent conflict resolution. Carl Sagan and Richard Turco (1990) theorized that smoke and dust from a large nuclear war would cause prolonged cold and darkness, decimating plant life and all that depend on it.

Like the threat of trials, the prospect of violence may moderate optimism that can separate the expectations and demands of parties to a dispute. When the

8 See www.cdfe.org/ecomurder.htm.

9 See www.csmonitor.com/durable/2000/07/21/p8s1.htm.

10 See Boffey (1998).

threat of war is not enough to foster acceptance of settlement offers, the force of combat can decide a dispute. Unfortunately, sometimes the battle must be fought to lend credibility to future threats. And worse, ego, pride, emotion, and greed can distract parties' priorities away from the efficient use of environmental resources.

The costly consequences of legal and military battles can be effective motivators for more cordial settlement when such alternatives are available. The use of violence has waned with the advancement of legal authority and alternative conflict resolution techniques. The courts deter some frivolous claims and encourage a large majority of claimants to settle before trial. By similar reasoning one might argue that trial should be more lengthy and expensive, thus inhibiting more lawsuits. Higher litigation costs encourage greater tolerance and discourage frivolous suits, but inhibit underfunded plaintiffs with meritorious suits, and may lead to vigilante justice if alternatives are not provided. If higher court costs are deemed desirable, an alternative to permitting inefficiency in the civil justice system would be to tax disputes and give the receipts to a worthy cause.

Decision Rules

Particularly in disputes with small stakes, parties sometimes acquiesce in decision rules as an efficient alternative to violence. The catalyst might be a third-party mediator or arbitrator whose decision each side has agreed to accept. Decision rules that are sometimes favorable include

- *Tradition (privilege to the first born)*
- *Rules of thumb*[11] *(women and children first, older is wiser)*
- *Strict adherence to religious teachings*
- *Precedent*
- *Arbitration*
- *Flipping a coin*
- *Drawing straws and similar games*[12]
- *First-come-first-served*

11 Sensitivity check: Although this phrase has been associated with the shocking idea that a husband can beat his wife so long as the stick is no thicker than his thumb, the more likely source is the historical use of body parts (like thumbs) as rulers to measure things. See www.worldwidewords.org/qa/qa-rul1.htm.

12 You may remember "grab the bat," "eny-meny-miny-mo," and "rock-paper-scissors."

All of these methods address a question of eligibility to receive certain benefits.[13] Sporting events, jousting, duels, fist fighting, wars, and related tests of strength or bravery have been used for the same purpose. None of these methods offers a panacea; the more harmless solutions often lack enforceability while the more violent solutions lack popular appeal.

The incentive to comply with unforced decision rules is inversely related to the size of the stakes. In small-stakes cases like a dispute over the removal of a tree straddling two lots, the transaction costs associated with trying to override a decision are likely to exceed the benefits. Large stakes motivate parties who are disadvantaged by traditional rules to forego the rules' convenience in favor of a more involved battle for privilege. In a dispute over national boundaries, it is likely that arduous settlement negotiations or a more authoritative determination will be needed to supplant unforced decision rules. The ease of dispute resolution under authoritarian rule is a strength among the weaknesses of dictators, kings, dominant spouses, and other autocrats.

Fair Division

Dividing a forest or other natural capital can resemble the cutting of a cake. The cake might represent the Middle East, a mineral-laden continental shelf, or the Arctic National Wildlife Refuge. Border disputes driven by interests in natural capital are commonplace. Looking only at Latin America and the Caribbean, the following disputes are ongoing at the time of this writing: Honduras and Nicaragua are feuding over fishing and oil rights in the Caribbean, and share a dispute with El Salvador over division of the shrimp-rich Gulf of Fonseca. Bolivia and Chile broke diplomatic ties in 1987 over access to the Pacific Ocean. Venezuela and Guyana have long disputed rights to land in the Essequibo River region of Guyana, which holds plentiful mineral and oil reserves. Neighboring Caribbean countries disagree over the division of Suriname, Belize, Aves Island, the Gulf of Venezuela, and the waters separating Venezuela, Trinidad, and Tobago. Mediation by Pope John Paul II settled a conflict between Argentina and Chile over three islands in the southern Beagle Channel, and Chile settled 22 territorial disputes with Argentina after civil rule was restored in 1990. There are many cakes to be divided.

Divide and Choose Simple solutions exist for simple conflicts. This is the case when equal division is the goal and the adverse parties have similar preferences. For natural capital that can be measured accurately, as with minerals or uniform land, fair division is straightforward. If the resource is not uniform or a reliable measuring device is not available, a divide-and-choose method can sometimes render an agreed-upon division between two adversaries. This solution allows one party to divide the resource into two parts and the other to choose between the two allotments. The divider has an incentive to divide the resource equally

13 See Brams and Taylor (1996) for a comprehensive review of decision rules.

Disputes over development are common. This sign arose during a dispute over new hotels planned for wilderness areas on the island of Oahu in Hawaii.

in order to maximize the value of the inferior (if not equal) part that will remain after the chooser makes a selection. The United Nations Division of Ocean Affairs and the Law of the Sea advocates the divide-and-choose method for dividing mineral-rich sections of the seafloor among neighboring nations.[14]

Some conflicts are not so simple. The equitable appeal of the divide-and-choose method diminishes when the preferences of the parties differ. Suppose that the Nature Conservancy (NC) and the American Petroleum Institute (API) are trying to divide part of the Arctic National Wildlife Refuge into a section to preserve and a section to tap for oil. The land in question contains mountains on one side, ocean on the other, and flat land in the middle. Suppose that the NC prefers to preserve the mountains while the API prefers to drill on the flat land near the ocean. If the NC makes the division, it will include more than half of the land in the section with the mountains, knowing that the API is still likely to select the section near the ocean. Likewise, if the API divides, it will include a disproportionate amount of land in the section with the ocean, knowing that the NC will favor a smaller section with mountains over a larger section on the sea. This dispute is not a good candidate for simple fair-division methods.

Say Stop The say-stop method can divide uniform but hard-to-measure assets among parties wishing to maximize their shares, and heterogeneous assets among parties with similar preferences. This method offers the advantage of being easier

14 See Division of Ocean Affairs and the Law of the Sea (1998).

to administer than divide and choose when more than two parties are involved.[15] Consider the ongoing dispute between fishers and environmentalists over giant cuttlefish living along reefs near Australia. Suppose that environmentalists, Australian fishers, and international fishers want to divide the cuttlefish habitat into three equally desirable areas, and that subjective estimates of cuttlefish densities at different points along the reefs prevent a simple division on the basis of kilometers.

A solution would be to have a boat travel the length of the reef, with a rule that the representative from any of the three parties can call out "stop" at any time, and the caller's share will be the stretch that the boat has already passed. After the first share has been claimed, the remaining two representatives will call out when they feel the boat divides the remaining reef into two equally favorable sections. If the boat had not reached the subjectively fair dividing point, calling out would leave the other party with the better side. If the boat were beyond the fair dividing point, both would want to claim the section behind the boat before the other captured the advantage. When the boat begins, the choice is thus between the section of reef behind the boat and half of the reef's natural capital not yet traveled. If less than one-third of the reef's capital has been traveled, then more than two-thirds (more than one-third for each of the last two callers) has not been traveled, and it pays to wait. If more than one-third has been traveled, less than two-thirds remains (less than one-third for each of the last two callers), and it pays to call out. Thus, the reef will be divided into three sections that do not elicit envy from the perspective of any of the recipients.

The theoretical result of the say-stop method with n participating parties is that a representative will say stop whenever, to the best of any party's knowledge, $1/n^{th}$ of the asset has been passed by the divider (in this example, the boat). The division may not be perfect, but when there is no satisfactory objective measure, this method divides an asset with minimal expense and to the satisfaction of everyone involved.

Like divide and choose, the say-stop method cannot assure an equitable outcome when dividing a heterogeneous resource between parties with differing tastes. The advantage will go to the party who prefers the characteristics of the asset on the side that the divider starts on. In the Arctic National Wildlife Refuge example, if the divider starts on the side of the refuge favored by the Nature Conservancy, the NC will wait to say stop until the divider has reached the point where the American Petroleum Institute is just short of indifference between the side with the mountains and the side with the ocean, at which point the side with the mountains will have a larger portion of the middle ground attached. Likewise, the API would gain the advantage if the divider started on the coast.

15 Divide and choose can indeed be applied with three parties. The first divides the asset into three pieces, the second trims what is in her perception the largest piece so that it is the same size as the second-largest piece, and the third gets the first choice of the three pieces. The trimmer gets the second choice and the divider gets the third choice. The result is a division that everyone is content with, but then the trimmings must be divided by the same method, and then the trimmings of the trimmings, and so on.

Strict Alternation Separable assets can sometimes be divided fairly by taking turns. This works particularly well when there are not an odd number of items with particularly high or low value, and when the parties' knowledge of each other's preferences cannot lead to an unfair advantage. Consider the dispute between Venezuela and Guyana over the environmentally rich region of the Essequibo River. There are many islands in the Essequibo's estuary, and we will examine a simplified version of the allocation of these islands with a goal of fair division. Let us assume that Venezuela and Guyana would each like to control as many islands as possible, and that they each favor control of the larger islands. If the islands in question are similar in size and location and even in number, strict alternation of island selection could yield a fair resolution. If, instead, there are three large islands and one small island, the first chooser will gain the advantage. The first chooser will select the first large island, the second chooser will select the second large island, the first chooser will select the third large island, and then the second chooser will select the small island. As illustrated in Figure 15.2 on the next page, the final tally in this case would be two large islands controlled by the first chooser and one large and one small island controlled by the second chooser.

To examine the role of known preferences, imagine there is one small, one medium-sized, and one large unpopulated island, and one large island populated by citizens of Guyana. Guyana is the first chooser and prefers to have larger islands. Understandably, it places the highest priority on the island already populated by its citizens. Venezuela is the second chooser. It likes the large unpopulated island the best and the small island the least, but would choose the medium island over the large island on which it would have to contend with citizens of its adversary. If these preferences are hidden and Guyana assumes that size is the primary selection criterion for Venezuela, Guyana will first select the populated island (because otherwise it has no assurance of receiving it). Venezuela will choose the other large island, Guyana will choose the medium-sized island, and then Venezuela will choose the small island. This provides each country with control over its most favored island, plus either a small or a medium island. The first chooser has a slight advantage.

If Guyana knows Venezuela's preferences, Guyana will begin by selecting the large, unpopulated island. Then Venezuela will select the medium island because, as Guyana knows, this takes precedence over the larger island populated by Guyanese. In the second round, Guyana will select the populated island and Venezuela will select the small island. This leaves Venezuela with the small and medium-sized islands and Guyana with the two large islands. The first-chooser advantage for Guyana is significant. Such an advantage is generally unfavorable from a policy standpoint, although it may be appropriate as a means of balancing other inequities, such as those between developed and developing countries. Strict alternation is applicable to divisions among more than two parties when knowledge of preferences and heterogeneity of assets are not a problem, although the opportunities for strategic manipulation increase considerably.

Figure 15.2 *Allocating Islands in the Essequibo Estuary: Order and Information Matter*

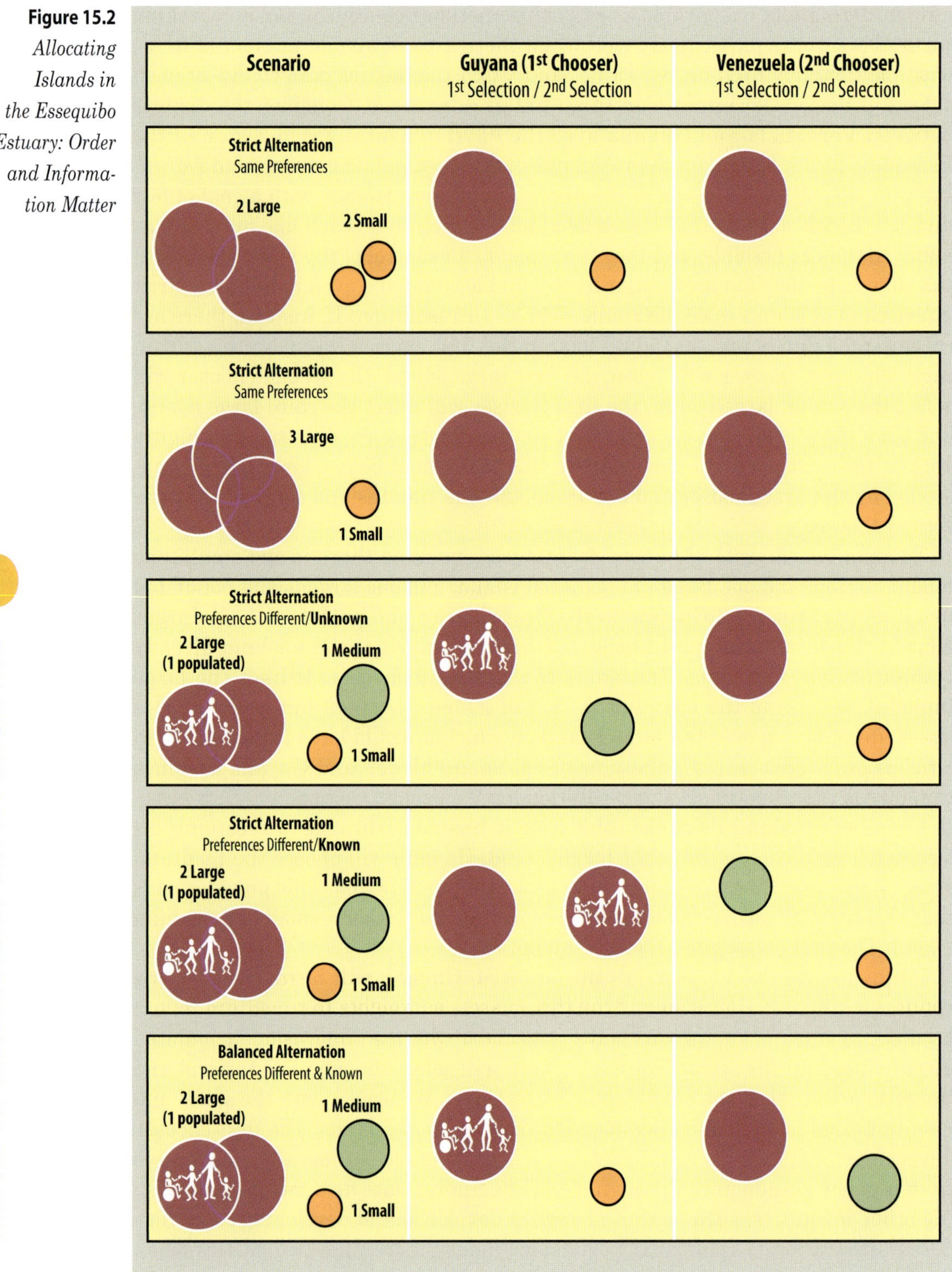

Balanced Alternation In some cases the inequities of strict alternation can be resolved by taking turns at taking turns. That is, in the island-choosing example, rather than selecting in the order Guyana Venezuela Guyana Venezuela, Guyana could choose first in the first round and Venezuela could choose first in the second round, making the order Guyana Venezuela Venezuela Guyana. This would prevent Guyana from garnering both of the large islands, but it does not guarantee the most equitable solution in every case. If there were one large island and three small islands such that control over all three of the small islands would give either party the same satisfaction as control over the one large island, it would then be more equitable to give the first chooser one selection and allow the second chooser to make three selections in a row. For example, Guyana Venezuela Venezuela Venezuela. In similar ways, balanced alternation can be customized to yield a fair solution in some situations when strict alternation will not.

Balanced alternation cannot provide balance when the parties value one asset by more than the others combined. It can also result in an inefficient outcome when preferences are unknown by those deciding on the balancing scheme. Suppose that Guyana cared only about the number of islands saved, and had unknown indifference between the large island and any one of three small islands, whereas Venezuela equated the one large island with all three of the small islands combined. The ordering of Guyana Venezuela Venezuela Venezuela that worked well in the previous example could result in Guyana choosing the large island and Venezuela choosing three small islands. Yet, both sides would be better off with a strict alternation of Venezuela Guyana Venezuela Guyana that would allow Venezuela to control a large island (subjectively equivalent to three small islands) plus a small island, and Guyana to control two small islands (subjectively equivalent to two large islands).

Adjusted Winner The adjusted-winner method can provide balanced allocations of resources in some cases when alternation cannot.[16] Take for example the dispute between Greece and Turkey over fish stocks in their contested territorial waters, land on the island of Imia, and rights to oil below the continental shelf of the Aegean Sea. An application of the adjusted-winner method would have each country assign 100 points among the three assets as weights to reflect the countries' preferences. Hypothetically, the outcome might be as follows:

Asset	*Greece*	*Turkey*
Land	25	25
Oil	**55**	50
Fish	20	**25**

16 See Brams and Taylor (1999).

In the first phase each asset is allocated to the country that assigns the largest number of points to it. If both countries assign the same number of points to some of the assets, these assets are distributed, one by one in any order, to the party with the fewest points worth of resources at the time when the distribution is being made. Thus, Greece starts out with rights to the oil for 55 points, and Turkey starts with rights to the fish stocks for 25 points. Both countries assigned 25 points to the land, and the tie goes to Turkey because it has received the fewest points worth of resources. With the land and the fish, Turkey receives 50 points worth of resources and Greece receives 55 points worth of resources, making Greece the winner of this phase of the process.

The first, "winner" phase is followed by an "adjustment" phase. For each item initially allocated to the winner, the mediator or authority in charge calculates the ratio of the winner's point allocation to the loser's point allocation for that asset. Since Greece won and received the oil, the relevant ratio is 55/50 = 1.10. Similar calculations would be carried out for any other items the winner received. Lower ratios indicate that fewer points will be lost by the winner relative to the points gained by the loser when an item is transferred from the winner to the loser. For efficiency, any transfers necessary to reach equality between the parties begin with the items with the lowest ratios of winner's to loser's point allocations and end with those with the highest ratios. If the transfer of the entire lowest-ratio asset would not give the initial loser more points than the initial winner, that transfer is made, and then the adjustment phase continues with the new lowest-ratio asset in the hands of the winner.

If, as in the story of Greece and Turkey, a transfer of the entire lowest-ratio asset would overcompensate the loser, a fraction of the lowest-ratio asset is transferred. Of course, indivisible assets cannot be selected for this purpose unless they can be sold or otherwise converted into divisible items. In order to determine the transfer of oil that would equalize the point allocations received by Greece and Turkey, the points received by each side can be set equal to each other, with x representing the fraction of oil that Turkey receives:

$$55 - 55x = 25 + 25 + 50x$$

The left side of the equation represents Greece's 55 points from oil minus the fraction of those points that will be transferred to Turkey. The right side represents Turkey's 25 points from land, 25 points from fish, and the fraction of the 50 points from oil that Turkey will receive. Solving for x determines that if Turkey receives 4.762 percent of the oil, each side will earn 55 – 55(0.04762) = 25 + 25 + 50(0.04762) = 52.38 points.

Strategic behavior can rear its ugly head in the midst of the adjusted-winner procedure. There is an incentive for parties to understate the extent to which they favor assets so long as they do not lose control of the assets they value more highly than the other party. By attributing fewer points to items they receive, parties are granted more compensation as the initial loser, or debited less as the initial winner. The best possible outcome for a party occurs when the party allocates just one point more than the adverse party for each item received. The worst possible outcome occurs when such misrepresentation leads to the parties receiving their least-favored assets. The strong incentives to lie at least a little, and the problems created when strategic behavior goes awry, make this method most useful when parties can be expected to be honest.

Sometimes environmental concerns, historical precedent, current possession, or broader social welfare objectives dominate egalitarian targets and make an unequal division appropriate. When equality is not the goal, the allocation process becomes more complex. If either the appropriate allocation or the measurement of the asset is in question,[17] subjective solutions may be necessary. Neutral third parties become valuable as facilitators and decision makers under remedies that include arbitration, mediation, negotiated settlement, and judgment at trial. As disputes intensify, attorneys are hired, claims are filed, and the costly process of discovery, demands, threats, and counterclaims may be forthcoming.

Agreement

Agreement mends disputes. Unfortunately, there can be much to agree on. Consider a dispute between the EPA and fictional MESSCO Corporation over the payment of cleanup costs for a Superfund site. Initially both sides expect that a jury would award $200 million from MESSCO to the EPA for cleanup. If trial would necessitate $40 million in additional attorney fees for the EPA and $60 million in additional fees for MESSCO,[18] there is $100 million to be saved by resolving the dispute beforehand. Even though they agree on the expected trial outcome, they may disagree over how to divide the $100 million of bargaining rent. The EPA expects to receive $200 million at trial minus $40 million in fees, so any settlement amount over $160 million would be better for the EPA than going to trial. MESSCO expects to pay $200 million plus $60 million in fees at trial, so any settlement amount below $260 million is preferred over going to trial by MESSCO. Where between $160 million and $260 million they might settle, or in other words, how they will divide the $100 million bargaining rent, depends on their relative bargaining strengths. Strategic behavior, misperceptions of bargaining strength, and undue optimism can prevent agreement over how to divide the savings from out-of-court settlement.

The uncertainty of jury awards impedes the alignment of parties' expectations. The wide range of possible outcomes also threatens risk-averse parties who cannot afford even a remote downside risk of paying an enormous award. In the past, multimillion-dollar awards were newsworthy. Exxon, General Motors, and Ford are among the growing numbers of U.S. companies facing damage awards in the billions of dollars. The risk burden of variations in judgments could be decreased with caps on damages, decisions made by judges rather than juries, or a standardization of awards for particular offenses or injuries.

17 Although measurement is seldom a problem with land, disputes can arise over the measurement of less uniform assets such as land with varying topography, improvements, or biodiversity.

18 Attorney fees in the vicinity of 30 percent of an award are common.

Alternative Dispute Resolution

The involvement of a neutral third party can foster settlement by removing barriers including differing information, biased expectations for trial, unrealistic perceptions of bargaining strength, and strategic behavior. **Alternative dispute resolution** (ADR) techniques couple assistance with these barriers with an abbreviated process that is faster and less expensive than trial. Under **decisional approaches**, the neutral third party has the authority to impose a solution on the disputants. Under **facilitative approaches**, the neutral party helps the parties achieve their own solution. And under **advisory approaches**, the neutral party renders a decision that is suggestive but nonbinding.

Decisional ADR Techniques

Conventional arbitration brings disputants before a neutral third party or panel to present evidence. The neutral(s) review the arguments and then render a final, binding decision that is not subject to court approval or appeal. The possibility that a neutral might offer a solution that splits the difference between the two parties' proposals provides incentives for polarized offers and discourages concessions. **Final-offer arbitration** (FOA) is meant to counter these incentives.[19] Under FOA, each side submits a last, best offer and the arbitrator selects one of the two offers as the final outcome. In contrast to the tendency for extreme offers under conventional arbitration, the incentive under FOA is to submit an offer that the arbitrator will deem fairer than the adversary's offer. FOA is sometimes called baseball arbitration because it is popular for settling baseball salary disputes. A variant of FOA under which the arbitrator selects an outcome prior to hearing the parties' offers has likewise been dubbed **night-time baseball** arbitration. The final outcome is that offer that comes closest to the arbitrator's selection.

Med-arb is a hybrid of mediation and arbitration. In an initial phase the mediator attempts to bring the two parties to agreement on an outcome, but if the impasse is not resolved, the dispute is referred to binding arbitration.

Facilitative ADR Techniques

Mediation involves no third-party judgment, but one or more mediators work with the parties to help them come to a settlement. The mediators help the parties clarify their differences and try to dovetail interests to the satisfaction of both sides. For example, Spain and Britain have disputed ownership of the environmentally sensitive Rock of Gibraltar—the headland on the southern coast of Spain that overlooks the entrance to the Mediterranean Sea—for almost

19 A number of economists, including Bazerman and Farber (1985), have found that the decisions of arbitrators are largely independent of the demands of the parties, lessening concerns about conventional arbitration.

300 years. The Rock is the European home for Barbary apes, and a rest stop for hundreds of thousands of birds migrating between their breeding grounds in Europe and their wintering areas in Africa. If Britain cared most about preventing further development on the Rock, and Spain cared most about ownership rights, a mediator might bring these mutually agreeable interests to light and foster a settlement that placed the Rock in Spanish hands with the stipulation that wilderness areas would be protected.[20]

Early neutral evaluation brings representatives of the two sides together with a neutral party shortly after a claim is filed to talk through the strengths and weaknesses of their arguments and clarify realistic outcomes. **Third-party consultation** focuses more on dissolving animosity between the parties than on specific issues under dispute. By attacking attitudes and issues at the root of repeated conflict, consultation can sometimes avoid many disputes that would otherwise crop up in the future. A **judicial settlement conference** brings lawyers representing the disputants together with a judge or magistrate to try to resolve the case short of trial. This is useful when settlement is deterred by at least one party having unrealistic expectations for trial because it helps bring everyone down to Earth.

Advisory ADR Techniques

Advisory attempts to bring parties closer together include explicit opinions from the neutral party or parties. A **mini-trial** provides litigants with a snapshot of what might happen in a real trial. A neutral panel presides over a hearing in which representatives of each side provide the highlights of their cases. The neutrals then offer an opinion regarding the appropriate outcome, and reflections on the strengths and weaknesses of each side. A **summary jury trial** is another abbreviated form of trial that provides litigants with an advisory verdict for guidance in their settlement negotiations. Summary jury trials are generally more formal and adversarial in spirit than mini-trials, and arguments are heard by a jury of peers resembling the jury that would hear the case if it proceeded to trial.

Court-annexed arbitration attempts to bridge the gap between disputants with a brief, non-binding hearing before a panel of attorneys or retired judges. With **neutral fact-finding**, a neutral party undertakes an independent investigation of a contested factual matter, such as whether a proposed road would endanger wildlife habitat. The issues in question are chosen by the parties themselves, and the decision is usually nonbinding. Alternative dispute resolution techniques such as these are required in some classes of civil suits and could be better utilized in others.

20 The dispute over Gibraltar was ongoing as of late 2009. For information on environmental interests on the rock, see www.gibraltar.gi/nature/.

Compatible Perspectives

Even when parties to a dispute lack the information necessary to share the same expectation, parties can reach settlement with differing but compatible expectations. Relative optimism regarding the expected judgment might be accompanied by relative pessimism regarding the appropriate division of the savings from avoiding trial, thus making a range of settlement offers acceptable to both sides. This opportunity arises because the judgment depends on the merits of each party's case, while the division of the savings depends on the parties' relative bargaining strengths. Either party might over- or underestimate either aspect of their situation. The task, then, is to bring parties close enough for compatibility.

Civil justice reform is in its infancy, with fledgling attempts at new rules of civil procedure that lower demands, increase offers, or otherwise satisfy one of the four conditions for settlement. Specific rules, including the American rule, the English rule, Federal Rule of Civil Procedure 68, and many parallel state court rules have met with limited success in encouraging parties to converge, negotiate, and tolerate.[21] These rules and some of their pitfalls are described here. The section that follows explains two alternative rules that could equitably resolve conflicts despite the parties' incompatible self-perceptions of their relative bargaining strengths.

The American Rule

As illustrated in Figure 15.3, the traditional "American rule" shifts court costs, excluding legal fees, to the "losing" party in civil cases. Under this rule, each party pays its own attorney fees regardless of the outcome at trial. The losing party—the defendant if there is a positive verdict in favor of the plaintiff, and the plaintiff otherwise—is assessed court costs other than attorney fees, including reasonable court fees, transcript costs, printing costs, and witness fees. This rule generally applies to litigation costs even when supplemental rules governing attorney fees are in effect. Court costs are typically negligible, making this rule a slap on the wrist for parties who fail to settle and fail in court.

The English Rule

The English rule places a greater burden on the losing party by shifting the payment of attorney fees, and not just court costs, to the losing party. Under the English rule the loser pays both court costs and reasonable attorney fees for both sides. This larger penalty for losing a case serves to discourage frivolous lawsuits. The downside is that the rule also discourages justified claims by parties who cannot afford the risk of an unfavorable judgment despite the merits of their cases. Related concerns have prevented acceptance of the English rule in the United States, although loser-pays rules have received considerable attention.

21 See Anderson and Rowe (1995).

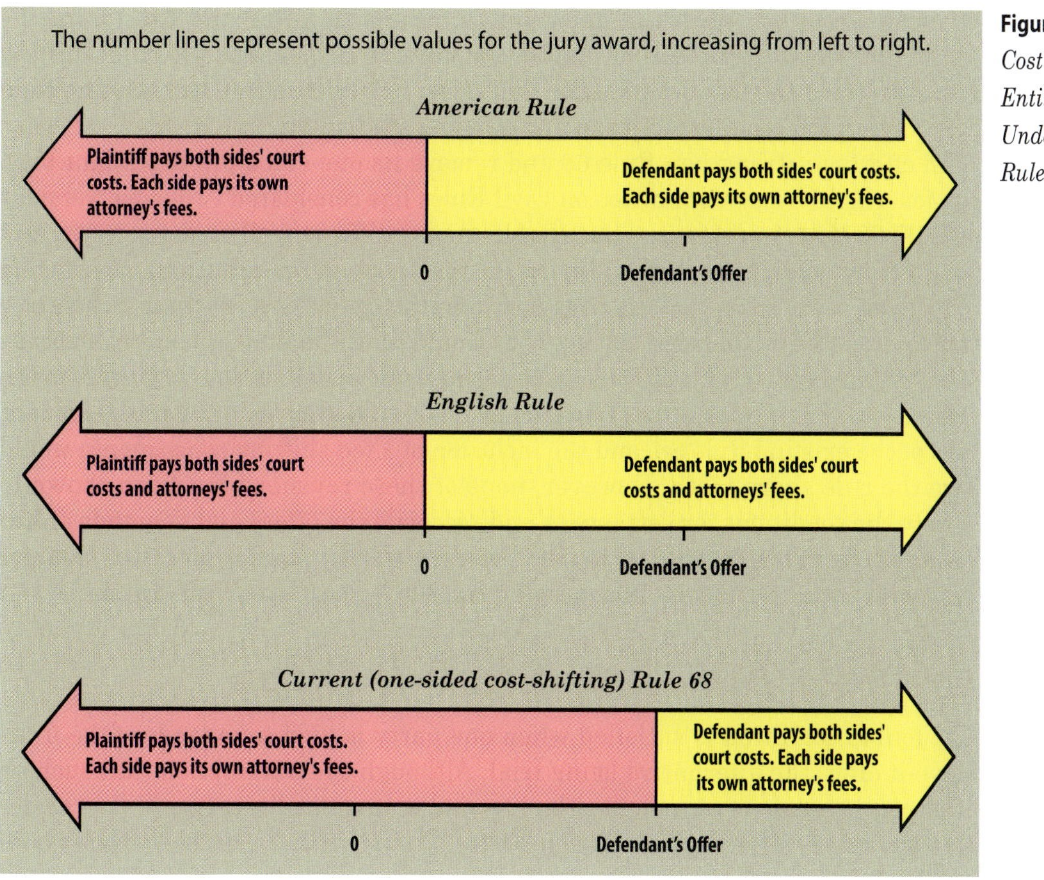

Figure 15.3 *Cost and Fee Entitlement Under Existing Rules*

The 1994 Republican "Contract with America" promoted legal reform measures including loser-pay provisions that continue to be discussed[22] but have not yet been adopted.

Federal Rule of Civil Procedure 68

Settlement rules, also called offer-of-settlement devices, are intended to encourage parties in litigation to settle out of court. A typical settlement rule allows a party in litigation to formalize a settlement offer. If the opposing party refuses that offer and does not improve on it at trial, the refusing party suffers a consequence. Existing Federal Rule of Civil Procedure 68 (Rule 68) mandates that defendants collect post-offer court costs, but usually not attorney fees, from the plaintiff if a refused offer is not improved upon at trial. In theory, because Rule 68 creates an added threat that the plaintiff will have to pay the defendant's costs at trial, the plaintiff is more likely to accept any given offer. Unfortunately, rather than making the same offers she would make in the absence of Rule 68, the defendant is likely to offer to pay less as a result of her improved bargaining

22 See, for example, www.legalreform-now.org/menu3_10.htm.

position. In effect, both the defendant's maximum offer and the plaintiff's minimum demand decrease by similar amounts in response to the rule, shifting but not closing the gap between the two sides. For this reason, the existing Rule 68 is underused and ineffective in encouraging settlement.[23]

In efforts to strengthen Rule 68 and remove its one-sided pro-defendant bias, the federal Advisory Committee on Civil Rules has considered two-sided versions of Rule 68 that would make it available to plaintiffs as well as defendants, and fee-shifting versions that would increase the sanction for refusing a reasonable offer from court costs to costs plus post-offer attorney fees. William Schwarzer (1992) proposed a two-sided variant that would limit the total amount of attorney fees shifted as the result of Rule 68 to the amount by which the jury verdict was superior to the rejected offer. Two-sided rules would eliminate the pro-defendant bias of the existing Rule 68, and the inclusion of a fee-shifting consequence would give the rule sharp teeth. However, none of these revisions has been shown to satisfy the conditions for settlement and reconcile the offers and demands of litigants who would otherwise go to trial. In other words, there is plenty of room for improvement in settlement-encouraging rules by you and your generation.

Credible Take-It-or-Leave-It Offers

The fourth condition is satisfied when one party is able to extend a take-it-or-leave-it offer, the alternative being trial. Although the assumption that such an offer can be made is common in the law and economics literature,[24] it is easier said than done. If a party had such power, assuming the parties were rational and seeking to maximize the expected value of their net gains, the offeror would make an offer slightly superior to the offeree's expected net outcome from trial. In the example of *EPA* vs. *MESSCO*, if such an opportunity existed, the EPA would make a final offer of $259.99 million or (alternatively) MESSCO would make a final offer of $160.01 million. Since bargaining cannot continue after this point by definition of the final offer, the offeree would choose the settlement offer over the option to continue to trial for lesser expected gain and greater uncertainty.

Fortunately for those who might receive them, purported take-it-or-leave-it offers are seldom credible because it is not in the offeror's best interest to carry them out. After the rejection of any offer that would make the offeror better off than going to trial, further bargaining over settlement values that fall between the rejected offer and the net trial outcome for the offeror would be beneficial to both parties. For example, if the EPA turned down a "final" offer of $160.01 million, MESSCO would be better off trying to bargain for a settlement above $160.01 million and below $260 million than ceasing negotiations and paying $260 million at trial. This means it can be difficult to make a credible final offer.

23 See Anderson (1994) for expanded theoretical explanations for Rule 68's inadequacies, and Anderson and Rowe (1995) for empirical evidence.

24 Examples include Bebchuk (1988) and Spier (1994).

From the standpoint of fairness, it is also undesirable for parties to be able to make take-it-or-leave-it offers because they permit the offeror to gain most of the benefits from settlement.

The Sincerity Rule

If enacted, the **sincerity rule** would provide a more equitable, yet relatively simple solution despite bargaining inequities. The rule was proposed to take advantage of the power of credible take-it-or-leave-it offers to bring settlement, while ensuring that such offers are fair.[25] The legal system has sufficient authority to enforce the finality of offers, although if unrestrained, this ability would convey a distinct advantage to the offeror. The rule is so named for its ability to elicit a "sincerely fair" offer in the face of impasse. Under this rule, either party may designate an offer as a sincerity offer. The offeree then either accepts this legally enforced take-it-or-leave-it offer, or rejects it, in which case the parties proceed to trial with no further opportunity to bargain and the *offeror* will pay the *offeree's* reasonable post-offer fees.

Those unable to stomach the high cost of a trial, or those facing unreasonable offers from well-positioned opponents, would have an incentive to make an acceptable sincerity offer. If the offeror offers an amount slightly better than the offeree's expected judgment, the offeree (unless risk-loving) will accept it. If the offeror offers an amount inferior to the offeree's expected judgment, the offeree can choose to proceed to trial at no additional cost, and the offeror must pay post-offer attorney fees for both sides. Acceptable offers are thus expected in the vicinity of the offeree's expected judgment and can be augmented to account for any possible risk-loving disposition on the part of the offeree.

The sincerity rule could provide equitable solutions to unfair demands among adversaries. Consider the hypothetical case in which the EPA and MESSCO dispute the payment of cleanup costs for a Superfund site. Knowing that the EPA has been criticized for its large legal expenses in the past and will not want to advance to trial, MESSCO may insist on a settlement near the EPA's threat point of $160 million. Rather than submitting to this unfair offer, as the EPA might with no better alternative, the EPA could make a sincerity offer to settle for $199 million. This offer approximates the expected jury award, and if MESSCO seeks to minimize its payment, MESSCO will favor the $199 million payment over the expected $200 million payment at trial (with fees paid by the EPA). Since sincerity offers are optional, there would be no reason to make such an offer to a seemingly irrational or spiteful adversary. If the offeree is risk averse, an offer exactly equal to the expected jury award, or even a bit inferior to it, will be acceptable as a means of eliminating the uncertainty associated with trial. Sincerity offers could be used in a variety of situations to avoid trial, an inequitable settlement, or prolonged strategic bargaining.

25 For more on this rule, see Anderson (1994).

Final Offer Auctions

Final offer auctions are another proposed method of avoiding negotiation deadlock by permitting a credible final offer, again adding a mechanism to avoid the potential inequities of unchecked final offers. A final offer auction allows the two parties to bid for the right to make the final offer. The amount of the winning bid is granted to the party who lost in the bidding phase. If the final offer is rejected, the parties must proceed to trial with no further bargaining, and each side is responsible for its own attorney fees.

In our Superfund example, with each side expecting a $200 million award at trial (from MESSCO to the EPA for cleanup costs), the EPA and MESSCO would save $40 million and $60 million respectively on attorney fees by settling out of court. Given the opportunity to make one final offer, each would offer the other an amount just better than the adversary's threat point—their expected trial outcome net of fees. The EPA would make a final offer to settle for about $259.99 million, and MESSCO would make a final offer to settle for about $160.01 million. Notice that the difference between what the EPA receives if it can make the final offer and what it receives if it cannot is about $100 million. The right to make a final offer conveys the ability to capture virtually all of the $100 million in bargaining rent. Each side would bid up to half of the bargaining rent, or $50 million, to receive $100 million, because the alternative is to receive the other party's bid. For example, after an EPA bid of $49 million, MESSCO chooses between not increasing its bid and receiving $49 million from the EPA, or bidding, say, $49.1 and either receiving a higher bid from the EPA or winning and receiving $100 – $49.1 = $50.9 million. It is rational for MESSCO to keep bidding until the EPA has bid $50 million, in which case MESSCO should stop and take the $50 million rather than bidding $50.1 million and receiving $100 – $50.1 = $49.9 million.

If the EPA makes the winning bid of $50 million, it will offer to settle for $259.99 and MESSCO should accept, rather than paying more in court with added uncertainty and the tribulations of trial. The net gain for the EPA would be $259.99 – $50 = $209.99 million. The net payment for MESSCO is the same: The $259.99 million settlement amount minus the $50 million bid received from the EPA. Thus, if both parties act rationally to maximize their net gains or minimize their net losses, the outcome will be halfway between the two parties' threat points. This is true whether or not the parties share the same expectation of the jury award. As with all of the existing and proposed rules, settlement is hindered when the parties' expectations for trial are unknown or differ by more than the total savings from avoiding trial.

Summary

The growing scarcity of natural capital exacerbates disputes over borders and use rights. Global industrialization increases the creation of toxic waste while environmental consciousness intensifies the calls for abatement. Litigation is a costly cure. This chapter highlights the causes of conflict, the conditions for settlement, and the variety of solutions available to avoid costly and prolonged disputes. Fair division techniques, including balanced alternation and the say-stop method, can apportion natural assets among consenting or submissive parties when preferences are similar or the assets are homogeneous. The adjusted-winner technique can accommodate both differing preferences and heterogeneous assets, but is subject to strategic manipulation. Alternative dispute resolution involves third-party neutrals who are able to handle complex and subjective issues. However, the trust of neutral parties, the adherence to nonbinding decisions, and the ability to enforce binding decisions are all more likely when conflicts are minor and domestic than when they are major and global.

In their intended role of resolving environmental disputes that would otherwise end in trial or violence, existing settlement rules are underused and ineffective. Stalemated and disadvantaged parties could benefit from the sincerity rule and final offer auctions, which show promise in theory and empirical testing. Use of the legal system to settle environmental disputes is not unlike use of fossil fuels to power automobiles and electric utilities. We lumber on with coal and oil for two-thirds of our energy needs despite the availability of techniques that, with wide acceptance, would provide inexpensive, renewable power and a lower environmental burden. Similarly, we often turn to the traditional approaches of trial and violence to settle conflicts over environmental assets and obligations when superior alternatives exist. The realm of environmental dispute resolution is one in which we stand to make great strides in economic efficiency.

Disputes are as natural as daylight, and arguably more common. Blades of grass abut each other in a competition for space, food, and water. Animals compete for all of the same resources. With boundaries established and stomachs swollen, animals further engage their adversaries in quests for mates and status. Wildlife has its own forms of conflict resolution. When neighboring ferns compete for sunlight, a race for height and breadth determines fate. Polar bears resolve conflicts over mates with contests of brute force. As parasites like the torsalo fly exceed the carrying capacities of their hosts, death makes space for those with endurance. Conflicts between water and rock are always won by rock in the short run and water in the long run.

Homo sapiens have a civil litigation system unequaled in nature, although we frequently revert to alternatives that resemble those in the wild. Height and breadth are favored in a fist fight. Brute force wins turf wars. Those with endurance live to see the end of conflict-laden regimes. Humans may yield temporarily to stubbornness in a standoff, but over time, progressive flows of intellectual capital have generally dominated rigid political and socioeconomic systems. A difference between the resolution of disputes over natural resources and the resolution of disputes between natural resources, one hopes, is the role of intelligence in the former. Thought contributes not only to the outcome of dispute resolution methods involving strategy, but also to the understanding and refinement of dispute resolution methods themselves. I hope this chapter, and this text as a whole, have enriched your thoughts about efficient solutions to our critical environmental and natural resource challenges.

Problems for Review

1. Suppose that in the punitive damages phase of the *Deepwater Horizon* case, both sides expect a jury award of $2 billion on appeal, and that if they proceed with the case without settling, the additional fees will be $100 million for the defendant (BP) and $50 million for the plaintiffs. On a number line similar to those in Figure 15.1, indicate the expected judgment (J), each side's threat point (T_p and T_d), and the settlement range.

2. Answer the following questions in the context of the *Deepwater Horizon* case explained in Problem 1.
   a) *What is the bargaining rent?*
   b) *What is the most either side should pay for the right to make a credible final offer?*
   c) *If the defendant can make a credible (non-sincerity rule) final offer, what should it be?*
   d) *If the plaintiff makes a sincerity rule offer, what should it be?*

3. Name the four conditions for settlement explained in this chapter. For one of them, explain a deterrent to reaching that condition and a remedy for that deterrent.

4. What do you think is the strongest deterrent to settlement in the dispute over the Rock of Gibralter?

5. What dispute resolution technique would you advise for Spain and Britain in their dispute over the Rock of Gibraltar?

6. Which dispute resolution technique would you advise for the residents and developers in the dispute over new hotels planned for natural areas in Hawaii?

7. Which dispute resolution technique would you advise for neighbors who disagree over homeowners' rights to replace lawns with un-mown native grasses.

8. What concerns might prevent Superfund litigants from pressing on to trial in the face of a seemingly unfair demand from the EPA? (*Hint:* From whom does the Superfund typically seek retribution and how might those parties' interests be affected by a trial?)

9. Do you feel that lawyers can bring justice to those who need it while stopping short of encouraging unnecessary litigation? Explain your answer.

10. Those who bargain ruthlessly and are intent on maximizing their personal gain are sometimes called "hawks." "Doves" give in easily, favoring peaceful accord over the potential gains from conflict. The presence of a "dove" makes settlement more likely. What is a possible drawback to settlement achieved because one party succumbed too easily? What are some other means by which to gain agreement?

11. What potential problem with conventional arbitration is resolved by final offer arbitration?

1. Find a description of an environmental dispute that was resolved using one of the techniques discussed in this chapter.

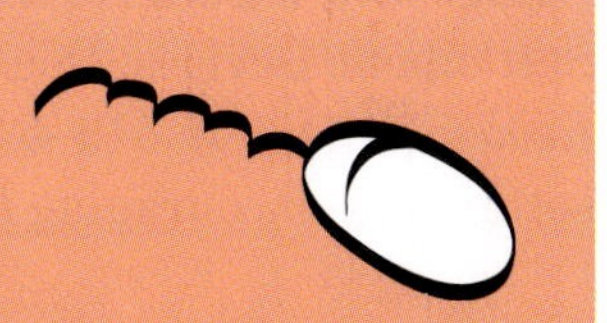

2. Find an argument for and against the English (fee-shifting) rule.
3. Find a website that advocates a specific measure of legal reform and critique its main argument.

Internet Resources

American Arbitration Association:
http://www.adr.org

Enviromapper Superfund site finder:
http://map3.epa.gov/enviromapper/index.html

EPA Superfund site:
http://www.epa.gov/superfund/index.htm

EPA Superfund Negotiations and Settlement Procedures:
http://www.epa.gov/compliance/cleanup/superfund/negotiate.html

Global Arbitration Mediation Association:
http://www.gama.com

Institute for Legal Reform:
www.instituteforlegalreform.com

Further Reading

Anderson, David A. "Improving Settlement Devices: Rule 68 and Beyond." *Journal of Legal Studies* 23 (1994): 225–246. A theoretical investigation of settlement devices and the conditions for settlement.

Anderson, David A. "The Fair Division of Natural Resources." *Journal of Natural Resources and Environmental Law* 15, no. 2 (2001): 227–245. An overview of decision rules applicable to the division of natural resources.

Anderson, David A., and Thomas D. Rowe, Jr. "Empirical Evidence on Settlement Devices: Does Rule 68 Encourage Settlement?" *Chicago-Kent Law Review* 71 (1995): 519–545. An empirical test of Rule 68 and several other settlement-encouraging legal rules.

Bazerman, M., and H. Farber. "Arbitrator Decision-Making: When are Final Offers Important?" *Industrial and Labor Relations Review* 39 (1985): 76–89.

Bebchuk, Lucian. "Suing Solely to Extract a Settlement Offer." *Journal of Legal Studies* 17 (1988): 437–450. A theoretical look at the incentives for litigation.

Boffey, Philip M. "Agent Orange in Vietnam, 30 Years Later." *New York Times* (September 8, 1998). An overview of the use of and subsequent problems with Agent Orange.

Brams, Steven J., and Alan D. Taylor. *Fair Division: From Cake-Cutting to Dispute Resolution.* Cambridge: Cambridge University Press, 1996. A comprehensive look at fair division techniques.

Brams, Steven J., and Alan D. Taylor. *The Win-Win Solution.* New York: Norton, 1999. A sequel to their previous book, with an emphasis on the adjusted-winner division technique.

Charness, Gary B. "Alternative Dispute Resolution and the Settlement Gap." In *Dispute Resolution: Bridging the Settlement Gap*, edited by David A. Anderson. Greenwich, CT: JAI Press, 1996, 205. An overview of many modern ADR techniques.

Division of Ocean Affairs and the Law of the Sea, Office of Legal Affairs, United Nations. *Oceans and Law of the Sea: Deep Seabed Minerals.* New York: DOALOS, 1998. Includes reference to how the divide-and-choose method is used to settle disputes over the ocean floor.

Harvey, Janice. "Ethyl Corporation v. Government of Canada." *Telegraph Journal*, New Brunswick, Canada, June 4, 1997, http://www.flora.org/library/mai/harvey3.html. An example of international environmental disputes.

Jacques, Kristi. "Texaco's Oil Production in the Ecuadorian Rainforest." *University of Michigan Environmental Justice Case Studies*, http://www.umich.edu/~snre492/Jones/texaco.htm, accessed November 22, 2002. Describes a sticky environmental dispute between a multinational corporation and indigenous tribes.

Rowe, Thomas D., Jr., and David A. Anderson. "One-Way Fee Shifting Statutes and Offer of Judgment Rules: An Empirical Experiment." *Jurimetrics Journal* 36 (1996): 255–273. An empirical test of three alternative fee-shifting rules that resolve the overlapping influences of pro-defendant rules and pro-civil rights rules.

Sablatura, Bob. "With Superfund, Lawyers Clean Up." *Houston Chronicle* (October 18, 1995). Discusses the downside of superfund litigation.

Sagan, Carl, and Richard Turco. *A Path Where No Man Thought: Nuclear Winter and the End of the Arms Race*. New York: Random House, 1990. Explains the stark realities of nuclear war.

Schwarzer, William. "Fee-Shifting Offers of Judgment—An Approach to Reducing the Cost of Litigation." *Judicature* 76 (1992): 147. A proposal to revise Rule 68 in search of efficiency.

Spier, Kathryn. "Pretrial Bargaining and the Design of Fee-Shifting Rules." *RAND Journal of Economics* 25 (1994): 1–18. An analysis of Rule 68 and its effects on settlement negotiations.

Stein, Mark S. "The English Rule with Client-to-Lawyer Risk Shifting: A Speculative Appraisal." *Chicago-Kent Law Review* 71 (1995): 603–624. A discussion of the "loser pays" English rule.

U.S. Department of Justice. *Justice Department Files Suit against Japanese Company over Air Pollution at U.S. Naval Base near Tokyo*. U.S. Embassy Press Release, Tokyo, Japan, March 27, 2002, http://usembassy.state.gov/tokyo/wwwhp022.html. An example of an international environmental dispute.

"Aim above morality. Be not simply good, be good for something."

—HENRY DAVID THOREAU

"We realize that in today's world, a business leader must be an environmental leader as well. Hence our determination is to analyze every aspect of our business in terms of its impact on the environment, and to take actions beyond what is expected if they hold the prospect of leaving future generations an environmentally sound world."

—MCDONALD'S CORPORATION

"The secret of success is honesty and fair dealing. If you can fake these, you've got it made."

—MARK TWAIN

"We seem ultimately always thrown back on individual ethics as the basis of conservation policy. It is hard to make a man, by pressure of law or money, do a thing which does not spring naturally from his own personal sense of right and wrong."

—ALDO LEOPOLD

16 Morals and Motivation

Some of our constraints come from the laws of science. In order to split hydrogen atoms from oxygen atoms in water, we must heat water to 2,800°C. Other constraints are imposed by our own will. We set public and personal policies and determine what is socially acceptable. We choose our goals and our paths toward them, and decide where to draw the line in terms of the burdens our lifestyle imposes on others. Although humans can be stubborn about change, the last two decades of the twentieth century brought the fall of the Berlin Wall which divided East and West Germany, the formal end of racially oppressive apartheid in South Africa, and "perestroika" in Asia that restructured the Soviet political and economic systems. So sea changes are possible, even when they involve teaching old humans new tricks. American philosopher and naturalist Henry David Thoreau (1817–1862) wrote, "I know of no more encouraging fact than the unquestionable ability of man to elevate his life by conscious endeavor." Given that society's treatment of the environment and natural resources is similarly subject to human discretion, this chapter explains approaches to the elemental ethical dimension of our choices.

How are ethical decisions made? Is any behavior unselfish? And what are the implications of selfishness on appropriate environmental policy? The allocation of environmental assets entails struggles between profits and preservation, and between people and wildlife. In the end, critical decisions about consumption levels, policy compliance, discount rates, and conservation come down to moral judgments. The trade-offs discussed in Chapter 5 and the sustainability questions of Chapter 8 force similar

A protester in Hawaii alleges unethical behavior by McDonald's.

moral dilemmas. What sacrifices should be made for future generations. Do our grandchildren deserve the same level of utility that we enjoy? Should they be left with the same natural capital that we have to work with? These questions are inseparably economic and ethical.

As we consider the selfishness of individuals we must also consider the obligations of firms. Business ethics has much to do with environmental economics and natural resource management. The Monsanto Chemical Company and its subsidiaries decided to produce PCBs, Agent Orange, Bovine somatotropin (BST), and dioxin. McDonald's is often harangued for excessive packaging and alleged animal cruelty.[1] And automakers must decide whether to oppose or surpass emissions and fuel-economy standards. If firms have no interest in ethics beyond visible efforts rewarded by customer loyalty, regulations may be necessary to promote ethical behavior behind the scenes. The refusal of McDonald's to permit rainforest destruction for its beef supply,[2] Toyota's development of hybrid vehicles,[3] and Starbucks' composting of coffee grounds[4] may simply be responses to the social conscience of the consumer. The leaders of these corporations may or may not weigh the costs of these changes against anything beyond profits. Taking moral behavior as that which is "right," whether motivated by unselfish individuals or firms that see beyond profits, gives it paramount importance. This chapter discusses models for personal and firm behavior and their implications for environmental and natural resource economics.

Morals *are standards for right and wrong, and* **ethics** *is the study of morals. In some contexts these terms can be used interchangeably.* **Ethical theories** *offer principles for the assessment of human behavior, and provide the guidance needed in many instances of decision-making and policymaking. The modifier "normative" in the title of the next section indicates that these theories refer to the way things should be, not necessarily the way things are.*

1 For a scathing attack on the ethics of McDonald's, environmental and otherwise, see www.mcspotlight.org.

2 See www.mcdonalds.com/corporate/social/environment/index.html.

3 See http://toyota.com/html/about/news/index.jsp#environment.

4 See www.starbucks.com/aboutus/enaffair.asp.

Normative Ethical Theories

Human behavior is motivated by our objectives. Economists generally assume that rational individuals maximize a subjective utility function that places weights on everything from the number of apples the individuals consume to the welfare of other people, the environment, wildlife, and future generations. For example, consider the hypothetical preferences of two individuals named Mark and Joan. Mark's utility function might be

$$\text{Utility} = 1{,}000 + 3(\text{apples}) + 17(\text{utility of friends}) + 2(\text{hours of television per day})\,(\text{utility of next generation})^2$$

while Joan's utility function is

$$\text{Utility} = 300 + 2(\text{number of animal species}) + 7(\text{utility of friends}) + 47(\text{square feet in house})/(\text{arsenic level in drinking water})$$

Every time Mark receives another apple, his utility increases by 3 utils. Mark places no weight on the number of animal species, and he places a greater emphasis on the utility of friends than Joan. Each individual's utility function influences his or her decisions regarding the allocation of time, money, and other resources. The makeup of one's utility function is subjective, meaning that individuals make choices regarding their underlying objectives. The function that firms try to maximize has similarly subjective weights on such variables as profits, market share, service to the community, and loyalty to employees.

Some decisions rest on a sense of duty or obligation. These may include choices not to litter, smoke around children, or hunt the bald eagle. The extent to which upholding perceived duties and obligations corresponds with utility maximization is subjective and debatable. On the one hand, it might be a burden to carry trash to the nearest bin, refrain from smoking, or forego a tempting kill. This suggests that utility maximization would lead interested parties to litter, smoke, and hunt whenever they can get away with it. On the other hand, if guilt would cause headaches and lost sleep for having carried out these activities, compliance with the perceived duties might be perfectly rational within a model of utility maximization. The role of moral duties in our behavior and in our utility functions depends on our own ethical stance. The ethical theories that follow offer alternative criteria for acceptable behavior that span from an emphasis on one's selfish gratification to a focus on social policies that are beneficial to everyone.

The **teleological**, or **consequentialist**, theories of ethical egoism, utilitarianism, and the common good focus on the consequences of actions and the achievement of a desired end, such as utility maximization. The **deontological**, or **nonconsequentialist**, ethical theories of rights, justice, and virtue focus on the duties and intentions of the decision maker. It is up to individuals and firms to decide which of the underlying principles to adopt.

Ethical Egoism

Ethical egoism, also known as **individualism**, is about "looking out for number one." It asserts that our moral obligation is to pursue personal interests, regardless of the effects of these pursuits on others. *Atlas Shrugged* author Ayn Rand embraced egoism as part of her larger philosophy of objectivism.[5] Rand summarized her view this way: "My philosophy, in essence, is the concept of man as a heroic being, with his own happiness as the moral purpose of his life, with productive achievement as his noblest activity, and reason as his only absolute."[6] *Wealth of Nations* author Adam Smith described how selfishness could lead to efficiency in a free market under the right assumptions. Critics of ethical egoism argue that excessive inward focus can result in needless interpersonal conflict, neglect of others and the environment, and outcomes that are inferior to cooperative outcomes for everyone involved. Rational and informed foresight would prevent egoists from missing opportunities to gain from cooperation, although problems with social efficiency remain, as the following examples suggest.

The suboptimal prisoner's dilemma outcomes in Chapter 3 illustrate ways in which selfish behavior can cause each party to be worse off than it would be under a cooperative solution. Land-use issues provide additional examples. Suppose that several parcels of land lie along a road in a county with no zoning ordinances. Should a go-cart track be erected on one of the parcels, the property values of the other parcels could fall precipitously due to objectionable noise and air pollution. As stated by a neighboring landowner in such a case, "[the go-cart] race engine is very, very loud and very, very annoying."[7] Acting selfishly, an ethical egoist might be inclined to make the socially *in*efficient decision to build a track even if the neighbors' losses would exceed the track owner's personal gains.[8]

Although ethical egoists are not looking out for society, they must be careful not to let their interests in personal freedoms cause personal losses. Sometimes that which is best for society is also best for the individual. The freedom to pollute can backfire, causing illness and environmental degradation that harms the polluters themselves. In the context of the go-cart track, opposition to zoning laws is a mistake if cooperative support for stricter zoning would make everyone's property more valuable. It may be the case that a go-cart track will bring in more money than the sale of an unzoned lot. However, since big-spending commercial and residential land shoppers are reluctant to purchase property that could end up next to scores of unmuffled race engines, the security of zoning restrictions might make each of the parcels more valuable than a go-cart track. For similar reasons, planning and zoning boards often place limits on billboards, swine farms, junk cars, the size of homes, and commercial development. Higher standards can benefit everyone involved.

Critics of ethical egoism point out that a narrow focus on self-interest can

5 The Objectivist Center website at http://ios.org provides detailed explanations of objectivism and Ayn Rand's views.

6 See www.aynrand.org.

7 "Hasty Grants Permit for Go-Cart Track," www.amnews.com/. Accessed March 2002.

8 This assumes the absence of successful Coasian bargaining, an assumption supported by the real-world case example.

lead to greater damage than that from go-cart tracks. A standard example is the opportunity to kill one's rich relative in order to obtain his or her wealth. Indeed, many an act of violence and destruction is carried out for personal advancement, neglecting the impact on others. Children really have been known to kill their families for wealth,[9] pharmacists have watered down chemotherapy drugs to save money at the expense of human lives,[10] the habitat of endangered species has been preemptively destroyed to avoid the need to comply with environmental regulations,[11] and deadly chemicals have been dumped into the air and waterways to avoid the cost of safer disposal.[12] These acts would not be justified by personal gain if foreseeable retribution would cause greater harm to those carrying them out. Nonetheless, there is much that individuals can (or think they can) get away with if they choose to. Ethical egoists could disavow hideous self-serving acts by operating within a broader ethical framework that provides boundaries for behavior. The challenge, in that case, is to define and defend this outer set of boundaries, which would likely resemble some of the following ethical theories.[13]

Go-cart tracks are fun, but please, not in my back yard!

Utilitarianism

Under utilitarianism, it is a moral obligation to steward the greatest good for the greatest number of people. Promoted by nineteenth-century economic philosophers Jeremy Bentham and John Stuart Mill, this criterion brings into the picture everyone who would be affected by a contemplated action. Rather than downplaying externalities as advocated by ethical egoism, Mill wrote that "the liberty of the individual must be thus far limited; he must not make himself a nuisance to other people." Bentham's utilitarian calculus called for a maximization of aggregate utility for all of society. Although difficulties with interpersonal utility comparisons make an actual summation of utility unrealistic, the goal of maximizing social welfare is sufficiently lucid to provide guidance for many

9 A famous example is the Menendez brothers, who were convicted for killing their parents in 1996 in the family's Beverly Hills home. See www.courttv.com/casefiles/menendez/. In Orange County, California, seven children have been accused of killing their parents since 2000.

10 For example, in 2002 a pharmacist admitted diluting cancer drugs for more than 30 patients, many of whom died shortly thereafter. See www.usatoday.com/news/nation/2002/02/26/pharmacist.htm.

11 This is called the **scorched earth** technique for avoiding regulations. See http://graphics8.nytimes.com/images/blogs/freakonomics/pdf/FreakPDF3.pdf.

12 As one of many examples, GE legally dumped over 1 million pounds of chemicals into the Hudson River; see www.cnn.com/2000/NATURE/12/06/hudson.pcb/. See also the Reality Check in this chapter.

13 For more on ethical egoism, see www.utm.edu/research/iep/e/egoism/htm.

individual and public decisions. According to Bentham, we are to let individuals define what "good" means to them, examine policy options with regard to their effect on every person, and subscribe to those policies that provide the greatest balance of what the public perceives as good and as evil.

Utilitarianism is implicit in everyday deliberations. When a plan for a new wilderness area is evaluated in terms of its benefits to nature lovers, its boost to nearby property values, and the resulting losses to those who would otherwise develop the protected area, this is essentially a utilitarian exercise. In regard to the case study in the previous section, utilitarianism would not permit the construction of a go-cart track that caused more harm from noise and air pollution than good from profits, whether or not the track owner would benefit personally. The utilitarian approach is egalitarian in its equal consideration for the interests of each person, and appealing to some because it does not rely on tradition, superstition, prejudice, or religious doctrine. It does not follow a strict egalitarian tenet that each individual should receive the same allocation of goods or utility.

Detractors point out difficulties with the classical interpretation of good and evil as pleasure and pain. The satisfaction of selfish and sadistic preferences could be consistent with a goal of utility maximization even if the preferences involved were, say, the torture of animals or the burning of forests. For this reason, utilitarians often speak of a range of acceptable preferences, or define good and evil in broader terms with less room for immoral pleasures. As an example, good can be defined as the production of **agent-neutral** or **intrinsic** goods such as health, beauty, or knowledge that every rational person values.

Utilitarianism is also criticized for permitting the unjust distribution of resources. Discrimination, exploitation, and concentration of wealth among a small number of individuals can all be justified under this theory, so long as they lead to the maximization of aggregate utility. If rich, healthy, and young people were found to receive more utility per dollar spent cleaning up nearby toxic dumpsites than poor, sick, or older people, no dumpsites would be cleaned up near the homes of the latter groups until every site had been cleaned up near all of the former groups. Contemporary philosopher John Rawls advocates an alternative **maximin** approach that targets utility improvements for those who are the worst off. The Rawlsian approach would have us devote resources to better the lives of the poor and downtrodden first, and continue to do so until they are as well off as the rich and healthy.[14]

Figure 16.1 illustrates hypothetical utility distribution curves and the favored allocation under each of the theories mentioned thus far. Each curve represents the set of achievable combinations of utility for Artemis and Brutus.[15] The point labels indicate the associated theory as follows:

14 See Rawls (1999) for more on this and related approaches.

15 In Greek mythology, the hunting goddess Artemis is the daughter of Leto and Zeus, and the twin sister of Apollo. She is known as the "Mistress of Animals," and is often found frolicking in the forest. Brutus was a Roman politician and general who conspired to assassinate Julius Caesar, and in another incarnation, is the nemesis of Popeye.

E = Egalitarian
R = Rawlsian
U = Utilitarian
A = Cooperative ethical egoism - Artemis
A' = Noncoop. ethical egoism - Artemis
B = Cooperative ethical egoism - Brutus
B' = Noncoope. ethical egoism - Brutus

The top curve does not necessarily resemble a real-world set of choices; it is constructed to differentiate the preferred outcomes among the various theories. An egalitarian allocation divides utility equally, so it is represented by a point on the 45° line between the two people's utility levels. Points to the right of that line give Brutus more utility than Artemis; points to the left favor Artemis.

The point that satisfies the Rawlsian maximin criterion

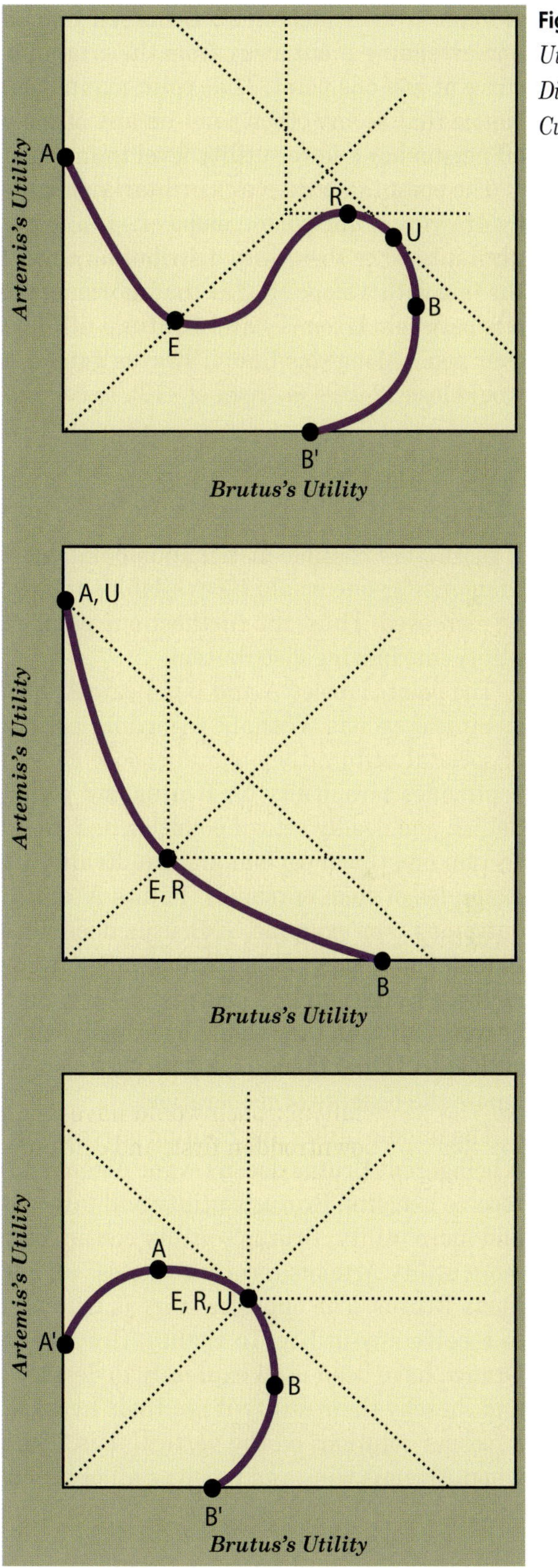

Figure 16.1 *Utility Distribution Curves*

These graphs show choices among utility levels for Artemis and Brutus. As indicated by the points labeled *E* in each graph, an egalitarian allocation divides utility equally, so it is represented by a point on the 45° line between the two people's utility levels. The points labeled *R* satisfy Rawls's maximin criterion, which yields an outcome on the highest point on an L-shaped line that has its kink on the 45° line and touches the utility distribution curve. The point that achieves a utilitarian maximization of utility, labeled *U*, is found at the point on the highest line with a slope of –1 that touches the curve. The points labeled *A* and *B* indicate Artemis's and Brutus's preferred outcomes as ethical egoists. Points *A'* and *B'* indicate the noncooperative egoist outcomes for Artemis and Brutus, respectively.

is found by considering an L-shaped line with its "kink" on the 45-degree line and extending it out away from the origin until it touches the utility distribution curve at just one point. That point maximizes the smaller of the two utility levels. Notice that at any other point on any of the utility distribution curves, the worst off person has a lower utility level than at point R.

The point that achieves a utilitarian maximization of utility, labeled U, is found by drawing a line with a slope of –1, and extending it out away from the origin until it touches the utility distribution curve at just one point. The significance of the line with a slope of –1 is that movements along it represent one-for-one trade-offs between Artemis's and Brutus's utility levels. Remember that slope is "rise over run." Along this line, if Brutus gained, say, 12 utils (a "run" of 12), Artemis would lose 12 utils (a "rise" of –12), to correspond with the slope of

$$\frac{rise}{run} = \frac{-12}{12} = -1$$

If there were possible distribution points *above* that line, then a trade-off of more than one-for-one would be available, and the sum of the two utility levels could be increased. Thus, the furthest-out point that touches that line represents the utility maximizing distribution.

The points labeled A and B indicate Artemis's and Brutus's preferred outcomes as ethical egoists. Without regard for equality, the worst-off person, or the sum of societal utility, they would choose these points. On the middle graph, point A provides zero utility for Brutus and point B provides zero utility for Artemis. Selfish and deadly acts of pollution and violence, including those described in the section on ethical egoism and the Reality Check in this chapter, are real-world examples of such outcomes. Points A' and B' are noncooperative ethical egoist outcomes. For example, if Brutus does not recognize that he gains by helping Artemis up to point B in the top and bottom graphs, he will suffer the same fate as those caught up in a prisoner's dilemma or mutual free riding. Everyone will be worse off than they would be at points above and to the left of points A' and B', such as at points R and U in both the top and bottom graphs, if Artemis or Brutus ignore the benefits of cooperation.

The middle utility distribution curve could tell a story of spite, jealousy, or war. A belligerent Brutus doesn't want Artemis to receive any benefits, and if she does receive benefits, Brutus's utility will fall considerably. As Artemis receives more and more utility, Brutus's utility continues to fall, but at a decreasing rate. The more utility Artemis receives, the less an additional increase in Artemis's utility hurts Brutus. The opposite story is true for Artemis: she does not want Brutus to receive any utility. In reality, fire and chemical defoliants including Agent Orange have been used expressly to destroy the forest environments of enemies, and thereby their utility if not their lives. Notice that the utilitarian outcome is a "corner solution" on the vertical axis. The greatest sum of utility levels occurs when Artemis wins and receives all of the utility. The egalitarian and Rawlsian solutions would be a draw that provided each party with the same level of utility.

The bottom curve could resemble the utility distributions between environmentalists and developers. Let Artemis be a developer and Brutus be an environmentalist on an otherwise deserted island. If Brutus prevents Artemis from developing any of the island at all, Artemis receives no utility and Brutus is without any shelter. This places them at point B'. The first few developments improve both parties' utility levels, providing Artemis with an occupation and both residents with shelter, and leading to point B. Additional developments make Artemis happy but cut into wilderness that Brutus would like to protect. The negative slope of the curve between points A and B represents these tradeoffs. For Artemis to restrict Brutus's utility below the level he receives at point A would decrease Artemis's utility as well. Such decreases in environmental interests would hinder the viability of hunting and fishing stocks, and detract from the natural beauty both castaways enjoy. Thus, a movement from A to A' would cause both Artemis and Brutus to suffer. The egalitarian, Rawlsian, and utilitarian outcome in this case would be to provide each party with the same level of utility. A scenario in which the Rawlsian and the egalitarian allocations are identical, but the utilitarian allocation is different, is left for you to discover in the problem set.

The Common Good

Originated in the ancient writings of Plato, Aristotle, and Cicero, the notion of the common good is that society is a community whose members share the pursuit of common goals. The welfare of individuals is inextricably bound to the good of the community. John Rawls wrote, "The common good I think of as certain general conditions that are in an appropriate sense equally to everyone's advantage."[16] Likewise, common-good policies are focused on outcomes that are beneficial to all, examples being clean air and water, health care, public safety, and stable global temperatures. This approach respects and encourages individuals' freedom to pursue private goals, but asks that we recognize and advance those goals we share in common.

Like many of the ethical theories, this approach leaves some ambiguities. Exactly which outcomes are considered to be for the common good? When may individual freedoms be exercised at the expense of others? How do we assess activities that benefit some people and harm others? While it may involve few absolutes, this approach clearly advocates a community mindset in which we recognize the interconnectedness of our utility, and act collectively and cooperatively in the interest of social welfare. Plato himself emphasized the social benefits of education in this regard. In the environmental realm, the maintenance of soils and climates suitable for agriculture and the protection of wildlife species that provide widespread benefits from their mere existence are further examples of allocations for the common good.

16 See Rawls (1999), p. 217.

Virtue

Deontological ethicists argue that we should focus on duties and intentions rather than on moral principles and outcomes. With roots in the writings of Plato, Homer, and Sophocles, the normative theory of virtue is the oldest ethical theory in Western philosophy. This theory asks us to reflect on the types of people we intend, or have the duty, to be. According to Aristotle, "That which is the prize and end of virtue seems to be the best thing in the world." He opined that a moral virtue is the mean between two vices. For example, courage is a moral virtue between the vices of cowardice and rashness. Modesty falls between the vices of arrogance and low self-esteem. Aristotle's theory of virtue enjoyed great popularity during the Middle Ages when it was endorsed by philosopher Thomas Aquinas. Despite the rise of competing approaches, virtue theory remains among the most prominent ethical theories of modern times.

Virtues are character traits, attitudes, and dispositions that influence our utility functions and actions. Examples include generosity, courage, compassion, temperance, fortitude, honesty, fairness, and self-control. Virtues must be learned and practiced, and virtue theorists place special emphasis on education and the exercise of self-discipline. The theory of virtue holds that once a character trait is obtained, it becomes characteristic of the acquirer. Those who have formed the virtue of benevolence tend to practice benevolence often. Those who have developed many virtues become predisposed to act in accordance with moral principles. In that way, the virtuous person is the ethical person.

Critics argue that virtue ethics fails to address several issues relevant to the quest for right and wrong.[17] The lack of specific behavioral guidelines leaves common ethical dilemmas such as whether to recycle or whether to contribute to habitat preservation open to interpretation. Seemingly virtuous people might engage in questionable behavior for lack of specified criteria or offenses. Is it moral to hunt? Is it moral to drive an SUV? There is little in virtue theory to assist with such determinations. There is also the possibility of moral backsliding. If virtues are maintained only with practice, individuals might fall out of practice, or temporarily deviate from the standards of their character traits. A focus on traits rather than conduct might overlook activities that would pass few other tests of morality.

Rights

Eighteenth-century German philosopher Immanuel Kant, like Aristotle, argued that the morality of an action is determined by whether its performance adheres to moral duties, rather than by the action's repercussions. Our moral duties, in Kant's view, include the treatment of individuals with dignity and respect.

Consider the U.S. Department of Health and Human Services' determina-

17 See Louden (1997).

tion that larger-than-expected portions of the nation and world were blanketed with nuclear fallout from Cold War nuclear testing, causing at least 15,000 cancer deaths in the United States alone.[18] One could make an "ignorance is bliss" argument that the withholding of information on this irreversible environmental disaster would permit higher levels of utility and do more for the common good than its revelation. Kant felt that individuals have the right to learn the truth, and would have applauded the U.S. government's 2002 report of these findings as duly honest treatment, regardless of the consequences. Other fundamental moral rights in Kant's theory include the rights of individuals to choose freely what they will do with their lives, to have privacy, to be free of punishment, and to receive what has been promised in a contract or agreement.

Is it moral to buy bottled baby sharks?

Kant advocated two additional principles that are relevant to environmental and natural resource economics. According to the **Principle of Ends**, one should never treat humanity as a means to an end, but always as an end in itself. This suggests that individuals should not be exploited in the pursuit of profits. Kant taught that we are obligated to act out of respect for the human worth of others. Many environmentalists advocate the same principles of respect for wildlife and natural resources.

Kant's **categorical imperative** states that we should choose only those actions that we would put forth as universal laws of nature. If we would not want everyone to build go-cart tracks in residential areas, we should not choose that behavior for ourselves. If we would want everyone to recycle and ride their bicycle to class or work rather than driving, we should do so as well. This view that moral behavior is that which we would rationally recommend to others provides a criterion for specific actions the morality of which other deontological theories leave as ambiguous.

18 See www.usatoday.com/news/nation/2002/02/28/usat-nuke.htm.

Chickens, some alive and some dead, on the way to market. Is our treatment of animals moral?

Justice

Aristotle and Plato saw fairness and justice as compelling measures of morality. These criteria for behavior have a solid intuitive foundation. Even young children call attention to actions they do not perceive as fair, with acuity that the actions are therefore not right. Aristotle's teaching that "equals should be treated equally" supports modern antidiscrimination and comparable-worth movements.[19] In regard to the environment, justice theory calls for decisions that are fair to present and future generations of humans. In the same way, justice for animals and other wildlife is central to the ethical theory of People for the Ethical Treatment of Animals (PETA), Citizens for Responsible Animal Behavior Studies (CRABS), and various environmental organizations. Perhaps the largest challenge in applying the theory of justice is to determine which actions are indeed fair and just. For example, the theory makes it clear that citizens should have equal access to national wilderness areas, but it is not clear how much pollution it is fair to impose on one's neighbors.

Environmental Ethics

Ethical theories are useful for guiding human decisions that affect other humans. Human decisions that affect the environment or natural resources, and in turn affect humans, are also within the purview of these theories. Apart from some modern adaptations, however, the traditional theories are anthropocentric. The approaches discussed in this section shed more light on ecocentric morality.

19 The comparable-worth doctrine states that those whose jobs are deemed equally important should receive equal compensation. See www.scu.edu/SCU/Centers/Ethics/publications/iie/v3n2/comparable.html.

Deep Ecology

Norwegian philosopher Arne Naess (1973) defined **shallow ecology** as the fight against pollution and resource depletion in order to improve the health and affluence of people in developed nations. **Deep ecology**, he said, adds to this fight the elements of ecocentrism and sustainability, and the intrinsic value of nonhuman nature. Naess and other deep ecologists believe that moral evaluations should rest on ecological principles, with scientific insight into the interrelatedness of all systems of life. They believe that greater respect for the environment is morally right, in part, because environmental peril could be the end of us all. In other words, that which is good for the environment is good for humans and all living things.

In contrast to ethical egoism, which is about individuals focusing on themselves, Naess suggests that we should identify with the ecosphere, and the plants and animals therein. Such a focus would encourage behavior that is consistent with what he feels science tells us is necessary for the well-being of life on Earth. Australian philosopher John Passmore, among other critics of deep ecology, feels that the emphasis it places on environmental concerns is not necessary, and that the risks of environmental neglect are less important to ego-based choices than individual rights.

Social Ecology

> *By so radically separating humanity and society from nature, or naively reducing them to mere zoological entities, we can no longer see how human nature is derived from nonhuman nature and social evolution from natural evolution.*
>
> —Murray Bookchin[20]

Bookchin's eco-anarchist theory of **social ecology** has inspired many environmental ethicists to connect environmental interests with socialistic ideals. Social ecologists promote social equality and ecological interests within a framework of revolutionary libertarian socialism. A common view among people with these leanings is that the concentration of economic and political power, the homogenization of culture, and the strengthening of social hierarchies are barriers to freedom and are the principal causes of what social ecologists see as an ongoing ecological crisis. Social ecologists ask people to play an active role in social evolution that will remedy these perceived imbalances of power, diversity, and equality. In the extreme, this can lead to vigilante justice as discussed in Chapter 12. The annexation of radical political views with environmentalism, valid or not, brings with it opposition from those with moderate and opposing political views. Critiques of the underlying political philosophies, aside from the brief coverage in the chapter on government, are beyond the scope of this text.

20 See www.spunk.org/library/writers/bookchin/sp000514.txt.

Ecofeminism

Ecofeminism, a term coined by French feminist François d'Eaubonn (1994), links environmentalism with feminism. The unethical domination of women is associated with the domination of nature. Ecofeminists see a common thread of immorality in varying levels of disrespect for women and for wilderness. Disregard for the feelings of other human beings and disinterest in the state of the environment may be rationalized in a similar manner, and conversely, the virtue of compassion may carry over from compassion for humans to compassion for animals. With a focus on the interconnected spheres of feminism, development, and community, ecofeminism has become a popular grassroots activist movement over the last three decades.

Respect for animals and the environment can be costly. Recycled materials often cost more to purchase than virgin products, and the expense of keeping livestock increases with the size of their living quarters. Theological ethicist Reinhold Niebuhr (2002) argues that corporations cannot be ethical because they have an essential vested interest in their own survival; they can only be coerced into respectful behavior by another institution that threatens their survival. For example, the Roman Catholic Church has said in effect, "We represent the second-biggest block of consumers in the United States (after the government), and we will no longer do business with any corporation that is not an equal-opportunity employer." In this way, even businesses that only respect the bottom line can be brought to address a broader range of concerns.

In keeping with the deep ecology and ecofeminism models, Swiss dairy farmers appear to take great pride in their treatment of animal resources. Switzerland has joined with other European countries and Canada to restrict the use of a lactation-enhancing bovine growth hormone, recombinant bovine somatotropin (rBST). Some American dairies have made the same decision. The Crescent Ridge Dairy in New England states, "Our farm manager does not feel it is in the best interest of the animals to inject our herd with rBST."[21] At the same time, the Monsanto Corporation reports that rBST is the best-selling dairy animal health product in the United States.[22] There is apprehension about the effects that hormones, and the increased use of antibiotics used to cure hormone-induced mastitis (udder enlargement), might have on cows, humans, and the ecosystem.[23] The decision by farmers to show respect for animals and forego a 10 to 20 percent increase in milk production for the well-being of other living things suggests that some business owners may have objectives beyond profit maximization. Can you think of other evidence of ulterior motives among entrepreneurs you have observed?

21 See www.crescentridge.com/displays/disp_noGrowth.cfm.

22 See www.monsantodairy.com.

23 For a collection of news items on this issue, see http://organicconsumers.org/rbghlink.html.

Resolving Ethical Dilemmas

Would you be able to sleep at night after illegally dumping hazardous waste where it might reach drinking water supplies? Is it conscionable to wash your car during a water-use moratorium, to pitch recyclables, to dump trash out your car window, or to buy unneeded material goods? Our daily ethical dilemmas as individuals, business owners, and policymakers are simplified by the application of decision rules that guide our resource allocation. Almost any behavior can be rationalized with arguments like, "other people are doing it," "it's legal," "it provides a product that people demand," or "if I didn't do it, someone else would." However, these statements take no account of the harm caused by the activity, possible alternatives for the activity, the likelihood that others will mimick the behavior, or the effect of the behavior on one's conscience.

Economics provides the guidance that behaviors should continue until the marginal cost exceeds the marginal benefit. Unfortunately, dilemmas still arise regarding which costs and benefits to consider. For example, ethical egoism suggests consideration only of one's own costs and benefits, while utilitarianism seeks aggregate utility maximization. As extensions of moral theories, the following criteria are available to assist with decisions governing environmental and natural resources:

Ethical Egoism: *Is this action good for me?*

Utilitarianism: *Does it bring the greatest good to the greatest number of people?*

The Common Good: *Is it good for society as a whole?*

Virtue: *Does this action reflect balance between vices?*

Rights: *Does this action respect the moral rights of everyone?*

Kantianism: *Would I want everyone to do it?*

Justice: *Is this action fair and just? Does it treat equals equally?*

Deep Ecology: *Is this action sustainable and ecocentric?*

Social Ecology: *Is it consistent with social equality and ecological interests?*

Ecofeminism: *Does this action show due respect for living things?*

The following are three additional questions that some people like to consider when facing ethical dilemmas:

1. **Would you like to see it in a headline?**
   The **front-page-of-the-newspaper test** promotes consideration of what other members of society would think about an action. The criterion is: Would you carry out the behavior in question if you knew that a description of it would appear in a newspaper headline? If you envision that the headline would be incriminating or make you feel embarrassed, that's a sign that the contemplated act is morally unsound.

   How would you feel if one of the following headlines appeared in the newspaper?

   > SMOKER RELEASES CARBON MONOXIDE INTO PUBLIC RESTAURANT
   >
   > STUDENT DRIVES CAR TWO BLOCKS RATHER THAN WALKING
   >
   > STRIP-MINING CONTINUES DUE TO LACK OF RECYCLING

   Your response could help you decide whether these actions are acceptable. Here are some actual newspaper headlines:

   > POISONOUS LEGACY: "BLACK VILLAGE" TESTIFIES TO COMMUNISM'S TOLL ON THE ENVIRONMENT
   >
   > INCO LTD. FACES LAWSUIT ALLEGING NICKEL REFINERY POSES A BIG HEALTH RISK
   >
   > EXPERT SAYS ALABAMA PLANT SHOULD PAY $8.6 MILLION FOR PCB DAMAGE
   >
   > STATES ASK FORD TO REMOVE MERCURY SWITCHES

   Do you think some of these decision makers would have behaved differently had they subjected themselves to the front-page-of-the-newspaper test in advance?

2. **How Does This Decision Make You Feel?**
   Intuitionism is the doctrine that, rather than applying an explicit formula to reach moral decisions, we should follow our own intuition. Intuitionists feel that while certain moral principles should be adhered to, the principles express self-evident propositions. Thus, as Jiminy Cricket said to Pinocchio, "Just let your conscience be your guide." This is a common approach, and it can work well for those with good ears for a strong conscience. Pinocchio, on the other hand, said, "What's a conscience?"

reality check

Killing More Than Two Birds with One Stone

In the 1970s, Times Beach, Missouri, was a small town of 2,800 residents on the Meramec River floodplain. The town of Times Beach contracted with a private waste hauler to spray oil on unpaved roads and parking lots to control the dust. Local chemical companies hired the same contractor to dispose of sludge containing dioxin. The issue of where to dispose of the contaminated sludge and that of where to find oil to spray on the roads allegedly came together as an unethical opportunity to kill two birds with one stone. Unfortunately, more than two birds died. Soon after the roads were sprayed with dioxin-contaminated waste in 1972 and 1973, 50 horses and hundreds of birds died.

In 1982, the Meramec River flooded the town. The floodwaters deposited contaminated soil into homes and yards. At the behest of the EPA, which had been monitoring the state of the environment in Times Beach, the Centers for Disease Control issued a health advisory recommending the evacuation of Times Beach. The town roads were blocked, security guards patrolled around the clock, and so began one of the most expensive Superfund cleanups in history. The EPA spent $33 million to purchase Times Beach property, relocate all of the town's residents, and tear down their homes and businesses. The site cleanup was completed in the end of 1997, and by 2000, a new 409-acre state park had opened on the property to commemorate the famous Route 66.

3. **What Would My Role Model Do?**
   Many people have heroes, spiritual leaders, or role models whose behavior they admire. When faced with an ethical dilemma, they imagine what that other person would do if faced with the same situation. Those who admire their parents, community leaders, clergy, or teachers, for example, may try to allocate resources the way those people would. Friends and neighbors influence each other in the same way. When a few people in a neighborhood start putting materials out for recycling, that decision can be contagious.

The answer to the question "Does it maximize profits?" provides one means of decision making. The questions listed here provide alternative criteria for all those who choose to consider morality among the factors that determine resource allocations. If you question the ties between environmental economics and ethics, consider whether externalities, social discount rates, or most non-use values for natural assets would matter in the absence of ethical considerations.

Summary

At the core of common debates over environmental and natural resource economics are moral dilemmas involving the appropriate treatment of flora, fauna, fellow humans, and future generations of the same. This chapter considers the motives behind our behavior and the composition of our utility functions. Ethical theories offer guidance in decision making, including criteria for the acceptability of resource allocations. These theories help individuals choose actions that are conscionable and provide firms with alternatives to simple profit maximization. Economists, too, must decide how assorted costs and benefits should weigh into measures of efficiency. The allocation of natural resources cannot be divested from ethical issues.

Suppose five organ transplant candidates could be saved with the benefit of organs from one healthy human sacrifice. Should the sacrifice be made? If each individual gained the same utility from life, the strict utilitarian response would be yes, in order to maximize social welfare. Rights advocates would say no, because the healthy person has the right to live. Would you sacrifice five lives in exchange for the right of individuals to earn profits from an enterprise that pollutes? Would you sacrifice five forests for the same purpose? How about five animal species? Unfortunately, economic decisions like these must be made routinely. Although ethical theories do not remove the pain from these trade-offs, they do provide structure for well reasoned decisions. Perhaps the assistance of these theories is the most that we can hope for, and the least that those whose lives hang in the balance should expect.

Problems for Review

1. Imagine a world in which individuals cared only about themselves. Choose two of the following types of people and describe, in one paragraph each, how you think their behavior would differ in this worst-case scenario of complete selfishness, relative to that of the average person in their position today: doctor, environmentalist, teacher, parent, minister, coach.

2. What criteria do you most often use when faced with an ethical dilemma? Which of the theories described in this chapter is the closest to your personal theory? Do you think any of the new ideas you picked up from this chapter will influence your behavior? If so, how?

3. The giant Asian pond turtle is endangered. It is also highly sought after for medicinal and food purposes. Would you hunt and kill one of these turtles for \$20? For \$10,000? At what price would you draw the line? What does this say about your environmental ethics?

4. Do you believe that many Swiss dairy farmers really care about their animals as suggested in the text? Do you believe that many McDonald's executives really want to provide for an environmentally sound future as stated in one of the opening quotes? What do you think are the strongest determinants of an individual's environmental ethic?

5. Rawls (1999, 205) writes that if government is assumed to aim for the common good, and if "some men can be identified as having superior wisdom and judgment, others are willing to trust them and to concede to their opinion a greater wealth." To what extent is government aimed at the common good? Can individuals be trusted to act on the behalf of society? Comment in a paragraph or two.

6. Consider one of the many dilemmas faced by the U.S. Food and Drug Administration. A National Academy of Sciences report estimated that 60,000 women in the United States put their fetuses "at risk" of brain damage from mercury in the fish they ate. FDA scientists have warned that a woman should eat only one can of tuna per week, and that "The action levels we have in place are not protective enough for this—the fetuses." Nonetheless, after meetings with the U.S. Tuna Foundation and other seafood industry representatives, the FDA decided only to suggest that pregnant women eat fish in moderation. Which ethical theories would support this decision?

7. Draw a utility distribution curve on which the Rawlsian and the egalitarian allocations are identical, but the utilitarian allocation is different. Label the points representing each solution with the name of the associated theory.

8. Utilitarian Jeremy Bentham argued that if utility is good, then it is good irrespective of whose utility it is, and thus the sum of societal utility should be maximized. In what ways do you feel this is true or untrue?

9. The tenets of ecofeminism suggest that those who seek to dominate or exploit women and those who seek to dominate or exploit the wilderness have a similar mindset. Do you agree? Are the people you know who do one or the other the types of people that you believe would do both? Are the people you know who would never do one also the types who would be unlikely to do the other? Explain your observations.

10. Which ethical theory do you feel has the strongest influence on policymakers in your family, local area, and nation? For which of these sets of policymakers would you most like to see a change in ethics, and to which theory would you want them to change?

1. Find a website that explains a general ethical theory *not* described in this chapter and summarize it in one paragraph.
2. Find a website that explains the view of a prominent ethicist and describe how her or his view could be applied to environmental economics.

Internet Resources

Ecofeminism on the Web:
www.ecofem.org

On Environmental Ethics:
http://plato.stanford.edu/entries/ethics-environmental/

Institute for Social Ecology:
www.social-ecology.org

International Society for Environmental Ethics:
www.cep.unt.edu/ISEE.html

Opensecrets.org:
www.opensecrets.org

People for the Ethical Treatment of Animals: *www.peta.com*

Further Reading

Anderson, David A. *Treading Lightly: The Joy of Conservation, Moderation, and Simple Living*. Danville, KY: Pensive Press, 2009. This book discusses environmental ethics and provides examples of relevant practices and lifestyles.

Aristotle. *Nicomachean Ethics*. New York: Oxford University Press, 1998. Aristotle's classic treatise on ethics and virtue.

Beauchamp, Tom L., and James F. Childress. *Principles of Biomedical Ethics*. New York: Oxford University Press, 2001. Despite the title, this book provides an insightful general overview of the predominant ethical theories.

Bookchin, Murray. *Toward an Ecological Society*. Montreal: Black Rose Books, 1988. This book outlines the social ecology perspective of its greatest proponent.

d'Eaubonne, François. "The Time for Ecofeminism." Trans. Ruth Hottell. In *Ecology*, edited by Carolyn Merchant. Humanity Books, 1994. An edited volume on the themes of deep ecology, ecofeminism, and environmental justice.

Kant, Immanuel. *Critique of the Power of Judgement*. Cambridge: Cambridge University Press, 2002. A taste of classical Kantian philosophy.

Katz, Eric, Andrew Light, and David Rothenberg (eds). *Beneath the Surface: Critical Essays in the Philosophy of Deep Ecology*. Cambridge, MA: MIT Press, 2000. Compares deep ecology's philosophical ideas with other schools of thought, including social ecology, ecofeminism, and moral pluralism.

Leopold, Aldo. *A Sand County Almanac*. New York: Oxford University Press, 2001. A collection of essays on conservation in which it is claimed that the source of the ecological crisis is philosophical.

Louden, Robert B. "On Some Vices of Virtue Ethics." In *Virtue Ethics*, edited by Roger Crisp and Michael Slote. New York: Oxford University Press, 1997. A collection of essays on virtue ethics by prominent modern philosophers from several Western countries.

Mount, Eric. *Professional Ethics in Context: Institutions, Images, and Empathy*. Louisville: Westminster John Knox Press, 1990. Mount spent his career guiding ethical discussions and shares his many insights in this book.

Naess, Arne. "The Shallow and the Deep, Long-Range Ecology Movements: A Summary." *Inquiry* 16 (1973): 95–100. The article with which this Norwegian philosopher started the deep ecology movement.

Nash, Roderick Frazier. *The Rights of Nature: A History of Environmental Ethics*. Madison: University of Wisconsin Press, 1989. A well-researched history of environmental thought and politics in the United States

Niebuhr, Reinhold. *Moral Man and Immoral Society: A Study in Ethics and Politics*. Louisville: Westminster John Knox Press, 2002. Argues that corporations cannot be ethical because they have an essential vested interest in their own survival.

Passmore, John. *Man's Responsibility for Nature*. London: Duckworth, 1974. This book argues that there is no need for an environmental ethic.

Rawls, John. *A Theory of Justice*. Cambridge, MA: Belknap Press, 1999. This remarkably influential contemporary philosopher explains his doctrine of "justice as fairness."

Index

C

D

F

H

I

J

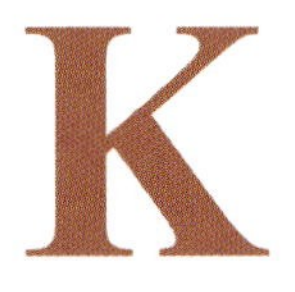

L

M

N

O

P

Q

R

T

U

V